PUBLIC UTILITIES
IN AMERICAN
CAPITALISM

THE MACMILLAN COMPANY
NEW YORK · CHICAGO
DALLAS · ATLANTA · SAN FRANCISCO
LONDON · MANILA
BRETT-MACMILLAN LTD.
TORONTO

PUBLIC UTILITIES
IN AMERICAN
CAPITALISM

Martin G. Glaeser
*Professor of Economics
and Commerce
University of Wisconsin*

The Macmillan Company • New York

Chapter XXXI under the title of "St. Lawrence Seaway and Power Project" (copyright 1954 by The Macmillan Company) appeared in slightly different form in *Land Economics* (November, 1954 issue).

Library of Congress catalog card number: 57-5970

To My Students

Sucht ich deshalb den Weg so sehnsuchtsvoll,
Dass ich ihn nicht den Brüdern zeigen soll?
Goethe-Zueignung

Preface

This book is an introduction to the problems associated with public utilities, including therein the various branches of the transport industries. It sets forth the economic and legal principles underlying public utilities and also traces the essentials in the development of the technology upon which these industries are based. Because public utilities are the principal foci in the utilization of our natural resources, particularly our energy resources, the text also deals with the growing interest in planning their regional and national conservation.

The writer has, of course, benefited from the work of others, whose conclusions have been combined with his own researches, experiences, and reflection in a gradually maturing point of view. Specific sources have been referred to in the text or in the Bibliography. But he owes more than the reader can appreciate to the never-failing challenge of generations of students whose fresh and ever-changing outlook has made him test and modify conclusions which so readily become traditionalized.

Nevertheless, the general point of view embodied in the author's earlier work, the *Outlines of Public Utility Economics,* did not need to be radically revised. The "going concern" idea is again basic and provides a frame of reference from which the problems and proposals for their solution may be judged. The author is more than ever satisfied with the general orientation in the study of social problems afforded him by his teachers, the late Professor John R. Commons of the University of Wisconsin, and Roscoe Pound, former Dean of the Harvard Law School. The former, an institutionalist in economics, and the latter, an institutionalist in the law, have provided him with a technique of investigation and of intellectual coordination which make theory and practice truly complementary.

Primarily, the book is designed to afford a general orientation to the college student beginning the serious study of public utilities. It is also written for those whose professional or citizenship interests require a general survey of the field. The book concerns itself with all industries subjected to economic regulation and may thus serve also as a basic text for courses in the relations between government and business.

Martin G. Glaeser

Madison, Wisconsin

Contents

Tables

Charts

1. ECONOMIC AND INSTITUTIONAL FOUNDATIONS

1. THE FUNCTION
OF PUBLIC UTILITIES IN
A NATIONAL ECONOMY

Introduction

The tremendous social importance of public utilities in the economic life of our times invites a study of these industries from an economic point of view. Within the period of the generation still living, the growth in volume and variety of their services has been little short of marvelous. This growth was accompanied, however, by the development of certain vexing problems which require more satisfactory solutions than have thus far appeared, if this progress is to continue.

Public Utilities [1] is a collective name covering diverse industries which it is common practice to group under this designation because certain common characteristics give them unity. At the same time public utilities are classified apart from other industries because they differ from them in certain fundamental respects. We propose in this introduction to public utility economics to subject these common elements and these distinctive elements to such special consideration as their uniqueness requires.

It is, however, a mistake to assume that public utility economics is a special brand of economics, the principles and rules of which differ markedly from the principles and rules with which the student has become familiar in his study of general economics. Public utility economics is in fact only a branch of the general study, just as public utility industries are only a sector in the broad field of industrial economics. What is significant and must be recognized at the outset is that all economic activity is conducted in accordance with certain social rules which give unity and coherence to economic conduct and which collectively constitute a framework within which such economic activity takes place. By recognizing the importance of these rules we make what has been called an institutional approach to the study of

---

[1] "Public Service" is sometimes used as a synonym of "public utility," in order to avoid offensive repetition. Common usage is beginning to accept this substitution.

economic problems. Of these the public utility problem is one of the oldest and most important and has developed for itself a special kind of framework which must, however, be articulated with the general framework.

A Preliminary View of the Field

In the world in which we live today the supply of economic goods and services and their distribution to users takes place by means of a process which functions differently, according to whether it depends upon the volition of the individual or rests upon the compulsion of government.

Governmental functions. The supply of certain goods or services in which the common benefit is dominant are furnished by the state or some of its subordinate units, and the rules in accordance with which they are used and distributed are laid down by law. The functions are, nevertheless, economic in character because scarce resources are handed over to government agencies with which they are expected to carry out their functions efficiently. The funds with which these governmental agencies work are apportioned to them by legislatures through budgetary allowances; their services are distributed and utilized under governmental rules, and the costs of service are met by means of compulsory governmental exactions upon all those who come within the jurisdiction of the government. In other words, these governmental functions represent collective interests which must be supported by *taxes*. No questions are asked as to how great or how small may be the beneficial use to the individual; it is enough that there be, or that there is presumed to be, a collective benefit.

The economic principles and rules relating to governmental expenditures and receipts are elaborated in the study of public finance, which is closely associated with political science. This science, in turn, is concerned with the way in which these governmental agencies are run. Under the system of constitutional democracy, government rests upon the theory of consent of the governed; practical politics approaches this ideal. Politicians elected by the people determine the nature and extent of these expenditures and how they are to be met by governmental income. The individual pays his share of that income as the member of a group, and there is no calculus of the extent to which he benefits from these expenditures. He participates as a member of a going concern, which is the political state, and he is made to conform to the collective rules of that state. Compulsion of the individual by democratically fixed rules dominates this scheme. Such activities as the maintenance and defense of the state, the administration of justice within the state, the preservation of internal security of life and property, represent, perhaps, the minimum unfolding of such governmental functions. They represent a social overhead whose cost is borne collectively.

Transitional functions in a twilight zone. There are economic activities which are clearly transitional, where collective interests and common benefits are dominant, but where we begin to take account of the special benefit to the individual. The supply of educational facilities best illustrates this transitional type. Although the church had controlled education for centuries, under modern conditions education has become a concern of the state. At the present time it is the general practice in the United States to provide education by means of a public school system which is an educational pyramid, with the primary school at the base and the university at the top. Education is free but compulsory to all children of school age, a limit which has been gradually extended to include the high school years. Taxes for the support of schools are paid by the childless bachelor in proportion to the assessed value of his property, while the head of a large family, if he owns no taxable property, makes his contribution indirectly in the rent he pays. That is to say, in the supply of educational facilities of this grade there is no *quid pro quo*. However, the children of poor and rich parents alike are required to pay fees when they enter the state university, and they pay in proportion to the number attending.

Why this shift from the economics of collectivism in the supply of primary education toward an economics of individualism in furnishing higher education? The answer is that under the consent theory of government, society has not seen fit to change the rules to provide for free matriculation at the university. Be it noted, however, that the incidental fee paid by students does not cover the cost of university instruction, as the legislative budgets for university instruction sufficiently attest. The policy of the state with respect to college education appears to be that it should be left to the judgment of the individual whether these educational services are worth the time and expense which they entail.

Moreover, government does not monopolize the supply of educational services as it does, for instance, judicial services. It permits and even encourages through tax exemption the furnishing of different and even superior educational services by private agencies of the most varied types. On the other hand, there are governmental activities, such as the filing and registration services of judicial agencies, which are monopolized by the government. Here the *fee* is supposed to cover the cost of the service. Monopoly by the government of an essential service in connection with the registration of mortgages serves to make the fee akin to a tax in that it is a compulsory exaction from all who need the service, though payment is limited to users alone. The principle of *quid pro quo* is much clearer in this case.

The emergence of special benefits.   One further illustration is needed in order to bring into fuller view the gradual emergence of the principle of individualism out of the original matrix of collectivism. Drainage and irrigation of land has long been a matter of collective interests. The ancient civilizations of Egypt and Chaldea were founded upon these works. Everywhere and in all times we find the government taking an interest in their collective supply.

In this country, acting under statutory authority, courts have advanced the collective interest in the economical drainage of lands, by approving the organization of drainage districts. They have been implemented with the compulsory powers of eminent domain and taxation, in order to bring within the control of a single agency all lands likely to benefit from the drainage improvement, and to give this collective agency a priority over private interests. Consent having been obtained from the court, the district is empowered to defray the cost of the improvement through the compulsory imposition of *special assessments* upon all the lands benefited and in proportion to the *special* benefit to each landowner. No profit is to be made by the district, no matter what the magnitude of the general benefit may be. Moreover, no special assessment to one landowner may exceed the special benefit estimated to accrue to him alone. By this process only the *cost* of a collective benefit is apportioned to the individual *in proportion* to his special capacity to benefit from the improvement. Drainage districts thus illustrate even more clearly the principle of the *quid pro quo*.

The supply of water under pressure may be taken as another example of a dominant collective interest where the service is supplied under conditions which make the individual user responsible for a share of the cost of the service. In this instance, we speak of the *sale* of the water and of the producer as being in a *business*. The supply of potable water under pressure for domestic, agricultural, commercial, and industrial uses has become such a *common necessity* that government has from time immemorial supplied water as a communal enterprise or has closely controlled a private supplier. If a potential private supplier of water feared he might not meet his costs, government has not hesitated to come to his assistance with a *tax exemption* or even a *subsidy* from the general taxpayers. The modern "big city" needs for fire protection, public sanitation, education, and recreation have made the government one of the larger users of water. Even the small householder, hitherto depending upon his own pumped supply, may be forced by public health and sanitary regulations to become a buyer from the common source. The *price* which is paid for this common necessity has achieved a name of its own, the *water rate*. This signifies that the basis of the charge is the special benefit upon which the consumer is peculiarly dependent.

In this illustration of the declining of collective interests and the growing of individual interests in economic functions, we select next the business of insurance. The essential function of insurance is to pool the risks of a collectivity of persons and to charge each one only with the average cost of this risk enhanced by a charge for management. Incidentally, the life, property, and casualty insurance businesses also administer the funds collected from policyholders as premiums, investing them in other undertakings in order to earn an interim return before paying them out to cover current losses of the insured. There is no doubt that a high degree of public interest inheres in these businesses, both on account of the function they perform of spreading risks and on account of their financial functions. Hence they have been subjected to increasing regulation by compulsorily imposed rules. Yet insurance is still dominantly a private business with competition the rule rather than the exception, and with the individual accorded freedom of choice as to whether he desires insurance and who his insurer shall be. The collective interest is present but not recognized as paramount.

The free enterprise economy. As we pass down the scale of commodities and services with waning social importance, we find that all are furnished by business enterprises under a system of price economics where, while there is always public control of these transactions, the price-fixing function becomes more and more free. We rely progressively upon the principles of competition and of the free functioning of the forces back of demand and supply to achieve that correlation between special benefits and costs incurred which are the hallmarks of the economics of individualism. In order to induce continuous supply under a regime of freedom of enterprise, we use the rules of what has been called a "profit and loss economy."

The Public Utility Sector of the Economy— A First Approximation

It may thus be said that these five economic terms—(1) the tax, (2) the fee, (3) the special assessment, (4) the rate, and (5) the price—express, as if in a declining magnitude, the social importance of an economic function, while the entire series recapitulates the social process of customary classification in accordance with some scale of social evaluation. These classifications are always in a fluid state, and we hazard them only as devices for preliminary orientation in social affairs. As Maitland, the great English legal historian, said with respect to the analytical study of history, "He who tears the fabric of history tears a seamless webb," so he who attempts to analyze social relationships will find that he is dealing with a fabric the threads of which are perplexingly interwoven.

We take it as the cardinal point of departure for this economic analysis that where the supply of a given commodity or service has become *monopolized* so that a given producer has achieved complete control over the same, and where the demand for such commodity and service is sufficiently general so that it has become a *common necessity,* the economic power of such a producer must be curbed by the application of political power so that he will deal reasonably with those who are dependent upon him for supply. This status of being required to "deal reasonably" has been called the *"public utility status,"* and industries so classified have been called public utilities. Within a more comprehensive legal framework, the public utility classification is designed on the one hand to distinguish industries best conducted as monopolies and on the other hand to assure that these industries will not, under normal conditions, look to government funds for support, but that they will be required to *sell* their services and look for support only to those who are the actual users. The supply of water may serve as a marginal case to show how on the one hand the public utility classification limits the spread of a legal framework of collectivist economics. On the other hand, the legal framework of public utility economics preserves the freedom of choice of the free enterprise system while it makes the necessary adjustments in the same to protect consumers against the exercise of monopoly powers. These classifications are brought together in Chart I.

In its most extended sense the term *public utilities* is designed to cover certain industries which in the course of time have been classified apart from industry in general and have likewise been distinguished from governmental services with which, however, they often are intimately related. The basis of the classification is essentially economic and technological, although the meaning of the term is derived from the law.

An Industrial Classification of Public Utilities

Bearing in mind what was said above about the difficulty of making rigid classifications because they are constantly in a state of flux, we may, nevertheless, enumerate public utility industries in accordance with the generalized function which they perform in the economy:

1. *Services of transportation or the common carrier function.* This may include the provision of the "way," as well as the transporting medium. Transport services are rendered by highway, railway, pipeway, waterway, and airway. A part of the plant may be furnished by the government, as in the case of highways, waterways, and airways. Certain ancillary services may be rendered, such as the providing of ports, docks, stockyards, terminals, elevators, warehouses, hotels, and specialized equipment. There is usually a bobtail of incidental services which cluster about the primary transport services. The area of service may be local, regional, national, or international in scope. Only those agencies, however, which "hold themselves out to serve all comers," the so-called common carriers, are true public utilities, which must be distinguished from private carriers and contract carriers for hire.

2. *Services facilitating communication.* Here are included the postal service, land telegraph and ocean cables, local exchange and long distance telephone service. Again there are communication devices and incidental services which cluster about the primary communication services and which may not have achieved the full status of public utilities. Examples are radio-broadcasting, stock-ticker, teletype, and television services.

3. *Facilities providing power, light, heat, and refrigeration.* These functions are carried out by artificial and natural gas works, electricity supply works, steam and hot-water heating plants.

4. *Facilities providing water, sanitation, flood protection, irrigation, and drainage.* This grouping is most likely to trench on public functions, ordinarily carried on by governments. Irrigation, flood control, and drainage works, which are facilities regulating water supply, are usually furnished as governmental services, but they can and have been treated as public utilities. Water works supplying water for fire protection, for domestic, commercial, and industrial purposes are truly public utilities. Sewage and garbage disposal plants are of the in-and-out variety, with a present tendency for sewage services to be treated as public utilities.

The difficulty of giving an exhaustive enumeration of public utilities is apparent.[2] This difficulty arises from the fact that the evolution of industry

---

[2] A somewhat more detailed classification is the following:
1. Services of transportation (common carriers)
   (a) Provision of highways, turnpikes, ferries, and bridges
   (b) Vehicular transport over highways by stage-coaches, taxicab companies, motor bus, and trucking companies

is constantly changing the technological foundations, while the evolution of institutional controls is also raising questions as to the propriety of placing a particular industry in a particular category. Thus the supply of rental housing, the retail distribution of fluid milk, banking, insurance, the petroleum and coal industries, and the meat-packing industry are closely controlled.

Are all these industries public utilities, and must we expand the concept to cover every case in which the government has undertaken to regulate the industry in some fashion? The answer seems to be that the public utility status is a sort of halfway house between strictly governmental functions on the one hand and private functions on the other, with the recognition that there are twilight zones between. As we pass down the scale from functions of the highest social importance we find first certain tax-supported public functions, whose administration is in accordance with the economic principles of collectivism. They subsist in a sphere or zone of compulsion where compulsory exactions by governments, that is, the tax, the fee, and

---

   (c) Provision of artificial waterways, canals, canalized rivers, harbors, and roadsteads
   (d) Water transport by tow-boat, sailing vessel, tramp steamer, and steamship companies having a definite schedule
   (e) Steam railway transport of freight, passengers, mail, and express
   (f) Provision of urban and interurban electric railway transit of passengers, freight, mail, and express
   (g) Provision of transport by airways of passengers, express, mail, and cargo freight
   (h) Pipelines for the transport of oils, gasoline, and natural gas
2. Services incidental to transportation
   (a) Supply of specialized equipment: sleeping, dining, parlor, refrigerator, etc., car service
   (b) Stockyards, warehouses, and elevators
   (c) Docks and terminals, transfer, lighterage, compress and freight forwarding services
3. Services facilitating communication
   (a) Postal service
   (b) Telegraph service with and without wires, including submarine cables
   (c) Local and long-distance telephone service, with and without wires
   (d) Stock-ticker, radio-broadcasting, signaling, and teletype and television services
4. Facilities providing power, light, heat and refrigeration
   (a) Artificial and natural gas works
   (b) Electricity supply works
   (c) Steam and hot-water heating plants
   (d) Artificial ice plants
5. Facilities regulating water supply and providing water and sanitation in urban communities
   (a) Sewage and garbage disposal plants
   (b) Water works supplying water for fire protection, domestic, commercial, and industrial purposes
   (c) Irrigation, flood control, and drainage works

the special assessment, record the declining magnitude of their social importance. A tax levied for general governmental purposes is premised on the general benefit to the taxpayer. An automobile registration fee and a special assessment levied by a drainage district record and measure the special benefit to the payer, though limited strictly to the cost of the service. Continuing down the scale of declining social importance, we enter the domain of price economics. It is in the borderland or twilight zones where public functions merge into public utilities or public utilities merge into industries which are imperfectly competitive that we meet some of the most perplexing problems of modern capitalism. On the one hand, on the side of government we meet problems of subsidization, and on the other hand, problems of trustified industry where the welfare assumptions underlying a freely competitive society certainly do not obtain. We have supplied this general orientation in Chart I.

	State Functions	No Marketing	Taxes
	Functions in a Twilight Zone	No Marketing	Fees Special Assessments Subsidies
Authorized Transactions	Public Utility Functions	Controlled Monopolistic Markets	Governmental Rate-making
	Functions in a Twilight Zone	Oligopolistic Markets	Administered Pricing
	Free Enterprise Functions	Open Markets	Competitive Pricing
Unauthorized Transactions	Prohibited Functions	Black Markets	Exploitive Pricing

Chart I   Segments of a Capitalistic Economy

Elements of a Capitalistic Economy

The present study bears the title "Public Utilities in American Capitalism." Something should, therefore, be said in a preliminary way as to the meaning of capitalism in this connection. Certainly the term *capitalism* is not being used in the way in which Karl Marx, who first coined the word, used it in his interpretation of the class struggle. We cannot do better than to quote briefly from a recent work by the late Professor John R. Commons, one of the pioneers in the study of the capitalistic process:

In modern capitalism, the most important stabilized economic relations are those of private property. But property relations are not something fixed and permanent. They are undergoing change all the time within the processes of collective action . . . Capitalism in its highest form, as found in the United States, is built upon this legal foundation of private property, latterly modified by the emergence of joint-stock corporations, holding companies, banks, labor unions and political parties seeking control of the sovereign power of the state . . . The main characteristic of this twentieth century economics and the reason why it can be distinguished as banker capitalism are the large amounts of savings of millions of investors that must be brought together in order to finance these huge aggregations of machinery, and armies of employees, made possible by science, invention and world wide markets.[3]

We may now place beside this view of capitalism the meaning of economy which is most current in the textbooks of the day. According to these formulations, economics concerns itself with the way in which scarce resources are allocated in human society. Pivotal in any such consideration of the administration of scarce resources is the formula of supply and demand; in other words, the functioning of markets. Economic activity in a capitalistic environment is thus concerned with transactions which concern themselves with scarce natural resources. These resources are manipulated by means of a technique of production to produce goods and services for purposes of consumption or exchange.

Capitalism is the legal ordering of this process by means of working rules which give primacy to the wants of individuals in households and of concerns in business. But it also recognizes working rules that minister to the collective wants of organized society which supply social services according to canons of public welfare. The carriers of these activities are social units—from the biological individual to the most complex creations of the social process—who are animated by what they regard as their future interests. Continuity and faith in the future is provided by the operation of working rules—guided by custom and sovereignty—which keep these individual or collective concerns going. Public utility functions are transcendently important in keeping the national economy going, as its history attests.

[3] Commons, J. R., *The Economics of Collective Action* (New York: The Macmillan Co., 1950), pp. 21, 67.

Something ought to be said in this connection with regard to the control exercised by government over all the elements of a national economy in time of emergency. When the free flow of consumer goods is interrupted, for instance, by a state of war, governments in all countries have converted themselves into an agency not unlike a giant public utility. The all-pervading scarcity of the means of livelihood and the imperious need of channeling productive resources into the manufacture of munitions make necessary a degree of interference with the system of free enterprise which enormously expands the area of collectivism. Under these circumstances the interventionist state will set up an emergency framework of wartime controls which extends price regulation into every important nook and cranny of the industrial system.

2. THE PROMOTIONAL EPOCH IN THE EVOLUTION OF PUBLIC UTILITIES

In order to gain perspective, it is sometimes convenient to attempt a historical interpretation of the detailed facts of technological, economic, and institutional changes in a particular country. This is peculiarly useful in the study of public utility economics in this country because, by virtue of the constitutional and common law foundations, these diverse industries have been held to a somewhat uniform course of development. This interpretation will be made in terms of the principal epochs through which the development has passed.

Historical Interpretation

We distinguish, for this purpose, four main epochs, the limits of which, with material overlapping, may be briefly characterized and chronicled as follows: (1) a promotional period extending from Colonial times to past the middle of the nineteenth century; (2) an essentially competitive period extending from about 1850 to the end of the century; (3) an essentially monopolistic period beginning gradually in the 1880's and extending to the beginning of the great depression in 1929; and (4) a period of national coordination and planning, with public ownership and public regulation jointly effective in achieving certain public ends, among which conservation of natural resources plays a leading role. We may briefly state some reasons for this delineation.

Until the Civil War the country was in a pioneering stage of development. While the frontier did not actually disappear until after the Civil War, the dominant note was that of the frontier in its westward movement. During this initial period, public utilities were primarily conceived as means for opening up and conquering a continent of unparalleled resources. Since capital was scarce, public utility investments, like all other investments, had to be induced by the hope of large financial rewards, while the regulatory and restrictive aspects of public policy were kept in the background. The methods of regulation were of three kinds: (1) regulation by means of the judiciary, using common law principles as derived from England and working them over to suit an American pioneer setting; (2) regulation by means of charters granted by special legislative acts which emphasized the privileges expressly conferred rather than the limitations tacitly implied; and (3) regulation by means of such sporadic legislation as the development of the industries most urgently required.

In this period falls the establishment of turnpikes, canals, and railways, and the competitive struggle between them. As communication utilities, the post office and telegraph were ready to offer their services. Only a few cities were large enough to boast of a central water supply, central gas supply, and omnibus or horse-car transit services. It was a period when ferries were still common and bridges were displacing them over only the most frequently used lines of travel. It was in most respects a period of beginnings in the establishment of facilities, in the exploration of their techniques, in understanding the economic principles of operation, and in adapting to them an inherited system of social control. Out of this period come certain leading constitutional cases, such as the Dartmouth College case and the Charles River Bridge Company case, which have given us a legacy of constitutional doctrine with which a growing appreciation of the importance of public interests has had to struggle ever since.

In the next period the extensive margin of natural resource utilization gives way to the intensive margin. In a technological sense the promotional impetus continues. Aside from continuous improvement in railroad and other transport, this period gave us the telephone, the ocean cable, the steam-electric and hydroelectric power plant, the cable and electric railway, and the beginnings of motor vehicle transport. Yet the significant fact is that the country had grown to such an extent in population, wealth, and urbanization that markets were available to support not only new establishments but also competitors of those establishments. It was a period when legislators, scourged by irate consumers who had gathered in Granger movements and antimonopoly revolts, were passing general incorporation laws to make easy the enfranchisement of all would-be competitors. It was a period when a policy of granting exclusive or monopolistic franchises was giving way to nonexclusive and competitive grants, when there was danger that even the courts would follow public opinion by throwing aside the inherited distinction between public utility industry and ordinary private competitive industry, treating them all alike, as was threatened in the famous case of *Olcott v. the Supervisors.*

After the competitive urge had done its worst by generating in turn all the evils of cutthroat competition, such as discrimination and rebating and the corruption of legislative bodies, there was a rebirth of regulation, the first phase of which was in terms of the Granger and Populist laws designed to control public utilities by means of revitalized direct legislation or by means of a new agent, the administrative commission, of which the Interstate Commerce Commission was the prime example. This was an agency designed to control monopoly, but actually it did more to control competition. Gradually, however, the truth filtered through that perhaps public utility industries were naturally monopolistic, that rather than enforce competition and seek to control its excrescences, it would be better to recognize the monopolistic character of these industries and regulate them accordingly. This was accomplished by the political movement variously named the progressive movement or insurgent movement. This meant a complete overhauling of the inherited regulatory structure, which was largely accomplished under the political leadership of men like President Theodore Roosevelt, Governor Hughes of New York, Senators La Follette of Wisconsin, Pingree of Michigan, Johnson of California, etc.

Finally, we come to the fourth period beginning with the Great Depression. World War I, with its high prices, had severely strained and tested the regulatory mechanism. Of almost equal importance was the decade of false prosperity of the 1920's. The accumulated pressures of three decades of experimentation with the regulation of private industry had raised such questions as whether the public regulation of private monopoly could be made effective, and whether certain emerging interests of conservation of natural resources did not require a more active public participation than regulation alone afforded. Sharpened by the depression, these questions have presented themselves for answers with increasing insistence. We are in the midst of providing these answers.

The Promotional Period

In this period, extending from Colonial times until 1860, the American economy acquired practically all its present territorial base. Excepting only the later purchase of Alaska, comprising 586,400 square miles, the original territory of approximately 900,000 square miles in 1783 was expanded into a land area of 2,973,965 square miles by the Louisiana Purchase of 1803, the Florida Purchase of 1819, the treaty of 1842 settling the occupation of the Oregon Territory, the Texas Annexation of 1845, the Mexican Session of

1848, and the Gadsden Purchase of 1853. Into this territory poured waves of settlers who followed the explorer, trapper, and fur trader in reducing to possession an inland empire. As fast as this public domain could be released from Indian control through tribal cessions and surveyed, the surplus population of the eastern seaboard and the increasing tide of north European immigrants, who were lovers of the soil, were induced to take up lands affording them new soil under a strikingly liberal land policy. At prices varying between $1.00 and $2.00 per acre and in amounts to suit the purse of all purchasers, great quantities of the public domain passed into private ownership. It was a period of land speculation, promotion of land colonization companies, and migration which moved the frontier of settlement ever westward, against a retreating line of Indian barriers.

Before we summarize the economic influences exerted by public utilities during this period upon the development of the expanding economy of the United States, we must take note of the romantic facts of population growth as revealed by the decennial census. In 1790 this enumeration revealed 3,929,214 persons living in a coastal strip of land area equaling 867,980 square miles, with an average population density of 4.5 per square mile. From this benchmark the population of the United States grew in ten-year intervals by percentages never less than 33 per cent to a total of 31,443,321 by 1860. For the expanded land area this meant an increase of 27,415,107, or 700 per cent. In view of the concomitant increase in land area of 2,105,-985 square miles, or 243 per cent, the average population density increased to only 10.6 persons per square mile. Thus, up to the Civil War this country was still preponderantly a little-inhabited wilderness.

Transportation Utilities

Of foremost importance in settling this territory have been our transport facilities. Colonial settlement followed the seacoast and navigable water courses. After the Revolution, German and Scotch-Irish pioneers, who made their way over the Allegheny Mountain barrier into the river valleys of the Mississippi watershed, likewise followed the water courses.

Water transport. Colonial authorities had constructed few roads and these only of local importance. Overland travel had to be on foot or horseback following Indian trails or "traces" blazed by the pioneers. Settlement and population growth in the new territory, therefore, had to follow in the wake of long-distance water transport—new media which made their appearance in overlapping stages.

In the stage of river transport, canoes, keelboats and flatboats were of most importance, the latter having the greater carrying capacity but incapable of making the return journey. Transport was slow, dangerous, and costly. Commodities shipped downstream, taking New Orleans traffic as an example, consisted of grain, flour, whiskey, pork, bacon, and cheese. Upstream there were carried coffee, sugar, molasses, and manufactured goods from the East. Thousands of flatboats continued to descend the Ohio and Mississippi Rivers even after the steamboat had put in its appearance.

Robert Fulton's successful run of the Clermont up the Hudson River from New York to Albany in 1807 introduced the steamboat to internal navigation. In 1809 it appeared on the Ohio River and in 1816 on the Great Lakes. In the period under consideration the steamboat took over the main burden of carriage after 1820 and continued to be the backbone of transport on the Mississippi system until the Civil War, which stopped all traffic to the South. Under the influence of its steamboat traffic, New Orleans in the 1840's was outranked as a port only by London, Liverpool, and New York. On the Great Lakes steamboating rose to importance by 1850 and continued its development to the present time, while on the rivers it began to fall prey to the competition of the railroads, who diverted traffic in the 1850's and finally overpowered the post-Civil War revival of steamboating by 1880. Rates charged by these agencies of river transport were sometimes monopoly charges or fixed by competition, depending on conditions, but generally speaking, their trend was downward.

The difficulties of river transport early suggested canals as a way out. The canal stage began in the 1780's, reached its peak after the completion of the Erie Canal in 1825, came to a halt with the crisis of 1837, but then continued on a smaller scale to the Civil War. First came short canals around waterfalls and rapids in streams, then longer canals connecting the longer watercourses or the anthracite coal fields with tidewater. Canals as main arteries of traffic date from the Erie Canal, constructed by New York from 1817 to 1825 at a cost of $7 million. With its connecting canals and watercourses, it provided a new waterway to the interior; through lower costs, it diverted traffic from the Mississippi–New Orleans route to its own terminal, New York City.

Commercial rivalry between New York and the other Atlantic seaboard cities (especially Boston, Philadelphia, and Baltimore) for this trade with the Middle West soon set up a series of parallel efforts to attract traffic by these competing centers. The immediate financial success of the Erie Canal induced a program of public spending by emulating states which had much to do with the financial crisis of 1837. Pennsylvania set up a system of railroads and canals known later as the Pennsylvania Public Works, with the canal mileage of 278 exceeding the railroad mileage of 117. The railroad links extended from Philadelphia to Columbia, with a portage railway over the mountains from Hollidaysburg to Johnstown. The system was completed in 1834 at a cost of $10 million. However, it never could compete successfully with the more favorably situated Erie Canal, and although of considerable local benefit, it failed of its real purpose and was finally sold to the Pennsylvania Railway.

Other canals were the Chesapeake and Ohio, canals built by Ohio, Indiana, and Illinois to connect the Ohio River or other rivers in the Mississippi basin with Lake Erie or Lake Michigan. Canals, combined with other internal improvements like highways and railroads during the boom era between 1820 and 1840, piled up an indebtedness of $200 million. Most of these debts were never paid, the states defaulting in part or repudiating them entirely. Even after the railway appeared, canal construction continued. However, in 1880 the closing of the canal era was signalized by a report of the Census showing that of the 4,468 miles of canal constructed, 2,000 miles had been abandoned and many of the remainder were not paying expenses. Only as modernized barge canals and ship canals do artificial waterways still have a continuing function to perform.

Domestic water transport was not restricted to canals or watercourses. An exceedingly important avenue of penetration during the period was the Great Lakes. Of glacial origin, this natural waterway had been improved by canals and locks, built to get around Niagara Falls in 1829 and the Rapids of the St. Mary's River (the "Soo") in 1850. The entire distance of 1,340 miles was navigable, however, only for small boats. The development of the steamboat, along with the sailing vessel over parts of the route, provided transport for bulk cargoes; first of grain, lumber, and copper, and later of iron ore and coal. There were also common carriers of passengers and general cargo freight.

Another growing branch of domestic water transport was "deep sea" navigation, both coastwise and intercoastal around the Horn. Since 1817 this traffic had been reserved to vessels flying the United States flag and had increased significantly with the growth of industry and commerce, and especially with the California Gold Rush.

International shipping, owing to the doctrine of "freedom of the seas," was in the hands of both foreigners and nationals and was highly competitive. Foreign-built ships were denied American registry. To promote shipbuilding and shipping by Americans, imports in U.S. flag vessels were early (1792) favored by a 10 per cent discrimination in the tariff. This concession was finally cancelled in 1858 because the American merchant marine had meanwhile entered the period of its preeminence in the design and operation of the famous clipper ship. The "clipper era" did not begin to decline until after the Civil War. A more direct means of fostering faster steam navigation was adopted with the introduction of systems of mail subsidies between 1845 and 1858. This type of promotion is best exemplified by the American Collins Line, which set out to compete with the British Cunard Line and achieved some measure of success until the subsidies were repealed. As a further aid to navigation, a Lighthouse Service and the Coast and Geodetic Survey were inaugurated. And finally, as a result of shipping disasters, federal safety regulation was begun which ultimately held American shipping to higher standards of performance.

Land transport.   We may now turn to a brief view of the development of land transport. There has never been a period when the need for improved means of transportation has not been pressing. With respect to overland transport, this need seems to have been felt first in New England. Here its evolution can be traced from Indian trails to widened bridle paths which ended in the unimproved wagon road, deep with dust in summer and heavy with mud in the autumn and spring. Although in Massachusetts the General Court had ordered each town to construct a highway to connect with that of the adjoining town, they were, nevertheless, constructed without system. Moreover, they were dirt roads without proper drainage. Bridges were few, and fords and ferries were common. Under such conditions ton-mile costs sometimes ranged as high as 35 cents and not much below the cost of transport by packhorse, the use of which had restricted traffic to only the most valuable and essential freight. In the Middle Atlantic colonies, conditions were about the same. Organized common carrier transport was therefore slow to arise. The first stage line between New York and Philadelphia was not established until 1756; that between New York and Boston in 1788. Even the construction of wagon roads was opposed by the packhorse operators, whose business they threatened. Violent altercations between common carrier wagoners and coachmen and the packhorse operators were not uncommon.

With the formation of the Union the political necessity of maintaining interstate communication was added to commercial and social requirements. This created an opportunity for private companies to build improved roads such as were being constructed in England. They were called *turnpikes* from the toll gate which turned on a pike. The turnpike period extended roughly from the Revolution to about 1830. The first important one was the Philadelphia and Lancaster Turnpike, finished in 1794. It was a complete financial success. This led to a turnpike movement in the course of which hundreds of turnpike companies were chartered by the states, who frequently purchased some of the stock or gave construction subsidies. Though some of the turnpikes were profitable, most of them yielded a meagre return or none at all, especially after the competing canals and railways or free state highways took away the long-distance traffic. In the course of time most of them reverted to the public.

The most important turnpike, the Cumberland Road, was constructed by the federal government between 1806 and 1838 and was intended to give Washington and Baltimore connection with the West. By 1818 it extended from Cumberland, Maryland, to Wheeling on the Ohio River, but though originally planned to reach Jefferson City, Missouri, it was terminated at Vandalia, Illinois, because the railroad was proving to be the better carrier. During Jackson's administration the road was handed over to the states. In this connection, mention should also be made of the Conestoga Wagons, much used by carriers on the turnpikes at the time, and of the inns and taverns supplying an ancillary travel service to such transportation.

The turnpike usually was a macadamized road, rather costly to construct. In the 1840's and 1850's and even later, another type of improved highway was tried, the plank road, constructed where timber was plentiful and cheap. It was a toll road, usually privately constructed and maintained. Besides halving the investment required for macadam, plank roads doubled or trebled the load to be hauled, as compared with ordinary dirt roads. They also were proof against the inclemencies of the weather. On the other hand, they did not last so long and their maintenance cost was high. In the end they, too, succumbed to the superior economy of the railway, although they continued in some cases to serve as feeders.

The final achievement of the period under review was the development of the railway into an independent carrier of persons and property. Railways, using animal power, had long been in use in England and elsewhere in coal mines. The lower resistance offered by the smooth rail, as contrasted with even the best highway, made possible the hauling of increased loads. Railways, or rather tramways, were constructed in this country, of which the 4-mile long Quincy Railroad of 1826 was the most famous because it hauled the granite used in constructing the Bunker Hill Monument to the waterside.

The first real common carrier railway, the Baltimore and Ohio Railroad, was chartered by the state of Maryland in 1827 and began operation in 1830, only five years later than the world's pioneer railway venture, the Stockton and Darlington in England. Using Peter Cooper's steam locomotive, the Tom Thumb, this railway started out first on its march to Wheeling on the Ohio River, which it reached in 1852. In South Carolina, the Charleston and Hamburg was started about the same time. Others were built in New York, Pennsylvania, and the New England states. The panic of 1837 scarcely affected the progress of railway construction. In fact, railways did not begin to compete with canals until the 1840's and did not completely master the situation until the decade ending in 1860. Railways had the advantage of not being tied to the previously existing routes of trade; whereas canals, besides being more dependent upon climatic conditions, were tied to river and lake routes. In supplying the demand for more and closer connections between the East and the West, canals were made still more ineffective because streams flowed prevailingly north and south. The railways diverted traffic into new channels running east and west. Moreover, they could carry both passengers and freight cheaply, safely, and expeditiously. Although much of the construction was experimental, crude, and disconnected, it soon became clear that the future in transportation belonged to the railroads.

Many of the early railways were supplementary to waterways. It was also assumed that they would be conducted as toll roads with shippers or common carriers free to haul their own vehicles over the tracks upon payment of tolls. But the adoption of steam as motive power, plus the difficulties of using specialized equipment and of meeting and passing on single lines of track, soon brought the realization that the toll principle of operation was ineffective and that monopoly of use was the superior principle. *Competition would have to be between lines.*

In the 1840's and 1850's additional all-rail routes were constructed in the East and the Mississippi Valley. The New York Central System connected New York City with Buffalo as a competitor of the Erie Canal route. The Erie Railroad made the same connection, using a route along the southern boundary of the state. "Through" rail routes were established between Boston and Albany and Boston and New York. The Illinois Central and the Mobile and Ohio provided all-rail connections with the Gulf, and the Hannibal and St. Joseph provided rail connections between the Mississippi and Missouri Rivers. Similar rail connections were provided between the lake ports of Chicago and Milwaukee and points of transshipment on the Mississippi River. As a result of this early expansion the railway network grew slowly from the 23 miles of 1830 to 9,021 miles in 1850. In the decade after its emancipation, 21,614 miles of road were added for a combined total of 30,635 miles by 1860.

The failure of state enterprises. One important result arising out of this period should be noted in passing. The investment by states [1] in internal improvements increased tremendously after 1820, growing from $12,790,-728 to $170,356,187 in 1838. Of this total, $6,618,868 was spent for roads, $60,201,551 for canals, $42,421,084 for railroads, $52,640,000 for banks, and the balance of $8,474,684 for miscellaneous purposes.[2] These sums were borrowed in part from domestic sources but in larger part from foreign capitalists. Soon, however, it began to appear that many of these enterprises were premature if not entirely unnecessary. They were often extravagantly and corruptly managed. The panic of 1837 ended the speculative mania and soon the debts began to press upon the debtors. At this juncture several of the states repudiated their indebtedness, though later paying in whole or in part. Meanwhile, however, the works were sold and the states withdrew from the field. All state-owned and operated railways, except those owned by Virginia and Georgia, were sold by 1857. State constitutions adopted after 1840 showed the changed attitude by prohibiting the use of state funds or the loan of its credit for internal improvements. The work of supplying all such facilities in the future was to be left to private initiative aided by grants from public sources. This represents in large part the historical explanation for the preeminence of the private corporation in the supply of public utilities in the United States.

Communication Utilities

The most important utility in the field of communications was the post office conducted by the federal government under a specific constitutional authorization. It used whatever transport facilities were at hand and was able to extend a regular though not too frequent mail service to all parts of the United States. The earliest media of transportation of the mails were the stage coach and the sailing vessel. Since speed is the essence of service of this kind, railways and steamships were quickly pressed into service. Railway contracts for the carriage of mail date back to 1834. By such means

---

[1] No estimate is available of the amount expended by local units. The amount of county and municipal bonds outstanding in 1870 was estimated at $185 million. The total amount issued will probably never be known.

[2] Bogart, E. L., *Economic History of the United States* (New York: Longmans, Green & Co., 1912), p. 214.

the development of the postal service, although strongly impregnated with political considerations from the beginning, was very rapid, with over 186,000 miles of post roads in operation before the Civil War. The romantic stories of the western stage lines and of the transcontinental stages, including the fabled pony express, testify to the difficulties, the importance, and the primitive nature of the services being rendered by these pioneer facilities. In a significant way, the post office in cooperation with transport facilities aided in breaking up the isolation of frontier life.

The promotional period also witnessed the first development of the telegraph industry, the oldest of the telecommunication industries. New public utilities centering in cities were destined to develop out of the industrial applications of a new form of energy—electric power. The electric telegraph and cable were its first offsprings. It was over a hundred years ago that Samuel F. B. Morse perfected this instrument sufficiently so that the United States Government could inaugurate commercial service between Washington and Baltimore, with the first public message being transmitted in 1844. Placed under the control of the Postmaster General, it seemed at first as if the postal and telegraph services would be developed together and under public initiative. However, the line did not prove self-supporting, and in 1847 it was sold to private interests. Before the close of the period under review, a multiplicity of companies was organized and licensed, most of them under the Morse patents. Among the others a printing telegraph using Roman letters instead of dots and dashes put in its appearance before 1850. Acquired by Ezra Cornell and others, this device became the basis for the activity of the Western Union Telegraph Company, organized in 1856. By constructing new lines and acquiring competitors, this company early in the next period became the dominant element in the telegraph field, with a line to California already completed in 1861. All told, about 50,000 miles of telegraph lines connecting all important cities had been built before the Civil War.

A beginning was also made in extending telegraph service into the field of international communication by the introduction of the first trans-Atlantic cable, which was operating experimentally for a few days during 1858.

Urbanization and Municipal Utilities

So far we have surveyed the development of utilities whose services were of a state-wide or interstate nature. Facilities of transport and communication have been for long periods the principal limiting factors in the development of a nation-wide market. They were of interest to all the people of the country. We come now to a class of utilities, sometimes called municipal or local utilities, which are of primary interest to the residents of populated places because it is here that they find their first natural markets. While the characteristics of expansion of markets and localization of industry tend to develop together, such regional specialization in industry is possible only if reliable systems of transportation and communication are available. Hardly less important has been the provision of reliable and adequate systems of power production, for localized industry has meant, ultimately, the concentration of industry into large units. Large scale and localized industry has stimulated population growth and its increasing urbanization.

The promotional or pioneering epoch did not yet afford that degree of concentration of population in cities which was necessary for a flourishing of these municipal utilities. The eighteenth and early nineteenth century village was to all intents and purposes still a self-sufficing community, made up predominantly of self-sufficing households. As the village grew into a town and the town into a city, it ceased to be merely a supply station for the farming population and became, instead, a manufacturing center. While some strategically located cities had always been important trade centers, it was the industrial impetus that dotted the land with cities.

The Census shows that the urbanization of population was not very rapid during the period under review. Using the Census standard, which classifies localities having a population of 2,500 inhabitants or more as urban areas, only 24 places with a population of 201,655 could be so classified in 1790. By 1860 their number had increased to 392, with a population totaling 6,216,518. If we take 25,000 as a convenient dividing line for cities urgently requiring municipal utilities, there were only two such cities in 1790, and their number had grown to only 35 in the 70 years intervening to 1860. Whereas in 1790, 5 in 100 persons were living under urban conditions, their number had increased to only 20 in 100 by 1860. At the latter date only nine cities had grown to real metropolitan proportions.

Local Transportation

In the smaller cities the travel between the home and the workshop, store, or place of amusement was within convenient walking distance. Horses and privately owned vehicles served the needs of the rich, halt, or fastidious.

In only a few of the larger cities was there any need for public transportation for hire, which began with the horse-drawn cabby offering a personalized service to occasional patrons. As cities grew in size, the horse-drawn omnibus line appeared in the 1820's with fleets of vehicles offering regular service over definite routes and operating on a more or less fixed schedule. In those days pavements were rough, and there was a widespread demand for smoother riding. Likewise, operators wanted to handle bigger loads. This led to experiments with tracks of various types of construction. The experiments extended over a long period, and the idea met with much opposition from those who thought that the presence of tracks in public thoroughfares would create a danger to other traffic. The experiments terminated in the street railway, using animals as motive power, with New York City boasting the first one of commercial importance on Fourth Avenue in 1831. It used the so-called John Mason cars. There and elsewhere improvements in the track and vehicles gained increased popularity for the street railway in all our larger cities before the Civil War, although service was still sadly lacking in speed, comfort, heating, and lighting. A beginning had, however, been made in local transit as an agency of mass transport.

Water Utilities

A new development in central water-supply systems was introduced by the municipality of London after the great fire. The first American waterworks plant was established in Boston in 1654 and was used for both fire protection and domestic supply. This early centralized public system, drawing its supply from springs, appears to have become inadequate; for in 1796, when Boston attained a population in excess of 20,000, an "Aqueduct Corporation" organized a private system which drew its water from Jamaica Pond, 5 miles distant. This development illustrates the older of the two types of water-supply systems that have become general. One captures a supply of surface water and impounds it in natural or artificial basins, whence it is conveyed by gravity through aqueducts and mains to customers. A second type secures its supply from underground sources (springs and wells) by means of pumps or from some low-level body of water (lakes and rivers) and forces the water into the mains by pump-maintained pressure. The second water-supply system in the United States at Bethlehem, Pennsylvania, as reconstructed by J. C. Christensen in 1762, appears to have been of the second type.[3]

[3] "The machinery consisted of three single-acting force pumps, of four-inch calibre and eighteen-inch stroke and worked by a triple crank and geared to the shaft of an

Early projects were both municipal and private enterprises. The earliest water-supply system for New York, begun in 1774, was a municipal enterprise; but it was never completed. In 1799, after the Revolution, a private corporation in which the city was interested through stock ownership built a system which, by 1823, had grown to 25 miles of main with 2,000 taps. About 1830 the city built its own works for fire protection purposes. Soon this developed into the Croton River System. The first successful municipal enterprise was begun by Philadelphia in 1798 when the city had a population of 80,000. This system secured its water from the Schuylkill River, using for the first time big steam pumps for pumping and cast-iron water mains for distribution. Other early water works were those of Worcester, Mass., and Portsmouth, N.H., completed in 1798, and of Albany, N.Y., in 1799. The need for a central water supply was recognized by different cities at different stages in their development. New Orleans, founded in 1718, had none until 1836; Buffalo, founded in 1801, had none until 1852; Cleveland, founded in 1810, had none until 1853; San Francisco, settled in 1776, had none until 1857. Chicago, on the other hand, incorporated in 1837, already had service in 1840.

The trend toward public ownership. Statistical data relating to this industry are scarce, incomplete, and not coordinated. Some information as to the development of this utility up to the Civil War may be gleaned from the following table:

Table I　Number of Water Works in the United States at End of Decade *

Year	Number Public Works	Number Private Works	Total	Per Cent Public
1800	1	15	16	6.3
1810	5	21	26	19.2
1820	5	25	30	16.6
1830	9	35	44	20.5
1840	23	41	64	35.9
1850	33	50	83	39.7
1860	57	79	136	41.9

* *Manual of American Water Works,* 1897.

undershot water wheel, eighteen feet in diameter, and two feet clear in the buckets. The water was raised by this machinery to the height of 70 ft., and subsequently to 114 ft. The works were in operation as late as 1832. The first rising main was made of gum-wood, as far as it was subject to great pressure, and the rest was of pitch-pine. In 1789 leaded pipes were substituted, and in 1813 they were changed for iron." *Engineering News,* October, 1875.

As shown by the table, however, a tendency toward public ownership and operation set in very early, dictated by economic necessity, by the need for fire protection, and by sanitary and hygienic considerations. Works for impounding a water supply, together with aqueduct systems, required heavy capital investments and large use of the power of eminent domain, expenditures which private enterprise often was unable or unwilling to risk.

Irrigation

Irrigation, sometimes spoken of as the wedding of the sunshine and the rain, is an ancient art which was practiced by the original inhabitants on the American continents long before the so-called discovery by Columbus. The remains of extensive irrigation works within the present confines of the United States can be seen in New Mexico and Arizona. In the eighteenth century the Spanish padres built irrigation canals in connection with their missions in California and along the Rio Grande River. However, their efforts, as well as those of other early settlers, were on a small scale. The first real irrigation developments of a community size were undertaken by the Mormons beginning in 1847 in the Great Salt Lake valley. From there they spread to other points in the arid portions of the United States west of the 100th meridian where the annual rainfall of less than 20 inches is inadequate to support crops. Mormon experiments with irrigated agriculture are important because here were first worked out the principles of cooperative action and of the law of prior appropriation as applied to water rights. By 1865 they had dug 277 canals, 1,044 miles in length, at a cost of $1,800,000, and were irrigating 154,000 acres of land. These Mormon agricultural settlements served as a way station for the replenishment of food supplies to the weary overland immigrants who trekked across the desert, particularly after the California gold discoveries of 1849. A beginning had thus been made in the development of this utility of conservation which dates back to the dawn of civilization.

The Development of Manufactured Gas Supply

If there is any virtue in the Darwinian formula, as applied to economic undertakings, that the struggle for existence is a pragmatic test of the right of an industry for survival, then surely the gas industry has proven itself. First came a period of experimentation. This began in 1609 when John

Baptist Van Helmont [4] discovered that fuels by combustion and fermentation give off a substance to which he gave the colorful name of "Geist," meaning spirit. It ended in 1812 when Frederick Windsor promoted the first commercial gas undertaking by securing from Parliament a charter for the London and Westminster Gas, Light & Coke Company. The first use of gas, in this instance coal gas, for illuminating purposes is credited to William Murdock, who began his experiments in England in 1792. In 1797 he lighted his home and later a factory in which he was interested. In 1813 Westminster Bridge was gas lighted.

"Inflammable gas" was then fighting for its right to survive even as a commodity which might be useful to man. Historically speaking, the gas industry should be crowned king in the utility group because it was the first to break the shell of the custom-controlled past. Lamps, lanterns, and candles had served civilization from time immemorial. The idea of securing better illumination, therefore, required a long period of incubation. It began as a private improvement and fought its way to the front, attaining the full status of a public utility some time during the middle of the nineteenth century.

A second period extending roughly from 1812 to 1850 may be characterized as one of early commercial undertakings. In this period falls the organization and upbuilding of the pioneer companies in this country as in Europe, which added gas as a feature of their municipal sociology. The first American gas utility was granted its charter in Baltimore in 1816. Boston followed the example in 1822, New York in 1823, Brooklyn in 1825, New Orleans in 1835, Philadelphia and Pittsburgh in 1836, Louisville in 1838, Cincinnati in 1841, and Albany in 1845.

At first, gas lighting was hardly more than a luxury or, at most, an expensive convenience. The industry had to "sell" its services to the consuming public and to establish its reputation for profitableness with investors. It had to experiment with production, transmission, and utilization problems in order to make service adequate, safe, and continuous. In spite of all efforts, the cost remained high and hence also the rates. As an illuminant, its use continued to be restricted to streets, public buildings, some shops and industrial establishments, and a few houses of the well-to-do.

The arguments of those opposed to the new illuminant were as fanciful as those which the steam railway industry was to meet a little later. One argument was that extensive artificial illumination was iniquitous because it constituted a worldly interference with the original divine plan that there

[4] Natural gas was first discovered by Thomas Shirley in England in 1659.

be night. Other opposition came from the custodians of public morals who thought that drunkenness and depravity would be increased. Not to be outdone, the medical profession claimed that the emanations of illuminating gas would be injurious to health. The principal obstacle toward an extension of the service, however, was the high rates, ranging from $6.00 to $15.00 per thousand cubic feet (Mcf).

We have now sketched the genesis and early development of those utilities which provided the basic structure of economic life during the Colonial period and for the first seventy to eighty years of our life as a nation. We must now turn to a review, however brief, of the main elements in the system of social control by means of which these public utilities were regulated in an era dominantly promotional and exploitive in temper.

3. PUBLIC UTILITY
CONTROL IN THE
PROMOTIONAL ERA

Throughout the promotional period the dominant system of *legislative* regulation was by means of the charter or franchise conferred by state governments. However, existing alongside this system, and extending indefinitely into the past, was a system of *judicial* regulation. In fact, it is well to consider that behind the successive adoption of the different agencies and instrumentalities of legislative regulation there is always a background of judicial regulation, which should, however, not be confused with *judicial review* of legislative regulation testing its conformity with constitutional law. Even now, should some legislature abolish the entire complement of legislative regulation, judicial regulation would still be there to step into this legislative vacuum. Discernible stages in the development of regulation are not unlike the geologist's rock strata with their outcroppings and residues. We may distinguish roughly four stages in this institutional evolution: a stage of judicial regulations; a stage of special charter regulation, supplemented by occasional special legislation, with regulation largely the concern of the states alone; a third stage in which federal and local governments have also become active, indicating the growth of problems of regulation arising on the one hand out of interstate commerce and, on the other hand, out of urbanization and the desire of cities for a greater measure of local self-government; a fourth and contemporary stage in which the regulatory jurisdiction is still divided between the three levels of government but in which the active work of regulating has been delegated to administrative agencies.

Judicial Regulation

Judicial regulation implies that courts and their decrees are respectively the agents and instrumentalities of control. We will return to this subject once more in Chapter 12 because it was in the course of the development of judicial regulation by the common law courts that the institutional basis for public utility economics was laid. It is sufficient to point out here that this basis is the "common law" right of customers to reasonable service at reasonable rates. During the promotional epoch, particularly that part of it which extended into the nineteenth century when ideas of laissez faire held undisputed sway, judicial regulation was the chief form of control. The police power lay dormant. The courts alone made a conscious effort to correlate utility regulation with the demands of the complex and dynamic industrial civilization then rapidly growing up.

However, the attempt to apply a policy of "regulation by lawsuit" failed. Judicial methods, certainly those of that period, were designed primarily to remedy past wrongs and visit punishment. It was a piecemeal process whereby individual grievances could be brought to trial. Regulation, in order to be effective, must be preventive and promotive as well as remedial and exemplary. This is a lesson which legislatures have not yet fully learned. Moreover, the machinery of the courts did not move with sufficient expedition and spontaneity. Altogether, the method proved too expensive for the use of the ordinary individual in securing redress for his grievances. After all, these grievances were petty and loomed large only when taken in the aggregate. But the central difficulty was the one referred to above, that judicial remedies were characteristically limited to acts already committed, whereas the situation increasingly required rules which would forestall future difficulties.

Another disadvantage of judicial regulation lay in the fact that the training of the judiciary was not sufficiently specialized and technical to assume the tasks of constructive regulation. The immediate tasks of regulation required rather a long look ahead instead of a long look into the past to conform to precedents. With legislative regulation now largely supplanting judicial regulation, the judges' field of usefulness has accordingly become restricted to that of judicial review of matters of law, leaving the determination of questions of fact and delineation of policy to quasi-legislative agencies.

Legislative Regulation by Charter and Statute

Since transportation utilities were everywhere the pioneers, they were the first to be made the subject of regulatory experiments by legislatures. This early history has shaped the development of regulatory systems for other classes of public utilities. Public utility regulation has also been con-

ditioned by the fact that the corporation soon displaced the single proprietorship and the partnership as the dominant form of legal organization
of the business unit. This accounts for the early adoption of the charter as
a regulatory device.

First of all it should be noted that the words *charter* and *franchise*
may be used interchangeably. We must, however, make these distinctions:
(1) the franchise *to be* which is the *grant of corporate life* from the state
and belongs to the members of the corporation and cannot be parted with
by the legal person, the corporation; (2) the franchise *to do* which is the
grant of corporate power from the state to carry on some business, public
or private in its nature, which belongs to the corporation; and (3) the
franchise *to use* which is the *grant* to a corporation, which already exists
and has authority to engage in a particular business, *of the right to use the
public streets* in carrying on such business. The first two of these elements,
the franchise *to be* and the franchise *to do*, have come to be known as the
general franchise or the *charter*, while the third element, the franchise
to use, is called the *special franchise*. The general and special franchise
were both used in regulating utilities.

The first charters created turnpike and canal companies. Early railway
charters were modeled after these because it was assumed that a railway,
like turnpikes and canals, was a public highway upon which shippers and
travelers would use their own conveyances. The principal feature of these
charters was the right to charge tolls. In later railway charters this became
the right to fix rates. In some cases the power to fix rates was granted to the
board of directors without restrictions. Usually, however, some limitations
were fixed, and these give charter regulation its distinctive character. The
regulatory program is embodied in charter provisions. Out of the great number and variety of such provisions only a few important ones will be mentioned.

In addition to the usual provisions relating to the legal and financial
organization of a company, the charters contained clauses granting the
power of eminent domain, specifying routes, controlling construction and
extensions, and prescribing some of the details of operation. Although most
charters were silent as to their duration of life, there were some whose life
was limited, the usual term being ninety-nine years. In some cases the state
reserved the right to purchase the facilities at a stated valuation. In order
to encourage the building of these facilities, many charters conferred privileges of tax exemption or of tax limitation, either for an indefinite period or
a limited period. But charters also restricted the variety of businesses that
a given corporation might enter as well as the amount of land it might hold.

Three kinds of provisions illustrate the range of expedients which were used in controlling rates. Usually they took the form of a prescribed schedule of maximum rates. Within the limits of these charter maxima, the carriers were free to fix their own charges. A second type provided that rates, fares, or tolls should not yield a net income greater than, let us say, 20 per cent upon the common stock. Any excess would have to be paid, for instance, into an internal improvement fund. A third type, typical of New England, stipulated that at the end of some definite period (often twenty-five years) and of each twenty-year period thereafter, the legislature had the power to prescribe rates if the net income was greater than a specified percentage of the capital of the concern. These restrictions often were such as to allow profits which would be deemed excessive today. Indeed, the charters sometimes went further in assuring promoters that the stipulated returns would be earned by conferring at least a limited monopoly through an exclusive charter.

The weakness of charter regulation.   It seems that maximum rate provisions soon lost their effectiveness because the prescribed rates were in excess of those actually charged by the companies. Under conditions of increasing competition between railways and waterways, and between railways themselves, the initial rates had to be cut. The decreasing unit cost of operation, brought about in part by increased utilization of plant capacity, in part by a decreasing level of prices particularly after the Civil War, and in part by continuous improvement in technique, made it possible for railways to render service at rates lower than those fixed in their charters and still earn substantial returns.

All early forms of charter regulation more or less assumed that the companies would voluntarily fulfill their charter obligations. Consequently, little attention was paid to securing proper *execution* of regulatory provisions except such as could be obtained by suits at law or by means of sporadic boards of railroad commissioners with limited powers. Rate control of the second and third types—ostensibly secured by reserving to the legislature the power to revise schedules when net income exceeded, for instance, 10 per cent on the investment or when dividends exceeded 20 per cent upon the stock—was avoided by padding investment accounts or by new issues of capital stock. The failure to provide adequately for financial and accounting control thus made these earlier forms of rate control ineffective.

As the first disposition to be liberal abated, the controls became stricter. In particular did legislatures grow cautious about granting exclusive franchises, the more so when the community began to feel that competition should be relied upon to protect the public. And so, whereas earlier charters protected carriers against parallel lines for a limited period of time or for a designated distance, railway charters later prohibited the purchase, lease, or joint operation of parallel or competing lines. However, while the East was emphasizing the restrictive aspects of regulation, the West, still in the promotion stage, continued to grant charters on the theory that inducements must be held out to secure transportation facilities.[1]

Even under charter regulation some supervisory control was exercised by means of special statutes, covering not so much the economic phases involved as those which fell under the police power in its narrower sense, that is to say, regulation in behalf of the public health and safety. Such supplementary regulation was conceived by the courts not to be inconsistent with regulatory provisions embodied in the charter. At this point administrative commissions were first introduced into our regulatory scheme of things.

An enumeration of some of the functions of these early commissions will give an idea as to their character. For instance, the commissions were required to appraise the value of private property when railroads exercised their charter power to take such property under eminent domain. They were required to inspect the roads and help in the enforcement of laws designed to prevent accidents. Upon them also fell the duty of apportioning revenues and expenditures to the state when operations of the railroad extended beyond state lines. This was necessary to determine whether the net income exceeded that authorized under charter provisions. Indicative of the prevalent spirit of parochialism, the commissions were required to investigate the conduct of these enterprises in other states to see that no greater advantage was given to citizens in other states. Such investigations were likewise necessary in order to determine whether the railroad corporations were violating their charters in other respects. In short, we may say that their duties were largely like those of the modern "fact finding" commission, consisting of the collection of statistical and other data relating to the financial affairs and operating methods of the companies, and designed either to serve as a basis for suits at law, or for further specific legislation. Such were the commis-

---

[1] "The legislative history of railways in the various states in the Union is essentially similar, and as we observe the movements of this legislation from east to west we may notice that in turn each state goes through, in the main, all the experiences and stages of advancement of other states which preceded it in railway development. An examination of the contents of these charters, as one observes their march westward, clearly indicates the fact that the restrictions of the earlier types granted in the east are gradually made milder if they are not altogether lost. Occasionally there is a reversion to type—a Western charter embodying all the salient restrictions and regulatory features of the severest Eastern charters." Meyer, B. H., *Railway Legislation in the United States* (New York: The Macmillan Company, 1909), p. 80.

sions established by Rhode Island in 1836, by New Hampshire in 1844, by Connecticut in 1853, by Vermont in 1855, and by Maine in 1858.

Charter Regulation of Local Utilities

In the field of the local utilities, that is to say, water, gas, and urban transit, policies of regulation went through the same evolution. Here the problem of franchise grants came to the forefront during the early part of the nineteenth century when cities had grown in population and area to such an extent that public services became not only essential but also profitable. It was at first customary to provide for such service by special acts of state legislatures. These acts incorporated public service companies and gave them specific rights in the streets of individual cities. Examples of such legislation were an act of the Territorial Legislature of Colorado in 1864, incorporating the Occidental Gas Light Company of the City of Denver and giving it for thirty years "the exclusive privilege of supplying the city of Denver with illuminating gas," and, again, the act of 1867 incorporating The Denver City Horse Railway Company and giving it for "a period of thirty-five years the sole and exclusive right and privilege of constructing and operating a horse railroad in the City of Denver."

In time public opinion began to oppose legislative grants of such rights without giving the city a voice in the choice of the company. The argument was that grants by a state legislature were less intelligent and consistent than those conferred by the cities themselves acting under delegated authority. Even after the authority had been conferred upon cities, conflicting grants were often made by the state and local authorities, owing to confusion regarding their respective powers. Or municipalities granted franchises which were subject to amendment and repeal by the legislature. In those cases the legislature might still make exceptions in favor of particular companies. These complications led to the adoption of constitutional provisions which forbade the granting of franchises and rights in city streets *without the consent* of local authorities. Such constitutional legislation terminated what may be regarded as the first period in the history of franchise regulation of local utilities in the United States.

Judicial Interpretation of Charter Regulation

The lessons of experience growing out of the first phase of charter or franchise regulation may now be summarized. Attention should first be called to the paradox that while the historical view was that corporate charters were special privileges of immense value, a situation was developing in which corporate charters, no longer the subject of special acts but increasingly issued under authority of general incorporation laws, were issued as a matter of common right. The conception of the franchise as a special privilege, conferred by government upon particular individuals or companies for their private profit, is derived from English constitutional history and is intimately associated with the grants of monopolistic privileges made famous by Queen Elizabeth.[2] Public opinion has carried this idea forward to the present time.

The franchise as a contract. In due course the courts were more and more forced to abandon the conception of franchises as monopolistic special privileges. The facts were that the charters were merely a thin disguise for bargains between the government and the franchise holders whereby the public secured service on the best terms possible. This transition came with the Dartmouth College case (1819) when the law was prone to regard all legal relations from the point of view of contract. Although this is not a case involving a public utility, it can nevertheless be placed at the threshold of our development of the public utility institution, the first of a series of landmarks by which the course of its evolution may be traced. In that case the court held that a charter is a contract between the state and the grantee, the obligation of which cannot be impaired by enactments of subsequent legislatures.

In order to establish this interpretation the court had to read the contractual element of *consideration* into the situation. The way in which it solved the difficulty appears from this citation: "The objects for which a corporation is created are universally such as the government wishes to promote. They are deemed beneficial to the country, and this benefit constitutes the consideration and, in most cases, the sole consideration of the grant."[3] Accordingly, the view has prevailed that a franchise granted by the state cannot be resumed, that there is an *implied contract* on the part of the state that it will not invade the domain of the franchise holder and on the part of the grantee that he will perform the specified service. In other

---

[2] Blackstone defines the franchise as follows: "Franchises and liberty are used as synonymous terms, and their definition is a royal privilege, or branch of the king's prerogative, subsisting in the hands of a subject. Being therefore derived from the crown they must arise from the king's grant; . . . . But the same identical franchise that has been granted to one cannot be bestowed upon another, for that would prejudice the former grant." *Blackstone's Commentaries*, Bk. 2 (Oxford: Clarenden Press, 1766), p. 37.

[3] *Dartmouth College v. Woodward*, 4 Wheaton, 518, 637 (1819).

words, a franchise is not granted as an honorarium but for a purpose supposed at least to be beneficial to the public.

The vice of the situation was that charters, which were loosely drawn
and freely granted with no adequate assertion of, or protection for public
rights to reasonable service at reasonable rates, came to be regarded as contracts the obligation of which would be strictly enforced. Attempts, therefore, to amend charters, and especially to change the faulty provisions relating to rates and service, were declared unconstitutional and void by the
courts because they came within the prohibition of the federal constitution
that "no state shall pass any law impairing the obligation of contracts." The
doctrine of the Dartmouth College case is firmly established and has been
extended to all types of corporate charters, to special as well as general
franchises. It has also been effective in securing to corporations the continuous enjoyment of such special privileges as exemption from taxation, rate
regulation,[4] or competition.[5]

The harmful effect of this doctrine was only gradually revealed. In
order to prevent the bartering away by contract of such important powers
as the powers of taxation and regulation, the courts set up the doctrine that
the terms of any contract conveying special privileges granted by the state
must be strictly construed, i.e., the abandonment of legislative power must
be expressly stated and cannot be implied. Any doubt or ambiguity was
resolved in favor of the state. Thus, in the famous case of *Charles River
Bridge v. Warren Bridge*,[6] the court held that an express grant of power to
build a toll bridge did not also imply that the state might not subsequently
charter a competing bridge. Similarly, it was held that the grant of special
privileges is to the grantee alone and may not be transferred unless expressly
permitted.

Effect upon Future Policies

As a result of the general laxity of the regulatory system that accompanied the promotional era, a reform movement set in which sought to
tighten up the system of public utility control. One group of reformers led
antimonopoly revolts and sought relief by means of the processes of competition. Another group put its faith in a mobilization of the police and inter-

[4] *Los Angeles v. Los Angeles Water Co.*, 177 U.S. 558 (1900); *Detroit v. Detroit Street Railway Co.*, 184 U.S. 368 (1902).
[5] *The Binghamton Bridge*, 3 Wall. 51 (1865); *New Orleans Gas Co. v. Louisiana Light Co.*, 115 U.S. 650 (1885); *New Orleans Waterworks Co. v. Rivers*, 115 U.S. 674 (1885).
[6] 11 Peters 420 (1837). See also *Blair v. Chicago*, 201 U.S. 400 (1906).

state commerce powers. By using the doctrine of strict construction of charters of the Charles River Bridge Company case, they tried to get concessions by way of bargaining when utilities wanted amendments to old charters. New franchises, on the other hand, were granted with the backing of constitutional or statutory provisions reserving the power to alter, amend, or repeal the terms of the new franchises. Moreover, an elected judiciary could be subjected to political pressures and thus made to consent to the enlargement of the police powers in derogation of private contractual rights. And when these alternatives failed, the power of eminent domain was available as a last resort to retire private enterprise and substitute public ownership. These were the issues of public policy which moved to the forefront of practical politics in subsequent periods.

4. THE

COMPETITIVE EPOCH

The banner period in the economic development of the United States begins after the panic of 1857 had run its course. This can again be seen best in the statistics of population increase for which the expanding agricultural, commercial, and industrial economy provided a steadily improving standard of life. Beginning with a population in 1860 of 31,443,321 for continental United States, the Census at the end of the century recorded a population figure of 75,994,575 in a land area, excluding the Alaska purchase, of 2,974,159 square miles. With no substantial accession in territory, the absolute population increase of 44,551,254, or slightly less than 142 per cent, spread itself unevenly throughout an immense area, with a steadily increasing average density from 10.6 to 25.6 persons per square mile. The striking phenomenon, however, was the increasing urbanization, since only 20,607,851 of the increase were living under rural conditions while 23,943,403 had taken up truly urban residence. For the country as a whole, while the agricultural way of life was still dominant, industrialization was on the way, with 40 per cent of the population classed as urban and 60 per cent as rural. This is best shown, perhaps, by the increased number of places with a population in excess of 2,500, which had grown from 392 to 1,737. Of the 30 million persons living in such places, 17 million were crowded into cities in excess of 50,000, with three cities alone showing 6.5 millions. Problems arising out of congestion of the population had begun to put in their appearance, with which the public utility industries are principally designed to cope. The period under review was thus the period in which the public utility problem grew to full maturity.

Transportation Utilities

The period from 1840 to the end of the century was, in all essentials, the great competitive period in the development of public utilities. Water routes and railway routes had developed a serious rivalry. The best illustrations were found in the competition between the Reading Railroad and the

Schuylkill Canal in the transport of coal, and between the New York Central and the Erie Canal in the carriage of grain and flour. This competition was, however, the beginning of a new development. At that time railways were still regarded as feeders to lake and river transport or as connecting links between inland waterways. By 1860, however, they attained complete independence. In the decade of the 1850's the railways carried a greater volume of traffic than did the canals. Yet freight traffic was particularly slow in developing. With the Civil War, however, the period of marvelous railway expansion began.

Decline of canal and river traffic. Canal traffic had practically disappeared by the close of the Civil War. Only the Erie Canal was able to maintain itself against railway competition by virtue largely of grain shipments which continued to move by way of the Great Lakes and the Canal. Drastic reductions in competitive railway rates, beginning in 1868, diverted the growing traffic to the railroads, and by 1872 traffic on the Erie Canal was on the decline. However, its competitive influence was prolonged at the expense of taxpayers by the abolition in 1882 of canal tolls.

River traffic followed canal traffic in its steady decline. The Mississippi trade was somewhat longer sustained by reason of the grain export trade through New Orleans. It reached its height in 1879 but when the railroads set out actively to compete with river traffic in the 1880's, the decline set in here also.

Railway expansion. The introduction of the iron rail and its manufacture in this country after 1844, together with the simultaneous introduction of the electric telegraph, did much to help the development of railways. The introduction of wrought-iron rails was followed by the development of the steel rail, first used in 1863, which rapidly displaced the iron rail. Greater speed, safety, and heavier loads were made possible thereby. New England developed her transportation systems in the 1840's, and the western states entered upon an era of rapid development shortly thereafter. This was facilitated by the policy of land grants. Beginning with the grant by Illinois to the Illinois Central Railroad in 1850, Wisconsin, Minnesota, Michigan, Iowa, Missouri, Arkansas, Alabama, Mississippi, Louisiana, and Florida, all in need of improvements, granted both state and federal lands in aid of railroad construction. Up to the outbreak of the Civil War, 31,600,842 acres of public lands had been given in aid of internal improvements.

There remains to be sketched the development of the railway system since 1860. Though retarded by the Civil War, construction in the upper Mississippi valley again became rapid during the years from 1868 to 1872.

Even though interrupted by periods of depression, railway construction proceeded, all too rapidly, in great swings of speculative building, alternately outrunning the growth in population, until at the present time the United States is better supplied with railroad facilities than any other country. The growth in these facilities is shown by Table II:

Table II   Miles of Railroad Constructed in the United States by
Decades, 1830 to 1900 *

Year	Total Miles of Road	Mileage Added During Decade	Per Cent Construction to Total at End of Decade
1830	23	. . . .	. . .
1840	2,818	2,795	99.2
1850	9,021	6,203	68.8
1860	30,635	21,614	70.6
1870	52,914	22,279	42.1
1880	92,296	39,382	42.7
1890	163,597	71,301	43.6
1900	193,345	29,748	15.4

* Source: Statistical Abstract of the United States.

At first construction was largely in the Northwest, then increasingly in the South and Southwest. The Civil War stressed the political and military necessity of uniting the Pacific states with the rest of the country. In 1862 Congress moved to aid in the construction of transcontinental lines. As amended in 1864, a federal charter granted the Union Pacific 12 million acres of public lands for a line from Omaha to Ogden. The Central Pacific was granted 10 million acres as its share for completing the line from Ogden to Sacramento. In addition, the two companies were authorized to sell $27 million of government bonds. Grants to the Northern Pacific, the Kansas Pacific, the Southern Pacific, and other corporations brought the total up to 33 million acres. The policy of land grants was discontinued in 1871, when over 130 million acres were actually patented to the companies by the federal government and almost 49 million acres through the medium of the state governments.[1] Although most of these grants reverted, the companies failing to fulfill the conditions of the grants, about 43 million acres had been certified to the land-grant roads by 1880. Other substantial forms of local aids were in stock subscriptions, the purchase or guarantee of bonds, cash loans and donations of cash, lands and other aids to construction.

The year 1869 is a memorable one in railroad annals. In that year the

[1] Federal Coordinator of Transportation, *Public Aids to Transportation*, Vol. II, p. 32.

construction of the first transcontinental line was completed, and the process of eliminating the last frontier in American history had begun. But it is also memorable because in the same year two eastern railways succeeded in consolidating lines held in separate ownership into two competing *routes*. Actual rail connections had been achieved earlier—New York to Chicago in 1853, and Philadelphia to Chicago in 1858. In 1869, however, the New York Central, with a line from Albany to Buffalo, consolidated with the Hudson River Railroad running from New York to Albany. By virtue of Commodore Vanderbilt's ownership of the Lake Shore and Michigan Southern, entrance into Chicago was assured. The Pennsylvania Railroad, operating from Philadelphia to Pittsburgh, leased the Pittsburgh, Ft. Wayne and Chicago, thus completing the second through-route to Chicago. To the competition between railways and waterways was now added the fiercer competition between the roads themselves, for other lines—the Erie, the Baltimore and Ohio, and the Grand Trunk—were soon to gain entrance to the same city.

After an interval of twelve years, that is, in 1881, a second transcontinental line, using a southern route, was opened. It was made possible through the junction of the Southern Pacific and the Atchison, Topeka, and Santa Fe at Deming, New Mexico. In rapid succession, in 1882 and 1883, two more transcontinental routes were opened by joining the Texas and Pacific with the Southern Pacific at El Paso and by the extension of the Southern Pacific from San Francisco to New Orleans. The latter, through its control over steamship lines, had a complete transcontinental route to New York. In 1883 a northern transcontinental route was opened when the Northern Pacific completed construction of a line from St. Paul, Minnesota, to Portland, Oregon and a little later to Seattle on Puget Sound. About the same time the Union Pacific completed construction of a connection with the Columbia River basin and a through-route to Portland, Oregon by means of the Oregon Short Line Railroad and the Oregon Railway and Navigation Company. In 1888 the Santa Fe entered Chicago; in 1893 the Great Northern opened its line between St. Paul and Seattle. Previously, in 1886, the Canadian Pacific Railway had completed a true transcontinental from Montreal, Quebec, to Vancouver, British Columbia. The decade of the 1880's also saw the speculative "paralleling" of lines in the East with the object of forcing the older road to buy out the newcomer at a profitable figure. The outstanding illustrations are the West Shore which paralleled the New York Central and the "Nickel Plate" which duplicated the Lake Shore.

These constructions and completions have made the 1880's the banner decade in the history of American railroads. Throughout the 1870's and

1880's, capital seemed to be plentiful. In spite of panics in 1873 and 1884, each yielding a crop of railroad bankruptcies, the expansion continued. When the prolonged depression following the panic of 1893 came, it may be said that the construction of the railway net, so far as its *extensive* development is concerned, was completed. The *intensive* development of the railway net, the double, triple, and quadruple tracking had begun. This is also true of the building of enlarged terminals, of lateral connections, cut-offs, branches and spurs.

Improvements in railway service.   The traffic over these lines had certain characteristics which differentiated it from the traffic over European roads. The largest tonnage consisted of heavy, bulky, and low-grade traffic which must be transported cheaply and steadily over long distances. This necessitated the reconstruction and improvement of the facilities by providing a standard gauge, heavier steel rails and bridges, larger cars and locomotives, and extensive and specialized terminal facilities. The permanent way was improved by reduction of grades, better alignment of track, improved drainage, and ballasting. Passenger traffic was made more comfortable, safe, and attractive by the introduction in the 1860's of Pullman sleeping, dining, and parlor cars, and later of air brakes and automatic couplers. Fast-freight companies (now largely discontinued) and special-car companies, catering to particular traffic demands, were organized.

In this same connection we should note the development of the express business, which came into existence in 1839 when William Harnden undertook to transmit valuable parcels between New York and Boston. This business developed gradually by taking out of the hands of the railroad companies the duty of transmitting high-class freight with greater speed and security than the railroads had undertaken to do. The five large express companies, which ultimately divided the field among themselves, were already in control of the situation by 1880. Since World War I they have been further consolidated into the American Railway Express Agency. A lone independent, the Southeastern Express Company, operated for a time over the lines of the Southern Railway, but it has now also been absorbed by the Agency.

In order to meet their own competition and that of water carriers, the railroads were induced to grant rate reductions. Beginning after the Civil War and continuing more or less uninterruptedly until 1900, the level of railway rates declined. With the decline of all prices, making possible decreases in the cost of construction and operation, and with advances in the technique of construction and operation, a progressive improvement of railway service was achieved with a continuously declining level of charges.

Railway abuses and the trend toward consolidations. Serious abuses arose in the construction and financing of the roads. A device frequently adopted was to place the actual building of the roads in the hands of construction companies which were separately incorporated, although leading stockholders and directors were the same as in the operating companies. By this means unduly profitable construction contracts were often entered into and these reacted to the disadvantage of the government and private investors, who had been induced to embark capital in the operating companies. The outstanding example of this practice was the "Credit Mobilier," functioning as the construction company for the Union Pacific. Irregular methods of financing, illustrated by the operations of Jay Gould and his associates of the Erie Railroad, served further to fasten public attention upon problems which were destined ultimately to lead to the adoption of a thorough-going policy of state control. Another abuse was the common practice of granting rebates and discriminatory rates to favorite shippers. The Standard Oil Company is the classic illustration of a company which benefited by means of these practices and used them to crush its competitors. Although the objection raised during and after the Civil War that rates were too high was soon met by the rate reductions of the 1870's, the complaint then was that rate reductions were granted preferentially to large shippers and to shippers located where there was water or rail competition. Also, in this connection should be mentioned the growing evil of the corruption and manipulation of government, particularly of the legislatures, which extended even into the administration of justice.

Such abuses were aided and abetted by the current morality of the times. The country was in a pioneer stage of development; the enterprises were urgently needed; ordinary business morality was low. The country was possessed by an easy optimism, where belief in freedom of competition unfettered by governmental regulation was deemed sufficient to protect the public interest. Great achievements were accompanied by national scandals. Public opinion was uninformed. Scientific methods of management and agencies of control were as yet undeveloped.

It is a mistake to assume that the men conducting these enterprises had no thought for better things. When they began to realize that the underlying difficulty was the competitive struggle of the roads for traffic, they sought to escape the evil results of the struggle by *combination*. This method of escape was also dictated by another consideration, namely, the demand for through-traffic arrangements. This tendency set in during the 1850's, but the larger combinations of connecting roads into great trunk lines did not occur until after the Civil War. The development of the grain traffic and other

East-bound business gave impetus to the work of men like Cornelius Vanderbilt, under whose aegis the New York Central, the Pennsylvania, and certain other systems had taken form by 1880.

Curiously enough, as we have seen, the first consolidation movement—frequently called end-to-end, or linear, consolidation—terminated, particularly after 1869 when Chicago connections were assured, in a period of rate wars between the several independent routes. Rivalry for the through-traffic between the Central West and the Atlantic seaboard resulted in drastic rate reductions in an attempt to attract traffic from rival lines. This gave rise to a new development, the railway pool, by means of which, after disastrous experiences, the rival lines divided earnings (the money pool) or traffic (the traffic pool) on a prearranged basis. This was the favorite method of eliminating competitive evils in the 1870's and 1880's. Writings in defense of the pool began to show a real understanding of the railway problem on the part of management.

The most significant result of the period under review was that the railroad had largely eliminated all other forms of inland transport. Highways, canals, and rivers, insofar as they still carried traffic, had become merely feeders to the rail lines.

Domestic and foreign shipping. Independent waterborne commerce continued to develop only on the Great Lakes, the New York Barge Canal system, and in the coastwise and intercoastal carrying trade. There was also some movement on rivers and canals of heavy and bulky commodities like sand, gravel, coal, and timber in localized transport.

The merchant marine, which had had an auspicious start in the clipper ship era, gave way to foreign competition, largely British, with the advent of the steel steamship. Aided by continuous and heavy subsidies, lower wage scales, and established trade routes, foreign shipping was able to displace American shipping from the high seas. An ineffective and small-scale policy of mailpay subsidy was revived in 1865 and again in 1891, but the promotional effort had little effect for the decline continued. Yet this was the period when the United States became an important factor in world trade and when the experiences of the country in the Civil and Spanish-American wars showed the need of acquiring a larger merchant marine.

The beginnings of another transport revolution. Certain significant events, hardly regarded as important at the time, did, however, presage a new era in the development of transport media. In 1859 the first oil well was sunk at Oil Creek, Pennsylvania. The first 2-inch pipe line for the transportation of crude oil a distance of only four miles was constructed in western Pennsylvania in 1865. Soon the oil fields in the Appalachian region were connected with railways or local refineries by short-distance pipe lines. In 1869 came the first use of the steam roller in road construction, followed by the first manufacture of Portland cement in 1871. The first high-wheeled bicycle appeared in 1877, and local units of bicycle enthusiasts organized themselves into the League of American Wheelmen in 1880 to promote better city streets. The year 1879 marked the awarding of the first basic patent for a gasoline-driven automobile to George Selden, and eventually, when New Jersey passed the first state-aid road law in 1891, the last foundation had been laid for the combined structure of the oil and automotive industries which have once more revolutionized transportation, just as steam power and the railway had revolutionized it in the period before the Civil War.

Communication Utilities

Postal service. We have already mentioned the fact that 186,000 miles of post roads were in operation before the Civil War. Since then, the development of postal service has been very rapid. The use of the mails was rapidly extended by reductions in service charges, the most important being the reduction of letter postage to three cents in 1863 and to two cents in 1883. The introduction of carrier delivery in 1863, of the railway mail car in 1879, and of postal money orders in 1884 greatly added to the convenience of the service and extended its popularity. Rural free delivery was authorized in 1890, but actual delivery did not begin until 1897. Although falling in the next period, parcel-post service was inaugurated in 1913 after much opposition from retail merchants and the five express companies.

Telegraph service. Land telegraph service even before the Civil War was in the hands of the Western Union Telegraph Company, the surviving company of some fifty smaller telegraph companies, which it succeeded in displacing through purchase and competition. The "wildcat" development of this earlier period was superseded by planned construction and purchases so that all the principal cities in the eastern part of the country were soon interconnected for telegraphic communication. This company also completed the first telegraph line to the Pacific coast in 1861, and by 1866 it had gained complete ascendancy by absorbing the remaining two large companies. About the same time, in 1865, international communication was greatly facilitated by the construction of the first commercially successful Atlantic cable. In the early 1880's, John W. Mackey and James Gordon Bennet broke up this monopoly by incorporating the Commercial Cable Company, which laid two transatlantic cables. In order to provide connections with internal points, they also organized the Postal Telegraph Company, with an extensive paralleling land-telegraph system. These two companies, the Western Union and Postal, dominated the field at the close of the century. In 1872 the field of telegraphic communication had been considerably enlarged by the invention of the duplex telegraph, which greatly reduced the cost of rendering service.

The telephone and local communication. Although the field of long-distance communications had already been developed by the postal service and by land and ocean telegraph systems, a new competitor in the field of wire communication appeared with the invention of the telephone in 1876. The development of the telephone industry is especially interesting to Americans because this industry has found its best opportunities in the United States. Speech transmission by electric impulse was first used to provide local communication. Later, long-distance lines appeared so that the industry is now divided into two departments: the telephone organized as a local exchange system; and the telephone as a system of long-distance communication, conducting its service on a message-toll basis. In the long-distance field this service soon rivaled the telegraph in national and international importance.

Local communication is carried on mainly by means of municipal telephone exchanges. For the sake of completeness, mention should be made of the local postal service, of municipal police and fire-alarm systems, and of electric signaling in burglar-alarm, night-watchman, taxi-call, and messenger services.

The technical and commercial development of the telephone, once called the "electric toy," is a most absorbing story. It recounts the struggles of inventors with technical problems and their efforts to overcome the early indifference of capitalists. It has been said that Chauncey Depew was offered a one-tenth interest in the Bell patent for $10,000 but rejected the offer on advice of experts. Of the greatest importance was the positive hostility of the organized telegraph industry. The history of the telephone goes back to experiments by Page in 1837, who discovered that an iron bar, if magnetized and demagnetized at short intervals of time, will emit sounds. In 1875, Alexander Graham Bell constructed his first pair of magneto telephones, receiving his original patents the following year. Improvements were soon made to which the versatile Thomas A. Edison, retained by the Western Union Telegraph Company, contributed his share. Emil Berliner,

David Hughes, and Francis Blake are some other names to be associated with the first patents and the legal struggles arising over them. It was the Bell Telephone Association, however, which first applied the idea of securing widespread and flexible intercommunication by connecting local telephones with central stations. The first local exchange was the Bell plant established in New Haven in 1878 with 21 subscribers. Other cities receiving local service the same year were San Francisco, Albany, Chicago, St. Louis, Detroit, and Philadelphia.

Telephone service rapidly gained favor, and by 1880 there were 34,305 miles of wire and over 50,000 receiving telephones in operation. This development was primarily in local exchanges. In 1879 the first commercial attempt at long-distance service was made between Boston and Lowell. The next step was the extension of service from Boston to Providence, R.I., a distance of 45 miles, made possible by installing a complete metallic circuit. In 1884 service was extended from Providence to New York. After this date, development was rapid and carried on primarily by the American Telephone and Telegraph Company, organized in 1885 to develop the long-distance service. The miles of line in operation increased to 140,000 in 1892 when Chicago and New York were connected.

It has been said that the telephone was a luxury up to 1894, when the original patents expired. It is undoubtedly true that the major expansion has come since that date. Before this date development was largely in the hands of the American Bell Telephone Company. Since then competition has set in, but the major share of the business was, nevertheless, that of the Bell companies. The dominating company was the American Telephone and Telegraph Company. In 1900 it absorbed the American Bell Company, was reorganized as a holding company of regional operating companies, and undertook the task of developing inventions, owning patents, handling legal, financial, and manufacturing problems, and operating a "long lines department."

Water Utilities

In 1860 when the Census showed 392 cities in excess of 2,500 population, there were only 136 water works in operation. The spread of centralized systems of supply is indicated by the fact that by 1896 this number had increased to 3,179 systems, with the 1900 Census showing only 1,737 such cities. This shows that public utility water supply had penetrated to even the smaller places. The trend toward public ownership, already noted, was continuing with 1,690 public plants, or 53 per cent near the close of the century.

Developments in water supply service. With the general advance in standards of living since the Civil War, the supply of water under pressure became very common. The technology of water supply changed rapidly, particularly improvements in pumping. Modern centrifugal pumps have displaced all other types. Electric power was being substituted for steam power.

At first, ordinary river, lake, and spring water was the most common source of supply. Because sewage systems were few and less extensive than they are now, the danger of pollution was not great. As the number of water works increased and their service expanded, sewer systems were likewise extended so that the danger of pollution increased. To this was added pollution from industrial wastes. The high and increasing death rate from typhoid fever, first noticed by health authorities in the 1890's, was traced to water pollution. This was the first practical application of bacteriology in the developing science of public health. Sanitary regulations, filtration, and chlorination were adopted as remedies. First introduced to remove color and turbidity, it was found that filters also removed a large part of the bacterial content. European advance in these practices was distinctly ahead of American. In some cases pollution was so serious that double filtration had to be resorted to in order to make headway against waterborne diseases. Where waters were hard, facilities for water-softening were added.

Another improvement was the water meter, but its adoption was tardy. Where water was scarce, however, as in the Southwest, great pressure was exerted to secure the installation of meters for greater economy in the use of the available supply.

Mention should also be made of the expansion of storage reservoirs. These served the double purpose of providing additional pressure for fire protection and of equalizing the demand upon primary sources by taking care of the fluctuations in the hourly, daily, and seasonal rate of draft.

Irrigation

In spite of the tremendous increase in the area available to agricultural production in humid regions, the westward movement of the frontier was so rapid and in obedience to so great a speculative urge that even desert lands had to be reclaimed for agriculture in those locations where crop production on the spot seemed to be economically feasible. This accounts for the spread of the Mormon principle of cooperative irrigation. In 1870, for example, the Greeley Union Colony was set up in northern Colorado to carry on its experiments in irrigation in imitation of the Utah prototypes. Similarly, in southern California at about the same time cooperative irrigation of the colony type was undertaken by the California Arcadians and by German colonists at Anaheim. By 1880 about a million acres had been irrigated, largely as a result of the rapid construction of small ditches by individuals and associations of farmers in the previous decades. The "boom" period in the construction of these works was the decade of the 1880's. Since returns from investments looked large, great enterprises were projected, organized as corporations, and money obtained from the sale of bonds and by stock subscriptions.

This era of "speculative irrigation" differed from the pioneer cooperatives because the capitalist project owner was not the "farmer under the ditch," although he looked to the crops produced by the latter for a return on his investment. This separation of the project owner and water user brought about more failures than successes in these commercial ventures. The reason was that company management did not take sufficient account of the stern necessity of securing earnest and competent settlers whose labor would have to make water payments. Other private irrigation companies were bankrupted because speculators, acquiring public lands under the Homestead Act, had no intention of working the land but merely holding it until the project was finished and then selling out at higher prices. Meanwhile, there was no sale for the water. Moreover, as irrigation was extended to reclaim the more difficult areas, the increasing cost per acre began to count against the success of the later undertakings. As suppliers of capital began to realize what the difficulties were, these sources of private capital dried up. Although earlier federal legislation was not notably successful, a new period in reclamation was ushered in when the federal government in 1902 set up the Reclamation Service as the agency to continue the work in the more difficult places. Meanwhile, the irrigated area had been expanded to 3,715,767 acres by 1890 and to 7,728,937 acres by 1900. All this irrigated area was in the arid West, except irrigation for rice in Arkansas, Louisiana, and Texas.

Artificial and Natural Gas Utilities

Rapid development appeared also in the field of gas supply, both natural and artificial. When, in spite of many business failures, the possibilities of acquiring a market in at least the larger cities was sufficiently demonstrated, gas companies multiplied in numbers. The period after the Civil War was also the great competitive period in the gas industry. The popular belief in the regulative power of competition was at the bottom of this shift from the comparative freedom from competition which had characterized the industry in the earlier period.

Competitive influences. The industry also had to withstand the competition of such substitutes as improved lamps using kerosene, and beginning in 1878, of electric lighting. In that year the electric arc for street lighting appeared, and the central electric station entered the field soon afterward. Within its own ranks the industry had to withstand rate wars and the handicaps of a high cost of production due to the competitive duplication of investment. Management tried to overcome these difficulties by the merger of competing companies. Efforts in this direction were hampered, however, by the prevailing distrust of large organizations, by the popular belief in competition to beget low prices, and by the courts, who held that the consolidation of competitors resulted in monopoly and was thus contrary to public policy as expressed in the Common Law. Nevertheless, under the influence partly of competition and partly of technical cost-reducing improvements, a decline in rates set in, which gradually expanded the market for this service. After 1873 the Lowe process of the manufacture of carbureted water gas was introduced, and this by 1880 won out over the coal-gas producers. This cheaper process was the more willingly used because the contest with electricity had just begun.

The new electric illuminant gradually displaced gas in residence and commercial lighting and made inroads also in the street-lighting field. A series of inventions by Thomas A. Edison and others raised a great furor of technical and popular discussion of the relative merits of the two competing systems. Gas company stocks fell in value. Slowly but irresistibly the great advantages of electric lighting in safety, steadiness of illumination, and ease of control demonstrated themselves. Meanwhile, gas lamps were improved. The old type of open-flame burners was supplanted by the more economical Welsbach type of burner which saved some of this business for a time. It was certain, however, that the industry would, in time, have to adjust itself to a complete change in the utilization of its service.

The opening of new markets for gas was accomplished through the introduction of improved processes of gas production which so lowered the cost that utilization was gradually extended from the lighting to the heating field. Gas was first used for cooking about 1859. But gas stoves and heaters in quantities did not appear until toward the close of the nineteenth century.

Natural gas and long-distance transmission. Although natural gas had been known for a long time and put to sporadic use earlier, the first utility of this type, The Fredonia Gas Light and Water Works Company, was organized in 1865. Confined largely to those sections in the East where there were petroleum deposits, the use of natural gas remained unimportant until the first boom in the oil industry of the 1880's and 1890's also started the natural gas industry upon its continuously upward climb. Until 1891 natural gas lines were short and of small diameter. When, beginning in 1872, the wastage of gas by the use of wooden pipes had been overcome by the use successively of cast-iron pipes, wrought-iron pipes and steel pipes, the Indiana Natural Gas and Oil Company finally succeeded in transmitting gas in 1892 by the use of mechanical compressors from its natural gas wells in Indiana to Chicago, a distance of 120 miles.

Urban and Interurban Transportation

As cities grew in population and area, local promoters and capitalists came forward to give cities improved systems of public transportation. The increasing separation of the home from the workplace consequent upon the development of the factory system, and the need of expanding the residential areas through new real estate developments, had much to do with the rapid development of urban transport after the Civil War.

By 1870 street railways operated with animal power were found in most of the larger cities. This form of urban transportation reached its peak in 1890. At that time there were 5,662 miles of track in operation, but the system was never entirely satisfactory. It was slow; it could not be operated to advantage on heavy grades; it was hard work for the animals. Accordingly, inventors all over the world turned their attention to the development of some form of power suitable to the service. Experiments were made principally with steam, cable, and compressed air. The cable railway proved to be the most efficient and was first used in New York City in 1869. It was especially useful in cities having heavy grades, as Pittsburgh, Seattle, and San Francisco; but it was also used in Chicago where grades were practically absent. However, the cost of constructing cable railways was high, and therefore they were self-sustaining only where traffic was heavy. This disadvantage militated against a wide adoption of the cable railway so that at the height of its popularity there were only 658 miles in operation.

Development of the electric railway. Finally, electric energy, already in use for lighting, was extended to the street railway. The honor of having demonstrated to the world for the first time that electricity could drive a car along rails is accorded Thomas Davenport of Brandon, Vermont. The experiment was made in 1836. According to investigations of the American Electric Railway Association, the first practicable line in the world was, however, not put into operation until 1874 in Berlin, Germany. It was demonstrated upon a commercial basis at the Berlin Exposition in 1879. The pioneer electric railways in the United States began operation in 1883 at Saratoga Springs, N.Y., and at Cleveland, Ohio, in 1884. The former used a third rail for power transmittance and the latter a conduit system. These were soon followed by other installations; Appleton, Wisconsin, figuring among the pioneers. The first electric railway using the modern overhead trolley and other features began operation on May 4, 1888, at Richmond, Virginia. This date is generally regarded as marking the beginning of the electric railway industry. The stimulating effect of the change was almost instantaneous. Within ten years the horsecar was practically extinct. The street railway plant of the country continued its rapid expansion until the outbreak of World War I. The development of electric transit for interurban traffic between nearby cities did not begin until 1895, and hence its discussion will be reserved for the next period.

Rapid transit.   In the meantime, the increasing traffic congestion upon the streets of our larger cities developed a new need for rapid transit. Since this service could not be obtained from surface lines operating in crowded streets, the elevated railway and, later, the subway were developed to meet this demand. The elevated road appeared in New York in 1878, using steam locomotives, and operated a station-to-station service. In 1901 the third-rail system of electric traction was substituted. The first use of an underground railway came in London in 1853. In this country the construction of subways was long delayed.

The Development of Electricity Supply

The large-scale application of electricity to the uses of man could not begin until technology had made practical and cheap the conversion of mechanical into electrical energy. This was made possible by the discovery of electromagnetic induction by Henry and Faraday about 1831. Other important links in the long chain of inventions culminating in the central station were the development of component parts of the generator by Siemens and Wheatstone in 1867, by Gramme in 1870, and by Hefner-Alteneck in 1873. The development of utilization devices was begun by Davy who built an arc lamp in 1812 and by Starr and King who produced the first crude low-resistance, incandescent electric lamps in 1845.

Steam-electric power utilities. Not until 1878, however, was it possible to develop a complete lighting system consisting of producing equipment (prime movers and generators), distribution lines, and utilization equipment. At that time three systems were designed, one by Jablochkoff in France, another by Brush, and a third by Edison, the two latter having been developed in the United States. The American systems used direct current; the French system, alternating current. The Jablochkoff and Brush systems introduced improved arc lamps, and the Edison system used the carbon-filament, incandescent lamp. The Edison system was commercially the most successful because it secured greater economy in distribution and utilization. The Brush system was most useful in street lighting; the Edison system, in interior lighting. Only the Edison system has maintained itself to the present day in serving congested districts where direct current is distributed over short distances. In the United States direct current is used in the operation of electric railways and of passenger and freight elevators. Alternating current is now used exclusively in long-distance transmission. The greatest improvement was made in generating devices where the development of the high-speed steam engine, the steam turbine, and the Francis hydraulic turbine [2] have been the cornerstone upon which rests the structure of modern central-station electricity supply.

The first central station, the Pearl Street Station in New York, started operation in 1882 with 5,500 lamps. Central stations were constructed soon after in Boston, Brooklyn, and Chicago. In 1886 there were forty-seven Edison illuminating companies. In 1890 there were more than 1,000 central stations. In fact, the development of electric utilities was phenomenally rapid.

The advantages of electric lighting have already been mentioned in our discussion of gas supply. For power purposes the superiority of electric energy consists in the fact that through the electric motor, first developed commercially by Tekla in 1884, power can be provided in units of any required size. It is adaptable to variations in load; it is portable over long distances; electric motor installations make for cleanliness about the plant, enhance the safety of operations, and are structurally compact. Accordingly, the main uses for electric energy are found in street, interior, and display lighting, commercial and industrial power and heating, electric power for urban and interurban transit, and in electrochemistry. The use of energy at high voltages has made safety a primary consideration. Also, as more resi-

[2] Two classes of hydraulic turbines are now in use. High-head, impulse turbines are used extensively in mountainous regions where the quantities of water are small but the falls very high; the other type is designed for large quantities of water and small heads.

dences, commercial establishments, and industrial plants have made themselves dependent upon central-station supply, *continuity of service* has become another primary requirement. In truth, the central station represents the heart of modern city life.

Hydroelectric power utilities. Electric power is derived primarily from energy stored in coal, natural gas, and oil, although the amount of electric power derived from the energy of falling waters has been steadily increasing. Devices for the utilization of water power for industrial purposes have been in use for over three thousand years. Technical development, however, was exceedingly slow. The chief reliance continued to be a modified type of the primitive undershot or overshot waterwheel. Development was remarkably quickened with the introduction of the turbine waterwheel. However, the utilization of this power was limited to the factory located at the source. Of the power used directly in industry in the United States, even as late as 1870, about 48 per cent was furnished by water-power plants. But steam power was in the ascendant. By 1919 the proportion supplied from water power had fallen to 6 per cent.[3]

In 1886 the Westinghouse Electric and Manufacturing Company began the commercial production of alternating current machinery on a large scale.[4] This made possible a great increase in voltage capacity and enabled operators by means of transformers and high-voltage lines to transmit electric energy over large areas. It also gave a new impetus to the water-power industry by transforming it into the hydroelectric industry.

The first hydroelectric plant was installed at Appleton, Wisconsin. It was placed in operation October 5, 1882, with 250 lamps of 16 candlepower. Thus the pioneer steam-power station in New York and the pioneer water-power station in Wisconsin were placed in operation scarcely a month apart. Another early hydroelectric station was located at Portland, Oregon, in 1884, which obtained its power from a site on the Willamette River, thirteen miles distant. In 1888 it was converted into a plant generating alternating current, and here was installed the first alternating current transmission line in the United States. The introduction in 1893 of rotary converters, which convert alternating current into direct current, removed another limiting factor in the development. Inventions and improvements, particularly in the direction of making possible the economical transmission of electric energy over long distances, have followed in rapid succession.

[3] Voskuil, W. H., "Water-Power Situation in the United States," *Journal of Land and Public Utility Economics*, Vol. 1, January, 1925, p. 89.
[4] The Westinghouse Company is credited with establishing the first regularly operated alternating-current plant in the United States at Greensburg, Pa., in 1886.

5. *REGULATION*

IN THE COMPETITIVE EPOCH

We must next consider the system of public regulation which developed along with the public utility plant of the country. In the interval between 1860 and 1900, the distinction between utilities whose market was local, and utilities whose market was state- and nation-wide, was clearly established. In fact, due to the increased urbanization of the population, local utilities were gaining in importance as contrasted with national utilities. This showed itself first of all in a pronounced home-rule movement which left in its wake a crop of statutes and constitutional amendments transferring powers of regulation to local governing units. On the other hand, the extension of markets was creating a movement also in the opposite direction, whereby powers of regulation were conceived to be best lodged in the hands of the federal government. In conformity with this trend, control of state-wide and nation-wide operations was lodged in state and federal governments, while utilities centering in cities were controlled by municipal governments.

Another important development of the period should be noted. We have seen that the regulation of common carriers by means of the charter was justified on the theory that a railway was a public highway. This doctrine of the courts reflects the notion, prevalent before 1830, that it is the duty of the state to provide for inland transportation, whether by turnpike, canal, or railway. At this point, a circumstance entered which accounts for the failure of policies of regulation to develop continuously in accordance with this principle.

As in 1830 the federal government stepped aside for state governments, so in 1850 the state governments assigned to corporations the duty of furnishing the means for inland transportation. The twenty years intervening were marked by a gradual decline of the theory that the development of a country through canals and railways was a public function, and the gradual rise of the theory that this duty was one which could with greater safety be entrusted to private enterprise.[1]

---

[1] Adams, H. C., in introduction to Dixon, F. H., *State Railroad Control* (New York: Thos. J. Crowell & Co., 1896), p. 6.

In other words, the opinion began to gain ground that the business of a common carrier was purely private.

General Incorporation Acts and Their Influence on Regulation

So long as each charter was a vehicle of special regulation, there was bound to be great diversity of restrictions. But there were nevertheless certain tendencies toward uniformity. In drafting charters, states copied largely from one another. When the work of granting charters by special acts became burdensome, the legislatures developed the custom of abbreviating railway charters by referring to charters previously granted in the same or other states. By this means a gradual transition to the policy of granting charters by general law was worked out. General legislation appeared in the early 1830's, although special charters continued to be granted as late as the 1870's.[2] The change to the new system was gradually completed but not until the passage of special acts in a perfunctory, indiscriminate, and even corrupt way had yielded a grist of charters that contained all manner of restrictions and of special privileges. By this time the corporation had become so favored a form of organization for economic enterprises that politicians began to advocate the free and unrestricted use of the device. In other words, the corporation had by this time become an expression of laissez faire. This explains the enactment of general statutes which prescribed the general manner and conditions of securing incorporation.

Typical of this situation are the following clauses in the Wisconsin constitution:

Corporations without banking powers or privileges may be formed under general laws, but shall not be created by special acts, except for municipal purposes, and in cases where, in the judgment of the Legislature, the objects of a corporation cannot be attained under general laws. All general laws or special acts enacted under the provisions of this section may be altered or repealed by the Legislature any time after their passage.[3]

In spite of such provisions, the legislatures continued to amend earlier special charters and even to grant new ones until the legal situation, in view of the consolidation of railways, became very complex.[4]

---

[2] Charters were originally special acts except in the case of a few western states (Arizona, California, Colorado, Idaho, Montana), which began with general laws.

[3] *Constitution of Wisconsin*, Art. 2, Sec. 1, 1871.

[4] As a leading authority writes, "The Pennsylvania Company, for instance, represents more than 150 original lines, each having its special charter or certificate of incorporation. Many of these charters represent conflicting, if not mutually exclusive

It is, accordingly, a mistake to assume that the adoption of general incorporation laws brought about an improvement in the machinery of regulation. As a matter of fact, the first effect was a recession in the vigor of regulation. Under such laws, a small number of persons, by simply filing a certificate, could organize a public utility corporation and be subjected to very little control in their operations. The era of free competition among utilities should really be associated with this system. It is small wonder that abuses crept into corporate organization and management. Even the power of eminent domain was often used by rival companies to defeat legitimate and sound enterprises by blocking construction or by forcing one of them to purchase needed properties at exorbitant prices. The reaction set in after it was recognized that the system involved social waste and that the inevitable outcome of competition would be consolidation. Thereupon, in response to public clamor, legislative regulation entered upon a new phase— control by "direct action"—which is known in history as the "Granger" movement.

In the regulation of municipal utilities, general incorporation laws brought the same result. Although companies were incorporated by general laws and obtained their special franchises from local governments, the result was an era of competition. This policy predominated during the latter half of the nineteenth century. Although the new method was believed to be an improvement in the procedure of granting franchises, it led to many abuses with which the history of these utilities is replete. The regulatory provisions in general incorporation laws were lax and ineffective. The familiar charges of fraudulent capitalization, over-capitalization, and exorbitant and discriminatory rates date from the practices that crept in during this period. Owing often to the lack of clearness in the general laws, serious questions arose whether a city, in granting the special franchise, was authorized to impose conditions upon applicant companies in addition to those imposed by general statute. There was as yet no definition of the powers of the cities and the rights of the companies. Cities tried to protect themselves by granting franchises to competing companies, often with no reservations or restrictions in the interest of the city and the consuming public. Thus here, as in the railway field, the belief prevailed that competition was the best regulative power and that governmental regulation was unnecessary where there

_____

privileges, and what the charter rights of such a corporation are is a question difficult of solution. Not only is there a possibility of conflict between the diverse provisions of different charters, but also between the charters and the general laws, although in many states the supremacy of general over special laws has been at least acquiesced in, if not publicly recognized." Meyer, B. H., *Railway Legislation In the United States*, p. 87.

was competition. Competition was destined, however, to have a shorter life in this area.

Denver again furnished an example of the practice. In 1880 its council granted a general electric franchise "to all comers" in a resolution which provided solely "that permission be granted to any company desiring to supply the city with electric lights, to erect posts and such other appliances as may be necessary to carry on their business; provided, that said companies do not obstruct the public thoroughfares." Such competition, of course, could not and did not persist, for the industries are inherently monopolistic. Consolidations and mergers placed upon the final incumbent an unnecessary duplication of investment, besides keeping alive in some of the cities the terms of the competing grants.

The Granger Movement

During the early part of this competitive period, i.e., before 1870, there was no great emphasis on regulation. The demand was usually for more railways to beget competition. The various forms of public aid (loans of public credit, subscriptions to stock) were supplemented by appeals to private parties, particularly to farmers along the right of way, who would be benefited by the new roads. Shares of stock were sold and frequently paid for out of funds obtained by mortgaging farms. When the promised dividends failed to materialize, and the new transportation facilities did not at once cheapen the price of transport, attempts were made to repudiate county and municipal railway bonds by having them declared illegal. The reason assigned was that they had been issued for the benefit of *private* railway corporations. Fortunately the attempt failed; the legality of the bonds was upheld by the United States Supreme Court in a famous decision on the theory that they were issued in aid of a governmental function.[5]

Other events of that period fanned the flame of public indignation. Construction rings and unscrupulous directors had wrecked some of the properties. Competition was being eliminated by consolidations. Rate agreements between trunk line carriers, the first railway pool in 1870, kindled an opposition which revealed vividly the extent to which faith in competition had penetrated public opinion. The uncompromising position of railway managers who shielded themselves with the Dartmouth College decision only added to the desire of legislatures to subject these corporations to rigid

[5] *Olcott v. The Supervisors,* 16 Wall. 678, 694 (1872).

control.[6] Absentee ownership was blamed for such lack of amenability to public opinion. Moreover, legislative and official corruption appeared in the shape of the free-pass system and the transfer to legislators of stock at less than its market value. What appeared to be unjustifiable rate discriminations between persons and places were the subject of public complaints, as was the high level of rates which made the shipment of farm products unremunerative. This was particularly true after the Civil War, when prices fell from the high level they had reached through currency inflation during the war.

When abuses, real and imagined, flowing from unrestricted activity by the pioneer utilities, had kindled "Granger movements" in the different states,[7] investigations of the "railroad problem" were begun by legislative bodies and temporary advisory commissions. The publication of their reports and the public discussion thus invoked accomplished a good deal of informal regulation. This was the atmosphere in which the police power was rejuvenated.

At this stage in the history of regulation appeared a plethora of laws and regulations, very precise and definite as to subject matter. Specific laws were aimed at specific abuses. The immediately important result was a wave of maximum rate legislation which centered in the four states of Iowa, Illinois, Wisconsin, and Minnesota, but which spread to many other states in the decade from 1875 to 1885. The state-wide classifications of freight and the maximum distance tariffs of freight rates, which were in effect in some of the Granger states until the beginning of the twentieth century, are relics of this period of legislative regulation.

The Establishment of Administrative Commissions by State Governments

Although the Granger movement began with legislation which prescribed maximum rates and fares and prohibited discriminations, it ended with legislation creating commissions with power to prescribe reasonable maximum rates. The commission as an *agency* of regulation has had a long history. But the great variety of historical conditions that lie back of this

---

[6] For an earlier attempt at regulation in Wisconsin, see Frederick Merk, *Economic History of Wisconsin*, Chap. 12, Publications of Wisconsin Historical Society Copyright 1916.

[7] *Cf.* Buck, S. J., *The Granger Movement* (New Haven: Harvard University Press, Copyright 1913).

movement for commission regulation in the different states makes it difficult, if not impossible, to generalize.

Without departing radically from the avowed purposes for which the earlier commissions of New England were established, New York in 1855 and Massachusetts in 1869 set up commissions with enlarged powers. More and more, as emphasis shifted to rates charged and particularly to discriminatory practices, the need for more detailed and authoritative information about the rapidly growing railroad business became evident.

In meeting this need the eastern states developed a policy that varied considerably from that of the western and southern states. In the East, in regulating the relations of railroads to one another and to the public, great reliance was placed upon *publicity* and the *force of public opinion* to correct abuses. Under this system the commission first investigated and made recommendations, and this was followed by legislation only when the companies proved unyielding. In the West, on the contrary, public opinion demanded legislation first and *set up commissions* later to make and enforce orders and collect penalties. This difference in approach was the basis for the distinction drawn between commissions of the advisory or "weak" type and those of the mandatory or "strong" type.

The Massachusetts Board of Railroad Commissioners of 1869 is the outstanding illustration of the former type. It consisted of three men appointed by the Governor with the consent of the Council. The term of office was three years, one person being appointed each year. This commission was empowered to investigate the operations of the carriers, to determine whether they were living up to the terms of their charters and of such special legislation as had been adopted to supplement the charters. It was likewise empowered to investigate complaints or begin investigations upon its own motion. It could hold hearings, summoning witnesses and examining them under oath. Its findings might be coupled with recommendations, which were usually accepted. As an incident to its supervisory powers, it could prescribe a uniform system of keeping accounts and had the power to inspect the books of account. It acted as a board of arbitration in settling disputes and issued an annual report to the legislature upon the general subject of railroad transportation in relation to the welfare of the state, in which report it suggested such additional legislation as seemed appropriate. Since this board early developed a reputation for courage and intelligence throughout the country, its example served appreciably to give the commission idea great vogue. Reasonably free from political influence, the commissioners set out upon their task of investigation, and by the force of facts and arguments succeeded in fathering much sound legislation. Among other things, it was able to prevent the construction of useless roads built only for speculative and blackmailing purposes.

It was to Charles Francis Adams, whose dominant personality on this board for so many years gave it preeminent standing, that many of the fecund ideas on regulation may be traced. The late Commissioner Eastman of the Interstate Commerce Commission, who hailed from Massachusetts, said of this board that it was distinctly the product of evolution and that it did much of the laboratory work by which the whole country has profited. Moreover, he found in the Massachusetts experiment the germ of "nearly every important power now exercised by the various public service commissions in the United States."

In the West and South the opposition of the carriers to the new legislation, particularly their ability in using the technicalities of legal processes to delay and emasculate its effectiveness, soon taught the lesson that the law on the statute books and the law in action are horses of a different color. Moreover, during the period of falling prices following the Civil War, statutory rate structures were left "up in the air" by the voluntary reductions of the carriers themselves, just as the maximum rates fixed in earlier charters had become "paper rates." Thus the statutes soon lost all their regulatory vigor. The increasing complexity of rate problems and the preoccupation of legislatures with many new problems in time brought a realization that statutory regulation should be general rather than specific; that the subject matter of statutes should be the statement of principles and standards, rather than the specification of concrete details; that the new policy of continuous legislative regulation required an effective agency, sufficiently "informed by experience" to carry legislative standards into effect. The administrative commission filled this need. It is, in one sense, a new political institution which has revolutionized, if not created, administrative law.

Thus, in the western and southern states, the Granger movement led to the establishment of commissions of the mandatory type. Illinois took the initiative; its commission may be taken as typical. A revised constitution, adopted in 1870, required the legislature to enact laws regulating the railroads and warehouses. Such legislation, prescribing maximum rates and fares and prohibiting discriminations, was passed in 1871. A Railroad and Warehouse Commission was set up to supervise railroads and assist in enforcement. Two years later, in 1873, this commission was given the duty of prescribing a schedule of maximum rates. The Commission also had to investigate operations and to prescribe the form of a report to be made by the railways. The new element, however, was its power to prescribe rates and to compel obedience. Between 1871 and 1874 a wave of maximum rate laws also spread over Iowa, Wisconsin, and Minnesota. Georgia followed in 1879. In the same year California took the unusual step of providing in its constitution of 1879 that the legislature establish a railroad commission with power to fix maximum rates.

Reaction against mandatory commissions. The panic of 1873 placed many of the roads in financial difficulties. Coming at the same time that these boards were being created, this fact was used to turn public opinion against the newer form of regulation. The commissions with power to prescribe rates and issue orders were abolished or changed into advisory commissions or into public bureaus presided over by a single commissioner whose functions again became merely investigatory, supervisory, and of a reporting character. The Michigan Commission of 1889, consisting of the Commissioner of Railroads, the State Treasurer, and the Secretary of State, is an example of what came to be known as an *ex officio* board whose duties were also largely ministerial. What is important in this reaction against strict legislative control is that it represents, as in Massachusetts, a declaration in favor of *publicity* as a remedy for abuses. The argument was that publicity together with enlightened self-interest could be depended upon to eradicate what was evil and to promote what was good. This policy was less of a break with the traditions of the past and was more adapted to the prevailing American psychology. A legislative statute enforced by an administrative commission, with hordes of inspectors prying into the sanctity of private affairs and issuing mandatory orders as to details of conducting business, was regarded as introducing into American institutions the agencies and instrumentalities of the continental European "Police-State." There appeared also the grave constitutional question whether the power to fix rates and set service standards *for the future* could be delegated to a commission or board.

Origin of a Federal System of Regulation

Meanwhile, the Granger movement had also begun to make an impression upon Congress. Before briefly sketching the origin of the federal system of regulation it will be well to recall certain background considerations which have conditioned our development during this part of the century. Our railway plant was built up by a speculative stimulus with the crest of each wave of speculation followed by a trough of depression. There was little thought of scientifically coordinating supply with demand. Much necessarily hasty and mistaken construction was undertaken. Fortunes were made and lost. It has been estimated that in excess of 70 per cent of American railway mileage has passed through receivership. In the end there emerged strong transportation systems, reorganized and consolidated by the energy and capacity of leading executives.

The importance of these conditions in any true estimate of the history of regulatory institutions has never been better stated than by Professor F. W. Taussig:

Historically, the course of development seems to have been controlled by a fated destiny. Given the impossibility of public ownership and management (and for the earlier stages of railway development in this country public operation was out of the question); given the eager desire of the community for ways of transportation and its willingness to encourage their construction in every way; given the looseness of corporation laws, the universal speculative temper, the laxness of business standards; given the periodic fluctuations in industry, the economic peculiarities of railways, the opportunities for large scale returns—and the harvest was prepared for the daring and able operator. Perhaps all the advantages of rapid construction, wide permeation of the land with railway facilities, from competition and consolidation and vigorous management, could have been gotten in some other way; but a train of deep-seated causes seems to have decreed that they should come in just this way and with just these checkered results.[8]

Other factors which have added to the complexity of the regulatory problem were the great expanse of the country with the accompanying diversity in local conditions and the extremely rapid succession of new inventions and improvements. Regulatory institutions could not be brought to that stage of maturity which alone affords a sufficient test of their adequacy before new conditions arising out of the country's growth or fundamental changes in the art confronted them and subjected them to the strain of altered circumstances.

After a community's first concern to get transportation facilities had been satisfied, its next concern was to get improved service at lower rates. To this end the competition of railroads with each other or with carriers by water was primarily relied upon. When at length the time arrived to assert a policy of governmental regulation of service and rates, it proved difficult to reverse the trend of at least a half-century. The Granger movement came during a period of linear consolidation of hitherto disconnected lines. And thus arises the circumstance that the regulation of interstate carriers has always been hostile to monopoly and colored with a desire in

[8] Taussig, F. W., *Principles of Economics,* Vol. II (New York: The Macmillan Co., Copyright 1920), p. 393.

some way to retain competition.[9] Even the carriers were anxious to retain the differential advantages arising out of strategic locations. This has kept competition alive even to the present time.

The first important step looking toward federal regulation of railroads was the report of the Windom Committee to the United States Senate in 1874. (Senate Report No. 307, 43d Cong., 1st Sess.) As already mentioned, this investigation was occasioned by Granger opposition to what were regarded as excessive railway rates. The remedy proposed reflected the spirit of the times, namely, further encouragement of competition by developing waterways and the construction by the federal government of parallel railways to the seaboard. Although the report argued at length that Congress had the constitutional power to regulate railroad rates, it actually proposed that regulation be brought about indirectly by the competition of government-owned railroads which could not be drawn into the vortex of the consolidation movement.

The next important step was the report of the Cullom Committee in 1886, likewise to the Senate. (Senate Report No. 46, 49th Cong., 1st Sess.) Instead of complaining about high rates this committee contended that the "paramount evil" in the conduct of the transportation system was "unjust discriminations between persons, places, commodities, or particular descriptions of traffic." Improvements in railway facilities, the growth of traffic, and particularly rate wars had in the time between the two reports changed entirely the incidence of the railway problem. Discrimination, as a new phase of the railroad problem, was the direct result of excessive railway competition, a competition which pooling was unable effectively to combat. Place discriminations arose out of the fact that railroads regarded themselves as adjuncts to the markets which they entered, and their rates were consequently adjusted to favor the markets which particular railroads desired to build up. Higher rates were also in effect upon local traffic, not subject to competition, as compared with rates applying on traffic moving between junction points where competitive influences were felt. Another type of discrimination arose between large and small shippers because the large shipper was able to secure a rebate or other preferential treatment on account of the larger quantity of traffic which he could offer.

Between 1874 and 1887 various bills were introduced looking toward

---

[9] A distinction must here be drawn between two classes of shippers. A railroad has certain inherent monopoly powers which enable it to discriminate between shippers local to a given line and shippers who are in a position to use a competing railroad or other common carrier. Hence the seeming inconsistency that regulation should seek to restrain monopoly by means of maximum rates and at the same time aim at the control of place discrimination originating in competition but affecting both classes of shippers.

federal regulation, but none of them became law. Finally in 1886 the United States Supreme Court, in the famous Wabash case, decided that state regulation must confine itself to intrastate traffic. In view of the growing importance of interstate traffic, this decision forced action by Congress, with the result that the Interstate Commerce Act regulating such traffic and creating the Interstate Commerce Commission was passed early in the following year.

The difficulties which stood in the way of the adoption of federal legislation illustrate well our policy of drift and of mental lethargy in thinking about these problems. Very little thought had been given to the proper selection of governmental agencies best fitted to carry on the work of regulation. The federal constitution provides that Congress shall have power "to regulate commerce with foreign nations and among the several states and with the Indian tribes." [10] The Tenth Amendment distinguishes the sphere of state and federal activity by providing that "the powers not delegated to the United States by the constitution, nor prohibited by it to the states, are reserved to the states respectively, or to the people." Largely as a result of the judicial leadership of Chief Justice Marshall, it was early established that within the sphere thus marked out by definitely delegated powers, Congress was supreme.[11] Similarly, each state under the police power regulates commerce within its own boundaries.

The successive steps in the interpretation of the commerce clause may be presented as follows: [12] During an initial period ending about 1829, the power of Congress over interstate commerce was interpreted by the courts to exclude regulation by the states. On the other hand, the power of the state to regulate its internal commerce (both beginning and ending in the state) was regarded as equally exclusive. But the arbitrary nature of the distinction between interstate and intrastate commerce became apparent when it was realized that in the regulation of intrastate traffic it was impossible, with the increasing volume of through-business, not to affect indirectly also interstate traffic. Yet the idea of States' rights was so strong that even as late as 1877 in the Granger cases it was held that "until Congress undertakes to legislate for those who are without the State, Wisconsin may provide for those within, even though it may indirectly affect those without." [13] The dominance of federal power was only potential. Naturally, this led to a situation where state control was more and more permitted

---

[10] Art. I, Sec. 8.

[11] *Gibbons v. Ogden*, 9 Wheaton (U.S.) 1 (1824).

[12] Coleman, Wm. S., "The Evolution of Federal Regulation on Interstate Rates: The Shreveport Rate Cases," *Harvard Law Review*, Vol. 28 (1914), p. 34.

[13] *Peik v. C. & N.W. Ry.*, 94 U.S. 164, p. 178 (1877).

to affect interstate commerce, until the decision in the Wabash case definitely stopped encroachment. The court's language in this case is significant: "It cannot be too strongly insisted upon that the right of continuous transportation from one end of the country to the other is essential in modern times to that freedom of commerce from the restraints which the state might choose to impose upon it, that the commerce clause was intended to secure." [14] This decision points to the first criterion upon which regulatory institutions must be judged; namely, Do they create an administrative area sufficiently large to cope with the expanding market of the industry itself?

The Act to Regulate Commerce—Its Emasculation

The Act to regulate commerce merely set forth principles already contained in most of the state laws. It provided, for instance, that all charges should be "just and reasonable" and prohibited the various forms of discrimination. It provided for the publication and posting of all rates and fares, required them to be filed with the Interstate Commerce Commission, and provided further that the Commission be promptly notified of all changes. Only the rates on file were to be considered lawful charges. Owing to the fierce competition between rival carriers, it came about that rates between competitive points were usually lower than rates to intermediate points. Accordingly, the so-called long and short haul clause made it unlawful "for any common carrier . . . to charge or receive any greater compensation in the aggregate for the transportation of passengers, or of like kind of property, under substantially similar circumstances and conditions, for a shorter than for a longer distance over the same line, in the same direction, the shorter being included within the longer distance." The Interstate Commerce Commission was given authority to suspend the operation of this part of the law if, after an investigation of the competitive situation, it appeared that a particular carrier would be injured by loss of competitive traffic were the clause applied to it. Another provision of the Act prohibited pooling, in deference to public sentiment represented most strongly in the House. The commission of five members created by the Act was authorized to make investigations upon complaint or upon its own motion and to make a report as to its findings of fact together with a recommendation as to the amount of reparation, if any, to which an injured party was entitled.

It was clear that the Act was aimed principally at discrimination and

[14] *Wabash, St. Louis and Pacific Ry. Co. v. Illinois,* 118 U.S. 557 (1886).

rebating. So far as the general level of rates was concerned, competition was relied upon as before to prevent extortion. Where competition was not effective, the long and short haul clause was depended upon to extend the benefits of competitive rate levels. Although, as Professor Locklin points out,[15] the Commission had prescribed maximum rates in 68 out of 135 formal cases, regulation of the worst forms of competition rather than the achievement of monopoly may be taken as the prime result of the interstate commerce law in its original form.

The first period of federal railroad regulation under the Interstate Commerce Commission ended in 1906. It was in large part an experimental period, in which much technical knowledge was gained as to how the railroad problem must be handled under regulation. Barring the first few years, it was a period marked by hostility between the companies and the commission; in fact, the commission worked in an atmosphere of contempt for its processes and of suspicion of its agents. Congress had not sensed the full import of the problem.

Some of the defects were remedied by amending legislation. While the original Act had stipulated that ten days' public notice be given when rates were advanced, the Act was silent in regard to reductions. Since the carriers continued to grant special concessions by means of "midnight tariffs," an amendment in 1889 required that three days' notice be also given of reductions. It proved, moreover, to be difficult to get witnesses to testify. This defect was remedied by the Compulsory Testimony Act in 1893. Delays in enforcement of the Act by the courts led to the passage in 1903 of an Expediting Act. Although the cash rebate was gradually eliminated, the practice of personal discrimination, of which the larger shippers were the beneficiaries, continued under cover of various "devices." This time the carriers themselves sought legislation to conserve their revenues. Public sentiment favored such legislation because it was believed to counteract one of the causes for the growth of "trusts." The Elkins law of the same year declared that *every* departure from the published tariffs should be deemed to be conclusive proof of discrimination. Liability under the Act was extended to reach corporations as well as their agents, and shippers receiving rebates were also made subject to penalties which the Act strengthened.

The principal difficulty, however, grew out of judicial interpretation of the law. Vital defects were uncovered by a series of decisions. It seemed as if the courts were jealous of the usurpation of functions that had been

[15] Locklin, D. P., *Economics of Transportation* (New York: R. D. Irwin, Inc., Copyright 1947), p. 224.

in their hands from time immemorial. Although the law assumed that the Commission's orders were prima facie reasonable, the courts took the position that they might review the evidence as in a new proceeding.

Again, for ten years the Commission assumed that it had the power to fix maximum rates. In 1897, however, the United States Supreme Court in the Maximum Freight Rate Case [16] held that since fixing rates was a legislative power, it could not be assumed to have been granted by general language regarding the reasonableness of rates but could be delegated only in unmistakable language. The court concluded, therefore, that this power to fix rates for the future was not among the powers granted to the Commission. This decision effectively destroyed the rate-making power of the Commission, which was not restored until 1906 and not vouchsafed by judicial decision until 1910. It reduced the Commission's power practically to the equivalent of that possessed by advisory commissions. The Commission might still find that a particular rate was too high, or discriminatory, but it could not name a specific rate to be substituted for the future. It could order reparations to be paid to shippers, but the rate-making function was left, as before, in the hands of the carriers so that there was no warrant that these practices would be discontinued in the future. As a particular rate might be discriminatory and thus injurious to competitive industry, so the entire schedule of rates might be excessive, unduly increasing the price of the product to consumers and enabling the carriers to collect an extortionate income.

Even the Commission's power over place discrimination was emasculated by judicial interpretation. The Commission had interpreted the "long and short haul clause" in such a way as to permit higher rates for shorter hauls than for a longer haul *only* when the competition of water carriers, or of rail carriers not subject to the Act, fixed the lower rate for the longer haul. Such competition was regarded as "constituting dissimilar circumstances and conditions" and therefore as affording relief under the law. The Supreme Court, however, in the Import Rate Case [17] of 1896 and the Alabama Midland Case of 1897 [18] overruled this interpretation. Even the competition of interstate railroads was held by the court to "constitute dissimilar circumstances and conditions." Because the carriers under this interpretation were generally able to prove that circumstances were dissimilar, the Commission's power to control this form of place discrimination was gone. As Justice Harlan said in his dissenting opinion in the Alabama

[16] *I.C.C. v. C.N.O. & Tex. Pac. Ry. Co.*, 167 U.S. 479 (1897).
[17] 162 U.S. 197 (1896).
[18] 168 U.S. 144 (1897).

Midland Case, these decisions had "made the Commission a useless body for all practical purposes." In other words, judicial interpretation had shorn it of power to accomplish the important objects which Congress had in mind.

At this juncture a new angle of the rate problem appeared. The Act of 1887 had declared illegal all pooling arrangements designed to eliminate cutthroat competition. As a consequence, existing pools were dissolved or reorganized. The next move on the part of the carriers in controlling competition was to enter into "rate agreements." In 1897 and 1898 these were held to be illegal in cases involving traffic associations brought under the Sherman Anti-Trust Law of 1890 [19] which declared illegal every contract, combination, etc., in restraint of trade. These decisions ushered in the great combination period among railroads extending from 1898 to 1903. It was then that E. H. Harriman, to take a typical illustration, built up the Union Pacific System in 1897; and J. P. Morgan, the Southern Railway System in 1901. So great was the degree of concentration among railroads that a report, made in 1905, showed that thirty-nine persons constituted a majority of the boards of directors of all railroads in the eastern part of the United States. With the railroads consolidated into great territorial and ownership groupings, the public mind was beset with fear of monopoly. The time-honored American tradition of individualism, which means in practice the principle of competition, was endangered by monopoly.

Regulation of Municipal Utilities

It is important to note the changing objectives of local regulation. As already indicated, the regulation of water, gas, electric, telephone, and urban railway utilities throughout the period under review was in the hands of cities which had been given the power to grant special franchises. At first there was a tendency to confer them without adequate restrictions when cities welcomed franchise seekers as public benefactors. Realizing that these utility services were important for the growth of cities and that they would greatly enhance real estate values, the promotional spirit here also showed itself by the ready grant of franchises with liberal terms.

With the advancing prosperity of the companies, however, municipal officials began to realize that the franchises were valuable. Increasingly, therefore, in the grant of new ones or the renewal and amendment of those

[19] *I.C.C. v. Trans-Missouri Freight Ass'n.,* 166 U.S. 290 (1897), also *I.C.C. v. Joint Traffic Association,* 171 U.S. 505 (1898).

already conferred, local authorities began to insist that cities should participate in the growing revenues. It was then that franchise-granting became a means of self-enrichment on the part of corrupt politicians. It was partly to clear civic life of this corrupting influence and partly to secure a share of the expected profits for the taxpayers that the demand arose throughout the country that franchises should be sold to the highest bidder, payment being expressed as a lump sum, or as an annual sum, or as a percentage of gross or net revenues.

But these policies, although supposedly benefiting taxpayers, left out of account that portion of the public most vitally interested in the utilities —the customers. Their interest was in lower rates rather than lower taxes, and hence the demand arose that rates be reduced. The large majority, it was argued, have no interest in arrangements designed to make a few franchise holders enormously rich or to relieve property owners from taxes.

But, after all, a company bent upon maintaining its net revenues in the face of rate reductions may also lower its operating costs by reducing wages and rendering poorer service. As a consequence the labor problem and service problem began to move into the center of attention. Later, the spread of the city planning movement called attention to the importance of keeping control over street uses in the hands of local authorities in order to prevent the overburdening of public highways and to coordinate public and private uses.

The problem of tenure—perpetual and long-term franchises. The question of tenure is a central, vexing problem that runs through the history of special franchise regulation. Many of the earliest franchises, particularly in the eastern states, were expressly perpetual or, lacking a definite time limit, were held by the courts to be perpetual.[20] Long-term franchises whose expiration dates were so far in the future, often 999 years, that utilities need not worry over them, had no regulatory effect. Even though they were not exclusive, competition failed to function because consolidations were the ultimate outcome. To be sure, in many instances companies had to await the growth in demand; in the more rapidly growing cities, however, substantial earnings began early and developed into true monopoly profits. The gas companies of New York City, consolidated in the 1880's, were perhaps the best illustrations of this tendency.

Short-term franchises. When the view became sufficiently general that the profits of a monopoly based upon a franchise should be limited, the terms of franchises were shortened. The short-period franchise ranged from

[20] Cf. *People v. O'Brien*, 111 N.Y. 1 (1888).

ten to fifty years. A New Jersey commission which investigated municipal franchises in 1905 recommended that franchises should not be granted for a longer period than thirty-three years, unless a majority of voters should authorize longer grants not to exceed sixty-six years. In Illinois the maximum period was fixed at twenty years, in Ohio at twenty-five years, and in Michigan at thirty years.[21] With the current popular opposition to exclusive franchises, indeed with express constitutional prohibitions against the practice in many states, it was hoped that the short-term franchise would prevent franchise holders from establishing rates at the point where they would yield monopoly profits. This position represents a middle ground between the opinion expressed by Mayor Tom L. Johnson of Cleveland that "the best franchise is a dead one" and the view of the Committee on Public Policy of the National Electric Light Association [22] that all franchises should be perpetual.

On the whole the short-term franchise was a failure. The original vice of awarding competing grants brought about a situation where there was such diversity in the termination of the different grants that at no time could cities exercise complete control over all of them so as to work out a uniform policy of control. This becomes peculiarly significant when we bear in mind that local utilities in the larger cities are an amalgamation of constituent companies. The Consolidated Gas Company of New York, for instance, is an aggregation of seventy gas and electric companies. The resettlement of franchise terms was thus made difficult. Some claimed that the public service companies "have not failed to see the advantage to be derived by them from franchises that are not co-terminous." Since cities could not successfully take over the system piecemeal or secure bids from competitors, the existing companies had an advantage in negotiating for renewals.

Another objection to limited-term franchises was that often such franchises did not specifically provide what should be done with the fixtures laid in city streets upon termination of the grants. This operated to handicap the cities because the companies claimed that by virtue of their *general charter* they might continue operation under revised conditions, or in the event of failure to agree upon a new franchise-contract with the city, continue under "day to day franchises" with such reasonable regulations as to rates and services as the city might from time to time enact.

[21] Wilcox, D. F., *Municipal Franchises*, p. 35 (2 vols. Eng. News Book Dept., 1910–11).

[22] *Report of Committee on Public Policy*, National Electric Light Association, June 1907, p. 8.

In the absence of specific provisions for service in the future, the courts as well as the communities were reluctant to have the fixtures reduced to scrap and service discontinued.

Short-term franchises have also handicapped the companies by creating uncertainty as to renewals. If the franchises were not extended under reasonable conditions, what would happen to their investment in street fixtures and other specialized properties? The piecemeal nature of franchise grants and their differing and uncertain tenure often created a situation which made refinancing difficult if not impossible. A bond issue running for a period beyond the expiration dates of important franchises is a difficult issue to sell. On the other hand, with franchises terminating in the near future the companies were unwilling to build needed extensions unless suitable arrangements could be made to insure a continuance of their right to operate and thus enable them to secure the necessary capital. Companies tried, therefore, to keep the expiration dates of important franchises sufficiently far in the future so that their investments would be secure. This served to keep the franchise issue in the foreground. One method adopted was to obtain a renewal of operating rights by consolidating all franchises in the renewal grant. According to the terms of one of these "blanket franchises" granted in 1900, the Milwaukee Electric Railway and Light Company was given an exclusive franchise until 1934. This time limit was likewise made to apply to all prior rights, privileges, and franchises granted to the company and its predecessors, whether or not a definite time limit had been specified. It was similarly provided that if the suburban territory in which the company held franchises should in the future be annexed by the city, the suburban franchises should likewise expire in 1934.

The common ground of experience.   Out of the welter of this experience finally came the conviction that franchises should be reorganized *into a system* with a definite period of tenure and a grant of monopoly rights, but with regulation of service and rates. As the Commission on Public Ownership and Operation of the National Civic Federation said in its report: "Public utilities, whether in public or in private hands, are best conducted under a system of legalized and regulated monopoly." [23] The impelling motive was the recognition that where competitors are bound to be few, consolidation is apt to follow anyway, while the difficulties of operation in crowded streets require that street facilities be used to maximum capacity. The advantages of unified operation of street railway, telephone, electric power, and gas utilities in giving better service to patrons and a lowered operating cost due to the economies of large-scale operations imperiously

[23] Part I, Vol. 1, p. 26 (1907).

dictated the change. Moreover, public policy required that, in addition to being as cheap as possible, the service should be extended over as wide an area geographically as the economic situation would permit. An early illustration was afforded by the transit situation in Boston. From December 9, 1897, when the West End Street Railway system was leased by the Boston Elevated Railway Company, the entire system of subway, elevated, and surface lines in this city and its suburbs was operated by one company.

Yet these term limitations, often without provisions for city purchase or purchase by some other grantee at the end of the period, had the effect of making investments insecure. As the termination date of franchises approached, there was no assurance that they would be renewed. Failing to obtain a renewal, the property of the company would be worth only its scrap value. The inducement was too great, therefore, to manipulate operations so as to enable investors to recoup their capital out of earnings. Improvements and extensions were not made; the service was restricted to the area where population was densest; replacements and necessary repairs were deferred; as a result, service deteriorated. The privately owned street railways formerly operating in Toronto and Detroit were good illustrations of the disintegrating effect of the term franchise.

Regulation of Rates and Service under Term Franchises

While a term franchise or a revocable franchise limits monopoly power in one dimension (i.e., as to time), it is even more important that monopoly power be limited in another dimension (i.e., as to the extent of power) by regulating the rate of charge. This was done by fixing maximum rates for the franchise period. Street railway franchises adopted the convenient five-cent cash fare with some provision for free transfers and lower ticket rates for regular customers. Similarly, maximum rates were fixed for gas, telephone, and electric service, but these maximum rates soon became obsolete because the growing business of the companies required more complex and flexible rates schedules, thus repeating the earlier experience with railways and other common carriers. Moreover, the companies began to appreciate that increased earnings, both gross and net, could be secured by means of rate reductions.

With franchises interpreted as contracts, this rate, whether maximum or specific, became an inflexible term in a binding agreement. In case of the long-term or perpetual franchise, this ruling was particularly vicious. Although franchise renewals or consolidations of companies provided some opportunities for modifications, yet the atmosphere was hardly such as to bring about substantial concessions in a spirit of mutual accommodation. The same difficulty arose in negotiating new, limited-term franchises. The hope of reaping an exceptional reward or the fear of a probable heavy loss were the imponderables that made bargaining a matching of wits between company and city representatives. An earning power guaranteed by a fixed rate was dependent upon the growth in traffic units and the changes in cost of operation; yet both were subject to favorable as well as unfavorable tendencies that could not be foreseen for all the years of even comparatively short-term franchises. Once agreed to, the parties were bound by the terms of the grant. Attempts by cities to change the terms were met by the objection that the change would violate a contractual obligation and confiscate the property of the companies. Only when the franchise was silent on rate questions or when the power to alter, amend or repeal the terms of franchises was reserved, could the power to regulate rates or service be exercised by state or local legislatures.[24] In other cases the rates could not be disturbed.

The suggestion was also made that cities reserve the power of adjusting rates periodically or at any time. The companies were not enthusiastic over the adoption of such provisions because they lacked faith in local councils. In any event, the controversy usually came to the courts. Beginning in 1896, the gradual increase in the cost of operation placed companies in a position where they in turn had to apply for increases in franchise rates. The courts, however, were consistent by holding that changes could not be made without agreement between the parties.

Discriminatory rates. An even greater evil that crept into the administration of these enterprises as a result of the ineffectiveness of control under the special franchise was that of discrimination in both service and rates. We cannot do better than to quote the late Professor B. H. Meyer, Interstate Commerce Commissioner, and also at that time a member of the Railroad Commission of Wisconsin.[25]

The whole state was literally streaked and plastered with discriminations in the rates of utilities; and in all the rest of the country where the extent of such discriminations has not yet been determined as it has in Wisconsin, it is quite probable that discriminations similar in character and extent likewise exist. For thirty-two of the reporting (telephone) companies, eight out of every one hundred subscribers received free or reduced service.

[24] In California the power to regulate the service of local utilities is reserved to the localities by constitutional provisions.
[25] Quoted from Holmes, F. L., *Regulation of Railroads and Public Utilities in Wisconsin* (New York: D. Appleton and Co., 1915), p. 295.

The same commission found the following situation with respect to other utilities.

Seven big consumers were served water in one city of 4,000 inhabitants without charge. In Madison, 1,360 telephone users out of 5,000 received reductions amounting to $1,120 a month. Discriminations also existed between public and private users, between metered and unmetered users, and between power and light consumers. In Ashland the city was paying about $8,400 less for water than its share.

Not infrequently the franchises themselves carried provisions for free service to the cities. Thus, electric utilities were required to furnish free power to swing bridges and to provide pole room for police and fire alarm wires. Street railways carried policemen, firemen, and other public employees free of charge. We will return to this subject of free service again in another connection.

Control over service. Term franchises were even less effective in securing control of service. Under dynamic conditions, service requirements were bound to change, for both technical improvements and growth of population change the character of demand. The common law formula of "adequate service" was found upon examination to be composed of so many elements that specification of concrete detail was not possible. Nor could the need for extensions be intelligently determined in advance. Some cities accordingly inserted provisions whereby the power to require extensions and to prescribe the characteristics of adequate service were reserved. These reservations were believed to be necessary in order to secure the administrative flexibility that is essential to efficient regulation. Particularly was it necessary to ensure that the utility in question would be operated in coordination with other public utilities and with municipal functions. This objective was not generally achieved in earlier franchises, although later franchises record some advance in this direction.

A most important aspect of good service is continuity. This was most likely to be destroyed by strikes and other labor disturbances. As a result, the powers of cities in the event of strikes and lockouts were made the subject of specific provisions. The principle at stake was that the public might reasonably expect uninterrupted service because under modern conditions communal life was dependent upon it. Obviously then, it was necessary to prevent strikes and lockouts, and in doing so the provocative causes had to be made the point of attack. Cities accordingly tried to obtain fair wages and fair treatment for employees, and to set up for the companies adequate protection against destruction of their property by recalcitrant workers. To bring this about, franchises stipulated the respective rights of employers and employees, and provided for boards of conciliation or arbitration to settle grievances.

Public Ownership and Operation as an Alternative

Although the earliest franchises usually made no provision for public ownership and operation, clauses intended to bring this about appeared oftener toward the close of the nineteenth century. The belief in competition favored this development. With the movement for the short-term, non-exclusive franchise went the demand for keeping the government in the position of a potential competitor. Moreover, it was felt that this purchase option would serve as a bargaining asset in renewing franchises and would forestall consolidations. Later, with the development of sentiment for monopoly, it was felt that the government itself might desire to undertake the service. Consequently, provision was made for the ultimate reversion of the plant to the city. Sometimes companies were allowed to accumulate out of earnings an amortization fund to retire investment when the franchise should terminate and the plant revert to the city. This method proved unsatisfactory. It complicated the regulatory machinery because, necessarily, the charges had to be increased during the life of the franchise, and this set up an inducement to a low standard of maintenance and to poorer service as the expiration date approached.

It is now agreed that the best mode of procedure is to grant either franchises of indeterminate duration or short-term franchises with the privilege of renewal but with a firm option to the city to purchase the plant. In the case of indeterminate grants, this purchase option may be exercised at any time, or at any time after a fixed period; in the case of term franchises, it may be exercised at succeeding expiration dates. Sometimes a new company may be substituted for the old company, but the former is obliged to purchase the existing properties. These methods obviate amortization charges and protect the investment. The purchase price is usually fixed by arbitration at the time, or the method of computing the price is definitely fixed in the franchise.

Although there was gradual improvement in conditions under exclusive local regulation by means of special franchises, the inflexibility of the system was not overcome soon enough to prevent the development of a movement whose object was securing exclusive state regulation by administrative commissions. The best known type of this form of regulation is that which accompanies the grant of an indeterminate permit instead of the term franchise. This will be discussed in a later chapter.

6. PUBLIC UTILITIES IN THE TWENTIETH CENTURY: THE MONOPOLISTIC EPOCH— PLANNING AND COORDINATION

In the present and subsequent chapters the economic development of public utility industries will be reviewed up to the present time. As already indicated, the period from 1900 to 1929 was dominated by the monopoly concept; but while the idea of monopoly persists, the great depression of 1929 clearly marks the beginning of a new epoch, the hallmarks of which are planning and coordination. During this half-century the United States became a dominant world power, both economically and politically. The period begins with the Spanish-American War which brought on the complications of overseas dominions. In the course of the next fifty years the country fought two victorious world wars. These and other complicating developments have completely reoriented its outlook.

In population *continental* United States grew from 75,994,575 in 1900 to 122,775,046 by 1930, but to only 131,669,275 by 1940, indicating a significant slowing down of the rate of population increase, especially after 1930, when it dropped to a mere 7.2 per cent during the depression decade. Meanwhile, the country remained almost stationary in land area, growing only from 2,974,159 square miles to 2,977,128 square miles. However, even the lesser rate of population increase meant a significant increase in average density from 25.6 to 44.2 persons per square mile. More significant still was the progress in urbanization, where the percentage of urban to total population changed from 39.7 per cent to 56.5 per cent.

During the decade of World War II the rate of population growth was once more accelerated. In 1950 the population figure stood at 150,697,361, with an average density of 50.7 per square mile, and with an urbanization trend of 62 per cent continuing. Our civilization is now dominantly an urban one, and while our rural dwellers are still increasing in absolute numbers, their relative importance is on the decline.

The number of places of markedly urban concentration (2,500 and over) have increased from 1,737 to 3,464, but here, too, the rate of increase is slowing down. Between 1930 and 1949, the increase was only from 3,165 to 3,464. It is also most significant that there has been no increase at all in the number (thirty-seven) of cities with population in excess of 250,000. New York, Chicago, Philadelphia, Detroit, and Los Angeles continue to be the leaders into which between fifteen and sixteen million people are crowded. Thus, there is a slowing down all along the line.

One new phenomenon of population distribution should be noted, however; there has been a rapid development of metropolitan areas, where the population density is 150 or more per square mile and where central cities tend to overflow into surrounding satellites with truly urban con-centrations. The Census lists 140 such districts in both 1930 and 1940, but their population has increased from 57,602,865 to 62,965,773, with the greatest rate of population growth in the areas outside the central cities. By 1950 there were 168 such areas with a population of 83,929,863. Our urbanized population is trying to escape the rigors of congested living conditions.

Local Transportation Utilities

We shall begin our discussion of transportation by tying up with the urbanization phenomenon just alluded to, namely, the growth of metro-politan areas consisting of the central city with its satellite suburbs. This development would have been unthinkable without greatly improved sys-tems of urban transportation, in which the motor vehicle, rapid transit, and the electric street and interurban railway figured most prominently. These carriers, together with the facilities for communication to be described presently, have also done much to break down the isolation of farm life. They have introduced higher standards of living by broadening horizons and by bringing the advantages of city life, such as schools, recreational, and marketing facilities, within the reach of the country dweller.

Urban, suburban and interurban railway transportation. Until World War I, the electric street railway was the unquestioned medium of mass transportation in all of our cities. After its first introduction in 1883 the mileage increased very rapidly to 1,260 by 1890 and to 22,576 by 1902. In fact, within a decade the horsecar and electric car exchanged places. The period since then has seen the rise and decline of the electric railway. The peak of its popularity came in 1922 when 12,666,557,734 revenue passengers were carried. In that year, of 43,932 miles of single track operated, 43,789 were operated by electricity, 46 by cable, and only 4 by animal traction. These figures also include electric interurban mileage of 17,807, and suburban mileage of 3,200. Operating revenues were in excess of $1 billion.

The development of electric transit for suburban and interurban traffic between nearby cities and intervening rural districts belongs almost entirely to the period since 1895, with most of the development coming during the first decade of the present century. It was then that many extravagant promotions were conceived, oftentimes referred to locally as somebody's "folly" because the more sanguine proponents of electric traction believed it would drive out the steam railway. Interurban service turned out to be merely an added convenience for transacting business and for social intercourse. It did make the electric railway an active competitor of the steam railway in short-haul passenger service and succeeded in diverting a considerable share of this traffic to itself, besides creating traffic of its own. At first the superiority of interurban electric transit consisted in the more frequent stops, the greater frequency of service by using the single car unit, and the lower fares due to greater economy in construction and operation. Beginning about 1907 the best service was being rendered by high-speed interurban lines operating nonstop between terminal points upon their own private rights of way. The later interurbans were equipped with cars of a more modern design calling for heavy motors, automatic brakes, and comfortable seats. Heavy rails laid upon well-ballasted roadways, train operation with regular schedules and fixed station stops, and block signals to ensure safe operating conditions made possible a quality of service approaching that of the better equipped steam railway lines. Mail and express business was solicited from the beginning. Later l.c.l. (less than carload) freight service, transport of milk and perishable freight, and even transport of bulk freight, like lumber, coal, and sand were added.

Most of this interurban development came in New England and the Central States. On the Pacific coast, the Pacific Electric Railway (centering in Los Angeles) did much to promote the intensive development of that part of southern California. Efforts were made by some steam railways, particularly in New England, to secure control of electric lines regarded by them as competitors.

Decline of the electric railway. World War I marked the beginning of the decline of the electric railway. For a time the industry fought rearguard actions in an effort to hold up the decline; but retreat was inevitable when substitute competition in the shape of the motor bus and the private motor car set in, aided and abetted by a highway and street improvement program. The decline in electric railway operations was most marked on interurban systems and in urban operations in the smaller cities, where they have practically disappeared. Interurban trackage declined from a maximum of 18,098 miles in 1917 to 7,995 in 1936. At the present time, interurban operations have become bus operations or have been merged into the rapid transit systems of our larger cities. Only to a lesser degree has the urban and suburban street railway accompanied the interurban in its decline. The coincidence of a depression period, beginning in 1914, with the availability of a first crop of second-hand motor cars put destructive and unregulated "jitney" competition alongside the streetcar on short, heavy traffic routes. Moreover, caught between the upper millstone of the customary and franchise-fixed fare of five cents and the nether millstone of rapidly rising wartime operating cost, the financial condition of the streetcar companies steadily worsened. The rising tide of bus competition and the enhanced cost of operating in streets because of vehicular congestion put the streetcar into a battle for self-preservation. Experiments with new fares and other traffic stimulating devices and attempts at coordinating electric traction with bus operations merely served to delay the descent of the hard-pressed industry into hard times, reorganization, receivership, and eventual abandonment. Street railway mileage declined from a peak of 44,677 in 1917 to 31,432 in 1932. Revenues declined from a peak of $1,016,719,092 in 1922 to $566,289,987 ten years later, while riding fell off from over 12½ billion passengers to less than 8 billions. An investment in excess of $5 billion was rapidly disintegrating. The villain in the piece was the new motor vehicle industry, at which it now is necessary to take a hasty glance, though the concrete facts are a matter of common knowledge.

Long Distance Highway Transport and the Motor Vehicle

The most far-reaching technological change affecting both local and long-distance transport has come with the invention of the gasoline-driven motor vehicle. After a brief period of experimentation, the first practical motor cars were introduced in 1893. By 1900 the new age of automotive transportation had definitely arrived, bringing in its wake a new era in road building. Beginning with New Jersey in 1891, all states have again taken up programs of state aid and state supervision in road building. This supplemented the work of highway and street improvements which counties and cities were also beginning to take up with renewed energy. Finally, federal legislation, first enacted in 1916, provided for a system of federal aid highways in each state, not to exceed seven per cent of its total road mileage. The plan included a national system of trunk-line highways designed to join together the various sections of the country.

Under the stimulus of these financial aids and influences, the total rural highway mileage increased from 2,151,379 in 1904 to 3,029,811 in 1954. In 1904, only 153,530 miles were surfaced, scarcely any of it of high type. In 1954 over one-half, or 1,905,871 miles were surfaced, with 291,000 miles of high-type surfacing.

Although railways and waterways have been the principal arteries of inland transport throughout most of our history, there always was great need for the maintenance of highway systems that would serve the purposes of local short-distance transport—the capillaries, so to speak, of our national system. They have come to be called "farm to market" roads. Local units of government have always had these local roads in charge. During the "horse and buggy" days, they were hardly a credit to the country; neither were street improvements in cities and villages. The universal adoption of the motor vehicle revolutionized all this.

Local taxes, which originally financed road improvement, quickly proved inadequate in face of the new demands. Roads were consequently classified into local-use highways and general-use highways. The former continued to be financed through local taxation supplemented by borrowing, while the latter were supported by a user tax in the form of gasoline sales taxes and motor vehicle registration fees, also supplemented by borrowing. By 1937 this system was producing $756 million from state gasoline taxes and $360 million from registration fees. Supplementary financing through borrowing by state and local governments had accumulated a highway debt of $1.3 billion by 1936. Federal aid funds in 1935 from gasoline taxes totaled $219 million. By this process the old-time turnpike is being reincarnated with the gasoline pump of the filling station doing duty as the turnstile.

The new highway system increased highway traffic enormously. The number of motor vehicles registered grew from a mere 8,000 in 1900 to 62,020,000 in 1955. Trucks and busses became significant parts of the total after World War I. Of the 1955 total, 51,989,000 were passenger vehicles and 10,031,000 were trucks.

With these developments, a new prime-mover engine, using a new form of power, has also come to the front and is challenging the older forms of power. The internal combustion engine, experimented with on the street railways of Chicago in 1892, has been developed to a high degree of efficiency and is being applied to cars that run on tracks. But its most significant development is by way of the motor vehicle industry which uses this network of improved highways and has put the old common carrier industries on the defensive.

At first the public carriers were unwilling to admit that danger threatened. In its first form as the so-called "jitneys" of 1914, it carried only urban passengers for short distances on heavy traffic routes at a five-cent fare. Although the "jitney" was unreliable, uncomfortable, and financially irresponsible, and hence was soon supplanted by the organized bus or coach company, unregulated substitute competition had its beginning with this episode. Ultimately, but tardily, electric railways were forced, one after another, to buy up these competitors or to start bus operations of their own. The improved bus provides a faster and more flexible service and has met most of the objections to the earlier types.

The most serious threat to electric railway patronage has come from the widespread ownership of automobiles (one car to every 4.1 persons in 1950 and one car to every 3.2 persons in 1955) which has radically reduced the "riding habit" (rides per capita) tributary to the common carriers. In one respect, however, the privately owned motor vehicle is succumbing to its own inherent limitation. It is most uneconomical in the use of street space. Since only 1.7 persons is the average load per motor car, a street car or bus carrying fifty passengers is the equivalent of twenty-nine automobiles occupying an entire city block. And to this must be added the inconvenience and expense arising from the well-known parking problem.

Despite economies and innovations, such as the "skip-stop," the one-man safety car, and the more recent Presidents' Conference Committee cars,[1] the electric railway is giving way. The number of companies declined from 1,260 in 1912 to 112 in 1952, with miles of line declining from 30,438 to 12,254 in the same interval. Meanwhile, motorbus route miles increased to over 99,600. In our largest cities, where the electric streetcar is maintaining a precarious foothold, there is a tendency to restrict the motor bus to intercity traffic, to city traffic on boulevard streets where tracks would be objectionable, to service in outlying districts, and to the supply of a special fare "de luxe" service. In such cities, the electric railway continues

[1] The PCC cars were the result of years of expensive research. They combined lighter weight, powerful motors, noiseless operation, attractive stainless steel interiors into a fast-moving vehicle designed to recapture traffic from the busses; but it seems to have come too late.

as an agency of mass transport, although even as early as 1926 the proposal was seriously made to eliminate all surface cars in New York, substituting a fleet of busses. Part of electric track abandonment is reappearing in mileage of trolley coach routes (1954) aggregating 3,630. These "trackless trolleys," first developed in Europe, might be called the electric railway in retreat.

The failure to extend effective regulation to the new motorbus industry has had much to do with the difficulties in which the traditional common carriers now find themselves. The taxicab company, rendering a public, though special, service, was not at first a serious competitor. However, the arrival of fleets of low-fare taxicabs cruising freely about on city streets is a renewed threat even to the organized bus or railway carrier, which must operate over fixed routes and with a definite schedule according to the terms of their franchises.

The motor truck operated as a common, contract, or private carrier has also brought motor vehicle competition to the steam railways. Particularly after 1929, these carriers began to make inroads upon the merchandise express, milk, and freight business.

These adverse conditions, made more stringent by the oncoming depression, have left their mark upon the electric railway industry in terms of receivership, foreclosure sales, and track abandonments. This record, as gathered by the *Electric Railway Journal* at the time, shows that in the eleven years between 1920 and 1931 an aggregate of 6,804 miles of track were abandoned, an average of 618 per year, with additional thousands of miles in financial distress.

Rapid Transit

As already mentioned, in this country the construction of subways was long delayed. New York, after a long period of agitation, authorized construction in 1891, but work did not begin until 1901 and the first project was not completed until 1904. In 1903, the Manhattan Elevated Railways were leased to the Interborough Rapid Transit Company which had been organized to operate the public subways. Other subway construction followed in 1908 and after. Since 1947 complete ownership and operation is in public hands. Other cities with elevated and subway lines are Boston, Philadelphia, and Chicago. The question has been more or less agitated in Cleveland, Detroit, St. Louis, and Los Angeles, but the heavy investment required has given all these cities pause. This kind of metropolitan mass-transport facility with 1,223 miles in operation, has remained static since World War II.

Philadelphia is unique in that under the former "Mitten Management" a completely coordinated urban transportation system has been achieved. It consists of elevated, subway, streetcar, trolley-bus, gas-bus, and taxicab service. In this country, as in Europe, the trend is toward complete integration of common carrier service. Only in this way can the tremendous daily movement of passenger traffic be effectively handled.

Present Status of the Transit Industry

Some pertinent facts as to the relative importance of the different branches of the transit industry for 1954 are summarized in Table III. Gasoline rationing and the scarcity of rubber during World War II gave all forms of common carrier transport a temporary surcease from the eroding effects of motor vehicle competition, where the government furnishes the right of way.

Table III   The Transit Industry,* 1954

Item	Surface Lines	Subway, Elev.	Trolley Coaches	Motorbus
Miles of route	5,547	1,218	3,630	99,000
Passenger vehicles	6,400	9,200	6,598	54,000
Investment (dollar, millions)	692	2,250	165	756
Oper. Rev. (dollar, millions)	204	269	142	857
Rev. Passengers (dollar, millions)	1,053	1,767	993	6,045
Employees	71,000	. . . .	18,000	122,000

* Source: *Statistical Abstract* of the U.S.

Our National Transportation System

We pass now to a discussion of our nation-wide transportation facilities. We shall not be concerned with the minutiae of the national transport problem but only with those general aspects which afford a picture of the changes that have come in the course of the present century. Although the transport function consists of the carriage of persons and property, we will use only their freight-carrying capacity to indicate the relative importance of the several classes of carriers at this point.

The size of our intercity transportation plant in domestic commerce is estimated from data derived from the Census as follows:

Steam railway miles of first track operated, 1954	234,497
Controlled civil airways mileage, 1954	134,354
Highway mileage, all types, 1954	3,029,811
Inland waterway mileage approximated (excluding Great Lakes)	27,933
Petroleum pipeline mileage, 1954	140,000
Total	3,566,595

The Bureau of Transport Economics of the ICC estimated that 1955 intercity ton-mile freight traffic, categorized according to kinds of transport agencies, was as follows:

Carrier	Billions	Percentage
Railroads	631.4	49.41
Motor vehicles	226.2	17.71
Inland waterways, including Great Lakes	216.5	16.94
Airways	0.5	.04
Pipelines	203.2	15.90
Total	1277.8	100.00

The most significant economic factor in the recent development of the transportation industry is the division between those branches of the industry who use their own rights of way and structures and those who use a public right of way furnished for joint use by both private and common carriers. This creates an economic problem of cost apportionment as a basis for user charges to be assessed against private carriers on the one hand and the common carriers on the other hand. Common carriers using this fixed transportation plant jointly with others compete with common carriers who supply their own fixed plant.

The financial magnitude of this fixed transportation plant, excluding the mobile equipment, was estimated by the Board of Transportation and Research set up by Congress in 1940. The figures for *unamortized public* expenditures and for *depreciated private* expenditures are shown separately. Public expenditures exclude land values. The estimates also are exclusive of the contemporaneous investment in mobile operating equipment.

Waterways, federal improvements	$1,230,000,000
Public terminals	700,000,000
Total	1,930,000,000
Highways	16,500,000,000
Federal airways	14,500,000
Public airports	236,500,000
Total air transport	251,000,000
Grand Total Public	18,681,000,000
Private airports	83,348,980
Pipelines reporting to I.C.C.	384,313,115
Pipelines not reporting to I.C.C. (est.)	65,686,885
Total pipelines	450,000,000
Railway fixed plant excl. oper. equip't.	16,000,000,000
Grand Total Private	16,533,348,980
Transportation, fixed plant only	35,214,348,980

The significance of the foregoing is that it establishes an estimate of the capital expenditures for fixed transportation plant provided by the public purse. The question as to how much of these expenditures are to be made recoverable through taxes, fees, or user charges while still providing an equitable basis for competition is one of the most vexing with which public utility economics has to deal.

Railway transportation. We will now add to the bare bones of the above statistical outlines such descriptive and historical facts as will provide a background for our later analyses and interpretations. Steam railways up to 1900 had already amply demonstrated their effectiveness in enhancing the production of goods by making possible an expansion in the occupational and regional division of labor. They had unlocked the natural resources of the country, and by reducing transportation cost, had enlarged the area in which goods could be marketed. This, in turn, had ushered in the economies of mass production. Railway managers, by adopting a theory of keeping everybody in business, had promoted the movement of goods and sharpened the competition among producers. The long-run influence of these procedures had been to help raise the standard of living. Although the movement of raw materials for producer and consumer goods required a variety of transport services, water transport in particular, the steam railway had become the backbone of our national transportation system.

Since 1900 only the following major expansions in the railway network

need to be chronicled: (1) the construction in 1905 of a line from San Pedro
—the harbor of Los Angeles—to Salt Lake City; (2) the expansion in 1909
of the Chicago, Milwaukee & St. Paul into a transcontinental line through
its Puget Sound extension; (3) the construction of the Western Pacific from
Salt Lake City to San Francisco, also completed in 1909; (4) the construction of 500 miles of railroad in Alaska by the federal government, completed
in 1923. The last named is the only important stretch of railroad, aside
from the Panama Canal Railroad, owned and operated by government in the
United States.

The expansion of the railway network ended in 1916 when the peak of
254,037 road-miles was attained. Since then, abandonments have exceeded
new construction, so that road mileage in 1954 had decreased to 221,098.
For a time there was continuous growth of trackage (multiple tracking,
sidings, terminal expansion), achieving a maximum of 429,883 miles by
1930. Owing, however, to the gradual and at first almost unnoticed growth
of competition from intercity highway transport and the effect of the depression of the 1930's in reducing the demand for transport, this mileage declined to 392,580 in 1954. Similarly, the investment by steam railways in
road and equipment reached a peak in 1931 of $26,094,899,000 from which
a decline set in. The effect of the decline is concealed, however, by the
growing inflation which set in with World War II. In 1954 the book value
of investment in road and equipment was $32,708,945,000, from which a
depreciation reserve of $7,152,098,000 should have been deducted to obtain
the net dollar value of the investment.

Despite a new era of consolidations after the depression of 1893 had run
its course, there were still 947 operating companies in 1925. Bankruptcies
and reorganizations reduced the number to 443 in 1954. Railroads are,
nevertheless, a coordinated national system, made so by standardization of
gauge, track and track structures, time zones, operating rules, joint rates,
joint use of equipment and terminals, and the interchange of traffic.

World War I severely strained the carrying capacity of the railroads,
and there was much traffic congestion along the eastern seaboard. The railroads were leased by the federal government and operated until 1920. Revised programs of operation instituted by the U.S. Railroad Administration
worked toward further integration of service and facilities. Nevertheless, the
railroads emerged from government operation in 1920 requiring extensive
improvements in its fixed plant and mobile equipment. The prosperity of the
1920's made possible much reconstruction of the railway plant, particularly
in the operation of heavier and longer trains, which required more powerful
locomotives, heavier rails, strengthened bridges, and modernized rolling

stock. But the diminished traffic of the depression 1930's, coupled with the growing highway and waterway competition which began in the 1920's, left the railways with an excess of facilities.

Like the urban common carrier had done, the railroads met the threatened motor vehicle competition by radical improvements in passenger and freight transport. Air-conditioned, streamlined trains powered by improved steam and diesel locomotives, together with a promotional fare policy, succeeded in slowing down the decline in patronage. Improved freight service with faster and more convenient schedules met the competition of motor vehicles for merchandise and livestock shipments. The tardy adoption of store-door pickup and delivery service for less-than-carload freight saved a portion of this traffic from further inroads by highway carriers.

With the rapid development of the defense program, the traffic using the rails began to accelerate rapidly. After Pearl Harbor the Office of Defense Transportation was set up for the conservation of all forms of transportation. By cooperating with this agency and with each other, the railroads were able to carry an immense war load of long-distance traffic, which came to the rails because of the diversion of coastal and intercoastal shipping to maintain overseas supply lines. Similarly, until the construction of the Big and Little Inch oil pipelines, the rails had to carry a great volume of petroleum traffic, taking the place of diverted oil tankers. The curtailment in the use of private automobiles due to tire and gasoline rationing threw upon the rails an extra burden of passenger traffic. As compared with immediately prewar volumes, the peak year of 1944 showed that freight traffic had more than doubled and passenger traffic more than quadrupled.

Since no significant plant expansion and maintenance was possible during the war, the railroads suffered great physical deterioration from deferred maintenance. Although the high earnings during wartime made possible the accumulation of working capital and the retirement of much funded debt, the resumption of the job of restoration and improvement, due to the prevailing high level of prices and wages, again produced such unsatisfactory financial conditions for most roads that the improvement programs had to be deferred. Meanwhile the carriers sought and obtained rate increases, which, when made permanent in December, 1946, averaged 17.6 per cent above prewar levels. Nevertheless, the earnings record of the railroads, on account of the division of traffic between new and old competitors, continued to be a precarious one.[2]

[2] Locklin, D. P., *Economics of Transportation.* See particularly Chapter XV, The Railroad Rate Level, pp. 363 *et seq.,* for statistics of annual railway earnings.

The most promising development on the horizon for the railroad industry is the growing "dieselization" of its motive power, with its resulting economies. In 1925 out of a total of 68,092 locomotives of all types, only one lone diesel electric locomotive was reported. In 1954 their number had grown to 25,256 in a total of 35,033. A technological revolution in power is safeguarding the status of railroads as the principal agency of mass transport.

Water transportation. Domestic traffic carried over waterways is of three types: (1) coastal and intercoastal through the Panama Canal, (2) traffic on the Great Lakes, (3) river and canal traffic. We are touching only lightly in this account on the development of shipping in foreign commerce which, aided by a subsidy policy, developed once more after World Wars I and II. In each case the revival of an American deep-sea merchant marine was materially aided by the sale at heavy discounts of vessels constructed by the government during the wars. United States flag vessels now carry American commerce over thirty-one trade routes to all parts of the world. The 1955 tonnage of the U.S. merchant marine engaged in foreign and domestic commerce was 29,958,000, the bulk of it, or 26,792,000 tons, being steam and motor tonnage and 3,133,000 tons in canal boats and barges. Hundreds of vessels were laid up in a reserve fleet for emergencies.

Owing to an abiding belief that water transport is inherently cheap, there has been a significant revival of interest in our inland waterways since the beginning of the twentieth century. With the tardy technological developments in water transport, and because the Interstate Commerce Commission had failed to restrain the railroads in their competition with waterways, water transport was at a very low ebb by the close of the nineteenth century. The revival of interest began with the convening of the first National Rivers and Harbors Congress at Baltimore in 1901. With support from the nation's chief executives, who were becoming interested in conservation, commissions were appointed to investigate and report on ways and means of improving our inland waterways. In 1903 New York voted $101 million to transform the Erie Canal into a modern barge canal. Intercoastal traffic was greatly stimulated by the completion of the Panama Canal in 1913. With the completion of facilitating canals at the head of Lake Superior and improvements at other points, shipping on the Great Lakes has grown to tremendous proportions. Growing out of the operation of barge lines by the U.S. Railroad Administration during World War I on the Mississippi and Warrior Rivers, the Inland Waterways Corporation (liquidated to private interests in 1954) was created in 1924 to carry on these promotional operations. Combined with motor carriers, air transport, and pipelines (to be considered presently), these water transport facilities are once more threatening the supremacy of railway transport.

Pipeline transportation. Although pipeline transportation was first associated with the early marketing of crude oil and natural gas, its development into a specialized carrier of liquids and gases of major proportions belongs almost entirely to the period since 1900. We will postpone the discussion of the transport by pipeline of natural gas and water to Chapter 7. In 1865 oil transport was begun successfully in a small way by Samuel Van Sychle in western Pennsylvania. It quickly spread through the Appalachian oil fields, at first our principal source of supply, carrying the crude oil either to nearby or more distant refineries. Gradually, the lines lengthened until in 1879 the Tidewater Pipe Company transported crude oil from fields in northwestern Pennsylvania to the seaboard. By 1892 numerous lines, aggregating 3,000 miles, connected the oil pools with distant refineries located in interior and seaboard cities.

The rapid development of the oil industry after 1901, particularly with the exploitation of the mid-continent, Gulf, and California oil fields, brought on an almost continental expansion in pipeline transportation. Since 1926, with the advent of better steel and alloy pipes, electrically welded joints and improved pumping engines, the technical conditions for economical and dependable transport over very great distances had been provided. After 1931 the same economies also induced the pipeline transport of petroleum products, notably gasoline, from the refineries to concentration points for further marketing. In 1946 a network of local gathering lines and of interstate trunk lines carried 68 per cent of all crude petroleum shipped, or 1,280 million barrels. About 25 per cent moved by tanker and the remainder by rail and motor truck. The mileage at that time was about 60,000 for crude gathering lines, 73,400 for crude trunk lines, and 16,300 for gasoline, making a total of 149,700 miles of pipeline transportation. The ocean tanker and pipeline can carry crude oil in wholesale quantities at costs with which the tank car and motor trailer simply cannot compete. As of 1942, according to the Bureau of Transport Economics and Statistics of the ICC, the cost range per ton-mile was 0.63 mills for the tanker, 1.98 mills for the pipeline, and 10.62 mills by rail.

Not all the mileage is in common carrier service; hence, coordinated figures covering the entire industry are hard to obtain. As regards common carriers, the Interstate Commerce Commission reported 138,962 miles of petroleum pipelines in 1954 with an investment of $2,501,330,000 and operating revenues of $617,463,000. Pipeline transportation is thus a substantial and growing segment of our national transportation system.

Other adaptations of the pipeline technique, which have been suggested and experimented with relate to the transportation of grain and pulverized coal, the latter in a water solution; but thus far they have been found impractical. Another adaptation of the idea of specialized transport is the carriage of single commodities like coal by means of a conveyor belt (the rubber railway). This method while demonstrably practical in a limited way, does not appear to lend itself to public utility service.

Air transport. The most recent accession to the transport family has been the airplane. After some experimental use of lighter-than-air craft, commercial development has settled upon the airplane as the most efficient carrier of passengers, mail, and merchandise express. Since the last war, its use as a cargo carrier has also given it limited importance in freight transportation. Beginning with the historic sustained flight by the Wright brothers at Kitty Hawk, N.C., on December 17, 1903, the principles of controlled flight were sufficiently developed so that in 1914, with the outbreak of war, the airplane could be used as a military instrument. After the war, with the availability of a surplus of planes and trained flyers, experiments were conducted in the rendition of special services which worked out the potentialities of air transport. The stunting "gypsies" and barnstorming aviators of that era helped the government in developing the foundations of the aeronautics industry.

The post office began its air mail service in 1918 with transcontinental service inaugurated the following year. These early air mail routes were operated by the federal government. But with the Air Mail or Kelly Act of 1925, authorizing air mail contracts with private companies, and the Air Commerce Act of 1926, extending the promotion of private air transport to the passenger and express business, commercial air transport on a common carrier basis was really begun. The Kelly Act inaugurated the policy of generous air mail contracts as a public aid to promote this infant industry because of its commercial promise and its growing importance to national defense. By virtue of the Air Commerce Act, the Bureau of Air Commerce in the Department of Commerce began the establishment of airways equipped with beacons, radio range finders, and emergency landing fields. With initiative passing to private enterprise through the provision of an assured income by way of air mail contracts, the air carriers tested the market for passenger and merchandise traffic. Municipalities and private capital cooperated by providing permanent airports.

In the late 1920's, despite unsatisfactory financial returns but encouraged by the epic transatlantic flight of Lindbergh in 1927, private capital inaugurated an air transport boom. With securities easy to sell, holding companies were set up to control both operating and manufacturing companies.

Air transport may be said to have come of age with the passage of the Civil Aeronautics Act of 1938. As amended, this Act now makes full provision for the regulation of the services and rates of common carrier airlines. It set up the usual independent regulatory agency comparable to the Interstate Commerce Commission. This five-man regulatory body, now called the Civil Aeronautics Board (CAB), is independent of the executive and is responsible directly to Congress. It regulates air transport to achieve certain objectives laid down by Congress as in the public interest: (1) to encourage and develop an air transport system adapted to the present and future needs of domestic and foreign commerce, the postal service, and national defense; (2) to so regulate air transportation as to recognize and preserve its inherent advantages, to assure the highest degree of safety and foster sound economic conditions in the industry, and to improve the relations between, and coordinate transportation by, air carriers; (3) to promote adequate, economical, and efficient service by air carriers at reasonable charges without unjust discrimination, undue preference or advantage, or unfair or destructive competitive practices; (4) to preserve competition to the extent necessary to assure the sound development of an air-transportation system properly adapted to the needs of the foreign and domestic commerce of the United States, of the Postal Service, and of the national defense.

The 1938 Act, as amended, also set up a Civil Aeronautics Administration (CAA) headed by an administrator within the Department of Commerce. To the CAA were committed promotional and developmental functions such as operating and maintaining the airways of the country, together with the various facilities for air traffic control and for the promotion of aviation safety. It also administered federal aid to airports.

The stimulus of a second world war and continuous improvement in equipment, service, and facilities has given us an airway system which grew from 2,041 miles in 1926 to 23,723 miles in 1938 and to 67,770 miles in 1955. In the latter year, 31 operators employing 1,212 aircraft operated 78,992 route miles. From its feeble beginnings, airport development of all classes in the United States has been most significant. However the federal aid program of the Federal Airport Act of 1946 has hardly achieved its objective—that of an integrated system of airports throughout the United States. States and localities have not shown the same responsibility for securing an integrated airport system as they had shown previously in building an integrated highway system. Federal aid began during the depression, but systematic aid was not forthcoming until the Act of 1946 authorized the expenditure of $500 million in matched grants to local governments over a seven-year period. The total number of airports and landing fields of all classifications increased from 1,036 in 1927 to 6,391 in 1950 to 6,839 in 1955. The 1950 total showed the following classification by type of ownership: commercial, 2,378; municipal, 2,243; CAA intermediate, 94; military, 328; miscellaneous governmental, 144; private, 1,204.

In 1955 the Civil Aeronautics Board estimated that certificated domestic air carriers could be grouped into these classifications: thirteen carriers operating major trunk lines; sixteen carriers operating feeder lines; two carriers operating territorial lines; and four carriers operating cargo lines only. This domestic system was supplemented with international extensions flown by fifteen trunk lines and four all cargo lines carrying the United States flag.[3]

The comparative distribution of traffic achieved by these air carriers for 1955, by significant traffic classifications, was as follows:

	Passenger Miles	Airmail, Ton-Miles	Express, Ton-Miles	Freight, Ton-Miles
Trunk lines	19,217,164,000	86,026,000	49,605,000	174,019,000
Feeder lines	523,941,000	1,348,000	1,435,000	1,358,000
International	4,410,400,000	52,407,000	. . .	90,828,000

SOURCE: *Air Transport Association of America, Quarterly Review,* Oct. 1st, 1956.

The foregoing traffic performance for 1955 illustrates the revolution in air traffic which has come since the inauguration of commercial service. The growth in business and shift in emphasis can be seen when 1931 is compared with 1945, a critical period in the development of the industry. The $24 million of gross revenues of 1931 had grown to $233 million by 1945. But even more significant was the shift in emphasis. Whereas in the former year 82.5 per cent of the total was derived from mail contracts, 17.2 per cent from passenger transport, and 0.3 per cent from merchandise express, in the latter year 76.5 per cent was derived from passenger traffic, only 18 per cent from mail contracts, and 5.5 per cent from express service.

The shift in traffic indicated above is explained by the dominant service characteristics of modern air transport. Its greatest asset is speed, especially

[3] For additional statistics and extended discussion, see Frederick, J. H., *Commercial Air Transportation* (Homewood, Ill.: Richard D. Irwin Inc. 4th edition, 1955).

on long runs. While the capacity of planes is limited, their potentialities in ton-miles and passenger-miles is great. Another asset is its flexibility in rendering and inaugurating service. Airlines can easily pioneer in the opening up of new territory. But its greatest advantage lies in long-distance service. Transcontinental runs can be made on fast airline schedules in less than 8 hours as compared with 60 hours by the fastest trains. In transatlantic and other overseas service the time advantages are equally marked. Transatlantic crossings can be made in 18 hours as compared with 3½ to 4½ days by the fastest ships. Jet propulsion holds the promise of even greater disparity.

However, there are significant disadvantages. One deterrent arises from the greater liability to delays on account of weather conditions as compared with other transport media. Another deterrent is the spotty accident record. Although the situation with respect to air safety is improving, especially for scheduled flights, there are still large numbers of travelers who prefer the safety and comfort of the Pullmans. It is true that insurance companies now proclaim that it is safer to travel by air than to cover the equivalent distance by motor vehicle; nevertheless, the accident statistics for air travel do not appear to weigh adequately the greater number of fatalities. It is not a question of mere number. The assumption of this risk, however, may be a matter of the personal equation.

7. PUBLIC UTILITIES
IN THE TWENTIETH CENTURY
(CONTINUED)

Transportation utilities were the first to respond to new technological developments and thereby achieve new spatial concepts. We have seen that transport problems are now local, regional, national, and international in scope. Other utilities, especially communication, have not lagged far behind in this respect. On the other hand, some utilities still find their principal markets in urban areas, but these too are becoming regional in the scope of their operations.

The Development of Electricity Supply

We will take up first the more recent development of electricity supply for heat, light, power, and refrigeration. By 1900 this industry was an economic reality. It had already fought and won its initial battles with gas and had established itself as a central station supply; but it had a decidedly limited local service area. With the opening of the twentieth century the infant electric utilities could look forward with considerable assurance to an expanding future in the lighting and power field based upon the incandescent lamp and the electric motor. However, the growing demand for electric energy was running into obstacles. Generator units seemed to have reached their practical limit in size with about 3,000 to 5,000 horsepower capacities because they were driven by low-speed steam engines. The invention of the steam turbine solved the problem so that a new phase of low-cost electric power generation was started. Combined into a single machine, the turbogenerator, the new unit was also much more economical of space and in fuel consumption. Beginning about 1903 the maximum output size of units increased from about 3,000 kilowatts to 250,000 kilowatts by 1954. This development put the industry in a position where it could induce manufacturing establishments to retire their own individual "prime mover" power plants and to purchase electric power from the enlarged

97

central station of the public utility. As a result old-fashioned steam engines, steam turbines, internal-combustion engines, hydroturbines, and water wheels were retired from service and electric motors driven by purchased energy were substituted. In 1899 the horsepower of electric motors driven by purchased energy, as reported by the Census of Manufactures, amounted to only 178,176. Ten years later this figure had increased to only a modest 1,669,226. By 1939 electric energy purchased from central stations produced 29,213,085 horsepower units of electric motor energy.

The increase in the size of central stations was also dependent upon technological advances in the wholesale transmission and the retail distribution of power in order to reach these enlarged markets. These have all been forthcoming, due in no small measure to the wizardry of Charles P. Steinmetz of the General Electric Company. Early alternating-current transmission distances of not over 25 miles drew energy from hydroelectric sites. Around 1900 most of the smaller cities had their own electric plants and the larger cities were served by a number of central generating stations, each plant owned by an independent utility and strategically situated with respect to its limited marketing area. Under the spur of these economies, competition set in for additional markets; the first phase of the movement was the merger and interconnection of the independents in a city-wide consolidation. Usually, the integration of electric plants was also accompanied by the integration of similarly isolated street railway plants into city-wide consolidations and their conversion from animal, cable, or steam traction to electric traction. The addition of the "electric railway load" to the lighting and commercial power load served to further spread out the requirements for energy from the "peak" hours of lighting demand to other hours of the day. If, perchance, it was possible to acquire also a publicly owned street-lighting and water plant, or at the very least negotiate a contract to supply electric energy for street lighting and water pumping purposes, the central electric generating supply could be put on a complete diurnal schedule, operating on a 24-hour day and a 365-day year basis.

The progressive expansion in the distance of electric transmission to the present limit of approximately 300 miles made possible a further step in integration of electricity supply, whereby neighboring cities and the intervening suburban and rural territory were interconnected into territorial consolidations. The aim was to achieve a compact service area which looked to the integrated power system for its source of supply. This situation began to raise the question as to the area for most economical production of electricity. Steam-electric power plants could be located anywhere, provided fuel and a supply of cooling water for condensing purposes was economically available. This fact had a tendency to locate steam plants at or near the largest market, called the "load center." Hydroelectric production could be located only at the most economical power site and depended on long-distance transmission to reach the market. The costs of transmission, besides those arising from investment in lines, were represented by the losses of energy in transmission, usually varying between 12 and 15 per cent. An economical source of electric power supply therefore consisted of that combination of hydroelectric and steam-electric power which, when integrated by means of transmission lines, provided electric power at the lowest unit cost at the point of supply. As a consequence, in the course of time, old, inefficient steam-electric plants were abandoned or converted into substations and production was concentrated in new, large, and advantageously located steam stations. The supply from hydroelectric plants was combined with that from steam plants if it could be delivered at the market at a cost equal to or less than the cost of steam-electric power.

Meanwhile, there were put forth continuous efforts to expand the use of electric power. The original electricity consumer, in particular, was being urged to increase his domestic use of lighting service, and by adding appliances, to expand his use of energy into the power, heating, and refrigeration field. Small appliances such as toasters, vacuum cleaners, ironers, and large appliances such as mangles, refrigerators, electric ranges, and water heaters, brought about an increase in average annual consumption by domestic customers from 264 kilowatt-hours in 1913 to 611 kilowatt-hours in 1932. A National Power Survey conducted by the Federal Power Commission reported that despite the depression, the capacity of appliances sold between 1929 and 1935 was 29 million kilowatts.

The territorial expansion of the network of electric service suggested the possibility of selling electricity to farmers. In favored locations, particularly in California where power could be used for irrigation pumping, rural electrification was begun by private utilities before World War I. However, most of the development has come since that war. Besides the uses characteristic of urban homes, farms can use electricity in farm operations if they can afford to buy the equipment designed for their use. The availability of electricity for farm use was actively promoted by federal agencies after the "New Deal" came to power in 1933. Through agencies such as the Rural Electrification Administration (1935) and the Tennessee Valley Authority (1933), the problems of the farmer in the use of electric energy have been studied, and the construction of rural lines has been promoted and financed. At present over 95 per cent of the nation's farms have been electrified.

Gas Utilities

During the first half of the present century the gas industry made another of its remarkable recoveries. When electricity replaced gas as an illuminant toward the close of the last century, gas shifted to the cooking and heating field. Followed by the electric utility, artificial gas plants sought to become the centralized suppliers of heat in domestic, industrial, and commercial markets. Natural gas, on account of its cheapness and higher Btu content (heating value), was already being extensively, even wastefully, used in natural gas regions for a variety of purposes, including house heating. In the race with electricity the gas industry developed newer utilization devices, particularly cheaper gas ranges, refrigerators, hot-water heaters, and gas furnaces, with air-conditioning units most recently added to this list.

Coal gas is made by heating coal in retorts, driving off the gas, and leaving coke, tar, and other substances as by-products. Water gas, now most commonly manufactured, is made by passing steam through incandescent coke or anthracite coal, but it must be enriched by spraying oil-gas into it. Another type of manufactured gas is coke-oven gas, which is in turn a by-product of the manufacture of coke by the steel industry. Finally, liquefied petroleum gas (LPG) in the shape of butane and propane, best known as "bottled gas," is supplied as stand-by or interim service by public utilities. It is transported under pressure in tank cars and containers and has found wide usage in recent years in rural territory beyond the reach of gas mains. The greatest expansion, however, has come in the use of natural gas with the growth of long-distance transportation from the extensive natural gas fields in the mid-continent and Gulf coast regions. This remarkable shift set in during the 1920's and has almost revolutionized the industry in the postwar years. The manufactured-gas branch now is a static if not a declining industry, while the natural gas branch is on the march. The following figures compare a depression year (1932), a war year (1945), and a recent postwar year (1950). The first part (A) of the tabulation shows what this shift means in terms of the number (in thousands) of customers serviced, and the second part (B) shows it in terms of gross revenues (in thousands).

(A)	Natural Gas	Mfg. Gas	Mixed Gas	Liquid Petrol.	Total
1932	5,499	8,476	1,557	0	15,532
1945	8,914	8,582	2,400	81	19,977
1950	14,267	7,618	1,789	327	24,001

(B)	Natural Gas	Mfg. Gas	Mixed Gas	Liquid Petrol.	Total
1932	$300,792	$359,884	$62,552	0	$723,228
1945	680,874	360,801	107,106	4,026	1,152,807
1950	1,361,005	454,436	111,214	21,347	1,948,002

SOURCE: *Gas Facts*, Amer. Gas Assoc. 1953 and previous years.

There have also been significant shifts within the manufactured-gas industry. The most important change is the virtual disappearance of production of retort coal gas, as apparent in the tabulation below.

Manufactured gas produced and purchased by gas utilities in millions of therms * was as follows:

	Carbureted Water Gas	Coke-oven Gas	Retort Coal Gas	Oil and oil Refinery Gas	Total
1932	954.3	763.9	171.3	62.6	1952.1
1940	962.7	794.8	82.8	101.1	1941.4
1945	1410.3	961.0	79.1	153.8	2604.2
1950	1611.3	860.5	20.9	166.3	2659.0

* A *therm* is a new unit of measurement based on heat content. It is being used increasingly in place of the old volumetric unit, the cubic foot. The wide introduction of natural gas, with more than twice the heating value of artificial gas, is making the change desirable.

Utility revenues of manufactured-gas companies are supplemented from the sale of by-products, amounting in 1950 to almost $62 million. Most of this, or $41 million and $11 million, is derived respectively from the sale of coke and tar, the remainder of it coming from ammonium sulphate, petroleum briquets, and other derivatives. Both manufactured and natural gas sales are dominantly in residential service. In 1950, of the 7.6 million customers of artificial gas utilities, 7.1 million were residence customers, consuming 33 per cent of the total gas produced. In the same year residential customers to the number of 13.1 million, out of a total of 14.6 million, consumed 30 per cent of natural gas distributed in utility service.

In recent years, with the flush production of oil (of which natural gas is a by-product) and the discovery of extensive dry gas fields, natural gas, with its high Btu content, has become a premium-quality fuel selling at a discount. Compared with the advancing prices of coal and oil, natural gas has been a bargain. Transportation and distribution by pipeline is relatively inexpensive. For the householder it is an ideal fuel for cooking, space heating, and water heating. It is clean, requires no storage, produces no waste products, and its utilization is flexible and easily controlled. Exact temperatures and high temperatures can be readily attained and maintained, making it also an ideal fuel for many industrial processes.

The natural-gas industry consists of three divisions, only two of which are presently treated as of a public utility character. The first, or field end, is essentially a production problem—collecting the gas from oil or gas wells and concentrating it by means of gathering lines, processing, and treating it preliminary to its sale to transmission companies. The second division consists of the transmission or transportation of the gas by means of large-diameter pipelines in intrastate or interstate commerce to major consuming centers. This step in long-distance marketing was aided by the development of automatic trenching machinery, and after 1926, by an electric pipe-welding process. If the gas moves in interstate commerce, its transmission and sale has since 1938 been subject to federal regulation. In some cases the transportation companies also own gas fields and gathering lines, thereby raising the question whether production and gathering are also subject to regulation. The third division, or local distribution in retail marketing areas, is similar to the manufactured-gas utility, and it is in this branch of the industry that rapid conversion is taking place in the distribution of natural gas or in the supply of mixed artificial and natural gas.

The miles of main employed in the first step between 1945 and 1950 had grown from 27,000 to 32,850. Between the same years in the second or transmission step, miles of main increased from 77,280 to 109,360, with the mileage and carrying capacity growing monthly. On the other hand, long-distance transmission of manufactured gas was declining from 3,410 to 2,230 miles of main between the same dates. The third step, indicating the growth of the retail gas industry as a whole, shows rapid increase from 201,480 miles of main in 1945 to 241,570 miles in 1950. Only the distribution of manufactured gas was declining from 68,590 miles to 53,190, while utilities distributing natural gas alone were growing from 113,720 to 172,270. This truly remarkable change finds its explanation in certain new developments in our energy economy, as will be explained in Chapter 10.

Water Utilities

Two problems dominate the history of the water utility in the twentieth century. The first, and in the long run most important, problem is the growing scarcity of supply both generally and in certain locations. We shall discuss this problem in Part III in another connection. The second problem is a growing concern for the quality of the water. Both problems, of course, have their origin in the growing urbanization and industrialization of the country. Since 1900 there has also been a tremendous increase in the number of central water-supply systems. By 1900, as we have already indicated, the number of systems had grown from 17 in 1800 to about 4,000 in 1900. According to a survey conducted by the U.S. Public Health Service in 1945, the number seems to have grown to 15,400, although the figures are hardly comparable because the survey included all population groupings in excess of 200, the systems serving 94,390,000 persons.

Statistical data relating to this industry are scarce, incomplete, and not coordinated. The President's Water Policy Commission of 1950 deplored the fact that the industry did not report to a single agency.

The trend toward public ownership already noted in both the promotional and competitive periods, continued after 1900. The 1920 Census reported that of 204 cities with a population in excess of 30,000, there were 155 that owned their water works. The New York system represented an estimated investment in excess of $350 million, which alone was 32.7 per cent of the total investment of $1,071,211,511 for the 155 cities. Indianapolis is the only large city supplied exclusively by a private system, though the number of private systems in 1950 still constituted about 20 per cent.

A tendency toward combination into larger units has also set in. Hitherto, this industry has resisted a consolidation movement, operating units restricting their retail sales to one municipality. The Hackensack Water Company is a private utility serving at present fifty-six separately incorporated communities in northern New Jersey and neighboring New York. A new type of public integration is now going forward. The Metropolitan Water District of Southern California was organized in 1928 under California law and represents an association of cities and water districts whose purpose is to bring water by means of an aqueduct to the coastal regions from the Colorado River over 340 miles away. The district sells the water in wholesale quantities to its members, after storing, purifying, and softening it. The sale takes place at the end of a transmission network which brings the water to the gateway of the distributors' systems. In the East, beginning with the creation in 1935 by Massachusetts for Boston and its environs of the Massachusetts Metropolitan Water District, other metropolitan areas and geographical districts have created agencies whereby cities and other unit areas have associated themselves to carry on water supply and sanitation operations over far-flung areas. The retail operations usually continue as local enterprises, but the change of pace in wholesale operations is made necessary by reasons of economy and water-shed planning.

The use of water has been slowly increasing, particularly after 1900, when industrialization started in earnest. By 1945, the U.S. Public Health Service reported an average per capita use in the United States of 127 gallons per day, made up of as little as 60 gallons in small communities of 500 population and of as much as 150 gallons in cities over 10,000. Some large cities whose water utilities are operating under special circumstances may show a per capita usage of as much as 300 to 500 gallons. This is accounted for not only by the growing commercial and industrial activity but also by the semiagricultural irrigation, lawn sprinkling, air conditioning, and garbage removal uses of water. These and other newer uses go with an advancing standard of living and of sanitation, and have much to do with this upward trend in per capita consumption. Even Los Angeles, where water is the scarcest of commodities and which operates a completely metered system, has shown an increase from 119 gallons to 156 in the ten years from 1941 to 1951. As examples of extremely heavy users we may cite the steel industry, with 65,000 gallons per ton of output; the wood pulp industry, with usages between 60,000 and 85,000 gallons per ton; the paper industry, with 39,000 gallons per ton; and oil refining, with 770 gallons per barrel.

Not all the water used is supplied under public utility conditions. Some of the largest users, like steam-electric generating plants, pump their own supply, which is often several times the requirements of the municipal water utility. Wherever possible, much sea water is used by industries for washing, cooling, and condensing purposes.

In 1950 the survey by the U.S. Public Health Service, previously mentioned, lists 4,446 cities with a population of over 21.5 million as deriving their supplies from ground water, while only 2,120 cities (but with a population of over 50.7 million) were dependent upon surface supplies. Except for the smaller cities there was a trend for ground-water supplies to prove inadequate. Only 22 cities in excess of 100,000, with a total population of about 3 million, used ground water, while 144 cities of that size, with over 30 million population, used surface water. This underscores the need of increased watchfulness to prevent contamination of supply. Practical measures of pollution control are needed for both ground and surface waters, but the latter are in greater danger of contamination. When cities and industries purify their own supplies but pour their untreated wastes into streams and lakes, they are adding to the problems of downstream water users. They may also be destroying the waters as a proper habitat for fish and wildlife and interfering with their use for recreational purposes.

It is not merely a figure of speech to say that water systems and sewer systems are two sides of the same coin. Although some cities began to construct sewers in the 1880's to forestall the danger of epidemics, and although their construction was generally accelerated with the turn of the century, *sewage treatment* lagged woefully behind. It was common practice to dispose of sewage and industrial wastes by discharging them untreated into any convenient body of surface water. The water utilities, particularly in the East, responded by installing purification plants, beginning with the pioneer filter plant at Poughkeepsie, N.Y., in 1875. Nevertheless, in 1900 over 23,000 people died of typhoid fever. At the present time, 16,000 water works serve purified water to two-thirds of our population, while 9,000 sewer systems serve one-half our total number. But of the 9,000 sewer systems, only 6,000 (serving one-third of our population) flow into treatment plants. Pollution control remains as one of the incompletely solved problems of our municipal sociology.

Land Reclamation

In the twentieth century it is fitting to substitute for the earlier irrigation and drainage functions the more inclusive term of *land reclamation* because it embraces (besides irrigation in the arid West and drainage in the humid East) flood control and river regulation and the clearing and preparation of cropland.

Irrigation. In the West a severe drought in the early 1890's had started a movement to organize first a National Irrigation Congress and later a more permanent National Irrigation Association. About 1900 these two groups coalesced into the National Reclamation Association. They found a political sponsor for their activities in Theodore Roosevelt who, when he became President in 1901, proposed a national program for the conservation of land and water resources in the seventeen arid states of the West. In his message to the Congress he placed these reclamation functions beside the historic navigation and flood control functions already in the charge of the Army Engineers in the following significant passage:

It is as right for the National Government to make the streams and rivers of the arid regions useful by engineering works for water storage as to make useful the rivers and harbors of the humid regions by engineering works of another kind. . . . Our people as a whole will profit, for successful homemaking is but another name for upbuilding of the Nation.

The Reclamation Act of 1902 set up the Reclamation Bureau in the Department of the Interior with a Reclamation Fund derived from the sale of public lands in these western states. These sums were to constitute a revolving fund and to be expended in the construction of water storage reservoirs and irrigation canals. The water was to be delivered to actual settlers with irrigable lands limited to 160 acres for each owner. The fund was to be replenished by repayments of an apportioned share of the cost of the project without interest in not more than ten annual installments.

The Act was amended by broadening and liberalizing its provisions. Beginning with the Salt River Project near Phoenix, Arizona, completed in 1909, much irrigated land has been added. Although there has been no return by way of interest on the capital employed, the Reclamation Service reports seven mature reclamation projects that have yielded income tax revenues between 1916 and 1949 of nearly $384 million, or over $350 per acre. The accrual of earnings subject to the federal income tax are an indication of the economic importance of the activities induced by the Reclamation Act and represent an indirect return on such construction expenditures by the federal government.

For the country as a whole, the Census of 1944 showed an irrigated land area of 21 million acres, of which 19.4 million were in the seventeen reclamation states. Much of this acreage represented private and cooperative effort; but after the less costly and more accessible irrigation opportunities had been exploited, further development of the irrigation acreage depended upon public assistance.

Drainage.   Drainage projects on a large scale have only become a part of federal programs since World War I. The over-all accomplishment in reclaiming agricultural land has thus been very largely the result of private and cooperative initiative under a framework of local and state authorizations. The results have, nevertheless, been impressive, particularly in the North Central States and in certain sections of the South. Only California shows a similar accomplishment. The Census of 1940 reports about 87 million acres in drainage areas, of which 75 million are reported as fully drained and fit to raise crops, while 5 million are only partially drained. Of this total, about 35 million acres are in drainage districts. The investment in drainage enterprises in 1940 is reported as about $700 million. Since the onset of the depression in 1929, acreage planted seems to have suffered a steady and quite general decline of about 5 million acres, with considerable acreage returning to its pristine condition. It is also important to note that drainage is as significant a feature of agricultural reclamation in the East as irrigation is in the West.

Communication Utilities

It seems to be a characteristic of the communications industry that its branches achieve integration more easily than any other utility. Certainly their development is in marked contrast with the slow and tortuous path of the various branches of the transportation industry.

The post office. Since 1900 the only significant addition to the services rendered by the post office is in the rendition of services which has placed it in competition with the banking interests. In 1910 Congress authorized the creation of postal savings banks. This new banking function, together with the issuance of money orders, the sale of small denomination bonds, the insurance and expediting of mail, and the collection of cash on delivery orders, all for an extra fee, rounds out the services of this oldest utility.

The major service continues to be the delivery, transfer, and collection of four classes of mail through some 44,300 post offices, using the transport facilities of railways, air lines, water and highway carriers, besides local transport equipment.

Congress has reserved to itself the power to fix rates on all mail except rates for parcel post (fourth class) which are fixed by the Postmaster General, subject to approval by the Interstate Commerce Commission. In making contracts for the *transportation* of the mails, the rates are fixed by the ICC for carriers under its jurisdiction and by the Civil Aeronautics Board for airlines.

It is well known, of course, that due to social and political considerations this publicly owned utility, except for its earlier years, has almost consistently failed to cover its costs. In an attempt to appraise the effect of this policy of rendering some services below cost, the annual report of

Table IV   Apportionment of Postal Revenues and Expenses by
Classes of Service, June 30, 1940

Class of Service	Revenues	Expenses	Surplus or Deficiency
First class mail other than			
local	$330,357,753	208,256,856	122,100,897 *
Local	82,715,355	59,219,595	23,495,760 *
Air mail	19,122,905	28,039,249	8,916,344
Total	432,196,013	295,515,700	136,680,313 *
Second class mail	24,949,510	110,330,537	85,381,027
Third class mail	75,105,950	101,397,936	26,291,986
Fourth class mail	133,693,509	155,503,379	21,809,870
Foreign mail	17,831,570	26,225,846	8,394,276
Penalty mail	. . . .	16,986,112	16,986,112
Franked mail	. . . .	746,110	746,110
Free for blind	. . . .	196,023	196,023
Special services	66,774,495	88,495,185	21,720,690
Unassigned and unrelated	17,464,281	14,843,858	2,620,423 *
Totals	768,015,328	810,240,686	42,225,358

* Indicates surplus.

the Postmaster General attempts to allocate the revenues and expenses by classes of service for each fiscal year since 1930. These allocations, together with the financial magnitude of operations for a recent prewar year, are shown in Table IV.

The telegraph. The oldest of the telecommunications industries was also caught up in the rush of technological achievement which marked the twentieth century. Led by the giants among them—Western Union and Postal Telegraph—innumerable companies had been consolidated into twenty-five systems by 1902. There was a steady increase in miles of pole line and miles of wire operated until 1932, when mileages of 256,215 and 2,259,827, respectively, were attained. The depression of the 1930's wrought the greatest havoc in the telegraph and cable industries. They had attained their peak in 1929, but by 1933 revenues of Western Union had declined 43 per cent and of Postal, 32 per cent. Since they are dependent upon the volume of business transactions for their own revenues, telegraph carriers recovered with the lifting of the depression; but the industry had suffered a blow which ultimately led to bankruptcy of the Postal Telegraph Company and a final consolidation when on Oct. 7, 1943, Western Union acquired Postal with Congressional approval. As a result of these financial vicissitudes, gross investment declined from about $383 million in 1935 to $300 million in 1954. Wire and cable mileage dropped to 1,129,000, although revenues recovered somewhat and now stand at $210 million.

When the railroad industry after 1908 shifted from the use of the telegraph to the telephone in train dispatching, a warning was issued that difficult times were ahead. This development resulted in improved and new equipment to compensate for the revenue loss by providing a wider area of service. The introduction of "carrier" systems and improvements in multiplier operations increased many times the capacity of telegraph wires to transmit messages. The sending of messages was also expedited by the installation of high-speed switching centers. The printing-telegraph and private leased-wire services were introduced. The revenue picture was further improved with the multiplication of private services, such as the 16,000-mile system of the General Electric Company, which with nine high-speed switching centers links 106 points in its nation-wide organization. The completion of a microwave, radio-beam telegraph system, linking some major cities in the East, has the promise of greater continuity and reduction in cost of service, particularly because it will eliminate the network of pole lines and miles of wire. Nevertheless, the economic future of the telegraph as a utility is clouded with considerable uncertainty. At least we may say that as a system of communication which records its messages, the telegraph has an advantage which gives it a competitive footing alongside its chief rival, the telephone utility.

The telephone. As a system of voice communication, the telephone is the most highly integrated of all public utilities. This was the outstanding achievement of the present century. An idea of the magnitude of this industry and its importance in knitting the nation into a social whole may be gained from a few statistics. In 1900 the Census reported all telephone systems to comprise 2,807,000 miles of wire, connecting 1,355,900 telephones. The Bell System alone reported a daily average of exchange conversations at that time (1902) of 9,322,951, and of toll conversations, 239,689. In 1955 wire mileage had expanded to 218,100,000 and telephones in service to 56,000,000, practically all Bell interconnected. Daily average use in local exchange service has swelled to over 169 million conversations and in toll service to over 6 million conversations. The A.T.&T. Company and its principal subsidiaries, doing over 80 per cent of the telephone business, represented an investment in plant and equipment of $15.3 billion, with operating revenues of $5.3 billion. Employees number 745,629 and stockholders 1,408,851. It is the largest, most outstanding example of corporate capitalism in the world.

The corporate structure of the Bell system is surprisingly simple. The holding corporation, A.T.&T. Company, is the parent organization of twenty-three operating telephone companies, and it is also the direct owner and operator of interstate telephone facilities (the Long-lines Department) connecting the exchange and toll facilities of its associated as well as outside connecting companies. It also owns the Western Electric Company, which is the manufacturer and supplier of equipment and materials for the system. A.T.&T. Company and Western Electric jointly own the Bell Telephone Laboratories, Inc., which does the research and development work for the group. These are the important units in the system, significant for its utility status. Besides stock control, the system is held together by contractual agreements whereby Western Electric has the exclusive right to manufacture telephone equipment which it sells to licensed subsidiaries as well as outsiders. In this way standardization of apparatus and physical interconnection has been achieved, which has lead to corporate integration of independents with the Bell system.

The idea back of these arrangements was that the telephone industry was naturally monopolistic, an idea injected by Theodore N. Vail, an early general manager of the Bell Company. After leaving the employ of the company for a time, he returned again in 1907 as head of the A.T.&T. Company. At this time he determined to carry into effect his original intention to secure a single, universal, nation-wide system of communication and to eliminate direct competition. The watchword of the new policy was "One System, One Policy, Universal Service." All this was practically accomplished by 1915.

The new era of commission regulation, beginning in 1907, closed a period of very bitter competition between the Bell companies and the independent telephone operators. The Bell interests had been backward in extending telephone service. Moreover, the public was still quite hostile to the idea of monopoly as being economically advantageous. Independent operators were therefore looked upon with favor in many cases. The Bell interests tried at first to eliminate these competitors by the method of cutting rates; by tying up the railways and the larger establishments, both private and semipublic, with special contracts; and by bringing suits against both competitors and outside manufacturers, charging them with infringement of patents. From 1907 to 1913 the Bell system adopted the policy of (1) "acquisition of competing systems" and (2) "the prevention of financing of competitors through the influence of the Baker-Morgan banking interests," which were the financial sponsors of the Bell system. These activities were modified somewhat in response to threats from the Department of Justice under the antitrust laws. Among other things the Bell system agreed to connect its toll facilities with all independent exchanges upon request.

The independents and their manufacturers countered by organizing themselves into an association for mutual protection and for improving their methods of doing business. For instance, the automatic telephone was pioneered by the independents while the Bell companies would have nothing to do with it until the period of the first world war. Machine switching is becoming well-nigh universal, and the industry is now upon a better plane of cooperation. Also, the change in public opinion which accompanied the development of commission regulation and which made monopoly appear less odious has worked in favor of further integration.

The competitive situation has been completely cleared up. There are fifty-four integrated independent systems of considerable size (representing an investment in plant of $637 million) and many small companies serving in small towns and thousands of rural lines. They still own and operate 18 per cent of the telephones in the United States. As the Federal Communications Commission (FCC) said in its 1937 investigation: "Attempts at this late date to develop a strong, independent telephone system to compete with the Bell System would be futile . . . Protection of that interest (the rate-paying public) must be accomplished through effective governmental regulation of the telephone industry."

Nevertheless, the independent operators performed a great service in the development of this industry by stimulating the Bell interests and by broadening the market through their own efforts. As one of the leaders among them writes: [1] "It seems a fair estimate to say that the Bell and its subsidiaries, during the period of monopoly through patents, relied too much on legal monopoly and not enough on service. The small towns and country districts generally were ignored. Even in the larger cities there was not the intensive development the field required."

Recent progress in the art has been considerable. Automatic telephones were perfected; the pay station and extension telephone were introduced. An automatic trunkage system and the vacuum tube, which makes possible the superimposing of four distinct telephone messages on one transmission line, are important recent improvements. Especially in toll service has the application of "phantom" and "carrier current" principles increased the carrying capacity of toll lines. The new coaxial cable makes possible the concurrent carrying of 480 telephone messages. In 1930 the Bell system obtained control of the manufacture and sale of the teletypewriter, thereby expanding its service in a new direction.

Since 1927 the development of the radiotelephone has made possible transoceanic communication without dependence upon wires and cables. Beginning with a circuit between New York and London, the expanding use of the radiophone has since brought the entire world-wide network of telephone lines within the reach of wireless conversation.

Radio communications.   For the sake merely of completeness of coverage, mention should be made of the radio broadcasting and television industries. While these add to the variety of our media of communication, they are not organized (in this country at least) on the basis of monopoly but subsist in the general atmosphere of competition. In so far as these industries are subject to regulation by the Federal Communications Commission, the central problem is one of the assignment of frequencies. In order to end a period of intolerable confusion in network broadcasting, the Federal Radio Act of 1927 set up a Federal Radio Commission with power to license stations and assign wave lengths, operating time, and power outputs. In 1934 it was merged into the Federal Communications Commission. But the Communications Act of 1934 does not give these industries the status of a public utility. As the United States Supreme Court pointed out in 1940 in *F.C.C. v. Sanders Brothers Radio Station* (309 U.S. 470), the Act does not regulate the business of licensees nor protect them from the effects of competition.

[1] Gary, Theodore, "The Independents and the Industry." *Telephony,* March 13, 1926.

8. REGULATION
IN THE TWENTIETH CENTURY

The extremely rapid and complex development of public utility industries which we have just portrayed was accompanied also by radical changes in regulatory policies. In order to gain perspective we shall condense our discussion, eliminating unnecessary minutiae; but we shall still retain the historical point of view. We are, however, telescoping the monopolistic epoch extending to the great depression with the current period, during which planning and coordination appear to have been the supreme goals because the former was gradually fused into the latter.

The facts of economic evolution which we have traced in previous chapters make it amply clear that the first goal of this evolutionary process was the suppression of competition and the achievement of monopoly. It was accordingly only a question of time until it would become necessary also to overhaul the regulatory machinery developed in the preceding period. Moreover, as the defects of the inherited systems of commission and franchise regulation became more apparent, it became increasingly clear that some better substitute for competition must be found. The main difficulties with franchise regulation seemed to be (1) its inflexibility when communities grew rapidly or when, as in recent years, underlying economic conditions changed radically; and (2) the absence of adequate administrative machinery to execute franchise terms. At the same time the commission system which developed during the 1870's and 1880's, while more flexible and administratively better equipped than the franchise system, had been undermined both legislatively and judicially. It is difficult to describe the transition to the existing system of regulation because its history must be traced in forty-eight states, not to mention the development of federal regulation and the changes taking place in the control exercised by local units of government. In this chapter we shall sketch the essentials only in the state and local spheres.

State Commission Regulation

A new reform and expansion movement set in about 1905 following the reestablishment in Wisconsin of a commission of the "strong" type under the political leadership of Senator La Follette, senior. New York, under Governor Hughes, adopted similar legislation. The movement to set up commissions under varying names spread rapidly from state to state. In 1911 alone, seven states adopted the commission system. By 1913 only Wyoming, Utah, and Delaware were without a commission. Even these states fell into line with the others by 1915, 1917, and 1950, respectively.

Before 1907, state commission jurisdiction was limited to utilities of the common carrier type, or those ancillary thereto, like express companies, telegraph companies, warehouses and grain elevators, freight line and equipment companies. Widespread dissatisfaction with franchise regulation after 1907 brought state commissions authority over street and interurban railways, and gas, water, electric, and telephone utilities. The latest accession is motor transportation. Many advocated municipal ownership and operation as a way out. The progress of this movement was, however, slow; and so it came to pass that the impatience of the reformers with public ownership induced them to adopt exclusive regulation by a state commission as a quicker way to the appointed goal. Even the Massachusetts railroad commission was converted into one of the strong type in 1913. Sometimes, state highway commissions were given jurisdiction over telephone and telegraph lines. Others, like Massachusetts in 1885, set up an independent Gas and Electric Commission. Increasingly, too, state boards of health have been assigned regulatory functions over water and sewage utilities. Old-style railroad and warehouse commissions were rechristened public utility or commerce commissions, their jurisdiction growing by accretion. Arizona, New Mexico, North Carolina, Oklahoma, and Virginia created corporation commissions, whose authority extended to public utility corporations, and to banking, insurance, and certain kinds of industrial corporations, thereby illustrating the all-inclusive scope of police power regulation. The jurisdiction of Congress over local utilities in the District of Columbia and the territorial possessions of Puerto Rico, the Hawaiian and Philippine Islands was vested in public utility commissions. In eight states, beginning with California, the commission system has been anchored in the constitution, thus giving it greater stability.

Statutory standards of reasonableness. The distinguishing characteristic of the new laws setting up commissions was that they considered regulation as a problem upon which continuous attention must be bestowed. Instead of periodic adjustments of rates by means of legislative acts or special franchises, the new legislation set up standards which were to be continuously operative. In this respect legislation concerning railways in states like Wisconsin, New York, and California was well in advance of legislation enacted by Congress, as will be explained later. The regulatory systems developed in these three states and in Massachusetts have served as models for other states, and the great degree of similarity between the model systems has given some degree of uniformity which makes possible the delineation of the scheme at least in rough outline for the country as a whole.

Instead of prescribing the *specific* rate for *each public utility,* as had hitherto been the case, the statute merely *lays down a general standard.* This general standard is legislatively declared to be the one to which all public utilities must conform. To this extent the new system represents a return to the relatively simple basis originally worked out in the common law. This does not mean, however, that there are no specific rates and service regulations; it merely means that they are not fixed by statute but are instead promulgated by administrative order of a commission. In exceptional cases the legislature may and often does override its administrative agent, as was true when many state legislatures after 1907 enacted two-cent passenger fare laws applying on intrastate business of railways, despite reduced rates already fixed by commissions. At common law the owners of public utilities had the right to fix their own rates and to render the quality of service which they felt obligated to render; but their acts were subject at all times to court review as to reasonableness upon application by an aggrieved customer. The new system adopted the common law *rule of reasonableness* and declared it to be the *legislative* standard. The administrative commission was then selected as the *agency* to *apply* this standard to the concrete facts in each case and to name the particular rate or service regulation reasonable under the circumstances. In the course of their investigations of particular situations, the commissions have gradually evolved standards of administrative policy which we will examine in detail in Part II. These subordinate administrative standards should constitute, if they have been well conceived, an organic theory of regulation.

The central problem with which this legislative standard deals has two aspects: (1) the furnishing of "reasonably adequate service and facilities"; (2) the collection of a charge for every service rendered which is "reasonable and just."

Another legislative standard contained in the public utility laws of practically all states prohibits discrimination in rates or service. Administrative commissions are given the power to prevent unjust and unlawful discriminations and to prohibit rates and practices unduly preferential. This legislative injunction has been made practically operative in connection with another one calling for publicity of rates and providing that only those rates and regulations which are on file and have been approved by the administrative authority are the lawful ones.

Peculiarity of the service problem. One word more should be said on the general subject of service regulation. The earlier legislation was very precise and explicit as to details. Gradually the realization came that, on account of the multiplicity of operating conditions, the constant changes and improvements in technique, and the very large number of elements that go to make up good service, it was necessary only to lay down such general standards of good service as would give commissions the utmost latitude and elasticity in carrying these standards into effect.

One outstanding purpose of service regulation is to secure the public safety in the use and enjoyment of the service and in the operation of facilities. The past practice of legislating in detail in regard to safety appliances has given way to the practice of setting forth in a legislative standard the criteria of good service, allowing commissions to determine specific standards by administrative regulations. Nevertheless, legislatures will, in obedience to public sentiment, frequently pass upon technical questions.

Individual consumers may often be unable to see attributes of unfitness in goods and service, just as the importance of safety and sanitary precautions are insufficiently appreciated. Private motives of gain constantly jeopardize the quality of the service. Even continuity is not assured where irregularity of service makes operation cheap and easy though inconvenient to the public. Extensions and improvements are often unremunerative in themselves though socially necessary and desirable. Regulation, therefore, seeks to overcome managerial inertia by forcing the extension and improvement of service to the limits of reasonable profitableness.

Scope of statutory regulation. The scope of state regulation under the commission system varies in different states. In its most developed form it applies to the following industries: (1) common carriers by rail, highway, and water, including such supplementary facilities as are provided by express companies, passenger and freight terminals, toll bridges and ferries, docks and wharves, freight line, equipment, and terminal companies; (2) telephone, telegraph, and cable companies; (3) utilities supplying water, electric light and power, electric railway and bus service (including subway and elevated lines), natural and artificial gas service, heating and refrigerating service. In a few states the scope of state regulation is still restricted to interurban utilities of the first two types mentioned above, leaving urban utilities to regulation by local authorities. These states are Nebraska, Arkansas, Iowa, Mississippi, South Dakota, and Texas. In other states certain utilities, more particularly urban transport utilities and water utilities, remain under local supervision. Other odds and ends are represented by canal companies, irrigation companies, signaling and messenger service companies, companies operating inclined-planes, warehouse, grain elevator, and booming and rafting companies. In Kansas regulation has also been extended to companies engaged in the shipping, marketing, and handling of livestock. Another state includes commission merchants. And so the line drawn by statute is a wavering and uncertain one, often drawn experimentally.

In another way the scope of regulation is, however, decreased, at least as far as the state commission system is concerned. State legislatures show a tendency to keep municipally owned utilities, especially the water utilities, entirely outside the scope of state regulation. Where these utilities are subject to commission jurisdiction, the boards have a tendency to tread lightly in exercising their regulatory powers.[1] Similar to this exemption is the exclusion of cooperatives and mutual associations carrying on public utility enterprises. The implication is, of course, that public and cooperative enterprise is sufficiently responsive to social needs without administrative guardianship.

The franchise problem under state commission regulation. Some legal doubt surrounds the validity of the above legislation where it supersedes the terms of franchises previously in force. There is no doubt where the original permit or franchise was issued by the state, as in the case of railroad, telegraph, and telephone franchises, and where such permit did not specifically name the rates to be charged. There is also little doubt where the state constitutions have reserved the power to revoke or amend franchises. In cases, however, where municipalities were authorized to grant franchises and where the power to revoke or alter these franchises had not been specifically reserved, either in constitutions, statutes, or the contracts themselves, this movement to substitute state for local regulation rests upon somewhat insecure foundations.[2] A local ordinance regulating rates may be operative for some time doing the work of a state commission before being

[1] A decision of the Wisconsin Supreme Court upholds this power of the Commission; *Pabst Corporation v. City of Milwaukee* (190 Wis. 349), 1926.
[2] *Quinby v. Public Service Commission of N.Y.*, 223 N.Y. 244 (1918); *cf.* also, 227 N.Y. 601 (1919).

set aside by a state law unless the state constitutions confer "Home Rule" upon cities.

The indeterminate permit. The best illustrations of commission regulation of local utilities are found in those states where the indeterminate franchise has been adopted. In considering this form of franchise we are limited in our field of inquiry, since only a few states, among which Wisconsin was one of the first, have substituted it for the special franchise.[3] From a historical point of view, it may be said that the indeterminate permit was the logical and inevitable outcome of the attempt to secure efficient regulation by commissions in states which had a constitutional reservation of power to amend or revoke special franchises. The *term franchise,* on the other hand, presented difficulty in commission regulation to enforce proper service and reasonable charges. If a corporation operated under such a franchise and did not set up nor maintain amortization funds to recover capital investment before the term expired, little assurance was given to either creditors or the public that satisfactory conditions could be expected over the life of the franchise.

The indeterminate permit offered a satisfactory alternative in that it recognized the monopoly character of the business, removed the need for amortization funds, provided for flexible accommodation in rates and service to changes in economic conditions, gave the municipality an option to purchase at a fair price, and protected the exclusive nature of the grant by requiring potential competitors to secure a certificate of convenience and necessity from the state commission. In this form it was adopted in Wisconsin and New York in 1907, largely because disinterested students of the subject (like Com. Milo R. Maltbie of New York and Prof. John R. Commons of the University of Wisconsin) advocated its adoption.

As a new development in the technique of regulation, the indeterminate permit is part and parcel of the commission system of regulation. It first came into prominence in 1898 when a special legislative committee in Massachusetts called attention to its advantages. In its Massachusetts form of a revocable license which does not require compensation to the companies for their property in the streets, it violated the spirit of the indeterminate franchise in its more developed form; however, in practical operation in Massachusetts, the properties of the companies have been secure.[4] The Congress of the United States likewise adopted the policy of granting

[3] These states are Arkansas, Colorado, Indiana, Minnesota, Ohio, Oklahoma, and Wisconsin.

[4] See Report of Committee on "Terminable Permit," American Elec. Ry. Assoc., 1924.

indeterminate franchises in the District of Columbia, as well as in the insular possessions of the United States (Puerto Rico, the Hawaiian and Philippine Islands).

Regulation and the great depression. Although certain weaknesses had appeared in the operation of the type of regulation initiated in 1905 by Wisconsin and immediately thereafter in most of the states, it was the great depression beginning in 1929 which generated a new movement for the more comprehensive reorganization of public utility regulation. Piecemeal amendments had sought to make minor improvements. An outstanding weakness was the absence or inadequacy of financial regulation and of control over the purchase and sale of properties in the process of consolidating them into city-wide and state-wide systems. Although these powers were shored up to some extent, on the whole they remained inadequate, as the experiences during the depression proved. Another deficiency, met in some of the states by amendment, was the absence of commission control over the water resources of the states. In the same way other powers over rates, services, intercorporate relations, accounts, and record keeping were inadequate or not clearly defined. Two influences, however, which the depression aggravated, were primarily responsible for a growing note of criticism of state commissions, and these generated the political energy which led to the more comprehensive reorganizations. The first of these influences had to do with the valuation or rate-base problem which is fundamental to the whole process of regulation of earnings. Commissions and courts were at loggerheads over how a rate-making rule laid down by the United States Supreme Court decision in *Smythe v. Ames* in 1898, at the very threshold of the monopolistic epoch, was to be applied. The second major influence was the growth of holding company control of operating public utilities which, besides creating certain difficulties inherent in a holding company setup, had the effect of undermining the regulatory powers of state commissions. Both influences worked to the common end of creating a wide-spread belief that state commission regulation had "broken down."

The reorganization movement had two aspects. In one aspect the commission system sought to purge and strengthen itself by internal reorganization and by adding to and more clearly defining its statutory powers. The other aspect led to a demand for a strengthening of regulation as a whole by filling a regulatory gap with a complementary system of regulation by federal commissions. Incident to this major objective was an oblique demand that regulation be further strengthened by mobilizing public ownership and operation as an alternative to regulation of private enterprise.

Scarcely a state commission remained uninfluenced to a greater or lesser degree by this third wave of regulatory advance. It was usually preceded by official investigations of the working of regulation in the past, with Massachusetts, Wisconsin, and New York again leading the way. An unusually thorough and competent report was made by the New York Commission on Revision of the Public Service Commissions Law in 1930. A Wisconsin statute of 1931, overhauling the regulatory laws, was again widely followed in many other states. We are reserving a discussion of these regulatory improvements for Part II.

Local Regulation

Contemporaneous with the development of state commissions since 1905 was a parallel movement to perfect local regulation without the intervention of state commissions. Conceding that the primary defects of the franchise system were centered in their inflexibility, it was felt that these defects might be overcome by adopting some new devices calculated to remedy them. At the same time it was believed that these reforms might preserve a greater measure of local control which fitted in with the home-rule aspirations of the growing number of our metropolitan centers. Even the New York commission law, while setting up two state commissions, provided that one should have a jurisdiction limited to the Greater New York area. It cannot be gainsaid that many aspects of rate and service regulation have both a state and a municipal setting. They require detailed knowledge of local conditions as well as cooperation between state and municipal officers. Nevertheless local regulation was subject to serious limitations.

One of these was that local councils often act without proper investigation and are unrestrained by legal and economic principles. The background of those favoring state commissions in the first decade of the twentieth century, both as regards the inefficiency of court processes and the helplessness of local councils, is well illustrated by two citations from the decisions of one court. Referring to a rate litigation involving the Des Moines Water Utility in 1911, Judge McPherson wrote:

It is now more than three years since the passage of this ordinance. This case illustrates the evils in connection with the fixing of rates by municipalities to govern public utility corporations, . . . by the time this case is decided by an appellant court, at least four years will have elapsed from the passage of the ordinance until the matter is put at rest by the courts. . . . The present expensive chaos should be brought to an end. It is well known by all informed men that city councils necessarily adopt rates with but little or no investigation as to what rates ought to be fixed. The result is that we have ordinances fixing rates based upon little intelligent effort for the ascertainment of the facts. Some of the states like New York, Massachusetts, and Wisconsin, have state commissions of competent men, who give public hearings, and who do nothing behind doors, nor in secrecy—a commission with no member interested as a taxpayer of the city, and with no member subject to influences other than the ascertainment of the truth and the facts. Rates are thus fixed with which most fair-minded people are ready to acquiesce.[5]

Shortly thereafter, in another rate case, the same judge returns to this subject in the following words:

This litigation has cost both the gas company and the city extravagantly large sums, most of which cannot be taxed as costs, nor recovered back by the party successful in the end. Much of this kind of litigation and practically all the expense would be avoided if Iowa, like so many of the others, including some neighboring states, had an impartial and city non-resident commission or tribunal, with power to fix these rates at a public hearing, with all interested parties present, with the tribunal selecting its own engineers, auditors, and accountants. Too often we have selfish, partisan, prejudiced and unreliable experts engaged for weeks at a time, at $100 or more and expenses per day, exaggerating their importance and making the successful party in fact a loser.[6]

These excerpts point out some of the reasons why exclusive regulation by state commissions has been advocated. Another argument has been the inability of local agencies to introduce a scientific basis for regulation by requiring accurate, uniform, and well-conceived systems of accounting and statistical records. This, undoubtedly, has been a development for which state regulation must be given much credit. It was also urged that the expense of maintaining a competent staff of administrative officials to supervise utilities would be prohibitive to all but the larger cities.

The most serious defect, however, was found in the fact that the incorporated city or village was no longer the natural unit of control as it ceased proportionally to be the natural economic unit of supply. This was recognized also by Dr. Delos F. Wilcox who best represented those who advocated enlarging municipal powers. In an early work [7] he writes:

After all, the day of walled cities is past and now an urban community is primarily a congested spot on the state map, a center of population and of industrial

[5] *Des Moines Water Co. v. City of Des Moines,* 192 Fed. Rep. 193, p. 194 (1911).

[6] *Des Moines Gas Co. v. City of Des Moines,* 199 Fed. Rep. 204, p. 205 (1912).

[7] Wilcox, D. F., *Municipal Franchises* (vol. II, The Eng. News Publ. Co., 1910), p. 704.

activity intimately related to the personal and property interests of all the citizens within its sphere of influence, which often extends to and beyond the boundaries of the commonwealth itself. Public utilities, although still comparatively simple industries, have grown far enough beyond merely local bounds to require complex governmental machinery to operate or regulate them.

The advocates of exclusive regulation by state commission pointed to certain facts in the development of public utilities to prove their claim that exclusive local regulation would be difficult if not impossible. One writer [8] explained that in his state (Wisconsin) at the time of writing (1914) more than 93 per cent of the telephone exchanges extended beyond municipal limits. It was becoming a matter of common knowledge that the expanding consolidation movement, combined with the technical progress in long-distance transmission of electric power, gas, and electric signals, had joined together under single corporate or administrative control the supply of public utility services hitherto rendered by organizations operating in separate cities and even in separate villages. This fact, undoubtedly, would make for an enlargement in the unit of control. For, after all, our incorporated cities and villages, since they are "public instrumentalities established in aid of the administration of the affairs of the state," have authority limited to the geographical area entrusted to them by the parent state. The paramount and original power of regulation is in the state, which may and does delegate that power to subordinate public corporations. It must, therefore, be admitted that the successful administration of a system of local regulation had a great handicap to overcome, imposed upon it by the economic evolution of these industries.

No unbiased student of the history of regulation will deny that in 1907 the system of franchise regulation required radical amendment. By no means were all willing to admit that the system of continuous regulation by state commission should be exclusively substituted for it. There were many who contended that public ownership in its varied forms would best secure the true objectives of the social economy. Others were insistent that a larger measure of local autonomy be left to cities in the control of their local utilities. They pointed out, for instance, that the concessions made to local regulation in Wisconsin and elsewhere, at the time the state commissions were created, brought forth no activity on the part of municipalities because of a fear that all determinations of consequence would be appealed to the state commission.

The problem of working out some measure of local autonomy under state regulation has been variously met in the different states. Where there

[8] Holmes, F. L., *ibid.*, p. 301.

were constitutional provisions granting home rule to cities, or where local
sentiment was strong in the legislatures, a good deal of authority was left
in local hands. The Colorado constitution, as amended in 1902, gave the
city of Denver "home rule" as to its municipal affairs. The city charter
provided for the initiative in legislation and for the adoption of franchises
by vote of all tax-paying electors. Arkansas, Texas, Iowa, Kansas, Kentucky,
Michigan, Minnesota, and Nebraska were states in which important local
utilities remained subject to local regulation. In Ohio, under a home-rule
provision, cities may fix both rates and service by ordinance as franchises
expire. But the ordinance provisions may be appealed to the state commission, which may determine reasonable rates and service.

Legislatures were particularly unwilling to grant to state commissions
regulatory powers over publicly owned and operated local utilities. Only
eleven states have such a provision. Some states make it the duty of the
state commission to advise these publicly owned utilities in their operation
and management.

Regulation of public utilities by local commissions.   The strong sentiment for local autonomy brought forth another line of advance which has
been pursued in some localities. This advance has assumed two forms: (1)
the redrafting of franchise provisions so as to make them service-at-cost
franchises; (2) the adaptation of administrative regulation to local conditions by setting up municipal commissions.

The Washington sliding scale.   We shall conclude consideration of
local regulation with a discussion of the Washington sliding scale which
alone survives from an era of local regulation and which uses the device of
flexible rate franchises.

Service-at-cost franchises were found to be peculiarly adapted to urban
transportation, particularly the electric railway, and may still find some
measure of usefulness in handling our urban transport problem. Assuming
that a city is unable or unwilling to take over its local transportation plant
as a public enterprise, some method must be devised whereby cities can
assure themselves that there shall be no breakdown in rendering this
necessary public service. This problem confronts all our larger cities. In some
of them it has become a metropolitan transportation problem in which
suburban steam railways, urban and suburban electric railways, busses,
taxicabs, elevated railways, and subways must be coordinated into a well-
articulated transportation machine. All now agree that we must have
monopoly; that elevated, surface, and subsurface lines must be combined

to give local and express service. This will in most cases involve the adoption of rapid transit programs, the facilities to be provided by public capital at least to the extent of the permanent way. Service-at-cost plans, when properly drawn, should also provide *in advance* for the operation of such rapid transit facilities, fixing terms and conditions.

Few, if any, service-at-cost franchises, in so far as they applied to urban transportation, have survived the collapse of the electric railway. Even the Taylor franchise of 1909 in Cleveland had to make way for public ownership. Nevertheless, the experience with their operation has yielded valuable insight into the functioning of regulated industry.

Commissions have used a combination of the sliding scale and service-at-cost plans as a device to secure both automatic and flexible regulation. In New Jersey, Memphis, Tennessee, and the District of Columbia, plans were set up by their respective commissions, of which only the Washington experiment survives. A somewhat similar arrangement is in effect in the province of Ontario, Canada, where municipalities cooperating with the Ontario Hydro-Electric Power Commission provide themselves with wholesale electric power supply by entering into a species of service-at-cost contracts, with sales under these contracts so adjusted as to repay these costs to the provincial government.

The Washington plan went into effect on January 1, 1925, after a prolonged period of litigation between the district commission and the Potomac Electric Power Company over the valuation of its property for rate-base purposes and the fair rate of return thereon. At the time, the North American Company (which was the parent holding company of the Potomac Electric Power Company and the Milwaukee Electric Railway & Light Company) was negotiating a service-at-cost plan for its Milwaukee properties; hence the suggestion was made that the seven-year-old Washington litigation might be terminated if the parties could agree upon a similar plan combining service-at-cost with a sliding scale of returns. After compromising on the rate-base question by adopting an initial figure about 33 per cent in excess of original cost as found by the Commission, but 26 per cent below reproduction cost as contended for by the company, a formula was devised which adjusted the rate base for additions to plant at cost. The formula also provided agreements on depreciation and other operating expenses and fixed a basic rate of return of 7½ per cent. It became the duty of the District commission to adjust rates upward or downward in accordance with a sliding scale if actual earnings yielded less or more than the basic rate of return. Under a somewhat complicated scale the company retained a stipulated portion of the excess earnings for its corporate purposes, the remainder being available for rate reductions. The plan was sanctioned in a consent decree of the Supreme Court of the District of Columbia.

Beginning with rates to consumers on a high level, the plan was unusually successful in bringing about a succession of rate reductions. Residential rates, for example, were reduced from a level where 100 kilowatt-hours cost $7.02 in 1925 to a level of $2.56 in 1942, thus achieving a price for electric energy among the lowest in the United States. Returns to stockholders under the plan were also inordinately high, and hence the plan was subsequently modified by dropping the sliding scale and reducing the basic rate of return to 5½ per cent. A similar plan was devised for the Washington Gas Light Company in 1935 and received the approval of the United States Supreme Court in 1944, though the Office of Price Administration protested an increase in rates by the commission. The New Jersey plan was discontinued after several years of operation as a result of disagreement over the operation of its rate-of-return formula. It is, however, a reasonable conclusion that modernized service-at-cost plans can be devised which will operate with a fair degree of success, affording both flexible rate structures and some measure of local decentralization of regulation. Each plan must be judged on the basis of its own special facts.

9. REGULATION
IN THE TWENTIETH CENTURY
(CONTINUED)

Owing to the growing divergence between the regulatory policies applied to intercity transportation and the policies used in regulating the other branches of the utility family, we are isolating the discussion of the former from the latter. A comparison of the different trends should prove illuminating and helpful, perhaps, in recognizing harmful tendencies. In the preceding chapter dealing with state and local regulation, we have only alluded to intercity transport in passing. Except for the regulation of intrastate motor transport by bus and truck, the regulation of railroads has become a very minor phase of state commission activities. Only in the interval between 1905 and 1920 was there any intrastate regulation of railroads worthy of the name. State commission activities relating to railroads are now limited—except for purely local rate and service matters—to the protection or promotion of the interests of the shippers of the state in proceedings before the Interstate Commerce Commission.

This chapter is devoted, therefore, to a discussion of transport regulation by the federal government. But the same technological innovations and marketing necessities which had first expanded rail transportation were also expanding the scope of operations by the electric, gas, and communications industries. This meant that, ultimately, federal regulation would also have to be extended to them. We shall also briefly survey these major developments.

Railway Transportation

The Interstate Commerce Commission in a new role. We shall first trace the regulatory developments in the railroad industry. About 1900 the cost of operating railroads was rising so rapidly that, unless rates were also increased, net earnings would be adversely affected. This fact once more changed the incidence of rate regulation. Whereas in the past applications had been principally by shippers to get reparations or adjustments in particular rates, from this time forward the initiative was taken by the carriers. A series of what appeared to be concerted rate increases caused widespread public criticism.

In 1904 President Theodore Roosevelt recommended making railroad regulation effective. The House was favorable, but the Senate delayed with investigations. However, Roosevelt persisted in his attempt to "put teeth in the law." The railroads loosed a tremendous publicity campaign. As an argument against giving increased power to the Interstate Commerce Commission, they pointed to its past inefficiency as shown by the reversals of its decisions in the courts. The principal issue was the power of the Commission not only to declare that an existing rate was discriminatory, and hence unlawful, but also to fix maximum rates, regulations, and practices to be observed *in the future*. Against this meddling in what they deemed their private managerial function, the railroads put up a "finish fight." But under the impetus of President Roosevelt's dynamic personality, the Act was changed in this respect by the Hepburn amendment and further strengthened by the provision that the decisions of the Commission should be final except as to questions of constitutionality and as to whether a specific order was within the scope of the delegated authority.[1] The year 1906 thus ushered in a new era in regulation by the federal government.

Startling disclosures in regard to further discriminatory practices in 1905 aided in securing the passage of the Hepburn Act. The most important provision was that *expressly* conferring upon the Commission the power to fix maximum rates for a period of two years, if existing rates were found to be unjust, unreasonable, or discriminatory. This power was further supplemented in 1910 by the Mann-Elkins amendment, which gave the Commission authority to suspend rate advances by carriers and to proceed either upon complaint or on its own initiative to hear evidence as to the propriety of such increases. This placed the burden of proof upon the carriers, while it tended to protect the shipper against rate increases. These provisions are peculiarly important because in progressive steps they deprived the carriers of their rate-making initiative, which was very important at a time of rising prices and wages. And they also went far to make the Interstate Commerce Commission an administrative authority with delegated powers comparable to those exercised by mandatory state commissions. It still lacked the power to fix minimum rates, which was important to prevent the rate structure from being constantly disturbed by competitive rate-cutting. Its request in the annual report to Congress of 1916 that this

[1] *Cf.* 215 U.S. 452, 470 (1910).

power be conferred was not acted upon until 1920.[2] It is important to bear in mind, therefore, that federal regulation lagged appreciably behind the best state regulation of railroads, as in New York and Wisconsin, as far as the perfection of the regulatory machinery is concerned.

Other amendments embodied in the Hepburn and Mann-Elkins Acts need only brief mention. In 1906 the jurisdiction of the Commission was enlarged to include express and sleeping car companies and pipelines. The terms *railroad* and *transportation* were redefined to include all manner of special facilities and services, terminal and otherwise, particularly those afforded by industrial railways and private car lines. Authority was conferred over joint rates. The Commission's power to prescribe the character of accounts and reports was enlarged. An antipass provision was incorporated. By eliminating the phrase "under substantially similar circumstances and conditions" in 1910, the "long-and-short haul" principle was reestablished without qualification, unless the Commission expressly authorized departures. The "commodities clause" of the Hepburn Act was directed against objectionable discriminatory practices engaged in by the railroads, relating particularly to the carriage of coal, owing to the ownership of coal mines by the carriers. This clause makes it unlawful to transport in interstate commerce any commodity, except lumber and its products, in which the carrier is interested as owner or producer.

Enforcement was measurably strengthened. The orders of the Commission became immediately binding, except that carriers might seek relief by applying to the courts for an injunction. Courts were not merely authorized, but they were *required* to enforce the Commission's orders with penalties accruing not less than 30 days after the effective date of the order. Between 1910 and 1912, in a series of decisions testing out the new legislation, it was clearly established that the courts could not and would not set aside the Commission's orders merely because of disagreement as to policy. The court recognized that it was not their province to decide where "reasonable men might well differ." In short, administrative regulation had also become an accomplished fact in the field of interstate commerce.

Other details regarding the history of federal regulation of interstate carriers will be taken up later at points where discussion of them will prove more illuminating. It should be added here that in 1910 a Commerce Court was created and given special jurisdiction over rate matters, but it

---

[2] The Commission first recommended that minimum rate powers be conferred upon it in the annual report for 1893, pp. 38–39. The recommendation was renewed in 1897 and 1898.

was abolished in a little over three years. This court was the special contribution of President Taft, who urged its adoption in order to expedite further the adjudication of cases and to secure a greater degree of uniformity in court decisions. The same idea had already been applied in some of the states in order to secure greater expertness on the part of judges by specializing their jurisdiction. However laudable the object, the members of the court reverted to the practice of unduly interfering with orders of the Commission. They proceeded to substitute their own judgment for that of the Commission. The temper of Congress and of the country was hardly such as to brook interference, judicial or otherwise, with the legislative purpose of establishing and perfecting administrative regulation; consequently, the court was abolished. The Panama Canal Act of 1912 gave the Commission power over the relations between rail and water carriers, and the Clayton Act of 1914 extended its power over intercorporate relations of railroads.

Development of its powers.   The Commission's control over rates is so crucial a matter that no mere enumeration of amendments can suffice to bring out its full significance. After 1906 the Commission began to have a true rate-making power. In order, however, to set this power in motion there had to be a complaint, and the complainant had to assume the burden of proof. Evidence substantiating the complaint had to be based upon experience with rates actually in effect. If the Commission found that rates were unreasonable, it might award the shipper reparation for his loss and secure a change of rates for the future. This remedy, however, would not meet the difficulty that shippers, engaged in competitive business, might suffer irreparable losses due to a falling off in business. Moreover, the working procedure was slow and costly. Nor is the question of rate reasonableness entirely a shipper's problem. Under competitive price-fixing, when consumers "pay the freight," it becomes also a consumers' problem. It was necessary, therefore, that the Commission have the power upon complaint, or *upon its own motion without complaint* to determine the justice and reasonableness of *new rates in advance of their going into effect.* This was accomplished by the Mann-Elkins amendment.

While the Commission's power over rates was thus tremendously enhanced, it did not yet have complete control. It could not name future rates to be effective as *minimum* rates as well as *maximum* rates. Competition or other considerations might still induce carriers to file, publish, and charge lower rates than those fixed by the Commission. Many influences were still at work tending to make the Commission's rate determinations inconclusive. Accordingly, in its 1916 report, the Commission also suggested that the interests of all concerned would be best served by enacting a law, like that in effect in Wisconsin, which declared all existing interstate rates, fares, classifications, rules, and regulations as reasonable for the past but also provided that no changes could be made except upon order of the Commission.

Significance of the "Advanced Rate Cases." Before this recommendation was acted upon, a series of events came which laid bare the true nature of the problem of regulation in the field of railroads, as it had long ago been demonstrated in the field of local utilities. It is necessary to go back a little to pick up the threads. As the unfavorable relation between income and outgo became more and more apparent, the railroads realized that applications for increases would have to be made not by individual carriers but by associations of carriers. In 1906, in connection with the Hepburn amendment, the carriers had learned the advantages of cooperation. Accordingly, in 1910 the Bureau of Railway Economics was founded to supply information, and an association of railway officers was formed to prosecute cases before the Commission.

In 1910 the first important case arose, simultaneously involving rates in eastern and in western territory. Due principally to increased labor cost, the railroads complained that a fair return upon the value of their property was not being earned. The application was denied early in 1911 by the Commission, which held that operating revenues were increasing sufficiently to absorb increased expenses and that efficient management could take care of the situation. This reflected the influence of the growing demand for "scientific management" which Frederick Taylor, its chief apostle, was then popularizing.

The next general application for an increase in rates was the so-called Five Per Cent Case of 1914. The Commission granted horizontal increases in class and commodity rates in Central Freight Association territory, but denied them in the rest of Official Classification territory. In doing so it again called attention to the fact that income could be increased by increasing the rates on special commodities, by securing increases in passenger fares from state legislatures, by the introduction of economies, and by the abandonment of wasteful and unremunerative services. With the outbreak of World War I and the traffic slump following it, the railroads decided they could not afford to wait upon the suggested reforms. They applied for a rehearing and in December, 1914, the Commission approved the 5 per cent advances with certain exceptions.

This decision marked a new departure in the handling of the railroad problem. The old standards of determining the reasonableness of rates, where the inquiry was not as to the reasonableness of the rate level of the carriers as a whole but as to the reasonableness of particular rates, were of no avail. It was now a question of the earning power of the carriers. In the Eastern Advance Rate case of 1911, 50 per cent of the tonnage and of the freight revenue of the whole country was involved in the application. Yet such was the conservatism of even those intimately associated with the work of regulation that the Commission was divided upon the question whether the need of carriers for earnings should be considered. It is significant that Commissioner Daniels, fresh from his duties with a state commission where most rate cases involved questions of earning power, was one of the group which argued for a "living wage" for capital and a margin of profit to attract new capital for extensions and improvements.

We must also import into this chronology the Valuation Act of March 1, 1913, the purpose of which was to furnish some standard by which to test the reasonableness of the general level of rates. The question of a physical valuation of the railroads had been raised sporadically in the past, but as long as the chief focus of attention was the problem of adjusting *particular* rates, it had not been seriously urged. In fact, the carriers contended that revenues did not depend upon the value of their properties. After 1910, however, when the general level of rates moved into the center of attention, their attitude changed. And when in 1911 the Commission refused to advance rates upon such evidence of general earning power as was available, but intimated that physical valuation would introduce a new element into the calculation which might lead to a different result, the carriers changed their attitude and favored valuation.

In the Western Advance Rate case of 1915, advances were granted on only a few commodities and in passenger fares. Commissioner Daniels again called attention to the importance of earning power, and while he admitted that financial mismanagement in the cases of the Rock Island, the Frisco, and the Alton had undoubtedly contributed to the bad showing, he also acknowledged that the time had come to look at the problem from the standpoint of the consumers. He contended that any attempt to punish all the roads on account of the shortcomings of a few was unjust; that mismanagement was traceable to those not now connected with the enterprises; and that the proper remedy was the prosecution and punishment of the individuals and not the withholding of adequate rates to the carriers as a whole.

A fourth application for a rate increase came in the spring of 1917 shortly before our entrance into World War I when an amount of 15 per cent was applied for. No country-wide emergency was deemed at hand and the Commission granted increases only in class rates and a few commodity rates. The trouble with the entire situation was that the period had passed when the railroads had unused capacity on hand for which they were actively seeking users. New problems of investment had arisen, calling less for extensions into new territory and more for increasing the capacity of existing plants. These improvements would have to be made in the congested districts of cities where enlarged terminals, yard tracks, sidings, warehouses, roundhouses, etc., could be acquired only at heavy costs. While there was a steady increase in the efficiency of handling traffic, as shown by steady increases in the number of tons per train and per car and in ton-miles per mile of road, operating expenses continued to increase. Expenses for other improvements such as grade crossing protection and safety devises, unproductive of additional revenues, were also multiplying. Although $4,625,000,000 of additional investment was made between 1908 and 1916, these improvements appeared not to be sufficient.

For the reasons so far outlined, the railroads entered the war period with inadequate facilities for handling traffic. The war traffic still further aggravated the situation so that the under-supply of existing facilities as compared with traffic requirements became a factor of grave public concern. The blame for this situation cannot be placed at the door of the Commission, as the railroads were inclined to do. The decline in railway credit was due to more fundamental facts than any that the Commission could control. Financial mismanagement, the cumbersomeness of the rate-making machinery to which the recalcitrance of the railways themselves had measurably contributed, and the existence of lucrative opportunities for investment outside were the chief reasons for the decline of railway credit.

We may summarize the period immediately preceding World War I by describing the condition that the railroads were in when the President requested Congress to authorize government operation of the roads as a war emergency measure. The net earnings of the railroads had been sapped by increasing costs of operation, particularly wage increases, and by the inability of the carriers to get horizontal increases in rates corresponding to the increases in cost of service. The credit of the roads was impaired by the widely publicized example of bad financial management. From the physical standpoint, the roads were in a condition where, in spite of increased efficiency, the traffic offered could not be handled adequately. The capacity of the plant had been reached and further increases in capacity could be obtained only at the cost of increased investment, for which no credit base appeared. While there had been several good years since the depression of 1907, these good years were by no means sufficient to offset the increasingly bad showing since 1900.

The fact of the matter appears to have been that regulatory policies developed differently in the field of national utilities as compared with local utilities. While monopoly was early recognized as the principle of organization in local utilities, competition was the principle under which railroads were developed, and to this principle regulatory policy was attuned. It was in accord with the traditional American belief that competition among railroads was the ultimate controller of earnings. Those members of the Interstate Commerce Commission who refused to concede that the earning power of rates was a consideration to be taken into account were at least consistent in applying this tradition. With such an objective in the background, regulation was designed merely to control competition, not to displace it. The limit of rate and service control ought to be the control of discriminatory practices and no more. This, it is submitted, roughly characterizes the implicit philosophy of railroad regulation previous to 1906.

But when in the piecemeal process of building up our national regulatory machinery so as to control discrimination more effectively, the provisions giving rate control to the Commission had been so maneuvered as to take the rate-making initiative away from management and to give it to a regulating authority, *the crucial step had been taken which represented a break with the traditions of the past.* Continuous development along this line was bound to usher in a new policy. Commissioner Daniels' position was therefore the correct one, albeit an advanced position, in this twilight period between the passing of an old epoch and the coming of a new.

Government Operation of Railroads during World War I

During the war period the motive which dominated all others in the management and regulation of railroads was unification.[3] For eight months under the Railroad War Board the aim was to "coordinate their operations in a continental railway system, merging during such period all their merely individual and competitive activities in the effort to produce a maximum of national transportation efficiency." Though this aim was realized only in part, significant administrative changes were introduced which were

[3] Cunningham, W. J., *American Railroads: Government Control and Reconstruction Policies* (New York: McGraw-Hill Book Co., Copyright by A. W. Shaw Co., 1922).

worked out more fully under federal control. These changes were retained in the Transportation Act of 1920 under which the roads were returned to the owners. The most important legislation during this period was the lodging of full rate-making powers in the hands of the President by the Federal Control Act of March, 1918; at the same time the Commission's power was reduced so that it could no longer suspend rates but would have to content itself again with reporting findings after investigating complaints. Even then the Commission was required to take into account that the transportation system was being operated as a unit, and that the Director-General could certify that the increased revenues were necessary to defray expenses. Speaking of the increases in rates made effective by the government, one writer [4] says,

The method by which the increases were accomplished must have won the envy of all railroad officials who had struggled through protracted hearings with federal and state commissioners, and had been obliged in the end to accept increases, if any at all, far below what they deemed necessary to meet their needs.

The over-all results of federal control during and after the war were well summarized by Director-General Hines in his final report:

It made practicable a war transportation service that could not have been otherwise obtained; its unification practices have increased the utilization of the inadequate supply of equipment so that an exceptionally large transportation service has been performed in the busy periods of 1919 with a minimum of congestion; it met the emergency of the unprecedented coal strike in a way which private control could not have done and absorbed a heavy financial loss on that account which would have proved highly disturbing to private control; it provided more additions and betterments and equipment than private control could have provided during the difficult financial period of 1918 and 1919; it dealt fairly with labor, and gave it the benefit of improved and stabilized working conditions which were clearly right; it not only did not cost more than private control would have cost during the same period, but cost considerably less on account of the economies growing out of unifications, and the total burden put upon the public (through rates and taxes) on account of railroad costs was substantially less than would have been necessary if the railroads had remained in private control and rates had been raised enough to preserve their credit; it protected the investment in railroad properties, whereas without federal control those investments would have been endangered; and it turned the railroads back to private control functioning effectively, with a record of exceptional performance in an exceptionally difficult winter, despite the disruption caused by the coal strike, and in condition to function still more effectively with the normal improvement to be expected in the weather and in other conditions.[5]

[4] Dixon, F. H., *ibid.*, p. 159.
[5] Hines, W. D., *Report to the President*, Feb. 28, 1920, pp. 45–46.

The Transportation Act of 1920. The Transportation Act of 1920 provided, first, for a transitional policy to be applied for what has been called the guaranty period, during which the nationally conceived system of railroad organization for war purposes was to be transformed again into an organization consisting of efficient individual units; and second, it provided for a revised system of commission regulation which was to obtain in the future. We will restrict the discussion to the second of these objects, and summarize only the provisions dealing with rate regulation because these are the hub of the wheel.

In this connection, the greatest significance attaches to the congressional declaration of policy in regard to rates. This statutory rule of rate-making provides:

In the exercise of its power to prescribe just and reasonable rates, the Commission shall initiate, modify, establish, or adjust such rates so that carriers as a whole (or as a whole in each of such rate groups or territories as the commission may from time to time designate) will, under honest, efficient and economical management and reasonable expenditures for maintenance of way, structures, and equipment, earn an aggregate annual net railway operating income equal, as nearly as may be, to a fair return upon the aggregate value of the railway property of such carriers, held for and used in the service of transportation.

Briefly, the new rule put upon the Commission the task of fixing rates which were reasonable relative to one another; also that of so adjusting the rate structure as a whole as to yield no more than a reasonable return on the investment. The Commission was still authorized to adjust specific rates, but the problem of adjusting the relativity of individual rates was subordinated to the requirement that rates as a whole should yield a reasonable rate of return. This provision brought federal railroad regulation more nearly in line with the practice that state administrative commissions had evolved in the control of local utilities.

For the first two years, beginning March 1, 1920, Congress fixed the fair return at 5½ per cent, to which the Commission might, at its discretion, add an amount not to exceed 0.5 per cent to be used for improvements, betterments, or equipment chargeable to the capital account. After this period the actual percentage upon property value, constituting the fair return, was to be determined from time to time by the Commission. In such determination it was to take into account the transportation needs of the country "and the necessity (under honest, efficient, and economical management of existing transportation facilities) of enlarging such facilities in order to provide the people of the United States with adequate transportation." In determining the aggregate value of carriers' property the

Commission was 'to give due consideration to all elements of value recognized by the law of the land for rate-making purposes, and it was authorized to make use of the results of the work, so far as available, of its Bureau of Valuation.

Minor changes in the rate-making power were the restriction of the Commission's suspension power from ten to five months and the conferring upon it of power to prescribe minimum rates. The former amendment was designed to expedite the work of rate control, while the latter sought to put an end to the competitive lowering of rates. The authority to grant relief from the long and short haul principle was surrounded with some restrictions, the most important being the requirement that the Commission may not "permit the establishment of any charge to or from the more distant point that is not reasonably compensatory for the service performed." Authority over joint rates was increased by a grant of power to fix them upon its own initiative as well as upon complaint, to fix them as minima as well as maxima, and to prescribe their division between participating carriers.

The development of railroads on a competitive basis had made some railroads financially strong and others weak. Although the Act contemplated that the reasonable earning power would be determined by rate-territories, in which strong and weak roads were commingled, this did not eliminate the competition of these roads with each other for traffic upon the basis of the rates fixed. Some carriers would therefore have earnings in excess of a fair return. To take care of these cases, the Act introduced the new principle that the public had a vested right in these excess earnings. The so-called recapture clause provided for the disposition of such excess, as follows: "Any carrier which receives such an income so in excess of a fair return, shall hold such part of the excess, as hereinafter prescribed, as trustee for, and shall pay it to, the United States."

The Act then provided that one half of all net operating income in excess of 6 per cent must be placed in a reserve fund by each carrier to be used in any year for making up deficits below a 6 per cent return. These sums were to be used only in meeting interest, dividends, and rentals. The reserve could be built up until it equaled 5 per cent of the total value of the carriers' property. Excess earnings beyond this amount were to be retained by the carrier and used for any lawful purpose. The other half of the excess earnings were to be paid to the Interstate Commerce Commission, which must use these funds to maintain a general railroad contingent fund. An exception was provided for in the case of those carriers that proposed to undertake the construction and operation of new lines.

These could secure permission from the Commission to retain all earnings derived from the new line for a period not in excess of ten years.

The Commission was authorized to use the sums in the contingent fund as a revolving fund for the purpose of making loans to carriers when the object of the loans was to refund maturing securities originally issued for capital account or to meet expenditures properly chargeable to capital account. The Commission could also purchase transportation equipment and facilities and lease these to carriers under certain prescribed conditions.

The arrangement just described met with much opposition, particularly from the strong carriers. It was, however, approved by the United States Supreme Court in the Dayton–Goose-Creek case.[6] The reason for such opposition is readily understood when we compare past traditions with the policy contained in the recapture clause; for the break with the past was striking. The arrangement is somewhat similar to service-at-cost franchises in the local utility field, which have already been described. What is of peculiar significance in a study of the comparative development of regulatory institutions is that in one way or another the inner meaning of regulation, both in the field of the local as well as of the national utilities, had come to be the control of earning power through the medium of rate control. Despite the significant changes of 1920 it was as yet imperfectly realized in the case of railways.

Extension in scope of jurisdiction of the Interstate Commerce Commission. Prior to 1906 the Interstate Commerce Commission had been almost exclusively a railroad commission. The Act of 1887 had included water carriers only when joint arrangements had been made for continuous shipment by rail and water. The Hepburn Act, as we have seen, added express and sleeping car companies and pipelines, as well as industrial railways, private car facilities, and terminal facilities of every kind by broadening the definition of the terms *railroad* and *transportation*. These extensions of the Commission's jurisdiction were as much for the purpose of ending the discrimination evil among railroads as to extend to new types of public service enterprises the prohibitions and requirements of the Act to Regulate Commerce. The Mann-Elkins Act of 1910, however, extended jurisdiction in a new and somewhat discordant direction by including telegraph, telephone, and cable companies.

Gradually, also, the Interstate Commerce Commission pared down the power of the states to regulate national utilities. The first step in this process was the previously cited Wabash case which induced federal action while

6 263 U.S. 456 (1924).

at the same time it checked state control. The next step in subordinating state to federal regulation was taken in the Minnesota [7] and Shreveport rate cases.[8] In both cases the railroads were under the competitive necessity of adjusting interstate rates to rates fixed by state authority, and the decision in the former foreshadowed the decision in the latter. Justice Hughes, who rendered the opinion in both cases, said in the Shreveport case:

Wherever the interstate and intrastate transactions of carriers are so related that the government of the one involves the control of the other, it is Congress, and not the state, that is entitled to prescribe the final and dominant rule. . . . It is for Congress to supply the needed correction. . . . So far as these interstate rates conform to what was found to be reasonable by the Commission, the carriers are entitled to maintain them, and they are free to comply with the order by so adjusting the other rates to which the order related as to remove the forbidden discrimination. But this result they are required to accomplish.

The Transportation Act of 1920 made the above a part of declared public policy. The law provided that whenever the Interstate Commerce Commission, after full hearings, finds that any rate, classification, or regulation imposed by the authority of a state (or fixed by the President during the period of federal control) causes any undue or unreasonable advantage or preference or prejudice as between persons or localities in intrastate commerce and those in interstate or foreign commerce, or causes unjust discrimination against such commerce, the Commission shall prescribe the rate, classification, or regulation thereafter to be charged or applied that will remove the discrimination or preference and which must be observed by the carrier "the law of any state or the decision or order of any state authority to the contrary notwithstanding." This provision as interpreted by the Commission deprived the states of any effective rate-regulating power. While the state commissions may be called upon to confer with the federal commission or to hold joint hearings, the latter is required merely to give notice and an opportunity to be heard. Operating under this clause the Interstate Commerce Commission has not only swept aside state-made rates where the claim was made that the rates discriminated against interstate commerce, but it has also held that rates of its own selection should be substituted for state-made rates where an insufficient amount of income, as measured by the Congressional standard, was being obtained from such state-made rates. In the regulation of interstate carriers the federal government was thus clearly in the ascendant.

[7] 230 U.S. 352 (1913).
[8] 234 U.S. 342 (1914); 23 ICC Reports 31 (1912).

The failure to achieve monopoly. From the foregoing it should be clear that only two general goals of policy were achieved: (1) the ICC acquired the status of a mandatory commission; (2) it achieved the goal by a combination of judicial interpretation and congressional action whereby it could supplant state regulation of the railroad industry. For the rest, although a beginning was made in achieving a monopoly status, the traditional faith in competition forced an abandonment of the policy considerably short of the complete monopoly goal. This appears best from two new provisions of the Act of 1920. Pooling had always been considered as inimical to competition, and hence was absolutely prohibited in the Act of 1887. After the evils of cutthroat competition had been more completely revealed, the 1920 legislation authorized voluntary pooling upon a showing that the particular pool would improve service or promote economy of operation but would not unduly restrain competition. The latter condition obviously limited the scope of pooling. The same conclusion can be drawn from the provisions of the Act of 1920 in relation to consolidations. It set aside federal and state antitrust legislation enforcing competition by legalizing consolidations when approved by the Commission. But again the cloven hoof of belief in competition appears from a specification of the conditions under which the Commission might approve the unification. Consolidation was permitted if the par value of the stocks and bonds of the consolidating agency did not exceed the value of the consolidated properties as determined by the Commission (a not unreasonable requirement), and if the consolidation was in accord with a complete plan of railroad consolidation as drawn up by the Commission (a requirement difficult if not impossible of achievement). The limiting effect arises from the fact that the section authorizing the drawing up of a plan of consolidation into a limited number of systems required that competition be preserved as fully as possible. Moreover, the proposal was bound to be stillborn because it was based on voluntary action by the carriers and not, as Senator Cummins demanded, upon compulsion.

Other provisions of the Act were merely helpful in restraining competition. Still others were designed to be helpful only in making headway on the "strong and weak road" problem by achieving a situation of stabilized competition in connection with the recapture clause and the rate-making rule embodied in the Act. As an example of aid to weak carriers was the new power of the Commission to determine the divisions of joint rates *on its own initiative,* whereby a larger share of the joint earnings could be made to accrue to the weaker road than would have been possible before 1920. Restraint of competition is represented by the newly acquired power of the Commission to prescribe minimum rates. The better state commissions had been given this power at the outset and Congress was only tardily falling into line. The fixing of minimum rates strengthened the Commission's power over discrimination and was an effective weapon in terminating rate wars, and had been so used by the older state commissions in controlling public utility rates for a long time. Other powers belatedly conferred in 1920 were those of regulating the issuance of securities (stocks and bonds) and of controlling extensions and abandonments of service by means of certificates of convenience and necessity.

Hardly had this federal agency acquired a reasonably effective modicum of power for the control of the developing monopoly situation, when the trend in the direction of monopoly was ended by new technological developments, namely a revival of water transport on canalized rivers and of highway transport by means of new motor carriers. Equally significant was the emergence of the hitherto unknown form of air transport. The inroads made by these new transport techniques were aggravated by the effects upon railway traffic of a gradually deepening economic depression. The miseries of Europe arising from World War I were beginning to engulf the United States also.

The first phase of the depression was agricultural. Congress sought to combat it by means of the Hoch-Smith Resolution, which attempted to afford relief by urging rate reductions on agricultural commodities in the guise of ending undue discrimination against the free movement of agricultural products. The suggested remedy, political rather than economic in nature, was ineffective, if not patently unsound in principle.

Meanwhile the rule of rate-making of 1920 was failing to stabilize earning capacity. Since the rule did not guarantee a fair return, its effective operation would have to depend upon the availability of traffic. The administration of the rule by the Commission was hampered by the prolonged controversy between the courts and the commissions over the "fair value" doctrine, which will be discussed at length in Part II. The recapture clause proved to be unworkable. But it was the business depression beginning in 1929, together with the development of keen transport competition, that caused the monopolistic epoch to end in an economic emergency affecting the whole transportation industry.

The movement toward transport coordination and planning. The first fruits of the depression was the passage by Congress of the Emergency Railroad Transportation Act of 1933 (recommended by the National Transportation Committee and the ICC). The purposes of the Act where: (1)

to study ways and means of improving the general transport situation; (2) to eliminate wastes due to the failure of railroads to coordinate operations and to avoid unnecessary duplication of service; and (3) to reduce fixed charges by means of financial reorganizations. To carry out these purposes machinery created by the Act consisted of a Federal Coordinator of Transportation (Com. J. B. Eastman) and three regional coordinating committees. The exploratory studies were made; plans to reduce losses through better coordination were suggested; financial reorganizations for 111 companies with 78,016 miles of line and $6 billion of securities were effected. These were accomplished through court proceedings under Section 77 of the Bankruptcy Act of 1898, which had also been added to legislation in 1933. But the economizing proposals were not carried out because of carrier opposition and because of the limiting effect of provisions designed to protect employees' earning capacity. All told, the positive results of the Coordinator's efforts were disappointing.

The most significant change traceable to the Emergency Act was the excision from the rule of rate-making (Section 15a) of the scheme of fixing the rate of return upon the "aggregate value" of carriers as a whole or in rate groups, which in turn was tied to the fair value and fair return standard. Along with it the recapture clause was repealed retroactively. The effect was to make the remainder of the rule more flexible because the Commission was still required to consider the need of the carriers for revenues and the effect of the rates upon the movement of traffic. Another forward step should be recorded. The railroad holding company was made subject to ICC regulation with respect to accounts, reports, and security issues.

The final step in this chronology of the development of railroad regulation was taken with the Transportation Act of 1940. With this legislation the main stream of railroad regulation is joined by two major independent streams of transport regulation, that is to say, by regulation of motor carriers and water carriers. Only air carriers still remain outside this charmed circle, which pipelines had already joined in 1906. The principal purpose of the Act of 1940 was to further stabilize competition, not to eliminate it. Since the Emergency Act of 1933 had failed to bring relief and the economic outlook continued to be precarious, Congress decided to make another attempt to bolster the transport industries. Buttressed by presidential committee reports in 1938 (The Committee of Three and the Committee of Six),[9] Congress enacted what seemed to be the consensus of the two reports.

[9] The "Committee of Three" consisting of Commissioners Eastman, Splawn and Mahafee was to submit recommendations for immediate relief, while the "Committee of

For the first time a national transportation policy envisaging all major transport media has been evolved. This undoubtedly marks a new departure in policy and signifies that in the end "coordination and planning" will become the new goal of regulation.

The importance of the rule warrants quoting it at length:

It is hereby declared to be the national transportation policy of the Congress to provide for fair and impartial regulation of all modes of transportation subject to the provisions of this Act, so administered as to recognize and preserve the inherent advantages of each; to promote safe, adequate, economical and efficient service and foster sound economic conditions in transportation and among the several carriers; to encourage the establishment and maintenance of reasonable charges for transportation services, without unjust discriminations, undue preferences or advantages, or unfair or destructive competitive practices; to cooperate with the several states and the duly authorized officials thereof; and to encourage fair wages and equitable working conditions . . . . all to the end of developing, coordinating, and preserving a national transportation system by water, highway and rail, as well as other means, adequate to meet the needs of the commerce of the United States, of the Postal Service, and of the national defense. All of the provisions of this Act shall be administered and enforced with a view to carrying out the above declaration of policy.

No noteworthy changes were introduced in the consolidation provisions of the Act except that unification, though requiring Commission approval, need no longer be in conformity with a previously existing formal plan and included provisions designed to protect labor. As in 1920, consolidation continues by means of voluntary action on the part of carriers.

The 1940 Act also created a Board of Investigation and Research of three members appointed in the usual way for a four-year period. It was instructed to investigate and report on all matters deemed important in promoting the national transportation policy; and, in particular, to determine the relative economy and fitness of rail, motor, and water transport, the extent of public aids to transportation in the past, and the nature and extent of carrier taxation. The report as submitted failed, however, to include comprehensive materials and specific recommendations on the vital question of relative economy and fitness.

The Reconstruction Finance Corporation was authorized to loan carriers up to $500 million after approval and certification by the ICC that the borrower could reasonably be expected to meet fixed charges without judicial reorganization. Finally, the railroads were relieved of the burden arising out of land-grant policies of charging reduced rates on government

---

Six" representing labor and management was to make recommendations on the general situation.

traffic for civilian purposes. In 1945 Congress also extended the same relief to carriers with respect to military traffic.

We must now draw together the remaining threads of the transportation story as it relates to the other branches of the transport industry, the oldest of which is water transport.

Water Transportation

The regulation of water carriers. Few states are concerned with the regulation of water carriage, which is usually for long distances and hence interstate in character. In fact, administrative regulation has been slow to develop because competition among carriers by water was widely prevalent. Until recently the protection afforded by this rivalry, supplemented by judicial regulation (admiralty law), was regarded as sufficient.

Owing, however, to the historic competition between rail and water carriers, Congress became more interested in the conduct of water transport when railroad regulation started in 1887. This Act applied to interstate traffic when transported over joint rail and water routes where the movement takes place under "a common control, management or arrangement for a continuous carriage or shipment." Under this Act, as amended, the ICC had power to establish through-routes and joint rates; it fixed maximum joint rates and determined the division thereof between rail and water carriers; it ordered physical connection and regulated terminal facilities operated in connection with such joint handling of interstate traffic. This was a very limited jurisdiction. It did not include the so-called port-to-port traffic of common carriers nor did it cover contract or private carriers. The Rivers and Harbors Act of 1882 had prohibited the collection of tolls on "any canal or other improvement of navigation belonging to the United States." This provision, of course, had stimulated the use of waterways by private and contract carriers as well as common carriers because the taxpayer was paying a part of the cost of transportation for them. It was all blessed and sanctified in the name of competition.

A further development of the policy to give full effect to competition came with the Panama Canal Act of 1912. This Act made it unlawful after July 1, 1914, for any common carrier subject to the Act to Regulate Commerce to own or operate any common carrier or vessel carrying freight or passengers through the Panama Canal. The same prohibition was applied to vessels operated by railways elsewhere, especially on the Great Lakes, unless the Commission permitted such operation as in the public interest and as not limiting competition. By virtue of such a permit the Morgan Steamship Company, controlled by Southern Pacific, could offer a joint rail-water route, in conjunction with the latter company, which was a complete transcontinental haul. Similarly, the railways could be required to make physical connections with water lines and establish joint through-routes and maximum joint rates. The Denison Act of 1928 carried this idea further by authorizing water carriers on the Mississippi River system to apply for certificates of convenience and necessity; thereupon the railways could be required to make similar joint traffic arrangements with these river lines, more particularly the Inland Waterways Corporation.

The United States Shipping Board and successor agencies. In 1916 maximum rate regulation and regulation designed to control discrimination was extended for the first time to common carriers by water operating on the Great Lakes and the high seas over regular routes and in interstate commerce. For this purpose a new agency, the United States Shipping Board, consisting of five members, was set up as an independent commission. Amendments in 1920 enlarged the membership to seven; and after various vicissitudes, including transfer to the Department of Commerce as a Bureau in 1933, it was revived in 1936 as an independent board of five members as the United States Maritime Commission. Once again it was abolished as an independent agency in 1950 and its duties transferred to a Federal Maritime Board of three members and a separate Maritime Administration, all in the Department of Commerce.

The preceding recital of changes in regulatory structure suggest something of the difficulties attending the regulation of water carriers in foreign as well as domestic shipping between 1916 and 1940. The details of the story are too intricate for portrayal in this summary. Ocean carriers have sought to limit and stabilize their own competition by adopting the device of the agreement or "shipping conference" for the pooling of earnings, the apportionment of traffic, and the control of rates. It was a species of cartel device which the law came to recognize as a means of preventing unfair competitive practices. When approved by the regulating authority, these conference agreements were exempted from the Sherman Anti-trust law as not employing certain unlawful competitive practices, such as deferred rebating and the use of discriminatory devices like "fighting ships" to drive competitors out of business. In domestic shipping of the coastal, intercoastal, and Great Lakes variety, the Board was given a limited jurisdiction over rates to stabilize competition there also.

The Transportation Act of 1940 gave extended powers over domestic water carriers to the Interstate Commerce Commission, but it opened the door wide to exemptions so that less than one-third of the domestic tonnage was subject to such regulation by the Commission. All private carriers and contract carriers of bulk cargoes and liquid cargoes like oil tankers were exempted, as was all transportation in terminal areas and all water carriage by craft of small size. All other common or contract carriers were subject to the Commission's jurisdiction. The Maritime Commission retained a regulatory jurisdiction over foreign shipping and continued its promotional functions with respect to merchant marine subsidies and the governmentally owned merchant marine. Common carriers were subject to a complete regulating power with respect to rates, certification, the Grandfather Clause, and service by the Interstate Commerce Commission. Contract carriers were subject to permit legislation and to the control of rates as reasonable minima. All were to be treated alike in accord with the policies laid down in the rate-making rule as finally modified and consolidated in the legislation of 1940.

Motor Transportation

Motor carrier regulation was begun by the states in the 1920's, but it was largely ineffective because interstate traffic was at once declared by the courts to be beyond the reach of state police powers. After more than a decade of agitation by the National Association of Railroad and Utilities Commissioners and the organized railway industry, Congress finally passed the Motor Carrier Act of 1935, following the recommendations of the Interstate Commerce Commission and a bill drawn by the Federal Coordinator in 1934. It was the intensification of competition during the depression which in the end brought federal action.

Again the list of exempt carriers is a large one. The Act exempted all farm vehicles transporting agricultural products; motor vehicles distributing newspapers, carrying livestock and fish; school busses, trolley busses, taxicabs, and the like. The Commission itself was authorized to exempt the transportation of persons and property in city and metropolitan service, and transportation for hire conducted casually but not as a regular business.

In general, provisions regulating rates, service, securities, accounting, safety, and consolidation of common carriers followed the railway model. With respect to rates, the Act required that they be reasonable and non-discriminatory, and the Commission was authorized to fix maximum and minimum rates in both passenger and freight service. Joint rates and the divisions thereof could be fixed for passengers only, though motor carriers might establish joint routes and rates voluntarily. Contract carriers, on the other hand, were required only to file their contracts and observe the minimum rates specified therein. Even these minimum rates could be reduced after thirty days notice. The most that can be said is that regulation of motor carriers was undertaken to preserve a level of competition deemed to be fair among motor carriers and not too disruptive and cutthroat when the competition was directed against the railway common carrier. Motor transportation by highway, like water transport, was to be encouraged to develop its inherent advantages. However, the Commission was somehow to encourage coordination among common carriers of the various types subject to its jurisdiction so as to preserve a transportation service of national scope. It was also the design of the 1935 legislation to preserve state regulation of motor vehicles to the maximum extent possible; to this end it provided for the establishment of joint boards composed of members appointed by the Interstate Commerce Commission from nominees of the states concerned. Decisions of the joint boards were made binding, with the privilege of an appeal to the federal commission. It was hoped in this way to preserve a measure of local decentralization in the regulation of motor carriers as well as to lighten the burden upon a federal agency in the regulation of an exceedingly complex and varying transport situation.

Air Transportation

A final and most disturbing element in an already complex transport situation was the arrival of air transport on a commercial scale and the need during the 1920's to stabilize its competition and to promote the expansion of this new industry by a tentative and sometimes fumbling program of social regulation. The initiative was taken by the Post Office, which had charge of the letting of air mail contracts and thus controlled the establishment of the major trunk lines. The Interstate Commerce Commission was ultimately called upon to fix the compensation for this type of service. With the development of passenger and merchandise express traffic, under the Air Commerce Act of 1926 and the establishment of the Aeronautics Branch (in 1934 consolidated into a Bureau of Air Commerce) within the Department of Commerce, the regulation of this industry was begun. Its principal concern in the beginning was with the important matter of safety, as well as with the exercise of certain promotional functions. But the regulation of rates, service, and securities, as usually obtained in

regulating other utilities, was conspicuously absent. And yet there was a
growing demand for full-fledged regulation, coming in this instance from the
air transport industry itself.

The Civil Aeronautics Act of 1938. Endorsed in principle by the Federal Coordinator of Transportation and by the ICC, a program of comprehensive economic regulation of air transport was begun in 1938 with
the passage of the Civil Aeronautics Act. A threefold organization was provided, consisting of (1) an independent commission, the Civil Aeronautics
Authority, of five members with six-year terms, selected in the usual way;
(2) an Administrator to promote development and enforce safety measures;
(3) an Air Safety Board of three to investigate accidents and make recommendations. In 1940 a reorganization was made by executive order which
abolished the Air Safety Board and transferred its duties to a newly
constituted Civil Aeronautics Board, a quasi-independent board within
the Department of Commerce. It reported to Congress and to the President
through the Secretary who, however, was not empowered to review its
decisions. An Administrator of Civil Aeronautics again headed a division
in the Commerce Department and carried on development work such as
the operation of airways, aircraft inspection, pilot training and licensing,
and enforcement of safety rules. The Authority was replaced by a board
which had a full regulatory jurisdiction over domestic common carriers,
including certification and a "Grandfather" clause to control right of entry.
It required the publication and filing of tariffs of rates and charges and
regulated their services. It prescribed accounts and reports and regulated
consolidations. Again, consolidations with other types of common carriers
were authorized if competition was not unduly restrained. It controlled
mail contracts and air transport rates, both as to their reasonableness and
their nondiscriminatory character. Like the Interstate Commerce Commission, it could fix maximum or minimum or exact rates.

A full regulatory jurisdiction was thus assured, with promotional features added. Air mail compensation was to provide an adequate income
over and above other commercial earnings. Even a rate-making rule, emphasizing the need of each carrier for resources and equivalent to that
governing surface transport, was provided. The principal criticism was that
regulation and coordination of air transportation with the other branches
of the transport industries was made difficult by failing to enlist the active
cooperation of the Interstate Commerce Commission except as cases involving joint rates between airlines and other carriers might be referred
to joint boards on which the two agencies had equal representation. The

development of separate regulatory institutions for air commerce was justified by the peculiar importance attached to national defense and the promotion of foreign commerce in the development of this youthful industry.

The Federal Power Commission (FPC)

The year 1920, besides witnessing an important expansion in power of the Interstate Commerce Commission over transportation utilities, also witnessed the development of federal policies in a new direction. On June 10, 1920, Congress passed the Federal Water Power Act, marking the climax of a long period of discussion in regard to federal water-power policies. Under previous legislation Congress itself had issued licenses for the development of water powers without properly safeguarding public interests. Theodore Roosevelt had vetoed such bills when they contained no time limit or made no provision for compensation to the government for the use of its property. It was also generally agreed that the terms and conditions of these licenses made the financing of development difficult.

Licensing provisions. The Act provides for the improvement of navigation, the development of water power, and the use of public land in connection with such development. It created a Federal Power Commission of unusual design, an ex officio commission comprising the Secretary of War as chairman, the Secretary of the Interior, and the Secretary of Agriculture. The Commission had jurisdiction over all projects involving the construction, operation, and maintenance of dams, water conduits, reservoirs, power houses, transmission lines, and other works associated with the development, transmission, and utilization of hydroelectric power. However, the jurisdiction extended only to the navigable waters of the United States, the public lands, and such other waters as were subject to Congressional authority under the Commerce clause.

The purpose of the Act was to enable applicants for a power project yet to be developed, or the incumbents of a grant under previous legislation, to secure a license for a term not exceeding fifty years. This license is a contract between the government and the licensee, the terms of which cannot be altered by the government without the consent of the licensee. It is, however, subject to cancellation by executive action if the licensee fails to begin construction. After construction has been started the license can be cancelled only through action by a court. When the license expires the property may be taken over by the federal government for its own use, or a new license may be issued to the old licensee or some newcomer. If the properties are taken either by the government or a new licensee, the old licensee is paid his "net investment." This is an amount equal to his actual legitimate dollar investment plus severance damages and less the sums set aside for depreciation and amortization. The Act also provides that renewals of the license must be upon reasonable terms. Most important, because it represents a new development, is a provision that the licensee must make his improvements conform to a plan of development which will secure the fullest reasonable utilization of the resources of the stream. In addition, he must keep the plant in good operating condition by making all necessary repairs and replacements; he must pay an annual rental for the use of public property and reimburse the government for the cost of administering the Act. The foregoing provisions govern the standard license and represent the heart of the Act.

The Commission is also empowered to issue preliminary permits of not more than three-years' duration for making preliminary plans, thus protecting the applicant's priority. It may also issue minor part licenses for which the conditions applying to standard licenses may be waived.

If the safety of the country demands such action, the President, acting under the war powers, may take possession of the projects for the purpose of manufacturing nitrates, explosives, or other munitions of war and of managing and controlling operations for such length of time as may appear necessary. The Commission is required to fix just and fair compensation to be paid the licensee for such use.

Other duties of the Commission relate to the regulation of rates, service, and securities where the facilities are used in interstate commerce or where, though the business is intrastate, there is no state regulating agency. In the execution of these objects, the Commission is authorized to make all needed investigations and may make others relating to water-power resources and electric energy requirements. Under recent conditions such investigations have become one of the most important aspects of its manifold duties.

At the end of the fiscal year 1955, there were 650 licenses of all kinds in effect, 227 involving major projects. The installed capacity of major projects aggregated 9,844,000 horsepower with an ultimate capacity of 15,545,000 horsepower, which would then represent a claimed investment of $2,440,000,000.

The reorganization of 1930. The original organization under which the Commission functioned proved to be both cumbersome and inadequate. Devoting only a small portion of their time to their duties as commissioners, operating with personnel borrowed from the other departments, and with only an executive secretary as a coordinating medium, the Commission fell chronically behind in its work. Moreover, the inadequate staff was torn by internal conflicts from which only the licensees benefited. Reorganization was overdue and absolutely essential. In 1930 Congress moved to make the Commission over into an independent administrative body of the type which had become standard in federal service. Five full-time commissioners, appointed by the President with the advice and consent of the Senate for five-year terms, with annual salaries of $10,000, took the place of the ex officio monstrosity. An adequate budget assured a competent permanent staff. Only three of the members could belong to the same political party, and all were required to divest themselves of financial interest in power utilities.

Meanwhile, operations of the electric utility industry had become increasingly interstate in character through expansion of the market area and of the power supply and transmission systems. These interstate activities, according to the logic of the doctrine in the Wabash case, were beyond the scope of state regulation. This was made abundantly clear by the Attleboro case of 1927. The Narragansett Electric Lighting Company of Rhode Island sold a small amount of electric energy to the Attleboro Steam and Electric Company of Massachusetts. Because the Rhode Island Commission believed that the selling price was so low as to constitute an unjust burden upon its other Rhode Island customers, it sought to raise the rate to the Massachusetts wholesale customer. But the U.S. Supreme Court held that the order of the Rhode Island Commission raising this specific rate constituted an unconstitutional burden on interstate commerce. This decision placed all transmission and sale of electric energy across state lines beyond the reach of state commissions. Since at least 20 per cent of electric energy generated was by 1935 moving across state lines, a further expansion in the jurisdiction of the Federal Power Commission was indicated.

An equivalent expansion in the production and transmission of natural gas across state lines had been going on for even a longer period of time. Particularly after 1925, with the development of the natural gas fields in Kansas, Oklahoma, Texas, and Louisiana, and the transmission and sale of state surpluses over a network of pipelines in thirty-seven states, did the problem of state commissions in regulating the rates for local distribution become acute. Because in this industry it was usual that interstate transmission was in the hands of a separate though affiliated company, the point of contact and sale was at the gateway of the local distributing companies. In a series of decisions, among which the Kansas Natural Gas Company case [*Mo. vs. Kas. Nat. Gas Co.*, 265 U.S. 298 (1924)] was outstanding, the regu-

latory power of states was restricted to retail rates and service. Inquiry into
the reasonableness of the gateway prices was beyond their administrative
competence. This decision revealed another of the growing weaknesses in
the state commission system of regulation for which only federal intervention could provide an adequate remedy.

The Federal Power Commission achieves maturity.   The election of
1932, bringing Franklin D. Roosevelt to the Presidency, had been fought in
part upon the issue of the failure of public utility regulation. We shall treat
this question in greater detail later. It is only necessary to say here that the
coming of the "New Deal" merely hastened the enactment of legislation
which was on the way in any event. The remedy was applied in two doses:
the Federal Power Act of 1935 and the Natural Gas Act of 1938. In most
respects the two acts are similar. Both are amendments of the 1920 legislation in expanding the jurisdiction of the Commission by giving it power to
regulate the rates and service of electric and natural gas utilities when the
transactions are in interstate commerce. This feature was intended to close
the gap in regulation disclosed by the court cases. In addition, the FPC was
given control over security issues, accounting, and consolidations of electric
utilities. It was also empowered to make special investigations of electric
rates, the interstate transmission of electricity, and national defense problems. With respect to natural gas, its jurisdiction did not extend to security
issues, consolidations and mergers, and the sale of property. Other amendments gave the Commission additional miscellaneous powers which we shall
set forth in other more appropriate connections.

The Federal Communications Commission (FCC)

It is a strange fact that in the field of wire communications, where a
high degree of monopoly was achieved rather early and where intercity and
even nation-wide service was quickly consummated, regulation by the federal government was not begun until 1910 with the Mann-Elkins Act. Telephone, telegraph, and cable companies transmitting messages in interstate
commerce were subjected to an inadequate system of rate and service regulation which continued until 1934, when federal regulation of the field of
wire and wireless communications was comprehensively revised. In practical
effect, except for certain aspects of accounting control, including a prescription of depreciation rates, the industry in its interstate phases remained unregulated. And in the matter of accounting control, owing to conflict in

policies with those of the better state commissions, relations between federal and state agencies were none too happy.

After the transmission of sound by means of radio waves had been technically perfected, and after litigation over patent control was settled and the patents consolidated by organizing the Radio Corporation of America in 1919, radio broadcasting was initiated by Station KDKA of Pittsburgh in 1920. The very rapid growth in popularity of this communications service and the intolerable confusion attending the more or less unregulated multiplication of broadcasting stations, finally required Congressional interference by way of the Federal Radio Act of 1927. A federal Radio Commission was empowered to license stations, assign wave lengths and power, and allot operating time. Network broadcasting is not organized as a public utility in this country (as it is in Britain). For control of earning capacity it is our policy to rely upon the principle of competition. Nevertheless, to preserve tolerable conditions of service, this competition must be restrained by regulation. It is this type of regulation of service without earnings control which was committed to a new Federal Communications Commission when the Radio Commission of 1927 was abolished by the passage of the Communications Act of 1934. The regulation of telephone, telegraph and cable companies was also given to the new Commission under a revised program. This change had been brewing for some time on account of the preoccupation of the Interstate Commerce Commission with the growing complexities of the railroad problem. The rise to importance of the motor vehicle and the airplane as new branches of the transport industry suggested that the ICC become a specialized regulating agency and that further neglect of regulating interstate communication be ended. Again the "New Deal" merely hastened a trend.

The FCC is composed of seven members with staggered terms of seven years. The salary is now fixed at $17,500, with the usual provisions as to party affiliation and for safeguards as to their administrative integrity. A new departure was the designation of the chairman by the President instead of his election by the members.

The new Commission has complete jurisdiction over the rates and services in interstate and foreign communications of telephone and telegraph companies. This covers questions of unjust discrimination as well as reasonableness of rates and adequacy of service. To extend service materially by the construction or acquisition of lines, the utilities must obtain certificates of convenience and necessity from the Commission. The Commission may require physical interconnections between telephone utilities and may establish through-routes. It also has adequate powers to control accounting and has joined with the National Association of Railroad and Utilities Commissioners in setting up a uniform system of accounts. Like the other federal commissions it is empowered to make investigations. It began its work by making the most comprehensive investigation ever made of the telephone industry at the special behest of Congress. On the other hand, its powers of financial regulation are inadequate. It may not regulate service companies nor can it control security issues. Also, its control over consolidations is weak.

The Securities and Exchange Commission (SEC)

Along with the growth in the interstate character of public utility markets there went an increase in the size of the business unit. It was a race between the technical achievement of the economies of mass production and the invention of legal devices for mobilizing entrepreneurship to make use of them. The individual proprietorship and partnership as business entities hardly counted in this race. Only the corporation with its flexibilities survived. By using the devices of the lease, the trust, the corporate merger, and the holding corporation, great pyramids of ownership and control of public utility markets were set up. These syndicated systems of ownership and control not only extended beyond state lines but ramified also through many states and even into foreign countries. Here we need record only the fact that the jurisdiction of state commissions could not reach all the facets of this developing problem. Aggravated by the depression, and by the fact that less than half the state commissions had adequate powers over security issues and over mergers and consolidations, the unsound financial structures of many holding companies collapsed in the financial storms which swept the country beginning in October, 1929. The administration of President Hoover in Washington temporized with the problem, and hence the control of these "pyramids of power" became an issue in the campaign of 1932.

With the election of Franklin Roosevelt, the "New Deal" program of political action quickly passed the Securities Act of 1933, the Securities and Exchange Act of 1934, and the Public Utility Holding Company Act of 1935. As the capstone of this legislative structure of federal financial regulation, the Securities and Exchange Commission was created in 1934. Excepting the ICC, it became the third in this triology of commissions designed to plug up the worst leaks in the structure of state regulation.

As to organization and functioning, the SEC is like other federal agencies that are bipartisan in character and have an independent status. Five members are appointed by the President and confirmed by the Senate for staggered terms of five years, with the Commission electing its own chairman. It has a substantial budget of its own, enabling it to sustain a staff of qualified technicians who function in three main operating divisions. These are a Trading and Exchange Division, a Corporation Finance Division, and a Public Utilities Division, the last named being our principal concern.

The Securities Act of 1933 gave it jurisdiction over the issuance of all securities to be sold in interstate commerce, both those of a utility and of a nonutility character. In this respect, it was the federal government following the example of the states, notably Kansas, which had established a so-called Blue Sky Law to prevent the exploitation of the public by the sale through misrepresentation of fraudulent and worthless securities.

The objective of the 1934 Act was to regulate stock exchanges engaged in interstate commerce. After securities had been issued for the first time, certain abuses crept into trading them on the security exchanges of the country, especially the abuses of market manipulations and trading "on margin." It was to control these practices on the organized exchanges and in over-the-counter markets, and also to supply accurate information about corporations whose securities are listed on these exchanges, that the Commission was given this extended jurisdiction. Together with the Federal Reserve Board, which sets margin requirements for banks, the SEC thus regulates the use of the nation's credit in securities trading.

The 1935 Act declares holding companies of gas and electric utilities to be affected with a national public interest because they sell their securities in interstate commerce and use the mails to transact business. For the purposes of the Act, a holding company is defined as one which directly or indirectly owns 10 per cent or more of the voting control of an operating public utility or another holding company. The Act applies to such gas and electric holding companies who, as a first step, were required to register with the Securities and Exchange Commission. The Act also applies to their subsidiaries, affiliates and mutual service companies.

For the protection of security holders and gas and electric consumers, the Commission is authorized to regulate the issuance of securities, the acquisition of financial interests in public utilities, contracts between intrasystem holding companies, operating companies, and affiliated service companies. The commission may prescribe accounting practices and can generally control relations between officers and directors. The heart of the Act is Section 11, which provides for the physical disintegration of holding company systems and which limits the corporate structure to two tiers of holding companies and the ownership of operating utilities to one physically integrated system. As to security issues, the Act provides for a simplified financial structure which would stabilize corporate credit and equitably distribute voting power. All told, the task set for the Commission was the structural reorganization of a $14 billion segment of the economy.

Financial regulation on a national scale by the SEC was further extended by legislation in 1939 and 1940. A Trust Indenture Act of 1939 requires that bonds, notes, and similar securities offered for sale by use of the mails or other instrumentalities of interstate commerce must meet certain statutory standards designed to safeguard the interests of the purchasers. Similar protection was accorded investors in 1940 by the Investment Company Act and the Investment Advisers Act by requiring registration of investment companies and investment advisers, and by setting up qualifications for them. By these various means the Commission functions to protect investors in public utility as well as other securities. It also advises with federal district courts in reorganization proceedings under the amended Bankruptcy Act, besides rendering general advisory assistance to the financial community.

10. PUBLIC UTILITIES
AND OUR ENERGY ECONOMY

From the foregoing historical survey it should be clear that public utility industries are in a technological sense at the very center of our advancing material civilization. It should also be clear that technological improvements affecting these industries are dependent upon the utilization of the various forms of energy which have become available to man. Without them our present machine age with its high productivity would be inconceivable. There has always been a close correlation between average real income and the quantity of energy consumed per capita in the different countries. In fact, the history of man's material progress has been the history of his exploitation of the various forms of energy. The world-wide realization of this interdependence has resulted in the founding, in 1924, of a World Power Conference devoted to a survey of the world's energy resources and a discussion of current developments in their exploitation.

Development of Technology in the Use of Power

The ancient world had to get along with only three forms of power, of which the oldest was the muscular power of man and animals. The fundamental means of applying energy through machines—that is to say, the pulley, inclined plane, lever, and wheel—had already made their appearance and muscular power was dominantly harnessed by means of them. Ancient public works like the irrigation canals of the Egyptians, Greeks, and Romans were monuments to this technique. They were hardly conceivable without a system of slavery. As a second form, wind power, applied through the sail and windmill, had become important and was used in transportation and in the industry of primitive workshops. Least important was hydraulic power in the shape of the water wheel, deriving its energy from a flowing stream, and known to have been in use in Egypt for irrigation purposes.

Some improvements were made in these power utilizations during the long period of time covered by the Middle Ages, and again they yielded their best results in transportation. The period of overseas navigation and explorations, and the establishment of European colonial empires, was one of the direct results and helped usher in the modern era.

In the sixteenth century new applications of science, particularly improvements in hydraulic power, became the basis of the early factory system which ultimately culminated in the industrial revolution. The invention of a most practical steam engine by James Watt in 1785, bringing coal into general use as a new form of energy, made steam the chief prime mover in the expanding economy. Both hydraulic and steam power were used in the early gristmills and sawmills of this country, in the woolen and cotton industries, and in many small shops and factories. Toward the end of the nineteenth century, the internal combustion engine was added to the list of prime movers, bringing into wide use another new form of energy, petroleum. These three energy sources and the various prime-mover engines by means of which they are harnessed were next given progressively wider scope by being hitched to a secondary machine, the electric generator or dynamo, which transmutes the resulting mechanical energy into electric energy. The age of steam has become the age of electricity.

The year 1945 witnessed the definite emergence of a new source of energy from the womb of science, the energy of atomic fission, which is now being made the subject of experiments looking toward the invention of safe, economical, and reliable means of using it. This new source of energy has brought the realizaton that, from the viewpoint of fundamental science, the ultimate source of all energy forms is the same, namely, solar radiation. The light and warmth of the sun reaching the earth are the necessary conditions for the development of animal and vegetable life. Over millions of years this solar radiation has been stored in plant and animal life and has thus become the source of the power produced from what are called the fossil fuels—coal, oil, and natural gas. Even water power, though regarded as a permanent and inexhaustible resource as compared with the limited reserves of fossil fuels in the crust of the earth, depends upon the heat of the sun. It is available only as long as the hydrologic cycle is maintained: evaporation of water into the atmosphere, condensation of the vapor as rain and snow, and run-off to the ocean. Chart II, reproduced from the 1950 Report of the President's Water Resources Policy Commission, illustrates this most fundamental of all cycles.

Researches in connection with the uranium atom and the use of its atomic energy for weapons purposes have explained this fundamental relationship. All matter is only a form of energy, and if the atomic structure of an element of matter can be changed so as to bring about a loss of mass, this change will be accompanied by tremendous releases of energy in the form

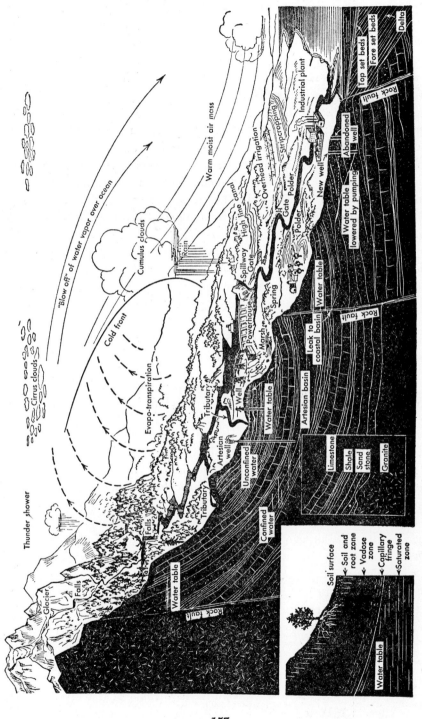

Chart II The Hydrologic Cycle. (President's Water Resources Policy Commission, Vol. I, 1950.)

Thunder shower

Cirrus clouds

"Blow off" of water vapor over ocean

Warm moist air mass

Cumulus clouds

Cold front

Evapo-transpiration

Glacier

Falls

Falls

Water table

Rock fault

Tributary

Tributary

Well

Artesian well

Water table

Unconfined water

Confined water

Soil surface

Soil and root zone

Vadose zone

Capillary fringe

Saturated zone

Water table

Rain

Spillway

Gate

High line canal

Powerhouse

Marsh

Spring

Overhead irrigation

Stripcropping

Gate

Polder

Polder

Industrial plant

New well

Water table

Leak to coastal basin

Artesian basin

Water table

Rock fault

Limestone

Shale

Sand stone

Granite

Abandoned well

Water table lowered by pumping

Rock fault

Top set beds

Fore set beds

Delta

157

of heat. The same reaction takes place when atoms of hydrogen are converted into helium, except that energy releases are on a much greater scale. Solar radiation is this continuous conversion of the radiation of the sun (which is largely composed of hydrogen) into helium, accompanied by tremendous releases of energy with loss of mass.

Less conventional forms of energy, important in isolated places and for special purposes, are: wood, still widely used for house heating; wind-power plants supplying electricity to small islands; and volcanic steam, used in Italy in the generation of electricity. Engineers have also attempted to harness the gravitational pull of the moon upon the oceans, giving rise to the energy involved in the rise and fall of tides. Experimentally, it has proven possible to trap the tidal waters in reservoirs and capture the energy as the waters run back to the sea.

Atomic energy, the most recent discovery of a source of power, is either the great hope or the great scourge of the twentieth century. If certain technical problems of heat transfer and of operating safety can be solved, the potentialities of power residing in the nuclear fission of the uranium atom may soon be demonstrated on a commercial scale. The significance of this new source appears from the fact that a single ton of uranium, destroyed by nuclear fission, is the equivalent in energy of three million tons of coal.

Hydroelectric technology. Hydraulic power is the oldest and best perfected of the more conventional forms of power. Development began with the old-fashioned water wheel or current wheel which is turned by the velocity of the stream. Examples may still be seen in out-of-the-way places of the Southern Appalachian highlands. Its efficiency varies between 3 and 5 per cent; that is to say, the wheel converts only that much of the energy residing in the flowing stream into the mechanical energy of motion. The next step was the location of the water wheel at a natural or artificial fall in the stream. Where there is a steep gradient in the stream, a dam may be located, the function of which is to provide the drop or "head" artificially. Dams also have the function of creating, according to their size, pondage or storage of water. The two types of water wheels used to develop power at these "heads" were, consecutively, the "undershot" and "overshot" water wheels. These are descriptive terms to show how the buckets arranged on the wheel catch and discharge the water. By means of these wheels gravitational energy is turned into mechanical energy. For the "undershot" water wheel the progress in design from the primitive to the more advanced types have brought about ranges in efficiency varying between 25 and 40 per cent. The "overshot" water wheel is now known as the turbine. It was first developed by Boyden in 1844 at Lowell, Massachusetts, with a capacity of 75 horsepower in one unit. Modern turbines develop efficiencies in excess of 90 per cent. Individual units, installed at dams where the quantity of water and the heads involved are large now develop more than 100,000 horsepower.

Naturally, there has also been continuous improvement in the dam structures, which have varied from earth and timber construction to solid masonry and concrete. They have become expensive structures because they must resist the pressure of ice and masses of water. Features appurtenant to dams are forebays, penstocks, navigation locks, fishways, and log-chutes.

Hydraulic power was dominant in the United States up to the Civil War. Thereafter, it fell in importance from about 50 per cent in 1869 to a mere 6 per cent by 1919. Its importance continues, however, as hydroelectric power. The first phase of the industrial revolution was tied up with hydraulic power when the factory was located at the power site. Now we locate factories at the market, near a labor supply or other raw material and transport the coal or transmit the electricity. The steam engine and internal combustion engine have now ousted hydraulic power from its supremacy.

Thermoelectric technology. Engines using the energy residing in mineral fuels—coal, oil, and natural gas (the use of wood and wood waste being clearly exceptional)—are generally designated as heat engines. They may be subclassified into fuel-burning and internal combustion engines. The steam engine may be based upon the burning of coal, oil, or natural gas in its boiler plant which produces the steam. Some plants are equipped to use either oil or natural gas, depending upon which is the cheaper at the moment. The original steam engines were of the reciprocating type in which the expanding steam pushes a piston back and forth (like the steam locomotive). Now the steam turbine has all but displaced this type. On the other hand, an internal combustion engine may be a gas or gasoline engine which requires no boiler because an electric spark explodes the gas mixture to push the piston. Similarly, a diesel or oil engine explodes the fuel oil by means of the heat of compression and needs no electric spark. The choice of heat engine is a matter of fuel efficiency and of over-all economy.

The following ratings afford a comparison of average efficiencies of the different engine types. It should be borne in mind, however, that modern exemplars of each type will develop higher efficiencies and that progress along these lines is continuous.

1. An old-fashioned but good steam locomotive,   5 per cent
2. A stationary steam engine,   17 per cent
3. A reciprocating marine steam engine,   22 per cent
4. A steam turbine,   28 per cent
5. A stationary gas engine,   30 per cent
6. A diesel oil engine,   30 per cent

After the Civil War, industry was increasingly powered by the steam engine, using a system of shafting, belts and pulleys for transmission to a localized point of use. With the advent of the electric motor the use of steam power became steam-electric power supplied by the industry's own plant or by some central station producing electric energy for public use. There was much scrapping of private steam and hydraulic plants, and more and more reliance was being placed upon centralized systems of steam-electric and hydroelectric plants having a public utility status. This was particularly true after the electric utilities shifted from the production of direct current to alternating current in order to expand the economical range of transmission. With the introduction of the transformer to raise and lower voltages, electric energy was mobilized as never before. About 1910 long-distance transmission by means of high-voltage power lines expanded the market for both steam and hydroelectric power and made possible the interconnection of these two classes of power supply. The further improvement of the electric motor was of transcendent importance in capturing and developing these new markets. The attainment of high speeds in motors, their adaptability in small and large sizes to a variety of tasks, their economy in the use of energy, and with all their compactness, cleanliness and safety, were the decisive factors in this expansion of use. In parallel fashion, new utilization devices and improvements in old ones expanded the use of electric energy also in the lighting and heating fields.

The effect of these transformations can be seen in the increased yearly production of electric energy. Dividing the growth between hydroelectric and thermoelectric generation, the amount of production for census years, in billions of kilowatt-hours, was as follows:

Year	Hydro	Thermo	Total
1902	. . . .	. . . .	6.0
1907	. . . .	. . . .	14.1
1912	7.4	17.4	24.8
1917	13.9	29.5	43.4
1922	21.3	39.9	61.2
1927	32.9	68.5	101.4
1932	36.0	63.4	99.4
1937	48.3	98.2	146.5
1942	69.1	164.0	233.1
1947	83.1	224.2	307.4
1950	100.9	287.8	388.7

The source of these data, as well as others we shall be using, can be found in the publications of the Federal Power Commission, especially

"Electric Power Statistics, 1946–1951" or a publication of the Bureau of the Census, "Historical Statistics of the United States, 1789–1945," unless the figures have already been gathered by some other authoritative source. The President's Materials Policy (Paley) Commission, which was set up in 1951 to study the availability of natural resources in the United States and other free and friendly nations of the world, is such a source.

Commenting on this rapid growth, the Commission points out that since 1920 the use of electric energy has doubled every ten years; that by 1950 electricity was being used for domestic purposes in 83 per cent of all rural homes and 92 per cent of all homes in the United States; that electric motors have provided 90 per cent of all mechanical power used in industry; that the use of electric energy per man-hour of labor increased from 2.61 kilowatt-hours in 1929 to 6.29 kilowatt-hours in 1950. Of the 388.8 billion killowatt-hours generated in 1950, losses in transmission and distribution absorbed 55.1 billion; while residential consumption accounted for 74.5, commercial consumption (small light and power) totaled 50.4, industrial consumption (large light and power) 198.1, and miscellaneous uses 10.7. A most significant fact is the great upsurge of consumption in the major electro-process industries (aluminum, magnesium, and similar production), which accounted for 37.5 billion kilowatt-hours, representing an increase in twenty-five years of 815 per cent. It is this type of use, so important for defense purposes in a "cold war" environment, which the Commission calculates must expand most rapidly and will require large blocks of low-cost electric energy.

With the aid of statistics gathered by the Edison Electric Institute, the Commission calculated that the 1950 generation in billions of kilowatt-hours showed the following distribution as to type of ownership:

Generated by	Thermo	Hydro	Total	Per Cent of Total
Private utility corporations	217	51	268	68.9
Private industry	54	5	59	15.2
Municipalities and cooperatives	15	7	22	5.6
Federal government	2	38	40	10.3
Total	288	101	389	100.00

It is important to note in the above tabulation that hydroelectric generation represents 26 per cent of the total, and that this kind of energy is most important in the case of public and cooperative agencies. Another fact of cardinal importance is that only 15.2 per cent of the grand total of energy generated is derived from private, that is to say, nonpublic utility sources.

Truly, the supply of this vital force in modern industry is an expanding public utility function.

Natural Gas

Rivaling, if not surpassing, the increase in use of electric energy has been the consumption of natural gas. The Paley Commission reports that five times as much was marketed in 1950 as in 1925 and that the increase in 1951 was the largest in history.

Natural gas now supplies more than 18 per cent of the energy used in the United States as compared with four per cent of a much smaller total energy use in 1920. . . . Extensive markets have been developed near the source of production where gas prices have been far below those of competitive fuels for the energy contained, while in more distant markets consumption has been stimulated both by the superiority of natural gas in specialized uses and by favorable prices . . . The future position of natural gas in the energy economy therefore depends on how much more of that fuel is discovered and how efficiently the nation recovers and uses that which is found.

Natural gas is drawn from two sources: gas wells and oil wells, with the former increasing in importance. In 1950, of an estimated gross production of 8.5 trillion cubic feet, 5.6 trillion were derived from gas wells and 2.9 trillion from oil wells. Because much gas vented or blown to the air is not reported, actual withdrawal from the ground is larger. Of the gross production, increasing amounts are now being returned to the ground to maintain pressure so as to aid in the recovery of petroleum or natural gas liquids in the future. In 1950, the amount so returned was 1.4 trillion cubic feet, leaving a net production of 7.1 trillion. Losses and waste of 0.8 trillion further reduced the marketed production to 6.3 trillion cubic feet.

The use of gas in repressuring operations is exceedingly important because it seeks to restore the original condition in which the gas dissolved in the oil or the free gas "associated" with the oil provided the driving force which caused the oil to flow. From the beginnings of the oil industry (as is still the practice in Venezuela at the present time and also in isolated oil fields in this country), after the gas (or water) has served its function in bringing the petroleum to the surface, the gas is blown into the air or flared. The tremendous quantities thus wasted in the past because no transportation facilities were available to carry the gas to distant markets, represents one of the economic paradoxes with which the history of exploitation of natural resources in this country is replete. Gradually, industries requiring large quantities of this cheap fuel were attracted to these locations. In 1950, of 4,440 billion cubic feet so used, 1,187 were consumed in field utilizations; 411 in plants producing carbon black; 455 in petroleum refining; 97 in Portland cement plants; 629 in electric power plants of a public utility character; and 1,661 in miscellaneous industries such as chemical and metallurgical industries, glass and clay products manufacturing, the paper industry, and food processing. But the rapid construction since the 1930's of gathering and transmission pipelines has expanded distant marketing for residential and commercial purposes. In 1950, this amounted to 1,842 billion cubic feet, of which 1,198 and 388 were absorbed by residential and commercial uses, respectively; 171 were lost in transmission; and 59 were stored in underground abandoned gas fields near terminal markets. Only 26 billion cubic feet were exported.

The oil and gas industry are intimately linked from both production and consumption viewpoints. It is estimated that, as a matter of discovery, about 4.6 thousand cubic feet of gas are now recoverable with each barrel of recoverable oil. The Paley Commission reports that as a result of deeper drilling for oil and of exploration for gas by itself, this discovery ratio will rise to 6 thousand cubic feet per barrel. This amount of gas has about the same energy content as a barrel of oil. In 1950, Texas was responsible for 52 per cent of the domestic gas production, Louisiana for 13 per cent, California for 9 per cent, Oklahoma for 8 per cent, while the entire Appalachian field, once the largest producer, supplied less than 6 per cent. The greatest concentration of local consumption is in Texas, California, and Louisiana, amounting to more than one-half of the total consumed throughout the country. About 40 per cent of the gas available for marketing in 1950 was sold in interstate commerce, compared with only 17 per cent in 1925. The benefits of this cheap source of energy are thus increasingly spread throughout the country.

The Adequacy of Our Energy Reserves

The unprecedented expansion in the use of energy has raised the question of the adequacy of these supplies. Since the use of each of these energy resources affects the others as well, it is necessary to understand these interlocking relationships. Some of these interrelationships raise questions of public policy that have to be answered within the ambit of the public utility problem; these will be reserved for later discussion. At this point we shall make only a few comments regarding the comparative adequacy of these energy supplies.

Our coal reserves, while exhaustible, are usually taken to be adequate. In 1937 the National Resources Committee estimated them to be 3,000 billion net tons, more than half of which was low-grade bituminous and lignite. Appalachian coals are of better quality than the coals of the central coal regions of the Mississippi valley. The latter are, however, adaptable to a wide range of industrial uses, including electric power generation and the production of synthetic fuels. About 70 per cent of the reserves are located in the semi-arid plains of the West or the Rocky Mountains, far removed from centers of industry and population. The drain on the remaining 30 per cent of reserves of the eastern and central regions is therefore heavy because 85 per cent of the present use is derived from them. Western coal will have to surmount greater handicaps, among them the long hauls to reach markets or the inadequacy of water supplies for local electric generation. The development of the coal-fired gas turbine may make such large-scale use of these low fuel-value Western coals possible because it would eliminate dependence upon water supplies.

Considering the prodigal way with which the American people have come to use their various energy resources, particularly in transportation, it is obvious from a long-run conservation point of view that inexhaustible water power should be substituted for the use of fossil fuels wherever feasible. The Federal Power Commission has estimated the long-range hydroelectric power potential at about 105 million kilowatts, or an average potential output of 478 billion kilowatt-hours. Of this potential, 16.5 million kilowatts of capacity, or 16 per cent, is now installed, leaving 88.5 million kilowatts of undeveloped hydraulic power scattered throughout the country. Of this total, 5,598,000 kilowatts is now under construction, almost 5 million of it in federal projects. Federal projects in the planning stage aggregate 12,652,000 kilowatts, leaving almost 70 million kilowatts of undeveloped potential, much of it in the Mountain and Pacific states. The best remaining sites are in the Pacific Northwest in the Columbia River basin and in the Great Lakes basin at Niagara Falls and on the St. Lawrence River. Depending upon the reliability of these estimates and upon the rate at which electric energy will be demanded by the economy in the future, it is fairly obvious that the rising energy costs of natural gas and oil (sawmill refuse being severely limited and localized) will ultimately force increased reliance to be placed upon thermal generation of electricity from bituminous coal, lignite, and even peat.

Energy Losses and the Conversion Problem

The fact that changing technology forces changes in the use of energy is in large part the reason why the primary sources of energy must be converted into secondary forms. The Paley Commission estimated that in 1947, when the amount of secondary use was 33 per cent, the conversion loss was 17 per cent. By 1975, when the secondary use will have become 39.2 per cent of the total, the conversion loss will have grown to 20.4 per cent. Whatever the real facts may turn out to be, it is certain that the conversion problem, due to the exhaustion of primary forms of energy and the shifting and development of new end-uses, will be the focal center of our energy economy and will vitally affect public utility industries. Since the conversion to electric power is the most important single form of conversion, this will be used for illustrative purposes.

Table V   Some Efficiencies in the Production and Delivery of
Electric Power

A. Carboelectric Generation

	Potential Horsepower	Losses Horsepower	Per Cent Efficiency
At the coal pile	4,968	. . . .	. . . .
Boiler plant	3,726	1,242	75.00
Electric plant			
Turbine	745.2	2,980.8	20.00
Generator	715.4	29.8	96.00
Station use	697.5	17.9	97.50
At station bus bar	697.5	4,270.5	14.04

B. Hydroelectric Generation

	Potential Horsepower	Losses Horsepower	Per Cent Efficiency
At the reservoir	1,000	. . . .	. . . .
Penstock	980	20	98.00
Electric plant			
Turbine	813.4	166.6	83.00
Generator	780.9	32.5	96.00
Transformation (step-up)	765.3	15.6	98.00
Transmission	711.7	53.6	93.00
Transformation (step-down)	697.5	14.2	98.00
At central receiving station bus bar	697.5	302.5	69.75

Table V (*continued*)

C. Local Transmission and Distribution

	Potential Horsepower	Losses Horsepower	Per Cent Efficiency
Local transmission	683.5	14	98.00
Substation	663	20.5	97.00
Local distribution	643.1	19.9	97.00
Distribution transformer	623.8	19.3	97.00
Electric pumping	561.4	62.4	90.00
Energy available for pumping	561.4		80.49
Distribution Transformer	610.9	32.2	95.00
Energy available for domestic consumption	610.9		87.58
Local transmission	683.5	14.0	98.00
Substation			
Transformation (step-down)	663.0	20.5	97.00
Conversion	610.0	53.0	92.00
Railway distribution	579.5	30.5	95.00
Railway motor	521.5	58.0	90.00
Energy available for transportation	521.5	. . . .	74.77

D. Comparative Over-all Efficiency (Power Source to Customer) of Steam and Hydroelectric Generation in Serving Typical Customers

	Domestic Customer	Pumping Customer	Electric Railway Customer
Steam	12.30	11.29	10.50
Hydroelectric	61.09	56.14	52.15

Charts III, IV, and V trace the steps which present-day technology of average efficiency requires in converting coal and water power to electricity. The efficiencies attained in the production and delivery of electric power by these alternative means are shown for each step in Table V. It is assumed that the hydro plant will require long-distance transmission in order to market its energy, while the coal-burning plant will be located at the market. Beginning with a potential horsepower of 1,000 as the energy residing in the stored water, the losses incident to each step are shown, until we arrive at the central receiving substation with 697.5 horsepower. This result as shown in Section B of Table V should be compared with the equivalent steps shown in Section A, where the same quantum of energy was derived from

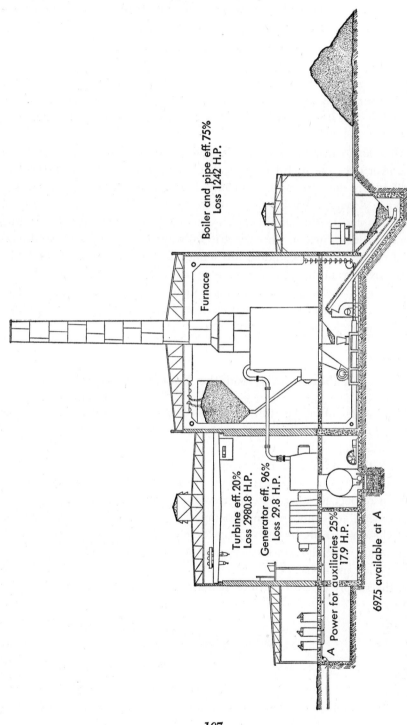

Boiler and pipe eff. 75%
Loss 1242 H.P.

Furnace

Turbine eff. 20%
Loss 2980.8 H.P.

Generator eff. 96%
Loss 29.8 H.P.

Power for auxiliaries 25%
17.9 H.P.

A

697.5 available at A

Chart III The Conversion Problem.

coal. In order to show the disparity in losses, the coal computation was made in reverse order. No special importance should be attached to the percentage efficiencies assumed. They are conventional values, *considerably below the best present-day efficiencies.* The principal difference is that the hydraulic turbine is able to capture 83 per cent of the energy in the falling water while the steam turbine captures only 20 per cent of the energy in the steam.

After losses in local transmission and distribution are deducted, 561.4 horsepower does the useful work of water pumping and 610.9 horsepower is available for domestic uses. Only 521.5 horsepower is available for electric traction in driving a car along the track. This greater loss in the case of railways is due to the additional step required in converting alternating current to direct current, since electric railways in this country use direct-current energy. These operations are summarized in Section C of the table. It is apparent from the table that greater potential economies are realizable in the case of carboelectric generation than in the case of hydroelectric generation. Section D of the table provides a summary of the comparative over-all efficiencies of the two forms of conversion.

Public Utilities and the Energy Economy

The essence of public utility service is centralized supply. The functions of supplying communication, transport, water, light, heat, power, refrigeration, and sanitation, if performed collectively, are of a public utility character. All the energy resources which we have surveyed are important if not indispensable in carrying on these functions. The same thing may be said with respect to other material resources, notably, steel, copper, aluminum, cement, and lumber. Any economies which may be achieved in the use of these materials by marshaling them in the service of man through public utility procedures are, therefore, of the greatest social importance. Public policy in the shape of conservational and other controls has influenced the supply of most of these materials.

A Technological Approach

In working out the facets of this far-reaching problem, the Paley Commission recognized that technology has important tasks to perform. It summarized these under six headings, some of which need only be stated:

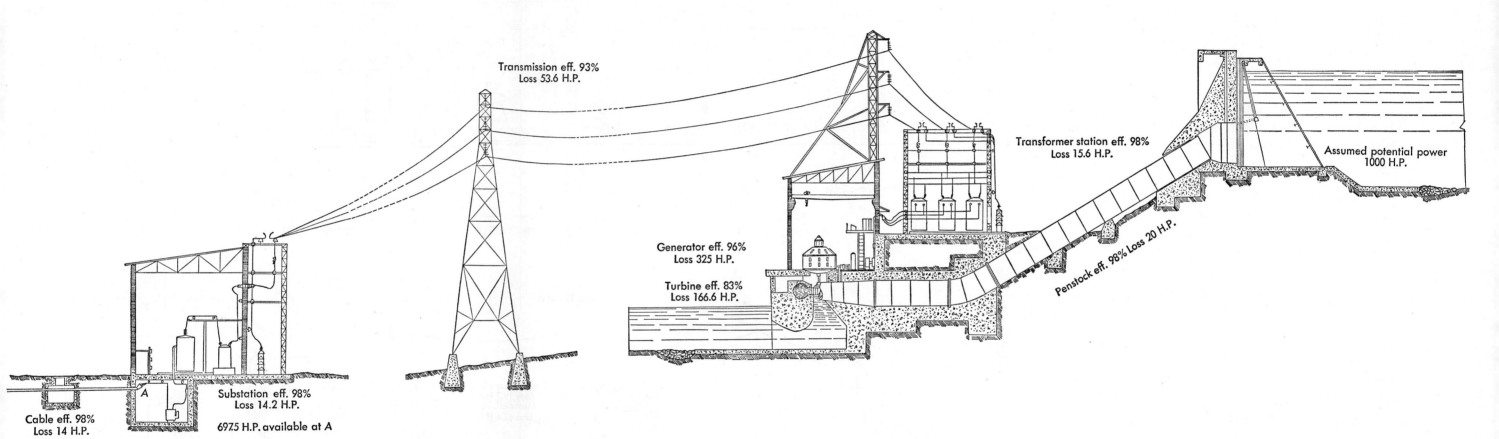

Transmission eff. 93%
Loss 53.6 H.P.

Transformer station eff. 98%
Loss 15.6 H.P.

Assumed potential power
1000 H.P.

Generator eff. 96%
Loss 325 H.P.

Turbine eff. 83%
Loss 166.6 H.P.

Penstock eff. 98% Loss 20 H.P.

Substation eff. 98%
Loss 14.2 H.P.

697.5 H.P. available at A

Cable eff. 98%
Loss 14 H.P.

Chart IV   The Conversion Problem.

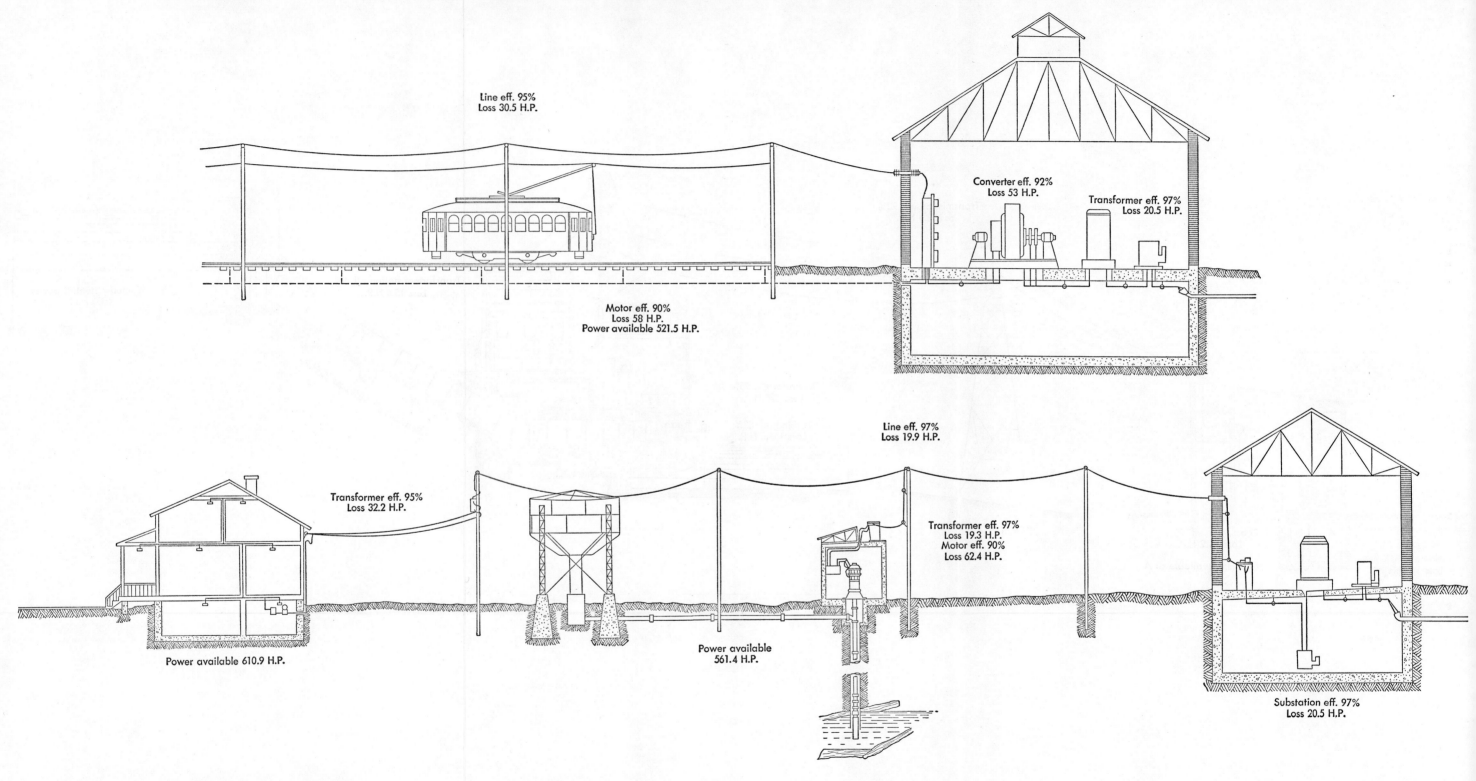

Line eff. 95%
Loss 30.5 H.P.

Converter eff. 92%
Loss 53 H.P.

Transformer eff. 97%
Loss 20.5 H.P.

Motor eff. 90%
Loss 58 H.P.
Power available 521.5 H.P.

Line eff. 97%
Loss 19.9 H.P.

Transformer eff. 95%
Loss 32.2 H.P.

Transformer eff. 97%
Loss 19.3 H.P.
Motor eff. 90%
Loss 62.4 H.P.

Power available 610.9 H.P.

Power available
561.4 H.P.

Substation eff. 97%
Loss 20.5 H.P.

Chart V The Conversion Problem.

1. To foster new techniques for discovery.

2. To bring into use new materials because we use only a fraction of the elements that surround us in the physical world, uranium being the most recent example of a new accession.

3. To apply the principle of recycling more and more broadly. This needs a brief explanation although it is illustrated by the familiar hydrologic cycle. As the Commission puts it:

> We wring material from the earth, we use it, and after its span of life it disperses by rot, fire or corrosion back into the earth, into the air, or into the sea. It may not again become sufficiently reconcentrated by natural forces to the point of industrial usefulness for geologic ages. Wherever we are able to shorten this cycle, we are able to use materials more intensively with less net drain on what the earth still provides.

4. To learn how to deal with low concentrations of useful materials. An example here would be the newer chemical industry which is now able to extract magnesium, a light metal, from sea water, where its concentration is only 0.13 per cent.

5. To develop and use more economically the resources that nature can renew. The direct use of solar energy would be an example, thereby obviating "the necessity for cycling it through stockpiles of fossil fuels millions of years old."

6. To lessen or eliminate the need for a scarce material by substituting a more abundant one. This is the great contribution plastics are making.

An Economic Approach—Dimensions of Economy

Another approach to the problem is to use more effectively the conventional measures of economy upon which we have come to rely in securing better utilization of our scarce, and hence costly, natural and human resources. We shall summarize these dimensions as (1) economies of the load factor, (2) economies of the diversity factor, (3) economies of scale, and (4) economies of joint cost. While these economies apply to all production, they are peculiarly important in public utility industry. We shall again use the electric power industry for illustrative purposes.

In explaining economies of the load factor by means of this industry, it is necessary first to understand certain fundamental engineering units of electrical measurement. We approach this subject first from the physical side, that is to say, from the point of view of plant operations. However, engineering operations are the alter ego of business operations because plants are run to produce output which can be sold. Plant operations thus reflect the meeting of demand and supply.

The unit of sale or output of electric energy is called the kilowatt-hour (kwh or kw-hr.). Energy requirements or the rates of output (demand) are measured in terms of kilowatts (kw).

The demand is registered by means of special demand meters and is usually recorded as an average demand for a short interval of time (15 minutes, a half-hour, or even an hour). The resulting curve is also known as *the load* carried by a generator, by a single power station, or by a power system composed of several power stations. It is the duty of an electric utility to supply the demand for service at the time when it is wanted. The exigencies of the use of electric power are such that there can be no delay in serving customers. In order to meet this demand at all times the utility must provide itself with a capacity which exceeds the greatest demand from customers. This extra capacity, called *reserve capacity,* is needed in order to ensure that energy supply can be continuous even if accidents or other contingencies put some power units temporarily out of commission. Such reserves are also necessary in order to provide for growth of the load. When the demand exceeds the capacity, as it often did during war years, the utility will proceed to ration service under proper regulatory safeguards. To be sure, since generating equipment is "rated" according to kilowatts, it may carry a greater load than the "rated capacity" for short periods of time, but not without danger of overheating or otherwise injuring it.

The kilowatt thus measures both the capacity of a power system to produce and the demand that customers make. In the former case it measures the maximum *potential rate* of supply, and in the latter, the *actual rate* of supply. A demand of one kilowatt, supplied for one hour, means that the plant has served some customer with an energy *output* of one kilowatt-hour.

Variations in demand or the load curve.   Actual rates of supply vary throughout the day. It is shown graphically by means of daily-load curves. The configuration of these daily-load curves will differ as between power systems that serve communities with different living habits and working characteristics. They will also vary from day to day in the same power system because of seasonal and other diurnal changes in the demand. A cloudy day and a holiday produce significant variations.

Typical daily-load curves of a metropolitan city for a winter day and a summer day are reproduced in Chart VI. It should be noted that the time of lowest demand comes in the early morning hours, while the highest demand (the station or system peak) comes during the late afternoon hours in the wintertime, and during the late afternoon and early evening hours in the summertime.

Another daily-load curve for a much larger city is shown in Chart VII. Other seasonal load curves for smaller communities with different charac-teristics (one principally residential, the other industrial) are shown in Chart VIII.

The load upon a power plant or system is, of course, the composite of the demand which different classes of customers make *simultaneously*. For instance, the street-lighting load represents an even load which is car-ried during the hours between the time of sunset and sunrise. Upon the street-lighting load will be superim-

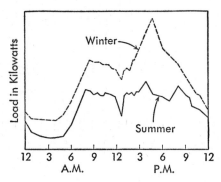

Chart VI   Typical Diurnal Load Curves.

posed the industrial load of such industries as operate on a night shift. Upon it also will be superimposed the electric railway load, which is com-paratively heavy during early evening hours and dwindles to nothing or to a slight demand for owl-car (now mostly discontinued) and work-train service after midnight, becoming heavy again when normal street railway schedules are resumed. (See Chart IX) At nighttime the lighting load of residences, restau-rants, theatres, etc., and the display lighting of commercial establish-ments will also swell the demand.

During the daytime the load consists of the composite demand for industrial and commercial power, for such residential, com-mercial, etc., lighting as may be required, for street railway and

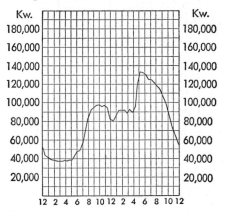

Chart VII   Daily Load Curve—Metro-politan Area.

trackless trolley power, for cooking, refrigeration, and other household uses, and for any other demands. The coincidence of these separate demands may be such as to build up to a morning peak, a recession in the demand during the noon hour, and to build up once more to the highest peak dur-ing the late afternoon. This peak is called the *maximum coincident demand*.

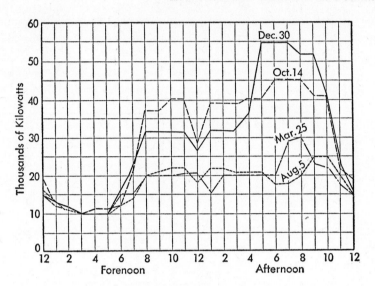

Chiefly Residential Consumption

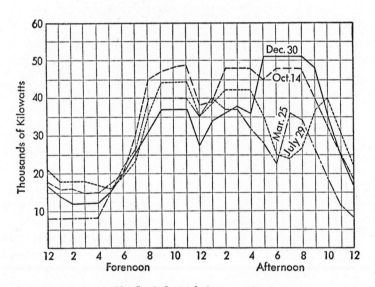

Chiefly Industrial Consumption

Chart VIII   Typical Seasonal Load Curves for an Electric Utility.

On account of the lighting load, the peak comes earlier in the winter and later in the summer. Also, on account of the Christmas traffic, it is likely to be higher in December than in any other month, thus constituting the highest maximum demand for the *year*.

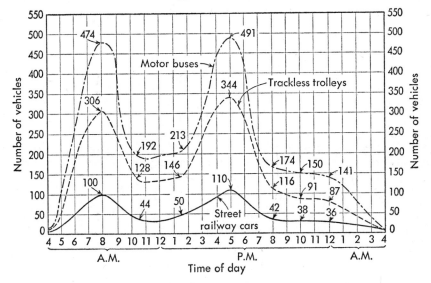

Chart IX   Load Characteristics of a Transit Utility.

Load curves are important aids in the design of rates as we shall see. The characteristics of the diurnal load curve and the changes it undergoes with the seasons and the growth of the business are most important from the standpoints of forecasting the need for additional power facilities and of the operation of power facilities now at hand. They are made use of by "load dispatchers" whose function it is to marshall the power sources available and thus to coordinate demand with supply from both an engineering and economic point of view.

The load factor.   The *load factor* has been defined as the ratio of the average power (average load) used to the maximum power (peak) used during a certain period of time. We may thus have load factors for a day, a month, or a year. The annual load factor is most important in cost analyses. A related ratio is known as the *utilization factor* and expresses the relationship of the average load to the rated capacity instead of the peak of the power station. Both ratios measure economy in the use of capacity already installed. Since the output in kilowatt-hours is the product of the demand in kilowatts and the time interval, a higher load factor expresses greater economic productivity than a lower load factor. This is true because the same fixed costs of the plant when divided by the greater output of the plant operating at a higher load factor will yield a lower cost per unit of output. Thus, a lighting load alone will represent a poor load factor. By filling up the valleys of the load with other kinds of utilization, better plant utilization and lower unit costs can be obtained. It should be noted that the load factor is independent of the size of the plant.

The diversity factor. Another dimension of economy is expressed by the *diversity factor*. It is an economy which relates to the installation of capacity and arises out of diversity in the time of individual peak demands. If the demand for service comes at different times, the same plant capacity can be made to serve different customers. The diversity factor has been defined as the ratio of the sum of the maximum power demands of the sub-divisions of any system, or parts of a system, to the maximum demand of the whole system, or of part of the system under consideration, measured at the point of supply. This definition certainly requires explanation.

We may illustrate with a numerical example. Let us assume three farmers who, desiring electric service, have the option of each installing his own electric power plant or of combining to use one jointly. Their separate installations of capacity must be sufficient to supply their separate maximum demands. But since these separate maximum demands do not come at the same time, it is suggested that they may be able to get satisfactory service from a jointly used plant which need not be of so large capacity as the sum total of their individual plants. These assumptions are shown in the following table.

Farmers	Separately Required Capacity, kilowatts	Time of Separate Maximum	Maximum Coincident Demand at 4:30 P.M.
A	35	4:30 P.M.	35
B	25	5:00 P.M.	5
C	20	6:00 P.M.	0
Total	80		40

Since the capacity of the separate plants would be 80 kilowatts, as compared with 40 kilowatts for the joint plant, the economy of the joint plant is expressed by the factor of 2 (80:40). The required capacity has been halved. By taking account of the diversity of use among the farmers, the required capacity needs to be equal only to the demand which comes at the same time, i.e., at 4:30 P.M. This is called the *maximum coincident demand*, to which the capacity of the plant must be attuned.

Analogous to the above illustration, it is not likely that the maximum demand of residential customers will come at exactly the same time. In fact, with respect to any very large group it is in the highest degree improbable that their individual maximum demands will come together. Just as there is diversity in the time of demand between customers in the residential class, so there is diversity between commercial customers and between power customers. However, the diversity factor for power and commercial customers is lower than for residential consumers because business practices bring it about that their installations are used with less variation as to the time when the maximum demand comes. But there is considerable diversity between the three classes. Substations in residential districts may carry a light load while substations in commercial districts are carrying a moderate load and those in industrial districts a very heavy load. Industries operating round the clock tend to have a diversity factor close to unity. They, therefore, show little or no saving in the installation of power capacity, but because of continuous operations, show a very high load factor and thus are economical in their use of capacity already installed.

It is this cumulative effect of the diversity factor in lowering the coincident demand upon the power source that is reflected in the daily load curves. It is also reflected in the capacity of the installations which serve them. Because there is diversity between customers, there can be a saving in the size of the transformer which is their common power source. Because there is diversity between transformers, there can be a saving in the capacity of their common substation; and because there may be diversity between substations, the common power station which supplies them can be of lesser capacity. The effect of diversity in bringing about savings in power installations can climb to a peak at which there is diversity between the demands upon individual power stations; these stations are then interconnected by means of transmission ties into a unified regional power system.

The necessary reserve capacity is indicated by the probabilities of growth of the load and the margin needed to meet contingencies, of which the utilization factor is the best indicator. This minimum reserve capacity, it is usually considered, should be at least equal to the capacity of the largest generator which is likely to be out of service due to accident. On the other hand the maximum required reserve capacity can be held down when there is interconnection with other regional electric systems, especially when there is diversity between the peaks of the two regional systems.

Economies of scale. The third dimension of economy has to do with the size or scale of operations. Load factor and diversity factor economies apply to small as well as large plants and are therefore independent of the scale of operations. With the expansion of business it is possible to secure fuller utilization of existing plants, but when this expansion becomes continuous it also becomes possible to increase the size of plants. Electrical operations started on a small scale, with plants serving customers only in the immediate vicinity. Soon the combination movement set in, with intervals of short-lived competition, but the end result was city-wide and later area-wide consolidations. Inefficient, high cost plants were retired from service or relegated to serve as substations or to carry only the peak load. Throughout the business, the aim was to carry the continuous or "base" load by means of the most efficient productive instruments available. Labor-saving machinery was introduced, provided there was enough use for that type of equipment to keep it fully employed. The standardization of equipment and of operations, which followed as a result of the standardized character of the service rendered by public utilities, was of real help in this connection.

It is difficult in a short treatment of this subject to make clear its many aspects involving both advantages and limitations. A few observations should nevertheless be added. With the enlarged scale of operations, it is possible also to specialize labor and managerial operations to obtain gains in efficiency and lowering of costs. Some economies are external to the plant or the business, such as economies in buying and selling. One of the most important are the advantages in financing that go with increased size. An economy of scale, important from a technological point of view, arises from the fact that larger units of equipment cost less per unit of capacity.

We shall have occasion to refer to these economies again later in our discussions of the organizational structure of public utility industries and of rate policies.

Economies of joint cost.   A final category of economies, distinguishable from the others we have discussed, is that of joint cost. Another way of stating it is to say that some products or services may be jointly produced. Where one of the joint products is of greater economic importance than the other, the other may be called a by-product, often rising to this economic status from being a waste product. The important point in this connection is, however, that the production of one product is technically so arranged that its production will of necessity lead to the production of the other. Wool and mutton and beef and hides are familiar illustrations from agriculture. Petroleum and natural gas is another from mining. But there is also an extension of this principle when it is cheaper to turn out two or more products or services from one central process or structure than to produce them separately. The bringing of water for irrigation or urban water-supply purposes from a distance and over mountain ranges may create "heads" for the production of hydraulic power, as was true in the case of the first Los Angeles aqueduct which we will discuss in Chapter 27. In this instance joint costs are of the by-product variety. Operations of the Tennessee Valley Authority, however, illustrate a productive process in which the construction of dams was so planned and designed as to control the Tennessee River for flood control, navigation, and power purposes as true joint products. The joint production of these services realizes certain economies because their separate realization would have been more costly, if not impossible of realization, if an attempt had been made to develop the river without using these multiple purpose structures. This also will be discussed later in Chapter 32.

11. THE STRUCTURE
OF PUBLIC UTILITY
CAPITALISM

We have arrived at the point where it becomes necessary to examine another institutional development: the agencies which society has employed in carrying on these public utility functions. Where the sovereign state has not itself engaged in these activities, it has given the power to conduct them to subordinate units of government and to private individuals or associations. Concessions or franchises to conduct public utility enterprises have been given to individuals, partnerships, joint stock companies, cooperatives, legal trusts, and corporations.

The Public Service Corporation

With minor exceptions, privately conducted public utilities are now organized as corporations. The world-wide adoption of this corporate form in the nineteenth century has changed and now conditions the entire character of public utility regulation. Not public utilities alone but all kinds of economic endeavors have been affected by this trend. It is important that the law recognize the continuous existence of groups and the social functions performed by them, and that it seal this recognition by investing forms of group life with legal personality. In the sonorous language of Chief Justice Marshall in the Dartmouth College Case, "a corporation is an artificial being, invisible, intangible, and existing only in contemplation of law."

Why is the corporate form of the business unit so well adapted to public utilities? It is a well-known fact that public utilities involve the large-scale use of capital. In spite of a public policy hostile to combinations, these enterprises—once scattered, unrelated, and competing—have been transformed into connected, correlated, and usually monopolistic units. There are still a number of small utilities, but they are gradually being absorbed. The basic cause is that the quest for efficiency in production has brought on the technological changes briefly surveyed in the preceding chapters, and these in turn have increased the importance of the capital factor in the organization of production. The public utility is among the most capitalistic of enterprises, and the corporate form of organization was its evolutionary counterpart.

Only public agencies or corporations can cope with the magnitude of the financial problem. The corporate form, with its capital divisible into shares and its limited liability of shareholders, was admirably adapted for gathering the savings, large or small, of numerous investors. By restricting the shareholder's risk of loss to the amount of stock subscribed, the corporate institution rendered a great social service during the developmental period. On account of the permanent need for the services rendered by public utilities, the corporation, with its continuity of life, is also better adapted to supply them than are other forms of business organization. An enduring function must be given an enduring organization. The corporation also has a high degree of flexibility in the administration of its affairs. By delegating responsibilities of management to directors, executive committees, and officers, it is possible to secure the intelligent initiation of policies, their approval by stockholders, and the speedy decision of important questions arising in the day-to-day administration of corporate affairs. This flexibility extends also to financing, for a corporation, by agreement among the shareholders and when authorized by the state, may classify its shares into common and preferred.

A corporation has the power to make contracts in the corporate name. It is this power which is important in all relations with creditors, with those from whom it buys, with those whom it hires as officers, agents, and employees, and with those to whom it sells service. Most important of all is the power of a public utility corporation derived from its charter or franchise to produce a certain commodity or service, to sell it to customers in a given market area, and to use the public highways in doing so.

A corporation has the power to borrow money if this is necessary and appropriate for the transaction of its business. But the state may limit the amount which it may borrow, or prescribe the conditions under which it contracts these debts. This is peculiarly true of public service corporations. In this connection the power of a corporation to pledge or mortgage its property in making loans becomes important. This power was specifically conferred by statute upon public service corporations and surrounded with safeguards because a mortgage or pledge may result in the sale of the property for the benefit of creditors and might thus prevent the companies from performing their public utility functions. Public service corporations have also been limited in their power to sell property needed in the public service.

The debts incurred are usually for long periods. Capital so obtained is used in the construction or acquisition of plant. The interest obligations assumed constitute for extended periods the fixed charges against the income of the corporation.

The voting power of capital stock is a very complex matter. By statute in most states all classes of stock have voting power, so far as concerns the sale of a substantial part of the assets of corporations. According to by-laws, most preferred stock has voting power when dividends are in arrears by certain specified amounts. In many cases preferred stock has equal voting power with common stock. Nevertheless, under normal conditions, there is a tendency to restrict voting power to common stock alone; in the 1920's, by a process of classifying common stock, this privilege was even further restricted.

The Holding Corporation

After the first establishment of public utilities, the integration movement was not long in coming. This developed in two rather distinct phases, again following closely the development of technology. The first phase was the consolidation of competing or scattered plants serving sections of our larger cities into local city-wide monopolies. This phase was practically completed by 1910. Some of the earlier holding companies were organized to facilitate this type of combination. With the development of superpower systems, the long-distance transmission of gas, the interconnection of hydro and steam stations, and the spreading out of the telephone and electric railway network, these localized monopolies were transformed into territorial monopolies, state-wide and even interstate in character. It was in connection with this second phase of the concentration movement that the larger number of our present-day holding corporations and giant operating companies were formed.

The holding company device is useful in effecting consolidations because it can build corporations into systems or groups so that all are subject to a single control. Speaking generally, holding companies are not operating companies; as the name indicates, they merely own the common stock and other securities of operating companies so as to control their policies. The advantage of the holding company over other forms of combination is that control may be secured with very much less difficulty by merely exchanging securities, and hence without the use of much capital. Control is assured by owning only a bare majority of the voting stock of a particular corporation, but *de facto* control can be exercised by minorities through the use of the proxy system.

American corporations, in their early history, were not permitted to own the shares of other corporations. Beginning with a New Jersey statute of 1888 most states now authorize such ownership, and it is customary to confer such power in a corporation's charter. Sometimes state laws provide that no foreign corporation may own real estate or carry on certain businesses such as banking and public utilities. By retaining or organizing a domestic subsidiary corporation, the parent company, though organized in another state, can obey the state law and still retain control. Subsidiaries are often created in order to carry on special lines of business which are conveniently run as separate enterprises because they are experimental or especially hazardous.

Historically, the chief purpose of holding companies has been to eliminate competition. Since local public utilities tend toward monopoly anyway, the organization of holding companies has not met with so much opposition in these industries as has the organization of railroad holding companies. Moreover, by retaining local representation upon the board of directors of each subsidiary, it has all the appearance and some of the reality of being a local enterprise.

The usual method of purchasing subsidiaries is for a holding company to offer its own capital stock in exchange for the capital stock of the companies which it seeks to control. If the exchange cannot be effected, the stock must be bought outright, but the holding company may in turn deposit this stock as security for collateral trust bonds which it sells to the public. By this means, a portion of the capital outlay is recouped. Or it may issue its own securities—preferred or common stock—and purchase control with the cash proceeds. This alternative, however, is open only to well-known holding companies having an established financial reputation.

The real capital of a true holding company, therefore, does not consist of physical property but of the stocks and bonds of other corporations. Holding companies own only a stockholder's equity in the operating companies. Their earnings consist of the dividends and usually some interest paid upon the securities of the controlled companies, and their financial standing is therefore only as sound as are these securities.

The real purpose lying back of the organization of a holding company usually is the desire to secure an increasesd profit by placing under common management the affairs of operating companies, without destroying their separate corporate existence. Regardless of the legal form which public utilities assume, they function as economic entities which have come to be known as "going concerns."

The Life History of Going Concerns

The operating subsidiaries of holding companies are the true "going concerns" with which we must deal. By taking a typical public utility organization and observing the various stages through which such an enterprise passes, the nature of a going concern will become clearer. It will also serve to lay the groundwork for an understanding of the valuation of public utilities. For, as we shall see later, a public utility valuation recapitulates the stages in the life history of these concerns.

The period of preliminary organization. The first phase involves the promotion of the enterprise and usually consists of three distinct steps: (1) the discovery of a business opportunity; (2) the assembling of the elements of a business, and (3) the securing of funds to put these elements to work at producing the commodity or service. This is the work of the promoter, who may perform all these functions himself or may and usually does call in others to assist him. Since a business opportunity is premised upon the effective demand for a particular service or commodity at a price which covers the cost of production plus a profit, the ideal promoter is an economist with an eye for exchange values. But the utilization of a business opportunity involves marshaling funds, assembling a physical plant for production, and formulating a plan to organize the human relations out of which productive work proceeds. He may thus have to call upon the specialized services of bankers, industrial engineers, and lawyers. Recently, promoters' activities have been chiefly concerned with reorganizations and consolidations, made necessary by the integration movement and the rearrangement of our transport facilities. Nevertheless, the promotion stage has been an important phase in building up these industries, the necessity and importance of which must be understood.

All these activities take place during an interval of time which we may call the *period of preliminary organization.* The significant parts into which this organization work divides itself may be presented as the drawing up of:

1. An economic and financial plan of promotion
2. An industrial plan of construction and operation
3. A legal plan of organization

The economic and financial plans of promotion. This phase of planning may be combined. Preparing an economic plan usually involves an estimate of probable revenues and expenses, and the casting up of the balance of prospective profits. These estimates, originally made by the promoter, are checked and verified by investment bankers. In order that the probabilities be estimated accurately and in order to do justice to the opportunity, promoters and bankers must possess experience and imagination. If the new utility, for instance, be a bus company, the tributary population must be determined and the number of bus riders estimated on the basis of rides per capita. The probable fare that may be charged must be ascertained. Together, these factors will yield an estimate of the probable revenues. Account must be taken of the probable growth in population and the possibility of developing traffic. Allowance may also have to be made for competition and substitute services, as well as for seasonal variations in traffic. If the enterprise is an intercity facility, the situation is complicated by the traffic flow between important centers, so that account must be taken of the relative amounts of through-traffic and of local traffic. In all these calculations comparisons with already established enterprises, similarly situated, may prove helpful. As far as possible, the calculation is made upon a unit basis; that is, the revenues and expenses are estimated per bus-mile or other convenient traffic unit. Meticulous accuracy is not necessary for a promoters' calculations.

As a basis for determining the amount and kinds of capital required, a financial plan of promotion must be drawn up. This will set forth the classifications of capital contributions and will thus give a clue to the probable cost in fixed charges. Of course, the amounts involved are determined by the size and character of the plant required. The estimates of cost are again based roughly upon some convenient unit, such as costs per mile of single or double track or per kilowatt of capacity of power plant. At this point the financial plan is dependent upon the industrial plan. Investment bankers will be helpful in determining the proportions of fixed and floating capital required and the form that security issues should take. They can provide estimates of the probable money rates in leading money centers and thus determine provisionally the burden of fixed interest charges. The composition of the financial plan will ultimately determine such important relations as the amount of bonds to be authorized and sold, as compared with stock authorizations and their subscription. The importance of these determinations cannot be overemphasized because the promoters are the financial architects of the future going concern.

The industrial plan of construction and operation. The drawing up of the industrial plan involves characteristically three important determinations. The first relates to a preliminary location of the plant. The site eventually chosen should be such as to meet the convenience of the patrons and should draw out the revenue possibilities of the territory. Safety and economy of service are other desiderata. Topographical, social, and legal considerations limit or determine the choice of location. City, county, and regional plans, in their present and future aspects, are often determining factors.

The second decision has to do with the choice and design of instruments. Equipment must suit the requirements of operation, must be safe and economical in operation, and should not be subject to early retirement because it is obsolete or inadequate. Experimental construction, which introduces an element of uncertainty into these calculations, is often necessary.

The final determination, namely, estimates of costs of construction and operation, flows from its two predecessors. Consulting engineers of wide construction experience usually cooperate with operating engineers in this part of the work. With all due allowances and safeguards, costs are frequently underestimated.

The legal plan of organization.   The last step will be the drafting of a legal plan of organization. This part of the preliminary work is not usually undertaken unless it is believed that financial success is reasonably assured and unless the investment bankers have shown their faith in the economic future of the enterprise by agreeing to underwrite the sale of securities. While important and vital, the legal plan is of a more formal and standard character, inasmuch as the law generally prescribes the form organizations must take. The work involves the securing of a charter of incorporation, the negotiation of franchises, obtaining indeterminate permits, certificates of convenience and necessity, permits to issue securities, and negotiations to secure rights of way. Dealings may be with private parties, but legal status is obtained primarily through public authorities. Definitive work consists of the examination and drafting of contracts, franchises, consents, mortgages and deeds of trust, and other important legal documents. Much time is usually spent in the examination of titles, statutes, ordinances, the decisions of the courts, and in other research activities.

The end product of these activities, a resultant of much experimenting and discarding of tentative plans, may be called the *going plan of organization*, since it is on this basis that the actual steps are taken which translate the theoretical conception into a practical, working reality.

The period of construction.   Having developed the conspectus of our economic enterprise, the next step is the construction of the plant, plans for which have already been worked out. When the work is completed we have what may be called a *going plant* capable of turning out the product. We shall call this the *period of construction*. The going plant refers only to the technical process of production and not to the sale of the product. Usually, when properties of substantial size are to be assembled, the work will be performed in sections so as to permit production to begin with the earliest section before all the construction work on the remaining sections has been completed.

The durable portion of the going plant. The physical plant consists of two elements: the durable element and the nondurable, depreciable element. The durable element, as the name implies, consists of the land, rights of way, or easements upon which the structures are erected. Two peculiarities should be noted here. Because of the necessity of obtaining land in strategic locations, or because the land must provide a continuous right of way, as in the case of railroad construction, the public utility is under the necessity of procuring the land considerably in advance of actual construction. The need for careful selection of land will be appreciated when one reflects upon the great importance to these enterprises of dock and transportation facilities on account of the quantities of raw materials that will be used. Similarly, the need of thermoelectric power plants for an abundant supply of good water limits the choice of sites. The second peculiarity is that private right of way, once dedicated to a particular use, cannot usually be reconverted to other uses.

It may not always be necessary to acquire land outright. It may be leased for long periods, or easements, representing a limited property right, may be secured. Easements are rights to build tracks, to erect poles, and to string wires or lay underground conduits. Much of the land, however, is purchased in the open market, often without disclosing the use to which it will be put, in order to secure it at the lowest possible price. When the price is believed excessive or the owner of the most appropriate site will not sell, the utility may proceed to condemn the property, in which case the utility must prove that the *particular* property best meets its needs. The price will then be fixed by a jury. To this must be added the costs of condemnation. The real estate departments of public utilities contend that the prices fixed by condemnation juries are in excess of market values (they call them *hold-up* values), which, when added to the costs of condemnation suits, make it advisable to purchase rather than to use the power of eminent domain.

Incidental revenues may make their appearance at this point. Rents may accrue from facilities bought in advance of immediate requirements, or they may accrue because the utility has purchased an entire holding—more than it requires for its public utility uses—in order to avoid the costs of severance when it buys less. In the past, an element of speculation has often entered into these purchases in that utilities may, by forehanded purchase of contiguous lands, realize upon resale the rise in market value often accompanying the construction of new utilities.

Not all the land used by public utilities is necessarily bought or leased. The land may be donated by private persons or by public authorities. The former may be impelled by considerations of civic spirit or because they expect advantages to accrue to them indirectly, as is often the case in new real estate subdivisions. The land grants to railroads are the classic illustrations of land obtained from governments. The right of way may be the public highway, permission having been obtained by the franchise. But it must not be lightly assumed that these grants are entirely without cost, since expensive street and paving improvements may be coupled with them.

The nondurable portion of the going plant.   The nondurable element of the plant involves buildings and structures, equipment, and facilities. Providing such facilities is usually the task of a separate construction organization. The work may be done by the company's own organization (force account) or by an affiliated but separately organized construction company. Again, all or some of the work may be performed by general contractors who will sublet portions of the work to subcontractors. The utilities will then render only general supervision and inspection services. Many ingenious bonus and premium plans have been worked out to secure rapid and economical completion of the project. The highly seasonal and temporary nature of the work is an added reason for the separate organization of construction work. The cost of the work accrues through payrolls, purchases of materials, and payments upon contracts.

At this point account should be taken of indirect construction costs, usually called *construction overheads.* These costs arise from emergency surveys, relocations, and the preparation of special designs; from the administrative control of construction, involving such items as superintendence, inspection, accounting, payment of insurance premiums, taxes, and interest during construction. Costs for work not covered by contracts may be enhanced by unforeseen contingencies such as strikes, cyclones, earthslides, fires, accidents, stream diversions, and delays in the delivery of material.

No very definite ratios can be set up in which these elements are combined. The land element may run from 5 to 30 per cent of total construction cost, depending upon the type of utility. Indirect construction costs have likewise varied between 8 and 30 per cent.

We have mentioned above that the work will, when possible, be constructed in sections so that a part of the plant may begin operations while the balance of the project is being finished. This divides the construction period into an earlier period of pure construction and a later period of mixed construction and operation. The construction work will continue until the plant, as originally planned, comes into being.

At this point a new need arises: the development of an operating organization to carry on the work of turning out the physical product or of rendering the service for which the plant is designed. This involves the assembling of an executive and supervisory personnel with a full complement of operating labor. Training, reliability, and efficiency are the qualities which must distinguish the operating organization. Some untrained or "green hands" may be employed in any public service undertaking, but there must always be present a substantial nucleus of "key men" of various grades upon whom the responsibility for continuity and efficiency in operation will fall. The *esprit de corps* which motivates an organization depends upon the loyalty, standards of performance, and devotion to duty exemplified by this nucleus. On this account seniority is given great weight in the preferments and assignments of responsibility within the operating organization.

A second requirement relates to the provision of *operating* materials and supplies as distinguished from those required for construction. While the latter must be obtained enough in advance to ensure steady progress in construction work, a larger store of *operating* materials and supplies are required in order to ensure not only steadiness of output but also provision for unexpected increases in demand and for prospective growth. Moreover, cash working capital is required to meet payments before receipts from customers come in. After the enterprise is well established, cash working funds may be relatively decreased in proportion as the credit of the enterprise enables it to borrow for short periods upon open account or by negotiating its notes payable.

At this point, accordingly, a distinction must be made between costs arising from the continuance of construction operations, and therefore chargeable to "fixed capital," and costs arising from the new phase of operation, and hence chargeable against the expected revenues from operation.

In a newly constructed plant it will be found necessary to incur certain expenditures arising out of what has been called the element of *adaptation and solidification*. This is a term borrowed from steam railway parlance which has since been given a wider meaning. It covers not only expenditures arising out of the realignment and adaptation of the roadway to actual operating conditions but also all other expenditures having to do with the extra ballasting of track, the rearrangement and adaptation of buildings, structures, and equipment to meet operating demands. The practical outcome is that operating and maintenance costs will be rather heavy at the outset until the plant has been "seasoned" or "shaken down" to operating conditions. These costs are usually treated as operating costs.

Our term *going plant* should accordingly be understood to refer to a plant, constructed in accordance with the going plan, adapted to actual operating conditions by an experimental period occasioning additional cost, and manned by an operating personnel trained to various assigned jobs.

The period of acquisition of a going business.   A going plant which has the capacity to turn out units of physical product may be a going plant in an engineering sense, but it does not become a true operating unit in an economic sense until it finds a market for its product at rates that provide for all costs of operation, and in addition, a satisfactory return to its owners. A plant which has acquired such a market is said to have attached to it a *going business,* where business means the satisfactory seller-buyer relationships usually comprehended under the term *good will.* We shall have more to say about the relevance of the good-will concept later. But these business connections, in the case of public service enterprises, are dependent on the franchise which the concern holds. It is upon the hypotheses: first, that the service is needed; and second, that the franchise to render such service within a defined service area has opened up a market sufficiently large to absorb in time the maximum potential output of the plant and that the cooperation of promoter, financier, and investor has been secured. Except as subsidies may provide them, the government has not *guaranteed* sufficient revenues. On this account all energies of the new enterprise must be set to work to develop the market.

Some peculiarities inherent in the operating and the marketing situation should be recalled. The enterprise is one which has involved large investments in fixed and specialized capital, usually providing a producing capacity in excess of immediate requirements. There is thus unutilized plant capacity which awaits the development of a demand. Incomplete utilization of producing capacity therefore results in high costs per unit of output sold. The unused capacity offers a great incentive to securing additional business. In other words, the going business, within the limits of the producing capacity afforded by the going plant, is subject to the law of decreasing cost or its correlative—the law of increasing returns.

We may therefore expect that the management will spare no reasonable costs in securing increases in patronage. Expenditures will be incurred in the solicitation of new business. Experimental and trial installations will be made. If the service is of a type which must be introduced by demonstration of its usefulness, everything will be done to acquaint potential customers with its virtues. Its superiority over substitutes or sources of private supply must be demonstrated. The doubts of the timid must be allayed, and the arguments of detractors met. All this means heavier initial costs than those incurred later on in order to get the expected growth in business. Under such conditions it is not surprising that the enterprise may fail during an initial period to meet its total outlays for operation. Under these conditions, not only will there be no dividends to stockholders but they may even be subject to assessments. It will be a cause for congratulation if the business should happen to "break even." It has been the fortunate circumstance of but few enterprises in their early days to have current income exceed current outgo, thus leaving some element of return. The normal situation in the acquisition of a going business is that the total cost of operation exceeds operating revenues and that these annual deficiencies below a compensatory return measure the costs of acquiring a going business.

At this point it is convenient to draw the distinction between operating costs in the sense of "variable operating outlay," or prime costs, which accompany the sale of product, and that part of operating costs which continues whether product is being sold or not, or the so-called *fixed charges*. The former consists principally of the wages paid and the materials consumed in operating the property or in maintaining it in a fit condition for operation. The latter is made up primarily of the outlays required to meet taxes and fixed interest obligations upon security issues. Sound business policy will therefore dictate that the initial prices be so fixed as to compensate for all outlays of the former class and cover as much of the fixed charges *as will not restrict the enterprise in the sale of additional product*. Outlays not recouped from customers will have to be met out of working capital or, eventually, out of assessments on stockholders.

As the business grows in volume the revenues are adequate to meet not only the variable operating costs but also more and more of the fixed charges. It then becomes necessary to take account of certain expenditures which, while not immediately necessary, will shortly be required in order to offset the disintegrating effect of operation and of the action of the elements upon the going plant. Thus, hidden costs like depreciation and reserve charges to cover losses from unforeseen contingencies begin to appear and imperatively to demand attention. Only after adequate provision has been made for these can surplus revenues be devoted to dividend purposes.

This line of thought tends therefore to develop in the owners of the enterprise a conception of deficiency in income, not only below actual outlays but below outlays necessary to ensure their willingness to continue in the business (alternative opportunity costs). The necessary income (the long-run necessary supply price) with which actual income is compared must be sufficient to meet all costs under normal conditions, including therein a reasonable profit for the entire time that the enterprise has been acquiring its going business. When this point is reached the enterprise has obtained, in the minds of its owners, the status of a *going business,* and it will be regarded by them *in its entirety* as a going concern. Looking backward, the owners have mentally *capitalized* the deficits below the expected reasonable return. The capitalization process has been one of cumulating the yearly deficits occasioned by noncoincidence in the accrual of what they regard as the true cost of the service and compensatory revenues.

The enterprise as a going concern.   Now the period of normal operation, the ultimate objective of past effort, begins. The utilization of the capacity of the going plant is sufficient to ensure that, with efficient management, earnings and expenses have reached normal proportions and are mutually compensatory. But, like Alexander, the owners may look about them for new worlds to conquer. They may seek an extension of their franchise into new markets, or they may seek to cater to new demands in the old markets. It will become necessary to make extensions of the going plant. Additional capital investments will become necessary, thus repeating upon a smaller scale the cycle of activities upon which the theory of the going concern rests. The process of successive enlargements of the physical plant goes by the name of *piecemeal construction.*

The ebb and flow of demand for the product, due to daily and seasonal variations together with variations due to the business cycle, will have developed the need for a permanent reserve capacity in the going plant so that customers' wants may not go unsatisfied. Transient new business, and temporarily increased demands by old customers, represent a service obligation which wise public utility management will seek to satisfy. In this way alone will public utilities be able to make themselves secure in their monopolistic position.

Accountancy and Financial Ratios as Aids in the Interpretation of Going Concerns

The fundamental purpose of accounting systems is to so organize the facts of outgo and income of pecuniary values that a basis for judging the comparative success or failure of business enterprises as going concerns is provided. For this purpose, accounts have been classified as balance sheet accounts, income accounts, profit and loss or surplus accounts. It will be seen that these classifications tend to reflect the varying stages in the life history of going concerns.

During the period of preliminary organization, accounting entries are concerned with the accounts showing the cost of intangible assets and organization expense and the corresponding capital liabilities. These entries reflect the cost of building up the financial, legal, and industrial structure of the concern as a whole. During the period of construction, entries are made in the various plant accounts which, after completion of construction, become the various detailed asset accounts and reflect the cost of the ready-to-go plant, including indirect construction expenses. The sources of the funds are indicated by entries in the corresponding capital liability accounts. Except as lands, easements, and water rights provide the durable part of the going plant, these assets are subject to replacement in the course of time, and their costs become the basis of depreciation or depletion reserves.

With the beginning of operations the two new classifications of income and expense accounts and surplus accounts become the repositories of debit and credit transactions. Income from sales are credited to revenue accounts, and outgo in terms of operation and maintenance costs are debited to the various expense accounts provided by the classifications. In the debit category belong the constructive expenditures for depreciation and depletion, as well as the fixed charges for taxes and interest. The balance between the credits and debits, whether positive or negative, records the progress which the concern is making in building up a going business. The surplus or profit and loss accounts will record these positive or negative balances, together with any other transactions reflecting the changing relations of the corporate equity (owners in their collective capacity) to the individual stockholders (owners in their individual capacities). Dividends paid or assessments levied upon stockholders are the ultimate determinants of success or failure. "Break even" charts are devices for recording the accrual of these incomes and outgoes.

The development of uniform accounting systems on a standardized basis throughout the country has also had a beneficial effect on the development of techniques of internal control for management purposes. Some of these are too detailed to be surveyed here. However, statisticians and economic analysts have long used certain financial ratios as tools in the investigation of public utilities from regulatory and investment points of view. These, too, have gained in importance with the new developments in standardized accounting. Only the more important of these will be discussed here and in the following order:

1. Ratios of turnover of investment in fixed property and plant
2. Ratios of operating expenses to operating revenues
3. Ratios of net operating revenues to total capital employed
4. Ratios expressing the cost of borrowed capital
5. Ratios expressing the return earned on stockholders' investment [1]

Ratios of turnover of investment in fixed property and plant. Most public utilities are now large-scale businesses. Their operations differ, however, from large-scale trading enterprises like the mail-order businesses. In the case of the latter, the annual volume of business done, as shown by sales, is large when compared with the capital employed; in the case of public utilities, this relationship is small. Mail-order merchandising shows a ratio of about $0.10 as the investment in fixed property per $1.00 of sales; water utilities show fixed investments of about $8.00 per $1.00 of sales; steam-electric utilities, about $4.50 per $1.00; and hydroelectric utilities, about $15.00 per $1.00 of sales or revenues. In fact, the utilities show a great range in dollars of fixed-property investment per dollar of sales, depending upon the technology of the industry and the extent to which a given business has saturated its market. A steam-electric utility is bound to have a lower ratio of investment to revenues than a hydroelectric utility because the latter has substituted dams, storage reservoirs, and water rights for the coal pile, which is constantly being renewed and charged to operating expenses. Another significant contrast is between electric and steam railways, which own their own rights of way and hence exhibit a high investment per dollar of revenues on the one hand, and motor transport utilities, which show a much lower ratio on the other hand because they use the public highways. In all utilities there is also a persistent tendency to substitute automatic machinery for labor, for example, when a telephone exchange changes from manual to automatic switching. This ratio of investment to revenues has been called the *capital turnover.* It is one of the most important financial facts to be known about any business. It measures the revenue producing efficiency with which the capital is employed and shows how important capital costs are in a given business.

Ratios of operating expenses to operating revenues. These ratios, called *operating ratios,* are logically next in the analysis of a business unit. They show the periodic cost of operation or the number of cents out of operating dollar-revenue absorbed by ordinary operating expenses, excluding all capital costs. Although variously defined, expenses other than material and labor costs ordinarily include depreciation, taxes, and rentals. So defined,

---

[1] A ratio of great importance to investors expresses the number of times fixed charges are earned to the number of times fixed charges are expended.

they comprise all the variable expenses and some proportion of the fixed expenses, and their relation to gross revenues must be closely watched. The reason is that there is an inverse correlation between the operating ratio and the ratio of capital investment to operating revenues. A high operating ratio is inseparably tied to a low ratio of capital costs to operating revenues because the small margin available above operating costs leaves little room for fixed charges. But as technological innovations permit the substitution of the machine for labor, operating ratios fall and the necessary margins become available to absorb the carrying charges on capital equipment. The process may again be illustrated in the telephone industry when machine switching takes the place of the telephone operator. After an enterprise has become technologically stable, an increasing operating ratio reflects either upon the efficiency of operations or upon the selling policies of the concern.

Operating ratios, however, fail to distinguish between fixed and variable expenses and are therefore open to misinterpretation. Maintenance expenses, for instance, may be deferred for a time, and costs may thus be understated. Nevertheless, operating ratios tend to become characteristic for industries or long-established business units, and much can thus be learned from them in a general way.

Ratios of net operating revenue to total capital employed. For purposes of regulation it is most important to know the financial return of the business unit, without distinguishing between capital contributed by owners and that obtained from creditors. This return is shown by bringing into relation with each other the net operating revenue and the *total* capital used in operation. This ratio measures the earning power of the concern as an *economic* unit. If the business carries on different kinds of operations—a joint utility operating an electric railway, an electric utility and a gas utility—it is then necessary to determine the net operating revenue for each utility and the total capital employed in operating each. This will involve the apportionment of joint expenses and may create some uncertainties. Nevertheless, both management and the regulating commission should know the earning power by departments because the sources of gain or loss should be disclosed.

Using the year as a convenient unit of time, the net operating revenue is the amount of operating revenue remaining after paying all operating expenses for the year. The total capital employed in operations consists of the total assets of the business less such assets as are not used by the concern in its utility operations. For instance, investments in securities yielding an income of their own should be deducted. This means that the corresponding revenues and expenses arising out of nonutility investments should likewise be eliminated in computing the net operating revenues. For practical purposes, the capital consists of the average investment in fixed assets for the period plus some allowance for working capital. Working capital may be taken (somewhat arbitrarily) as current assets diminished by current liabilities. The resulting ratio has come to be known in the parlance of regulation as *the rate of return*. It measures the over-all yield upon the capital factor employed by the concern. This ratio and its derivative has become the touchstone of regulation. It will be further discussed in Part II.

Ratios expressing the cost of borrowed capital.   The rate of return does not distinguish between owned and borrowed capital. Some utilities operate without borrowed capital; others, usually publicly owned ones, because they have taxing power behind them, need invest no capital of their own. Whatever the variance between these extremes, the cost of borrowed capital represents the leverage between returns going to creditors and returns to owners. Usually, the cost of borrowed capital constitutes a major portion of the over-all return. The interest rate paid on borrowed capital does not alone make up this cost. To the nominal interest should be added the cost of bond and note discounts applicable to the period under consideration, as well as expenditures in connection with bond and note issues. By adding together for the year the nominal interest paid and the expenses of issuance and discounts (deducting any premiums that may have been received), the true cost of borrowed capital may be ascertained. The total, divided by the *average* amount of capital borrowed during the accounting period, expresses the cost of borrowed capital. This cost is usually less than the over-all rate of return because creditors trade their security and continuity of income against the risks assumed by the owners. Because owners hold an umbrella over creditors they get the residue of the over-all return.

Ratios expressing the return earned on stockholder's investment.   The stockholder's investment consists of his original capital contribution (in pecuniary terms) plus earnings retained in the business and not *paid out* in dividends. If the "pay out" ratio is low, more earnings belonging to stockholders are retained as earned surplus. The equity of stockholders therefore consists of original capital plus surplus. The over-all rate-of-return may therefore conceal a lower cost of borrowed capital and a higher return on owned capital. The differential between the two ratios is a measure of the degree to which the concern has "traded on the equity" of stockholders. If nonparticipating preferred shareholders agree to accept a fixed dividend, the residue of earnings goes to the common shareholders. This may further enhance the return available to common stockholders.

12. EVOLUTION OF
THE PUBLIC UTILITY
CONCEPT

Public utility enterprises are regulated by governments throughout the civilized world. We must not think of public utility regulation as a new device invented by disgruntled American farmers about 1870. It is, in fact, only one aspect of the social control of all economic activity and depends, in the last analysis, upon the social philosophy which people profess as a result of their experience. Since the law has long recognized the separate classification of certain businesses as public utilities, we must, if we would gain a complete understanding of this sociological process, trace the historical development of certain cultural ideas that have, in the course of time, provided us with an institutional development which we now call a public utility.

The Historical Background of Regulation

In this historic process we must recognize the operation of two elements: One is a customary element which has been a result of long social evolution and which changes only very slowly; the other is a statutory or political element which represents the social pressures of the present and which works changes upon the received traditional element. Here again, the courts, as arbiters in this process of institutional development, guide it along channels which appear to them productive of the greatest good. This process is well illustrated by the recent attempts to regulate the fluid milk industry. The first step comprised a long period of agitation to subject this industry to some kind of legislative regulation on account of the appearance of certain evils. The next step was the development of a legislative program of specific regulations, designed to reach and correct the evils complained of, and its enactment by the legislature. The third step—and here is where guidance by the courts is introduced—consisted of judicial review of the legislation in the light of constitutional principles of "due process of law." We will first exam-

195

ine the historical, customary element in the development of this regulatory institution.

Doctrine of just price. Public utility regulation grew out of the general matrix of governmental regulation until it developed certain procedures and objectives which are characteristically its own. Regulation of private industry has been attempted by government from the earliest times. All attempts at such regulation owed much to a very ancient ideal of social justice, which, as applied to economic life by the early Church Fathers, became their very famous doctrine of *justum pretium*, i.e., "just price." They opposed this idea to the contemporaneous doctrine of *verum pretium*, i.e., "natural price," which the Roman law had derived from Stoic philosophy. As contrasted with the doctrine of natural price, which justified any price reached by agreement in effecting exchanges between willing buyers and willing sellers, the "just price" doctrine drew attention to the coercion which may reside in economic circumstances, such as a food famine where a buyer is made willing by his economic necessities. Hence, in order to draw the sting of coercion, the early Church Fathers, following St. Augustine, considered only that trading to be legitimate in which the trader paid a "just price" to the producer, and in selling, added only so much to the price as was customarily sufficient for his economic support. There was to be no unjust enrichment. A good illustration of the practical effect of this doctrine may be seen in the two price edicts of Emperor Diocletian of the years 285 and 301, during the period of the decline of the Roman Empire, when Christian theology was beginning to exercise some influence. The reason for the legislation was fear of revolution. Prices were high and unsteady due to the debasement of the currency; taxes were heavy under conditions of political insecurity and declining trade; and the cost of living for the poorer classes was rising. Without now considering how ineffectual the measures may have been, the aforementioned imperial legislation to relieve these conditions fixed maximum prices for from seven to eight hundred articles upon the basis of their estimated cost of production.

The doctrine of "just price" was passed on by the Church Fathers of the Roman period to the Schoolmen of the Middle Ages. When adopted by the scholastic philosophy of the Middle Ages, it was given a somewhat revised interpretation by St. Thomas Aquinas, the greatest of the Schoolmen and one of its principal exponents. He said, in substance, that buying and selling were established for the *common advantage* of both parties, each requiring that which belonged to the other. But the exchange must take place at a "just price," not at what is fixed in the market. But what is a "just price"? It is a price which will repay the expenses of production. These expenses include labor and material costs, costs of transport including compensation for dangers and risks, and costs of storage. Even interest, in spite of the general condemnation of usury, was included as an expense of production on the theory that there must be compensation for the loan of money which involved the possibility of loss to the lender or the forgoing of an advantageous use of the money on his part.

This medieval reinterpretation of "just price" continued to be effective well into the modern era. In fact, as the ethical element in the present-day pricing problem, the doctrine is still basic. In the medieval regulation of industry and trade by the guild societies and the town authorities, this ethical doctrine can be observed at work. The historian Cheney has well summarized them for us:

In those occupations that involved buying and selling the necessities of life, such as those of the fishmongers and the bakers, the officers of the fraternity, like the town authorities, were engaged in a continual struggle with regraters, forestallers, and engrossers which were appellations as odious as they were common in the medieval town. Regrating meant buying to sell again at a higher price without having made any addition to the value of the goods; forestalling was going to the place of production to buy or in any other way trying to outwit fellow-dealers, by purchasing things before they came into the open market where all had the same opportunity; engrossing was buying up the whole supply, or so much of it as not to allow other dealers to get what they needed, the modern "cornering of the market." These practices which were so objectionable in the eyes of medieval traders were frequently nothing more than what would be considered commendable enterprise in a more competitive age.

The "just price" doctrine has thus served as the main stem upon which other institutional developments were grafted.

The Medieval concepts of status and common calling. The first graft upon this main stem of the just price doctrine was legal in nature and was added by the English common law, which is in its essence judicial custom. These grafts are made up of two shoots, each a distinct contribution in the gradual evolution of the public utility institution. The first graft is the medieval principle of social organization called *status;* the second graft is the legal concept of a *common calling.*

De Quincey once wrote:

It is a natural resource that whatsoever we find it difficult to investigate as a result, we endeavor to follow as a growth. Failing analytically to probe its nature, historically, we seek relief for our perplexities by tracing its origin. Thus, for instance, when any feudal institution eludes our deciphering faculty from the imperfect records of its use and operation then we endeavor conjecturally to amend our knowledge by watching the circumstances in which that institution arose.

Does not this apply with special force to our problem here?

As an institutional development, the concept of a public utility has had a long growth; but as an analytical tool it is of comparatively recent origin. As a matter of origins, it stems from the Middle Ages, which termed the then correlative a *common calling* or a *public employment,* as distinguished from a *private employment.* No one has done more to explain in detail the nature of the law governing public employments than has Professor Bruce Wyman in his book, *Control of the Market.* (See Bibliography) But it was the genius of Dean Roscoe Pound in his illuminating lectures on the "Spirit of the Common Law" that first developed the central principle running through this long historical development which constitutes the other legal graft upon the main ethical stem of the just-price doctrine.

Dean Pound, in his exposition of the spirit of the common law, distinguishes its two characteristics. One is its extreme individualism; the other is its treatment of individuals as members of a group. The latter is the medieval idea of status.

It is the second characteristic which is of importance to us here. Quoting Dean Pound's own words:

On the other hand, it [the common law] is characterized by another element tending in quite another direction; a tendency to affix duties and liabilities independently of the will of those bound, *to look to relations rather than to legal transactions* [author's italics] as the basis of legal consequences, and to impose both liabilities and disabilities upon those standing in certain relations as members of a class rather than upon individuals.[1]

His explanation of this characteristic is that it represents the feudal element in our law and owes its origin to the fact that, when the common law was in process of formation, the principal social and legal institution of the time was the feudal relation of lord to man.

Here the question was not what a man had undertaken or what he had done but what he was. The lord had rights against the tenant and the tenant had rights against the lord. The tenant owed duties of service and homage or fealty to the lord and the lord owed duties of defense and warranty to the tenant. And these rights existed and these duties were owing simply because the one was the lord and the other was tenant. *The rights and duties belonged to that relation.* [Author's italics.] Whenever the existence of that relation put one in the class of lord or the class of tenant, the rights and duties existed as a legal consequence. The first solvent of individualism in our law and the chief factor in fashioning its system

[1] Pound, Roscoe, *The Spirit of The Common Law* (Boston: Marshall Jones Co., 1921), p. 14.

and many of its characteristic doctrines was the analogy of this feudal relation, suggesting the juristic conception of rights, duties, and liabilities arising, not from express undertaking, the terms of any transaction, voluntary wrong-doing, or culpable action, but simply and solely as incidents of relation.

This cultural contribution of the medieval period is so important to our modern conception of a public utility and its probable evolution that a greater development of this theme is imperative.

Public Utility Origins in Medieval Economy

It is not wrong to speak of the medieval ideal as that of an ordered society where each had his place, for this appears to have been in large part true. Life was cast in a regime of custom and status, and economic wants were viewed from this narrow outlook. Ordinary buying and selling in incorporated towns was controlled by the guilds. Exceptions were found in the market towns and at fairs. A similar system of control and exclusive jurisdiction obtained in the villages, where the feudal lord was the center of the manorial economy. His control was exercised in person or through bailiffs sitting as judges in the manor courts. Prices and quality of services were thus controlled. This was the approach, peculiar to the political economy of feudalism, which medieval courts applied to those economic transactions of which our modern public utility dealings are the lineal descendants.

It must not, however, be lightly assumed that the distinction between a public and private calling, drawn in modern times upon some theory of monopolistic as against competitive undertakings, was the basis of the medieval distinction. As E. A. Adler has shown,[2] to import this meaning into the medieval term of common carrier, common innkeeper, common tailor, common surgeon, common blacksmith, common barber, and common miller would be to read into simpler economic conditions the complexities of modern economics. The term *common*, when used by the medieval lawyer, indicated rather that the employment was public in the sense of availability to all who might want to be served. In the self-sufficing economies of that distant time there were many craftsmen who were employed by feudal lords and others entirely on private account. Such employment required them to be distinguished from the plying of a craft for the common use and for account of the craftsmen. Viewed in this light, guild regulations and judicial regulations are illustrative merely of the all-pervading spirit of authoritarian control of industry and life.

[2] Adler, E. A., "Business Jurisprudence," 28 *Harvard Law Review*, 135, December, 1914.

The peculiar nature of guild organization, which assembled all members of the same trade or craft into separate associations and granted them a local monopoly of plying their trades or crafts, and the restricted, self-sufficing character of the manorial or town economy was effective in giving to these public or common callings a status that required close regulation.

The Regulation of Industry under Mercantilism

With the development of feudal society into modern state structures a change came in the source of regulatory policies. In England this development is shown best on its legal side, where the guild, town, and manor authority was being displaced by the authority of the common law courts. The existence of a national parliament, enacting laws for the commonwealth as a whole, did much to break up the sense of local control. More and more appeals were being taken in trade disputes from the local courts to the king's court. As Professor Ashley has said: "The royal authority secured for society trustworthy instruments of exchange; and by helping to break down the privileges of isolated town economies, prepared the way for the idea of a *national economy* to make its appearance in the sixteenth century." [3]

This brings us to a discussion of the system of mercantilism, a policy associated with Colbert, the famous finance minister of Louis XIV. To him money appeared as the index of national wealth and its acquisition as the loadstone of national policy. To this end, he contended, all agencies of national control should be shaped. Where the medieval ideal of control had been that of a (*self-conscious*) *local economy*, mercantilism was that of a (*self-conscious*) *state economy*. Economic wants began to be viewed from the national instead of the local standpoint. Markets, as in Roman times, had again widened. Accordingly, Colbert advocated, not the *trade restrictions* of the guilds and towns but the *tariff restrictions* of states. Industry should be regulated, but it should be the regulation of the state, in order that industry might promote the strength and power of the state. He advocated tariff and manufacturing restrictions so imposed that a favorable balance of trade (excess of exports over imports) might be obtained. The favorable balance would tend to bring precious metals into the country, and thus eventually provide the national treasury with the sinews of war. The export of gold was forbidden. National regulations, such as the navigation Acts, were devised to build up a merchant marine and to promote a colonial system calculated to produce the raw materials for manufacturing.

[3] Ashley, W., *Introduction to English Economic History,* Vol. 1 (New York: Longmans, Green & Co., 1913), Chap. 3, p. 49.

Public franchises—a contribution of mercantilist policy. The element of mercantilist policy which is of the greatest importance in this background for public utility regulation, is the practice of granting royal charters to trading and plantation companies which carried on their functions under a system of national regulation. It was the old idea of the grant of exclusive privileges to perform functions of social importance, formerly applied in a manor or town economy, but now applied in the wider field of national economy.

These private enterprises, organized in a modern corporate form instead of a medieval guild society, were conceived to be performing a quasi-governmental function and hence were clothed with responsibilities of government. Thus, the grant of monopoly was regarded as a method of accomplishing social results. Since franchises were royal grants, they conferred the special privilege of performing functions which the state itself, for various reasons, did not care to undertake, but which the mercantilist authorities conceived to be governmental in character. These grants of monopoly provided an incentive for the investment of capital and the assumption of risks. That they turned out, in many cases, to be extremely profitable to their grantees, and would in turn need curbing, should not conceal the fact that they were originated by the state as a means of attaining public objects. No distinct line can be drawn between the guilds, the regulated commercial companies of the fourteenth and fifteenth centuries, and the new, joint-stock companies that sprang into being in the sixteenth century with the discoveries and colonizations. In this development, however, is to be found the origin of our modern notion of a public service corporation. Historical continuity, important for all economic institutions, is especially important in this connection.

Opposition to domestic monopolies as special privileges. Another social movement of this period is important because to it may be traced the antagonism of the law to monopolistic privileges. It finds its best exemplification in Queen Elizabeth's policy of granting to her favorites patents of monopoly that gave exclusive rights to deal in certain articles of common use *within* the country. Exorbitant prices were charged for salt, iron, vinegar, lead, and paper—to mention only a few articles thus monopolized. This policy aroused widespread public condemnation. It ran counter to the tendency of the times, which was away from medieval industrial restrictions. Finally, by act of Parliament in 1624, all monopolies, except patents, which controlled the buying, selling, and manufacturing of goods, were declared to be null and void. The practices of laissez faire as a legal theory had preceded its economic formulation by Adam Smith at least one hundred and fifty years. Historically, the legislation was a swingback to the "natural price" doctrine of Stoic Roman law.

The Common Law Concept of "Business Affected with a Public Interest"

The next step in the process is not clear. Why certain occupations or callings, conceived to be carried on under peculiar conditions, were subjected to special regulation, is worthy of intensive historical study. Wyman asserts that it was due to the undeveloped state of the law of contract. He also refers to the existence of virtual monopoly in such callings, as that of the common carrier and innkeeper. It is certain that justices in the royal courts decided cases involving these callings upon a theory that the individual customer was in a position of dependence and required protection. In the cases of the ferrymen and wharfingers, presumably occupations requiring a license, we have the authority of Lord Hale in his treatise *De Portibus Maris:*

If the king or subject have a public wharf unto which all persons that come to that port must come as for the purpose to unlade or lade their goods, *because they are the wharfs only licensed by the queen,* according to the statute of I Eliz. cap. II or because there is no other wharf in that port, as it may fall out where a port is newly erected, in that case there cannot be taken arbitrary and excessive duties or cranage, wharfage, pesage, and so forth, neither can they be enhanced to an immoderate rate, but the duties must be reasonable and moderate though settled by the king's license or charter. For now the wharf and crane and other convenience are affected with a public interest and they cease to be *Juris privati* only. As if a man set out a street in new building on his land, it is no longer bare private interest, but it is affected with a public interest.

The Modifications Introduced by Laissez Faire

The reawakening in the seventeenth and eighteenth centuries of Stoic ideals of laissez faire brought forward the open market once more as the predominant exchange mechanism, whereas the guild and manorial system had relied upon the controlled market. Competition and individualism as social forces gained ever wider applications. Legal monopolies were restricted. The callings once closely controlled by guild regulations were freed. The philosophical presuppositions of laissez faire need now to be examined.

Compared with the predominant thought of the preceding period, they represent a revolution in ideas. The ideal which came to the forefront, particularly in the latter part of the eighteenth century, was for liberty, for freedom from governmental and authoritarian restraints in economic and social life. Within the realm of economic interests this meant freedom for individuals to make a living in any way they saw fit.

This theory and the system of social control which it explains found its chief exposition in Adam Smith's book, *The Wealth of Nations,* published in 1776. Historically, the theory represents a recrudescence of Stoic belief in the existence of natural laws. The evils existing in the world, it was believed, arose from artificial interference by human agencies, primarily governments, with the working of natural law. A return to a "state of nature" would again set things right. As Adam Smith wrote:

The patrimony of a poor man lies in the strength and dexterity of his hands; and to hinder him from employing this strength and dexterity in what manner he thinks proper, *without injury to his neighbors,* is a plain violation of this most sacred property. It is a manifest encroachment upon the *just liberty,* both of the workman and of those who might be disposed to employ him. As it hinders the one from working at what he thinks proper, so it hinders the other from employing whom they think proper.

It is perhaps somewhat difficult for us, accustomed as we have become to the beneficent interference, on the whole, of government in private affairs, to realize that an ideal of the general welfare underlay this seeming insistence upon private benefit. The thought was of an *unconscious* realization of the general welfare through the *conscious* striving of individuals for individual welfare. As put by Adam Smith in language which has become classic: "By preferring the support of domestic to that of foreign industry, he intends only his own security, and by directing that industry in such a manner as its produce may be of the greatest value, he intends only his own gain, and he is in this, as in many other cases, *led by an invisible hand to promote an end which was no part of his intentiton.*" [Author's italics.] The functions of government in this system were limited to those of umpire in the struggle. State regulation was to prevent merely force and fraud.

In contrast with mercantilism, this theory viewed economic wants from a cosmopolitan instead of a national standpoint. Its typical institution was the *open market,* as distinguished from the *controlled market.* Competition was not to be artificially limited to the members of a guild subsisting under common rules, or to international rivalry for foreign commerce, but was to be given the utmost scope. On its legal side the system called for a development of the institutions of private property and contract and for a release of the individual from legal restraints affecting his person. Hence it was that Sir Henry Maine, the noted student of the history of law, writing in the early nineteenth century, epitomized social progress as the evolution of man from status to contract.

Although price regulation by public authority continued to some extent, industry, taken as a whole, was placed in a position where it fixed its own prices. The old conception of "just price" was displaced, and a new conception of "natural price," now called "market price," was substituted. The new explanation of natural prices was based not upon cost of production but upon the existing state of the demand for, and supply of, commodities in a particular market (modified, however, by the concept of cost of production in the long run). It is clear that such a theory of price is premised upon competition or free access to markets.

The tendency for competition to displace public authority in the control of industry was stopped, however, when the turn came to apply the prevalent notion of unrestrained competition to certain public callings. Here the laissez-faire period served, in general, as a test of the merits of the restrictive system. Thus, in the case of these public callings, the essential elements in the medieval framework of regulation survived its general collapse. They continued to be businesses "affected with the public interest." Their legal duty to provide adequate service and facilities was not abated. Even more than under conditions of a restricted market was it incumbent upon them to render services to all applicants without discrimination. The law continued to require that the prices charged be reasonable.

American Colonial Legislation

Within the period of mercantilism fall the voyages of discovery of North America which resulted in the colonization of these territories and their incorporation into European state systems. European, that is to say, British control over colonial policies lasted long enough to transplant not only the English system of common law jurisprudence but also the idea of legislative control of price. The scarcity of food, the isolation of the settlements, the difficulties of colonial trade, provided the requisite conditions for cornering the market. Enough of the guild spirit survived to transplant also some of its conceptions of local and trade autonomy. And so we find the colonies attempting to control prices. Massachusetts in 1635 and Plymouth in 1668, to mention only two instances, forbade the charging of excessive prices by shopkeepers for corn, tobacco, beer, bread, beef, etc. The Revolution tore the political fetters that tied America to Europe, but it did not place us outside the influence of the sweep of ideas and wants that characterized an industrialized Europe and that brought forward a liberalized and competitive economic policy.

Another factor peculiar to the United States tended to emphasize competition and, although not affecting the legal status of these common law callings, to hold the exercise of legislative restrictions regarding them in abeyance. Along with the political demand to free American industry from colonial restrictions, there went the cultural demand of pioneer communities to give individual initiative free scope. As we have seen, facilities of transport and communication were agencies of the first order in taking possession of a continent. Multiplication of these facilities thus gave to competition, when it did arise, much greater scope than the same industries experienced in Europe. Early charters testify to public liberality. Courts were seldom called upon to adjudicate customers' complaints. It was not until after the Civil War, when complaints about discrimination and high rates arose where railroads had already been introduced, and when it was found that competition was not working satisfactorily, that a demand came for supplementary legislative regulation. Pioneer communities still needing these facilities did not take part in the agitation and continued to be friendly.

The courts, however, by going back to the historical elements of our jurisprudence before the Revolution, adopted the concept of a public calling worked out in the mother country. When the epoch-making case of *Munn v. Illinois* was decided, the court took it as a maxim of the law that, since to serve all at a fair price was immemorial practice with respect to these public callings, the legislative regulation of price was in accord with "due process of law." With this brief sketch of the general historical background of regulation, we may turn to a consideration of certain legal opinions by the United States Supreme Court, which give us the constitutional basis of public utility regulation.

13. THE
CONSTITUTIONAL BASIS OF
PUBLIC UTILITY
REGULATION

Judicial Consideration of the Meaning of Public Utility

The Munn Case. In the United States, judicial consideration of public utility regulation begins with the famous decision in *Munn v. Illinois* in 1877 (94 U.S. 113), which has, by common consent, been placed at the threshold of our modern treatment of the public utility problem. *Munn v. Illinois* involved the validity of an Illinois statute fixing maximum rates for storing grain in elevators at Chicago. Munn and his partner Scott had been engaged in the elevator business since 1862, long before the enactment of the statute. They had been in the habit of charging rates fixed by agreement among the elevator owners in Chicago and had continued to charge these rates although they were in excess of those fixed by the Act. They were convicted and fined in the state courts and appealed to the United States Supreme Court upon the ground that the Act violated the Fourteenth Amendment in that it deprived them of their property without due process of law.

Chief Justice Waite, in upholding the validity of the statute, said in substance that under the circumstances in which the elevators were being operated in Chicago (that is, standing "in the very gateway of commerce and taking toll from all who pass"), they had become a business "affected with a public interest and had ceased to be *juris privati* only." The mystic formula was not his own language but was quoted, as already mentioned, from Lord Chief Justice Hale who had penned it some two hundred years before in England. This legal doctrine, Justice Waite said, had been a rule of the law of property ever since; that under this rule and in the exercise of the police power of the state, "it had been customary in England from time immemorial and in this country from its first colonization to regulate ferries, common carriers, hackmen, bakers, millers, wharfingers, innkeepers, and so forth," and to fix maximum charges.

Justice Field, in his dissenting opinion, objected that the rule applied only in those cases where the business was based upon a governmental franchise or license, or upon an implied franchise claimed by prescription through long usage and consent. The warehouses here in question had always been a private business and had not been operated under governmental franchises nor had they received governmental privileges. He ridiculed the idea of calling them public warehouses.

There is no magic in the language, though used by a constitutional convention, which can change a private business into a public one . . . A tailor's or a shoe-maker's shop would still retain its private character, even though the assembled wisdom of the state should declare, by organic act or legislative ordinance, that such a place was a public workshop, and that the workmen were public tailors or public shoemakers.

Justice Field was undoubtedly right if the expression is to be given the narrow interpretation for which he contends. But, as Professor Commons has clearly pointed out, the right of government to regulate prices is made by the majority opinion to depend not alone upon "a special grant of sovereignty" but also upon a recognition of the fact that private property rights bear within themselves the germ of coercion which becomes apparent when *economic conditions* create a state of facts which the majority felt was virtual monopoly.

But what is the meaning of the phrase "affected with a public interest"? It means in the none-too-clear language of Chief Justice Waite that private property is being used

. . . in a manner to make it of public consequence, and affecting the community at large. When, therefore, one devotes his property to a use in which the public has an interest, he, in effect, grants to the public an interest in that use, and must submit to be controlled by the public for the common good, to the extent of the interest he has thus created. He may withdraw his grant by discontinuing the use; but, so long as he maintains the use, he must submit to the control.

The importance of the Munn case resides in this: that Justice Waite's definition of the "public interest" concept was a dynamic one, and that the limitation of the Fourteenth Amendment with its due process clause was not deemed to be inconsistent with this customary element providing for the regulation of private property.

Another step in the delineation of the public interest concept was taken in 1914 when a closely divided court upheld the regulation of the business of fire insurance. This time, the state of Kansas, through its superintendent of insurance, had ordered a 12 per cent reduction in fire insurance premiums.

The German Alliance Insurance Company on appeal[1] contended that the business of fire insurance was private, a matter of natural right and not dependent upon special privileges derived from the state, that there was no physical property in the sense of *Munn v. Illinois* which had been devoted to a public use. Once more the court refused to limit regulation under the police power to a closed category of enterprises, contending instead that "a business, by circumstances and its nature, may rise from private to be of public concern and be subject in consequence to governmental regulation."

The Wolff Packing Company Case

After the upheaval of World War I, the state of Kansas undertook to extend the public interest concept in a new direction. Impressed by Australian experience with compulsory arbitration of wage disputes, the legislature, in the Industrial Relations Act of 1920, abolished its public utility commission but reconstituted it as an industrial court. It was empowered to fix not only prices but wages and other terms of employment in the event of labor controversies imperiling the peace and health of the public in all businesses affected with a public interest. The Act declared the following to be so affected: the manufacture and preparation of food for human consumption; the manufacture of clothing; the production of any substance in common use for fuel; the transport of the foregoing; common carriers and other public utilities. With its implication of extension to the common necessities of food, clothing and shelter, it is certain that this was the most far-reaching application by modern legislative act of the doctrine of public interest in the United States. The Act was challenged by the Wolff Packing Company on the ground of conflict with the Fourteenth Amendment.[2]

Chief Justice Taft, in considering the question, divided businesses affected with a public interest (and thus justified some public regulation) into three classes:

1. Railways, other common carriers, and what he termed *public utilities.* These he characterized as businesses carried on under authority of a public grant either expressly or impliedly imposing the affirmative duty of rendering a public service demanded by any member of the public.

2. Certain exceptional occupations, so recognized and surviving from the earliest times when arbitrary laws by Parliament or Colonial legislation regulated *all* trades and callings. Examples are innkeepers, cabs, and gristmills.

---

[1] *German Alliance Insurance Co. v. Kansas,* 233 U.S. 389 (1914).
[2] *Charles Wolff Packing Co. v. Court of Industrial Relations,* 262 U.S. 522 (1923).

3. Other enterprises which, though not public at their inception, may have become such, and thus be subject in consequence to some government regulations. "They have come to hold such a peculiar relation to the public that this (regulation) is superimposed upon them. In the language of the cases, the owner, by devoting his business to the public use, in effect grants the public an interest in that use and subjects himself to public regulation to the extent of that interest." No illustrations of business falling within this class are cited, but the grain elevators of the Munn case are implied.

It is apparent that this first classification is an inductive generalization from legal history. It accepts without question, as one class, industries based upon the franchise, in regard to which both the majority and minority in the Munn case were in agreement. It distinguishes, as a second class, callings that now fit with difficulty into the rubric of public utilities. Even the minority accepted these as survivals of the regulated economy of feudalism and mercantilism. The third classification represents the element of growth as evidenced in the Munn case, the Budd case,[3] the insurance case, the pipeline cases,[4] and the rent cases.[5]

By way of warning that the conception of public interest be not taken too literally, Justice Taft added:

In a sense, the public is concerned about all lawful business because it contributes to the prosperity and well-being of the people. The public may suffer from high prices or strikes in many trades, but the expression "clothed with a public interest" as applied to a business, means more than that the public welfare is affected by continuity or by the price at which a commodity is sold or a service rendered. The circumstances which clothe a particular kind of business with a public interest, in the sense of *Munn v. Illinois* and other cases, must be such as to create a peculiarly close relation between the public and those engaged in it, and raise implications of an affirmative obligation on their part to be reasonable in dealing with the public.

He might have added, as legal writers frequently do when dealing with problems of this character, that the distinction is one of *degree* which is raised to one of *kind*.

Although giving us a classification of the businesses treated by courts as affected with a public interest, the court rather leaves us in the dark as to its conception of a public utility. It does make the helpful suggestion that,

[3] *Budd v. State of New York*, 117 N.Y. 1 (1889). See also *Brass v. North Dakota*, 153 U.S. 394 (1894).
[4] *United States v. Various Oil Companies*, 234 U.S. 548 (1914).
[5] *Block v. Hirsh*, 256 U.S. 135 (1921); see also *Holding Co. v. Feldman*, 256 U.S. 170 (1921); *Chestleton Corporation v. Sinclair*, 264 U.S. 543 (1923); *Summons v. Winters*, 21 Oregon 35 (1891) (water utility); *Cummings v. Hyatt*, 54 Nebraska 35 (1898) (irrigation utility).

in the case of industries in the dynamic group, "the thing which gave the public interest was the indispensable nature of the service and the exorbitant charges and arbitrary control to which the public might be subjected without regulation." The court also explains that the classification of a business as a public utility "is not a matter of legislative discretion solely"; that the need of regulation depends upon "abuses reasonably to be feared"; that the intensity or the degree of regulation may reasonably vary with different kinds of business. Indeed, Chief Justice Taft sensed the delicacy of the problem when he said:

It is very difficult under the cases to lay down a working rule by which readily to determine when a business has become "clothed with a public interest." All business is subject to some kind of public regulation; but when the public becomes so *peculiarly dependent* upon a particular business that one engaging therein subjects himself to a more intimate public regulation is only to be determined by the process of exclusion and inclusion and the gradual establishment of a line of distinction.

The opinion throws some light upon the problem indirectly because it tells us what a public utility is *not*. The constitutionality of the Kansas Act had been urged upon the analogy of the doctrine of public use as exemplified in condemnation cases and tax suits. But the court did not regard these as "especially helpful." That doctrine was conceived to have a wider application inasmuch as *public use* may "cover almost any private business if the legislature thinks the state's engagement in it will help the general public and is willing to pay the cost of the plant and incur the expense of operation." The court probably had in mind the North Dakota legislation involved in *Green v. Frazier*,[6] where the state had engaged in competitive business.

The Public Interest Doctrine in Recent Cases

Certain cases have come before our highest court in recent years which tend to throw some additional light upon this vexing though most fundamental problem. The first one is the case of *Tyson & Brother v. Banton*,[7] in which the court in a bare majority decision of five to four refused to accord the public utility status to ticket brokers in the city of New York. The argument is given in two pertinent paragraphs:

A theatre or other place of entertainment does not meet this conception of Lord Hale's aphorism or fall within the reasons of the decisions of this court based upon it. A theatre is a private enterprise, which, in its relation to the public,

6 253 U.S. 233 (1920).
7 273 U.S. 418 (1927).

differs obviously and widely, both in character and degree, from a grain elevator, standing at the gateway of commerce and exacting toll, amounting to a common charge, for every bushel of grain which passes on its way among the states; or stock yards, standing in like relation to the commerce in live stock; or an insurance company, engaged, as a sort of common agency, in collecting and holding a guaranty fund in which definite and substantial rights are enjoyed by a considerable portion of the public sustaining interdependent relations in respect of their interests in the fund. Sales of theatre tickets bear no relation to the commerce of the country; and they are not interdependent transactions, but stand, both in form and effect, separate and apart from each other, "terminating in their effect with the instances." And certainly a place of entertainment is in no legal sense a public utility; and, quite as certainly, its activities are not such that their enjoyment can be regarded under any conditions from the point of view of an emergency.

The interest of the public in theatres and other places of entertainment may be more nearly, and with better reason, assimilated to the like interest in provision stores and markets and in the rental of houses and apartments for residence purposes, although in importance it falls below such an interest in the proportion that food and shelter are of more moment than amusement or instruction. As we have shown, there is no legislative power to fix the prices of provisions or clothing or the rental charges for houses or apartments, in the absence of some controlling emergency; and we are unable to perceive any dissimilarities of such quality or degree as to justify a different rule in respect of amusements and entertainments.

On similar grounds a majority of the court opposed the extension of the public utility category to employment agencies whose fees a New Jersey statute sought to regulate.[8] Again the court held that the interest of the public in the matter of employment is not "that *public interest* which the law contemplates as the basis for legislative price control." Justice Stone in a dissenting opinion tried to distinguish employment agents from other types of brokerage, especially ticket brokers, when he said:

There the attempt was made to limit the advances which brokers might charge over box office prices for theater tickets, an expedient adopted to break up their monopolistic control of a luxury, not a necessity. Those affected by the practices of the ticket brokers constituted a relatively small portion of the population within a comparatively small area of the state of New York. They were not necessitous. The consequences of the fraud and extortion practiced upon them were not visited upon the community as a whole in any such manner as are fraud and imposition practiced upon workers seeking employment.

Again it would seem that the majority was thinking of the public utility category in a strict sense, while the minority was not.

The following year, on January 2, 1929, the court held unconstitutional a statute which sought to fix the prices at which gasoline may be sold within the state of Tennessee by declaring that the business of dealing in gasoline

[8] *Ribnik v. McBride*, 277 U.S. 350 (1928).

was affected with a public interest. [*Williams v. Standard Oil Co.* 278 U.S. (235)] In this case there was no significant dissent.

We come now to the famous case of *New State Ice Co. v. Liebmann.*[9] Here an Oklahoma statute declared that the manufacture of ice for sale and distribution is a "public business" and confers upon the Corporation Commission in respect to it the powers of regulation customarily exercised over public utilities, including the power to license new enterprises upon a showing that they are necessary to meet the public need. Liebmann started in competition with the New State Ice Company, contending that he was not engaging in a public business but in a common calling, the right to engage in which being one of the fundamental liberties guaranteed by the due process clause. The majority of the court agreed with the defendant.

We are not able to see anything peculiar in the business here in question which distinguishes it from ordinary manufacture and production. It is said to be recent; but it is the character of the business and not the date when it began that is determinative. It is not the case of a natural monopoly, or of an enterprise in its nature dependent upon the grant of public privileges.

It should be noted how the court rests its argument upon the absence of monopoly.

We know, since it is common knowledge, that today, to say nothing of other means, wherever electricity or gas is available (and one or the other is available in practically every part of the country), anyone for a comparatively moderate outlay may have set up in his kitchen an appliance by means of which he may manufacture ice for himself. Under such circumstances it hardly will do to say that people generally are at the mercy of the manufacturer, seller and distributer of ice for ordinary needs. Moreover, the practical tendency of the restriction, as the trial court suggested in the present case, is to shut out new enterprises, and thus create and foster monopoly in the hands of existing establishments, against, rather than in aid of, the interest of the consuming public.

It is important to note how the conservative majority sought to prevent the extension of the public interest concept to an industry on the borderline of monopoly by taking the initial step of requiring a license. It treated the public interest concept as antagonistic to the sphere of liberty, as appears from these concluding remarks:

And it is plain that unreasonable or arbitrary interferences or restrictions cannot be saved from the condemnation of that Amendment (19th) merely by calling them experimental. It is not necessary to challenge the authority of the states to indulge in experimental legislation; but it would be strange and unwarranted doctrine to hold that they may do so by enactments which transcend the limitations imposed upon them by the federal Constitution. The principle is

[9] 285 U.S. 262 (1932).

imbedded in our constitutional system that there are certain essentials of liberty with which the state is not entitled to dispense in the interest of experiments. This principle has been applied by this court in many cases . . . The opportunity to apply one's labor and skill in an ordinary occupation with proper regard for all reasonable regulations is no less entitled to protection.

With this view of the case, the minority of Brandeis and Stone in one of Justice Brandeis' famous dissents takes issue:

Unless the Court can say that the Federal Constitution confers an absolute right to engage anywhere in the business of manufacturing ice for sale, it cannot properly decide that the legislature acted unreasonably without first ascertaining what was the experience of Oklahoma in respect to the ice business . . . Our function is only to determine the reasonableness of the legislature's belief in the existence of evils and in the effectiveness of the remedy provided.

The minority concluded: "We cannot say that the legislature of Oklahoma acted arbitrarily in declaring that ice is an article of primary necessity, in industry and agriculture as well as in the household, partaking of the fundamental character of electricity, gas, water, transportation and communication." According to the minority, making entry into this business dependent upon the grant of a certificate of public convenience and necessity was a method chosen to make the industry pass from a competitive to a monopolistic category. The essentially economic character of the argument should be noted:

Such a certificate was unknown to the common law. It is a creature of the machine age, in which plants have displaced tools and businesses are substituted for trades. The purpose of requiring it is to promote the public interest by preventing waste. Particularly in those businesses in which interest and depreciation charges on plant constitute a large element in the cost of production, experience has taught that the financial burdens incident to unnecessary duplication of facilities are likely to bring high rates and poor service. There, cost is usually dependent, among other things, upon volume; any division of possible patronage among competing concerns may so raise the unit cost of operation as to make it impossible to provide adequate service at reasonable rates. The introduction in the United States of the certificate of public convenience and necessity marked the growing conviction that under certain circumstances free competition might be harmful to the community and that, when it was so, absolute freedom to enter the business of one's choice should be denied.

The minority counters the contention that customers are no longer dependent upon ice manufacturers by stating:

The question whether in Oklahoma the means of securing refrigeration otherwise than by ice manufactured for sale and distribution has become so general as to destroy popular dependence upon ice plants is one peculiarly appropriate for the determination of its legislature and peculiarly inappropriate for determination by this Court, which cannot have knowledge of all the relevant facts.

The business of supplying ice is not only a necessity, like that of supplying food or clothing or shelter, but the legislature could also consider that it is one which lends itself peculiarly to monopoly. Characteristically the business is conducted in local plants with a market narrowly limited in area, and this for the reason that ice manufactured at a distance cannot effectively compete with a plant on the ground. In small towns and rural communities the duplication of plants, and in larger communities the duplication of delivery service, is wasteful and ultimately burdensome to consumers. At the same time the relative ease and cheapness with which an ice plant may be constructed exposes the industry to destructive and frequently ruinous competition. Competition in the industry tends to be destructive because ice plants have a determinate capacity, and inflexible fixed charges and operating costs, and because in a market of limited area the volume of sales is not readily expanded. Thus, the erection of a new plant in a locality already adequately served often causes managers to go to extremes in cutting prices in order to secure business. Trade journals and reports of association meetings of ice manufacturers bear ample witness to the hostility of the industry to such competition, and to its unremitting efforts, through trade associations, informal agreements, combination of delivery systems, and in particular through the consolidation of plants, to protect markets and prices against competition of any character.

That these forces were operative in Oklahoma prior to the passage of the Act under review, is apparent from the record. Where there was competition, it often resulted to the disadvantage rather than the advantage of the public, both in respect to prices and to service. Some communities were without ice altogether, and the State was without means of assuring their supply . . .

The most recent decision of the court seeking to clarify the notion of a public utility came in 1934 in *Nebbia v. New York*.[10] This was a five to four decision in which the so-called liberals were in the majority. It is deemed by some to be a victory for the views advanced by Brandeis in his dissenting opinion in the New State Ice Co. case.[11] The legislature of New York had declared the production, distribution, and sale of milk to be a business affecting the public health and interest and had created a Milk Control Board charged with the duty of fixing *minimum* wholesale and retail prices for fluid milk and with power to fix *maximum* prices *if necessary*. The Board also was empowered to issue and revoke licenses to milk dealers.

Upheld in the lower courts, the court of last resort likewise could find no basis in the due process clause of the Fourteenth Amendment "for condemning the provisions of the Agriculture and Market Law here drawn in

[10] 291 U.S. 502 (1934).
[11] Mr. Justice Roberts wrote the opinion with Hughes, Brandeis, Stone, and Cardozo concurring and Van Devanter, Sutherland, and Butler joining in Justice McReynolds' dissent.

question." We are chiefly interested in the argument of the Court. The decision points out that the production and distribution of milk is a paramount industry of the state affecting the health and prosperity of the people. It pointed to the demoralization of milk prices caused by the general price decline, an oversupply of milk, and the prevalence of unfair and destructive trade practices in distribution. The Court also found that "the fluid milk industry is affected by factors of stability peculiar to itself which call for special methods of control."

We may best summarize this evolutionary process by calling attention to the fact that the very indefiniteness of the "public interest" concept requires us to substitute for it the more modern "public utility" concept which draws a sharper distinction between public services and public utilities on the one hand and private services and public utilities on the other. As contrasted with public services supported by taxes, fees, and special assessments or combinations thereof, public utilities are self-liquidating enterprises which look to the sale of their product or services to consumers. At the same time, as contrasted with other business enterprises, public utility enterprises represent the monopolistic segment of the economy where for reasons of public policy monopoly rights are accorded them. On this account, a business may remain for a long time in a twilight zone where competitors are few because there is uncertainty whether monopoly or competition should be the major premise.

The Public Utility as a Legal Institution

Another conclusion to be drawn from this process is that the real significance of the public utility status is not that there be provided an unerring guide to correct classification of industries but rather that the nature of this complex of rights and duties be understood, for we are dealing here with an institutional development. The core of it is represented by the *feudal conception of relation,* which has been hardened into a social habit by becoming commonly accepted. The conception, thus generalized, has been given greater solidity and rational, coherent form by being organized into a definite mode of legal procedure. There was a persistent need for developing such forms of procedure, and as a consequence, these forms have crystallized into an institution which controls the continued performance of the function.

It must be clear that the conduct of public utility enterprises, subject to these legal obligations, exhibits a strange mixture of volition and compulsion. The use of compulsion was a characteristic of feudal times and of the system of mercantilism, while the use of persuasion, the touchstone of laissez faire, was a characteristic of the system of industrial liberty. The legal rights and duties to be observed by individuals toward one another in feudal times flowed as a result of the *relations* that individuals bore to one another, whereas in the freer atmosphere of laissez faire the rights and duties were a result of express undertakings or *contracts*. The public utility institution, originating in feudal times and modified by laissez-faire doctrines, combines the compulsory affixing of rights and duties as a consequence of "relation" with the voluntary procedure of entering into a "public utility" relationship. Persons are free to conduct a public utility enterprise, but having entered upon an undertaking of this character, they are constrained by its peculiar system of rights and duties. Persons are free to consume the products or use the services of a public utility or not, as they choose; but having voluntarily agreed to take such service, they also are bound by its peculiar system of rights and duties. Thus, volition and compulsion are combined in the elaboration of a scheme which collectively constitutes the law of public service companies.

There are many types of undertakings, relationships with which, either as producer or consumer, bring about the legal consequences described above. The nature of the institution itself—the complex of legal rights and duties—is singularly fixed and unvarying, changing only as rights and duties are multiplied, or as they become more clearly defined. It is an institution not solely of economic significance but also one of large political importance; for while, on the one hand, it is concerned with the material needs of individual economic life, it serves, on the other hand, to strengthen and make possible socioeconomic life. Out of its institutional character arises the public interest in its maintenance and development.

From this point of view, the term *public utility* does not refer to any specific industry but is used as a collective name for an entire group of industries. It becomes a highly abstract conception of certain relationships, embracing certain definable rights and duties. What the medieval jurist, as well as the modern jurist, means when he says that certain employments are public employments is this: that the objects of property engaged therein are "affected with a public interest" and that he wants these employments to be cast within the mold of relationships which will ensure their being carried out successfully. If one would know the nature of the institution, one must understand the rights and duties which compose it. If one would understand the rights and duties, one must appreciate the public interests which these rights and duties are to conserve. If one would be convinced that the preservation of these public interests must become a matter of rights and duties, molded and enforced by the state, one must be aware of the process of social evolution. The state lends to the institution the coercive power of its sovereignty. It is not without significance that some modern French writers [12] have discussed even the state itself in terms of a great public service corporation, on account of the great public interests which both of these protect.

Legal Tests of Classification

In determining whether an industry is subject to this coercive law, or in other words, whether it is a public utility, the courts have adopted certain practical tests to aid in making the distinction between a public utility and a private utility. These tests are both legal and economic in character.

The problem arose first in connection with turnpikes. The law here had no difficulty, since the turnpike was simply a highway and that had always been a public utility. In the absence of a franchise grant to private persons to build the highway and charge tolls, the highway would have been a public facility and free to all users. When bridges began to replace ferries, the charters of bridge companies similarly authorized tolls, the provisions in some cases being that when the tolls had been sufficient to repay, in addition to operating expenses, the entire first cost of the bridge and a designated annual profit, the bridge should become free. Bridge companies were treated as successors to the ferryman. With the coming of the canal and the steam railway, the same legal principles were brought into play, until it seemed that the common carrier relation would exhaust all types of services to which this special system of rights and duties might be applied. The test was the logical one of analogy.

The first break in the development came with the telegraph and gas-light company. At first telegraph companies were treated as common carriers of messages. Soon it was perceived, however, that the analogy was misleading in that the legal category of public utility might cover other than transport industries. It was then that the various economic tests began to appear in the decisions.

The clearest economic test is the one which bases the classification upon *natural limitations as to source of supply*. A water company which utilizes the most advantageously situated watershed in gathering its water supply is classified as a public utility. Under the same head would fall an irrigation

[12] Duguit, Leon, *Law in the Modern State* (New York: B. W. Huebsch, 1919), Chap. II.

company which impounds the only available stream and a water-power company which utilizes the only available site for a dam. Gas companies drawing their gas supply from natural gas fields are similarly classified.

A second economic test relates to the *conditions under which the product is supplied.* If these facilitate control of the market, the courts have conceded that this constitutes a basis for separate classification. Thus, artificial gas plants and electric plants sell a service which must be taken by customers directly connected with the plants. In view of the difficulties of granting occupation of the streets to competing concerns, the customer may, in effect, be dependent upon a single source of supply.

Another test looks to the *scarcity of advantageous sites,* such as sites for stations and terminal companies, for elevators, and for wharves. Another emphasizes *limitations of time* as a factor in the situation. Thus, innkeepers, cab companies, telephone and telegraph companies are held to come within a situation in which their customers are placed in a position of dependence, since their demand for service is urgent.

A less satisfactory test is based upon the broad ground that where a product or service is *supplied under conditions which deter effectual competition from entering* the market, the industry may be specially classified. In elaborating these conditions the courts have pointed to the large initial cost of the plant and to the tendency of costs to decline with increases in business as deterrents to potential competition. Unsatisfactory as some of these tests may appear to the logician looking for refinement in analysis, they have, nevertheless, been of great aid in the process of classification.

Rights and Duties of Public Utilities

Finally, what is the precise nature of this peculiar system of rights and duties? A public utility is under the extraordinary duty to render reasonably adequate service to all who apply. Persons engaged in private business are at liberty to refuse to serve any or all. As to those in private business, the law assumes that their own private interest and the ability of customers to seek out others are self-corrective of any failure to provide service at all or to provide it adequately. Again, a public utility is required to serve up to the limit of its capacity, where capacity is more and more being defined, not as mere physical capacity but as the limit of profitableness. It may not let customers' wants go unsatisfied. Nor may it attach unreasonable conditions to contracts for service which in effect negate its duty "to serve all comers." Furthermore, it must serve without discrimination all customers similarly circumstanced. Finally, a public utility must observe more than ordinary care in the rendition of service in view of the generally hazardous nature of the circumstances surrounding the service and the dependence of the public upon such care.

On the other hand, the law conceded the public utility the right to collect a reasonable price, to render service subject to reasonable rules and regulations, and to withdraw service under prescribed conditions after giving notice to customers. While customers are given the right to demand that a public utility live up to its duties, they are, on the other hand, required to accept reciprocal obligations. These general terms are the rules of law outlining the rights and duties of public utilities toward their patrons.[18]

[18] *Cf. Shepard v. The Milwaukee Gas Light Co.,* 6 Wis. 526 (1858).

14. *GOING CONCERNS*
AND CONTROL OF
THE MARKET

The organizational structure of public utility capitalism consists in the main of corporations, public and private. Examining the life history of such a typical business unit, we traced in Chapter 11 the significant phases through which it passes in the course of its history. But these aspects of the legal structure do not give an adequate picture because an analysis of the legal framework must be supplemented with an analysis of the economic framework, which likewise conditions its activities. Such activities are manifested in the negotiation of transactions for which the legal organization supplies only the nucleus or starting point.

Bargaining and Managerial Transactions

The production and sale of public utility services involves solving three types of problems: (1) purchasing, (2) manufacturing, and (3) marketing. Purchasing problems begin with the sale of stocks and bonds when the utility bargains for the input of money funds. We may call these transactions *investment bargains,* since they are concerned with the terms controlling the input of capital by owners and creditors. The next step is the transmutation of these money funds into fixed plant, employee's services, and circulating capital by bargaining for these goods and services in the open market. We shall call certain transactions *labor bargains* that control the input of the labor force as a production requisite. Others controlling the input of raw materials and manufactured products we shall call *price bargains.*

Next comes the manufacturing problem or the conversion of labor and material into a going plant and its operation as a part of the engineering process of producing an output of public utility services. These are *managerial transactions,* signifying a command-obedience relationship. They are not volitional in character because the individual or collective contracts have already been made. Management in this sense consists of the marshaling of natural resources and labor power in a scientific process of production. This is the field of "scientific management." In this engineering process input and output are characteristically measured in physical units—such as product per man-hour, or pounds of coal per kilowatt-hour—rather than in financial terms. Computations in physical terms are a part of the *engineering efficiency* concept of production. As such, they belong to the *going plant* phase of the going concern.

However, input and output must also be reckoned in monetary terms because units of output must be sold at prices at least equal to their costs of production. Units of outgo and income, reckoned in computations of cost of production and of revenue sales, are measures of *economic efficiency*. They belong to the economic process of buying and selling; again these are bargaining transactions, a part of the *going business* of the *going concern*. The flow of these bargaining and managerial transactions gives us a concept of both a money cost of production and of a real cost of production, according as we reckon them in bargaining terms, using money, or managerial terms, using physical units of measurement.

Thus the marketing problem consists also of a selling phase where the going concern operates as a selling organization. These involve bargaining transactions with customers which determine the *outflow* of beneficial services from the concern to customers in return for the *inflow* of revenues or income. We classify these transactions as *rate bargains*. From them we derive a concept of pecuniary *income* which, combined with the concept of pecuniary *outgo*, make up the going business phase of the going concern. This parallels the input and output of goods and services measured in engineering terms, which make up the going plant phase of the going concern. While these ideas are as old as business, the analysis of these transactions has recently come to be called microeconomics.

Rationing Transactions

We have passed over or taken for granted a distinct type of transaction between utilities and governmental units. This represents the political and legal nexus between business and government. By means of these transactions the economic status of the concern with respect to its buying and selling and tax relationships is determined. In this chapter we will be primarily concerned with those transactions that ration out to the concern the degree of control of the market which it will enjoy. Other transactions of this type determine the compulsory or quasi-compulsory contributions such as taxes, fees, and special assessments which must be made by utilities in return for governmental services. Government is here the "sleeping partner" in every business concern. Only in a Pickwickian sense could they be called tax *bargains.* Here, definitely, are relationships between superior and inferior, between sovereignty and subject, which Professor Commons has called *rationing transactions* of government. In the same category fall the price fixing functions of the state. The common element in all is that they are transactions between sovereign and subject whereby benefits and burdens, powers and immunities, liabilities and disabilities are apportioned through the working rules of the paramount concern, the state itself. They best exemplify the meaning of institutions as collective action in the control, liberation, and expansion of individual action.

The Theory of a Going Concern

We have reduced these relationships, as they affect the utility model, to diagrammatic form in Chart X. Transactions, distinguished as investment, price, labor, and governmental, provide the volitional or compulsory basis for the beneficial inflow on the one hand of money, goods, services, and governmental protection, and for the outflow of goods and services on the other hand. With respect to selling transactions, since customers are not charged a uniform rate, but for the purposes of rate-making are divided into classes with a different rate schedule applying to each class, the total receipts or gross revenues are determined by the schedules as a whole (the level of rates), while the separate schedules determine how much is received from each classification of customers (discriminatory rates). We will discuss these cost and income bargains and how they are regulated by means of the rationing transactions of governments in Part II.

The primary purpose of governmental regulations is to secure the balance of cost and income because the business unit is an organization within which resides the economic nexus of cost and income. If for any appreciable length of time cost is not balanced by income, the beneficial inflow of funds, goods, and services will cease, and the beneficial outflow of services to customers must cease also. The economic health of a going concern is thus dependent upon securing this long-run equilibrium.

This does not imply that the income must be sufficient to cover all costs, no matter what they may be. A public utility is under the legal duty to render reasonably adequate service at reasonable rates. Reasonableness implies reasonable efficiency in production and the exercise of reasonable skill in nego-

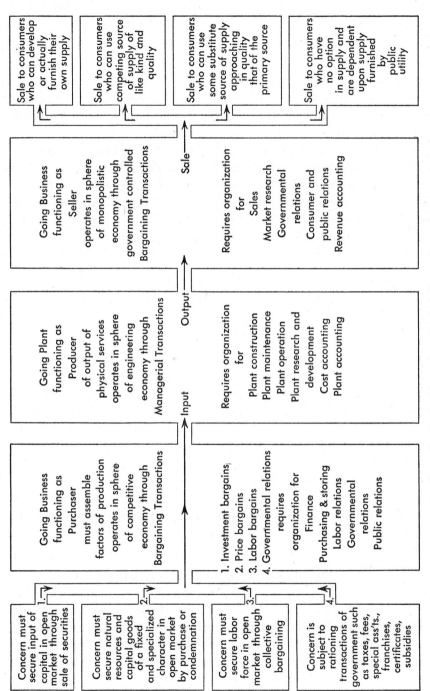

Going Business functioning as Purchaser must assemble factors of production operates in sphere of competitive economy through Bargaining Transactions

1. Investment bargains,
2. Price bargains
3. Labor bargains
4. Governmental relations requires organization for
   Finance
   Purchasing & storing
   Labor relations
   Governmental relations
   Public relations

Going Plant functioning as Producer of output of physical services operates in sphere of engineering economy through Managerial Transactions

Requires organization for
Plant construction
Plant maintenance
Plant operation
Plant research and development
Cost accounting
Plant accounting

Going Business functioning as Seller operates in sphere of monopolistic economy through government controlled Bargaining Transactions

Requires organization for
Sales
Market research
Governmental relations
Consumer and public relations
Revenue accounting

Input — Output — Sale

Concern must secure input of capital in open market through sale of securities

Concern must secure natural resources and capital goods of a fixed and specialized character in open market by purchase or condemnation

Concern must secure labor force in open market through collective bargaining

Concern is subject to rationing transactions of government such as taxes, fees, special ass'ts., franchises, certificates, subsidies

Sale to consumers who can develop or actually furnish their own supply

Sale to consumers who can use competing source of supply of like kind and quality

Sale to consumers who can use some substitute source of supply approaching in quality that of the primary source

Sale to consumers who have no option in supply and are dependent upon supply furnished by public utility

Chart X   Transactions of a Typical Going Concern.

223

tiating cost bargains. Government price-fixing thus involves the investigation of investment, wage, price, and tax transactions. Collectively, these transactions provide the so-called *cost-of-service* basis of regulation because the government in fixing rates must pass upon these going business transactions and also upon the efficiency with which the engineering organization of the going plant conducts its managerial transactions. Only reasonable costs may be passed on to customers in the rates they pay.

The parties to such transactions are always the legal concern on the one hand; the stockholders, bondholders, directors, officers, employees, and customers taken in their individual capacities, on the other hand. At the same time that the interests of these second parties conflict, they are aware that, so far as the continued security of their property, loans, offices, jobs, services, and markets is concerned, they must cooperate.

Detailed consideration of public utility management belongs elsewhere than in a general work. A word should be added, however, about the bearing of the idea of a going concern upon managerial policies. Cooperation or the lack of it may make or mar any business. From this point of view a going concern is an administrative scheme whereby rules of practice are applied in a manner which will correlate the different economic activities, compose and control nascent conflicts of interest, and keep these elements in a state of cooperation. This applies also to the so-called public relations. The important relations here are with employees, consumers (actual and potential), and public authorities. A public utility executive is in a sense a quasi-public official. In his dealings with customers and others there is need for a judicial temper and a disposition to hold the balance even. Moreover, the needs of regulation tend to throw upon the business a burden of routine in reports, hearings, inspections, and litigations. This restraint upon managerial initiative may be chafing; yet it is a mode of procedure arising out of the aspects of publicity which surround these businesses, requiring special talents and a broadened point of view.

Meaning of Control of the Market

What most distinguishes public utilities from other businesses is that they have achieved a high degree of control of their marketing areas. This manifests itself primarily through the exercise of economic power in selling transactions where, unless restrained by regulation, they would have monopoly powers over price. Yet there are some distinct limits other than those imposed by government within which this bargaining advantage is confined.

In the market for producers' goods and services, that is to say, in the case of cost bargains, utilities operate in what is dominantly an open market. But even in these purchasing transactions a given utility may be operating in a partially controlled market. That is certainly true of labor markets where, as a consequence of labor unionism and collective bargaining, there has been substituted for the indispensability of the individual, the indispensability of the group; that is to say, a utility in its bargaining is now up against collective action instead of individual action. The processes of vertical integration, particularly as promoted under the aegis of holding companies, have also tended to eliminate competition in whole or in part, as illustrated in the relations between the American Telephone and Telegraph Company and the Western Electric Company, the supply organization of the system. However, it would be exceptional if a given utility had a complete buyer's monopoly (monopsony). Least of all is this true in the market for loanable funds, which continues to be one of the most open markets with which the utility business is surrounded. Regulatory pressures, therefore, tend to be relaxed in proportion as the bargaining, whether of buying or selling, takes place in an ambient atmosphere of free and working competition. Regulation thus rests in the main upon the norms of competitive costs and reflects what has been called *arms-length bargaining.*

As was said above, a public utility's power over price is manifested primarily in selling transactions. While the *horizontal* integration movement has made most public utilities, with the outstanding exception of transportation, into single sources of supply in a given market area, some important elements of direct and indirect competition remain. We distinguish four strategic situations in which the seller of public utility services may find himself. (See Chart X.)

One is typified by sales to consumers who are in a position to develop their own source of supply. This potential or actual competition resides in consumers themselves, who may go back to their own original source of supply or undertake to supply themselves with a new or substitute facility. They then operate in accordance with the all-important economic principle of substitution which provides a limit beyond which even a monopolist, regulated or unregulated, may not go in his power over price. This alternative opportunity is open especially to customers who consume large quantities and can, therefore, take advantage of some of the economies of the load factor and of large-scale operation.

The railway transportation industry has become peculiarly subject to the inroads of substitute competition with the development of new technologies. Highway transport by motor car, motor truck, and motor bus competes with the urban and intercity railway, powered by the electric motor, or the steam or diesel engine. From another direction, and undermining particularly the market of the intercity railway, have come new carriers by waterline, pipeline, and airline. Of these only the pipeline, like the railway, supplies its own way and structures while the remaining two share these costly fixed facilities with other carriers—facilities which the government has supplied for them in the first place. It is in this connection that the distinction between private, contract, and common carriers becomes important, since only the common carriers are now subject to economic regulation as public utilities.

A second situation in which a producer may find himself is one in which he shares the market with competitors who furnish a supply of the same kind and quality. Although historically it was once quite prevalent, such competition is now much less important. Through exclusive franchises and certificates of convenience and necessity, the government now rations these competitive opportunities, providing either monopolistic markets or markets in which the competitors are strictly limited. In both commercial highway and airway transport the federal and state governments are following a policy of limited but balanced competition. A public utility properly so-called has complete control of the market so far as this form of competition is concerned. However, the public utility status has been accorded common carriers by motor vehicle and by air in order to preserve a condition of stabilized competition and to prevent the outbreak of cutthroat competition. To be sure, competition may even arise between two monopolistic utilities at the periphery of their service areas where customers are so located as to take service from either of them. Such "raids" are usually controlled by regulating commissions through certification, particularly if the conflict arises between public utilities and cooperatives. One form of indirect competition is, however, bound to persist where consumers are free to locate in any one of several monopolistic markets. Such competition in the location of industry is primarily interregional and thus ineradicable.

A third situation confronting a given utility may be that some consumers are in a position to use some substitute service furnished by another utility. Such interutility competition is common enough, as we have already noted, between the various branches of the transport industry. It also obtains over the rest of the utility field, as when electric service competes with gas service and telegraph service with telephone service. This form of competition is effective to the extent that the substitute service approaches in convenience and cost the primary service. Unless technological progress is to cease, this form of competition is also largely ineradicable, although it may need to be coordinated.

As a fourth and dominant segment of public utility markets we must distinguish sale to consumers who are dependent upon the supply furnished by the public utility enfranchised in a given service area. This is the market situation for which the public utility institution was developed. There are no competitors because the franchise is exclusive. Customers cannot supply themselves nor are adequate substitutes available to them. They are compelled by the essentiality of the service to buy in a controlled market.

When a public utility has thus achieved complete economic and legal control over its market, it has eliminated a principal cause of insecurity of investment. The nature of the franchise, and the degree of economic control vouchsafed a utility by its certificate to do business, is here determinative. Yet, a utility may be so entrenched in a particular market that, even if it did not have an exclusive, indeterminate franchise, its financial power to meet competition through rate reductions, its record of having rendered adequate service at reasonable rates, and its prior ownership of the best located sites may deter effective competition from entering a field not legally closed to a newcomer. The history of public utility expansion into new territory provides many illustrations where construction was undertaken to forestall competition. Under these conditions effective regulation must do the work of competition.

A New Concept of Control of the Market

The reappearance of competitive elements since the early 1920's in the market for mass transportation in our metropolitan areas has enforced a realignment of the concept of monopoly in order to achieve a tighter control of the market, both legally and economically. Here common carriers, usually owned by the public, have tried to preempt the supply, not only of a single transport medium but also of all major substitute mediums. Besides some foreign examples which could be cited, like the London Passenger Transport Board, an outstanding case in this country is the Philadelphia Rapid Transit Company. This utility has combined under common control all passenger transport by electric street car, elevated and subway, motor bus, taxicab, and for a time, by airplane. In Chicago in 1947, a public agency, the Chicago Transit Authority, took over the independently operated surface lines and also the elevated lines and combined them with the municipally operated subways. When a single utility thus controls all competitive services, the monopoly is complete, and public service can be fully planned and co-ordinated. Customers have only two alternatives: either to serve themselves or go without service, neither of which may be an accessible or reasonable alternative opportunity. Under such arrangements control of the market is complete. The dependence of the consumer upon a single monopoly and the weakness of the consumer vis-à-vis the economic power of the producer constitute the overpowering reasons for interference with the bargaining and managerial transactions of the utility by means of the rationing transactions of governments.

It is sufficient at this point to refer back to what was said in Chapter 8 regarding security of tenure as derived from the various types of franchises, including the indeterminate permit. Particular attention should be directed to the way in which antiduplication and certificate of convenience and necessity legislation, as administered by commissions, controls extensions into new territory. By this means, commissions not only prevent competition from arising but they also try to restrict the investment of capital to markets where there is a reasonable promise that a remunerative business can eventually be built up. This is best illustrated by the certification powers of the Civil Aeronautics Board. By granting or withholding certificates, commissions stand at the gateway to markets, rationing out these economic opportunities. Only utilities rendering adequate service at reasonable rates get these guaranties.

Control of the market is further strengthened by safeguarding the power of governments to take over these private enterprises by paying "just compensation" for them. Paradoxically, an exclusive franchise, terminable only by exercising such a purchase option, has much to commend it. This has been the law in Wisconsin and some other states that have adopted the indeterminate permit. In these states the ever present threat of public acquisition strengthens the hands of the commissions in enforcing proper regulatory standards.

The competition of publicly owned utilities with privately owned ones, when once established, is not as readily eliminated. Uneconomical competition, with its duplication of investment, has damaged both incumbents. For some time a municipally owned street railway divided the Detroit market with a private company until finally municipalized. In San Francisco the two tracks of a municipal electric railway paralleled the double tracks of the Market Street Railway Company, the four tracks creating a public nuisance even on phenomenally wide Market Street. Los Angeles, California, and Seattle, Washington, suffered the "slings and arrows" of public versus private competition for a time until public acquisition finally provided monopolistic control of the market, thus ending the needless duplication of facilities and making possible an economical supply of standardized service that was area-wide. From the long-run point of view the policy of competition is destructive of market stability and is a preventable cause of insecurity of investment.

The Control of Abandonments of Markets

If it is important to protect the public interest in connection with a procedure by means of which control of the market is built up, it is equally important to protect these same public interests in connection with the surrender of these markets. Public utilities assume the obligation to render service when they secure a franchise or a certificate of convenience and necessity, which is again the subject matter of dispute when utilities request permission to abandon service in whole or in part. The Transportation Act of 1920 for the first time provided that "no carrier . . . shall abandon all or any portion of a line of railroad or the operation thereof unless and until there shall first have been obtained from the Commission a certificate that the present or future public convenience and necessity permit of such abandonment." Some state utility commissions had obtained such powers to control railway abandonments even earlier. Owing to the small investment involved, Congress did not, however, see fit to give the Commission power to compel motor carriers to continue operations if a route turned out to be unprofitable.

Abandonment applications usually arise when railways, originally constructed to market some natural resource like lumber or mineral products, lose the economic basis for their support as these resources approach exhaustion and no other adequate supplementary traffic has developed in the meantime. Other applications for abandonments have come from urban and interurban electric railways and from the branch lines of steam railways, all alike suffering from motor vehicle competition.[1] Usually they are coupled with requests to substitute motorized service. In the period since the depression, the ICC has authorized the abandonment of over 3,500 miles of trackage.

Authorities are divided upon the question of abandonments. No more vexing problems arise because, in working out a solution, commissions enter the borderland of regulation. At one time utilities contended that they could surrender their charter, cease operations, and sell their properties without

[1] MacDonald, T. H., "Commercial Vehicles on Free Highways," *Journal of Land and Public Utility Economics*, Vol. 1, p. 385, October, 1925. See also Trumbower, H. R., "Abandonments of Railway Service," *Journal of Political Economy*, February, 1926.

securing the consent of public authorities. A Connecticut court,[2] however, held very early that a corporation had no right to abandon a public service enterprise against the will of the state. The court concluded:

Upon principle it would seem plain that railroad property, once devoted and essential to public use, must remain pledged to that use, so as to carry to full completion the purpose of its creation; and that this public right, existing by reason of the public exigency, demanded by the occasion, and created by the exercise by a private person of the powers of a state, is superior to the property rights of corporations, stockholders, and bondholders.

The foregoing does not imply that public utilities may not abandon unprofitable undertakings; to hold otherwise would amount to a "taking" of property without due process of law. It merely means that the consent of the state must first be secured. This conclusion harks back to the fundamentals of the public utility as a legal institution. Although the obligation to serve the public is voluntarily assumed, these duties are subject to future public regulation.[3] This includes regulation of the liberty to slough off obligations assumed under charters. Abandonment of service is thus not made to depend merely upon the consent of two-thirds of a company's stockholders; otherwise, as one commission said, a "State's economic structure would be on a shallow foundation." It was also felt that protection should be given to bondholders who had purchased bonds upon the faith that service would be continued. In this connection attention is always called by protestants to the public aids afforded these enterprises in the past and to the benefits derived by them from the taxing power and from the power of eminent domain.

It would seem that the weight of authority has settled this question so that there can be no doubt that public utilities may not abandon operations without governmental consent. But the further question must also be answered, whether administrative commissions may decide what abandonments are proper, or whether the legislature must be consulted. This problem had not arisen heretofore because abandonments were very rare, and hence statutes were silent upon the subject. In one case, the Georgia Supreme Court decided that since the Railroad Commission of Georgia did not have express statutory authority, it did not have the implied power to permit abandonments. Legal obligations to serve under a charter are different from those merely determining the quantity and quality of the service.[4]

The Ohio and New York Commissions[5] have taken the stand that the

<hr/>

[2] *Gates v. Boston & N.Y. Air Line R.R. Co.*, 53 Conn. 333, p. 343 (1885).
[3] Re: *Lima Elec. Lt. and R. Co.*, P.U.R., 1915 C. 871.
[4] *Railroad Com. v. Macon Ry. & Lt. Co.*, P.U.R., 1921 C. 540.
[5] Re: *Lake Erie B.G. & N.R. Co.*, P.U.R., 1916 F. 553; cf. *Day v. Tacoma R. and Power Co.*, P.U.R., 1915 C. 593; Re: *Charleston Interurban R. Co.*, P.U.R., 1916 F. 338.

question is one which must be settled by a court. Kansas, on the other hand, decided through its Supreme Court that service may not be abandoned without Commission consent.[6] In a few states this power is directly conferred by statute, and the courts have there upheld it. In other states the power to control abandonments is inferred from the power to control service, and in these its constitutional validity is in some doubt.

Economic Limitations upon the Power to Control Abandonments

We see in such moot questions the workings of legislative and judicial empiricism as these sovereignties experiment with the best mode of developing the public utility institution. Certainly, if these industries perform public functions and have undertaken them voluntarily, they can be made to continue rendering service either until the community is willing to undertake the service itself or until there has been time for some other adjustment.

As long as they are conducted as business enterprises with no coercion of the consumer, the economic nature of public utilities involves risks, since the demand for their services may decline. The question is: Who shall assume these risks? Certainly, the community is not required to underwrite them. But there are also economic limitations with respect to private companies who cannot be required "to throw good money after bad money." If the market as a whole in which the utility has a monopoly can economically support the enterprise, abandonments in a part of the field of service are a matter of public convenience; that is to say, they become a matter of reasonable or unreasonable discrimination. Such questions are a concern of public policy and must be decided by a public agency; they may not be left to the discretion or private policy of utility management.

However, if the entire enterprise becomes unprofitable and moribund, the problem becomes one of striking a balance between public and private interests; that is to say, determining the amount of economic loss which a utility may be made to suffer in view of the superior public interest in the continuance of service. In the long run and under "due process," the state cannot compel the rendition of a service which is uneconomical.[7] The confidence in, and credit of, such an enterprise would have been destroyed long before its operations would have to be wound up. Though the question of complete abandonment of service would have to come before a court, the

---

[6] *State ex. rel. Caster v. Kansas Postal Teleg-Cable Co.*, P.U.R., 1915 E., p. 222. Other states taking the same position are Cal., Colo., Ill., La., Me., Mont., Neb., Utah, Va., and Wis.

[7] 271 U.S. 153 (1926) and 320 U.S. 685, 690 (1944).

public interest in continuing an uneconomical service would have to give way before economic necessity after owners had lost their equity. Bondholders would then step into the shoes of the stockholders. It would not be "due process of law" to compel stockholders or bondholders to furnish additional sums in order to maintain unremunerative service. Only a detailed analysis of the equities of each case will reveal when, from a social point of view, further losses to investors should be prevented by authorizing the surrender of a franchise.

Residual Risks

After everything possible has been done to assure a utility legal control of its market, there remains a residuum of risk which cannot be eliminated. The decline of the electric railway in interurban transport and in urban transit in our smaller cities is everywhere demonstrating that mass transportation as a marketable service has disappeared. Consumers simply will not use the outmoded vehicle. Such utilities are no longer going concerns. Even the telegraph as a means of communication has also lost some of its original essentiality of service.

When in our larger cities a public carrier is nevertheless required to serve at least that part of the market which remains, only two policies remain as alternatives: either the privately owned common carrier must be freed from taxation and eventually subsidized or he must become public-owned with deficits met by taxation. This generally means receivership, bankruptcy, and financial reorganization, with losses to both owners and creditors.

The financial fate of the transportation facilities of Chicago affords an outstanding object lesson of these residual risks. Utilities once characterized by the muckrakers of an earlier period as the domain of "traction barons" have passed "under the hammer." In the forty years between 1907, when resettlement franchises were negotiated, and October 1, 1947, when the transit facilities were sold to the Chicago Transit Authority, they lost their going-concern characteristics, and their control of the mass transportation market had to be radically reorganized. In 1913 five electric railways were consolidated for unified operation purposes into the "Chicago Surface Lines." Similarly, five companies, each operating parts of an elevated rarilway system, were merged into the Chicago Rapid Transit Company in 1918. Eventually, these companies passed through receivership and bankruptcy, with the federal court fixing the extent of the losses to be sustained by the bondholders. According to a study made by the Vice-Chairman of the Chicago

Transit Board, the aggregate losses in principal and unpaid interest, after the trustees in bankruptcy had distributed certain payments, were as follows:

	Total Debt	*Distribution*	*Net Loss*
Surface lines	$201,295,101.28	$ 91,287,929.89	$110,007,171.39
Elevated lines	168,705,944.98	19,191,965.82	149,513,979.16
Total	$370.001,046.26	$110,479,895.71	$259,521,150.55

The same authority estimates that, not counting unpaid dividends some of which had not been paid since 1927, stockholders had lost an additional investment conservatively estimated at over $12 million. He also points out that the federal government through the Public Works Administration had contributed $25,967,000 as a grant in aid of subway construction by the city. We quote from a summary of his findings as to the reasons for these financial reverses, among which those growing out of inadequate control of the market should be noted:

Lack of good public relations; the failure of the companies to protect themselves against new bus lines, with the result that some of the choicest potential routes were taken by the companies that developed this new field; inadequate rates fixed by regulatory commissions; the lack of an adequate depreciation reserve fund which in turn is based upon inadequacy of rates; the supplying of off-hour service, particularly nighttime service, at a great loss; the rendering of service in areas which did not pay the cost of operation; duplication of services and expenses by the Surface Lines and Elevated System; the spread of population and industrial plants into outlying areas and the suburbs; and above all, the competition of the privately owned automobiles.

Conclusion. We conclude upon consideration of the foregoing history that the essence of the public utility problem from an institutional point of view resides in the degree of essentiality of the service and the degree of control of the market accorded a given concern. Stated in another way, it is a question of the degree of economic power to which the consumer is exposed under given marketing arrangements, which may have to be balanced by the exercise of political power either to promote or to restrain.

2. ADMINISTRATIVE ASPECTS OF PUBLIC UTILITY REGULATION

15. THE
ADMINISTRATIVE
COMMISSION

We have already placed the commission in its historical context. In the present chapter we shall take a closer look at its legal status and proper functioning. We have distinguished between the investigatory, advisory, and mandatory commission. They may also be classified as federal, state, and local commissions in accordance with the framework of government in which they serve. Local commissions are no longer of much importance; we will therefore restrict ourselves to state and federal commissions.

Legal Status

It is the duty of commissions to carry into effect the policies laid down by the legislative branch of the government. In doing so they exercise legislative power, in fact if not in law, under a broad delegation of authority to make rules and regulations. Such delegation of authority was promptly attacked as unconstitutional, but it was as promptly upheld by the courts if there was a reasonable definition of the legislative purpose of the commission. In applying principles or standards derived from the legislature as definitions of legislative purposes, the commission lays down rules of conduct for the future by issuing general orders or specific orders, the former addressed to a designated classification of utilities and the latter to specific utilities. A general order may require all electric utilities of a certain size to use a certain classification of accounts, while a specific order may require utility X to charge certain rates for service after a given date. The commission may not, however, enforce its own orders because utilities have a constitutional right to due process of law. This means that the order may become the subject of controversy before a designated judicial tribunal where the case will be decided upon its merits. If the order is sustained by the court, judicial machinery is available for its enforcement.

While commissions are an arm of the legislature, the original intention was to free them as much as possible from direct political influences. By this means it was believed that, with their expert staff and broad investigatory and rule-making powers, they could combine scientific research with flexible administration and thereby assist the legislatures in achieving sound public policies. It is not straining the facts too much to think of a commission as being a permanent legislature with a specialized jurisdiction. To be sure, a legislature, being a representative body, is a cross section of the public and tends to express public opinion on matters of public policy; but it needs a technical body as an aid in the investigation of facts and in securing administration and enforcement.

As stated, the creation of commissions was opposed on the theory that they constituted an unlawful delegation of legislative powers. But the United States Supreme Court overruled this objection in the case of the Interstate Commerce Commission by pointing out that a government which is empowered to do an act must also be allowed to select the means. In essence, this means that while a legislature cannot delegate its power to make a law, "it can make a law to delegate a power to determine some fact or state of things upon which the law makes or intends to make its own action depend."

In the early days, objection was also raised to giving the commissions' power to compel the attendance and testimony of witnesses, the production of records, etc. as being a usurpation of judicial power and an invasion of personal liberty. This barrier has also been leveled, since it was held that these powers were merely incidental to its duty to investigate and did not constitute a delegation of judicial power nor an invasion of personal liberty.

Commission Organization

The many years of experimentation with commissions has afforded certain conclusions as to their internal organization which we will survey briefly. No useful purpose is served in burdening this account with needless detail, which is subject to constant change in any event as new political administrations come to power. Only what appear to be the most abiding and useful features will be stressed. It should be recalled that in addition to commissions in each of the states, in the District of Columbia, and in the Territories of Hawaii and Puerto Rico, the important federal commissions regulating utilities are the Interstate Commerce Commission (ICC), the Civil Aeronautics Board (CAB), the Federal Power Commission (FPC), the Federal Communications Commission (FCC), and the Securities and Exchange Commission (SEC). Differences between them will reflect the size of their respective tasks and the exigencies of their local or functional setting. Only two examples of internal organization of state commissions—one functional (Wisconsin), the other by utilities (California)—are shown in Charts XI and XII.

Selection, number, and qualifications of members. The universal method of selection for membership on federal commissions is by appointment of the President with the advice and consent of the Senate. At times furious political battles are fought over confirmation of individual appointees on account of their espousal of policies or political affiliations. State commissions, some thirty of them, are appointed by the Governors and confirmed by the Senate, with the remainder elected at large or by districts. Appointment seems to have a better effect upon the caliber of membership because competent men often cannot be elected nor will they stand for election. There is something stultifying in the spectacle of candidates making campaign promises when it may often be necessary to apply the law in the teeth of widespread public disapproval.

The number of members varies between one and eleven, with federal commissions never having less than five members, while the modal state commission has three members. Among federal commissions, the FPC, the CAB and the SEC have five members; the FCC, with its jurisdiction over the telephone, telegraph, and radio industries, has seven members; and the ICC, with its flar-flung jurisdiction over transportation, has eleven members. It is important that the number be an odd one to secure a majority if the commission should be divided over some important question. The larger boards also offer an opportunity to secure variety in training and experience. It is most important that the members be able to work together despite division on questions of policy.

Statutory qualifications for membership have become less important because the experts on the staff supply the qualifications once deemed to be so important for the members. The possession of common sense and political discretion can be a more important qualification than a high degree of expertness. Wisdom in council and a capacity to size up alternatives and to choose between them may be the real hallmark of a good commissioner. It is, however, a common requirement, especially of federal commissions, that the membership be bipartisan in character. Commissions as policy-making and enforcing bodies must strike a balance between continuity of policy and response to changing political pressures. Staggering the terms of office is also important in this connection because of the experience available from holdover members.

On an entirely different basis is the usual statutory requirement that

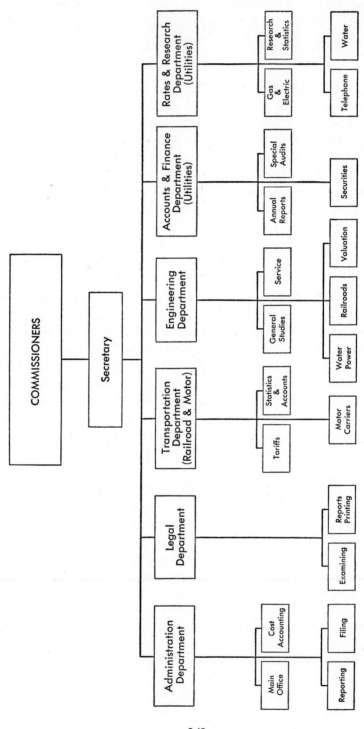

Chart XI Organization Chart of Public Service Com. of Wisconsin. (Prepared by Commission.)

240

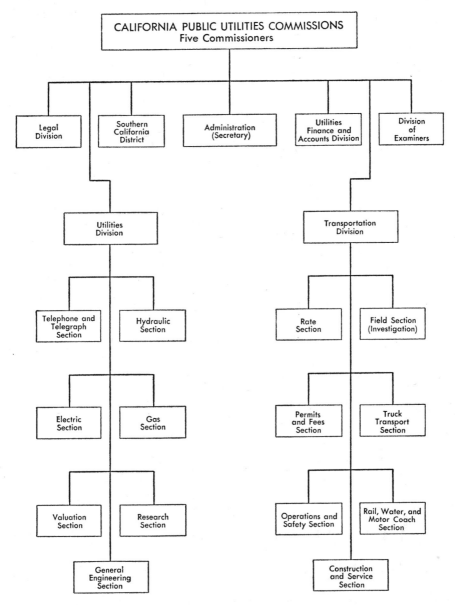

Chart XII Organization Chart (California). (Prepared by Commission.)

the members of boards and commissions have no official connections with, or pecuniary interest in, the public utilities under their jurisdiction. Usually, they are also required to devote their full time to the job. With the magnitude of the financial interests at stake, the part-time commissioner should now be an anomaly. Moreover, the absolute necessity of maintaining public confidence in the disinterestedness of the regulatory process requires that the membership, and the staff as well, be screened against the importunities of those who might be tempted to subvert them. Since commission regulation is a substitute for competition, the public interest must always be kept paramount.

Tenure, salaries, and removal from office. The term of office varies between two and ten years, the most usual tenure being six years. The principle of overlapping terms has also proven useful because it assures some continuity of policies and the holdover of some commissioners after each election. Biennial gubernatorial elections restrict any other than a three-term governor from completely altering the political complexion of the modal commission. With the better commissions, there has always been more turnover in the membership of the commissions than in the membership of the staff, so that the staff has "carried" the commission. Nevertheless, the longer tenures are definitely to be preferred along with reappointments, for the experience which comes to even the most uninitiated appointee has value. There can, of course, be no statutory prescription ensuring competence.

Salaries adequate to attract and hold qualified men are as important for commissioners as for staff members. The honor and distinction going with public office and with a career of public service are insufficient incentives in the long run. Regulation also has some of the aspects of management; hence the spectacle of underpaid commissioners, with uncertain and short political tenures, attempting to meet the highly compensated representatives of management is not a reassuring one. As a matter of empirical fact, the annual salary range now lies between $2,000 for the poorer state commissions and $17,500 for the better ones, with all federal commissions in the higher salary brackets.

For effectiveness in administration there must be the power of removal from office. This is usually lodged in the executive and is accomplished by executive order. The alternative of impeachment is too cumbersome. The removal of a commissioner must be justified by a cause such as incompetence, neglect of duty, or malfeasance or misconduct in office. The commissioner is entitled to due process, such as notice and opportunity to be heard; but the executive has the last word if the duties of a board or commissioner are purely ministerial. If the power of removal exists, it does not usually need to be exercised. However, this power of the executive is circumscribed in the case of the so-called independent commissions where the commission is an agent of the legislature and the removal of a commissioner may be a result of conflict between the policy espoused by the executive and that of the commissioner. For instance, the court refused to sustain the removal power of President Franklin Roosevelt in the case of Commissioner Humphrey of the Federal Trade Commission [*Rathbun v. U.S.* (295 U.S. 602)] because of differences over matters of policy. Such changes in personnel must await the end of the period of statutory tenure.

Staff organization. Almost universally, employees of commissions are appointed and continue to serve under civil service rules. This means permanent tenure, with promotions and compensation in accordance with procedures of classified civil service. Here, also, the adequacy of the level of compensation must comport with the responsibility and importance of the job. Commissions must be willing to pay the price for excellence. On occasion, outside experts will be retained on a consulting basis, though the larger and better commissions will rely upon their own permanent, nonpolitical staff. An efficient and loyal bureaucracy is the *sine qua non* of good governmental administration. Here, as elsewhere, career men protected by civil service and pension plans are the substance of government in a democracy.

Little need be said regarding the way in which the work of the typical commission is divided. It usually follows functional lines, the degree of subdivision depending upon the size of the commission, which is commensurate with the funds available, and the extent of the commission's jurisdiction. The smaller state commissions operate with as few as ten to twenty employees; the larger ones employ hundreds, while federal commissions will have several thousand employees.

Functioning beneath the commission executive will be the Secretary, who usually is the chief administrative officer. The bulk of a commission's work, arising from its investigatory and case-handling functions, is usually divided into an engineering department, a legal department, an accounting and finance department, and a rate department, all with their corresponding technical experts and supporting personnel. The essence of the job is the ability of the chief to coordinate the work of accountants, engineers, lawyers, economists, and technicians of different descriptions. The annual reports of commissions, with their wealth of descriptive information, should be consulted for a clear understanding of commission organization, since constantly changing details make specific delineation impossible. However, see Charts XI and XII for typical examples.

Commission Procedure

Generally speaking, authority is conferred upon commissions to adopt rules and regulations governing hearings, investigations, and proceedings before them. The more vital regulations are, however, specifically provided for by statute. A new movement to standardize and modernize procedure for all administrative agencies was begun by certain studies of the American Bar Association and first enacted into law by North Dakota in 1941, followed in 1943 by Wisconsin. These are known under the title of Uniform Administrative Procedure Acts. Some of the statutory provisions are highly technical and will not be discussed; only the more important procedural steps and the spirit which animates them will concern us here.

The original reason for the grant of authority to adopt rules of practice and procedure was to ensure administrative flexibility and to prevent the burdening of procedure by technical rules of evidence such as courts require. For instance, in some states it was early provided that "no informality in any hearing, investigation or proceeding, or in the manner of taking testimony shall invalidate any order, decision, rule or regulation made, approved or confirmed by the commission." Something of this spirit still obtains in administrative proceedings, although the rules of practice have been tightened up. The rules of practice of commissions are usually published and are available to the public. They are subject to petition for amendment or repeal and may be appealed to the courts if they impair legal rights.

Rules of procedure must, of course, provide for the two essentials of "due process of law"; that is to say, reasonable prior notice and a public hearing.

Investigations—formal and informal. Since commissions are primarily agencies for hearing complaints, the procedure for bringing complaints is definitely fixed by statute. A *formal complaint* may be made by either public utilities or their customers. One or some specified larger number (often twenty-five) of customers comprising persons, firms, corporations, or associations may make a complaint; or any body politic or municipal corporation may bring a complaint in its capacity as representative of consumers generally. Commissions early introduced the practice of initiating investigations upon motion of the commission, without the intervention of a formal complaint. This procedure was believed to be in the interests of timid customers or those who feared retaliation at the hands of the utilities. It has now been expanded into a method whereby investigations may be so organized as to scope and subject matter in a manner designed to meet specific situations.

Investigations may likewise be started by *informal complaints* of *single individuals*. These will also be attended to promptly and may, if the matter is deemed important enough, be made the subject of a formal complaint upon the commission's own motion. The purpose of informal procedure is to make investigation and redress of grievances easy, inexpensive, and sufficiently comprehensive to reach the real difficulties in any situation.

Usually, upon receipt of a complaint, commissions are directed to make a preliminary investigation. If the facts appear to warrant further proceedings, a public hearing is held, with due notice (usually ten days) to all interested parties. The new rules of procedure provide that in any contested case the parties are to be given a clear statement of the issues involved so that the parties will not be confronted with charges they are not prepared to answer. The statement of issues usually accompanies the notice of hearing, with the statement repeated by the examiner before beginning to hear testimony. This modification arose out of the Kansas City Stockyards case [*Morgan v. U.S.*, 304 U.S. 1 (1938)], in which the company had not been informed as to the precise nature of the contentions and findings. The hearing had been conducted through an examiner, but the Secretary of Agriculture had issued the price-fixing order. The United States Supreme Court insisted that whoever made the order had to appraise the evidence, although the evidence might be taken by an examiner. This relaxed somewhat the earlier position of the Court that he who decides must also hear. What the Court wanted was to give the opposing parties an opportunity to know and meet the contending arguments, if they could.

The course of the proceeding is charted by keeping a complete record of the evidence. This consists of (1) the stenographic report of the testimony and exhibits of witnesses, (2) the oral arguments and printed briefs of the opposing attorneys, and (3) the scientific or technical facts of which the commission is permitted to take "official notice." Enlightening discussions of an informal nature, usually between commissioners or examiners on the one hand and attorneys or witnesses on the other, may take place, but these are kept "off the record." Evidence is introduced by the commission's staff as well as by the interested parties. Hearings may take on the character of mass meetings for "blowing off steam," or they may be somnolent proceedings where some of the participants fall asleep.

In order to facilitate investigations, commissions are empowered to summon witnesses and compel the submission of documents and records.

They are authorized to inspect and have access to all the properties and records of public utilities. The staff may prepare limited or extensive accounting audits and engineering surveys and appraisals. From the beginning, commissions were empowered to require the submission of annual or other periodic reports upon prescribed forms. In order that these reports and the records upon which they are based may be most effective in aiding the process of regulation in all its phases, commissions are empowered to prescribe uniform systems of accounts and accounting records. From these and other authoritative sources relevant statistical and economic data are derived. They may be published with interpretive comment in official reports. These data or abstracts therefrom may also be submitted as evidence in proceedings. With respect to material of which the commission takes "official notice," the Uniform Administrative Procedure Act requires that all interested parties be informed of such notice so that the parties may contest the validity of the facts so noticed.

It was common practice, and under the Uniform Procedure Acts it is obligatory, that all materials which may be used in arriving at a decision become a part of the record. This formalized procedure represents somewhat of a departure from the greater freedom of procedure in the past when commissions used materials outside the record, notably staff reports submitted to them privately, in reaching their conclusions. Now, reliance upon such outside evidence would be cause for reversal of an order if it should be judicially reviewed. Nevertheless, the impinging of outside considerations upon the minds of commissioners in reaching their decisions may be incapable of being compressed into an articulate major premise by some witness.

Administrative orders. In a functional sense the burden of complaints always is that the existing rates, services, or practices do not measure up to the legislative standard of reasonableness. After the investigations and hearings are concluded, the commissions are directed to make appropriate findings and issue orders either applying the appropriate remedies or dismissing the complaints. These are embodied in written opinions which summarize the evidence and the arguments, and which finally lead up to the "findings of fact" and "conclusions of law" which are the bases of the "administrative orders."

As already indicated, should commissioners find it impracticable to hear and read all the testimony, examiners may be authorized to conduct the hearings, to summarize the evidence, and to present the appropriate findings and orders in a report to the commission. The report is mailed to all interested parties, who may file exceptions. The commission will then make its own determinations. Unless the commission specifies a different date, its orders usually go into effect twenty days after the order is filed and communicated to the parties. The effective date of the order is usually left to the discretion of the commission and is fixed for each case. It is the statutory duty of the public utility and its agents to carry out the orders; penalties are provided for failing or refusing to obey.

Unless a regulating commission is also a court—as is the case in California—it does not have the power to enforce its own orders or impose fines and penalties, but it must seek the appropriate writ of mandamus (to compel) or injunction (to restrain) from a court. To be sure, the statutes also give the utility the opportunity to start proceedings for review of the commission's order in the courts. In such a proceeding, however, the commission's order is given the status of being "prima facie reasonable," which means that the burden of proof of unreasonableness rests upon the appealing party.

Some additional flexibility has been introduced by providing for rehearings, usually within a period during which an appeal to the courts must be effected. Any party to the case may apply to the commission for a rehearing on any or all issues decided. The commission may grant the application to rehear all the issues or only those it chooses to rehear, provided that, in the judgment of the commission, sufficient ground for rehearing has been shown to exist. The commission is thus given an opportunity to modify, amend or rescind its orders. This procedure takes the place of earlier arrangements whereby, if new evidence had been introduced upon appeal, the case was automatically returned to the commission. If, after rehearing, the new order is again appealed to the courts, a more effective judicial review of the issues can be obtained.

Judicial review. Orders of commissions were made subject to judicial review so that regulatory statutes might pass the vigilant eyes of the state or federal supreme courts as guardians of the respective constitutions. They are usually first appealed to courts of subordinate jurisdiction, called *trial courts*. In the case of the state commissions, the "record" is examined in these trial courts, and questions of fact are gone into. However, the decision of the commission as to the facts is taken as prima facie correct. The practice in some states of designating special courts as trial courts has been helpful because it tends to make these courts familiar with many technical details. These appeals for review of state commission orders have been called actions *de novo* when the appeal is to a lower federal court where a "special master" is appointed to take new evidence and a new record will be built up (usually with inordinate delay and expense). Appeals to federal courts are made when the orders of state commissions involve questions within the scope of the federal constitution, or when the case involves diversity of citizenship. When the appeal is from the order of a federal commission, the federal courts alone have jurisdiction, and the review is based upon the record before the commission.

An appeal may be taken from the lower state court to the supreme court of the state or to another state court that has final appellate jurisdiction. The final step in the process of judicial review of either federal or state commission orders is an appeal to the United States Supreme Court. No legal problem is finally disposed of until passed upon by this court.

In the 1920's when utilities were disposed to ignore judicial review of state commission orders in state courts and resort instead to the federal courts with their actions *de novo,* in the belief that the federal courts would afford a more conservative handling of the issues, the state commissions joined to secure passage of the Johnson Act of 1934. This was sponsored by Senator Hiram Johnson of California, the former governor, under whose leadership the California Railroad Commission had been reorganized in 1912. This federal law provided that no federal district court should have jurisdiction to restrain the enforcement of any rate order of any state commission where a "plain, speedy and efficient remedy" is available in the state courts. The effect of the statute, while helpful, was limited by judicial interpretation to states whose judicial practices conformed to the standards set by the federal courts.

More effective in securing speedy and impartial review of state commission orders may be the results achieveable under the Uniform Procedure Acts like those now in effect in Wisconsin and North Dakota. Under these, judicial review is not available unless application for rehearing has first been made, and then application for review must be made within thirty days after rehearing. The court may grant an injunction to stay the commission's order, but the utility must post sureties to cover the damages and costs involved. The review is based solely upon the record before the commission. Reversal or modification of the order may come (1) if contrary to the constitutional guaranties of the appellant, (2) if the commission has exceeded its statutory authority or jurisdiction, (3) if the procedure before the commission was unlawful, (4) if the order is not based on substantial evidence, and (5) if the decision is arbitrary or capricious. Most important is the requirement that the court take into consideration the experience, technical skill, specialized knowledge, and discretionary authority of the commission. This applies in particular to the commission's findings of fact, where reasonable men may differ and where the courts are now less willing to substitute their judgment for that of the commission's. Practice with respect to federal commission orders is similar.

Financing Commission Regulation

The three essentials for success in the regulation of public utilities are adequate powers, adequate personnel, and an adequate purse. The commissions which have built up the best reputation in their work over the years are those in which these three elements have been present in some degree. Most important, of course, has been the influence of men with capacity, vision, and integrity. But even men of this stamp on the boards and on the staff will be starved out if their reasonable financial requirements are not met. The present writer has studied and observed the operations of commissions for many years, and it is his conclusion that the most important one of the three is adequate financial support.

Appropriations and assessments. The principal means of support until the third decade of the present century have been legislative appropriations. The Interstate Commerce Commission has, on the whole, received more adequate support, although some of its activities, notably the physical valuation of the railroads of the country, was unduly delayed by the failure of Congress to make appropriations. The development of transport policies might well have taken a different direction if Congress had implemented the Commission with adequate appropriations before World War I. The Federal Power Commission was practically without a budget of its own until its reorganization in 1930. Depressions and periods of financial stringency bring cuts in appropriations, often at a time when the case work of commissions calling for rate reductions is on the increase. While the situation has improved to some extent, state commissions were notoriously underfinanced. All who have investigated the facts [1] testify to the inadequacy of commission budgets and recommend that more funds be made available.

The most effective step toward this end was taken by Wisconsin in 1931 and New York in 1934 when legislation was enacted which assessed the costs

[1] Glaeser, Martin G., *Outlines of Public Utility Economics* (New York: The Macmillan Co., 1927), p. 749.

Mosher, W., and Crawford, F., *Public Utility Regulation* (New York: Harper & Bros., 1933), pp. 69–70.

Proceedings, 1937, The National Association of Railroad and Utilities Commissioners, pp. 204, *ff.*

Ruggles, C. O., "Aspects of the Organization, Functions, and Financing of State Public Utility Commissions," Harvard Business Research Studies, No. 18.

of investigations against the utilities investigated. It is entirely proper that these costs of regulation be borne by the ratepayers instead of the taxpayers because the services are for their special benefit. By this means all regulatory activities of the commission necessary to carry out its statutory duties can be directly charged against the utilities affected. This power to levy special assessments is most important in connection with the comprehensive investigation of specific utilities, necessary from time to time; such revenue covers the cost of both regular and additional staff engaged in accounting, statistical, engineering, and other relevant studies.

In Wisconsin the rate of assessments is limited to four-fifths of one per cent of the gross intrastate revenues of the utility for the preceding year. This special assessment relates to expenditures which can be isolated and applies to electric, gas, telephone, water, and other utilities, whether publicly or privately owned. In order to defray the costs of regulation which cannot be isolated, the commission is authorized to make "remainder assessments" against *all* Wisconsin utilities up to one-fifth of one per cent of the gross intrastate operating revenues of the preceding year. Certain overhead costs, such as the salaries of the commissioners and the general costs of running the office, continue to come out of legislative appropriations. Depending, therefore, upon the amount of investigatory work undertaken, the budgets of commissions will vary from year to year. Making costs impinge upon the utility investigated has a salutary effect in achieving efficiency and a reasonable level of operating costs.

The way in which this dual system of financing operates by means of appropriations and special assessments is illustrated in Table VI, where certain figures from a recent biennial report are assembled.

Research activities. By implementing the commissions' investigatory and regulatory powers with adequate financing, the commissions are not only put in a position where they can do their job of fact-finding most efficiently, but they can also keep themselves and the utilities informed as to progress in the industry. Special investigations of a research character are continually necessary; the commission may carry these on by means of its own staff alone or in cooperation with the staffs of other commissions through the medium of their national association, the NARUC. In these activities they should and do cooperate with the managerial employees of the utilities.

This raises the question of the relationship between regulation and management. To avoid trenching on the prerogatives of management, investigations and orders affecting certain subject matters involve drawing a line proverbially difficult to determine. Investigatory activities, particu-

Table VI   Finances of Public Service Commission of Wisconsin

Fiscal Years	1950–51	1951–52
Appropriations and receipts		
General legislative appropriations	$227,115.00	$227,432.00
Cost of living bonus appropriations	22,366.59	29,924.95
Emergency board appropriations	2,320.25	. . . . . .
Total appropriations	$251,801.84	$257,356.95
Utility receipts		
Direct charges	$ 50,019.94	$ 57,854.12
Remainder assessment	249,693.24	310,445.06
Total	$299,713.18	$368,299.18
Railroad transportation receipts		
Direct charges	$ 4,357.08	$ 5,200.61
Remainder assessment	68,147.24	90,292.69
Total	$ 72,504.32	$ 95,493.30
Fees for removal of material from outlying waters	$ 30.00	$ 5.00
Total appropriations and receipts	$624,049.34	$721,154.43

larly if cooperative in nature, are not likely to involve direct interference with management. They may suggest or even lead to specific regulatory orders, but such orders (like those involving accounting) usually can be kept free from the element of compulsion. In any event each commission order must rest upon its own special facts as to whether it constitutes encroachment upon the domain of management. The significance of research investigations is that they may forestall conflicts between regulation and management and enable the two phases of social control to work together. Worth-while activities of trade associations, such as the Edison Electric Institute, American Water Works Association, and American Gas Association, could well be coordinated with these researches.

Some Current Criticisms of Commissions

In order to understand some current criticisms of commissions, it is necessary to recall something of the legal status of commissions and the nature of the regulatory problem. While it is true that commission orders create legal rights and duties, these narrow legal adjudications do not touch the heart of the regulatory problem. It is less important, for instance, that a rate fixed by a commission be nonconfiscatory than that it be a rate which adjusts the conflicting interests of owners, lenders, and users into a mutuality which achieves the proper balance between these interests, preserving and advancing the economic health of the going concern. The regulatory process in advancing the public interest is a unity of saving, risk-taking, and managing in the production and sale of goods and services. It involves cooperation between legislatures which lay down policies, administrators who carry the policies into effect, and courts which finally adjudicate the rights and duties. For best results the regulatory agency should be accorded an independent status within the area of its responsibility. The regulatory agency is subject to legislative investigations; it must operate within the limitations of its budgets; it cannot be unamenable to the appointing and removing power of the executive. For these reasons, a criticism made (particularly of federal commissions) in 1941 by the President's Committee on Administrative Management, to the effect that independent status of commissions makes them irresponsible and a "headless fourth branch of the government," misses the point of the investigational function of the commissions and their capacity as experts to contribute, with a minimum of political interference, to the solution of long-run problems of the industries. To be sure, commissions could be fruitfully relieved of certain housekeeping duties and of some irrelevant ministerial functions, but one must be sure that these do not contribute in some measure to a fuller understanding of the problems confronting the commissions before handing them over to an executive agency. In correlating the commissions' budgetary, personnel, and housekeeping problems with those of executive agencies, the practice has been introduced of letting the President designate the chairman of the newer commissions and making him responsible for housekeeping functions instead of having him elected by the membership or serving on the rotational principle. This practice could be extended to state commissions and give the governors some additional control over administrative agencies without sacrificing their essential independence.

The Peoples' Counsel. In 1930 the majority report of a New York Commission on Revision of Public Service Commissions Law came forward with a proposal that a deputy attorney-general be appointed whose entire time would be devoted to representing the public before the commission. The idea back of the proposal, since acted upon in a few states, was to emphasize the judicial character of the commission's activities and to meet the criticism that the commission could not possibly act as prosecutor and judge in the same proceeding. Whether called a "Public Counselor" (as in Indiana) or a "People's Counsel" (as in Maryland), this officer would be independent of the commission, although attached to it, and would be authorized to use the services of the staff in carrying out his duties. He would appear in behalf of customers and the public in all commission hearings and in all proceedings before courts where the commission is a party. Proponents of the scheme claim success for it but it has not been greeted with a great deal of enthusiasm by the generality of commissioners and staff members, who dislike the criticism implied therein. The better commissions contend that such a functionary is unnecessary and that his presence tends to exaggerate the political element in the work of the commission. The present writer holds the opinion that commissions should not exaggerate the judicial aspects of their duties, which the segregation of their investigational activities would tend to induce. After all, hearing complaints, initiating investigations, and actively promoting improvements in the public services was the original public purpose in setting them up. It will not advance this purpose to strip them of their precarious and hard-won independence; neither will it help to make them into judicial slot machines.

16. *ACCOUNTING*
METHODS AND
REGULATION

The purpose of accounting systems is to set forth the sources, utilization, and disposition of pecuniary values. Every business unit which becomes a going concern has an accounting and record-keeping organization which can supply, more or less adequately, the current facts with regard to income and expenditure and the historical record of these transactions. Accounting as a practical art is, of course, as old as business, but as a science it dates from the attempts of Italian merchants in the sixteenth century to apply certain mathematical principles to their bookkeeping. From these beginnings accountancy has developed into a separate discipline which is being systematized and elaborated by specialists. In the nineteenth century the science of statistics was developed as an aid in the interpretation of mass phenomena. Now the methodology of accountancy and statistics is combined to aid business management in solving business problems. With the coming of regulation, governments have seen the need of further expanding these accounting and record-keeping activities and of making them serve also the needs of governmental agencies in their work of exercising control over business.

Development of Accounting Regulation

At first there was much opposition to publicizing the information that accounts could give; hence also, there was opposition to their regulation by government. The information was deemed to be properly available only to management and not to be revealed to outsiders, especially not to competitors. The first breaches in the wall of secrecy were made when charters or special legislation required early railroads to submit annual reports. The breach was widened when utilities were required to reveal facts in connection with the sale of securities. But these reports were often inaccurate and misleading and their nonuniformity did not permit comparisons. Only by going back of the reports and into the accounting systems themselves could the real facts be obtained. This step was first taken by Massachusetts, which in 1876 directed its board of railroad commissioners to "prescribe a system on which the books and accounts of corporations operating railroads or street railways should be kept in a uniform manner." It also gave the commission power to inspect books of account, to make sure that the regulations were being obeyed. These requirements were extended to gas companies in 1885 and to electric companies in 1887.

The ICC in 1887 was authorized to draw up a uniform system of railway accounts, but it could not order it into effect. With the new movement for the establishment of mandatory state commissions in New York and Wisconsin, inquisitorial powers embodying control over accounts were given. The Hepburn Act of 1906 and the Transportation Act of 1920 gave equivalent powers to the ICC. The Federal Power Commission was authorized to prescribe a uniform accounting system for its licensees. Meanwhile, many state commissions were empowered to adopt uniform accounting classifications for utilities under their jurisdiction, modeling them upon those adopted in New York or Wisconsin. In addition to the power to prescribe the form of all accounts, records, and memoranda, it was made unlawful to keep any other accounts or records than those prescribed or approved, to alter, mutilate, or destroy them, or to make false entries. Commissions and their agents were given access to all accounts and records for purposes of supervision. Heavy penalties were imposed for violations. All state and federal commissions now require annual reports to be filed and published. They are public records available to all. *Only those who worked in the earlier atmosphere, when facts were hard to obtain, can appreciate the improvements in regulatory processes made possible by the new legislation.*

The movement for national uniformity. In the early 1920's, despite considerable similarity between the various state-wide and federal systems of accounts, the need for nation-wide standardization of accounting and record-keeping was becoming apparent. Utility companies operating in different states felt the burden of this diversity. The increasing size of the ownership unit, particularly after 1900 with the development of holding company control, called attention to this inconvenience when utilities were operated in adjoining as well as widely scattered states. The National Electric Light Association (NELA), active in this field since 1900, published a standard classification in 1914 which was adopted in part by a few of the state commissions. The American Electric Railway Association cooperated with the ICC in drawing up its classification of accounts for electric railways doing an interstate business. A final step in reaching national uniformity was taken, it was thought, by the National Association of Railway and Utilities Commissioners (NARUC) in 1919 when a resolution was passed at its annual convention instructing its Committee on Statistics and Accounts of Public Utilities to formulate and present to the Association a uniform system of accounts for all public utilities other than railroads. With the NELA and American Gas Association (AGA) aiding and guiding the process, a classification for gas and electric utilities was drawn up and approved in 1922 and was recommended for adoption by individual states

Some of the states, notably California, and the Federal Power Commission refused to adopt the recommended classification because (1) it provided for retirement instead of depreciation accounting, and (2) the fixed capital account did not provide for showing the original cost as required by the Federal Water Power Act of 1920. National uniformity was thus not achieved. The mounting note of criticism in these respects, induced by the extravagances of the holding company consolidation movement and the virtual breakdown of effective regulation in the 1920's, led to a new attempt at achieving both accounting reform and national uniformity. Wisconsin again led the way with a revised system in 1932, and New York followed in 1934. Meanwhile, the jurisdiction of the FPC was extended to include interstate commerce in electric power in 1935. In the same year the Securities and Exchange Commission was given jurisdiction over holding companies and their affiliated service companies. The Federal Communications Commission was set up in 1934 to take over from the ICC the regulation of telephone and telegraph companies serving in interstate commerce. Certainly the time had come for another effort at achieving national uniformity under the leadership this time of the federal commissions and the NARUC.

The new regime in accounting control, with practically complete national uniformity, was inaugurated in 1936 and 1937. In November, 1936, the NARUC recommended the adoption by states of new classifications for electric and artificial gas utilities. It also approved for adoption a new classification for telephone utilities prescribed by the FCC. The SEC prescribed a classification for holding companies and mutual service companies under its jurisdiction in 1936. The FPC prescribed its accounting system for electric utilities effective January 1, 1937, and after securing jurisdiction over them in 1938, a system for natural gas companies, effective January 1, 1940. National uniformity was thus achieved because the variations between the accounting prescribed by the various state and federal commissions is minor and no greater than necessary to take account of the technical differences between the various branches of the utility industries. Federal agencies like the TVA have been required to follow these accounting classifications as far as possible, and most of the municipally owned or other publicly owned utilities do so voluntarily.

The most essential characteristic of accounts should be their comparability from year to year, and from utility to utility. In these respects, results of operation may be compared not only for the same company over time but also for different companies and for the industry as a whole. It is now possible to compile a financial history for individual companies and for an entire industry, and on the whole, to vouch for the honesty with which the transactions have been recorded. Classifications for motor transportation were added as a matter of course when regulatory jurisdiction was extended to them. Some work still needs to be done in connection with water and sewage utilities, where standardization is least advanced.

The largest measure of benefit from accounting control has accrued to the smaller utilities, especially the publicly owned ones, whose standards of practice in accounting matters were markedly improved. It is doubtful if anything but compulsion and assistance from government would have brought the desired result. The use and effectiveness of the classifications was furthered among the smaller companies, and particularly among the small public-owned enterprises, through advice and assistance in the installation of accounting systems by commission accountants.

In order that the work of record-keeping should not become unduly expensive for the smaller utilities, the commission introduced a practice of building the classifications around certain standard accounts which are required of all utilities, large as well as small. For utilities with larger operating revenues the standard accounts are subdivided into subaccounts, giving further details. This policy has made the system sufficiently flexible to meet a variety of operating conditions.

Expanding Uses of Accounting Systems

There are two fundamental approaches to the problem of ascertaining the facts with respect to a particular enterprise. One is the physical approach, which is primarily the job of the engineer. It concerns itself primarily with physical appraisals of properties, engineering studies and surveys of service characteristics and costs of production, and investigations of the basic natural resources available and of the changing technologies. In so far as this approach deals with problems related to the rate base, we shall discuss it in a later chapter. Paralleling this is a second approach, that of ascertaining the pecuniary income and outgo, which is primarily the job of the accountant. Mediating betweeen the accounting approach and the engineering approach lies the task of the economist and business analyst whose objective is the reconciliation of the cost approach of the accountant with the service approach of the engineer. These reconciliations, and the theories—both analytical and institutional—by means of which they are interpreted and applied, are the main subject matter of Part II. However, they must be grounded in accounting and engineering facts. Accounting systems are the primary sources of these pecuniary facts.

Functional cost accounting. The need of disclosing the cost at which different operations are being carried on is an extremely important objective of accounting control. Management and regulatory authorities are alike interested in costs per unit of service. This means that the accounts must be organized in such a way that the cost of major operations may be ascertained from them. It is then possible to judge the efficiency with which the different operations have been carried on, and if necessary, to start measures for economy. Securing comparability in accounting and statistical data is the essence of the problem. With such information as a basis, cost may be made a factor in fixing relative rates. This objective has been only partially attained. The ICC failed at first to take into account the needs of cost finding, but this is now recognized as one of the purposes which accounting classifications should serve.

Taxation and budgetary controls. Another use of accounting facts is associated with the administration of tax laws. Wherever the base of taxation is some financial fact, such as gross revenues, net operating income, the fixed capital accounts, or the capital stock outstanding, there an adequate accounting system is a prerequisite for tax assessment.

Accounting facts also serve as a basis for budgetary control. Under a budget, each department of a utility is allotted a certain expenditure for a future period, the amount of which is determined by its past requirements modified by such factors as future plans call for. Budgetary control is exercised by checking the actual expenditures against past allotments. In this way economy in expenditures is emphasized and reasons for over-running allotments are definitely established.

Financial accounting and accounting statements. The primary interest of regulating authorities in accounting control is, however, to ascertain the true earning capacity of the utility as a whole. Both management and commission must be able to determine when rates yield a reasonable return to compensate all the factors in production. This involves determining all the detailed facts of a complex financial history, best revealed in its accounts. All the phases in its life history (as we have outlined them in Chapter 11) leave their impress upon the accounting record. We have distinguished the period of time during which the prospective business matures its *going plan* from the ensuing period when it obtains its *going plant*. Expenditures made during these periods, chargeable to accounts as fixed and circulating capital, must be distinguished from those made during the following period when the concern obtains its *going business*. The latter are chargeable to operating expense accounts and are offset in whole or in part by incoming revenues creditable to operating revenue accounts. Indeed, the same necessity of separating expenditures on behalf of plan and plant and of those involving the future from expenditures arising out of the rendition of service in the present, obtains throughout all future time when the business operates as a *going concern*. The business maintains itself, goes backward, or is extended. There are always expenditures premised upon the continued existence of the business. They represent the hostages to fortune which every concern must give if it looks for a future return. Accountants classify these *outgoes* and *incomes* by dividing accounts under the general headings of Balance Sheet Accounts, Income and Expense Accounts, and Profit and Loss or Surplus Accounts.

General Character of Balance Sheet Accounts

An explanation of the fundamental conceptions underlying public utility accounting in their relations to economics and to regulatory policy appears to be necessary for a real insight into public utility problems. A balance sheet records the economic status of an enterprise and reflects the cumulative net result of investment and operations on a certain date. The accounts summarized in a balance sheet record the investment (shown in greater detail in the classification) which the concern has made in getting ready to serve and in keeping itself in readiness to serve. Accounts showing how funds were used are called *asset* accounts (shown on the left-hand side of the sheet), and they represent the cost of the physical things which the concern owns as property. Expenditures for nonphysical items of property are also shown as assets, such as investments in other companies or notes and accounts receivable representing the obligations of others which the concern owns. Under the theory of double-entry bookkeeping, balance sheet accounts also include liability accounts and accounts showing net worth (shown on the right-hand side), whence came the funds with which the concern acquired its assets.

Fixed property accounting. The most important asset account is variously called "Property and Plant" or "Fixed Capital." Here are charged the money costs to the enterprise of the various forms which fixed capital may take. It is divided into *intangible* and *tangible* fixed capital. The former consists of such items as franchises, patents, and organization expense, all important in working out the "going plan." The latter consists of land, structures, equipment, and the so-called overheads or indirect construction costs. Overheads include engineering, superintendence, taxes, insurance, interest, and legal expenses during construction.

Fixed capital has been defined by an official classification as "the property both tangible and intangible which is devoted to the accomplishment of the principal purposes of its business and which has an expectation of life in service of more than one year from date of installation in service." This definition calls attention to the fact that these properties are held for operation, that they are the very essence of the enterprise, and that their destruction or withdrawal from service results in the abandonment of operations unless replaced by equivalent property. Under the revised classifications of the 1930's, these accounts are shown in greater detail than formerly. The properties may, of course, be sold, and the amount realized may be more than cost, but as long as they are used for operating purposes by a going concern, this higher potential market value is of no particular significance.

However, in the course of the development of utility and railroad industries most of these original concerns were acquired in their entirety by the purchase of their voting stock by new concerns and were merged with others in large ownership groupings, usually taking the form of holding companies. This combining and recombining of properties as operating entities created a situation where the sales did not always take place between concerns at "arms-length bargaining prices" but at prices arbitrarily fixed by the holding companies as transactions between affiliates. Because state commissions did not have control over these transactions and federal commissions were as yet nonexistent, the earlier accounting classifications permitted the recording of these transactions in terms of the cost to the final acquiring utility. Sometimes these properties were reappraised at higher figures because their replacement costs had increased as a consequence of the price increases which accompanied World War I. The cost of the properties on the books would then be "written up" without the intervention even of a sale between two concerns.

The number and complexity of these purchase and sale transactions, together with the amounts of property involved, often created a condition wherein 50 per cent and more of the fixed property of a utility had been so acquired and was represented on the books as a single unclassified sum. Unless the books of account of the selling utility were available and had been properly kept, the task of classifying these properties would be costly and time-consuming; it was usually not attempted. It was to facilitate this process of reclassification and of determining the equity of these purchase and sale transactions that Wisconsin and New York, and later on the new federal commissions, undertook the setting up of fixed property accounting upon a new basis. The revelations of the Federal Trade Commission investigation, begun in 1928, had much to do with the adoption of the new procedures.

The new system of accounting is exemplified by the Federal Power Commission's classification for electric utilities. It spreads out the amounts involved in a series of interrelated accounts, most of which are self-explanatory.

    Account 100   Electric Plant
        Account 100.1   Electric Plant in Service
        Account 100.2   Electric Plant Leased to Others
        Account 100.3   Construction Work in Progress
        Account 100.4   Electric Plant Held for Future Use
        Account 100.5   Electric Plant Acquisition Adjustment
        Account 100.6   Electric Plant in Process of Reclassification
    Account 107   Electric Plant Adjustment

Account 100 is divided into six subaccounts of which 100.1, 100.5, and 100.6 are the important ones. Account 100.1 records the actual legitimate cost of electric plant to the person devoting it to public service, no matter how far back the chain of transfer may reach. This was the reason why its critics called this process the ascertainment of *aboriginal cost*. If the property had cost the final incumbent a sum in excess of the original cost and such cost was the result of arms-length bargaining, this excess would be recorded in Account 100.5 as an *adjustment* and might be kept in the rate base and subject to depreciation or amortization charges at the commission's discretion. On the other hand, excess amounts arising out of write-ups or property transfers between affiliates were to find lodgment in Account 107, where they could be excluded from the rate base and perchance be amortized by charges to the surplus account, which would be at the expense of the owners. It should be clear that the underlying purpose of such financial accounting is to establish an actual cost rate base. This will be discussed at greater length in Chapters 18 to 20.

Depreciation of fixed property. Since properties wear out in the course of time, only those capable of use for more than a year are classified as *fixed*. The definition is thus one of accounting convenience. Properties estimated to last less than a year, or which may be consumed in the very act of serving (like fuel) are classified as *current assets*. Materials and supplies subject to current use are not deemed subject to depreciation though subject to theft or loss and hence are charged as a *contraction of inventories*. When used up in the productive process, they are charged off as an *operating expense* of the accounting period and set off against the current revenues. The cost of fixed capital is also ultimately chargeable against the revenues of an accounting period, but it is classified as an *estimated* depreciation expense. Depreciation is, therefore, also a function of the dissipation of assets, but it must be divided up into accounting periods. As R. B. Kester (*Accounting Theory and Practice,* Vol. 2, The Ronald Press Co., Copyright 1918, p. 103) points out:

The distinction made . . . between capital and revenue draws attention to the fact that the depreciation factor arises only because the fiscal or other period, when information concerning values and costs, i.e., financial condition, is desired, does not coincide with the expiration of service life of the properties used in production. If the information just referred to were not desired at intermediate periods between the date of acquisition of the asset and the date of its discard or obsolescence, its cost could be treated solely as an expense of operation to be charged to the whole period in the same way that the fuel consumed, the raw materials used, etc., are regarded as revenue charges, or costs of manufacture.

While certain primary asset accounts thus set forth the facts as to the growth of the property of a public utility, showing as of succeeding definite dates the pecuniary investment in the properties which the concern owns, we must look to other primary accounts, called *liability accounts,* for an estimate of what the concern owes, either to its legal owners or to those associated with its economic fortune as creditors. This, too, can be shown historically by setting up a balance sheet at different times. Here again we meet the parallel distinction, drawn by accountants as a matter of convenience, between capital liabilities representing fixed obligations with a long-term date of maturity or without any definite date of maturity, and current liabilities representing obligations that mature frequently, usually within a year.

The account "Capital Stock" in its various classifications of preferred and common, for instance, usually represents the "permanent full paid interests in the accounting company, or interests which, if terminable, are so only at the option of the company." The par or stated value of the stock plus premiums represents the subscriptions to corporate capital by its legal owners and has thus been irretrievably committed to this enterprise. The capital may also be enhanced through stockholders' paid-in surplus. The account "Long-term Debt" in its various classifications represents the total par value of all debt "which, by the terms of its creation, does not mature until more than one year after date of creation. This covers bonds, notes, mortgage certificates, and all other forms of acknowledgment of indebtedness." As distinguished from the above, other primary accounts, such as "Notes Payable" and "Accounts Payable," represent outstanding obligations payable either on demand or after some interval of time, usually less than one year. Thus the concern may secure working capital in part on the basis of its current credit while it secures its fixed capital by a joint contribution of owners and from long-term creditors.

There are other types of primary asset and liability accounts, but since these grow out of technical accounting requirements, they will not be discussed here. We must, however, say a word about one of these types. In the development and upbuilding of a business, funds may come from four sources: (1) They are contributed by the joint owners; (2) they are borrowed from long and short term creditors; (3) they are secured from public or private sources as contributions and gifts; (4) they are derived from earnings.

Funds derived from the fourth source give rise to at least one peculiar type of balance sheet account. Gross earnings less expenses and less fixed charges represent net income available for distribution to owners. When net income is not distributed to owners as dividends but is retained in the business, it is credited to the surplus account. As long as these earnings remain in the business, they are analogous to the capital funds originally contributed by owners. They may be used for corporate purposes, as for the extension or improvement of the fixed property. Often they are used for the creation of casualty or insurance reserves or sinking fund reserves to pay a specific long-term debt. They are then taken out of the surplus account and credited to these special reserve accounts. Simultaneously, the actual cash may be transferred from the cash account to appropriate special funds carried as asset accounts.

By way of summary we may say, therefore, that balance sheet accounts and their marshaling in the form of a statement are designed to afford a picture of the financial condition of the concern at any given time; let us say, at the end of a calendar year. Another parallel statement will be prepared at the end of the next calendar year. In this way balance sheet accounts show, historically, the important economic facts in regard to a concern in so far as they have become a matter of accounting record. Changes, both favorable and unfavorable, can be noted by an examination; and comparison of these parallel statements can be made either as a whole or account by account. The surplus (sometimes also called *profit and loss account*) is the critical account in such an analysis and comparison because in it are supposed to be reflected the net changes in financial condition. If these changes show favorable tendencies, provided earnings are not paid out in dividends, the surplus will be growing or the deficit diminishing. Such a concern is what we have called here a *going concern,* or it is on the way to become one. On the other hand, a declining surplus or, worse still, an accumulating deficit is indicative of a concern whose economic future is not assured. It may develop into a going concern if the losses or recessions in surplus are but temporary. On the other hand it may be definitely on the way to receivership and eventual dissolution or reorganization. At this point there is a temptation for concerns to masquerade these deficits into the semblance of a surplus. To determine, therefore, what is and what is not a going concern is a complex task not to be lightly inferred from any one balance sheet or even a series of them because, after all, accounting facts must be translated into economic causation by an analysis of detailed operations to which balance sheets give but a clue. Yet they are the starting point in the process of diagnosis.

General Character of Revenue and Expense Accounts

We have said that a comparison of the facts disclosed by two successive balance sheets will show the extent and character of financial changes that have occurred in the interval between these two definite points in time. Such cross-sectional views of a particular business are supplemented by an income statement which summarizes the results of operation as disclosed by these accounts. They record changes during a period of time, such as a year or a month.

The classification of revenue accounts in the income statement begins with a primary account called *Operating Revenues.* Like the fixed capital account, this is a control account in which the several classes of revenues are summarized. The detailed revenue accounts are classified in accordance with the types of service rendered. Revenue classifications vary primarily with the character of the utility and secondarily with the classes of service rendered by each utility. As far as possible each single revenue source is related to one or more similar schedules of rates in order that the yield in earnings under each rate schedule may be readily ascertained. Miscellaneous revenues incidental to operation, as well as revenues arising from operations outside the primary purpose for establishing the utility, are likewise shown.

From operating revenues are deducted operating expenses. The general accounting classifications provide for detailed operating expense accounts, those for electric utilities including generation, transmission and distribution expenses, customer accounting and collecting expenses, administration, and general expenses. The general account is a summary. Operating expenses must also allow for the estimated amount of fixed capital consumed in operation, in addition to the direct outlay for labor and material consumed in operation. However, the fixed plant must be kept up and repaired. Minor renewals of small tools or of parts of larger units of equipment become necessary in order to maintain operating efficiency. Since these repair and renewal costs occur, on the whole, with regularity and are tolerably proportional in amount from one year to the next, they are called *maintenance expense* and charged against the revenues of the period when they occur. When, in order to maintain the efficiency of the going plant, it becomes necessary to replace major units of plant and equipment, the time for the prognosticated retirement from the accounts of the cost of these fixed capital assets has also arrived. *Depreciation* is merely a technical term for measuring the gradual wastage or consumption of such long-lived plant. If the full cost of the fixed assets about to be retired were charged against the revenues of the current accounting period, there would result an uneven flow of net earnings, or perchance, their complete disappearance. Because the physical and functional causes of depreciation (see p. 347 *infra.*) have been operating over long periods of time, the accountants introduced the practice of estimating this probable wastage of capital in advance. Then, by spreading these costs annually over a period of time equated with the probable life of the particular asset, the cost of service is more accurately allocated to each year's customers, and the distortion of the annual net income is avoided.

Similarly, taxes are a definite charge levied by governments annually against public utilities. The tax account is debited with the *estimated* amount of these contributions deemed to accrue *monthly*. A deduction for taxes is thus spread over the year on a monthly basis and adjusted to the *exact* amount at the end of the *year*. An estimated charge is also made monthly to an expense account for "uncollectible accounts." Usually the amounts charged off as depreciation and for bad debts are segregated in reserves, while amounts charged as taxes are carried in an accrued account on the liability side of the balance sheet.

It is often convenient for a particular utility to lease a portion of its physical plant or to divide with some other utility the cost of owning and operating a facility jointly used. Such lease rentals and joint facility rents are also provided for in the accounts and constitute a deduction from revenues. They are set off from other expenses because the rental is in the nature of a fixed charge for the use of capital provided by some other business unit.

Frequently, a concern may engage in operations outside of its purely public utility service. Or, again, it may operate several types of public utilities as a joint enterprise. It is then important that accounts and income statements be so arranged as to show separately the operating revenues and operating expenses attributable to each of these separate enterprises. The income statement of such a consolidated enterprise should therefore show: (1) the net income derived from the several types of public utility services, and (2) separately therefrom, the net income from nonutility operations. The latter usually takes the form of revenues derived from investments made by the corporation in the securities of other companies. These investments may be made solely for financial purposes, or they may be made in order to secure or retain the control of another utility.

These different streams of net income are now combined into a gross corporate income. The corporation then proceeds to take care of its fixed charges for which the enterprise as a whole is liable.

The deductions from gross corporate income give rise to another class of accounts, of which the "interest on long-term debt" is the most important. Other interest payments (on notes payable, for instance) are shown in an account called *Miscellaneous Interest*. Discounts and expenses incurred in floating long-term debts are prorated as an annual charge over the life of the security. Discounts represent prepaid interest, and the portion written off for the accounting period is charged as amortization of debt discount and expense. Other similar items, compulsory in character, are likewise accounted for and added to the other deductions. These deductions having been made, the result is the true corporate net income available to the corporation and subject to voluntary appropriation for corporate purposes by vote of its board of directors. If cash is or can be made available, the chief items here are appropriations of income to sinking fund reserves (sometimes required by mortgage provisions) and appropriations of regular dividends upon the preferred and the common capital stock. These appropriations are at least semicompulsory in that they are necessary to maintain corporate credit. The balance of unappropriated net income is transferred to the profit and loss or surplus account.

The control of operating expenses. The facts regarding operating expenses in the past are thus derived from the expense accounts summarized in the foregoing operating statement. In determining what allowance should be made for these costs in the future, however, it is necessary to modify the record of past experience by conditions to be expected in the future. The test period of the last year, or the last two or three years, may well be the starting point for these future prognostications.

In regulating operating expenses it would first be necessary to scrutinize all items of expense as to their allowability as a part of the "cost of service." The initiative in making these expenditures in the first place belongs to management, but regulatory authorities may substitute their judgment for that of management with regard to their normality, legal propriety, and reasonableness. Nonrecurring expenditures, such as those relating to litigations before courts and commissions, may well be eliminated except by way of an amortization allowance. All told, management must meet the market costs of labor and material. There are some expenses, such as taxes and wages (the latter negotiated in collective bargaining contracts), over which management has little control. In fact, management should represent the interests of consumers in these negotiations. Items often subject to question are managerial salaries and bonuses, payments to affiliated interests for financial and engineering services peculiar to holding company structures, promotional (advertising) and political expenditures, expenditures in connection with employee pension plans and employee welfare activities, costs attributable to nonutility business such as the sale of appliances, company contributions to community welfare agencies, and expenditures of like tenor.

General Character of the Surplus Account

We return once more to the earned surplus account on the liability side of the balance sheet. This is the collective title for a small group of accounts which form the connecting link between the income statement and the balance sheet. These are designed to give a summary explanation of the changes in financial condition that have come about since the date of the last balance sheet. In order to do so, the surplus statement carries the balance of profit or loss on the last balance sheet at the beginning of the fiscal period. To this is added the net change as indicated by the current income statement. Out of this total come additional appropriations of dividends, or if the current year's net income was inadequate, the regular dividends. Other items might be sundry appropriations to reserves not provided for as a matter of accounting routine. There might be other abnormal items of profit or loss, such as profits or losses from property sales, which would seriously distort the income statement if they were there included in whole or in part. They are therefore taken care of through this earned surplus account.

Expenditures disallowed as not properly chargeable to the cost of operation (that is to say, not chargeable against rate payers) may be charged against the earned surplus or capital surplus. Here is where the commission may direct that amounts segregated in adjustment accounts like Account 107 be charged off *below the line* because they will then come out of the stockholders' equity and have the effect of deferring or restricting the payment of dividends. They will also have the effect of reducing the pay-out ratio.

Reports and Statistics

As we have seen, the regulation of accounting began by making reports compulsory. At first these reports were neither uniform nor standardized. In fact, standardization and uniformity had to wait upon the perfection of accounting control. At the present time, all regulating commissions require annual reports upon prescribed forms.

These reports contain schedules which call for an annual balance sheet, an income statement for the year, and a surplus statement. They are supplemented by other schedules calling for further details with respect to particular items. Among these should be mentioned details concerning the fixed plant, revenues and expenses, capital stock and dividends, long- and short-term debt and interest payments, and appropriations of revenues to reserves and charges against these reserves. Without such annual (or even monthly) reports, customers and public authorities would have difficulty in keeping currently informed. In the event of actual litigation, and for certain specific purposes like special or general investigations, additional reports may be called for.

Audits. The ultimate in accounting control is reached, however, in the periodic audits of accounts and records which are undertaken on behalf of commissions by their own accounting and engineering staffs or by designated staffs of accounting and engineering examiners. On such occasions the examination extends into such refinement of detail as required by the specific purpose of the investigation. Particular attention is then bestowed upon the way in which the accounts have been kept and upon the fidelity, accuracy, and technical proficiency with which the prescribed accounting regulations have been carried out.

Statistics. Schedules calling for statistics of ownership and operation are a distinctive feature of annual reports. These statistics are of a miscellaneous character, not readily classified or described. In general terms they relate to (1) units of output of service, (2) units of performance in production, and (3) units of fixed plant. It is clear, therefore, that these statistics are not only fiscal in character but may also relate to purely physical items, or they may be of a mixed physical and financial character. Load factors, diversity factors, plant utilization factors, and other efficiency ratios may be derived from them. By means of these and other statistical units, efficiency in construction, operation, and financing is best judged. Statistical units of cost of service or of revenue receipts are the best means of relating rates paid to service consumed, and hence, of finding a basis for rate adjustment in economic facts.

We must also mention in passing that the regular reports give information regarding the legal history and corporate organization of the utility, its official and operating personnel, the territory served, the number and classification of customers, units of input and output, and the character of the service. The reports are used for a variety of purposes. All these miscellaneous matters have become important because they aid in making effective a system of regulation which has varied objects, a far-flung frontier, and which does a good deal of its work at long range.

17. THE PROBLEM
OF THE RATE BASE

The legislative process of rate-making is, as we have seen, inseparable from the process of determining the reasonable earning capacity of public utilities. After determining reasonable operating expenses, it is necessary to allow also for a reasonable return upon the fixed investment in a utility's property. The reasonable return has also been called the *fair return* and represents a calculated sum of dollars obtained by applying a "fair rate of return" (that is to say, a percentage) to a basic sum designed to represent the "fair value for rate-making purposes" (that is to say, a rate base). Thus the rate base and rate of return are interdependent functions and are of strategic importance in this pricing process.

The Movement for Physical Valuation

Prior to 1870 legislatures did not use their power to fix rates. The system of regulation then in force was regulation by charter. These usually granted the power of fixing rates to the board of directors. Competition was relied upon to keep rates down, if, indeed, any thought was given to the matter at all. Some charters named only maximum rates or maximum dividends. Regulation was experimental and primitive. But, withal, there was economic need for expansion of the new facilities. Particularly were conditions right for speculative development of railroads. This in turn engendered overcapitalization, excessive competition, useless duplication, and hasty construction. The reaction came in the Granger movement which challenged the validity of the old policies. The dormant power of regulation, using the police powers of the states, was asserted in the maximum rate laws of the Grangers. This was the starting point of the modern movement for legislative regulation.

Emergence of judicial review. The roots of the doctrine that "value" is the cornerstone of rate regulation go back at least to the Granger legislation. It will be recalled that the legislative power to regulate not only grain elevators but also railroads was called into question in these cases, and that

270

the Supreme Court of the United States decided that fixing reasonable rates is a legislative function not inconsistent with the Fourteenth Amendment. But it was unavoidable that in limiting *rates* under police powers the legislature might also limit earnings. This fact brought about a train of consequences not at first appreciated. It meant first of all a gradual relaxation of the ideal of competition as applied to public utilities and the gradual substitution of regulated monopoly. This should have entailed a redefinition of private property for public utilities under the Fourteenth Amendment, which differentiates itself sharply from private property subject to competition. The latter must seek its value content in commercial markets under competitive conditions, while public utility property receives its value content under regulated rates.

At first the courts did not clearly perceive their duty under the constitution of protecting private property "affected with a public interest." When later on this duty was assumed, they failed for a long time, specifically until 1923 in the Southwestern Bell Telephone Company case, to draw the institutional distinction between ordinary private property and public utility property.

The development of judicial review as affecting public utility rates may be traced in the opinions of the United States Supreme Court. In the Granger cases of 1877 the court assumed a position of *judicial noninterference*. It held that once the public utility status is recognized, the fixing of public utility rates is a prerogative of the legislature and that there may be no interference with legislative discretion. Complaints by public utilities against low rates should be addressed to the legislature and not to the court.

Ten years later, in 1886, after much urging by lawyers appearing for the public utilities, the court finally recognized this duty. In the Railroad Commission cases (116 U.S. 307, 331) it said that the power of the legislature to fix rates is not without limits. In the language of Chief Justice Waite, "This power to regulate is not a power to destroy, and limitation is not the equivalent of confiscation." At this point one may ask what it is that is being destroyed. In any real sense it must be the economic value of property, the right to derive a reasonable income from economic transactions. Without this right, property would be without substance.

Finally, in 1890, in the first Minnesota Rate cases [*C.M. & St.P. Ry. Co. v. Minnesota* (134 U.S. 418)] the court clearly asserts the doctrine of judicial review as applying also to public utility rates. In this instance, rates for the transport of milk had been fixed by the Minnesota Railroad and Warehouse Commission, acting under delegated authority. The court held that "due process of law" involved not only legislative discretion but also considerations of reasonableness which may be tested by the courts for confiscation. The Supreme Court of Minnesota had held that the commission's determination was final and conclusive; but the Supreme Court of the United States objected that this interpretation deprived "the company of its right to a judicial investigation by due process of law, under the forms and with the machinery provided by the wisdom of successive ages for the investigation judicially of the truth of a matter in controversy." This opinion affords the first characterization of reasonableness that rates fixed without the possibility of judicial inquiry are unconstitutional. Four years later, in 1894, in *Reagan v. Farmers Loan and Trust Co.* (154 U.S. 362), the enforcement of a commission rate order was enjoined for the first time because the rates fixed were too low to afford a reasonable return, but the court was not yet ready to elaborate its standard of reasonableness.

Emergence of valuation as a legal doctrine. The first definite adoption of the valuation doctrine as the fulcrum of reasonableness in rate regulation came in 1896 in a case in the lower courts. In *San Diego, etc., v. Jasper* (74 Fed. 79, 83) the court said that it is "the actual value of the property at the time the rates are to be fixed that should form the basis upon which to compute just rates." Two years later, in 1898, this idea was accepted by the federal Supreme Court in the famous case of *Smyth v. Ames* (169 U.S. 466), in which the doctrine of "fair value" was announced in the form in which it has been operative until the present time. It is now recognized that limitation of rates results in limitation of earning power and thus also involves the question as to what constitutes a "reasonable rate of return." The court's answer is that it must be a *fair return* on a fair valuation of the property used and useful for the convenience of the public. An earning power large enough to allow this return is the chief test of constitutionally reasonable rates.

Valuation as a device of legislative policy. The origin of the notion that there is something basic and equitable in the use of the value of property as a "rate base" is to be found in our traditional policy of taxation, which uses the value of property owned as a "tax base." "Valuation," or assessment, of property was therefore developed first by tax officials. It was also used in measuring the compensation to be paid in condemning private property for public uses. The legal principles of "valuation" were thus derived largely from cases arising under the powers of taxation and eminent domain. Since rate-fixing may be confiscatory, it was argued that the measure of compensation to public utilities under the police power should be the same as when private property is "taken" under eminent domain. This condemnation analogy has been responsible for much of the confusion in legal theory which identifies value under eminent domain with value for rate-making. The chief purposes thus are:

1. Valuation for taxation
2. Valuation for public purchase under eminent domain or under charter and special franchise provisions
3. Valuations in connection with the validation of security issues
4. Valuations for accounting and insurance purposes and for private purchase and sale
5. Valuation for rate-making purposes

These purposes must be carefully distinguished. Here we will treat only valuations for rate-making.

As far back as 1888 the Interstate Commerce Commission, in its 2nd Annual Report to Congress, discussed valuation as a basis for railroad rates. Since 1903 it regularly referred in annual reports to the need of having a basic valuation in its work of rate regulation. As the powers of the commission were extended and its influence upon the rate structure grew, the problem of the reasonableness of the general level of rates moved into the center of attention. This factor was of peculiar importance in the general rate-advance cases beginning in 1911. In that year the Hadley Railroad Securities Commission also advocated valuation of the railroads in its report to President Taft. Finally, in 1913, the requirements of the situation had become such that what was once a controversial issue was accepted by Congress, practically without opposition, in the La Follette Valuation Act, which required the commission to ascertain and report to Congress the valuation of the railroads of the United States. This official valuation was completed at an estimated cost (as of 1938) of $208 million. It was consolidated with the rate-making rule of the Transportation Act of 1920 and became an issue in a celebrated case before the United States Supreme Court, which we shall discuss later.

Meanwhile, the states had also espoused the valuation doctrine. Michigan in 1900 and Wisconsin in 1903 had passed ad valorem tax laws placing the taxation of railroads upon the basis of a so-called physical valuation. Railroads had been escaping an equitable share of the common tax burden, and it was believed that centralized assessment by state tax commissions, using a physical approach to the problem, would prevent tax evasion. In 1905 and again in 1907 when Wisconsin and New York passed laws regulating both railroads and local utilities, their commissions were empowered to make valuations for rate-making purposes. The practice has spread to all the states in the Union, so that valuation has become one of the most discussed subjects in public utility literature.

The Valuation Doctrine and the Theory of
the Going Concern

One of the most important consequences of the attempt to apply physical valuation to the properties of public utilities has been the recognition that there are other elements besides the existing physical property that must be considered. The financial history of properties was explored, and it was found that physical property had disappeared, although the books still recorded the investment. Expenditures had also been made in building up a financial and legal structure for these enterprises. It was further shown in consolidations that losses had been sustained on account of the scrapping of property and that deficits had developed during the years when the enterprise was building up its business. These items have been lumped together under the term *intangible* or *nonphysical* property. It is now recognized that valuation must take note not merely of the tangible physical property but also of the intangible nonphysical items. This has served to broaden the scope and purpose of valuations.

This broadening of the scope and purpose of the valuation doctrine can best be seen in a further development of the meaning of intangible property. In assessments for taxation, a theory was developed which has profoundly influenced the development of this subject. This theory is embodied in what is known as the *unit rule* of assessments. The traditional American policy of local assessors had been to assess real and personal property on some basis related to its selling value. This was not difficult so long as assessors dealt only with property which had a ready market, like city residences, machinery, equipment, and stock-in-trade. Steam railroads, however, offered difficulties because these properties seemed to be unique in character. Moreover, it was a form of property not regularly sold. At first assessors based their assessment only upon the *physical* property of the roads within their jurisdiction, valuing it on the traditional basis. As the roads grew beyond the limits of any one taxing jurisdiction, difficulties multiplied, particularly when mobile property like rolling stock had to be assessed. Tax officials then saw the need of assessing the physical property of the road as a whole. This was usually done by State Boards of Equalization, and the amount assignable to local tax jurisdictions was determined upon some basis such as the miles of track. In other words, adequate assessment required recognition of the fact that corporations are single business units and that their property must be assessed as a unit and then apportioned for local taxing purposes.

In 1894 an important case was decided in which this method of assessment was an issue. It was *Cleveland, Cincinnati, Chicago and St. Louis Railway v. Backus* (154 U.S. 439, 444). Referring to assessment of railroads, the court there said:

> The true value of a line of railroad is something more than an aggregation of the values of the separate parts of it, operated separately. It is the aggregate of those values plus that arising from a connected operation of the whole, and each part of the road contributes not merely the value arising from its independent operation, but its mileage proportion of that flowing from a continuous and connected operation of the whole. The value of property results from the use to which it is put, and varies with the profitableness of that use, past, present, and prospective, actual and anticipated. There is no pecuniary value outside that which results from such use. In the nature of things it is practically impossible, at least in respect to railroad property, to divide its value and determine how much is caused by one use to which it is put and how much by another.

That the economic value of an assembled plant is controlled by its earning power, and that the ordinary selling value of component property units has no relation to a value created when property is joined in a unified use, appears even better from a consideration of the assessment of express companies. When the Ohio State Board of Assessment, for instance, assessed the property of the Adams Express Company, it found a figure of $449,377.60, although the tangible property in the state was assessed at only $23,400. In other words, the term *property* was interpreted by the Ohio tax authority to include certain intangible elements. It used as the basis for its assessment the market value of the capital stock, the bonds of the entire company, and a value-per-mile amount proportional to the mileage in the state of Ohio. The rule was thus applied to both tangible and intangible property.

In appealing to the United States Supreme Court in 1897 [*Adams Express Co. v. Ohio* (164 U.S. 194, 222); rehearing (166 U.S. 185)], the Company contended that its Ohio property subject to taxation consisted of the horses, wagons, safes, and other personal property at their piecemeal market values. It argued that there was no unity between its physical property in Ohio and that in other states except in a "unity of ownership"; that stock and bond values reflected this physical property value but included in addition "the skill, diligence, fidelity, and success" with which its properties were used and the reputation and good will of the Company among its customers. The Company claimed further that express companies were not analogous to railroad and telegraph companies because these had a connected physical plant and could be taxed under the unit rule. In the express business the unit rule was a mere "intellectual fiction," a metaphysical or intellectual relation. But the majority of the court took the view that there was "unity of use" in the conduct of one business and that this gave a value to the separate items of property. The court pertinently asked: "Considered as distinct objects of taxation, a horse is indeed a horse; a wagon, a wagon; a safe, a safe; a punch, a punch; but how is it that $23,430 worth of horses, wagons, safes, and punches produce $275,446 in a single year?" The court answered the question by holding that where there is unity of use, the physical property must be assessed as that of a going concern.

Whenever separate articles of tangible property are joined together, not simply by a unity of ownership, but in a unity of use, there is not infrequently developed a property, intangible though it may be, which in value exceeds the aggregate of the value of the separate pieces of tangible property.

This is what, in Massachusetts taxing parlance, was called the "corporate excess," or in other states, "the value of the franchise." Here it was called good will, and the court ruled that, "If a state comprehends all property in its scheme of taxation, then the good will of an organized and established industry must be recognized as a thing of value."

The significance of this decision cannot be overestimated. Professor John R. Commons, in his *Legal Foundations of Capitalism* (see Bibliography), sees in this a change in the definition of property from that of *tangible things* to one of *business relationships*. Consequently, the inference is that all values are intangible. The significance of this case in the development of the valuation doctrine is that it lays the foundation for the valuation of the objects of property owned by public utilities. The case is precedent for the view that objects of property should not be appraised at their market value as *separate instruments* of production for *any use* but should be valued as productive instruments on the basis of their *integrated use* for the particular public utility service for which the corporation was created by the state. This is what we call the *going concern theory* in valuation and regulation.

Before proceeding to a discussion of valuation standards in detail some further general observations should be made. Gradually, physical valuation was deemed to be of such importance as to be favored by both of the major political parties. It was believed that valuation would put an end to controversy. In the course of long and involved financial histories most public utilities had lost the ideal relation between asset accounts and liability accounts. This is well set forth in the report of the Railroad Securities Commission:

Insofar as the value of the property is an element in rate regulation, the outstanding securities are of so little evidentiary weight that it would probably be of distinct advantage if courts and commissions would disregard them entirely, except as a part of the financial history of the property, and would insist upon direct evidence of the actual money invested and of the present values of the properties. For this and other reasons discussed in the body of the report, your Commission recommends that the Interstate Commerce Commission should have authority and adequate funds to make such a valuation of the physical property of railroads wherever the question of the present value of these roads is, in the judgment of that Commission, of sufficient importance.

Except in the case of Massachusetts, where financial transactions had early come under state control, neither the capital stock accounts nor the property accounts could be relied upon to show the true cash investment. The seat of the trouble lay in American methods of corporate promotion and of legal organization. Without official scrutiny of transactions and official regulation of accounting, the companies were permitted to capitalize not only the cash investment in existing properties but also the prospective future value of an assumed increased earning capacity. It was this reckless inflation of security issues that gave American public utilities of that period their top-heavy financial structures and their unreliable investment accounts. In this extremity it was believed that physical valuation would prove a helpful remedy and would place these industries again upon a sound financial basis. The valuation process at the very outset has thus been beset with all the difficulties that a confused and troublous history brings forth.

The Rate-Making Rule of *Smyth v. Ames*

The rule of rate-making as applied to public utilities was first announced, as we have seen, in the leading case of *Smyth v. Ames* in the following paragraph:

We hold, however, that the basis of all calculations as to the reasonableness of rates to be charged by a corporation maintaining a public highway under legislative sanction must be the *fair value* of the property being used by it for the convenience of the public. And in order to ascertain that value, the original cost of construction, the amount expended in permanent improvements, the amount and market value of its bonds and stock, the present as compared with the original cost of construction, the probable earning capacity of the property under particular rates prescribed by statute, and the sum required to meet operating expenses are all matters for consideration and are to be given such weight as may be just and right in each case. We do not say that there may not be other matters to be regarded in estimating the value of the property. What the company is entitled to ask is a fair return upon the value of that which it employs for the public convenience. On the other hand, what the public is entitled to demand is that no more be exacted from it for the use of a public highway than the services rendered by it are reasonably worth.

The foregoing rule may be interpreted as follows: The fixing of rates under a legislative act should be based upon a calculation of the gross revenues which given rates may reasonably be expected to yield. From these estimated earnings must be deducted the anticipated operating expenses. The balance of the earnings must be related to the *fair value* of the property which thereby becomes the *basis of the calculation*. In determining what is the fair value, that is, in fixing the basis of the calculation, the rate-making authority must take into account the following:

1.   The original cost of construction, which can refer only to the first cost of the original plant with which the enterprise began operations. To this may have been added, in the course of time, extensions and improvements of the fixed plant. Consequently, there must be added the amount expended in permanent improvements. Together, these items constitute what has come to be known as the *historical cost* of the tangible property.

2.   The amount and market value of its bonds and stock, which is the third item in the above enumeration. The *amount* of bonds and stock can refer only to the aggregate par value of capital stock, actually issued and outstanding, plus the par amount of the outstanding long-term debt. The *market value* of bonds and stock can be obtained from the current market rates at which the corporation's bonds and stocks are being sold upon the exchanges. These figures have been taken as indicating, respectively, the *capitalized value* and the *commercial value* of the business.

3.   The interpretation of the present cost of construction as compared with the original cost of construction meets an ambiguity in the language of the court. No useful purpose would be served by comparing the original cost of construction alone with the present cost of constructing a plant which in the course of time has been materially extended and improved. A study of the report of the case reveals, however, that what the court had in mind was that present costs of constructing a similar plant should be compared with the actual construction costs. Whether the present cost of construction was to be ascertained in order to provide a check upon actual cost, as some surmise, or whether the court was cognizant of the effect of price changes and improvements in technique, cannot be determined. Be that as it may, in order to make the suggested comparison, rate-making authorities have generally determined a figure which would represent the cost of reconstructing the plant as it stood at the date when rates were being fixed. This has been called the *cost of reproduction new* of the property.

These various measures of the cost of the plant, together with the capitalization and commercial valuation of the business, should then be considered as evidentiary facts, which must be "given such weight as may be just and right in each case." In the end they are to be combined in a final judgment or "finding" as to what sum represents a "fair value." This final sum must then be related to the estimated earnings (after deducting estimated operating expenses) by arithmetically computing the per centum of return. If the estimated rate of return is deemed to yield a reasonable amount, that amount becomes the "fair return," and the tentative rates may become the prescribed rates. The court then adds to this rate-making rule an element which might be termed a judicial *factor of safety*. "We do not say that there may not be other matters to be regarded in estimating the value of the property."

Making all due allowances for judicial ineptitude in describing a technical rate-making process, the rule may fairly be criticized because it was based upon an inadequate analysis of a very complex problem. The last two sentences, for example, are a good illustration of logical dualism. The rights of consumers and the rights of producers are stated but not harmonized. If consumers, *collectively* called the public, should be charged *individually* and *collectively* only what services are *reasonably worth*, this reasonable worth must find its fundamental basis of measurement in what the company is entitled to ask, which is, in addition to reasonable operating expenses, a fair return upon the fair value. In the absence of such an interpretation, reasonableness is referable either to the economic needs of the producer or to the necessities of the consumer. As stated, the rule calls attention to the conflicting claims, but it offers no basis for their reasonable reconciliation. Nevertheless, rate-making by public authority was constrained to develop with this rule as a constitutional guide.

The Investment Standard

Broadly conceived, three standards of valuation are suggested in that portion of the rate-making rule which deals with the valuation doctrine. The first standard may be called the *investment standard* because it deals with the amount of cash or cash value of property and services that have been contributed to the capital of the concern. The investment standard is best evidenced by the books of account, if these have been correctly kept. The amount of the capital investment can be obtained by looking either at the asset side or the liability side of the balance sheet.

On the asset side the fixed capital accounts should show the amount that has been paid for the fixed properties. But considerations may arise which will render this evidence less probative. Properties grow, diminish, or change in character. Ordinarily, growth is taken care of by increased investment which should be recorded on the books by debiting the increased cost to the proper accounts. Properties diminish through losses, sales, and abandonments. These should be recorded on the books as retirements by crediting the cost of the property lost, sold, or abandoned. Properties also change their identity by being renewed after depreciation has made such replacement necessary. At such times identical units of property or units more or less different will be substituted. The significance of these changes for us is not the technological one by which a generator of one description is displaced by an improved one of another description, but rather is the pecuniary one that the new generator costs more or less, or as much as, the displaced generator. If their respective costs are the same, the capital cost of the enterprise has not been enlarged; if the former costs more, the investment has been enlarged; if it costs less, the investment has been diminished.

Amid all these vicissitudes of property changes, especially in a complex property having a long history, it may well happen that the pecuniary cost will not be accounted for with the fidelity that the investment theory assumes. It may be that important accounting sources have been lost or destroyed so that the historical continuity of the investment accounts is broken. At other times the same physical property has passed through different ownerships. Corporation A, the first owner, may have sold the property to corporation B at a price that had no relation to cost; still, the investment of B will be represented by this figure. Or corporation B may have purchased the property at a receiver's sale, the price again being fixed without relation to construction cost. Very often the opening entries in property accounts represent merely the offsetting entries to adjustments in stocks and bonds at the time of reorganizations. In all these various ways the determination of the correct historical cost may prove difficult if not impossible.

This difficulty may be partially circumvented by recourse to a physical appraisal. Although the books of account are gone or are incorrect, the property is still there and may be inventoried. By determining, then, for each unit of property on hand, the cost of its acquisition, the sum total of these inventory items will give a measure of the cost of *existing items of property*. This procedure, however, does not do full justice in the determination of the investment cost of a particular concern which may have failed, on account of insufficient earnings, to retire the full cost of such property items—lost, sold, or abandoned—by charging them to the depreciation reserve or by charging them against surplus revenues. And yet these particular changes in the property have been a part of the integral growth of the business taken as a unit.

Another problem that enters into the determination of the investment is the wisdom or lack of wisdom with which expenditures were made. From one point of view, all that is necessary is to determine the amount, regardless of any questions involving managerial discretion; but having found the actual investment, it is still necessary to determine whether such investment was prudently made.

The considerations advanced above should make it tolerably clear that the application of the investment standard may require one or all of the following: (1) an audit of the accounts of the company in order to determine the *historical* cost of the fixed properties; (2) an engineering survey or appraisal of the *existing items* of property in order to ascertain from accounting records or by means of engineering estimates the investment costs; (3) a financial history of the business in order to ascertain from an economic and operating point of view whether any deduction should be made from the present investment as determined under (1) or (2) above to cover imprudent expenditures, or whether an additional allowance should be made to cover past financial losses on equitable grounds. We shall discuss these matters in greater detail later.

We must, in passing, stress a further point; namely, that investment could also be ascertained by scrutinizing the source of investment funds, that is, by examining the liabilities of the enterprise. The par value of bonds, provided there have been no discounts or premiums, should indicate the sums available from this source. Stock subscribed, and fully paid for, represents another principal source. The shares of capital stock represent the legal capitalization of the enterprise. With this must be included reserves set aside and invested in property, and the surplus account. To it should also be added the par value of notes or other evidences of indebtedness. This combination (stocks, reserves, surplus, and bonds) represents the economic capitalization of the enterprise. The satisfactory recognition and protection of these legal interests gives the business its going concern character. Under proper conditions there should be little variation between these two measures of investment, one derived from assets and the other from liabilities plus the net worth.

Unfortunately, however, before the regulation of securities had become widespread, the nominal or par value of security issues could not be relied upon as a measure of investment because of the practice of distributing stock as a bonus to encourage the purchase of bonds. Par value may thus represent investors' future expectations rather than past investment.

The Capitalization of Income Standard

The second standard suggested by the rate-making rule is that of the market value of outstanding securities. The market prices of bonds and stocks reflect the desirability of these securities as investments. However, as the going-market rate on borrowed capital changes, the market value of a given security with its fixed interest rate will also reflect these changes, rising as the market rate falls and falling as it rises. The market value of stocks is affected most directly by the present and prospective income yield and the customary dividend pay-out. Under some circumstances the market value of voting stock may, however, also reflect contests for control. It is apparent, therefore, that the summation of the market value of securities is not a measure of the invested capital, and its use for rate-base purposes is vitiated by the fact that its value depends upon the very income the reasonableness of which is being called into question. Besides moving in a logical circle, the market value standard *imputes* to all securities outstanding the market prices paid from time to time for the limited number actually sold on the security exchanges.

Although not mentioned in the rate-making rule, another variant of this standard has from time to time been suggested and also applied. This assumes that the value of an enterprise can be determined by capitalizing the net operating revenues at some rate which is assumed to be reasonable. The capital sum so derived is also clearly dependent upon the existing earning capacity, and in addition, upon the assumed capitalization rate. It is as defective for rate-making purposes as the market value of outstanding securities, whatever may be its usefulness for purposes of private sale or tax assessments. The market value of outstanding securities does, however, offer some clue as to what the market thinks of the credit of the enterprise and particularly of its future prospects. This may prove helpful in cases where the economic future of these businesses is beclouded by imprudent investments in the past.

The Cost of Reproduction Standard

A final standard for rate-base determination takes its departure from an assumed present cost of construction of the fixed properties. It has been called the *cost of reproduction theory.* We are accustomed to speak about "stubborn facts." Yet nothing proves more stubborn at times than a theory widely held. This is peculiarly true of this standard. It has found persistent advocates and has maintained itself until the present time.

First we must get in mind clearly what cost of reproduction means. This standard also has two variants. It may mean what it would cost to reproduce the *service* at the present time, the new producer being free to choose and coordinate his factors of production; or it may mean what it would cost to reproduce the service rendered by an existing plant where the new producer assembles and coordinates a plant like the existing one. These two hypotheses will be referred to respectively as "the substitute plant" hypothesis and the "equivalent plant" hypothesis. The value of the fixed plant for rate-making purposes may thus equal what it would now cost to assemble (1) the component parts of the present plant or (2) the component parts of a substitute plant capable of rendering the same service.

It is clear in the first place that this standard is free from the defect of the standard based upon income. As distinguished from the investment standard, it uses as its basic calculation not costs actually incurred in the past but one or the other of these estimated present costs of construction. We will give a critique of these standards in a subsequent chapter.

Purpose of the Judicial Rule of Rate-Making in Legislative Regulation

In order that the rate-making power may escape constitutional limitation under judicial review, the United States Supreme Court had set up these standards as a constitutional guide. It should be noted that the rule of rate-making fixes what may be called a *line of confiscation* and a *line of extortion*. The procedure is illustrated in Chart XIII. A rate must not be so adjusted as to bring it within either of the zones of unreasonableness there shown. The diagram arbitrarily assumes gas rates varying from 60 cents per thousand cubic feet to $1.30 per thousand cubic feet. Under the rate-making rule, a rate of less than 70 cents is confiscatory and a rate in excess of $1.00 is extortionate; that is to say, in the latter case the cost to the consumer is more than the service is reasonably worth.

This "reasonable worth" in the eyes of the customer means the cost of some alternative *substitute* service or the expense which some customers would be forced to incur themselves in order to supply the same service. It is at this point that the distinction must be drawn between public utilities and other industries. Public utilities are industries that have control of the market. There are no competitors from whom customers may get the identical service.

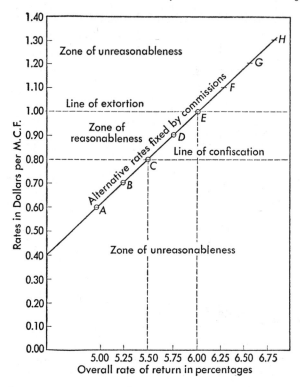

Chart XIII   Gas Rates Illustrating Zone of Reasonableness.

There may be *substitute* services, to be sure; but this involves a resort to services which are either inferior in quality or else rendered by enterprises which are themselves public utilities.

Clearly, rates may vary between 80 cents and $1.00 and yet be within the judicial zone of reasonableness. Except under abnormal conditions, the court is not so much concerned with rates that are extortionate. This is left to the legislature and its agent, the commission. It has concerned itself principally with rates that are *unreasonably discriminatory* as between customers. It also watches particularly the line of confiscation, leaving the determination of rate levels above the line of confiscation to the discretion of the commission. In 1913, in the very important, second Minnesota rate cases (230 U.S. 352, p. 433), this is explicitly recognized. The legislature is there given the choice of varying degrees of limitation of earnings as long as limitation is not clearly confiscatory. It is the zone of reasonableness which Justice Hughes had in mind when he wrote: "The rate-making power is a legislative power and necessarily implies a range of legislative discretion. *We do not sit as a board of revision to substitute our judgment for that of the legislature,* or of the Commission lawfully constituted by it, as to matters within the province of either."

Modification of the Rule by Administrative Commissions

The fair-value doctrine of the courts ushered in a long period of discussion, which was largely concerned with the development of methods of appraising and placed very little emphasis upon the philosophy of the subject. The eclecticism of *Smyth v. Ames* was taken for granted. Later, more attention was given to the meaning and significance of valuation, and it was then that standards of valuation, now partly clarified as to method of determination, came in for an *increasing measure of criticism.* The concrete result of this period of criticism was the definite elimination of standards based upon existing revenues as a measure of value. It was recognized that a commercial valuation predicated upon earning capacity had no place in a process of price determination whose objective was the determination of the reasonable exchange value of services produced under regulated monopolistic or semi-monopolistic conditions. The establishment of theoretically correct criteria of valuation has been made more difficult by the persistence of competition. In intercity transportation particularly, legislative policy continues to favor the maintenance of at least some elements of competition. It was felt that regulation could not be perfected to do the *full* work of competition. Opposition to consolidations was such that the combination movement could not bear its full fruit.

A good deal of truth, it must be admitted, is on the side of those who contend that the cost of service does not determine even the general level of rates as long as competing carriers must meet each other's rates and as long as there are differences in the cost of service among competing carriers. The so-called strong and weak road problem is one of the legacies of our laissez-faire past which makes the selection of any *one* standard of valuation difficult.

The situation may thus be summarized as follows: In the progressive development of valuation principles and practice, rate-making authorities soon recognized that the capitalization of income standard was inapplicable. Choice was thus narrowed down to the investment and cost of reproduction standards. As far as the investment standard is concerned, the par value of securities was infrequently used for the reason given above. Until 1942, when the courts began to give commissions more rein, they gave lip homage to all the evidentiary facts, but their main reliance has been upon investment, as evidenced by accounting records and cost of reproduction ascertained by appraisal, giving "due weight" to each.

In applying the cost-of-reproduction standard, a host of embarrassing questions was soon raised, all pertaining to the hypothetical character of the theory that any plant has a value equal to its cost of reproduction. We shall discuss these in the chapters which follow. The upshot of the matter was that commissions came to rely more and more upon cost of reproduction, which could be obtained at any time and for all properties by ordering that the properties be appraised. Historical cost, on the other hand, was neglected. The reason was well stated by Professor Ripley in 1912:

It has been neglected in part because of the inchoate condition of accounting principles and practice, and in part because of misunderstanding by laymen of such sound distinctions between capital and income as were well recognized among experts. Great confusion is everywhere apparent as to what the term implies. "Book value" or cost of property . . . seldom represents anything even approximating the facts. The meagreness of corporate records, either because of carelessness or bad faith, is indeed a severely practical objection and yet experience has already shown that original cost can be unearthed.

18. THE PLACE OF
APPRAISALS IN PUBLIC
UTILITY VALUATIONS

An appraisal consists of four operations: (1) making an inventory of units of property; (2) determining unit prices; (3) computing a figure representing the appraisal of the property as if new, which is the sum of the products of the number of units times the relevant unit prices; (4) determining the accrued depreciation for each unit of property in order to ascertain the so-called present value (cost new less the accrued depreciation).

An inventory is primarily the work of an appraisal engineer. It consists of the marshaling of the tangible elements of property in accordance with some convenient and logical classification of items. The listing now usually follows the classification of fixed-capital accounts. The determination of the unit prices and of the existing depreciation are the joint contribution of the engineer and the accountant, functioning as statisticians and price analysts. The final collation of the appraisal figures is a purely arithmetical operation in which statistical and engineering experience are combined.

Great divergencies often appeared in the figures offered by appraisers hired by the public utility companies and those hired by cities or consumers. This induced commissions to organize their own expert staffs for appraisal purposes. Their findings were used in order to check up on the appraisals submitted by litigants as evidence, as well as to conduct appraisals of their own. It was assumed, and the assumption is largely true, that official appraisers occupy an unbiased position. Such appraisals by their own organizations have accordingly been given great weight by commissions in fixing the rate base.

The Purpose and Cost of Appraisals

Why, it may be asked, are appraisals required if public service corporations are controlled in their accounting practices? The chief reason for making appraisals at the present time is that some states continue to require that an estimate of the current, or present, cost of construction be submitted as evidence in determining the fair value.

Historically, appraisals have been most important in establishing a basis for regulation, though they have now declined in importance. In the days preceding commission regulation, the accounts of public utilities were seldom, if ever, so kept as to lend assurance that investment costs could be determined. Thus, appraisals were undertaken in order to check investment costs. To some extent they took the place of accounting records where these were wholly unreliable. Upon the basis of such appraisals, properties were consolidated, securities were issued, and accounting systems reorganized. Sometimes appraisals served only the purpose of supplying particular deficiencies in accounting records. For instance, it was possible by means of appraisals to test the adequacy of the depreciation reserves of old properties. When properties were purchased or constructed without detailed records of cost, an appraisal could supply this deficiency. Sometimes appraisals were necessary in order to clear property accounts of entries that ought not to have been made. In the days before correct accounting principles were widely known and applied, and when depreciation reserves were inadequate or nonexistent, a company that desired to show a high net income might charge renewals to the property accounts when they should have been charged as retirements against depreciation reserves. Another defect was that the cost of maintaining property was often charged to the property accounts instead of treating it as an operating expense. On the other hand, particularly in growing properties, construction costs might be incorrectly charged to operating expense accounts instead of to the fixed capital accounts.

In setting up or reorganizing an accounting system, appraisals will provide the basis for the apportionment of property in accordance with a detailed classification of property accounts. Usually this also involves allocations by political subdivisions and by departments of the business. By this means the way is cleared for the installation of cost accounting records as an aid in rate-making. The segregation of the property by political subdivisions assists in the apportionment of taxes, which are assessed to the corporation as a whole under the "unit rule." Such taxes must be subdivided and apportioned to those local units in which a portion of the property is located and where it conducts a part of its business.

The cost of making appraisals varies with the extent of the properties and with the detail that a particular appraisal is designed to show. Appraisals for rate-making purposes and for use in condemnation proceedings are usually very detailed and hence more expensive than appraisals conducted to validate securities. Where plants are large and consist of properties of uniform types, the inventories are brief and the unit prices few. But where properties are complex, widely scattered, and of many classifications, the procedure becomes involved and time-consuming.

On this account, appraisals ought to be resorted to only infrequently. Not only must the direct expense to commissions and the litigants be considered but the disorganization incident thereto is reflected in the cost of the service. The time consumed in preparing appraisals and in hearings before commissions and courts has slowed up the process of regulation. Therefore, from the standpoint of the over-all efficiency of regulated industry, appraisals should be subordinated to accounting and should be resorted to only under exceptional conditions. Regulation can also be simplified, and its processes can be made more readily understandable to the layman if the accounting records and the capitalization of the companies are made to conform to the results of a thorough-going appraisal and the subsequent finding of a rate base. The mystery of a rate-base divergent from accounting records could thus be resolved, thereby furthering good will and mutual understanding between the going concern and its customers.

The Inventory

For most purposes the inventory should represent a *complete* listing of *all* the tangible property which the corporation owns. In certain cases it may also become important to know what property the concern leases. For rate-making purposes, however, the inventory should, strictly speaking, be limited to property used in public utility operations. This is usually accomplished by setting up two classifications, (1) operating property and (2) nonoperating property. In passing upon appraisals submitted to them as evidence in rate proceedings, courts and commissions have set up the standard that the inventory should include only *property used and useful in the service of the public*. The words *used and useful* were chosen in order to make clear that the inventory should include not only property that is used *continuously* but also property used *intermittently* or held for use in the immediate future.

In applying this standard to concrete situations, many problems have been encountered. The more important of these center around the following:

Nonoperating property
Property retired from service but not yet sold or otherwise retired from
  the fixed capital account
Improvident acquisitions of property
Engineering mistakes

Reinvested earnings and donated property
Omissions and contingencies

Nonoperating property. This class of property includes, for instance, facilities and appliances of merchandise sales departments. The line between operating and nonoperating property is, of course, difficult to draw. The principal reason for drawing one in this case is that trading in these appliances has developed upon a competitive basis. The same is true of wiring and installation services rendered by electric utilities to their customers. Where prices for incidental services are determined by competitive forces, properties used and useful in these services should not be included in the rate base and must, therefore, be excluded also from the inventory of operating property.

Property retirements. Old and established utilities, which have passed through periods of considerable changes in the art and in the development of their markets, will often have on hand property which has been discarded or which should be discarded from service. Historic illustrations were afforded by horsecars which had been superseded by cablecars and these, in turn, by electric cars. The rapid changes in the type of electric car equipment have added further items to the list of discarded properties for electric railways. The question arises: Should such property be excluded from the inventory as property no longer used and useful? Viewed from the standpoint of service alone, the property is certainly no longer useful. It should be, and usually is, eliminated from the inventory unless some equitable claim can be made that it be included. For instance, if the utility has been unable to set aside sufficient funds with which to provide for the retirement of such discarded equipment, on account of the rapidity with which the property has become obsolescent or inadequate; then on equitable grounds it may be included in the rate base as property used and useful. This would certainly be proper if the utility has not earned a reasonable return, and future business can carry these amortizations. Each instance would have to be judged in the light of its own special facts. In such cases, provision has sometimes been made for the gradual elimination of such elements from the rate base by suitable amortization payments. Examples are again afforded by the amortization of acquisition adjustments. In any event, no general rule can apply under all circumstances.

Improvident acquisitions of property. Public utilities must stand ready to supply service when the demand for service arises. They will, therefore, anticipate these demands by having spare facilities ready. Forecasting the future demand and making provision for it is ordinarily not difficult where facilities may be had upon call. However, in purchasing land in strategic locations the cost may be unduly enhanced, unless utilities are forehanded in the matter and make their purchases in advance of need. Other illustrations of facilities whose acquisition has been challenged are surplus stocks of materials and supplies and extra capacity for future needs in tunnels and conduits. Within reasonable limits, such spare facilities may be included in the rate base. Sometimes, however, these transactions may savor of speculations in commodities or real estate. In doubtful cases some utilities have adopted the commendable policy of applying for commission approval of such contemplated purchases or installations. Under modern conditions of accounting and investment control, the prudence of these expenditures can be left to commission approval. This has served to protect utilities against criticisms if reasonable calculations as to future needs or future prices prove later on not to have been so well founded.

Planning for the future is peculiarly difficult under conditions when investments are contemplated during periods of boom, or in communities whose economic livelihood depends upon some wasting natural resource. An element of administrative discretion must necessarily enter into the determination of such questions by commissions. Reasonable expectations may not materialize, and the utility may fail to establish a paying business. Under such conditions, substantial portions of property may have to be excluded from the inventory of used and useful property. Regulation should also protect consumers against improvident investments made by public utilities.

Engineering mistakes. Closely akin to the problem just discussed is that which has to do with property in the acquisition of which some engineering mistakes have been committed. The general standard applied in all such cases is that the management is required *to use ordinary care and foresight.* Property may prove to be useless, due to faulty design. Or the difficulties may arise out of faulty construction or mistakes in location. All these may lead to premature obsolescence or inadequacy. Each case must be examined in detail and a decision reached whether or not the investments represent palpable engineering blunders.

Omissions and contingencies. The chief requirement in preparing a classified inventory is that it be *accurate* and *complete.* The classification should be so detailed as to make the inventory useful in as many directions as possible. This is more likely to be accomplished if the appraisal is the work of an experienced and well-coordinated organization. Even the best organization, however, will make errors and omissions in an inventory. In order to allow for this deficiency, a percentage addition is usually made to cover "omissions and contingencies." From 3 to 5 per cent has been added on this account. In an appraisal of the properties of the Milwaukee Electric Railway and Light Company, the Railroad Commission of Wisconsin in 1910 made an allowance of 3 per cent. A reappraisal under better conditions in 1914 showed errors and omissions equal to an estimated allowance of 7.75 per cent, the difference amounting in this case to $1,521,662.

Unit Prices

The inventory gives details regarding the number of units of each class of property. For each, a unit price must be determined. The composition of the unit price is such as to include (1) the cost of material and labor (sometimes called *specific construction*) and (2) the cost of the units in place (sometimes called *specific overhead*). Little need be said here as to the method of ascertaining these prices. Appraisers have special facilities for the ascertainment of manufacturers' prices and their special discounts, and they organize this statistical information so that an appraisal may be made at prices prevailing over a wide range of time and area. Local prices and wage rates are important. Much information is derived from the accounts and records of the company and from the cost records of other similar enterprises. The specific overhead allows for freight, storage, handling charges, and in fact, all supervision and overhead cost that can be definitely allocated to specific units of property.

If the work has been done through a general contractor who may in turn employ subcontractors, the unit price will include the contractor's profit, which has sometimes been fixed at 10 per cent of direct costs. Much dispute surrounds this element in unit costs. It is generally conceded, however, that the contract system of construction is economical because the accumulated experience of contractors and their use of special facilities enables them to do the work more cheaply than when it is done through a utility's own construction organization. If the utility is large enough to employ its own construction organization, the arrangement is known as "force account." It is therefore important to distinguish between unit prices which include an allowance for contractors' profit and unit prices for so-called piecemeal construction. The advantages of the contract system are greatest in the wholesale construction of public utilities and less significant as far as concerns the smaller annual additions or reconstructions. In piecemeal construction, unit costs are generally higher, but no allowance is necessary for contractors' and subcontractors' profit.

The question of unit prices and their influence upon appraisals, and thus upon rate-base determinations, is so important that we shall return to it again later on. At this point it is only necessary to make clear what unit prices are, how they are arrived at, and how they are combined with other elements into a final appraisal figure.

General Overhead Charges

After the physical property has been inventoried and the proper unit prices have been applied to the unit-quantities, the resulting figure is called the *specific construction cost*. It then becomes necessary to make certain additions to the specific construction cost in order that the appraisal may embody all elements that go to make up the completed plant. The significant phases in the life history of a going concern were sketched in Chapter 11. It was there shown that the first period is one of preliminary organization during which the legal, financial, and industrial plans of organization of the going concern are set up. Since the appraisal is, in essence, an attempt to recapitulate the costs, either original costs or reproduction costs which have been or would have to be incurred, it must not confine itself to construction costs alone.

Reconstruction of the plant should not, in theory at least, bring new overhead costs. Presumably, under proper accounting, overhead charges associated with units of property retired have been charged to the depreciation reserve along with the cost of the old units and have consequently disappeared. New overhead charges associated with the new units of property have taken their place in the accounts.

There is some difference of opinion also as to what should be considered a proper *general* overhead charge. From an economic and accounting point of view it does not appear to be correct to consider uncompensated costs incurred as overhead charges during the period of building up the business. According to accepted accounting principles, all costs involved in solicitation of new business are charged to operating expense accounts. If revenues do not cover the operating outlay plus the necessary fixed charges, the result is a *deficit from operation,* which certainly should not be charged as *capital.* If stockholders have been obliged to forgo dividends during the early years of operation, that is a risk which they have assumed, and no process of accounting legerdemain should raise these failures of early returns to the level of *capital costs.* If, in the process of rate regulation, these losses are to be recognized, it must be by means of an accounting process which is *independ-*

ent of the accounting arrangements set up for the business as an economic entity. In this way alone can accounts serve their fundamental purpose of disclosing the balance between cost and income; that is to say, whether costs exceed income, or vice versa. It is, therefore, better accounting and appraisal policy that all costs incurred during the period when business is being built up be rigidly excluded from the category of "overhead charges." This would eliminate the so-called going value, or better, "going cost" from consideration at this point.

There remain the following classifications of cost:

1. *Preliminary expenditures associated with the going plan.* These include promotion expense, expenditures in financing, expenditures in preliminary engineering, and expenditures incurred in effecting a legal organization and in attending to all other legal matters appropriate during this period of preliminary organization. The last named item includes costs in securing franchises, examining and drawing up contracts, securing permits and consents from public authorities and private owners, etc.

2. *Expenditures during the period of construction.* The purpose of these is of so general a character that they cannot be associated with particular units of the plant but must be associated with the going plant as a whole. These include all salaries and expenses of the administrative, legal, clerical, and engineering staff during the *period of construction.*

A word should be added in explanation of certain items of overhead construction cost. These items include property insurance, injuries and damages, taxes, and interest during construction. They are designed to cover losses or insurance against losses due to personal injuries, floods, fires, accident, and other causes. Taxes are assessed against land, buildings, structures, and equipment, even though the plant has not yet commenced operation. The conditions of financing are usually such that interest-bearing bonds are immediately sold to cover a substantial part of the construction cost. Some allowances for interest should therefore be made for capital tied up in construction, whether the capital was derived by borrowing or from stock subscriptions. These items of cost may be capitalized during the construction period because they are as much a part of the completion of the going plant as the cost of construction of the physical property.

The best practice in dealing with general overheads is to apply varying percentages to the several primary classifications of property in the inventory. In the case of omissions and contingencies, for example, there is not likely to be any omission of land nor more than relatively small omissions and contingencies in some types of properties as compared with others. It has not always seemed advisable or possible to go to such lengths in refining the process. This was particularly true of earlier appraisals, and it is still customary to make allowance for overhead charges by general percentage additions to the total "specific construction." On account of the divergence in classification and practice, it is difficult to illustrate the magnitude of these allowances. The following classification which has been used shows the probable limits within which these percentage allowances fall.

Classification of Overhead Charges	*Range of Allowance*
Interest, taxes, and insurance during construction	6% to 12%
Engineering, superintendence, and administration	3% to 10%
Organization and legal expenses	3% to 5%
Omissions and contingencies	1% to 3%
Total	13% to 30%

Cases in which the allowance will be as low or lower than 13 per cent or as high or higher than 30 per cent are rare and unusual, but the range indicates how construction and other conditions will affect the size of the allowance. Appraisals of large properties tend to show lower percentage additions than appraisals for small properties. A conventional allowance is 15 per cent. It is well to call attention to an error which must be guarded against. Care should be exercised that there is no duplication of allowances, first in unit prices and again in the general overhead.

Ascertainment of Final Appraisal Figures

Ascertainment of a final appraisal figure consists primarily of the arithmetical process of multiplying the number of units of each class of property by the relevant unit price in order to get the total appraised price for each class of property. If general overheads have been determined by property groupings, overhead allowances must be added in order to give the total appraised price, including the overhead. If the general overhead has been fixed for the property as a whole, the appraised prices may first be added and the general overhead allowance computed as a total. The two will then represent the grand total appraised price of the tangible property which has been classed as operating property.

The foregoing considers the tangible property as if it were new. It is also necessary to determine, by means of an appraisal estimate, the annual rate at which the units of property depreciate both by classes and for the property as a whole. For this purpose appraisers have set up certain concepts that are of a mixed physical and financial nature. The first of these is "scrap value."

Scrap value is an engineering *estimate* of what might be the value of each unit of property in a disintegrated condition, after its useful life in service has expired. The "scrap value" is deducted from the total appraised figure, and the difference is called the "wearing value" or the depreciable part of the appraised figure for that class of property.

It is true of course that some properties are durable in character. From the standpoint of their own inherent physical or chemical qualities they may render service indefinitely, as long as they constitute a part of the going plant. They therefore have neither a scrap value nor a wearing value in the appraisal sense of these terms. Other properties have only a limited "service life." During this period it is assumed that the wearing value is dissipated. Old properties may thus be said to have a wearing value (1) which has already been dissipated, and (2) which still remains as a future service life "expectancy." The ratio of unexpired life to total life expectancy is sometimes called the *condition per cent* of the unit. Borrowing certain accounting terminology, we may speak of the expired life as the *accrued but unmatured depreciation,* and of the unexpired life as the *unaccrued and unmatured depreciation.* When the full service life has expired, the depreciation has matured. We may thus set up two equations which exhibit the relationship of these concepts in the case of new and old properties. (1) In new properties the cost new equals the estimated wearing value plus the estimated scrap value. (2) In old properties the cost new equals the accrued depreciation plus the remainder of wearing value plus the estimated scrap value.

It may also be necessary to show the proportion of the grand total of the appraised figure which is assignable (1) to different geographical locations and (2) to the different departments of a given enterprise. This is known technically as the process of *apportionment.* The latter is particularly important in the cases of corporations rendering more than one class of public utility service. Convenience and the purpose for which the figures are being compiled will dictate the degree of refinement and character of the apportionment.

The Appraisal of Accrued Depreciation

We have noted above that appraisers have defined certain concepts which are useful in their work of estimating accrued depreciation. They assume, for instance, that nondurable property may command a certain price in the open market—when such property is in a disintegrated condition. They call this *scrap* value, and it represents the minimum beyond which property does not depreciate. Some nondurable properties like ties and concrete foundations have little or no scrap value. In fact, the cost of removal and transportation of these materials to scrap markets might make the scrap value a negative figure. Such properties will therefore depreciate by the amount of their entire costs.

Let it now be assumed that appraisers have picked out the properties that are depreciable, and that they have assigned to them an estimated "scrap value." In any given plant, however, the properties, though no longer new, may still be in good working condition. Nevertheless, because they are units combined into a working whole, they are *in time* nearer the date when they will have to be retired *as units* and replaced by new units of the same or different description. The accrued depreciation is this estimated accrued cost of a future liability to replacement—not in terms of the cost of new units but in terms of the cost of existing units.

The first step in the ascertainment of accrued depreciation, therefore, must be the specification of an assumed length of life for each unit. This life expectancy must be based upon experience with such property units under actual operating conditions. It should be recalled that this length of service life is premised upon a policy with respect to repair which will keep the units in good working condition. Failure to make repairs in season creates a condition of undermaintenance and shortens the service life. Again, *local* operating conditions must be taken into account in the assessment of service life. In many instances, units of equipment will be found whose years in service have exceeded the estimated life. Perhaps easy operating conditions, a careful maintenance policy, a few improvements or rearrangements have made it economical to retain the unit in service. The determination of accrued depreciation is, in consequence, not a matter of mathematical accuracy, although it uses mathematical formulae. Any provisional determination of life expectancy upon the basis of life tables ought, therefore, to be tested out for its applicability to the individual case by an actual inspection and survey of the entire property from a service standpoint. Only engineers thoroughly familiar with such properties and using their best judgment can make a final assignment of lives. Complete accounting and statistical records showing dates of installation, operating data indicating past, present, and prospective intensity of use, important events in the life history of the units, all will give the requisite background for the exercise of a sound engineering judgment. From time to time as operating conditions change, or as additional experience is gained as to length of useful life, the estimated remainder lives may have to be changed, as was recently done by the Public Utility Commission of California.

One mode of procedure is to ascertain the condition of the property by a score-card method, assigning to property in *good* condition 100 per cent of the estimated remainder life, to property in *fair* condition 90 per cent, to property in *poor* condition, 80 per cent. If, then, the finally assigned life of a unit is taken to be twenty-five years, its age is ascertained to be five years, and the condition of the unit at the time of inspection is scored at 100 per cent. Its remainder life is assumed to be twenty years, indicating that 20 per cent of the wearing value has become accrued depreciation. The unit is said to be in 80 per cent condition, and that proportion of the wearing value plus the estimated scrap value is its cost new less depreciation. Without discussing at this time the bearing that these estimates have upon the final valuation of properties for rate-making or purchase purposes, we should note that the weakness of the procedure is again the lack of certainty that the prospective life will be attained. And yet some estimate of the accrued liability for replacement of the units should be made in order to test the adequacy of the financial provision that has been made. To condemn the entire procedure as theoretical, impractical, and academic seems to the writer to be running away from inevitable facts, and ostrich-like, burying one's head in the sand.

The Appraisal of Working Capital

In addition to the tangible elements thus far considered, a utility must have working capital in order to conduct its business. We have seen that the going plant is not complete until it is fully constructed, an operating organization is assembled, and operating materials and supplies are provided. Working capital consists primarily of these *materials* and *supplies*. A distinction must be recognized here between materials and supplies which are needed for plant extensions and those required merely for continuous operation of the existing plant. Continuous operation means adequate supplies of coal, coke, oil, ties, rails, poles, meters, small tools, and other equipment, an endless list of commodities. These materials are in part consumed in the very production of service, and in part they are needed to keep fixed properties in good state of repair; consequently, they must always be kept in stock. Materials and supplies are also required for new construction and reconstruction. In so far as they are required for the latter purpose, they too represent true working capital because continuity of operation in a broad sense is dependent upon a policy of timely plant renewal. It will be difficult in practice to separate materials for new construction from those for reconstruction. Still, the distinction is one that exists at least theoretically and ought in practice to be approximated. Since capital will be continuously employed for these purposes, working capital in the shape of materials and supplies constitutes a proper addition to the rate base. Appraisal engineers have accordingly included materials and supplies in their inventories and priced these along with other physical items.

Public utilities also distribute their product to customers in advance of payment. Only in the transportation of passengers do they perform a cash business. In the sale of streetcar and bus tickets a transportation company actually performs a cash-in-advance business so that some funds are obtained from customers in advance of actual expenditures. Taxes accrued in advance of actual payment constitute another source of cash working capital. Other utilities do not collect compensation until from thirty to sixty days later. An allowance is therefore made which, in the judgment of the regulatory commission, constitutes the amount of capital thus continuously tied up in unpaid bills or in advance expenditures. The determination is a difficult one but not very important in comparison with other items in the rate base. As rough measures, the average balance of cash and accounts receivable or two months' normal operating expenditures, may be taken. In strict theory, some allowance ought, however, to be made for noninterest bearing accounts payable because enterprises of established credit are in turn "carried" for short periods by producers from whom they buy.

19. RETROSPECTIVE
REGULATION—1898 TO 1923

Regulation of public utilities in the United States has been a matter of long growth. Our historical survey has shown that public utilities, excepting only transportation utilities, are best distinguished from other industries by two criteria: (1) they render services which are necessities of civilized life in an exchange economy, and (2) they are best developed under monopolistic conditions. It has taken a long time to wring this conclusion from the historical circumstances which have attended the development of these enterprises. With respect to transportation, the second criterion has never proved wholly acceptable. The Granger movements were regulatory in nature and based upon a recognition of the fact that railroads were instrumentalities necessary for the development of economic life but not at all that they should be organized as monopolies. An era of consolidations has brought about some changes in this point of view, but intercity transportation still reflects this policy of repugnance to monopoly and of encouragement of competition between transport agencies of the same kind, as well as between the various different forms of transport services. In the balance of the utility field, however, there has come a general recognition that public regulation must more and more do the work of competition. The only forms of competition which still remain are historical remnants of this competitive past and the competition of substitute services.

The doctrine of "a fair return upon the fair value," when announced by the court in 1898 as the fulcrum of regulation, came at the close of the prevailingly competitive period and at the beginning of a newer era of consolidation and monopolistic combination. The contradictory nature of the standards of valuation which the rule of rate-making embodied (as we explained these standards in Chapter 17) bears testimony to the transitional character of the period of its origin. It is, therefore, necessary to recognize that the rate-base problem had two aspects, one arising out of historical conditions and another having to do with conditions which were to obtain in the future. These divergent tendencies had to be somehow reconciled. One aspect would have been to take account of competitive origins, while the other aspect would need to envisage these monopolistic developments. A bridge would have to be erected by means of which these industries might pass under equitable circumstances from one period to the next. This bridge was provided by the commissions of the new era in what we call *retrospective valuations*.

Fair Value as a Basis for Reconciliation

From 1898 to 1923 the fair-value doctrine continued to serve as a basis for reconciliation of the past with the future. The Southwestern Bell Telephone Company case of 1923 marks the end of the period when the fair value was more or less generally accepted by commissions. In a general work of this kind we cannot attempt to deal with the varying circumstances under which the rule was applied by commissions nor to explain the expedients adopted or the compromises proclaimed. However, we will attempt to sketch the essentials.

During the period under review, the conflict between investment and cost of reproduction was not so apparent as it became later on. The reason is to be found in the course of wholesale prices as reflected in index numbers and as combined by statisticians in a single curve to represent the changing general price level. This general index is shown in Chart XIV. Beginning in 1865 the trend of the price level was steadily downward until 1897, followed by a gradual rise until 1914. In 1915 the price level began to mount in successive sharp increases, attaining a maximum peak in May, 1920. During 1920 and 1921 came a sharp recession, reaching its lowest point in October, 1921. Between 1921 and 1929, although the price level was slowly rising, it had, nevertheless, achieved a certain stability, then often referred to as a "new plateau of prices."

As pointed out in Chapter 17, commissions used reproduction cost in such a way as to give it preponderant influence. In doing so, however, they came upon a host of perplexing questions. The United States Supreme Court had ruled in 1909, in *Wilcox v. Consolidated Gas Co.* (212 U.S. 19) that the fair or reasonable value must be the value *at the time of the inquiry in regard to the rates.* Doubt as to the meaning of this phrase was finally resolved by adopting the practice of averaging prices over a period of years, usually three or five. It was assumed that this would smooth out the range of price fluctuations occasioned by the business cycle. Soon it was discovered that for some commodities like lumber and its products, in view of our gradually receding supply of the basic natural resources, prices were generally increasing. On the other hand the prices of many manufactured commodities showed a decided downward tendency. In these cases the "trend price" (i.e., the price computed as a moving average for the date of the inventory) was taken. An appraisal based upon these practices was usually called a *normal cost of reproduction appraisal* and was identified with the normal-value concept of neoclassical economics. So interpreted, cost of reproduction was believed to afford a stable standard, akin to the normal exchange value of competitive economics. Given the difficulty, if not the impossibility in many instances, of ascertaining historical investment costs, as well as the un-reliability (except in the case of Massachusetts) of using security issues (more particularly the watered stock) as a rate base, normal reproduction cost looked like the answer to the problem. Although utility representatives before 1914 inclined to favor investment, if not book, costs, while representatives of consumer's interests favored reproduction cost (which often was the lower figure), normal reproduction costs and investment cost were not too far apart. "Physical valuation," thus interpreted, looked like a reasonable starting point.

Other reconciliations, vaguely alluded to in the fair-value rule as "other matters" stemming from the varying financial history of the utilities, were also needed. In *Knoxville v. Knoxville Water Co.* (212 U.S. 1), also decided in 1909, the Supreme Court denied the claim of the company to an unde-preciated rate base. The earnings of the company had been sufficient to cover the accrued depreciation, but it had failed to reserve them, paying them out in dividends. It was a case of "eating its cake and having it too." The Court pointed out that it was not only the right of the company but also its duty to security holders and the public to earn a sum sufficient to make good the annual depreciation. Under the conditions obtaining in this case, the Court ruled that the accrued depreciation must be deducted from the rate base.

Another type of reconciliation grew from the hypothetical character of the reproduction cost theory. Two cases illustrate these modifications. We have already noted that in choosing between the substitute plant and identical plant variants of this theory, it was the trend of commission practice to use the identical plant hypothesis because it more nearly reflected the historical conditions. In the second Minnesota rate cases of 1913 (230 U.S. 352), the railways claimed that land values should be based upon the present cost of acquiring or condemning such lands. This value was to be found by ascertaining the present value of contiguous lands, with additional allowances by way of a multiplier for what was called the *railway value* of such lands. The multiplier was to reflect the present cost of hypothetical severance damages, court costs, and other extravagant claims, even though no such costs would ever be incurred. Justice Hughes, with some insight into the problem as a result of his New York experiences, refused to accept the multiplier and ruled that the railway should be satisfied if reproduction cost was based upon the fair average values of similar land in the vicinity. In most instances the lands had actually cost much less or had been a free grant. This also modified the reproduction cost theory in the direction of greater reasonableness. Similarly in 1915, in *Des Moines Gas Co. v. Des Moines* (238 U.S. 153), in applying the reproduction theory to a distribution system, the Court refused to allow for the cost of cutting through pavement over mains where the street had been paved *after* the construction of the gas mains.

Intangible Elements of Value

A further type of reconciliation has to do with intangible elements. These can be summarized under the headings of good will, franchise value, and going value.

Good will value. The question was soon raised whether public utilities are entitled to an allowance in the rate base for "good will." The value of good will may be tersely defined as that portion of the total value of a business undertaking which may be imputed to the patronage that the particular business enjoys. Ordinarily, in purchase and sale transactions, the element of good will—the disposition of customers "to return to the old stand"—is paid for as a distinct property right, apart from the right to physical property. The seller is usually placed under some reasonable restraint as to his right to engage in the same line of business. He has sold a portion of his "liberty." In the case of public utilities, however, commissions supported by the courts repeatedly refused to recognize good will. While they agreed that good will could be property, as such it was premised upon freedom of access to markets and upon competition. When the consumer is confined to the service of a single public utility, there is no economic basis upon which the value of good will may be predicated. This was early brought out by Judge Hough in *Consolidated Gas Co. v. City of New York* (157 Fed. 849,872) and later affirmed by the United States Supreme Court. Said Judge Hough in trenchant language:

There is nothing in the nature of its business enabling it to acquire good will in the property sense or indeed in any other. It is required by law to furnish gas to all demanding it within certain distance of the mains, and it owns the mains, service pipes and meters . . . I think it apparent that the conceivable good will of a gas company in this city is about equal to that of the street cleaning department of the municipal government.

This case settled the matter except as related considerations reappeared under claims for franchise value and going value. We need add only that if commissions desire to stimulate and reward exceptional skill in developing markets and in maintaining good customer relations, they may do so by making a suitable allowance in the rate of return.

Franchise value. In earlier discussions of franchises it was usually contended that substantial allowances should be made for their value in rate cases. Since franchises were property, so the argument ran, and taxed as such, their value should also be included in the rate base. But the argument was not accepted by commissions. The position of the commissions was well stated by the Railroad Commission of Wisconsin in 1910 in *Appleton v. Appleton Water Works Co.* (5 W.R.C.R. 215,281):

> The contention often made that the value of franchises should be included as an element for consideration in determining the present fair value of the active property of a public service corporation for rate-making purposes, though supported by judicial sanction in certain jurisdictions, does not appeal to us as either sound or practical. The only measure of franchise values recognized by the courts is the earning capacity of the property to which the franchises give vitality. Earnings are dependent upon the rates that are exacted, and, hence, the higher the rates the more valuable are the franchises, and *vice versa*. Obviously, therefore, it would be futile to attempt to determine the reasonableness of a rate by any standard which is at all dependent upon franchise values for its dimensions.

It is now current practice to include all reasonable and legitimate expenditures in securing franchises in organization expenses. But during the period of transition from the franchise system to the commission system of regulation there was considerable uncertainty in the treatment of the item. An older view was adopted by Justice Brewer in a purchase case and then was usually cited as a precedent in rate cases. As stated by Brewer in 1893 in *Monongahela Nav. Co. v. U.S.* (148 U.S. 312,329):

> The latter [franchises] can no more be taken without compensation than can its tangible corporeal property [of a Bridge company]. Their value depends upon their productiveness. If they yield no money in return over expenditures they would possess little if any present value. If, however, they yield a revenue over and above expenses they possess present value, the amount of which depends in a measure upon the excess of revenue.

This is true enough in a condemnation case where there may be an unexpired term of a franchise. In a rate case involving the police powers rather than eminent domain, the correct view was also first stated by Judge Hough in 1907 in the Consolidated Gas case:

For these reasons I believe that on principle a franchise should be held to have no value except that arising from its use as a shield to protect those investing their property upon the faith thereof; and that considered alone and apart from the property which it renders fruitful, it possesses no more economic value for the investor than does an actual shield possess fighting value apart from the soldier who bears it.

Statutes now frequently provide as did the Public Service Commission Act in New York, that

. . . the Commission shall have no power to authorize the capitalization of a franchise in excess of the amount (exclusive of any tax or annual charge) actually paid to the state or any political subdivision thereof as the consideration for the grant of such franchise right.

Going value. The judicial opinion which gave the going value concept its first formulation was, as in the case of franchise value, an opinion in a purchase case. In 1894, in *National Water Works Co. v. Kansas City* (62 Fed. 853), the Court said:

Nor would the mere cost of producing the waterworks plant be a fair test, because that does not take into account the value which flows from the established connections between the pipes and the buildings of the city . . . A completed system of waterworks such as the company has, without a single connection between the pipes in the streets and the buildings of the city, would be a property of much less value than the system connected as it is, with so many buildings and earning in consequence thereof the money which it does earn . . . Such a system would be a dead structure rather than a living and going business . . . It [the city] steps into possession of a property which not only has the ability to earn but is in fact earning. It should be paid, therefore, not merely the value of a system that might be made to earn, but that of a system which does earn.

Space does not permit giving in detail the nuances of meaning with which the term was used. It was often confused with franchise value and good will. It was quite an accomplishment when, due very largely to a Wisconsin formulation which we give below, it was distinguished from good will and franchise value and given a reasonable meaning for rate-making purposes as distinguished from acquisition proceedings. There was a common-sense appeal in the contention that a property with an established and profitable business should be valued at a higher sum than its structural or physical elements.

The Wisconsin concept of going value. In 1909, in *Hill v. Antigo Water Co.* (3 W.R.C.R. 623,709), the Commission had before it a company where it was possible to reconstruct a complete financial history from the books of account. In this opinion it formulated a *going-value* concept (perhaps better called a *going-cost* concept) and a method for quantitative measurement which is distinct from other formulations. Although it is usually represented as having been discarded by the authority of Justice Brandeis in the Galveston case of 1922, we reproduce it for historical reasons because the validity of this formulation in connection with retrospective valuations was not clearly perceived by the Court. We quote the Commission at length from the opinion written by Commissioner Halford Erickson:

The cost of developing a business of waterworks may be made up of many different kinds of expenditures. It may include the cost of advertising, soliciting, demonstrations showing the advantages of having water under pressure in the houses, or making free connections, of the granting of lower than regular rates, and of many other outlays of this character in order to secure customers. It may also include losses to the investors because of the fact that the plants in their earlier years failed to earn enough to meet all the requirements for operating expenses, including depreciation and reasonable return upon the investment. If the direct outlays for securing business are charged to operating expenses, as they should be, instead of to the capital account, then the cost of acquiring a paying business would be represented by the deficits, or by the amounts by which the gross earnings fall short of covering the cost of operation, as stated, including fair returns to the investors . . .

Just how long it takes for a properly adapted and reasonably well-managed plant to become self-sustaining is not entirely clear. Some reach this point within the first few years; others, again, require as many as ten or even more years, before they approach it. There are also those which never reach this point at all. Much depends upon the local conditions by which each plant is surrounded, and which vary from one place to another.

In order to determine the situation in this respect, it is therefore necessary to make a separate study of each particular plant, and of the conditions under which it was established and is operating. Where conditions are not favorable, the plants may never become paying enterprises. There are many reasons why, even under favorable conditions, it takes time to develop a paying business. The town, while growing, may not be large enough at the time. It may lack sewers and street-sprinkling systems. It may require less water for fire protection than was expected. It may have good wells for domestic purposes which the people are slow to abandon. These and many other conditions of a similar character often tend to keep the earnings of plants on a lower than normal basis for several years after they have been put into operation.

As to whether the cost of building up the business should be included in the value of a plant or gradually charged off from the earnings when these earnings become large enough to warrant it; or rather when they have so increased as to cover operating expenses, including depreciation and a reasonable return upon the investment, and, besides this, leave a surplus, may not be entirely clear. When added to the original capital upon which interest and profits should be earned, it becomes a permanent charge upon the consumers. This charge, however, is low; as low, in fact, as it very well can be made. When gradually written off, it results in a high annual charge that will terminate when the cost has been wiped out.

Either plan may be feasible. As to which one is preferable is a question that depends upon the circumstances in each particular case.

The method has come to be known as the *net deficits* method. By projecting into the past an assumption that the utility was entitled at all times to a reasonable return and no more, an estimate may be obtained, based upon historical evidence of the amount of the uncompensated loss which the owners assumed in developing a paying business for the first time. The net deficits may be negligible or even entirely absent. Or they may, in the judgment of the Commission, have been excessive in amount. Under these circumstances, either no allowance was made or only a reasonable amount of the net deficits were recognized. The latter was not done in the Galveston case as we shall see. It resolves to this: *Reasonable expectations* of investors should not be disappointed in a judgment process which takes past losses into account in fixing rates under a new dispensation for the future. An additional allowance by way of going value is made on equitable grounds and is within the discretion of commissions operating within the zone of reasonableness. Thus interpreted, going value is a legislative concept of reasonableness and is not a judicial concept of confiscation. Meanwhile, the U.S. Supreme Court in a series of cases, beginning with *Des Moines Gas Co. v. Des Moines* (238 U.S. 153) in 1915, ruled that going value was a property right entitling utilities to some return. Although the doctrine has since been considerably weakened, what is left of it comes close to being the "reasonable net deficits" method of the much maligned Antigo case.

Significance of the Galveston case. The specific question whether the Wisconsin formulation of going value and its quantitative measurement is necessary in order to escape the charge of confiscation was obliquely raised in *Galveston Electric Co. v. City of Galveston et al.* (258 U.S. 388). The method had "fallen among thieves." Certainly its use by the experts in this case was a travesty of the original design. In this case, rates fixed by ordinance of a local council were attacked by the company as confiscatory. Experts appearing for the company had made two estimates of going value, one of $575,300, another of $2 million. The city's expert had calculated a going value of $212,452. All these calculations were based upon a capitalization of net deficits. A special master, appointed by the lower court to make advisory findings, had included the sum of $520,000 for development cost. Justice Brandeis, in writing the opinion of the Supreme Court, carefully distinguished this item from another of $202,000 which was allowed to cover the overhead costs of construction. Included therein was $73,281 for "expenses of organization and business management." Brandeis said that these overhead items were "to cover the cost of establishing the system *as a physically going concern.*" The former item ($520,000 development cost), he therefore concluded, must be an allowance to cover the cost of developing the railway "into a *financially* successful concern."

The Court pointed out that these estimates were the result of calculations going back thirty-nine years in one case, when the original horsecar line was built; in another case, fifteen years, when the present owner purchased the property as a going concern. In both cases the calculations allow 4 per cent as a depreciation annuity and an annual rate of 8 per cent compound interest upon the value of the property. The net deficits were claimed to constitute a measure of the going value, and the question was raised whether an allowance based upon such evidence should be included in the rate base *in order to test whether the rate prescribed in the ordinance was confiscatory.*

The Court pointed out that accepting the allowance so ascertained

. . . would imply substantially a guaranty by the community that the investor will net on his investment ultimately a return of 8% yearly, with interest compounded on deferred payments; provided only that the traffic will, in the course of time, bear a rate high enough to produce that amount.

Should constitutional limitations protecting the property of public utilities be so interpreted as to force legislatures or commissions in fixing rates to take deficits into account? The Court's answer to this query is explicit:

A company which has failed to secure from year to year sufficient earnings to keep the investment unimpaired and to pay a fair return, whether its failure was the result of imprudence in engaging in the enterprise, or of errors in management, or of omission to exact proper prices for its output, cannot erect out of past deficits a legal basis for holding confiscatory for the future, rates which would, on the basis of present reproduction value, otherwise be compensatory.

Such allowances may be considered to make rates *reasonable* in the eyes of the legislature, thinks the Court; but, "Going-concern value and development cost, in the sense in which the master used these terms, are not to be included in the base value for the purpose of determining whether a rate is confiscatory."

So interpreted, the recognition or nonrecognition of going value as a retrospective element in these initial rate-base determinations under the rate-making rule of *Smyth v. Ames* becomes a matter of public policy. This was the point of view of Chairman Halford Erickson of the Wisconsin Railroad Commission, who left the impress of his thought upon its policies during the years when they were in the formative stage. No one can read the excerpt from the Antigo opinion without realizing that the aim was to build up a workable scheme of rate-control which would enable a commission to find a reasonable solution for the difficulties and incongruities of the past. Someone has well said that the definition of reasonableness is doing justice in hard cases, and it was in the service of reasonableness that the Wisconsin concept of going value was given scientific application.

An economic interpretation of going value. An economic principle is involved in these considerations which has not been adequately brought to bear upon the question at issue. Since public utilities are subject to the law of decreasing cost, there results a periodicity in the flow of net income. It would be rare indeed if these projects could be self-supporting from the beginning. According to careful investigations by F. W. Doolittle, a consulting engineer, it took the elevated railways of Chicago five years before the business attained reasonably full development. The plant as an original proposition or as a dynamic thing has to be so designed as to provide an efficient capacity. The exigencies of finding suitable locations and of long-run economy in construction and operation are such that public utilities must anticipate a future demand. If full development is therefore to be achieved, the service must be priced to comport with this eventual high load-factor development. Such developmental pricing policies necessarily mean low unit revenues during early years while total average unit costs are high. On this account the following statement of Justice Brandeis in the Galveston case is something less than the whole truth: "The fact that a sometime losing business becomes profitable eventually through growth of the community or more efficient management tends to prove merely that the adventure was not wholly misconceived." It may be true enough in those instances where public utility plants were constructed during boom periods and where the community failed to develop to boom expectations. Receiverships and reorganizations have usually liquidated such losses, and legislative policy need not be required to go behind that return.

But what about such mistakes in public policy as those which insisted upon dividing the business among competing plants? It is, of course, a risk inherent in all economic enterprises that they must adjust themselves to an all-embracing economic equilibrium which adjusts supply price to the demand. However, many utilities were started as a matter of public convenience and necessity, but required a period of preliminary waiting, of readiness to serve accompanied by solicitation for increased custom, before the requisite demand could be developed. Professor Richard T. Ely called them *ripening costs.* In such cases a legislative rate policy would be economically unjust in that it would not permit some recoupment of early losses to investors through increased earning power when full utilization has been attained. Such a procedure would, of course, require the exercise of judgment. It could not be reduced to a formula applicable in all cases. But this is no valid objection because the whole policy of regulation is based upon the exercise of official judgment in matters of economic concern.

If, in periods of transition, the rules of the game can be revised by an all but omnipotent police power, should not a wise public policy give this degree of discretion to an administrative commission, since it bears the responsibility for providing service in the future? The Wisconsin concept of going value was calculated to round off the edges of these changes by recognizing an equitable claim on account of past losses. Contrary to the current opinion of the effect of the Galveston case, it is our interpretation that Justice Brandeis' opinion merely pointed the way by eliminating going value as a judicial concept, an integral part of the confiscation doctrine. So conceived, this going-value element, along with the other elements of adjustment in a program of retrospective valuations, enabled administrative commissions in dealing with particular facts in each case to build a bridge from rate control under the latitudinous rule of *Smyth v. Ames* to rate control when the standards of regulation were more clearly revealed, and when, consequently, the delineation of a new rule of rate-making might become feasible.

The Fair Rate of Return as a Basis for Reconciliation

If the rate-making rule as laid down in *Smyth v. Ames* was to secure for public utilities a reasonable earning power, reasonable rates would have to yield earnings sufficient to cover reasonable operating expenses and leave a fair rate of return upon the fair value. The two concepts are thus interdependent. The fair rate of return has reference to what some economists have called the *wages of capital*. It thus takes into account the several types of investment bargains which going concerns make in financing themselves. There are, first of all, interest bargains with those who have loaned funds to the concern. Then comes the paid-in capital of preferred and common shareholders, with their preferred dividend requirements and the payment of dividends to the owners of the common stock equity. It is also usual to allow for some contribution to the surplus by way of a cushion to equalize fluctuations in earning power and to serve as a buffer against contingencies.

Since it has always been realized that utilities must compete for capital in the open market, there has been much less argument over the question of what constitutes a fair rate of return. Interest rates paid depend upon the going rate for loans involving similar risks. If, by means of certain institutional arrangements within the public utility sector of the economy, risks attending investment are eliminated or reduced, going rates will come to reflect them. The same considerations apply to the required payments to shareholders. In order to pass these benefits on to customers, the over-all rate of return should reflect these reductions in the costs of capital. The reasonable or fair rate of return should therefore be fixed with reference both to risks which may be eliminated or absorbed in operating cost and the risks which cannot well be eliminated or absorbed on account of their nature but which must be borne by shareholders, particularly the common shareholders.

In the period under review, commissions fixed an over-all rate of return without specific reference to the way in which net earnings are applied by public utilities in compensating investors in accordance with investment bargains. Some estimated allowances for the cost of capital, not necessarily related to the actual transactions of the utility under review, were usually the criteria for fixing the fair rate of return. There was a reason for this somewhat hypothetical, or *pro forma,* procedure. It was widely believed and generally true that all public utilities were overcapitalized. Hence the existing capital structure could not be used as a rate base, with the possible exception of utilities in the Commonwealth of Massachusetts where the issue of securities and their prices had been controlled since the 1880's. As the Commission of that state said in 1925 in the New England Telephone and Telegraph case: "It is the money honestly and prudently invested and devoted to the public service that is entitled to earn a fair return." Elsewhere, returns to capital could not be differentiated between that going to the various classifications of bond and stockholders. Commissions thus followed the eminently human course of least resistance and set up a single, undifferentiated or over-all rate of return (say, 6 per cent), which was applied to an undifferentiated or single-sum rate base obtained from a consideration of items on the asset side of the balance sheet or obtained independently of all books of account from the physical appraisal process. This also was a feature of retrospective regulation. It was a method of calculating the fair return to capital which would leave the financial structure undisturbed, thereby protecting a given utility's credit and rendering financial reorganization less threatening. Instances were by no means few where practically the entire undifferentiated return upon the fair value was needed to pay interest charges, leaving owners only the bare control with powers to keep themselves in executive positions. We shall reserve the more detailed consideration of the problem of the fair return for Chapter 23.

Judicial standards for the rate of return.　Since rate regulation may so limit earning power as to render the return confiscatory, the courts have attempted to define the boundary line of confiscation. The view of the courts is that any legislative limitation of earning power which escapes being confiscatory is a legitimate exercise of the police powers of the states or of the interstate commerce power of Congress. It may be unwise, but it is not confiscatory. Using language which suggests the eminent domain analogy, the courts say that utilities may not be "deprived" of their property without "just compensation." Whatever may be the origin of this seeming confusion, the courts have certainly opened the way for an interpretation whereby eminent domain begins where the police power leaves off.

The problem of extending constitutional protection to public utility property could be stated in another way. If governments, in protecting the public interest, limit and restrain the use of private property, they must do so in accordance with "due process of law." Due process of law involves defining what constitutes the "private property" of "public utilities." At this point the institutional differentiation of the unique property concept for public utilities may be said to emerge. It must be defined in terms of the *entire process* of rate-making under regulatory powers. If this process allows an earning capacity, that is to say, a rate of return, which does not place public utilities at a disadvantage in bidding for capital, the requirements of due process, considered from an economic point of view, have been satisfied.

The United States Supreme Court has definitely said, as early as in the Reagan case of 1894 (154 U.S. 362) that rates to be reasonable need not provide a return under all circumstances. There may have been extravagant expenditures in operation and poor judgment in the location and construction of plant. An early case seeking to define the fair return with some particularity was the opinion in the Wilcox case of 1909 (212 U.S. 19), where a return of 6 per cent was approved:

There is no particular rate of compensation which must in all cases and in all parts of the country be regarded as sufficient for capital invested in business enterprises. Such compensation must depend greatly upon circumstances and locality. Among other things, the amount of risk in the business is a most important factor as well as the locality where the business is conducted and the rate expected and usually realized there upon investments of a somewhat similar nature with regard to the risk attending them.

Initial rates of return as fixed by administrative commissions.　The first curbs upon the monopoly powers of public utilities by administrative commissions were developed under the rule of *Smyth v. Ames* and its later modifications. So much of their energy, however, was devoted to rate-base questions that the fair return received relatively little attention. For the period from 1905 to the outbreak of World War I in 1914, commissions fixed rates of return varying between 6 and 10 per cent, the usual range being between 7 and 8 per cent. Most states recognized some differences in the rate-of-return allowances as between the different classes of utilities (the differences varying from 0.5 to 3.0 per cent), but the variations did not appear to follow any fixed principles, except as municipally owned utilities and mutual companies and water utilities were accorded lower returns. With the outbreak of war and the acceleration of price increases, management tried to induce commissions, along with the automatic operation of coal and wage factor increases in rate schedules, to increase rate-of-return allowances. This effort was only partially successful. In the period from 1915 to 1918 the most noticeable difference seems to have been that the range of variation was eliminated and that all utilities were more nearly given the maximum rate. In the postwar period of price-level adjustment from 1919 to 1924, a few states increased their allowances by 0.5 of 1 per cent, but more often the trend was toward the introduction of uniformity in the rate of return. So great was the absorption with problems centering in the rate base, depreciation, and security issues during the 1920's that commissions usually contented themselves with quoting the guiding principles laid down by the Supreme Court in the Bluefield Water Works case.

The Interstate Commerce Commission showed no greater concern because of its preoccupation with the physical valuation of the railways of the country. To be sure, under the rule of rate-making in the Transportation Act of 1920, it was required to establish rates which would earn a "fair return" upon the "aggregate value" of carrier property. But Congress itself had fixed the minimum return at 5.5 per cent until March 1, 1922. However, it had authorized the Commission to allow an additional 0.5 of 1 per cent to be used for improvements and betterments, which was promptly done in July, 1920, making the rate 6 per cent. Due to the severe industrial and agricultural depression which began in the fall of 1920 and continued during 1921, the carriers were able actually to earn only 3.3 per cent during 1921. In May, 1922, the Commission fixed the fair return at 5.75 per cent, allowing, however, for the deduction of federal income taxes. This rate was appreciably lower than that which was being contemporaneously allowed by state commissions, since up to that time the railroads had been able to secure debt capital at lower effective interest rates than the local utilities. It was also hoped that with the lifting of the depression, actual earnings would equal or exceed this administrative standard.

The Bluefield case. All the various ideas affecting the rate of return as they had been developed were brought to a focus in an opinion in 1923 in *Bluefield Water Works and Imp. Co. v. West Virginia Pub. Serv. Com.* (262 U.S. 679,692). It should be noted that the emphasis is upon the dynamic aspects of the problem and that the dominant criterion is the credit of the utility; that is, its ability to attract capital under efficient and economical management. Justice Butler summarized as follows:

What annual rate will constitute just compensation depends upon many circumstances and must be determined by the exercise of a fair and enlightened judgment, having regard to all relevant facts. A public utility is entitled to such rates as will permit it to earn a return on the value of the property which it employs for the convenience of the public equal to that generally being made at the same time and in the same general part of the country on investments in other business undertakings which are attended by corresponding risks and uncertainties; but it has no constitutional right to profits such as are realized or anticipated in highly profitable enterprises or speculative ventures. The return should be reasonably sufficient to assure confidence in the financial soundness of the utility and should be adequate, under efficient and economical management, to maintain and support its credit and enable it to raise the money necessary for the proper discharge of its public duties. A rate of return may be reasonable at one time and become too high or too low by changes affecting opportunities for investment, the money market and business conditions generally . . .

General Summary

The fair-return on the fair-value concept dominated regulation until the 1923 decision of the Southwestern Bell Telephone case by the U.S. Supreme Court. We will consider this case in the next chapter and portray its meaning in the further development of regulation. In most cases, commissions with the support of the courts were able to work out reconciliations between investment costs and reproduction costs by so modifying the reproduction-cost concept as to make it a check upon investment. That these standards yielded results which were not far apart in terms of a fair-value rate base was demonstrated in those instances when evidence of reasonable investment costs and reasonable reproduction costs could be placed alongside each other. For example, an appraisal of normal reproduction costs by the Wisconsin Commission as of Jan. 1, 1914, of the Milwaukee Electric Railway & Light Company, when compared with investment cost as ascertained by commission audit, yielded $36,459,537 and $36,268,944, respectively. The difference of $190,593 was inconsequential. No really devastating criticisms were thus directed against the workings of regulation until the 1920's.

20. REGULATION

AND THE THEORY OF

THE GOING CONCERN

The major conflict during the 1920's and 1930's continued to center in the investment bargain because it controls the input of capital into public service industries and is inseparable from questions of over-all earning power. The rate-base problem was aggravated by a new development which had its origin in the wartime inflation of prices and wages. This issue of inflation or deflation, first raised in the Southwestern Bell Telephone case, has been running like a red thread through the fabric of our regulatory institutions ever since. The other issues of major consequence had to do with the depreciation problem and with the control over the financial policies of public service enterprises.

Origin of the Inflation Aspect of the Rate-Base Problem

The question as to what standard in the long run is best calculated to serve as a basic determinant of the rate base was raised previous to World War I, but no definitive answer was forthcoming. *Smyth v. Ames* made it a matter of giving "such weight as may be just and right in each case." We may best illustrate the effect of wartime inflation by giving the evidentiary facts which were submitted in 1919 to the Public Service Commission of Pennsylvania by a board of appraisers in connection with a rate case involving the Pittsburgh Railways Company. Without taking account of the accrued depreciation, the historical investment cost, based upon audited book figures and including $11,271,458 of superseded property, was $59,-069,382. The superseded property consisted of horsecar and cable systems and early electric equipment. The original cost of the active property was estimated at $49,324,791. At average wartime prices of 1914 to 1918, the estimated reproduction cost was $73,560,300, while at prices ruling at the date of valuation, April 1, 1918, the reproduction cost had more than doubled over the original cost to $192,842,274. Surely, investment costs and reproduction costs had parted company, signaling the advent of this new problem to plague the commissions.

The opening gun of the new battle was fired in 1920 by a District Court of the United States in *St. Joseph Ry., Lt., Ht.,* and *Pr. Co. v. Missouri Public Service Commission* (268 Fed. 267). The Commission had used as fair value a hybrid of investment costs and reproduction costs at average wartime unit prices, with the lower investment element predominating. Influenced by arguments regarding the decreased purchasing power of the dollar, the Court's opinion was unequivocal: "It is my judgment that the great weight of authority is against the adoption of a standard of original cost as a controlling basis for determining value."

The Southwestern Bell Telephone Company decision. In 1923, in *State of Missouri ex rel. Southwestern Bell Tel. Co. v. Public Service Com. of Mo.* (262 U.S. 276), the Supreme Court had to pass upon evidence which for the first time induced two members of the bench, Justices Brandeis and Holmes, to question the workableness of the historic rate-making rule. The state commission had fixed the fair value in this case at $20,400,000. This finding was based upon prior appraisals of constituent properties in 1913, 1914, and 1916, prepared by the Commission's engineers, plus the actual cost of additions subsequent to these dates at wartime prices. It was, in effect, the same as the "split inventory method" of appraisal, a device which the commissions were using to escape the effect of wartime price inflation by splitting the inventory into (1) a prewar part, to which prewar prices were applied, and (2) a wartime and postwar part, to which either book costs or inflated war costs were applied. Was this giving "due weight" to the several standards? The company produced evidence purporting to show that the property, inclusive of working capital, had cost $22,888,943. The company's engineers estimated, as of June 30, 1919, that the cost of reproduction new of the physical property, inclusive of working capital, was $29,506,052, with $25,760,859 depreciated. The majority of the Court criticized the Commission's finding because it

. . . undertook to value the property without according any weight to the greatly enhanced costs of material, labor, supplies, and so forth, over those prevailing in 1913, 1914, and 1916. As a matter of common knowledge, these increases were large. Competent witnesses estimated them as 45% to 50%.

Upon this issue the court divided.

We shall first give the view of the majority.

It is impossible to ascertain what will amount to a fair return upon properties devoted to public service without giving consideration to the cost of labor, supplies, and so forth, at the time the investigation is made. An honest and intelligent *fore-cast of probable future values* made upon a view of all the relevant circumstances is essential. If the highly important element of present costs is wholly disregarded, such a forecast becomes impossible. Estimates for tomorrow cannot ignore prices of today. [Author's italics.]

The universal interpretation of this decision was that "the law of the land" as laid down by the Supreme Court required a finding of the cost of reproduction at current prices for all the property and that the "split inventory" method had been disapproved. In fact, a new evidentiary fact was injected when the court said that "an honest and intelligent forecast of probable future values . . . is essential." Fair value now assumed aspects of futurity. Not only past considerations but future price levels should cast their shadows before.

The Court cites as a precedent the Wilcox case, where the sentence occurs: "If the property, which legally enters into the consideration of the question of rates, has increased in value since it was acquired, the company is entitled to the benefit of such increase." It also quotes with approval from the Minnesota rate cases that

. . . the making of a just return for the use of the property involves the recognition of its fair value if it be more than its cost. The property is held in private ownership and it is that property, and not the original cost of it, of which the owner may not be deprived without due process of law.

The fact of private ownership, not that it is public utility property, appears to make a universal rule of property law applicable in that the owner is entitled to have them valued as they stand in the markets of the world.

Views of the minority. The minority seemed to start from an entirely different premise. Although the valuation doctrine is accepted as the *starting point of calculations* to determine whether rates are constitutionally compensatory, the analysis does not proceed on the assumption that we deal here with ordinary private property. Instead, it goes back to the common law rights and duties of public utilities toward those whom they serve. After stating that he regards the so-called rule of *Smyth v. Ames* as "legally and economically unsound," Justice Brandeis gives this interpretation of a rule of rate-making which will afford private owners the protection of the Federal Constitution:

The investor [*i.e., the private owner*] agrees by embarking capital in a utility, that its charges to the public shall be reasonable. His company is the substitute for the State in the performance of the public service; thus becoming a public servant. The compensation which the Constitution guarantees an *opportunity* to earn is the reasonable cost of conducting the business. Cost includes not only operating expenses, but also capital charges. Capital charges cover the allowance, by way of interest, for the use of the capital, whatever the nature of the security issued therefor; the allowance for risk incurred; and enough more to attract capital. The reasonable rate to be prescribed by a commission may allow an efficiently managed utility much more. But a rate is constitutionally compensatory if it allows to the utility the *opportunity* to earn the cost of the service as thus defined. (Author's italics.)

In this view, what becomes of the concepts of "private property" and of its "value" for public utility purposes? Justice Brandeis answers this question in distinctly modern fashion. A public utility is no longer a medieval wagoner or ferryman, devoting his carriage or his ferry to a use in which the public has an interest, but it becomes a corporation empowered to raise money to carry on a business in which the public has an interest. He says: "The thing devoted by the investor to the public use is not specific property, tangible and intangible, but capital embarked in the enterprise." This capital, while protected against unreasonable exercise of the police power, is subject to this limitation:

The Constitution does not guarantee to the utility the opportunity to earn a return on the value of all items of property used by the utility or any of them. The several items of property constituting the utility, taken singly, and freed from the public use, may conceivably have an aggregate value greater than if the items are used in combination. The owner is at liberty, in the absence of controlling statutory provisions, to withdraw his property from the public service, and, if he does so, may obtain for it exchange value. [Cases cited.] But so long as the specific items of property are employed by the utility, their exchange value is not of legal significance.

Evidently, abandonments of service for which the permission of the state must be obtained are the "provisions" which the Justice has in mind as controlled by statute. Ordinarily, the right to abandon service and to devote fixed and specialized capital to other uses is wholly illusory.

The above statement of a new rule, championed by Brandeis and Holmes, has now come to be known as the *prudent investment rule.* The divergence in the legal premises from which the argument of the majority, on the one hand, and of the minority, on the other hand, proceed is too deeply seated to be explained by subjective differences. What shall be done with this challenge?

The competitive model. During the period of time we are now considering, i.e., the years from 1923 to 1929, the issue between replacement costs and investment costs was squarely joined. On the whole, commissions, especially the better commissions, were on the side of investment cost, while the utilities were either defending fair value with its uncertain weighting of reproduction costs or had completely gone over to reproduction costs. Massachusetts, with its approach to the problem from the liability side of the balance sheet, and New York, Missouri, Wisconsin, Indiana, and California, to mention only the bellwether states, were typical of the commissions who felt that the effectiveness of regulation was tied up with the ultimate adoption of the investment standard.

Two issues were embedded in this conflict, which were only dimly perceived by even the few economists who were concerning themselves with this problem at the time. One issue had to do with the institutional difference between the utility sector and the rest of the economy. As we have shown in Chapters 13 and 14, the fundamental difference that sets public utilities apart from other businesses is the degree of monopoly vouchsafed them by the state. Utilities operate not in an open but in a controlled market. Rate regulation by government is designed to take the place of the competitive mechanism. The policy of price regulation must, therefore, be adjusted to the degree of monopoly or competition obtaining in a particular market. The so-called competitive model cannot be applied in judging the reasonableness of consumer prices in the public utility field, but it must be recognized that capital is obtained in a competitive market.

We have seen that reproduction costs based upon a substitute plant hypothesis had never been seriously considered by commissions when the reproduction-cost standard was being emphasized in the period before World War I. Brandeis' challenge, and that of the state commissions, was designed to eliminate this interpretation of the reproduction-cost hypothesis in any future adjustment of the rate-base problem.

But there was another aspect of the matter which constituted the second, though concealed, issue involved in the rejection of reproduction cost. This issue arises as a consequence of price inflation or deflation. The investment standard (either as an original or historical cost doctrine) is tied to the *purchasing power* of our standard of value *at the time* the investment is first made. This institutional foundation subjects all price phenomena (regulated, as well as competitive prices) to changes in the value of money. Value here means changes in purchasing power; yet the investment standard freezes the rate base in terms of the dollar expenditure when it was first made. The effect of this *nominal dollar* doctrine, as it has been called, was only dimly perceived at the time. These considerations will be pointed out in connection with a series of court decisions.

The Waukesha Gas and Electric Company case. The case which has come closest to recognizing the fallacy of reproduction cost and approving what may be called a *going concern* approach to the regulatory problem is *Waukesha Gas and Electric Co. v. Railroad Commission of Wisconsin* (P.U.R. 1923 E634). In this case, with Justice Rosenberry writing the opinion, the Supreme Court of Wisconsin set itself apart from other courts by deciding that where public utility investments are made under the indeterminate permit law, the rule in *Smyth v. Ames* is susceptible of an interpretation which gives prime weight to investment costs.

The split inventory scheme of avoiding inflation was at stake. In a previous case the Commission had fixed the fair value of the utility in 1913 at $156,800. In this rate proceeding it adopted the procedure of bringing the 1913 valuation down to date (1920) by adding the cost of additions made in the interim. This resulted in a finding of $424,868. Engineers for the utility made an appraisal of reproduction cost of $595,904, using five-year average prices. The court stated the issue as follows:

It is contended that the present fair value of the property used or useful in affording the public service is the measure of the reward to which the owner of that property is entitled for the service rendered, such value to be established as of the time when the inquiry in regard to the reasonableness of the rates charged by the utility is under investigation.

Besides the argument of the parties directly concerned in the case, the court had before it a brief submitted as *Amicus Curiae* (friend of the court) by a committee appointed by the Mayor of Milwaukee. At this time the Committee was negotiating a "service at cost" contract with the Milwaukee Electric Railway and Light Company, using the investment standard as a basis. It was concerned lest the decision of the Court should establish reproduction cost as the "law of the land." [1] At the same time Justice Rosenberry became familiar with the manuscript of a study which Prof. John R. Commons was about to publish, his *Legal Foundations of Capitalism* of 1924. In it Professor Commons also gave expression to the going-concern point of view. These interpretations reappear in the decision of the Justice from which we quote below.

After citing certain recent decisions of the Supreme Court of the United States, among them the Southwestern Bell Telephone Company decision, the Court concludes that "these decisions have not entirely clarified the situation." The Court's criticism is that there is no indication of the weight to be accorded to the cost of reproduction new, less depreciation factor. "*It cannot be that the repetition of a mere legalistic formula* before the declaration of

---

[1] The author, as Executive Secretary of the Committee, helped to prepare this brief. The argument against the use of the reproduction-cost standard was in terms of the analysis presented in this chapter.

the trial court's final determination is *sufficient to bless and sanctify the re-sult, no matter what it may be.*" [Author's italics.]

The Court next reviewed the law under which public utilities operate in Wisconsin, as follows: (1) that the property of the utility is held under an indeterminate permit; (2) that by its terms the municipality has the power to take the property of the utility upon paying just compensation as fixed by the Commission; (3) that under the public utility law a company is required to furnish adequate service for a reasonable charge and that it may therefore be required to make additions to its property by public authority "'without regard to past, present or future price levels"; (4) that the state guarantees a monopoly to the utility by prohibiting the competition of both municipalities and private corporations, except it be established upon a public hearing that public convenience and necessity require a second utility.

In giving his reasons why the cost of reproduction should not be given controlling weight the Justice argues as follows:

In the first place, it ignores the fact that under *Munn v. Illinois* (94 U.S. 113) 1876, when a person dedicates his property to a public use by investing it in a public utility, he divides with the people the right to control the use of the property so dedicated and thereafter the public has an interest in the use of the property which it may within constitutional limitations assert. That so investing his property the investor has given to it a status is now well established and recognized in the law. He withdraws it from the great mass of property not so situated and subjects it to a degree of public control from that time on.

Second: Cost of reproduction new can be established only theoretically. Even in the case of a structure about to be erected, every-day experience confirms this. When applied to the property of a public utility, purchased under conditions which no longer exist, and incorporated into the property of a public utility under circumstances that cannot be reproduced, it is not only theoretical, but highly speculative.

Third: *The property of a public utility cannot be valued as is other property, not devoted to the public use, which is subject to the laws of competition and therefore is in an entirely different class.* [Case cited. Author's italics.]

Fourth: In the competitive field the cost of reproduction new is given minor consideration in fixing the value of property because in that field the value is determined largely by its usability. For instance, would any one claim that the cost of reproduction new is even a guide to the present value of a defunct brewery plant? In the valuation of an office building the amount which it earns is a much larger factor in determining its value than cost of reproduction new. The usability or earning capacity being in a competitive field a dominant factor in the ascertainment of present fair value and the cost of reproduction new being at least a minor factor, how can it be said that it is entitled to great weight in valuing the property of a public utility when the earning power is limited by law? [Case cited.]

Fifth: If the cost of reproduction new is to be accorded any considerable weight when the price level rises, it must be accorded the same weight when the price level falls. Utilities in Wisconsin, however, are not permitted, except within very narrow limits, to consider price levels, but are required to furnish an adequate service when and as needed irrespective of price levels. It would seem to be rank injustice to compel a public utility to make an investment and then after the investment is made hold that although the public compelled the utility to make the investment when prices were high, prices having fallen, the utility is entitled to earn a return only upon the present cost of labor and material. Utilities must grow and expand with the needs of the public. They have very little if any option in regard to the matter.

Sixth: If a public utility, which has during a twenty year period earned and distributed a reasonable return upon the investment value of its property, is permitted to increase its rates by reason of the fact that labor and materials have advanced in price in the open market, the earnings derived from such increase in rates will constitute an addition to its prior earnings and the utility will thus be permitted to earn more than a reasonable rate upon its investment . . .

Seventh: The materials—brick, stone, copper, etc.—which enter into the construction of the plant of a public utility lose their identity as such and become a part of a new whole and must be valued as such. It does not seem reasonable to say that the value of a cast iron pipe in a water main rises and falls in value with market fluctuations of pipe which is offered for sale in the open market. After material is incorporated into a public utility plant its value must be determined as a plant, not as material not so incorporated.

. . . None conceive that it was one of the fundamental objects of the public utility act not to stabilize investments in public utility property, in the interest of the public primarily, and secondarily, in the interest of the investor, so that the public would not be subjected to the hazards and exactions of a speculative enterprise in a field where it undertook to furnish a monopoly. The rates were to be just and reasonable. If the public wishes to purchase the property, it must pay just compensation therefor.

Under our statute, it may be well argued that with increasing prices, increasing interest levels, increasing cost of operation, the utility investor is in justice entitled to a larger return than formerly, but this argument is more properly urged to secure an increase in the rate of return rather than in the rate base upon which the return is to be computed.

Then follows a discussion of the "prudent investment" theory from the point of view that it is administratively best calculated to afford owners a reasonable return; that it will best enable the Commission to perform some of its other functions such as the control of security issues; that it will tend to stabilize investments, reducing risks and lowering capital costs to consumers.

The conclusion of the Court is reached in the following:

In determining the present fair value of a public utility operating under our public utility law, it is our view that justice as well as sound economic practice requires that controlling weight should be given in the valuation of the plant of a public utility to the investment cost, where the investment has been prudently made. In determining the present fair value of the property of a public utility for rate-making purposes, but little, if any, weight can be given to capitalization of earnings, or to stock and bond values for the reason that these are dependent almost entirely upon the rates charged, the reasonableness of which is the very subject under investigation . . .

The foregoing opinion represents the high-water mark of institutional theory, combining both legal and economic analysis. It fails, however, to take account of the effect of changes in the value of money upon the different contributors of capital to the capital fund of the concern. Should this be measured on both sides of the balance sheet in terms of the dollar amounts of such contributions, or should it be measured in terms of the present money cost of the assets? In other words, is the capital concept a pecuniary one or is it physical? We should here note the effect of the financial structure upon the theory of the going concern.

It is clear that at the inception of an enterprise subject to regulation, the charges should under normal conditions be so fixed as to yield in addition to operating expenses: (1) the interest on its funded and floating indebtedness, (2) the stipulated dividends upon the capital contributed by the preferred shareholders, and (3) a fair return by way of dividends upon the pecuniary capital contributed by the common shareholders. The exact amounts will depend upon conditions surrounding each enterprise. Additional investments should be treated likewise. The real concern of investors is with the security of this principal sum and the relevant rate of return. If interest rates increase during the period for which creditors have accepted a fixed return, they must await the end of the period before a readjustment in interest rates may be secured. Creditors do take potential changes in interest rates and the purchasing power of fixed income returns into account and try to anticipate them in the prices and terms of the securities. Similarly, the corporations, as debtors, embody premium payments for "call privileges," making it possible to refinance themselves upon a more favorable basis before maturity of the loan. Of similar import would be the wide adoption of purchasing power bonds or of preferred stock with escalator clauses. These have, however, found only a very limited application. These are expedients adopted as "insurance features" against changes in interest rates and the value of money, and could be recognized as legitimate features in corporate financing by commissions, as some have been.

We may assume the not uncommon capital structure of 50 per cent in long term debt, 15 per cent in preferred stock, and the balance of 35 per cent in common stock equity. This degree of trading on the equity places 65 per cent of the holders of a utility's invested capital subject to a fixed return and hence their interest in maintaining at par the security of their investment. They forgo all chance of gain and expect therefore to be protected from all chance of speculative loss. Let us first gauge the effect of the adoption of a reproduction cost standard (in terms of the identical plant) upon the return of these different classes of capital contributors. Whether the price level rises or falls, the application of replacement costs as a valuation standard would leave the contractual return to bond and preferred-stock holders unaffected, unless perchance a decline would wipe out the margin of the common stock equity. Residual claimants, like common stockholders, would gain or lose more than proportionally, depending upon the extent to which trading on the equity (65 per cent in our illustration) operated upon the familiar leverage principle. If the given public utility had built or expanded its plant during periods of high prices, a decline of 35 per cent in the rate base would wipe out the equity of common stockholders and jeopardize the investment of preferred stockholders and bondholders. Can it be assumed that conservative investors would be willing to furnish money for investment in plant if that investment ten years hence might be reduced to conform with replacement costs of the plant? It is this risk which it was the primary aim of regulation to eliminate. The only satisfactory solution is to treat the utility as a going concern requiring continuous investments of capital and not as a concern which must continuously refinance and reequip itself, reshaping both its financial plan and its operating plant as if a new entity, in accordance with the cost of reproduction of an "identical plant" or some mythical "substitute plant." Certainly, this is what the monopoly principle means and requires if a policy of regulation is to be successfully applied.

We come now to the decision which represents the high-water mark of the reproduction-cost standard. In *John W. McCardle, et al. v. Indianapolis Water Co.* [272 U.S. 400 (1926)], the United States Supreme Court, speaking through Justice Butler, criticizes a valuation of this outstanding private water utility as fixed by the Indiana Commission. The appraisal in this instance was based upon the following interpretation of unit prices by the Commission:

Considering all the facts, including all the appraisals and the other evidence concerning the trend of prices, the Commission is of the opinion that in this case the average of prices for the 10-year period ending with 1921, the last full ten years available, most nearly represents the fair value of petitioner's physical property.

Commenting upon this conclusion, Justice Butler says:

But in determining present value, consideration must be given to prices and wages prevailing at the time of the investigation; and, in the light of all the circumstances, there must be an honest and intelligent forecast as to probable price and wage levels during a reasonable period in the immediate future. In every confiscation case, the future as well as the present must be regarded.

This language is strongly reminiscent of the majority opinion in the Southwestern Bell Telephone Company case. Later on in the opinion, Justice Butler makes his special contribution to interpretations of the fair-value rule. He says:

It is well established that values of utility properties fluctuate, and that owners must bear the decline and are entitled to the increase. The decision of this Court in *Smyth v. Ames* (169 U.S. 466, 574), declares that to ascertain value "the present as compared with the original cost of construction" are, among other things, matters for consideration. But this does not mean that the original cost or the present cost or some figure arbitrarily chosen between these two is to be taken as the measure. The weight to be given to such cost figures and other items or classes of evidence is to be determined in the light of facts of the case in hand. By far the greater part of the company's land and plant was acquired and constructed long before the war. The present value of the land is much greater than its cost; and the present cost of construction of those parts of the plant is much more than their reasonable original cost. In fact, prices and values have so changed that the amount paid for land in the early years of the enterprise and the cost of plant elements constructed prior to the great rise of prices due to the war do not constitute any real indication of their value at the present time. Undoubtedly, the reasonable cost of a system of waterworks, well planned and efficient for the public service, is good evidence of its value at the time of construction. And such actual cost will continue fairly well to measure the amount to be attributed to the physical elements of the property so long as there is no change in the level of applicable prices. And, as indicated by the report of the Commission, it is true that, if the tendency or trend of prices is not definitely upward or downward and it does not appear probable that there will be a substantial change of prices, then the present value of lands plus the present cost of constructing the plant, less depreciation, if any, is a fair measure of the value of the physical elements of the property. The validity of the rates in question depends on property value January 1, 1924, and for a reasonable time following. While the values of such properties do not vary with frequent minor fluctuations in the prices of material and labor required to produce them, they are affected by and generally follow the relatively permanent levels and trends of such prices. The fact that original cost was probably 12–20 per cent less than the estimate of the Commission's engineer based on the average of prices for the ten years ending with 1921—two years before the rate order became effective —does not tend to support the Commission's adoption of that estimate. The cost of reproduction on price levels prevailing January 2, 1923, was found to be 30 to 35 per cent or from $4,500,000 to $5,000,000 more. The average of prices in the ten years ending with 1923—the effective date of the rate order—was shown by the testimony of the Commission's chief engineer to produce a result nearly 14 per cent higher than the figure adopted; and, on the basis of prices prevailing on the effective date of the order, cost of reproduction less depreciation would be about

32 per cent higher than that taken by the Commission. The high level of prices and wages prevailing in 1922 and 1923 should be taken into account in finding value as of January 1, 1924, and in the years immediately following. Moreover, there is nothing in the record to indicate that the prices prevailing at the effective date of the rate order were likely to decline within a reasonable time—one, two or three years—to the level of the average in the ten years ending with 1923. And we may take judicial notice of the fact that there has been no substantial general decline in the prices of labor and materials since that time. The trend has been upward rather than downward. The price level adopted by the Commission—average for ten years ending with 1921—was too low. And it is clear that a level of prices higher than the average prevailing in the ten years ending with 1923 should be taken as the measure of value of the structural elements on and following the effective date of the rate order complained of.

Justice Brandeis dissented from the decision. Justice Holmes concurred in the result but presumably did not agree with the theory advanced. In his minority opinion Justice Brandeis significantly remarks:

Nor do I find in the decisions of this court any support for the view that a peculiar sanction attaches to "spot" reproduction cost, as distinguished from the amount that it would actually cost to reproduce the plant if that task were undertaken at the date of the hearing. "Spot" reproduction would be impossible of accomplishment without the aid of Aladdin's lamp. The actual cost of a plant may conceivably indicate its actual value at the time of completion or at some time thereafter. Estimates of cost may conceivably approximate what the cost of reproduction would be at a given time. But where a plant would require years for completion, the estimate would be necessarily delusive if it were based on "spot" prices of labor, materials and money. The estimate, to be in any way worthy of trust, must be based on a consideration of the varying costs of labor, materials, and money for a period at least as long as would be required to construct the plant and put it into operation. Moreover, the estimate must be made in the light of a longer experience and with due allowances for the hazards which attend all prophecies in respect to prices. The search for value can hardly be aided by a hypothetical estimate of the cost of replacing the plant at a particular moment, when actual reproduction would require a period that must be measured by years.

The further history of the cost-of-reproduction theory before the onset of the Great Depression is most revealing and supplies one of the reasons for the widely accepted view in the 1930's that the policy of public utility regulation had broken down. Even in Wisconsin, in the so-called *second* Waukesha case [191Wis. 565 (1927)] the Wisconsin Supreme Court modified its decision in the earlier Waukesha case by conforming to the ruling of the majority of the United States Supreme Court.

The O'Fallon decision of the Interstate Commerce Commission. The conflict between these valuation standards came to a head again in the excess income case of St. Louis and O'Fallon Railway Company decided by the ICC on Feb. 15, 1927. This case, sometimes called the *billion dollar law suit*, arose under the recapture clause of the Transportation Act of 1920. The cleavage of opinion is shown by the differences between the majority and minority. The decision of the majority, written by B. H. Meyer, formerly Professor of Economics and a Commissioner at Wisconsin, attempts once more to lay bare the issue and to secure a modification in the ruling by the Supreme Court, since it was generally recognized that the proceeding would serve as a test case of the validity of the valuation work upon which over $100 million had been expended. As stated by the Commission:

> The statute directs that in determining values pursuant to section 15a we shall "give due consideration to all the elements of value recognized by the law of the land for rate making purposes." In the methods of valuation which we have followed in this proceeding we have endeavored to give heed to this direction, having in mind not only the conditions existent upon these particular carriers, but also the necessity, in the application of these methods to the carriers generally, of protecting the private owners of railroad property in their constitutional rights and at the same time of assuring to the public the continued maintenance and operation of a transportation system capable of rendering efficient service at reasonable rates.

The Commission's investigation of the facts in this case through the medium of an accounting report disclosed the complete corporate and financial history of the O'Fallon Railway. However, evidence of the original cost to date of the property, as a whole, could not be obtained because accounting records from the date of incorporation, June 1, 1896, to June 1, 1908, were missing; but the evidence of the net cost of property additions from June 1, 1908, to June 30, 1919, the inventory date, was available, as was also the net cost since that time.

With respect to the appraised cost of reproduction the Commission had this to say:

> The underlying engineering report, on which the tentative valuation in the 19a proceeding is in part to be based, contains estimates of cost of reproduction new and cost of reproduction less depreciation as of June 30, 1919, based upon 1914 unit prices. These unit prices have been determined, as explained by us in numerous reports in valuation cases, by consideration of the prices for labor and materials and the cost of constructing and equipping railroads, in most instances during a five-year period ended June 30, 1914, but in certain other instances during periods of 10 years or more ended June 30, 1914. *Texas Midland Railroad*, 75 ICC 1.

In determining the value of the property of the O'Fallon Railway, the Commission adopted a method which is analogous to the "split inventory method" of fixing the rate base. This method had already been disapproved by the United States Supreme Court in the Southwestern Bell Telephone Company case. Nevertheless, the Commission felt that the valuation problem:

> . . . is divided into two parts, which can be clearly distinguished, and the date when our valuation work under section 19a began marks roughly the division line between these two parts. Since that date we have required the carriers to report in detail all property changes and their costs, and these costs can be verified and checked. In the case of all property which came into existence prior to that date we have an inventory made by our own engineers, but no complete, reliable information as to original costs. The first part of our problem, therefore, is to determine upon a fair single-sum value for this older property. The second part of our problem is to bring this value down to any subsequent date, in the light of the property changes since our valuation work began, of which we have complete reports . . .
>
> From this accumulated information we have formed our judgment as to the fair, basic single-sum values, not by the use of any formula but after consideration of all relevant facts. In our opinion, these judgments have been reasonably liberal to the carriers. In all probability they are above rather than below the amounts which would have resulted if complete records had been available and the investment theory of valuation had been employed. But the public, as represented by the government, must bear some of the responsibility for the absence of records, and it is fair, under all circumstances, that the basic valuation should be reasonably liberal . . .

In adopting this method of valuation the Commission considered that its problem in the administration of the valuation and recapture provisions was "national in its scope and in its consequences," and that it was "affected by a vast variety of considerations that either do not enter into, or are less easily perceived in problems incident to the regulation of local public utilities." It concluded, therefore, that "limitations of issues, facts, or viewpoints impair many of the precedents which we are asked to follow by routes as divergent as the interests of those who make the requests."

Although the Commission was urged to take "cost of reproduction new at prices current on valuation date" as the basic measure of "fair value" to the exclusion of all other factors, it did not see fit to do so. Neither did it augment this figure "by an allowance for something called 'going value,' which is vaguely defined in many different ways," as it was also urged to do. The Commission used, instead, the cost of reproduction new, less depreciation of property as inventoried on June 30, 1919, based upon its interpretation of 1914 unit prices, plus the *adjusted* net cost from 1914 to date of additions to property, plus the fair average market value of lands at the recapture date, plus an allowance for working capital.

In rejecting the cost of reproduction as the sole standard of public utility valuation, the Commission set forth the usual objections. Its treatment of the question is marked, however, by concreteness in illustration and by a marshaling of common-sense considerations which reveal the responsible administrator. The majority of the commission said, for instance:

If it had been applied in 1920, the current reproduction cost doctrine would have required general increases in rates very much higher than those which we authorized. The latter ranged from 25% to 40%. It is quite conceivable that with the then current reproduction cost as the rate base, increases of from 75% to 90% might have been necessary. Neither the country nor the carriers could have endured such a rise in freight charges. Even now, when the general price level is materially lower than it was in 1920, a rate base so determined would in all probability require rates which the carriers would as a matter of self-interest hesitate to charge. *This amounts to saying that under such a doctrine of fair value the carriers would as a matter of self-interest choose confiscation. Plainly a doctrine which leads to such a conclusion is irrational.* [Author's italics.]

As if in answer to Justice Butler's statements that values of utility properties fluctuate and "that owners must bear the decline and are entitled to the increase," the Commission recounted what this would mean to owners of railroad property, where approximately one-third of the investment is represented by common stock, while the remainder is represented by bonds, notes, or preferred stock, the holders of which are limited to a fixed or maximum return. The benefits of an increased rate base resulting from a rise in the general price level, assuming that traffic could bear an increase in freight rates, "would involve returns to the common stockholders grotesque in their proportions." The Commission conceded that "theoretically the holders of common stock would suffer corresponding losses if the general price level should shift downward rather than upward, and this risk of loss is urged as justification for any gains that might accrue." But this theoretical possibility would be without practical consequences because "the country would hardly, for the sake of consistency in theory, permit stockholders to suffer losses which in their effect upon railroad credit would react disastrously upon all industry." The only persons to whom such prospects might appeal would be stock-market speculators. "It would be difficult," said the Commission, "to conceive of any plan more conducive to the encouragement of unrestrained speculation in railroad shares than such a method of valuation. In all probability it would provide a feast superior to anything which the bulls and bears have enjoyed since the creation of stock exchanges."

The Commission did not blink at the problem that changing price levels bring about a change in the purchasing power of money. It was suggested, however, that necessary adjustments be made through the "fair return" so that "investment in railroad facilities will be encouraged and promoted and the companies maintained in good credit."

The minority in this case, all lawyers by profession, although agreeing with the soundness of the economic argument, were disposed to follow the majority of the Supreme Court. This attitude was attacked by Commissioner Eastman in a concurring opinion, particularly the minority's objection that it is the duty of the Commission to apply the law of the land as laid down by the Supreme Court. He contended that the Court had wisely avoided a crystallization of the law with respect to public utility valuation and that it was the duty of the Commission, where interpretation of the law involved fundamental issues of public policy, to give the Court the benefit of its experience and judgment. For, while the Court is the final authority, "what it decides in one case to be the law may with further light and under certain conditions be superseded in a subsequent case by a modified or different conclusion." Moreover, administrative commissions are in a peculiar position to be helpful because they occupy "a daily front seat upon the stage, while the Supreme Court of necessity is only an occasional visitor in the balcony."

Commissioner Eastman also called attention to the inconsistency in the standard valuation procedure which adjusts the value of land in the rate base to its market value as of the valuation date. It should be noted that the inconsistency occurs again in failing to look upon land as an integral part of the going plant. Commissioner Meyer had used the analogy of a river system when he wrote:

The structures of a railroad system may be compared to a great river like the Mississippi, in which the main stream represents lines of railroad in the system and the branches represent the perpetual flow of new material into it. At New Orleans the Mississippi River is a composite of a vast multitude of waters contributed by a corresponding number of tributaries, big and little. Similarly, at any moment a railroad system is the result of contributions made by many different streams of materials, some wearing out rapidly and others slowly, but all requiring replacements from time to time. All are indispensable to keep the main stream efficient for service. Unless these collateral streams of materials maintain an uninterrupted flow into the railroad structure, the railroad system deteriorates and service to the public suffers. Each kind of material is acquired at prices prevailing when the purchases are made, either at the time of installation or prior thereto, when materials are drawn from accumulated stores, and during periods of time varying by days, months, and years. Just as the water of the Mississippi at New Orleans is composed of waters from myriads of different sources, so a railroad system is a composite of materials acquired at myriads of different prices and at infinitely varying periods of time, and put into the plant at many different levels of wages. Neither the highest price nor the lowest, nor the average, nor any price between, represents the outlay made for the system. The only thing that does and can represent what the investor has contributed to the value of the property is the aggregate amount which was paid for the many different items in the perpetual stream of metamorphosing railroad structures.

With this decision the fair-value doctrine had clearly arrived at the crossroads. In developing the doctrine it was as important in Eastman's phrase to know "the pertinent facts" and to have had the "experience which makes it possible to visualize probable results of a particular public policy" as to have the requisite "familiarity with the law books." As Justice Holmes long ago said with respect to the rational study of legal rules in general, so here it had become necessary

. . . to get the dragon out of his cave on to the plain and in the daylight, where you can count his teeth and claws, and see just what is his strength. But to get him out is only the first step. The next is either to kill him, or to tame him and make him a useful animal. For the rational study of the law . . . the black-letter man may be the man of the present, but the man of the future is the man of statistics and the master of economics.

But the hopes of those looking for a modification were doomed to disappointment. In May, 1929, with Brandeis, Holmes, and Stone dissenting, the Court, speaking through Justice McReynolds, agreed with the minority of the Commission and refused to modify the law of the land. Flatfootedly, the Court said, "In the exercise of its proper function this court has declared the law of the land concerning valuations for rate-making purposes. The Commission disregarded the approved rule and had thereby failed to discharge the definite duty imposed by Congress." The upshot of this episode in legal economics was that Congress in 1933 abrogated both the recapture clause and the rule of rate-making with its reference to the "law of the land."

The Fair Value and Fair Return Doctrine during and after the Depression

The agricultural depression had come in 1920, and efforts were being made to revive agriculture. Late in 1929 the stock market collapsed, signaling the onset of the industrial phase of the Great Depression. With the advent of the "New Deal," new and more vigorous policies were adopted by Congress to fight the depression. When some of these policies, notably the Agricultural Adjustment Act, were declared unconstitutional by the same majority which it was believed had already hamstrung the effectiveness of regulation, there arose a mounting flood of criticism of the Court, epitomized in the label of "The Nine Old Men." Though the attempt by President Roosevelt to convert the minority into the majority by means of his so-called court-packing bill was thwarted, inducements to secure voluntary retirement were held out to the aging members of the Court. The accelerated turnover of the membership through death and retirement by 1941 had significantly changed the dominating social philosophy of the Court. This change ushered in a new era in the interpretation of the doctrines of confiscation and reasonableness which were believed by many to have completely undermined the "fair value–fair return" rule.

Some transitional decisions. There ensued a period of transition during which Chief Justice Hughes sought to bolster the old rule with a display of political acumen. In the Los Angeles case of 1933 [*Los Angeles G.&E. Corp. v. Cal. R.R. Comm.* (289 U.S. 287)] the Chief Justice, speaking for a divided court, sustained a 1929 rate order of the California Commission. Since this Commission had used the actual or estimated investment as a rate base throughout its history, it seemed that the hold of reproduction cost on the Court had been broken. The Court was aided in reaching its conclusion by the fortuitous fact that the results of the rate-base determination by the Court and the Commission, though different in principle, came to about the same figure. The Commission had used an undepreciated, investment rate base, agreeable with the sinking fund method of financing depreciation, which permitted no deduction for accrued depreciation. It had also made little or no allowance for going value. In conformity with precedent, the Court had used cost of reproduction new, less depreciation, plus going-concern value. The Court discovered a margin of $5,500,000 which could be attributed to going value, saying: "The fact that this margin in the rate base was not described as going value is unimportant, if the rate base was in fact large enough to embrace that element."

Another decision by Justice Hughes in 1938, in *Railroad Comm. of California v. Pacific Gas and Elec. Co.* (302 U.S. 388), reinforced the generally held opinion that the Court was leaning toward a recognition of historical cost or prudent investment. In this case the Federal Power Commission submitted a brief as "Friend of the Court" urging the acceptance of the investment standard and the rejection of replacement cost. The FPC was at the threshold of its "original cost" determinations which had been embodied in the new national uniform classification of accounts promulgated in 1937. Because the lower court had upheld the claim of the company that the California Commission had used a historical cost rate base and had refused to consider the "fair value" by giving some weight to the company's estimates of reproduction cost, it was felt that the judicial trend toward the investment standard was once more jeopardized. In reversing the decision of the lower court the opinion again gave promise that the replacement-cost doctrine was weakening, as indicated by the following excerpt:

While the Court has frequently declared that "in order to determine present value the cost of reproducing the property is a relevant fact which should have appropriate consideration" we have been careful to point out that "the Court has not decided that the cost of reproduction furnishes an exclusive test" and in that relation we have emphasized the danger in resting conclusions upon estimates of a conjectural character.

It had always been considered one of the objections to appraisals of reproduction cost that they were time-consuming and costly. To expedite the procedure the Maryland Commission had used a previously determined rate base of the Chesapeake and Potomac Telephone Company for 1923, and then, by adding the additions for each subsequent year, had established the rate base for 1932 by using as a translator a series of index numbers which corrected the nominal amounts for each year to the level of 1932 prices. [*West v. Chesapeake and Potomac Tel. Co.* (295 U.S. 662; 1935)]. Since the trend of prices was downward, the effect of the procedure was to reduce the nominal amounts for the undepreciated value from $57,450,606 to $39,928,-413. In language bristling with judicial censure, Justice Roberts, though with a divided court, rejected the procedure as "inappropriate." The compelling reason for rejection, however, was that in 1932 the reproduction-cost shoe was on the other foot. Said the Court: "A more fundamental defect in the Commission method is that the result is affected by sudden shifts in price level. It is true that any just valuation must take into account changes in the level of prices."

The Court here alludes, though not too definitely, to what is the most telling argument which has been brought forward by those who champion cost of reproduction, either as the sole standard of value or as an important element in fair value. Unless cost of reproduction is taken into account in rate-base determinations, the owners of public utility properties will be deprived of a fair return. Periods of high prices, particularly those induced by war and reconstruction disturbances, with their attendant credit inflations, usually are accompanied by a fall in the purchasing power of that return. Under these conditions a constant monetary return represents in fact a declining return which is a complement of the decline in its purchasing power. How this factor may be taken account of under a going-concern theory will be discussed later.

The Natural Gas Pipeline Company Case and
the Dawn of a New Era

In March, 1942, the Supreme Court handed down its decision in *Federal Power Commission v. Natural Gas Pipeline Go.* (315 U.S. 575). This case was generally hailed as marking the downfall of the forty-four-year-old doctrine of fair value and the dawn of a new era in commission regulation. Acting under powers conferred by the Natural Gas Act of 1938, upon complaint of the Illinois Commerce Commission and on its own motion, the FPC had issued an interim order reducing the wholesale rates which the pipeline company charged retail distributors in the Chicago area. The Circuit Court of Appeals had vacated the rate order because the Commission should have included $8,500,000 for going-concern value in the rate base and should have made more liberal provisions for amortization of the investment. Both the Company and the Commission appealed the decision of the lower court. The Commission had reluctantly adopted as a rate base the estimates of replacement cost new of physical properties by the company's own witnesses. Also included therein were the value of gas reserves, estimated future capital additions up to Dec. 31, 1942, and an allowance for working capital. The total sum was $74,420,424, all items representing liberal allowances, with replacement costs of the physical property in excess of the actual construction cost by upwards of $6 million. The Company was willing to concede a deduction of $2,866,758 for "viewed depreciation," but the Commission used an undepreciated rate base with the usual allowances for "overheads" in assembling the plant as that of a going concern.

Scope of judicial review. The Court began consideration of the scope of judicial review by appealing to a juridical custom, i.e., that commissions in applying the statutory standard of reasonableness may range over a zone of reasonableness "within which the Commission is free to fix a rate varying in amount and higher than a confiscatory rate." (See Chart XIII.) The lower limit of this zone of reasonableness is marked by the "lowest reasonable rate," which the Court characterized as "not confiscatory in the constitutional sense." It is significant that in this interpretation the Court relied upon the precedent (among others) set in the recent cases arising out of the work of the California Railroad Commission, which was well known for its emphasis upon investment rather than reproduction costs. The federal Act regulating gas companies had provided in Section 5(a) that the Federal Power Commission might order a decrease in rates where existing rates are "not the lowest reasonable rates." The Court drew from this the following conclusion:

> It follows that the Congressional standard prescribed by the statute coincides with that of the Constitution, and that the courts are without authority under the statute to set aside as too low any "reasonable rate" adopted by the Commission which is consistent with constitutional requirements.

Thus the real import of the decision from the point of view of constitutional law is that, by accepting the device of the "zone of reasonableness," the Court has confirmed the self-denying position so often advocated by Mr. Justice Holmes, namely, that the Court should not substitute its judgment as to the best public policy for that of the legislature or of its administrative agent, the Commission, particularly if that agent is one "informed by experience."

The following paragraph in the opinion confirms this interpretation. In substance this paragraph refers to the entire course of judicial decisions from 1898, the date of *Smyth v. Ames,* to the date of the present decision. From this experience the Court, following in the wake of the opinion of 1913 written by Mr. Justice Hughes in the second Minnesota Rate cases, draws the conclusion that constitutional legislation is a matter of setting economic limits for legislative experimentation, of preventing the abuse of discretion, and of *proper* versus *improper* investigation. The United States Supreme Court does not abdicate the position assigned to it by that far-seeing student of institutional economics, Professor John R. Commons, when he said that it was the only *authoritative* faculty of political economy in the world's history. In the paragraph quoted below the Court finally admits administrative commissions to significant partnership in the work of public utility regulation:

> The Constitution does not bind rate-making bodies to the service of any single formula or combination of formulas. Agencies to whom this legislative power has been delegated are free, within the ambit of their statutory authority, to make the pragmatic adjustments which may be called for by particular circumstances. Once a fair hearing has been given, proper findings made and other statutory requirements satisfied, the courts cannot intervene in the absence of a clear showing that the limits of due process have been overstepped. If the Commission's order, as applied to the facts before it and viewed in its entirety, produces no arbitrary result, our inquiry is at an end.

Going-concern value. The Company had urged that expenditures incurred in the establishment and development of the business during the period from 1932 to 1939, prior to regulation, should be included in the rate base as an additional allowance. These claimed allowances were for expenditures to secure additional business and for fixed charges (interest, taxes, depreciation, fixed expenses) on excess plant capacity. It was estimated that, owing to depletion of gas reserves, the property had a limited life of twenty-three years for earning a return.

There was testimony that larger gas mains and facilities had been constructed in anticipation of business growth. In fact, however, only the first two years showed a book deficit, while the average annual return for the entire preregulation period was at the rate of 8 per cent on the undepreciated investment. The Company had been able to pay average annual dividends of 33.6 per cent on common capital stock issues of $3,500,000. The balance of the financial structure, consisting of $67 million in bonds, had been decreased by one-fourth through bond retirements out of earnings. All actual expenditures for building up the business during the formative years had thus been properly brought to book. Under these circumstances with regard to past financial history, the Commission had declined to include going-concern value as an additional item in the rate base.

After reviewing the facts of financial history, the Court significantly pointed out that the claimed additions to capital value would constitute "synthetic figures." It states and confirms the legal position maintained in recent cases that "there is no constitutional requirement that going concern value, when it is an appropriate element to be included in a rate case, must be separately stated and appraised as such." If the rate base now includes what was once excess capacity, because at the time of installation such excess capacity was reasonably held for future use, the property has been treated as a going concern. "When that has been done the burden rests on the regulated company to show that this item has neither been adequately covered in the rate base nor recouped from prior earnings of the business." [*Des Moines Gas Co. v. Des Moines* (283 U.S. 166)]. This qualification is, in effect, a rephrasing of the well-known Brandeisian rate-base standard, i.e., that the investment must have been prudently made.

The constitutional requirement of making an allowance for going-concern value is clear. It is a problem of economic limits beyond which the Court will not permit the constitutional doctrine of due process to be pushed. This appears from the following language:

It is only on the assumption that excess capacity is a part of the utility's equipment used and useful in the regulated business, that it can be included as a part of the rate base on which a return may be earned. When so included the utility gets its return not from capitalizing the maintenance cost, but from current earnings by rates sufficient, having in view the character of the business, to secure a fair return upon the rate base provided the business is capable of earning it. But regulation does not insure that the business shall produce net revenues, nor does the Constitution require that the losses of the business in one year shall be restored from future earnings by the device of capitalizing the losses and adding them to the rate base on which a fair return and depreciation allowance is to be earned. [*Galveston Electric Co. v. Galveston*, (258 U.S. 388) and *San Diego Land & Town Co. v. Jasper* (189 U.S. 439; 446–47).] The deficiency may not be thus added to the rate base for the obvious reason that the hazard that the property will not earn a profit remains on the company in the case of a regulated, as well as an unregulated business.

After pointing out once more the high average return earned during the preregulation period, "which included the severest depression in our history," the Court concluded its discussion of the bearing of the facts of the financial history of a public utility upon its claim to a separate and additional allowance for going-concern value as follows:

Whether there is going concern value in any case depends upon the financial history of the business. [*Houston v. Southwestern Tel Co.* (259 U.S. 318, 325).] This is peculiarly true of a business which derives its estimates of going concern value from a financial history preceding regulation. That history here discloses no basis for going concern value, both because the elements relied upon for that purpose could rightly be rejected as capital investment in the case of a regulated company, and because in the present case it does not appear that the items, which have never been treated as capital investment, have not been recouped during the unregulated period.

We cannot say that the Commission has deprived the companies of their property by refusing to permit them to earn for the future a fair return and amortization on the costs of maintenance of initial excess capacity—costs which the companies fail to show have not already been recouped from earnings before computing the substantial "net profits" earned during the first seven years. The items for advertising and acquiring new business have been treated in the same way by the companies and do not in the circumstances of this case stand on any different footing.

We may conclude from the foregoing that this case clears up the misinterpretations of the Galveston case with respect to going value.

The amortization issue. The second contention of the Company was that more liberal provisions should have been made for amortization of the investment. In order to appreciate the full significance of this branch of the case, it is important to clear up a question of terminology. The Court here used the term *amortization* as the practical equivalent of depreciation. The specific problem was what should be the base upon which annual allowances of operating expenses are computed which will restore from current earnings "the amount of service capacity of the business consumed in each year." The Commission used as its base the sum of $78,824,009, which represented the total investment in fixed capital to the end of 1938, the beginning of the regulatory period, plus the estimated future net-capital additions through 1954, the predicted end of the project, less salvage. It was conceded that an annual allowance of $1,557,852, computed on a 6½ per cent sinking-fund basis, would restore this investment.

The Company's contention was that the base should be $84,341,218, using reproduction costs less observed depreciation, and on this premise it included going-concern value. Consistent with its previous conclusion that the constitutional requirement of due process does not require the Court to choose between investment or replacement costs, the Court approved the use of investment cost, as a matter of reasonable administrative discretion. "When the property is devoted to a business which can exist for only a limited term, any scheme of amortization which will restore the capital investment at the end of the term involves no deprivation of property." The Court put to one side the precedent of its decision in *United Railways v. West* (280 U.S. 234,265), where reproduction costs were approved as a depreciation base, by refusing to consider it.

It was necessary also to consider the length of the amortization period because the lower court had held that unless the total investment were restored within the regulatory period of sixteen years, from 1938 to 1954, the rate of return would be confiscatory. The Court held, however, that under the decision in *Lindheimer v. Illinois Tel. Co.* (292 U.S. 151) and in conformity with established business practice, the entire life span of business assets was available for the accumulation of amortization charges and had been so considered by the company. Moreover, earnings for amortization were available and were adequate during the preregulatory period to absorb its due share of the annual consumption of capital in operations. The Court concludes, with surprising fidelity to accepted accounting procedures, that:

> The companies are not deprived of property by a requirement that they credit in the amortization account so much of the earnings received during the prior period as are appropriately allocable to it for amortization. Only by that method is it possible to determine the amount of earnings which may justly be required for amortization during the remaining life of the business.

What makes this case so important is the consistency with which the Court applies an underlying theory of rate regulation and the discrimination in its use of technical terms, especially accounting terms. The long years of argumentation and discussion of this general subject appear finally to be bearing fruit. Nowhere is this more apparent than in the Court's treatment of the subject of the proper interest rate to be applied in setting up an amortization reserve on a sinking-fund basis. The Commission had used a 6 per cent compound interest rate which the Company contended should be more nearly 2 per cent, the presumptive rate at which a hypothetical sinking fund would now be able to derive income. To this contention the Court gave the following complete answer:

> But the argument ignores the fact that the amortization method adopted by the Commission contemplates not a sinking fund of segregated securities purchased with cash withdrawn from the business, but merely a sinking fund reserve charged to earnings and not distributable as ordinary dividends. Under this method there is no deduction of the amortization allowances from the rate base on which a fair return—6% under the current interim order—is to be allowed during the life of the business.

Gone is the hoary contention that a sinking-fund theory of accumulating depreciation must use an interest rate which is less than the full rate of return.

The fair rate of return. Without much ado the Court accepted the Commission's finding of 6 per cent as a fair annual return upon the rate base because it was "supported by substantial evidence." It pointed out that most of the securities of natural gas companies were selling to yield between 3 and 4 per cent, and that the interest on large loans ranged from 2 to 3¼ per cent. In considering the risk factor, which is wrapped up in the single, all-inclusive allowance of a fair rate of return, the Court followed the reasoning of the *Bluefield* and other cases in establishing the degree of risk assumed. It pointed out the exceedingly favorable conditions of sale of output, with 90 per cent distributed under long-term contract to the Chicago District Pipeline Company, back of which were the three distributing companies who owned 26 per cent of the investment in the pipeline company. With respect to the risk of gas field depletion, the Court referred to the complete amortization of investment as affording "a security to the investment which is lacking to those industries whose capital investments must be continued for an indefinite period." Since the Company was in at least as favorable a situation with respect to all other elements of ambient insecurity as are other similar businesses, the Court concluded that it could not say on such a record "that the Commission was bound to allow a higher rate."

Historical importance of the case for the meaning of due process. The majority opinion was delivered by Chief Justice Stone. Four Justices wrote concurring but separate opinions. Since the current belief, that the rule of *Smyth v. Ames* was definitely discarded in this case, seems to have had its origin in the separate opinion concurred in by Justices Black, Douglas, and Murphy, these separate opinions, including a cryptic one from the pen of Mr. Justice Frankfurter, are also important.

The issue between the majority and the concurring minority appears in the very first paragraph:

> But insofar as the Court assumes that, regardless of the terms of the statute, the due process clause of the Fifth Amendment grants it power to invalidate an order as unconstitutional because it finds the charges to be unreasonable, we are unable to join in the opinion just announced.

In other words, the minority desires to push abstention from judicial review of commission rate orders to the point of abdication.

The minority opinion, not content with dissent on the question of the scope of judicial review, insisted that the instant case provided an opportunity for the Court to rid the regulatory process of the incubus of "the fallacious fair value theory." This seems to have been the portion of the opinion which, for political reasons, was given the fullest publicity, thereby detracting from the much more substantial values inhering in the majority opinion.

The most quoted portion runs as follows:

> But we are not satisfied that the opinion of the Court properly delimits the scope of that review under this Act. Furthermore, since this case starts a new chapter in the regulation of utility rates, we think it important to indicate more explicitly than has been done the freedom which the Commission has both under the Constitution and under this new statute. While the opinion of the Court erases much which has been written in rate cases during the last half century, we think this is an appropriate occasion to lay the ghost of *Smyth v. Ames* (169 U.S. 466), which has haunted utility regulation since 1898. That is especially desirable lest the reference by the majority to "constitutional requirements" and to "the limits of due process" be deemed to perpetuate the fallacious " fair value" theory of rate making in the limited judicial review provided by the Act.

Many years ago this writer was persuaded that the rate-making rule had obvious limitation, but that the vice of the situation was to be sought rather in the unimaginative and perverted use made of the same than in the historical circumstances which gave it birth. In the hands of legal practitioners, the use of the formula degenerated into a species of ritualistic incantation, not inaptly described as the "trance method," which deprived the formula of such logical development and refinement of which it was inherently capable. In keeping with the tradition of exorcizing this evil spirit, begun by Mr. Justice Brandeis in the Southwestern Bell Telephone Company case, the minority undertook once more to joust with this windmill. Following a cue given by Professor Hale,[2] they condemned it because it "derives from princi-

---

[2] Hale, R. L., "Conflicting Judicial Criteria of Utility Rates," *Columbia Law Review,* Vol. 38, p. 959.

ples of eminent domain"; because "fair value" obviously cannot be a composite of such discordant elements as security values, reproduction costs and historical costs; because it has proved "unworkable" in practice. What it all sums up to is that "the Commission is now freed from the compulsion of admitting evidence on reproduction cost or of giving any weight to that element of fair value."

By way of guidance to "the expert administrators charged with the duty of regulation," the minority then offered their own interpretation of "just and reasonable." This consists of protection of the investor interest by allowing the utility an opportunity to earn a reasonable cost of the service. However, this general rule finds its limitation in a *caveat*, expressing the consumer interest and his point of view, "that a return on historical cost or prudent investment though fair to investors would be grossly unfair to the consumers." This led the minority to make the confounding announcement that the "correct principle" had been discovered as long ago as 1896 in the Covington Turnpike Company decision (164 U.S. 578,596) by the same Justice Harlan who wrote the decision they protest.

It cannot be said that a corporation is entitled, as of right, and without reference to the interests of the public, to realize a given percent upon its capital stock. When the question arises whether the legislature has exceeded its constitutional power in prescribing rates to be charged by a corporation controlling a public highway, stockholders are not the only persons whose rights or interest are to be considered. The rights of the public are not to be ignored. It is alleged here that the rates prescribed are unreasonable and unjust to the company and its stockholders. But that involves an inquiry as to what is reasonable and just for the public. If the establishing of new lines of transportation should cause diminution in the number of those who need to use a turnpike road, and, consequently, a diminution in the tolls collected, that is not, in itself, a sufficient reason why the corporation, operating the road, should be allowed to maintain rates that would be unjust to those who must or do use its property. The public cannot properly be subjected to unreasonable rates in order simply that stockholders may earn dividends.

The importance of the decision in giving administrative commissions the right of way requires that these contrasting observations be added. The minority said that "the decision in each case must turn on considerations of justness and fairness which cannot be cast into a legalistic formula. The rate of return to be allowed in any given case calls for a highly expert judgment. That judgment has been entrusted to the Commission. There it should rest." But, in reading these lines of the minority opinion, it will be well for commissioners to remember the injunction of the majority that the courts will intervene if there is a clear showing "that the limits of due process have been overstepped." The majority, like the minority, is willing that the baby be washed; but unlike the minority, it is not willing that the baby be poured out with the bath water.

The Hope Case

Since the *Smyth v. Ames* case, no single decision of our highest court has evoked more discussion of its bearing on the regulation of earning capacity of public utilities than has *Federal Power Commission v. Hope Natural Gas Co.* (320 U.S. 591; 1944). The Commission had ordered the company to reduce its wholesale rates, using as a basis for determining reasonable earning capacity the "actual legitimate cost." After deduction for accrued depreciation and depletion, the rate base in round numbers was $33 million, upon which the Commission allowed a rate of return of 6½ per cent. The Commission had failed to include some $17 million of well-drilling and other costs because these had already been charged to operating expense. The capitalization was $28 million, of which $11 million had been issued as stock dividends. The allowed, net operating income of $2,191,314 per annum represented a return of about 8 per cent upon the stock. Since the bonds of other natural gas companies were selling to yield only about 3 per cent, the Commission felt that with this return, the well-managed, mature utility would be able to attract all the fresh capital it needed.

The Circuit Court of Appeals set aside the order because the rate base did not reflect the "present fair value" and because depreciation and depletion should likewise have been computed on the "present fair value" basis. The company had claimed a replacement-cost rate base of $66 million, with a rate of return of 8 per cent. In light of the decision in the pipeline case two years before, it seemed as if the "fair return on fair value" doctrine was making its last stand, at least in a federal jurisdiction.

In a five to three decision, the Supreme Court of the United States reversed the Circuit Court and upheld the Commission. In view of the facts of the case and the language of the opinion, it is generally believed that the Court has broken new ground. It not only reiterated the principle of judicial noninterference with the rate-fixing powers of the Commission, if the latter remained within the zone of reasonableness, but it announced the new doctrine of the "end result." We shall let the Court speak for itself.

Under the statutory standard of "just and reasonable" it is the result reached not the method employed which is controlling . . . It is not theory but the impact of the rate order which counts. If the total effect of the rate order cannot be said to be unjust and unreasonable, judicial inquiry under the Act is at an end. The fact that the method employed to reach that result may contain infirmities is not then important. Moreover, the Commission's order does not become suspect by reason of the fact that it is challenged. It is the product of expert judgment which carries a presumption of validity. And he who would upset the rate order under the Act carries the heavy burden of making a convincing showing that it is invalid because it is unjust and unreasonable in its consequences . . .

As we have noted, the Commission fixed a rate of return which permits Hope to earn $2,191,314 annually. In determining that amount it stressed the importance of maintaining the financial integrity of the company. It considered the financial history of Hope and a vast array of data bearing on the natural gas industry, related businesses, and general economic conditions . . .

Rates which enable the company to operate successfully, to maintain its financial integrity, to attract capital, and to compensate its investors for the risks assumed certainly cannot be condemned as invalid, even though they might produce only a meager return on the so-called "fair value" rate base.

What conclusions can be drawn with regard to the effect of the Hope case? Did the Court abandon "judicial review," and are we back again at *Munn v. Illinois* with unlimited discretion in the hands of the legislature or its agent? What has become of the doctrine of "confiscation"? What concrete test did the court embody in the "end result" doctrine? On this score, later decisions of the Court have not been particularly enlightening.

Implications in later decisions. In 1945, in *Market Street Railway Co. v. Railroad Commission of California* (324 U.S. 548), the Court had before it the unusual situation of an order by the California Commission reducing passenger fares in order to stay within the value of the service to the customers. Despite a book value of $41 million, an investment cost determined by the Commission as $25 million, the rate base used was $7,950,000. This was the price at which the privately owned railway, in active competition with a municipally owned street railway, had been offered for sale. Upheld by the Supreme Court of California, the Commission's order was likewise upheld by the U.S. Supreme Court because it recognized the shift in the consumer demand for urban transport from the streetcar to the motor vehicle, which had occurred since the 1920's. Under these conditions even the "fair value" might amount to little more than "scrap value" and yet the charge of confiscation could not be sustained.

As to the evidentiary value of the usual testimony introduced in rate cases, the Court, speaking through Justice Jackson, pointed out:

No study of the present cost of reproduction is shown, no present fair value is suggested. Nor do we think it important. Apart from familiar objections to the reproduction cost method, no responsible person would think of reproducing the present plant, consisting in substantial part of cable cars and obsolete equipment.

There is no basis for assuming that anyone, in the light of conditions which prevail in the street-surface railroad industry generally, would consider reproducing any street railway system. It was no constitutional error to proceed to fix a rate in disregard of theoretical reproduction costs.

In the same year, in two cases involving Federal Power Commission orders reducing rates, the Court upheld the use of actual legitimate costs and the new procedure of looking at the situation "in its entirety" and of measuring the order "by its end results." Said Justice Douglas with respect to "end result" in the Colorado Interstate Gas Company case (324 U.S. 581):

That is not a standard so vague and devoid of meaning as to render judicial review a perfunctory process. It is a standard of finance resting on stubborn facts. From the investor or company point of view it is important that there be enough revenue not only for operating expenses but also for the capital costs of the business. These include service on the debt and dividends on the stock . . . By that standard the return to the equity owner should be commensurate with returns on investments in other enterprises having corresponding risks. That return, moreover, should be sufficient to assure confidence in the financial integrity of the enterprise, so as to maintain its credit and to attract capital.

In the Panhandle Eastern pipeline case (324 U.S. 635), the Court followed the same procedure of measuring the "end result" by the test of the "return to the equity owners." In that case the Court was satisfied with earnings of 12 per cent on the stated value of the common stock, or 9 per cent on the same measure plus surplus.

In construing this new approach, since generally known as the *cost of capital* approach, in 1947 the Wisconsin Commission, in the Two Rivers case (70 P.U.R. NS 5), took the position that no findings of value for rate-base purposes were necessary; that the end-result doctrine merely required a finding that the sum of $12,500 constituted a reasonable profit available to the Company. In a decision bristling with criticism of the "due process" aspects of this summary and arbitrary procedure, the trial court set aside the Commission's order and was upheld by the State Supreme Court.

We may summarize the evolutionary trend in the decisions by pointing out that the doctrine of the Hope case has shifted the standard of investment from the undifferentiated measure of a fair return, based on the asset side of the balance sheet, to a differentiated measure, based on the liability side, with the return to equity owners taken as critical. The new procedures will be explained more fully and criticized in Chapter 23.

21. DEPRECIATION
POLICIES

The construction of a going plant converts capital, in the economic sense, into capital, in a physical or engineering sense. In a monetary economy we measure these transactions in terms of the monetary unit which we use as the medium of exchange. Businessmen operate with this unit in measuring relative scarcities. Revenues and expenditures are recorded in books of account in terms of this money of account. The instruments of production which comprise the going plant are recorded in the accounts as capital assets; the sources of the funds, as capital liabilities. The going plant, as an engineering organization, is concerned with preserving these productive instruments in a state of operating efficiency by which the relationship between the *input* of physical capital and the *output* of physical units of products or services are kept at a maximum. The going business, on the other hand, in recording these engineering transactions, measures them in terms of the monetary unit as units of outgo (costs) and units of income (revenue). It is the purpose of the going concern to keep the going plant as physical capital and the going business as monetary capital in a functioning relationship to each other.

Our monetary unit of scarcity, that is to say, of exchange value, has been the dollar. Our economy, until disrupted by the consequences of wars and depressions, has enjoyed a money of account of comparatively stable purchasing power. Short-term fluctuations due to the business cycle have tended to balance each other and have not been serious causes of disturbance. But since World War I, and especially since World War II, the measuring capacity of our unit of scarcity has been seriously disturbed by inflation. We shall concern ourselves with the effect of this phenomenon later on.

The Meaning of Depreciation

Depreciation is a device adopted for measuring the exhaustion or disintegration of physical capital in terms of monetary or pecuniary capital. It is by means of depreciation estimates that the going plant and going business are kept in right relationship to each other.

Let us consider the purpose behind depreciation policies. Each of the productive instruments, such as an electric meter or an electric generator, must be replaced from time to time so that the plant as a whole may keep on going. Only a going plant has the capacity for continuous service. Units of physical property or capital assets must be replaced as units because certain natural and social causes make them unfit for continued service. This phenomenon has been called *depreciation.*

In the sense in which the term is used here, depreciation also refers to the capital cost which accrues when productive instruments become unfit for service. If they could continue to render satisfactory service indefinitely, capital goods, once produced, would not need to be replaced. Cast-iron pipe in water mains, and lands as sites or standing room for operations, come close to this description. Saving or the accumulation of capital would then be a very much less important economic function. But capital as a whole must be replaced if production is to continue, and hence saving and reinvestment become a continuous process. Providing for depreciation is therefore one of the aspects of providing for continuity of saving and investment.

Each industry which undertakes to keep its productive instruments replenished is keeping its physical capital intact. But we must distinguish between physical and pecuniary capital. In the latter sense, capital represents the investment of present purchasing power, or of dollars. The latter is also the measure of capital in an accounting sense. One productive instrument, say, a bus, may cost $6,000. When the time arrives to replace this bus it may be found that one of exactly the same design will cost $9,000. In a physical sense, capital is maintained when one bus replaces another, but in a pecuniary and accounting sense, capital has been increased from $6,000 to $9,000. It would require an expenditure of $9,000 to maintain physical capital, while pecuniary capital would be maintained by the expenditure of only $6,000. The $3,000 of additional expenditure is necessary so that the enterprise may have a going plant, but this involves increasing the pecuniary capital of the going concern by that sum. Provisionally, let us take depreciation from an accounting point of view as relating only to the maintenance of capital in this pecuniary sense. The problems arising from inflation and deflation affect both the rate base and the depreciation base. We will, however, ignore them for the time being.

The Causes of Depreciation

After long investigations into the various causes of depreciation by engineers and accountants a consensus has been developed which may be compressed into the following classification:

1. Physical Causes
   a. Wear and tear
   b. Action of the elements
2. Functional Causes
   a. Obsolescence
   b. Governmental requirement
   c. Inadequacy

Wear and tear summarizes a grouping of causes that relate to the use or operation of properties. Friction, vibration, electrolysis, overheating, etc., at once come to mind as illustrations in point. Action of the elements, or a *weather factor,* produces deterioration with the passage of time. It may be due to such phenomena as rust, rot, decay, heat, washing, and freezing. These physical causes operate concurrently, and it is only by means of an abstraction that we distinguish them. Even if a plant is not being operated, the weather factor continues effective, while the wear and tear factor makes depreciation accrue faster.

Functional depreciation exists when there is a lack of adaptation to function of the parts of the going plant so that a need for earlier retirement arises. Quantitatively, functional depreciation is more important than physical depreciation. L. R. Nash, a utility engineer, estimated that retirements due to functional causes in the past have run as high as 80 per cent. This is not surprising when the meaning of obsolescence, inadequacy and governmental requirement as causes of depreciation is made clear.

Obsolescence occurs when a unit of physical property, though still fit for service from the points of view of the "weather" and "wear and tear" factors, must be retired from service because a new productive instrument is available which will improve the quality of the service or reduce the cost of the service. Technical advances in the art may have even produced an instrument which is superior to the old one in both respects. A new electric generator of greater efficiency illustrates the former, while a bus of better riding characteristics illustrates the latter. The requirements of adequate service at reasonable rates dictate that the old unit be replaced by a new one of more modern design. This is the *progress factor* in depreciation.

Closely akin to obsolescence as a cause of depreciation is one which has been named *governmental requirement*. Much utility plant occupies the public highways, and government, in caring for these highways, may require that alterations or improvements be made in such structures. Earlier retirements of old properties, when not due to progress in the art but to the need of bringing about better coordination between public utility uses and ordinary common uses of streets and highways, are occasioned by governmental requirements. The repaving of streets because of their effect upon track structures and the substitution of an underground distribution system for the pole lines of overhead distribution systems are familiar illustrations. This may be summarily described as the *social factor* in depreciation.

Again, a unit of property may be physically fit for service and of recent design but may not be of the requisite size or capacity for efficiency in production. The population of the community, and hence its service requirements, may have increased faster than was anticipated since the unit was first installed. These causes have been grouped together under the heading of *inadequacy*. Larger gas and water mains and increased size of electric and telephone cable suggest that there is a *market factor* operating among the causes of depreciation. In the case of both inadequacy and obsolescence, the shift of property units to new locations where these causes are not operative may prolong their useful life in the same or another going plant.

Attention should again be called to the fact that these causes of depreciation operate concurrently. As far as the ultimate need for retirement of the unit is concerned, their effect is mostly noncumulative. The immediate cause bringing about replacement may be any one of the five types enumerated. It is then the *limiting factor* conditioning further production.

For purposes of illustration only, let us take a productive instrument like a steam boiler capable of serving in a given going plant. If account be taken of the causes bringing about the retirement of this equipment, then for each of the five factors enumerated we have these prognostications:

Weather factor	50 years
Wear and tear factor	15 years
Social factor	12 years
Market factor	10 years
Progress factor	5 years

In this illustration the functional cause of obsolescence would bring about retirement five years before inadequacy, or ten years before physical deterioration would have required replacement. Reliable estimates of service life, as far as physical depreciation is concerned, can be based only on past experience. Functional depreciation cannot be foretold. Obsolescence is especially unpredictable. Who could have predicted the coming of atomic energy before World War I, or who can even now predict when and where it will be substituted for the conventional steam-boiler plant (although one hears that it will be a commercial reality in one year)?

We are now ready to give a definition of depreciation as suggested by the Depreciation Committee of the National Association of Railroad and Utilities Commissioners (NARUC) in 1943:

(a) Depreciation is the expiration or consumption in whole or in part, of the service life, capacity, or utility of property resulting from the action of one or more of the forces operating to bring about the retirement of such property from service.

(b) The forces so operating include wear and tear, decay, action of the elements, inadequacy, obsolescence and public requirements.

(c) Depreciation results in a cost of service.

We should place alongside this definition one derived from Chief Justice Hughes nine years before in *Lindheimer v. Illinois Bell Telephone Co.* (292 U.S. 151):

Broadly speaking, depreciation is the loss, not restored by current maintenance, which is due to all the factors causing the ultimate retirement of the property. These factors embrace wear and tear, decay, inadequacy, and obsolescence. Annual depreciation is the loss which takes place in a year. In determining reasonable rates for supplying public service, it is proper to include in the operating expenses, that is, in the cost of producing the service, an allowance for the consumption of capital in order to maintain the integrity of the investment in the service rendered.

Obviously, these definitions have the same import. They stress that depreciation (1) is the loss of service life not restored by current maintenance, (2) represents the gradual consumption of capital which must be charged to current output as a part of the cost of production. The cost concept is, on the one hand, a consumption of physical capital, and on the other hand, a consumption of pecuniary capital.

Maintenance and Depreciation

It is a matter of common knowledge that all productive instruments must be maintained in good operating condition by careful use and attention and by a timely replacement of minor parts. But the distinction between repairs and depreciation is difficult to draw because it depends upon what one considers a unit of property. The unit may be so minute, like small hand tools, that its identification as a unit in the accounts is impractical. In the end, expenditures to repair and replace units of equipment serve the same purpose of maintaining the unit and indirectly, the going plant in a state of operating efficiency. Engineering economics, which relates production costs to quantity and quality of output, will determine the amount of these expenditures for repair. Accounting practices will determine what may be considered a unit of property for depreciation purposes. What is most important is that both maintenance and depreciation as costs must be properly accounted for and their relation to past, present, and future output established. If this is not done, the economic nexus between cost and income will be lost and with it the economic basis for pricing. For this reason, according to current practices, the cost of repairs is charged currently as an operating expense, while depreciation is distributed as a cost over the period of time during which the unit of property is in service. The two costs are, however, interdependent. If repairs are made when needed, the productive instrument will remain in service longer than when repairs are delayed. The estimate of the length of useful life of a unit of property thus depends upon a definite standard of maintenance. If this standard is not maintained, the service life of the unit is shortened. Such shortening has been called depreciation due to *deferred maintenance.*

Foreshortened life. In the illustration used earlier the difference between fifteen years and five years represents what has been called *foreshortened life* and is due to functional depreciation. The limiting factor in rapidly growing communities like Los Angeles usually is inadequacy, while in dynamic industries like electric power it is obsolescence. The foreshortened life is chargeable to functional depreciation.

Other Causes of Loss of Capital Assets

With the exception of land as standing room, all productive instruments are irretrievably on the way to the scrap heap. There are, however, other causes of the loss of capital dependent more largely upon chance. Small tools, materials and supplies of all kinds in storerooms are subject to wear, loss, theft, breakage, or spoilage. These capital losses are spoken of as "contraction in inventories" and currently charged to special accounts. They are not so important in amount nor so irregular in occurrence that current charges to operation or construction cannot be made to cover them adequately. As a form of depreciation, however, they must not be overlooked.

More important are chance causes of capital loss due to unforeseeable contingencies. We need only mention explosions, fires, floods, earthquakes, and sleet and wind storms to call to mind the not infrequent and costly catastrophes which have brought large capital losses in their train. Similarly, wars, strikes, and riots have resulted in infrequent but severe property losses. Against most of these contingencies provision may be made through the various forms of property and casualty insurance. Premiums paid are charged as an operating expense. Some of the larger companies undertake to carry their own insurance, particularly on property where the hazard is a remote one. Uninsurable losses may be covered by contingency reserves or charged directly to surplus. The residuum of risk which remains must be borne by stockholders or other owners of the enterprise. It is for this assumption of final risks that the owners of the equity are accorded a higher differential return than other contributors of capital.

The Purpose of Depreciation and Insurance Charges

The ultimate objective of depreciation procedure is to charge against consumers the cost of maintaining intact the capital fund of a going concern. In so far as other losses of capital are covered by systematic insurance plans, the costs of insurance become a part of the cost of production and the concern has been protected against this risk of loss. Thus, depreciation and insurance charges are practical devices for shifting the incidence of risk from owners to consumers.

A sound public policy has recognized the validity of these practices in order to afford the going-concern security of investment. Whether capital is contributed by lenders or owners, they are both protected against the risk that their investment might be impaired, provided only that the market for the service will support the charges. We shall again reserve for later discussion the problem of whether investment should be kept intact against changes in the value of money. To be sure, bondholders are protected at law in that both interest and principal must be paid at their due dates, whether or not the utility has exacted depreciation charges from its customers. Such protection may, however, turn out to be an illusory safeguard when the shareholder's equity is small in amount or nonexistent. Certainly, it is the better policy for financial management and regulation to unite in fixing rates upon a basis of cost which includes both insurance and depreciation charges.

Properly understood, there is no conflict between the utility and the rate payers with respect to this procedure. There is mutuality of interest between them. The customer is interested in securing continuity of adequate service while the utility is interested in preserving its credit; that is to say, continuity of investment of capital at reasonable rates of return. Both objects are accomplished by means of such charges. By so doing, the utility preserves its productive instruments for continuous service (provided price levels have not changed radically), thus ensuring a continuous flow of income. By preserving its physical assets and business relations with customers, the capital assets can continue to function as security for the repayment or refunding of debt. With a reasonable margin of investment by stockholders similarly maintained, and with the assurance that any accretions in the capital fund due either to the increased cost of replacements or to new capital additions for extensions and improvements will be protected by the same price-fixing and depreciation policies, the financial credit of the enterprise can be continuously maintained.

We repeat: The central purpose of depreciation charges is to keep the capital fund unimpaired. If a less than adequate charge is made, the fund is impaired and dividends may have been paid out of capital. If the charge is more than adequate, the capital fund has been increased.

The Financing of Depreciation

We begin with two conclusions: (1) depreciation is a cause of insecurity of investment against which some systematic provision must be made; (2) depreciation is a part of the cost of operation chargeable as an operating expense and must not be considered a reservation of surplus.

In accordance with the second conclusion, annual net operating income is not ascertained until annual depreciation is deducted from operating revenues. There has been, and still is, real danger that a policy will be adopted making it the obligation of the corporation to provide for depreciation out of net income. In advertising the sale of securities, it is not unusual for corporations to publish figures of net income which are claimed to be available to meet interest, dividends, and *depreciation*. In this way an extra margin of net income above that required to meet either interest or dividend requirements can be shown. Justification of this practice is based upon the fact that interest must be paid, while property retirements may be deferred. It is true that this can be done temporarily, but if the practice continues, the plant which is security for the loan becomes physically impaired, service deteriorates, and the earning power of the concern diminishes. Unless abnormal conditions intervene, such as the deterioration of an entire industry, the policy should thus be to consider depreciation as an operating expense.

The depreciation base. The first step in financing depreciation is to measure its amount. From a financial point of view, depreciation relates to the pecuniary capital and not to the physical capital of the concern. Therefore, the financial problem involved is not that of ensuring the replacement of one unit of property by another unit. That would be interpreting capital in the physical sense. Rather, it involves collecting enough funds from customers through rates to replace the cost of the retired unit. The basis of the calculation for depreciation, or the depreciation base, is therefore the *cost of the units of property now installed,* not their cost of replacement. A very practical accounting consideration also points to the use of the cost of the old unit because the replacing unit is seldom of exactly the same design, capacity, and efficiency as the old one. Depreciation accumulations should represent the cost of the plant now in service.

Salvage and scrap value. Although property may be unfit for continued service, it is not necessarily valueless. Retired units may have either a *scrap value* or a higher *salvage value.* These amounts, when recovered, would reduce by that much the amounts chargeable as operating expense. It is the *net amount* that is chargeable as depreciation against the output of service during the time that the units of property were a part of the going plant.

The time factor. This brings us to a consideration of the time factor in depreciation. Over how long a period will units of property remain in service? At the moment of retirement, dictated by reasons of engineering economy, this time interval becomes definite. With adequate accounting for the various classifications of fixed capital and the maintenance of property records, the service life of units of property can be definitely determined as a matter of historical fact. The difficulty in the situation is that service life must be *estimated beforehand* if advance provision is to be made systematically by charging the annual aggregate consumption of service life as operating expense.

It has become current practice to estimate the life expectancy of units of property by property classifications and by means of life tables on the analogy of life insurance. At this point, opinion on the subject divides. There are those who have been extremely critical of these so-called theoretical estimates of depreciation. They contend that it is impossible to forecast the service life (not the physical life) of property accurately and that therefore estimates of annual depreciation are worse than useless. It must be admitted that service life cannot be estimated with accuracy; neither can the life of an individual, and yet the great business of life insurance has been built upon this foundation. Public utility regulation will be confronted with great difficulties if it abandons the depreciation concept on this account. The fact of the matter is that *accuracy* is not the essence of the problem. The real purpose of depreciation procedure is to make some provision for currently charging the accruing cost of capital retirements to the cost of the service. These charges should be as correct as possible, and the estimates should be brought to increasingly higher standards of accuracy. Past inaccuracies are always subject to corrections.

The renewal method.   Three methods of financing depreciation have been devised, of which two do not use the life-expectancy approach to the problem. The first of these is the so-called renewal method. When a unit of property is retired, the cost of the new unit installed in its place is charged to operating expense. There are no periodic charges to depreciation and hence no building up of a reserve for depreciation. The method was best exemplified by the former practices of the steam railways who renewed track and equipment whenever it was worn out and charged the cost to operating expenses.

Let us note the effect of this procedure. Presumably, the cost of the first unit of property remains charged in the fixed capital account. Whether the cost of replacement is greater or less, the customer pays only for the cost of replacement. If a physical appraisal of the cost of the existing plant were made at any time, it would reflect both higher and lower replacement costs together with the cost of any uncapitalized improvements. The objection at once comes to mind that the new unit may be one of greater capacity or efficiency for which the renewal method fails to account. This will be particularly true where inadequacy or obsolescence are the limiting factors in bringing about replacement. Accountants have therefore sought to correct the procedure by estimating the additional cost of the improvement and charging the excess to the appropriate fixed capital account, a difficult matter in any event. However, if this were not done, the fixed capital accounts would bear no relation to the actual cost of the plant in service.

Another result of the renewal method is that depreciation becomes a part of cost of operation only as it matures. A stretch of track completely renewed in any one year is charged to operation in that year alone. This is obviously contrary to fact with regard to the accrual of depreciation. The practice was defended on the statistical ground, however, that in the case of large and seasoned plants like railroads, the amount and cost of property replacement remained approximately the same from year to year and thus would not seriously distort the net income for the year.[1] This was true to the extent that large plants were composed of many units of varying sizes,

[1] Allison, J. E., *Should Public Service Properties be Depreciated to Obtain Fair Value in Rate or Regulation Cases,* Report to St. Louis Public Service Commission, September, 1912.

ages, and life expectancies. The generalization, however, was not, and is not, now applicable in the case of plants where the replacement of large units like power stations would seriously distort the net income for the year. By reason of these accumulating difficulties, the method was generally abandoned even in the case of the steam railways. In its place the second method of not depending on service life estimates was proposed.

The retirement expense method. This method, known as the *retirement expense method,* while not definitely based upon forecasts of the length of service life, does make some periodic allowance for retirements in advance of their actual occurrence. A retirement reserve is accumulated by means of charges to "retirement expense" which exceed in amount the cost of current retirements. After the reserve has accumulated to an amount which will take care of all fluctuations in the cost of retirements, it may be kept at a safe figure by means of periodical charges to operating expense, which will vary in amount with years of good and poor income flow. This method avoids the difficulty of a fluctuating cost of operation due to uneven retirements inherent in the renewal method. A reserve is accumulated equal to about 10 per cent of the cost of fixed capital, the amount and rate of accumulation from year to year being left to the discretion of management.

The retirement expense method was embodied in the uniform classifications of accounts for gas and electric utilities of the 1920's. It was adapted to these utilities because individual units of property represented so large a part of the total cost of the fixed capital that their retirement would have unduly distorted operating expenses unless their cost of retirement were spread over a period of years. It should be noted that this method relieves (credits) the fixed capital accounts of the cost of the retired units by charging this cost to the retirement reserve. The new replacing units of property, whatever their cost, will then be charged to the relevant fixed asset accounts. In this way these accounts will always reflect the actual cost of the active plant. In this respect the method represents a distinct improvement when contrasted with the renewal method; but the retirement reserve does not adequately reflect the elapsed service life in terms of the accrued cost, which is generally understated.

The life expectancy method. The third method proceeds by way of a detailed calculation of life expectancies for all the different classes of properties and accumulates a true depreciation reserve out of operating expense charges which, together with salvage recoveries, is estimated to provide for the full cost of the retired items. If the estimates as to lives and salvage values have been correctly made, the reserve will be more than adequate at all times to provide for the financing of replacements in an amount exactly equal to the actual cost of the *displaced* physical capital. The method achieves the same result as the retirement expense method, but the depreciation reserve is maintained at from 30 to 50 per cent of the cost of the fixed capital and measures the accrued depreciation on an "age-life" basis. The estimating of service lives should be done by experts who are familiar with the different classes of physical property, the local climatic and operating conditions, the standards of maintenance, etc., and who are in a position by periodical inspections and by current observation of the retirement process to make the necessary adjustment in life expectancies and hence in depreciation rates. The so-called life tables are only the starting points of more definitive investigations.

Straight-line depreciation accounting. There are two variants of the life expectancy method of providing for depreciation which have been in most general use. One is known as straight-line depreciation and the other as sinking-fund depreciation, with the former now in almost universal use among public utilities. To illustrate how straight-line depreciation is accounted for, let us assume that a unit of property costing $1,000 has no salvage recoveries and is estimated to have a life expectancy in service of 10 years. If this estimate proves correct, then $1,000 ought to have been collected from customers at the end of the ten-year period by either method of accounting. Straight-line accounting collects this sum in equal annual installments of $100, which are simultaneously charged to depreciation expense and credited to the depreciation reserve.

Unlike other expenses, such as wages paid out to labor, depreciation expense is usually retained in the business and used to finance extensions and improvements. After, let us say, five years of this process of accumulation, when the reserve contained $500, this sum has been invested in extensions; but there has been no increase in the capital liabilities because customers contributed these depreciation charges in advance of the need of financing *pro tanto* the replacement requirement. From the point of view of its capacity to render efficient service, the plant has been maintained in 100 per cent operating condition; in fact its capacity to render additional service has been increased by the unencumbered investment of depreciation reserve funds. For rate-base purposes, however, the pecuniary capital has not been increased but has merely been maintained; hence, if the rate base is measured from the asset side of the balance sheet, the investment in fixed capital must be reduced by the amount of the accrued depreciation as shown in the depreciation reserve. If the rate base is measured from the liability side of the balance sheet, the amount of the capital fund is equal to the capital liabilities (stocks, bonds, notes, etc.) plus or minus the surplus or deficit.

Let us now assume that the end of the service life of the unit has been attained so that the retirement will have to be made and a new unit installed. The accounting entries for this transaction are a credit to fixed capital for the full cost ($1,000) of the old unit which is being retired and a concurrent debit to the depreciation reserve which will in the meantime have grown to $1,000. The advantage of this method of accounting for depreciation and for fixed capital appears when the cost of the new properties differs from the cost of the retired properties. The fixed capital accounts are always credited with the full cost of the property retired, while the depreciation reserve is correspondingly debited. The depreciation reserve account thus records the turnover of the pecuniary cost of fixed capital. As prices change, the provision for depreciation changes because it is always based upon the cost of the active property. The influence of changing price levels impinges only when property purchased at higher or lower prices enters the fixed capital accounts and thereby becomes a part of the basis upon which future depreciation charges are calculated.

Sinking-fund depreciation accounting. The sinking-fund method of accumulating depreciation is in most respects analogous to the above except for the procedure in financing. The sinking-fund method assumes that as the reserve is accumulating, the cash represented by the reserve will be invested in outside securities and segregated in a separate fund (hence the name) or invested in the utility's own plant. In either case interest earnings from securities or earnings from property are allowed to accumulate, thereby reducing the annual depreciation allowance by the amount of the interest earnings. Depreciation expense is debited for the amount of the depreciation annuity and interest expense for the required interest, compounded at some definite rate (now usually taken as equivalent to the over-all rate of return). The depreciation reserve is correspondingly credited. (See p. 265.)

The difference between the straight-line and sinking-fund methods of accumulating depreciation is illustrated in Table VII, using the assumptions made in the text for property having a ten-year service life, a cost of $1,000 with no salvage, and an interest rate of 6 per cent, with the reserve invested in the property and not in outside securities.

We may now pass to a discussion of the public policy aspects of the depreciation problem, where, as already indicated, the practices of individual utilities and the policies of the different commissions have varied widely.

Table VII   Comparison of Straight Line and Sinking Fund Methods

| Year | STRAIGHT LINE | | SINKING FUND | | |
	Annual Depreciation Expense	Depreciation Reserve Accumulation	Depreciation Annuity Expense	Annual Interest Expense	Depreciation Reserve Accumulation
1	$100	$100	$75.87	$	$ 75.87
2	100	200	75.87	4.55	156.29
3	100	300	75.87	9.37	241.53
4	100	400	75.87	14.58	331.98
5	100	500	75.87	19.90	427.75
6	100	600	75.87	25.66	529.28
7	100	700	75.87	31.74	636.89
8	100	800	75.87	38.20	750.96
9	100	900	75.87	45.05	871.88
10	100	1000	75.87	52.25	1000.00
Totals	1000		758.70	241.30	

Aspects of Public Policy

Before 1900 depreciation charges as a cost of operation of public utility industries were, generally speaking, within the realm of managerial discretion, as they had always been in competitive industry. In fact the problem was but imperfectly understood because engineers, accountants, and economists had not made more than a beginning in their study of the problem. The law, proverbially lagging behind in its consideration of questions of public policy, had little to offer. *Smyth v. Ames,* for instance, had nothing to say upon the subject. The definitive choice of the commission system of regulation as a substitute for competition in the field of natural monopoly changed all this. Only a little later the adoption of state and federal income taxation of corporations also brought about significant changes with respect to depreciation policies in competitive industry. We shall discuss these policies first under the heading of depreciation as a cost of operation and next as depreciation in relation to the problem of the rate base.

Depreciation as a cost of operation.   With the adoption of the commission system it was necessary first to have the law recognize that depreciation is an operating expense and that some provision must be made to ensure the renewal of plant. This was accomplished by means of statutory provisions to this effect, however imperfect and tentative they may have been. Details of accounting policy were embodied in the first state-wide classifications of accounts prescribed by the pioneer commissions.

However, here as elsewhere, we are in danger of losing a sound footing unless we make the distinction between competitive and monopolistic industry. In competition, a private undertaking may fix such prices for its output as it can obtain in view of the option its customers have of buying elsewhere. Any profits above operating expenses and fixed charges belong to the owners. In the absence of statutory or other restrictions they may ration out profits in the form of dividends or keep them on hand in the form of surplus. The surplus may be used to create depreciation reserves, but there is nothing sacred about these reserves. The directors are empowered to use them in any manner that may promote the best interests of the undertaking. Some limitation upon this discretion may arise on account of the protection of the interests of creditors in connection with mortgages. When inadequate provision is made for depreciation reserves and most of the surplus is paid out in dividends, no funds will be on hand to provide against the deterioration of capital assets. Such dividend payments are then said to have been made out of capital. The inevitable result will be impairment of service. In competition, however, where the necessity for self-preservation will prevent the quality of the service from falling below the standard fixed by the trade, good business management will provide for keeping the capital assets intact.

Under public utility regulation, on the contrary, adequate depreciation charges had to be made compulsory. Since consumers do not have the option to get service elsewhere, there exists no automatic check upon deterioration of service. All this is now self-evident. Yet as late as 1902, a state supreme court in *Cedar Rapids Water Co. v. Cedar Rapids* (118 Iowa 234, 263) failed to recognize the true meaning of depreciation charges when it held:

We see no reason why plaintiff, in addition to operating expenses, repairs and other ordinary charges, should be allowed to reduce the apparent profits by deductions for a restoration or rebuilding fund. The setting aside of such a fund may be good business policy, and, if the company sees fit to devote a portion of its profits to that purpose (though, as we understand the record, no such fund as yet has been created) no one can complain; *but it is in no just sense a charge affecting the net earnings of the works.* [Author's italics.] To hold otherwise is to say that the public must not only pay the reasonable and fair value of the services rendered, but must, in addition pay the company the full value of its works every forty years—the average period estimated by plaintiff—for all time to come.

Fortunately, the Supreme Court of the United States dispelled such confusion when in 1909 in the Knoxville Water Company case (212 U.S. 1, 13) it held:

It is not only the right of the company to make such a provision, but it is its duty to its bond and stock holders, and, in the case of a public service corporation, at least, its plain duty to the public. If a different course were pursued, the only method of providing for replacement of property which has ceased to be useful would be the investment of new capital and the issue of new bonds or stock. This course would lead to a constantly increasing variance between present value and bond and stock capitalization, a tendency which would inevitably lead to disaster either to the stockholders or to the public or both. If, however, a company fails to perform this plain duty and fails to exact sufficient returns to keep the investment unimpaired whether this is the result of unwarranted dividends upon over-issue of securities, or of omission to exact proper prices for the output, the fault is its own.

If the policy of creating depreciation reserves is adopted, it must be applied consistently or it will break down. The difficulty of estimating these periodical accruals in advance calls for a treatment of depreciation reserve balances which keeps them inviolate and dedicated only to the purpose for which they were intended. The amounts charged to operating expense as a part of the cost of service must not be regarded as a part of the free surplus of the concern, much less as a part of operating profit. In theory these sums are set aside to compensate the utility for the consumption of capital as finally evidenced by asset retirements. The reserve is therefore susceptible to both overreservations and underreservations for the specific units of property, and hence adjustments will become necessary.

This requirement was not recognized either by the Commission or by our highest court in the New York Telephone Company case of 1926 (271 U.S. 23). The Company had set up depreciation on a straight-line basis. The depreciation reserve stood at $16,902,530 for a property valued at $76,370,-000. The reserve was not segregated in a separate fund but was invested in the going plant. The New Jersey Commission found that the reserve was excessive by $4,750,000 and directed that this amount (quoting the court)

be used by the company to make up deficits in any year when earnings are less than a reasonable return as found by the board . . . The effect of the order is to require that if total operating expenses deducted from revenues leaves less than a reasonable return in 1925 or a subsequent year, there shall be deducted from the expense of depreciation in that year and added to the net earnings a sum sufficient to make up the deficiency; then by appropriate book entries, the resulting shortage in depreciation expense is to be made good out of the balance in the reserve account built up in prior years.

The Company contended that depreciation charges in prior years were not excessive and that the Company could not be compelled to make up deficits in future net earnings out of past accumulations of depreciation reserves. It seems that the Company had not been earning an excessive return in the past. Upon the question thus raised the Court ruled:

It may be assumed, as found by the board, that in prior years the company charged excessive amounts to depreciation expense and so created in the reserve account balances greater than required adequately to maintain the property. It remains to be considered whether the company may be compelled to apply any part of the property or money represented by such balances to overcome deficits in present or future earnings and to sustain rates which otherwise could not be sustained.

The just compensation safeguarded to the utility by the 14th Amendment is a reasonable return on the value of the property used at the time that it is being used for the public service. And rates not sufficient to yield that return are confiscatory . . . Constitutional protection against confiscation does not depend on the source of the money used to purchase the property. It is enough that it is used to render the service . . . The customers are entitled to demand service and the company must comply. The company is entitled to just compensation and, to have the service, the customers must pay for it. The relation between the company and its customers is not that of partners, agent and principal, or trustee and beneficiary . . . The revenue paid by the customers for service belongs to the company . . .

Customers pay for service, not for the property used to render it. Their payments are not contributions to depreciation or other operating expenses or to capital of the company. By paying bills for service they do not acquire any interest, legal or equitable, in the property used for their convenience or in the funds of the company. Property paid for out of moneys received for service belongs to the company just as does that purchased out of proceeds of its bonds and stock. It is conceded that the exchange rates complained of are not sufficient to yield a just return after paying taxes and operating expenses, including a proper allowance for current depreciation. The property or money of the company represented by the credit balance in the reserve for depreciation cannot be used to make up the deficiency.

With all due respect for the opinions of our highest court, this interpretation of depreciation does not appear to be sound. It may be conceded that the board erred when it sought to divert depreciation reserve credits to make up expected deficits in future net earnings at a time when the company had been earning less than a fair return in the past and particularly when there was dispute as to whether the depreciation rate was excessive. But the Court's conclusion that excessive depreciation reservations are the unqualified property of the Company, so that equitable adjustments in depreciation rates for the future become impossible, appears equally unsound. It tends to make unworkable the reserve method of providing for property retirements when the economic life of units of assets together with their salvage values can never be definitely predictable. It fails to take into account the going-concern character of operations where, in the course of time, the conflicting interests of owners, creditors, and customers may be equitably reconciled. To this end a policy of continuous accounting is necessary, and this cannot be done unless the reserve is kept inviolate. An amendment of the Wisconsin law in 1931 definitely gives depreciation reserves this status of inviolability.

Depreciation and the rate base. We have already referred to the policy adopted by the early commissions of deducting the accrued depreciation from the cost of reproduction new in ascertaining the initial rate base. Unless a utility's plant had been constructed after commission regulation began, the corporations were the owners of depreciated plants, usually with inadequate reserves to provide for the retirement of assets no longer used and useful. If past earnings had been insufficient, the deficiency in the reserve requirement was a measure of the uncompensated losses sustained. If dividends had been paid in the past, it was necessary to determine whether they were excessive or whether they had been paid out of capital and at the expense of inadequate depreciation reserves. The depreciation reserve, its adequacy or inadequacy, was peculiarly the focus of all questions of retrospective valuations which would have to be resolved in the fixing of an initial rate base.

In their efforts to sustain the earning capacity of their properties, utility managers attempted to secure from the commissions generous allowances of depreciation as operating expense. As a rule the commissions obliged by assigning shorter lives to units of equipment as compared with the longer lives now in vogue. What was perhaps even more important, the depreciation charge set up on the books was usually less than that fixed in rate cases. It was not until the 1930's that some order was introduced into the chaos of depreciation charges by commission requirement that accounting entries be made to correspond with commission determinations. Similarly, in protecting their revenues, utilities attempted to argue with fine inconsistency that the accrued depreciation set up on an age-life basis was a theoretical quantity and did not measure the true depreciation deductible for rate-base purposes. Only depreciation observed and testified to by engineering experts after an actual inspection of the properties constituted deductible depreciation in any real sense.

In thus looking at the problem from an engineering point of view, depreciation was in effect identified with decline in operating efficiency. True depreciation in this view sets in only when there is a failure to maintain operating efficiency, something akin to "deferred maintenance." Depreciation in the economic sense, i.e., recording the wastage of capital and the need to keep the capital fund or investment intact, was wholly disregarded. The misconception of the nature of depreciation—which takes its cue from the fact that service has deteriorated and that additional expenditures will be necessary to restore normal operating efficiency—is best illustrated by a plausible analogy much used at the time. Just as a fresh egg laid by an old hen (so ran the argument) is not sold for less in the market than an egg coming from a young hen, so the reasonably adequate service rendered by an old but well-maintained plant should not be priced for less than the equivalent service rendered by a new plant. The misconception is, of course, that depreciation is a measure not of the cost of one single unit of output but of the cost of maintaining the *flow* of the requisite units of output in a going business. The egg dealer with a preponderance of old hens had better look to his hennery if he wants to stay in business.

The engineering interpretation of accrued depreciation as a deduction from the cost of reproduction new is best exemplified by Justice Butler's opinion in the Indianapolis Water Company case (272 U.S. 400,416), where in 1926 it became a part of the law of the land:

> There is deducted approximately 25 percent of estimated cost new to cover accrued depreciation. The deduction was not based on an inspection of the property. It was the result of a "straight line" calculation based on age and the estimated or assumed useful life of perishable elements . . . The testimony of competent valuation engineers who examined the property and made estimates in respect of its condition is to be preferred to mere calculations based on averages and assumed probabilities.

From the engineering interpretation of depreciation also stems the adoption during the 1920's by the NARUC of retirement expense, instead of depreciation expense, and of the "retirement reserve" as a substitute for the depreciation reserve in its uniform classification of accounts for gas and electric utilities. The retirement expense method with its inadequate reserve has been compared with the practice of "kiting checks." When checks are drawn on banks without a full balance at the bank to cover them, relying for their validity upon the fact that they will not all be presented for payment at the same time, this kiting deviousness is analogous to retirement accounting. Like observed depreciation, it slides over the primary object of depreciation charges, which is to ensure that purchasers of service during an accounting period pay for the estimated cost of the contemporaneous journey of physical capital to the scrap heap, even though its physical retirement may be years distant. It cannot be asserted that the annual depreciation requirement, and hence also the reserve requirement, is something which can be estimated with exactitude. The assignment of lives is complicated, of course, by the difficulty of fixing upon the "unit of property." It is further complicated by including obsolescence, public requirement, and inadequacy among the factors controlling life and by the common practice of rebuilding units of property so that their lives are prolonged. These difficulties are, however, amenable to treatment if a continuous property record be kept.

This engineering perversion of the depreciation concept was not reversed judicially until the Lindheimer case of 1934. In the meantime, however, it bore other strange fruit in 1930 in *United Railways and Electric Co. of Baltimore v. West* (280 U.S. 234). The doctrine was somewhat modified in the *Smith* case the same year by Justice Hughes who, while agreeing that as a matter of law the reserve was the property of the company, was willing to concede that depreciation rates might be changed for the future as a result of experience of the past. As the Court said: "The recognition of the ownership of the property represented by the reserve does not make it necessary to allow similar accumulations to go if experience shows that these are excessive." But the acme of reliance upon present value or reproduction cost new for both rate-base and depreciation-base purposes came with the aforementioned West case. It should be noted that this extension of the reproduction cost standard was announced before the price level took the plunge to the low levels of the last depression. Speaking for the majority (with a vigorous dissenting opinion, which we shall discuss later) Justice Sutherland said:

The allowance for annual depreciation made by the commission was based upon cost. The court of appeals held that this was erroneous and that it should have been based upon present value. The court's view of the matter was plainly right. One of the items of expense to be ascertained and deducted is the amount necessary to restore property worn out or impaired, so as continuously to maintain it as nearly as practicable at the same level of efficiency for the public service. The amount set aside periodically for this purpose is so-called depreciation allowance. Manifestly, this allowance cannot be limited by the original cost, because, if values have advanced, the allowance is not sufficient to maintain the level of efficiency. The utility "is entitled to see that from earnings the value of the property invested is kept unimpaired, so that at the end of any given term of years the original investment remains as it was at the beginning . . ." This naturally calls for expenditures equal to the cost of the worn out equipment at the time of replacement; and this, for all practical purposes, means present value. It is the settled rule of this Court that the rate base is present value, and it would be wholly illogical to adopt a different rule for depreciation.

The effect of the Court's opinion upon Commission practice was to establish the conflicting evidence of experts with respect to "observed depreciation" as the measure of accrued depreciation to be deducted in contested cases. As far as possible, however, commissions continued to use the actual reserve balance or the estimated reserve requirement. The complexity of the situation was not alleviated when in 1934 the Supreme Court disapproved the use of index numbers in another Maryland case where the Commission sought to apply the reproduction-cost standard in both rate-base and depreciation-base determination in the Chesapeake and Potomac Telephone Company case.

The foregoing comedy of errors was not relieved until the Court definitely reversed itself in 1934 in setting forth the proper method of estimating depreciation accruals in *Lindheimer v. Illinois Bell Telephone Co.* (292 U.S. 151). The issue between "reserve accumulations" and "observed depreciation" was squarely joined in this case when, despite a reserve accumulation in excess of $48 million, the Company contended for a deduction of only about $16 million. The Company had attacked the rates fixed by the Commission as confiscatory. The lower court had upheld the Company. In reviewing the evidence submitted by the Company, the Supreme Court, in effect, rested its decision on the disparity between the claims of the Company for annual depreciation expense which had resulted in the large book reserve and its contemporaneous claim that the existing depreciation in the property, physical and functional, did not exceed 8 per cent, or the $16 million referred to above. The Court held that the Company had not sustained the burden of proof in its elaborate estimates and computations but had "overshot the mark"; that is to say, it had proved too much. The Court's revised view of depreciation appears from the following extract from its opinion:

Broadly speaking, depreciation is the loss, not restored by current maintenance, which is due to all the factors causing the ultimate retirement of the property . . . In this instance, the Company has used the "straightline" method of computation, a method approved by the Interstate Commerce Commission . . .

While property remains in the plant, the estimated depreciation rate is applied to the book cost, and the resulting amounts are charged currently as expenses of operation. The same amounts are credited to the account for depreciation reserve, the "Reserve for Accrued Depreciation." When property is retired, its cost is taken out of the capital accounts, and its cost, less salvage, is taken out of the depreciation reserve account. According to the practice of the Company the depreciation reserve is not held as a separate fund but is invested in plant and equipment. As the allowances for depreciation, credited to the depreciation reserve account, are charged to operating expenses, the depreciation reserve invested in the property thus represents, at a given time, the amount of the investment which has been made out of the proceeds of telephone rates for the ostensible purpose of replacing capital consumed. If the predictions of service life were entirely accurate and retirements were made when and as these predictions were precisely fulfilled, the depreciation reserve would represent the consumption of capital, on a cost basis, according to the method which spreads that loss over the respective service periods. But if the amounts charged to operating expenses and credited to the account for depreciation reserve are excessive, to that extent subscribers for the telephone service are required to provide, in effect, capital contributions, not to make good losses incurred by the utility in the service rendered and thus to keep its investment unimpaired, but to secure additional plant and equipment upon which the utility expects a return.

Finally, in 1944 (and this sums up the present status of the depreciation question as far as the law of the land is concerned), the Supreme Court in *FPC v. Hope Natural Gas Co.* (320 U.S. 591) fully approved basing depreciation charges on cost. Said the Court: "By such a procedure the utility is made whole and the integrity of its investment is maintained. No more is required. We cannot approve the contrary holding of *United Railway and Electric Co. v. West.*"

22. THE CONTROL
OF FINANCIAL POLICIES

One central difficulty running through most of the history of public service enterprises is the failure of governments to control adequately the security issues of public service corporations. Given the state of the law and public opinion when these enterprises were in the formative stage, such laxity is not surprising. While this condition is now greatly improved, it is necessary to review briefly these historical facts of financial policies in order to understand and properly evaluate the reasons back of the gradual adoption of present-day policies of government control.

Early Corporate Financing Affecting
Security of Investment

The power to borrow money has always been conferred in corporate charters. It was exercised by the board of directors after an affirmative vote by stockholders. In the absence of statutory restrictions, only such safeguards attended these borrowings as the creditors themselves insisted upon. Similarly, within the rather wide limits of charter authorizations, corporations were likewise free to use their own discretion as to the *amount* of capital stock issues and the *consideration* for which they were issued. Also, at law, the issuance of these securities is not a right but a privilege to which the state creating the corporation can attach such restrictions as it deems to be necessary. This is particularly true of public service corporations on account of the public purposes which they serve.

It is a general rule of corporation law that funds derived from stock and bond issues may be used only for corporate purposes. This rule operates to render *ultra vires* only the most palpable diversion of funds to noncorporate purposes. In the absence of statutory restrictions it did not affect the discretion lodged in boards of directors to determine whether the issuance of the stock or the sale of the bonds was in return for adequate and valuable consideration, thus opening a door for financial manipulation.

The trust fund doctrine.   The courts did their best to curb some of the evil results flowing from these manipulations. In order to protect the interests of *creditors,* they evolved what has been called the *trust fund* doctrine. According to this doctrine, in the event of receivership, the receiver may seek to recover by suit from the stockholders the amount of the difference between the par value of the stock and the value which had actually been paid in money, services, or property. In the view of the courts, this difference constituted a trust fund for the benefit of creditors, which was in the hands of stockholders but which was available to be levied upon in case of insolvency. This method of procedure of proving value deficiency was not very effective. It was an expensive and difficult process, benefiting only creditors, and often doing an injustice to stockholders unaware of such legal consequences.

Overcapitalization.   If all the capital thus obtained had always been in the form of cash, the financial history of utilities would have been quite different. The fact is that securities were also issued to pay for physical properties (especially in consolidations and reorganizations), for promotional services, for franchises, and other forms of intangible property. In negotiating these transactions, directors had to appraise, on the one hand, properties and services, and on the other hand, the present value of securities offered in exchange. Honest errors and frauds committed in gauging the *consideration* which passes in such transactions brought on the evils attendant upon *over-capitalization.*

The first opportunity to overcapitalize came with the need for new industries in a new country. It gave to promotion activities in the United States that optimistic impress which has made America a byword for "unlimited possibilities." New enterprises were usually speculative. With respect to them, "nothing was certain except uncertainty." In the first place they were capitalized without regard to the monetary cost of the fixed plant. It is a matter of common knowledge that the construction cost was financed by means of bond issues, with shares of stock issued as a bonus to those who purchased the bonds. Franchises and the services of promoters and financiers were appraised by agreement between promoters and financiers themselves and paid for with bond and stock issues. There was thus no correspondence between the par values of security issues and the cost of the fixed properties.

Another occasion for overcapitalization arose out of the failure to distinguish between capital and income. In order to pay some return, particularly upon the bonus stock, maintenance was neglected, and little or no provision was made for property renewals. When the time for making replacements came rather suddenly, due to the rapid growth of the country, or when it became necessary to take care of the deferred maintenance, funds for these purposes had to be secured by more security issues. Indirectly, dividends were thus paid out of the proceeds of security issues.

The rapid development of the arts of production offered a third opportunity for excessive security issues. In order to keep the properties abreast of the times, old plants had to be abandoned faster than their cost could be written off as an operating expense. Additional securities were thus issued in order to secure funds for rehabilitation and modernization.

Consolidations also bred overcapitalization. Where the constituent companies had already developed the earning power of their properties, it would seem that the future prospects of their consolidation might be less uncertain. Yet the benefits and costs of such consolidations could not be accurately foretold. Moreover, they were usually prompted by the need of modernizing the plants in many respects. Security issues based upon such future estimates were also likely to prove excessive. Even where held down to consolidation costs, the figures were often excessive because prices paid were based upon oversanguine prospects of net earnings.

A fifth opportunity came when enterprises that had gone into receivership emerged again with a greater load of security issues which, while cutting down fixed charges, made up for this by increasing the amount of equity securities.

The basis of reasonable capitalization. The five historical factors enumerated above are the principal reasons why capitalization and investment costs have so often parted company. This raises the question as to the meaning of overcapitalization. The usual way of stating it is illustrated by Eli Clemens in his recent valuable treatise: [1] "In general, overcapitalization exists when the stated value of a company's securities is greater than the value of the assets behind them." The word "value" is obviously the critical one in this definition. To the accountant, for record-keeping purposes, value would be reasonable investment or acquisition cost. To the *economist*, value will have an entirely different connotation. It is not based upon the cost of property alone but also upon its prospective earning power.

The reasonableness of the particular value base thus has reference to the purpose of the analysis. To the accountant, investment costs are a reasonable basis because he uses them as a point of departure in recording the initial capitalization. A standard of valuation, based upon the net income available as a return upon the securities taken collectively, is simply a way of ascertaining economic value as it varies from the accountant's original bench mark. Both are reasonable for their respective purposes.

[1] Clemens, E. W., *Economics and Public Utilities* (New York: Appleton-Century-Crofts, Inc., 1950), p. 464.

It thus appears that over a period of time the question of what is a reasonable capitalization depends upon the net income-producing power of corporate assets as limited by regulation. The capitalization of net income is therefore the proper standard of valuation to be applied by investors in buying public utility securities or in estimating the commercial value of the entire going concern *as an investment opportunity.* The government, on the other hand, in fixing rates or in controlling capitalization will use the investment-cost standard because its object is the determination of that reasonable earning power which investors later capitalize when they choose between different investment opportunities.

Methods of Utility Financing

In order to appreciate the major problems of present-day financial policy, it is necessary to review briefly the methods used in the past for financing public utilities.

The very earliest method of financing appealed chiefly to the stockholding group of investors. Comparatively few people provided the funds for the original construction of public utilities, and these few were stockholders. Where the utilities were badly needed, the state and its political subdivisions often subscribed to shares of stock, or loaned the utility public funds secured through public credit, or made contributions in the form of land grants. In order to expand the scope of operations, earnings were very largely reinvested in the business. The original owners were content to receive a limited present income and to accept, as a substitute for higher present yields, an increased future value of their holdings and the promise of higher returns.

As the demand for extensions increased and as existing facilities had to be abandoned to make room for improvements, the original sources of capital supply proved inadequate. At this point these industries began to resort more extensively to the use of borrowed funds. The mortgage bond, secured by the creation of liens upon the existing physical property, was introduced as a method of corporate financing. This created the class of securities having a prior lien upon property and earnings, and relegated the capital stock to a subordinate place as junior securities. With its potentially wider distribution, the mortgage bond gradually became an important vehicle of corporation finance.

The next important step in the financial history of public utilities came with the consolidation of connecting properties, in the case of railroads, and of connecting and competing properties, in the case of the local utilities. These consolidations usually involved the discarding of considerable amounts of old property, its replacement by new property of an improved character, and the extension of service into new territory. This meant that many of the junior securities had to suffer large losses in their equity, some of the financial structures collapsing under these cumulative burdens.

The original financial plans had not foreseen the large amounts of capital that would be required in order to meet the need for expansions, improvements, and replacements. The early bond issues were usually limited to definite and often relatively small amounts. The funds which could be borrowed under these closed mortgages were exhausted before the need for improvements and extensions had been fully met. Because the enterprises often had not yet attained maturity and a settled earning power, such increased capital requirements could not be met by the public sale of stock. As the need for consolidations became more pressing, the fact that additional funds could not be obtained by the old means led to the introduction of new types of securities. The refunding bond and extension bond were an outgrowth of this condition. The latter became a second mortgage, with a lien junior to the lien of the underlying bonds. Wherever possible the outstanding closed mortgage obligations were eliminated by paying off the bonds. When this was impossible, provision had to be made in the new mortgages for refunding these securities as they matured. Because these refunding bonds offered only the security of a second mortgage, inducements had to be held out to give them a wider marketability. The era of consolidations thus brought new issues of preferred and common stock, in addition to the refunding bond, which were offered to prospective purchasers of refunding bonds. In some cases refunding mortgages provided for the deposit of bonds of underlying issues in escrow, thus giving refunding bonds partial first liens.

At this juncture the holding company appeared as a vehicle of public utility financing. Its characteristic mode of financing was the issue of collateral trust bonds. By combining the bond and stock issues of subsidiaries and offering them as collateral security, the bonds of holding companies could be sold to investors. Large amounts of capital were thus acquired from foreign sources, particularly England and Germany.

With the object of securing the advantages of unified operation, holding companies sometimes paid more for the stocks of subsidiaries than was warranted by their earnings or the value of their physical assets. If such excess purchase price properly measured the advantages which might accrue in time by introducing economies in operation (that is to say, if the income yield of the securities purchased would increase), the capitalization of the holding company was not inflated. Otherwise, the excess price represented nothing in the way of hoped-for economies, but merely served the desire of a financial group to extend the range of its power or to rid itself of costly and irksome competition.

Improvements in financing. Despite the accumulating difficulties, utilities were able to finance their improvements and extensions. Manufacturing companies were able to sell their equipment by taking the bonds, notes, and shares of utility companies in payment. The marketability of the debt securities was improved by substituting the "open end" mortgage with series financing for the "closed end" mortgage. Adjustment to lower interest rates in the open market was made possible by making the debts callable at premiums ranging up to 5 per cent. Properly drawn mortgages or trust deeds give assurance of safety of principal and income, not only by providing a lien upon *all* the property of the creditor (the after-acquired property clause) but also by including other specific terms in the contract under which the money was loaned. These terms usually include the specific nominal interest rates, the character of the lien, the date of maturity of the bonds, the conditions under which the bonds may be redeemed, sinking fund and conversion privileges, provisions relating to minimum maintenance and depreciation requirements, and the legal remedies available to bondholders in case of default.

The freedom vouchsafed utility companies in the adoption of financial policies finally raised the question whether such latitude in financing was not reacting unfavorably upon the security of investment and hence upon the credit of these enterprises. Legislatures, in response to public opinion, answered the question in the affirmative by conferring the power of regulating security issues upon administrative commissions.

The financial plan. Before discussing the outstanding features of such regulation, it may be well to discuss, however briefly, the general principles in accordance with which the securities should be parceled out to different classes of investors, i.e., the principles which constitute the financial plan or financial structure of the corporation. In its essence the financial plan consists of the amount and classifications of stocks and bonds which the corporation proposes to issue at the time of organization or reorganization. This is a very important step because, as Professor Dewing said in his pioneering work, *The Financial Policy of Corporations*, "the promoter-banker is here the architect of the new corporation. The form of the financial plan with which he endows it determines the lines which its whole future financial policy must follow." [2]

[2] Dewing, A. S., *The Financial Policy of Corporations*. (New York, The Ronald Press Co.) 1926.

In summary, the general principles upon which the financial plan should be constructed are as follows: Bonds should be issued only when the prospective earnings promise to be both substantial and reasonably certain or constant in amount from year to year. Preferred stock may be issued when prospective earnings, although likely to be irregular, nevertheless amount to so much that, when averaged over a period of years, they provide a safe margin above the fixed dividend requirements called for by the preferred stock certificates. If the earnings promise to be both unpredictable and fluctuating in amount, the safest policy is to issue only common stock.

Purposes of Security Regulation

The chief aim of security regulation, certainly the aim that appealed to the popular imagination when regulation was first instituted, was to protect *consumers* by putting an end to overcapitalization and stockwatering. It was believed that high rates and poor service were a direct result of such practices. The later extension of control to nonpublic utility securities (the so-called blue sky laws) had for its purpose the protecting of private *investors* against financial loss. It was undertaken with the view partly of conserving the capital fund of the country and partly of encouraging habits of thrift and industry.

The real purpose of security regulation for public utilities is the preservation of their credit. This means that security of investment must not be undermined by financial malpractices which may lead to at least two unfortunate results. The first result is the increased cost of capital arising from unsound security issues. This was certainly one of the consequences of unrestrained holding company financing before the great depression of the 1930's. The increased cost of capital has a very direct effect upon the "rate of return," as we shall see, and hence upon the cost of service. It is a sad state of affairs when a public utility must sell its bonds at heavy discounts or finds its stocks quoted at merely nominal figures. The second unfortunate consequence is that these practices lead inevitably to unsatisfactory service. In order to pay interest and dividends upon overissues of securities, a constant inducement is set up to divert earnings from maintenance and improvements.

The need for securities regulation is now conceded. It did not come, however, without overcoming much pettifogging opposition, such as that represented by the Federal Railroad Securities Commission of 1910, headed by President Hadley of Yale. This investigating commission contended that the proper remedy was publicity rather than strict control. They voiced the objection that the government should not be put in the position of guaranteeing the soundness of securities which it approves as investments. The report of the committee said:

We are told that if it was possible to standardize food by a pure food law, it ought to be possible to standardize railroad securities by a securities law. It is possible—to the same extent and no more. The pure food law enables a man to know what he is buying. It does not certify that the thing he buys is good for him. That is left to his intelligence. The government cannot protect the investors against the consequences of their unwisdom in buying unprofitable bonds any more than it can protect the consumers against the consequences of their unwisdom in eating indigestible food.

This was hardly a valid argument against security regulation, for the commissions specifically disclaim all implications that their authorizations are a guaranty. Though investors may get the advice of investment counselors, the final decision rests with them.

First steps in securities regulation.   During the earlier and primitive stage of the control of security issues, it was believed that general statutory provisions would suffice and that capital stock alone should be regulated. Hence we find that the hitherto unrestricted power of corporations to issue stock was at first restrained by pious injunctions that shares should be issued only for money, services actually performed, and property received. The proceeds were to be used only for the lawful purposes of the corporation.

Massachusetts merits recognition as the first state to undertake seriously the task of controlling capitalization. Since public utilities in that state were financed largely by means of stock issues, its policy centered upon controlling the issue price of capital stock, with the aim of making the par value equal to the investment. Legislation was early enacted to prevent the issue of bonus stock and also its issuance at less than par. This was the situation up to 1871. After that date Massachusetts' law provided that stock be sold at public auction. This violated the traditional rights of stockholders to preference in subscribing for new capital and opened the way to contests for control between rival interests. Finally, in 1894, security regulation entered upon its modern phase with legislation that the share capital be issued at a market price to be fixed by regulating commissions. At the same time the bonded debt was limited to a figure not in excess of the par value of the share capital.

Other states, among them New York and Texas, soon followed the example set by Massachusetts, all determined to stop overcapitalization. Texas in 1893 started the control of security issues, restricting itself, however, to railroad corporations alone. The law forbade the issue of securities—bonds as well as stock—without the *approval* of its railroad commission. The amount of the issues were to be held down to the reasonable value of the property as determined by the commission. Wisconsin and New York undertook the regulation of security issues as a part of their program of public utility regulation in 1907. The provisions of the Wisconsin stock and bond law were weak and ineffectual. A more effective law was enacted in 1911 and further amended in 1913. With the spread of the new movement for regulation by state commission, twenty-five commissions were given varying degrees of control over public utility security issues by 1928.

General character of state control of security issues. In the 1920's, securities regulation was generally assumed to be limited to the objective of holding down the issue of securities to the amount required to finance a utility's program of expansion and improvement. The legal basis of control was the statutory statement that the issuance of securities by public utility corporations is a "special privilege" which may be exercised only with the approval of the commission. Securities were usually defined as stocks, bonds, notes, or other evidences of indebtedness payable in periods of more than a year. This definition excluded the "floating debt" (maturing in less than one year) of corporations from such control. The purposes to which the proceeds from such security issues may be applied were generally as follows:

1. For the acquisition of property
2. For the construction, extension, and improvement of plant
3. For the improvement or maintenance of service
4. For the discharge or lawful refunding of obligations
5. For the reimbursement of money actually expended from income for the above purpose.

It should be noted that the enumeration of purposes does not include the payment of dividends. The treasury may be reimbursed by the proceeds of security issues for funds originally derived from depreciation reserves and earned surplus and expended for the statutory purposes. The authorization or certificate issued by the commission usually states the purposes to which the proceeds must be applied. Unauthorized issues of securities were declared by statute to be void. The laws did not leave much to the discretion of commissions. If securities were reasonably required for the purposes specified, commissions were required to authorize them.

Commissions were empowered to examine into and give publicity to all the facts surrounding each issue. They could assess penalties of fines or imprisonment upon those who caused unauthorized securities to be issued, who diverted the proceeds to other purposes than those authorized, and who made false statements or representations in hearings or filed incorrect statements.

Control of the prices at which securities are issued.   The most difficult problem in connection with the control of security issues is that of the price at which they should be sold. The Indiana and Wisconsin law met the problem by fixing the minimum price at which securities may be issued, which in the case of stock was the par value, and in the case of bonds was 75 per cent of their face value. In 1894 the Massachusetts' law provided that the stock be sold at a price fixed by the commission. Difficulties in administering this provision brought an amendment in 1908 which permitted the issue of shares at a premium but not at less than par, the exact issue price to be determined in each case by the corporation in the first instance but approved by the commission. Most state commissions fixed minimum sales prices by taking the price specified in the company's application. These were usually arrived at as a result of informal negotiation between the companies and underwriters, while the commissions were kept informed and were consulted during the progress of the negotiations.

A related problem has reference to the type of capital structure to which the utilities may be required to conform. Some statutes, as in Massachusetts, specified a definite ratio of bonds to stock. However, the law of most states, as in Wisconsin, merely provided that bonds should bear a reasonable proportion to stock, thus leaving the determination of the relative quantities to the commission after an investigation of the facts in each application. This provision was designed to prevent undue burdening of properties and operations with bond issues and fixed charges. It was also designed to make ownership and management reflect a substantial financial interest in the corporations. It should be pointed out, however, that the failure to distinguish between preferred and common stock tended to defeat the intent of the law when the widespread sale of preferred and common stock, usually without voting rights, to customers and employees in the 1920's constituted a borrowing of funds in all but in name.

The failure in many states to give commissions control over the reorganization of public service companies and over the consolidation of public utilities had an indirect effect upon securities regulation. Unless the commissions are authorized by statute to limit security issues to the reasonable value of the property concerned in such reorganizations and consolidations, the value represented by such security issues cannot be kept under control in the interest of investors and customers. As Commissioner Erickson said when such powers were finally conferred upon the Railroad Commission of Wisconsin:

Consolidations of operating properties are sometimes a very prudent and econom-ical move, but there are times when consolidations are effected with a view solely to profit on the part of those promoting the consolidation . . . The opportunity to combine two corporations and issue securities exceeding the combined value of their properties is so tempting that, in the absence of the regulation of security issues, public utility managers have often availed themselves of it in the past, much to the detriment of the public.

The Transition to a Modern System of Security Regulation

The decade of the 1920's was a supreme test of the efficacy of the system of security regulation which had grown up piecemeal under the historical condition just portrayed. In this decade following the price revolution of World War I, the utility industry was caught up in an expansion and integra-tion movement requiring unprecedented amounts of utility financing. Begin-ning with a low of almost $500 million, the yearly amount climbed progres-sively to a peak of almost $3 billion in 1927, remaining at the approximate level of $2,500 million until 1931, when it dropped to about $1,500 million. About 80 per cent of the security issues floated represented new capital issues, with the balance in refunding issues. During the depression years, until re-vival came again in 1935, the amounts dropped precipitously to a low of $92 million. This period represented the flowering of the holding company.

Because most holding companies did not possess franchises, they were not public utilities according to the statutes and were usually incorporated in states where regulation was conspicuous by its absence. State commissions therefore had no jurisdiction over their operations and their security issues. With the details of security issues and the initiation of financial policies left to the discretion of the management of the operating utilities, the commis-sions were in no position to control the financial excesses of holding companies with respect to their financial affiliates and their operating subsidiaries. More-over, it was not a matter of common knowledge, until revealed by the Fed-eral Trade Commission investigation of holding companies in 1928, that they would use their control over operating public utilities to profit from the sale and distribution of their subsidiary's securities. Similarly, it was not generally realized that state commissions had no control over contracts be-tween operating public utilities and their financial, management, construc-tion, engineering, and manufacturing affiliates within the same holding-company system. In particular, there was no control over dividend payments and over short-term borrowings—the so-called upstream and downstream loans.

The decade of the 1920's was also the period of exfoliation of reproduction costs as the dominant element in the rate-making rule of *Smyth v. Ames.* The new postwar plateau of inflated prices could be urged under this theory as a basis for rate increases, thus putting substantive earning values behind security issues equated with reproduction-cost appraisals of property acquisitions.

The state commissions, with rare exceptions, had also failed to correct the stockwatering and property write-ups of the past, as reflected in the existing security issues and in the fixed capital accounts. Regulation of securities and of accounting was restricted to current and future security issues and current and future accounting practices. With the coming of the depression and the collapse of the price structure of the economy as a whole, the stage was set for a political drama, the prologue of which was the collapse of holding company empires, followed by the public utility legislation of the "New Deal" era.

Reorganization of state control. Under the leadership of Wisconsin, New York, and Massachusetts, a thorough-going reorganization of public utility regulation was begun. In 1931 Wisconsin revised the section of its public utility law, giving the commission greater power over security issues, accounting systems, depreciation policies, dividend policies, and contracts between operating companies and their holding company affiliates. The most important amendment authorized the commission to stop the payment of dividends if such payments were actually made with the capital of the corporation. In order to keep this capital fund intact, the commission was also authorized to require utilities to submit reasonable depreciation rates for the several classes of property. When approved by the commission these rates were to be used thereafter in keeping the depreciation accounts. In controlling the financial structure, the commission was empowered to distinguish between preferred and common stock and to keep all classes of capital securities in reasonable relationships to each other. From these reforming states, including also the California Commission, more vigorous regulation of rates, service, and securities spread to an increasing number of other states. However, the new movement did not come soon enough to forestall the coming of federal regulation, if indeed the control of security issues by holding companies could have been accomplished at all without the intervention of Congress.

Federal Regulation

In shifting the emphasis to federal regulation of securities, a beginning was made with interstate carriers. Due to the impotency of state governments in handling utilities with national markets, security regulation for interstate carriers was more often perfunctory than otherwise. The conflict in state statutes and the variety of state jurisdictions presuming to regulate the issuance of such securities had engendered an intolerable situation. It was further aggravated by the delay and confusion attending the securing of permits from several states by the same interstate carrier. With control vested in a single authority, the Interstate Commerce Commission, it seemed that the character of regulation might be made uniform and the administration more effective.

After much agitation the *exclusive power* to regulate the issuance of such securities was finally vested in the Interstate Commerce Commission by the Transportation Act of 1920, combining in one body the preponderant power to fix rates, to control consolidations, and to control the issue of credit instruments. Commission approval is required for the issue of stocks, bonds, or other evidences of indebtedness except notes maturing in two years or less. Such short-term issues, however, are limited to 5 per cent of the par value of all capital liabilities. Unless operated as part of a steam railway system, electric railways are exempt, as are sleeping-car companies. The Commission is also required to certify to the courts and to approve security issues in connection with plans for reorganization under section 77 of the Federal Bankruptcy Act of 1933.

The Securities and Exchange Commission. The principal duty to regulate security issues other than railroad devolved upon the SEC. Under the Securities Act of 1933 it ultimately received a limited jurisdiction over all corporate securities issued and sold in interstate commerce, not merely those of public utilities. This act was aimed primarily at assuring "full disclosure" of all material facts so that investors might be better able to judge the value of any particular security. The Securities Exchange Act of 1934 extended the Commission's jurisdiction to organized stock exchanges and over-the-counter markets, in order to eliminate manipulation and certain other abuses associated with trading in securities *already issued.* But it was the Public Utility Act of 1935 that gave the Commission jurisdiction over all registered holding companies and their subsidiaries with respect to security issues. The Act required that the issuance of securities conform to certain broad standards of good financial management, which may be summarized as follows: (1) Securities issued should be reasonably adapted to the financial structure and earning power of the issuing company; (2) their financing should be necessary and appropriate to efficient and economical operation; (3) fees, commissions, and other remuneration for the sale of securities should be no more than reasonably necessary under competitive conditions; and (4), applying a most general standard, the terms and conditions of sale must not be detrimental to the public interest or to the interest of investors and consumers. These statutory standards have been translated into specific administrative standards that obtain their meaning from specific situations which cannot be detailed here, particularly when they arise from the financial reorganizations of companies which were likewise contemplated by the Act. It is important to note that the issuance of securities by subsidiary gas and electric utilities must continue to have the approval of state commissions, with whose standards the federal agency may be in conflict. A further objective of securities regulation by the SEC is to achieve an equitable redistribution of voting power among security holders. By 1945 some 54 holding company systems, comprising 118 registered holding companies, and 943 electric, gas, and non-utility subsidiaries were subject to the Commission.

The Federal Power Commission. Regulation of security issues by the FPC was designed to apply only to those utilities that were operating in states without securities regulation of their own. Hence the provisions were much like those in state laws, i.e., requiring utilities not to issue any security or assume any financial obligation without first securing an order from the federal commission. Only those securities are approved for sale where the issue is for some lawful purpose and reasonably necessary or appropriate therefor. The proceeds may be spent only for purposes specified in the Commission's order. No lease, franchise, permit, or contract for consolidation may be capitalized at a sum in excess of the amount actually paid.

Some Important New Financial Procedures

In regulating security issues, commissions can so guide the development of financial structures as to achieve these fundamental objectives: (1) adequacy and low cost of capital supply; (2) protection against an inequitable distribution of voting power; (3) the use of the securities as a base for determining the reasonableness of earning power. In the remainder of this chapter and in Chapter 23, relating to the "rate-of-return," we shall deal with these fundamental objectives by discussing and analyzing some important new financial procedures designed to achieve these ends.

"Competitive bidding" versus "negotiated sales." It had become customary in the gradual evolution of corporation finance that railroad and other utilities looked to specific investment banking houses for the sale and distribution of their securities. This financial relationship became a continuing one and was hardened into a system called *banker management* or *finance* *capitalism* by making bankers members of the board of directors and of the "finance committee" of the board. The system was further extended into the highways and byways of public utility finance through the practice of arranging for interlocking directorships. Under these arrangements, sales of securities did not take place in the open market but were "negotiated sales" without "arms-length" bargaining. The arrangement was defended as one which made the members of a particular banking house intimately acquainted with the problems and operations of their client utilities so that they could give better financial advice in their professional capacities. Financial plans could be so devised as to make financing immediately available and at propitious times. If the investment banking house was an affiliate of a holding company, which in turn controlled the operating companies needing the capital, the relationship was an identity: the right hand dealing with the left hand. These arrangements were nevertheless defended as being of a trusteeship type, and in the joint interest of the bankers, utility companies, and ultimate investors.

Commissions generally, including the ICC but the SEC in particular, objected to negotiated sales because it was impossible to determine the reasonableness of fees paid to underwriters and dealers. Since there was no open market, the competitive cost of selling and distributing the securities could not be ascertained. The suggestion that the securities be put up for "competitive bidding" did not meet with approval from the utilities or the bankers because the former were reluctant to abandon the old connections and the latter showed an inherent reluctance to compete with each other. Only independent investment bankers, anxious to extend their operations, welcomed the new procedure under a rule requiring that all security issues in excess of $1 million be put up to competitive bidding. According to reports of the SEC, the competitive procedure had eliminated long and costly investigations into the status of affiliated interests to determine whether there has been arms-length bargaining. It had also apparently reduced the average underwriting spread by 1949 from 2.95 points ($ per $100 bond) for negotiated sales to 2.46 points for competitive sales. There has also been a swing back to private placement of loans.

Equitable distribution of voting power. The integration movement for public utilities had not only been aided by the creation of holding companies but the need for concentration of control was made apparent by classifying the stock into common and preferred stock with limited voting rights. Sometimes the full voting rights were concentrated in a comparatively small issue of classified common stock, with the rest of the common and preferred shares having only limited voting rights. The SEC has attempted to restore and redistribute voting rights among those who have contributed the risk capital of the concern in some more reasonable proportion to the risks assumed. The opportunity to do this was afforded when new issues of junior securities came before them for approval or when the entire capital structure, but especially the equity portion, was revamped in connection with corporate reorganizations and corporate simplifications. The Commission has in particular sought to overcome the practical disfranchisement of the preferred stockholders by increasing their limited voting participation. Since the solicitation of proxies has also been an effective method of divorcing control from ownership, some limited control over proxies was secured. This was done in connection with SEC approval and report upon reorganization plans as they came before that Commission.

Internal financing.   As public utility industries became technologically more mature, it was not only possible for them to sell their securities in the open market but it also became possible to use retained earnings as a means of financing plant expansion and meeting new capital requirements. Such internal financing is derived primarily from net income not distributed as dividends and from accruals to operating expense reserves. Net income available in excess of dividend payments, especially during periods of cyclical or wartime prosperity, can be used to meet financial requirements and has been increasingly so used since the 1920's. The growing reservations of revenues in depreciation reserves, particularly after the shift from retirement to depreciation accounting, has made these sums available for more or less permanent financing. Similarly, the time lag between the accrual of taxes and their actual payment illustrates how smaller amounts may become temporarily available for financing through the process of operating expense accruals.

Institutional financing.   Although not a new development in public utility finance, the growing importance of the holdings of securities by insurance companies, banks, foundations, investment trusts, pension and retirement funds, and similar "savings" institutions should be mentioned. Life insurance companies may serve as an example. As reported by the Life Insurance Association of America, investments by forty-nine legal Reserve companies in 1952 aggregated $3.2 billion in railroad bonds and $10.8 billion in public utility bonds but only $0.1 billion in railroad stocks and $0.7 billion in utility stocks. The crucial importance of utility securities in the financial planning of the custodians of our life insurance benefits is further attested by the fact that the above railroad and public utility bonds constituted 5 per cent and 16.9 per cent, respectively, of their total investments. It is also significant to note that while the dollar amount of railroad bonds held by them has been relatively static since 1929, that of utility bonds has grown from $1.4 billion in 1929 to $10.8 billion in 1952.

Hiatus in Security Control

Although the need for security control is recognized in regulated industries, there are some exceptions, due, no doubt, to the low fixed investment in plant in relation to annual operating revenues. The Interstate Commerce Commission has no power whatsoever to regulate the issue of securities of water carriers, nor is its power to regulate the security issues of motor carriers very important. While it has the full power to control the financing of motor carriers of passengers and property, both common and contract, the scale of operations of highway carriers is so small in the case of most of them as to put them in the exempt class. Short-term notes up to $200,000 are exempt, while long-term issues, usually three- to five-year equipment trust certificates or notes secured by chattel mortgage whose par value does not exceed $1 million, are likewise exempt. Most loans are negotiated to buy or rehabilitate equipment or to provide working capital, and the funds are obtained directly from banks, insurance companies, or equipment manufacturers without public sale of securities.

Similarly, while it has asked for this authority, the Civil Aeronautics Board has no control over airline security issues, although the long-term debt in 1950 of domestic trunk airlines was in excess of $135 million and equaled about 35 per cent of their net worth. The reason assigned for this lack of control is that CAB would occupy an equivocal position if it had to approve security issues and also exercise its power to meet annual deficits by increasing the subsidy under total air-mail payments.

23. FIXING

THE FAIR RETURN

Economists have classified wealth into the two categories of capital and income. Wealth as income has been further classified in accordance with the factors of production (nature, capital goods, labor, and management), to whose cooperation in the productive process income may be attributed. At any rate, this is the analysis that has come down to us from the classical economists. A more recent analysis of productive functions classifies them as working, saving, management, and risk bearing. The difference in these classifications arises from a difference in point of view, which institutional economics has tried to surmount by taking a legal and hence transactional approach that uses instead certain legal categories. Accounting has followed this legal approach and adopted the fundamental legal classification which distinguishes only between owners and creditors.

Legal Categories and the Institutional Approach

All creditor incomes, whether called rent, interest, wages, or salaries, become *costs* because they are compulsory when based upon contract. All incomes in excess of costs accrue to owners and are called *surplus* or *profits* or *net income*. Accounting classifications attempt to follow the legal organization of the business unit. The business corporation recognizes and tries to harmonize the functions of working, managing, saving or waiting, and risk-bearing in its internal organization and in the distribution of legal rights, duties, powers, and immunities. Profits may thus cover forms of income which the classical analysis would consider interest or wages of management because capital and managerial services contributed have an alternative price, which might have been obtained elsewhere as a creditor's income. However, by contributing capital, owners become the risk bearers, and their status in the going concern must be judged from their position in this hierarchy of risk-taking. As common stockholders they have the full powers of management and select the directors who in turn select the officers. As the risks assumed by other classes of capital contributors decrease, their powers over management are likewise decreased, as was explained in the preceding chapter.

The management function is thus for the account of primary risk bearers, but it is delegated by them to elected or appointed officials. It should be recalled that risks are measureable, not only as the failure of the expected return to be realized but also as the loss of investment whether as owner or creditor. Even specialized employees, who have grown old in the service of a particular enterprise, incur the risk of loss through temporary or permanent unemployment, loss of retirement pensions, and other fringe benefits in the event of bankruptcy and general collapse. Only a conceptual line can thus be drawn which will separate working, saving, risk-taking, and managing. Nevertheless, in analyzing the problem of fixing the fair rate of return upon the rate base, it will conduce to clearness if we use the accounting and legal approach. Moreover, commissions and courts have always used it and have defined the fair return as an amount sufficiently in excess of reasonable operating expenses (including therein depreciation and taxes) to cover allowances for interest payments, dividend payments, and a margin for surplus.

The question of excessive salaries. This means that the question of fair salaries to management must be considered. While classed as operating expenses, excessive salaries paid to executive officers may be said to include an element of income which should be considered as part of the fair return. Commissions have been careful to examine salary schedules because a deficiency in the fair rate of return on the rate base may masquerade as excessive salary payments. Under the holding company form of organization, management services may be performed by the holding companies or by specially created service companies. The cost of rendering such services, including an element of profit, will be charged to the operating subsidiaries as a contractual fee. The fee becomes an operating expense of the subsidiary. These arrangements must likewise come under the scrutiny of rate-regulating authorities. It was one of the major functions of the Securities and Exchange Commission to assist state and federal commissions in regulating these intercorporate relationships.

Components of reasonable or fair return. After accounting for all elements of return that may be buried in operating expenses, it is necessary next to adopt some standard for measuring the reasonableness and fairness of the return to those contributing capital. These determinants of a fair rate of return have usually been said to include the following elements: (1) an interest payment to compensate the investor for parting with the control of his savings by investing them in the evidences of indebtedness of a given concern; (2) dividend payments to compensate the investor in the equity securities of a given concern; (3) payments to brokers and underwriters covering the costs of transferring monetary capital between buyers and sellers, which consist of commissions and discounts, call premiums, costs of engraving certificates, legal and accounting costs, and other expenses of flotation; such transfer costs enhance the average annual cost of both debt and equity capital and are usually prorated and amortized over the life of the security; (4) payments into the surplus account to meet certain contingencies. As suggested by the last named element, the payments demanded will vary with the degree of uncertainty and risk assumed by the contributor of capital.

Public utilities, like other enterprises, in bidding for capital in the open market must pay some competitive price which will constitute its "cost of capital." It is no less true of its share capital than of its borrowed capital. There is this difference, however, that while borrowed capital must be repaid, stockholder's capital may not be collectively withdrawn so long as the concern preserves its legal life. To be sure, the individual stockholder or bondholder may seek to sell his stock or bond in the open market, but his desire to sell must then find its counterpart in the offer of someone else to buy at a price mutually agreeable. It is by such operations that the degree of good credit or credit failure is best measured and established.

In this country public utilities have been constantly in need of more capital. Since utilities have an indefinite life, their financing had to be based upon a *continuing inflow of investments,* not only to balance the outflow but also to provide for their increasing capital requirements. Their good credit standing should thus be in the forefront of regulatory solicitude, and has been so regarded by the commissions. They have rightly adopted this general standard: *The rate of return should be high enough but not higher than may be necessary to attract capital and to hold it there.* In applying this standard, regulation pulls the teeth of monopoly by keeping returns within a zone of reasonableness. Neither consumers nor investors are coerced.

Judicial Standards

Since most of the controversy regarding adequacy of earnings has centered on the rate base, there has been a comparative paucity of judicial pronouncements on this question. By common consent the leading and most frequently cited case has been *Bluefield Water Works and Imp. Co. v. West Virginia Public Service Com.* (262 U.S. 679, 692) of 1923:

What annual rate will constitute just compensation depends upon many circumstances and must be determined by the exercise of a fair and enlightened judgment, having regard to all relevant facts. A public utility is entitled to such rates as will permit it to earn a return on the value of the property which it employs for the convenience of the public equal to that generally being made at the same time and in the same general part of the country on investments and in other business undertakings which are attended by corresponding risks and uncertainties . . . it has no constitutional right to profits such as are realized or anticipated in highly profitable enterprises or speculative ventures. The return should be reasonably sufficient to assure confidence in the financial soundness of the utility and should be adequate, under efficient and economical management, to maintain and support its credit and enable it to raise the money necessary for the proper discharge of its public duties. A rate of return may be reasonable at one time and become too high or too low by changes affecting opportunities for investment, the money market, and business conditions generally.

The foregoing opinion by Justice Butler was written at a time when the fair-value rate base emphasized reproduction costs which were generally in excess of actual investment costs. With the shift to original cost as the dominant standard in rate-base determinations by the Federal Power Commission, the judicial standard for a fair rate of return was laid down by the United States Supreme Court in 1944, in *Federal Power Commission v. Hope Natural Gas Co.* (320 U.S. 591, 603). Speaking through Justice Douglas, the Court explains:

From the investor or company point of view it is important that there be enough revenue not only for operating expenses, but also for the capital costs of the business. These include service on the debt and dividends on the stock. By that standard the return to the equity owner should be commensurate with returns on investments in other enterprises having corresponding risks. That return, moreover, should be sufficient to assure confidence in the financial integrity of the enterprise, so as to maintain its credit and to attract capital. The conditions under which more or less might be allowed are not important here. Nor is it important to this case to determine the various permissible ways in which any rate base on which the return is computed might be arrived at. For we are of the view that the end result in this case cannot be condemned under the act as unjust and unreasonable from the investor or company viewpoint.

The Capital Structure

The new element confronting the court in this case was that the rate of return had been computed in terms of the historical cost of capital by dividing the rate base into its components as derived from the capital structure. This was, in effect, the Massachusetts mode of procedure. We may illustrate with an example:

A utility with a rate base of $10 million has an offsetting capitalization of the following:

1. $5 million of 4 per cent bonds, requiring $200,000 in interest payments
2. $1 million of 5 per cent preferred stocks, requiring $50,000 in dividend payments
3. $3 million of common stocks, the amount of dividends depending upon declaration of dividends by the board of directors
4. $1 million of surplus or retained earnings, available as a cushion to protect the dividends of the common stockholders

The common stockholder's equity of $4 million thus represents a component in the capital structure which has no contractual basis for determining "cost of capital." If the regulating commission should impute a "cost of equity capital" of 8 per cent, based on the earnings-price ratio of the regulated company, and because evidence indicates that this was the return earned by the equity capital of public utility corporations with a corresponding degree of risk, the earnings requirements upon this segment of capital would be $320,-000. Applying the standard of the Hope case would thus mean that such rates would be just and reasonable whose *end result* would be revenues sufficient to cover operating expenses, plus the actual or imputed costs of capital. The cost-of-capital formula on this historical cost basis would require revenues of $570,000, or an over-all return on total capital of 5.7 per cent. This method is known as the *differentiated rate of return* because it builds up the total or over-all rate of return from the components of the capital structure.

The uncertainties surrounding the future earning power from rates so fixed are such that directors will not declare dividends on common stock at rates which will absorb most of the available earnings. Let us assume that prudence dictates a stable dividend policy of 7 per cent, or a requirement of $210,000. Dividend payments would thus absorb about 65.6 per cent of the year's earnings available to the common equity. This is known as the *pay-out ratio*. The balance of retained earnings is credited to surplus and serves to augment this component of the capital structure.

Estimating the Cost of Borrowed Capital

By trading on its common-stock equity, a utility is in a position to secure a portion of its capital requirements at lower prices per unit of capital through negotiating the sale of its bonds and other evidences of indebtedness and the sale of preferred stock. For practical purposes in estimating the fair return, a commission will include contractually fixed dividend rates on preferred stock as a part of the cost of borrowed capital. If it did not do so it would destroy the credit of the enterprise in so far as the payment of dividends on the common stock is concerned. In addition to the nominal rates of interest and dividends, in order to determine the actual experienced cost of borrowed capital, allowance must be made for the net costs of financing, such as discounts and premiums on sale and call premiums paid when bonds and preferred stocks are retired before maturity. There are also other flotation costs. Properly amortized, these adjustments enhance or diminish the actual cost of this capital to the company per unit of time. Projected into the future, these items provide the best evidence of what these fixed charges will be with respect to outstanding or contemplated issues. For outstanding issues the costs are a matter of statistical fact, while for contemplated issues they are a matter of judgment based upon current costs as evidenced by the market place.

Any attempt to reestimate what might be the *current* costs of securing all such borrowed capital *de novo* is entirely inadmissable under the going-concern theory of regulation. Such procedures would reintroduce the principles of competitive replacement cost, an alternative not actually available to a given utility. However, the yields at which utility bonds and preferred stocks of the same or other enterprises with similar risk characteristics are currently sold on the market will be, with proper adjustments for the costs of financing, the best evidence of the probable cost of fresh capital. Moody's and Standard and Poor's financial reports are the most convenient sources of the relevant information.

Estimating the Cost of Common Stock Capital

The most difficult problem in fixing the fair rate of return arises in connection with fixing the return to be allowed on that component of the capital structure which represents the equity of the common stockholders. In the absence of a fixed contractual rate of dividend, the rate actually paid is a matter of corporate policy, in light of the earnings available and of the effect on the capital market where this junior capital is to come from. Sometimes corporate policy has hardened into a customary dividend policy, presumably admitting of no variation, as in the case of A.T.&T. Company's 9 per cent dividend which has been declared since 1922, despite alternating periods of prosperity and depression, wartime inflation, and peacetime deflation. Like the laws of the Medes and Persians, it changeth not!

In our previous illustration of an imputed return of 8 per cent upon common stock equity, this imputation would have to be based upon the evidence of payments necessary to attract this classification of venture or risk capital. Costs per unit of capital would rise or decline with risks and uncertainties. Statistical evidence of such changes in cost can be derived from two sources: dividends-price ratios and earnings-price ratios. These are merely statistical techniques for measuring such costs. They reflect investor opinion of the attractiveness of the common stock as investments for their savings.

1.　The dividend-price ratio ($D/P = x \%$) measures investor opinion as to the comparative continuity of dividend policy and rate of dividend payments of the given opportunity for investment of capital as compared with others. Here the courts have held that the comparison should be with industries such as utilities where the risks are similar. The ratio of the particular company whose rate of return is the subject of investigation is compared with the ratio of other regulated companies representing other investment opportunities.

2.　Earnings-price ratio ($E/P = y \%$) measures investor opinion as to the future prospects with respect to earnings and dividend policies of a given investment opportunity as compared with others. This ratio depends in part upon the percentage of retained earnings (the pay-out ratio) and upon the percentage of common stock equity in the capital structure. Obviously, the risks will be higher and the ratio higher if the given utility is trading on a thinner equity.

In an article in the *Journal of Land Economics* for May, 1954, Professor Lionel Thatcher adduces this piece of evidence, exhibited as Table VIII.

Table VIII　Dividends-Price and Earnings-Price Ratios as Affected by the Percentage of Capital Structure Represented by Common Stock and Surplus

Percentage Common Stock and Surplus	No. of Companies	Average Common Stock and Surplus	Average D/P ratio	Average E/P ratio
Up to 30	51	26.7	6.57	9.52
30 to 40	40	34.5	6.33	9.28
Over 40	24	48.3	5.99	8.10

The ratio also measures investor opinion as to future dividend policies as shown by pay-out ratios in the past. Here again (Table IX) we can bring some evidence as presented by Professor Eli Clemens in an article in the same *Journal of Land Economics*, Vol. XXX, p. 97. The figures, arranged in tabular form and manipulated statistically, seem to indicate that market prices of utility common stocks are influenced more by dividend policies than by earnings. However subtle this conclusion, there seems to be no doubt that investor opinion regards certain common stocks of higher quality as evidenced by lower dividends-price and earnings-price ratios. We reproduce the table, but the entire article should be consulted.

Table IX   Dividends-Price and Earnings-Price Ratios as Influenced
by Pay-outs

MEDIUM QUALITY ELECTRIC OPERATING UTILITY COMMON STOCKS
(RATED "B" BY FITCH'S)

Group	No. of Companies	Average D/P Ratio	Average E/P Ratio	Average Pay-Out Ratio	Average Common Stock Equity
1	9	6.20%	7.78%	79.7%	33.9%
2	10	5.63	7.80	72.2	31.7
3	10	5.54	8.50	65.2	31.9
4	9	5.24	9.65	54.3	33.5

HIGH QUALITY ELECTRIC OPERATING UTILITY COMMON STOCKS
(RATED "BB" OR BETTER BY FITCH'S)

Group	No. of Companies	Average D/P Ratio	Average E/P Ratio	Average Pay-Out Ratio	Average Common Stock Equity
1	5	5.72	6.20	92.3	42.9
2	6	5.62	7.05	79.7	40.5
3	6	5.52	7.63	72.3	37.2
4	6	4.96	8.37	59.3	38.8

The determination of the proper pay-out ratio has been generally conceded to be a function of management, at least in the first instance. Commissions have not hesitated to substitute their judgment for that of the management in assuming a pay-out ratio in fixing the level of allowable earnings. The reason for this is that under revised accounting procedures inaugurated by commissions, charges have been required to be made to surplus, especially in connection with the writing down of book values resulting from the institution of original cost accounting by federal and some state commissions. These and similar direct charges to surplus have been called an *erosion* of surplus, but they have been found necessary to make corrections and adjustments for mistaken managerial policies in the past. Sometimes these were necessary in order to lead a given utility out of some financial wilderness in which it was wandering.

Another reason for the retention of earnings has been to facilitate a stable dividend policy. The alternation of the prosperity and depression phases of the business cycle has made this necessary, as have also good and bad water years and other contingencies. Public utilities have been less subject to these vicissitudes and uncertainties than have other business concerns (the so-called feast and famine industries), but they have not been free from them.

A final reason for considering pay-out ratios in connection with dividend policies and the allowable level of earnings is that the surplus can and has been used to meet new capital requirements by internal financing. Regulatory commissions must pass judgment upon these practices in their final determination of an over-all earning capacity deemed to be reasonable.

The Fair Rate of Return

The regulatory necessity of retaining some flexibility in the determination of the "fair rate of return," in light particularly of the evidence adduced in support of the historical and present cost of moneyed capital, has been well stated by the Public Utilities Commission of California in its decision in the Pacific Telephone & Telegraph Company case of July 6, 1954.

Earnings-price ratios and dividend-price ratios merely reflect the prospective investors' appraisal of the market value of stock and as such are influenced by prevailing market and economic conditions and the individual requirements of the purchaser. While useful for comparative purposes and of value in presenting background information, they are not conclusive in themselves in the determination of the allowable fair return on investment in operative properties. It is one thing to say that these ratios indicate the terms under which a new investor might devote his money to the business; it is another thing to say that these terms represent or limit the return the applicant is entitled to receive on the Capital committed to the service. It seems to us that reliance on ratios of this nature results in a restricted view of the subject of rate-of-return. Obviously, the price at which a security is bought on the market reflects anticipated earnings rather than past results of operations and it by no means follows that the rates at which present market sales prices are related to the past earnings represents the returns the purchasers at those prices are willing to accept in the future.

With the wide range in the claims now before us and with the opposing opinions of the witnesses to be considered, it is apparent that our final determination of [the] rate of return must represent the exercise of judgment on our part, having in mind the lawful interests of the ratepayer and the utility.

Thereupon the Commission fixed the reasonable return at 6.25 per cent, which would place the company in a position to meet its capital requirements. The new return represented an increase from the 5.6 per cent found reasonable in 1948.

The Inflation Problem

The most controverted question in connection with the rate of return concerns the effect which the decline in the purchasing power of our monetary unit should have upon the fair rate of return at the present time. Opinion is divided upon this question, and no conclusive answer has been forthcoming from the commissions.

Present policies of the commissions. We have seen that since the decision of the United States Supreme Court in the Hope case of 1944, both state and federal commissions have been free to devise their own procedures of rate-making. Speaking generally, federal commissions and most state commissions have since followed the "net investment" (original cost less depreciation) rule of determining the rate base to which is applied a rate of return designed to be adequate to attract the necessary capital. Owing to the renewed price inflation during and subsequent to World War II, this procedure is questioned by those who contend that preinflation stockholders are unfairly treated. Under the Fifth and Fourteenth Amendments, are they entitled only to the protection of the "dollar amounts" of their investment, or does the constitutional protection extend also to the "real values" of these investments? Since the purchasing power of today's dollars is roughly only one-half of their prewar purchasing power, the use of a dollar-investment rate base should be converted into an equivalent *present dollar value* rate base by applying some purchasing power index. This could then be translated into a definite percentage or inflation component to be *added* to the rate of return otherwise deemed fair and reasonable. Such an adjustment of the rate of return (usually computed to be from 0.5 to 1.5 per cent) would allow for the loss in purchasing power of the common stockholders if expressed only in nominal dollars. No commission has as yet granted such an adjustment for price inflation. However, owing to recent increases in the cost of pecuniary capital, in 1954 some commissions increased their previous rate-of-return allowances in which some purchasing power adjustment could be concealed. The Oregon Commission increased the rate of return from 5.6 to 6 per cent, the Rhode Island Commission from 5.3 to 6.25 per cent, and the California Commission, as we have indicated, from 5.6 to 6.25 per cent.

A different approach to the problem of price inflation is taken by those commissions which have never abandoned the "fair return on fair value" formula of rate-making, of which the jurisdictions of Pennsylvania and Ohio are examples. In these states the weight accorded replacement costs in terms of current prices in fixing the fair value above original costs (the nominal dollar amounts) automatically recognizes to that extent the factor of price inflation. A decision of the Supreme Court of Illinois in 1954, in *Illinois Bell Telephone Co. v. Illinois Commerce Commission* (414 Ill. 275), is particularly significant because it held that the use of a "net investment" rate base by the Commission is confiscatory and required instead the use of the "fair value" formula.

This entire problem of the effect and treatment of inflation in regulated industry is worthy of intensive and continuing study in order to determine what institutional rearrangements, if any, may be required in our present procedures. Here we shall explore only the major contending arguments.

Arguments against adjustment for inflation.[1] Those opposing an adjustment for price inflation in either the rate base or the rate of return take the position that such an adjustment is not necessary to attract capital. Professor Lionel Thatcher has presented for the postwar period the facts concerning the new capital raised by corporate security issues in the United States.

A perusal of Table X shows that public utilities have certainly had no difficulties in attracting the requisite capital, both borrowed and equity capital, at reasonable rates. With respect to common and preferred stocks it should be noted, however, that this type of capital is definitely committed to a given enterprise and that difficulties of financing by means of such issues would be slower in developing.

An adjustment for inflation in favor of the common stock alone leaves out of account an adjustment in favor of the holders of fixed income types of securities, i.e., preferred stocks and bonds. Professor J. C. Bonbright's comments [1] are particularly apposite in this connection.

On the one hand, price inflation, in its very nature, is grievously unfair and disorderly in its impacts on different classes of people. But on the other hand, any attempt to save one particular class against its inequities runs the risk of imposing

---

[1] Significant articles relating to this subject have appeared in many journals. We shall mention here only a series appearing in *Journal of Land Economics,* a publication devoted to the institutional aspects of economic problems. Because price inflation has a definite bearing on the working of our institutions, this series is of special importance and should be consulted for details:

James C. Bonbright, "Public Utility Rate Control in a Period of Price Inflation," Vol. 27, p. 16; February, 1951.

Walter A. Morton, "Rate of Return and the Value of Money in Public Utilities," Vol. 28, p. 91; May, 1952.

E. W. Clemens, "Some Aspects of the Rate-of-Return Problem," Vol. 30, p. 32, February, 1954.

Lionel W. Thatcher, "Cost of Capital Techniques Employed in Determining the Rate of Return for Public Utilities," Vol. 30, p. 85, May, 1954.

Table X New Corporate Issues in the United States: New Capital

(in thousands)

Item	1946	1947	1948	1949	1950	1951	1952 *
STOCKS							
Total †	$1,480,347	$1,233,089	$ 912,286	$ 973,643	$1,232,397	$1,651,654	$1,578,901
Public utilities	142,884	283,637	378,979	706,794	725,098	774,504	766,036
Per cent public utilities to total	9.65	23.00	41.54	72.59	58.84	46.89	48.52
BONDS AND OTHER DEBT							
Total †	$2,084,093	$3,597,956	$5,351,738	$4,186,986	$3,338,142	$4,478,657	$5,088,420
Public Utilities	674,919	1,751,564	2,506,526	1,849,531	1,608,566	2,058,197	2,171,661
Per cent public utilities to total	32.38	48.68	46.84	44.17	48.19	45.95	42.67
TOTAL STOCKS, BONDS AND OTHER DEBT							
Total †	$3,564,441	$4,831,046	$6,264,025	$5,160,629	$4,570,539	$6,130,311	$6,667,322
Public Utilities	817,804	2,035,202	2,885,505	2,556,326	2,333,665	2,832,701	2,937,698
Per cent public utilities to total	22.94	42.13	46.06	49.54	51.06	46.20	44.06

* For eleven months, ending November 30, 1952.

† Includes railroads; public utilities; iron, steel, coal, copper, etc.; equipment manufacturers; motors and accessories; other industrial and manufacturing; oil, land, buildings, etc.; rubber; shipping; investment trusts, trading, holding, etc., and miscellaneous.

Source: *The Commercial and Financial Chronicle*, Volume 173, No. 4993, dated March 12, 1951.

Source: *The Commercial and Financial Chronicle*, Volume 176, No. 5165, dated November 3, 1952.

even more cruel burdens on unprotected classes. It also runs the risk of adding fuel to the inflationary fire.

Both of these criticisms can fairly be made against the escalator clauses in the recent union-wage contracts. They can be made with even greater force against escalator provisions in public utility rate control. Of necessity these provisions can redound to the benefit of only one class of investors—the holders of common stock. Of necessity, moreover, the burden of protecting these stockholders would fall on consumers in general, including those consumers who have been unable to provide themselves with escalators. The problem, then, is that of choosing whichever form of unfairness is the least unfair.

At least two commissions have taken the stand that it is not within their legislative mandate to make adjustments for inflation. In 1953, in the Mountain States Telephone & Telegraph Company case, the Utah Public Service Commission, in refusing to make the adjustment, said: "Nor do we believe it was the intention of the legislature in writing the public utilities act to empower or require this Commission to take action that would make utility stockholders free from the impact of the economic forces at work in this country." Similarly, the New York Commission in 1954, in the New York Telephone Company case, definitely held that there is nothing in the regulatory statute to guarantee stockholders against the effects of economic forces in the form of price inflation.

A final major consideration running against an adjustment for inflation, especially of the type which would mean a return to the fair-value rule of rate-base determination, is that it would upset the orderly, expeditious, and definite procedures of rate regulation which have flowed from the adoption of the net-investment rate base. This argument weighs most heavily with the federal commissions and state commissions like Wisconsin, New York, and California, whose leadership in promoting stable utility relationships has long been recognized. We will use the California Commission to exemplify the argument. In the Pacific Telephone & Telegraph Company case just mentioned, the Commission had before it the testimony of a consulting engineer "with long regulatory experience" to testify "to the stability and advantages of the historical cost method of determining the rate base which has been consistently followed by the Commission in [the] regulation of utilities. Such method has been consistently followed during the periods of deflation as well as inflation."

Though recognizing that a serious inflationary trend has set in since 1941, the Commission pointed out that of the $1,235 million of plant at the close of 1952, only $220 million had been installed prior to 1941; that is to say, 18 per cent represented preinflationary dollars. It then went on to say:

The law contemplates that people who buy securities are charged with the knowledge that certain risks will be attached to their ownership and that one of the risks is the possibility of the decline in purchasing power of the dollar . . .

The record shows that the applicant has been able to finance itself under reasonable terms during the inflationary period, that the shareholders have been compensated to some extent through the rights which have been offered them with regularity and that the company itself has been authorized to charge rates which have been based on operating costs at prevailing prices rather than on the preinflationary price levels. It has been authorized to recover in depreciation charges the inflated dollars it has invested in its business. It, therefore, appears that the Commission has given adequate consideration to inflation in fixing rates for this company.

The Commission then concluded its discussion of the inflation problem by stating:

[We] find no reason to depart from our long established and stable method of computing [the] rate base on the basis of the actual dollars in plant, unadjusted up or down for changes in the purchasing power of the dollar, and allowing expenses at the full current rate adjusted for foreseeable near-future conditions. Applicants' inflation testimony is designed to support its request for extensive increases in rates, which would result in considerably higher earnings and increased common stock dividends compared with the Commission's traditional allowances. Such action would protect only one class of security holder, the common stockholder, against the risk of loss of purchasing power and not benefit the bondholder or preferred stockholder. It would penalize the ratepayer without a concomitant consideration. We will proceed to analyze applicant's operations in the traditional manner.

The case for an inflation adjustment. The most moderate statement of the case for making an adjustment for inflation is in the article (*op. cit.*) by Prof. Walter A. Morton, entitled *Rate of Return and the Value of Money in Public Utilities.* This proposal restricts the inflation adjustment to the component of the capital structure represented by the common stock equity. After determining the historical cost of borrowed capital, including preferred stock capital in the usual manner, and after determining the *current* cost of common equity capital by the use of cost estimates derived from dividend-price, earnings-price, and pay-out ratios, the cost of common equity capital would be further adjusted upward or downward by an allowance for the changing value of money. Under present conditions the adjustment would be upward through the use of a general price level index, with 1946 as the base year, and would be estimated to increase the over-all rate of return by 0.7 per cent. This procedure would assure common stockholders, new as well as old, if continuously applied, an income of relatively constant purchasing power.

Professor Morton contends that the prudent net-investment procedure introduced by the Hope case means that the previous emphasis upon fair value has been displaced by a concept of economic necessity. To use his own words:

Instead of giving a utility a reasonable return because it is just, we now ask what rate is necessary to maintain it as a going concern and to attract new capital. Justice is a moral concept. Necessity is a power concept. The demands of fairness are not always those of power. We have already shown that a utility will continue to function as a going concern and attract new capital even if no compensation is made for inflation to capital already irrevocably committed. An inflation adjustment is not necessary to maintain the financial soundness and integrity of the concern. As long as necessity is the sole guide to action, the property of a utility can be taken without compensation by means of inflation, provided the will to do so is accompanied by legal and political power. Under these circumstances, holders of utility property can hardly be expected to submit to expropriation without trying to use political power to protect themselves. Within the constitutional framework, political power is, after all, the ultimate arbiter of all rights to liberty and property.

The erroneous notion that the market somehow automatically compensates for inflation rests on the belief that economic power is capable of protecting itself. In unregulated industry this is true. Any interest having economic power to compel a fair return can exert that power; it does not need resort to the courts. Appeal to the courts under the 14th Amendment (and 5th) is made when the individual is incapable of defending himself against arbitrary action. A utility cannot protect itself against inflation by its power to control the supply of services because that power is limited and circumscribed by regulation. Potential investors can exert some economic power by withholding capital but past investors are wholly dependent upon constitutional interpretation.

The foregoing quotation raises the major issue involved in the problem of inflation as it affects regulated industry in contradistinction to unregulated industry. Does the existing institutional arrangement by means of which natural monopoly is now regulated require some institutional rearrangement which will protect the owners of common stock equities from the effects of changes in the value of money? Put in more direct fashion, is the correct position of the California Commission when it said that, "the law contemplates that people who buy securities are charged with the knowledge that certain risks will be attached to their ownership and that one of the risks is the possibility of the decline in purchasing power of the dollar."

Inferentially, Professor Morton recognizes that from an equitable point of view, the issue applies also to the fixed-income type of security. Only when continuous inflation is widely expected will interest rates and yields on fixed-income securities be raised automatically. In American investment markets many barriers stand in the way of such a discount, the chief of which are the usury laws and those institutional investors (life insurance companies, for instance) and banks who have no direct interest in protecting the purchasing power of their assets because their liabilities are in terms of nominal dollars.

The suggestion was made long ago by Professor Irving Fisher during World War I that the fixed-income type of security be protected against inflation by a purchasing-power adjustment clause. Professor Morton makes this adjustment for public utility industries in the article from which we are quoting, although he doubts that institutional investors with fixed monetary obligations would be interested in such a security. He also doubts whether such a bond would be feasible for the federal government because it has no means of automatically raising revenues from taxation. Professor Sumner Slichter proposed that the federal treasury issue savings bonds payable in terms of a specified purchasing power, but as Professor Bonbright points out, the proposal received a cold reception from the financial press and outright condemnation from Russell Leffingwell of J. P. Morgan and Company because it might accelerate the inflationary spiral.

Further study needed. The ramifying effects of wartime and postwar inflation upon the well-being of different segments of our population are giving pause to regulating authorities who might otherwise be willing to accord a measure of compensation to the common stockholders. They are also reluctant to accord relief because granting it in wholesale fashion to all stockholders of record would not discriminate between the bona fide preinflation stockholder and those "Jonnies came lately" who have purchased their shares with inflated dollars, for whom an inflation adjustment would represent a "windfall profit."

Under these circumstances, commissions do not feel that they have been authorized to embark upon a new legislative policy to protect against inflation under the guise that such action is "reasonable." The attitude of commissioners is that they would prefer a direct mandate from the legislature before taking such a step.

Making an adjustment for the effect of inflation upon utility common stockholders is selective and in no sense remedial. The basic factor in inflation was the enormously expanded money supply in circulation which, in turn, was a direct outcome of the lodging of billions of dollars of federal debt in our commercial banking system during and after the war.

Another psychological impediment to an adjustment for inflation is the fact that all proposals so far made would leave out of account the creditor classes whose capital contributions have been a major factor in building the structure of public utility capitalism. Made up principally of the claims of those who had invested their savings in life insurance, annuities, trust funds, and retirement plans in order to provide themselves with some security for the vicissitudes of life, they are, as far as the impact of inflation is concerned, the really "forgotten men" of the capitalistic system. Even Professor Morton, who correctly stresses the equitable as distinct from the legal basis of in-

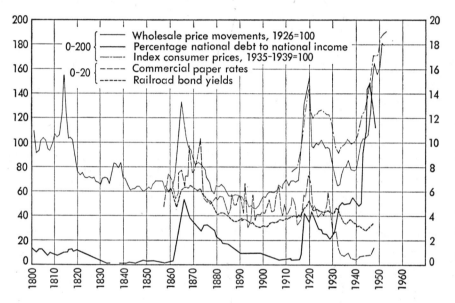

Chart XIV   Indices of Changing Economic Conditions.

flation adjustments as part of a rate of return allowance, relegates most of what he has to say on this subject to a footnote. Yet this author believes that, like mercy, the quality of equity should not be so strained.

In their valuable study of our national debt, a Committee on Public Debt Policy points out that our present debt is of "unprecedented size, incurred in fighting an unprecedented war." Although the national debt at the close of the Civil War had grown until it amounted to 50.2 per cent of the national income, it was steadily reduced after that. Before World War I, with our faster growing national income, the debt was only 3 per cent of the national income. Since then (World War I), deficit financing of the Great Depression and expenditures of World War II lifted the debt enormously, so that by 1946 it was 160 per cent of the national income. (See Chart XIV.)

Because the Committee found that the ultimate remedy for the inflation problem is in the adoption of wise policies of debt management, their summary [2] of the essentials of such policies is herewith reproduced:

1. We must exercise careful watch over the budget. A budget deficit creates debt, and a budget surplus makes debt reduction possible. Therefore, the Number One task of debt management is to control the huge overall total of government spending. This is partly a problem of improving the quality of government, by more effective administration and by attracting and holding able people in public service. It is partly a question of our philosophy of government—of what to expect from the central government and what should be left to local government and to individual initiative and self-reliance.

2. We must plan a debt reduction policy which is related to the state of business activity of the country. A heavy retirement of debt in time of prosperity would tend to check overexpansion and inflationary tendencies, while less retirement in times of adversity would relieve the burden of taxation and aid recovery. A reasonable tentative program is to agree now on an annual amount that seems feasible in relation to national income, and if necessary adjust it later.

3. We must distribute the debt as widely as possible among non-bank investors, and so reduce the inflationary money supply that accompanies a national debt heavily concentrated in the hands of the banking system.

4. We must restore flexibility to interest rates so as to give monetary authorities more freedom in determining credit policies. Rates must have more scope for performing their economic function of adjusting the supply of savings to the demand for investment funds. This will help to discourage extremes of boom and bust.

5. We must take every possible step to preserve and to increase the dynamic energy of our economic life, for it will make the burden of debt easier to bear and will help to maintain our American tradition of freedom. Because high taxes are one of the greatest handicaps to productivity in this country, they should be reduced as rapidly as sound fiscal policy permits. Since such reductions should be tuned to the swings of business, prices, and the budget, this emphasizes the need for cutting expenditures enough so that both debt and tax reduction are possible.

· In 1927, almost three decades ago, with the example of hyperinflation in Europe before him, this writer in his *Outlines of Public Utility Economics* recognized the demoralizing effect of monetary inflation. Although the position taken was opposed to the use of replacement costs, he recognized the need of keeping the rate of return instead of the rate base flexible. The relevant paragraphs are quoted: [3]

The most-telling argument which has been brought forward by those who champion cost of reproduction, either as the sole standard of value or as an important element in fair value, takes this form. Unless cost of reproduction is taken

[2] Committee on Public Debt Policy, *Our National Debt* (New York: Harcourt Brace & Co., Copyright 1949), p. 164.

[3] Glaeser, M. G., *Outlines of Public Utility Economics* (New York: The Macmillan Company, Copyright 1927), pp. 479, 480.

into account in rate-base determinations, the owners of public utility properties will be deprived of a fair return. Periods of high prices, particularly those induced by war and reconstruction disturbances with their attendant monetary inflations, usually are accompanied by a fall in the purchasing power of that return. A constant monetary return under these conditions represents, in fact, a declining return which is the complement of the decline in its purchasing power. This argument has unquestioned economic merit. It addresses itself, however, to the question of what is an adequate return under such circumstances. Everyone, even the economically illiterate, have learned that the economic value of money resides in its purchasing power, its power in exchange for commodities and services. The rate of return should therefore be made flexible to correspond with some index of purchasing power. If the choice is between a relatively fixed rate of return which is applied to a rate-base varying with the cost of reproduction, and a rate of return varying with some index of purchasing power which is applied to a fixed rate base, it is easier to choose the latter alternative. To commit regulation to the cost of reproduction standard is sure to have consequences that are far-reaching in unsettling the machinery of regulation and in disturbing the accounting and credit structures of going concerns.

Administrative commissions should, therefore, take steps to make the rate-of-return flexible, and, particularly, to make the amount available as a return upon the risk capital of public utilities bear some constant relation to the varying purchasing power of the most fundamental of all standards of pecuniary value the dollar.

24. THE ECONOMICS
OF REGULATED
MONOPOLY PRICE

Our introductory chapter made a distinction between economic functions carried on by governments, which are supported by taxes, fees, and special assessments, and economic functions conducted as business enterprises which must sell their services at a price. Utilities belong in this second class. Except under crowded conditions of urban and suburban living where the residents are required to take water and sewage services, utility consumers are not required to take service. There is consumer's sovereignty in that he has freedom of choice as to what, when, and how much to buy. Utility services command a price, however, because they are both useful and scarce. Where prices control production and exchange, and these prices, as in the case of public utilities, are fixed by government, an analysis of the economic conditions which are the determinants of the demand for and the supply of such services is most important.

Economic Characteristics of Public Utility Industries

Tendency toward monopoly. Public utilities are best organized as monopolies. This seems to be an inductive generalization from their technological and economic history. They grow with expanding markets, try to bring competition among themselves under control, and usually, though not necessarily always, consolidate until they have monopolized their respective markets.

A seller's monopoly (there can also be a buyer's monopoly, as in the case of the sale of uranium ore to the Atomic Energy Commission) has been defined as the organization of production so that a single agency has control over supply. An approach to monopoly is attained when several concerns which have hitherto supplied service as competitors combine in such a way that they follow common price tactics. This was true of the Chicago grain elevators in the Munn case. Such monopolies by agreement, since the Sherman Act, are unlawful because they are in restraint of trade. Public service industries soon discovered also that such contracts were particularly hard to maintain. Monopoly by agreement was thus changed into the monopoly of full ownership. When technical considerations made it appear advisable that supply be integrated, the policy of the law was changed so as to favor monopolization. In the absence of regulation we would be confronted with a situation where a seller's monopoly would be bargaining with a multiplicity of buyers. Public utility markets would be sellers' markets. While regulation redresses the balance of power between sellers and buyers, public utility economics remains monopoly economics and must be distinguished from competition and oligopoly (competition among the few). But even monopolies must recognize limitations upon their power over the supply price because of the degree of substitution obtaining in a given market, as was explained in Chapter 14.

Peculiarity of service characteristics.   Few, if any, business enterprises are as important to our economic well-being as are the public utilities. They minister to wants which are regarded as basic. The supply of water, light, heat, refrigeration, power, transport, and communication is essential to everyone for civilized and comfortable living. They are also essential from a social point of view because they are the bases for the local and regional division of labor. Without, for instance, a transport and communications system, national and international in scope, our present complex mechanism of production and exchange would disintegrate into its primitive, self-sufficient components.

Of equal importance is the requirement that service must be adequate as well as essential. Under the common law, it should be recalled, those engaging in public callings are required to furnish reasonably adequate service and facilities. Statutory regulation has taken over this legal standard, but it has also gone beyond it by providing regulations relating to specific matters of service. In competitive industry the theory is that these questions of adequacy will be solved automatically. Increased demands bring higher prices which stimulate production. In monopolistic public service industries the initiative of producers has been supplemented by administrative determinations of what constitutes reasonable service. The law in a number of states makes it the duty of the Commission to establish *standards of service*. It should also be noted that the law makes reasonable service and reasonable rates interdependent. Even if a poorer grade of service could be supplied at a lower rate, it is the Commission's task to determine what would be the reasonable grade of service under the circumstances and then fix rates accordingly. Rates are thus a resultant, at least in part, of a *regulated demand*. In fact, in times of prosperity or war emergency, when the productive facilities of a nation are being utilized to their utmost capacity, the service-rendering capacity of public utilities may be the limiting factor in business expansion.

Commissions were empowered to investigate conditions upon their own motion or upon complaint of customers, to determine what was reasonably adequate service, and to make and enforce any necessary rule, order, or regulation. By this process, service was standardized and a code of perform-ance provided with which the performance in individual cases could be com-pared. The widest adoption of such standards has been by the local utilities, particularly those supplying water, gas, electric, and telephone service. The work was carried on by a few pioneers among the commissions, beginning about 1908. They were usually promulgated after general state-wide or nation-wide hearings, attended by representatives of the industry, and after considerable preliminary study by technical experts of performances in the states and cities of this country and even of foreign countries. Such standards must be revised from time to time to take into account the changes in the art. This task of standardization, supplemented by an inspection service, has brought about a high degree of homogeneity in service characteristics, and has promoted safety and continuity throughout the country. These results do not "just happen."

Demand characteristics.   Because public utilities are in the center in-stead of at the periphery of our national economy, demand as distinguished from supply does not represent the problem that less centrally placed in-dustries meet in disposing of their product. They are important from the point of view of satisfying the demands of ultimate consumers as well as of consumers who need these services in production. The increasing im-portance of the exchange features of our capitalistic economy has also mag-nified the importance to organized society of public utilities as collectively organized units which operate as a monopoly in the production and sale of their services. Reference should be made here also to our discussion and chart of the typical market situation of a public utility in Chapter XIV.

As a consequence of the technical and economic evolution of these in-dustries, the demand for their services is increasingly a derived demand. All are still important in the domestic economy of consumers, where they con-stitute a backlog of continuing demand even in times of depression and un-employment. Their importance in our exchange economy has been growing. Transportation, communication, water, light, heat, and power are increasingly demanded where they become a part of the cost of production of goods and services. The demand thus depends upon wants which express themselves both directly and indirectly.

It is also true, of course, that the demand for service is not *effective* unless combined with the necessary purchasing power. On this account, even though public utilities tend to become monopolies and to have a monopolist's control over supply, their prices must be adjusted so as to stay within the limits of customers' effective demands. This raises problems of pricing when an entire industry, a region, or the national economy suffers a relapse. Nevertheless, public utility services are subject to the general law of price which expresses the interaction of the relative cost of producing these services and of the relative intensity of the demand of consumers for them.

The Theory of Monopoly Price

Because public utilities are business enterprises whose purpose it is, certainly when privately owned, to earn a profit, it is necessary to consider how they could fix prices in the absence of governmental control. It is familiar doctrine that a monopoly can, if it will, so adjust supply as to enable it to sell upon terms that will yield maximum net revenue. Public utilities have not always followed this practice. They may have been restrained by the desire to aid in the development of the community. Custom, as in the case of the long maintained nickel fare of the street railways, may have kept prices constant despite changing costs. They may have been restrained by the triple threat of inviting competition, stringent regulation, or public ownership. But the potentiality of charging *all* that the traffic would bear was certainly inherent in a monopolized market where the maximum rates fixed in charters or franchises afforded plenty of room for the deployment of such managerial talents.

The principle of diminishing utility and the calculus of demand. Since a monopolist has only indirect control over the demand, he will so adjust the quantity supplied or the price to the point which he thinks will assure him the maximum excess of earnings over the total cost of production. But it is as true under monopoly as under competition that the higher the price, the lower will be the quantity of service demanded at that price. The utility per unit tends to decrease as the supply in the hands of a single customer increases. *This principle of diminishing utility, or calculus of consumer preferences* (however it may be phrased), has certain far-reaching consequences upon the demand. How much less the quantity demanded will be with the increase in price will depend upon the *elasticity* of the demand. Elasticity is affected by the degree of essentiality which the service has attained in the eyes of the consumer. It will depend upon the factor of custom or habit in the fixing of living standards. Much also depends upon the availability of substitutes and how good they are. It is also affected by the variety of uses to which, with expanding technique, the service may be put. Illustrations were given in earlier chapters.

Each consumer has a demand price which represents the maximum that he will pay for any given quantity. The *maximum* price which he is willing to pay for the *minimum* quantity represents the maximum intensity of his want for the service supplied. Economists have called this the *marginal demand price*. If the quantity a consumer demands increases more than proportionately as rates decrease, demand is said to be elastic, while a less than proportionate increase in the quantity demanded with a decline in rates indicates inelasticity.

Over a period of time the elasticity of a given consumer's demand may change substantially. A consumer may be very "rate conscious" when he decides, for example, whether or not to install an electric hot-water heater. However, once the installation has been made, a previously elastic demand for electricity may become decidedly inelastic.

The classification of customers. On account of the large number of consumers and the great variety of uses to which public utility services are put, the determination of consumer marginal demand price is a difficult experimental process. For the sake of administrative convenience, utilities deal with their many customers by classes instead of individually. In disposing of supply they will fix a rate for each of these classes which approximates the maximum demand price of the consumers taken as a group. But each utility will be careful to have in the same class only those customers whose marginal demand price is at least equal to the class price. In this way the rate schedules will be so adjusted as to enable the utility to discriminate among its customers upon the basis of their marginal demand prices. As a monopolist, it need fear no competitive source of supply to which customers may turn who dislike these discriminatory price tactics.

It is necessary to recall here what was said in Chapter 14 about the *limits* of monopoly power. Some consumers may be able to use more or less adequate substitute services, or they may undertake to supply themselves. Except in the case of gas and electricity, the legal grant of monopoly in the hands of the same company does not usually extend to available substitutes. The effect of the divestment proceedings before the SEC of holding companies has been to increase the number of single-service utilities and to decrease the number of joint utilities. Another important limitation comes from those customers who are in a position to supply themselves. Alternative costs of service must thus be recognized even by monopolistic producers.

Cost of production and the adjustment of monopoly price. Thus far, nothing has been said regarding the monopolists' own cost of production. Again excepting some transportation services, utilities must make large investments in fixed capital of a highly specialized character. Upon this fixed investment the business must yield a return. In addition, there will be operating expenses. Because the producer has alternative choices as to quantity of service to be produced, he must determine what these alternative conditions of price, revenue, and costs may be.

For this purpose total costs are divided into fixed, or constant, and variable costs. Fixed costs are interest and dividends, taxes, insurance, and depreciation associated with the plant. Close analysis will reveal that some kinds of operating outlay, such as salaries and expenses of administration, also remain relatively constant. These costs must be met if the plant is to be kept ready to serve at all times. They accrue even if operations are temporarily discontinued. Since these expenses are common to all units of output and remain constant whether the output be large or small, they have also been called *overhead costs.*

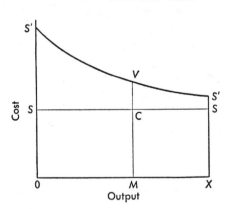

Chart XV   Constant and Variable Unit Costs.

The presence of large overhead costs make such a business subject to what economists have called the *law of decreasing cost;* that is to say, as output increases the average total costs per unit become less. (See Chart XV.)

But decreasing costs are of significance to the profit seeker only to the extent that a sustained demand makes fuller utilization of the plant with its concomitant reduction in unit costs more profitable, i.e., when the price, minus average cost per unit, times the volume of sales approaches a maximum profit. This maximum profitability is achieved at an output where marginal cost equals marginal revenue.

The law of decreasing costs affects industries differently, depending upon (1) whether the industry must cut its rates in order to secure increased business; (2) whether in cutting rates it must do so upon *all* units of output; or (3) whether it need cut its rates only upon the additional units of output, leaving the rate upon the original units of supply at the old level. This practice of cutting rates only on the increment in output has been referred to as "fixing rates upon the additional business basis."

A qualification must be introduced at this point. The law of decreasing cost does not operate indefinitely. If an increased volume of business can be secured only at the expense of an enlargement of the plant, the additional amount of business is secured at an increasing cost per unit. Large additional overhead costs, constant in amount, arise at this point because the capacity usually cannot be increased by small increments. The large number of units of new potential supply raises the problem of securing increased utilization of the enlarged fixed plant. Only when a regular and dependable increase in sales is anticipated will managers ordinarily expand the plant and incur increased overhead costs. Once the capacity of the plant has been increased, only a financial reorganization of the business can decrease them. It is therefore important to recognize that the law of decreasing costs in the short run operates only within the limits of the capacity of the fixed plant. In the long run, as the firm expands capacity, there may be decreasing, increasing, or constant costs of production depending respectively upon the

realization of net economies, of net diseconomies, or of neither of these categories with the new proportions of the resources of production. It is quite possible that new economies in production will be achieved with expansion of capacity up to a point. Beyond this point, however, net diseconomies would be incurred with further plant expansion. This is demonstrated in Chart XVI, which indicates that average unit costs reach new lower minimums as capacity is expanded a first and then

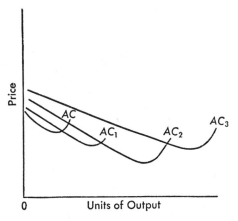

Chart XVI Changes in Average Cost with Successive Changes in Capacity.

a second time. However, a third expansion of plant is accompanied by an increase in minimum average costs. It is perhaps also worth while to note that, with successive changes in capacity occurring at different times, changes in the price level may be of considerable importance in determining whether expansion will result in decreasing, increasing, or maintaining constant costs.

Out of pocket costs.   A contrasting type of cost, usually called *variable cost,* includes all other operating expenses that are said to vary directly with changes in the volume of business. (See Chart XV.) These costs, also called *direct* or *out-of-pocket* costs, tend to increase proportionately with output. Fuel costs of an electric utility are a good example of operating outlays which vary with output. This classification is more or less of an approximation. Fuels consumed by banked boilers, for instance, are chargeable to variations in the *rate* of output. Refinements of accounting and statistical analysis enable one to go much further than was once thought possible in segregating costs chargeable to different outputs. But when all that one can possibly do in tracing costs to output has been done, large elements of cost remain that cannot be definitely assigned.

Marginal cost.   This cost is a unit cost derived from a comparison of the cost of successive increments in output. It has also been called *incremental cost,* since it is the cost of an additional unit of output measured (as the difference in total costs) at successive points on the total unit-cost curve. It is usually compared with the incremental or marginal-revenues curve to determine where the marginal revenue equals the marginal cost. This locates the point of maximum net returns. The expansion of sales beyond this point would begin to show reductions in net revenues because marginal costs exceed marginal revenues.

It should be noted that cost characteristics, like demand characteristics, make necessary a policy of classifying output for purposes of price differentiation, as will be more fully explained in Chapter 25. It is necessary, however, to discuss briefly the considerations upon which the policy rests.

We have seen in Chapter 10 that the demand for utility service is not uniform throughout the day but tends to grow to a peak. It also fluctuates from month to month in accordance with certain seasonal variations. This also raises the problem of securing better utilization of productive capacity with reference to the time when the demand is *not* at its maximum. If fuller utilization can be obtained at these other times, more gross revenues will be available to meet the same quota of overhead costs. If the increased business comes at the peak, so that the capacity of the plant must be increased, these additional units of supply may be produced under conditions of increasing cost per unit. Particularly is this likely to be the case if the load factor is lowered when the plant has expanded. A utility may not turn down these applications for service. The normal condition, however, which usually underlies its cost computations is one of decreasing cost. Utilities must also seek *to prevent the loss of business,* particularly that which comes at off-peak times, because that would mean that costs would rise on the remaining output. The need of price discrimination is therefore a continuing economic necessity in order to *maintain* maximum utilization of existing fixed plant.

Some Effects of Monopolistic Price Discrimination

If all units of a given supply could be produced by a monopoly at constant unit costs, the producer may sell them at a uniform price without incurring losses. If he sold at lower prices to some customers, he would, in order to avoid losses, have to sell at higher prices to others. This would be discriminating arbitrarily among his customers, and while of no special advantage to himself, it would injure consumers who pay higher prices, particularly if they compete with the other customers who pay less. The same public policy considerations should underlie discriminatory pricing under conditions of decreasing cost. Customers should not be granted rate reductions which go below the level of short-run out-of-pocket costs and thus fail to make at least some contribution to overhead costs. Classifications of customers for price discrimination purposes should take both cost and competitive considerations into account. Utilities should hold the balance *even* between competitors, in order to make our competitive organization of industry workable.

The dominant economic basis for differential price policies may thus be stated as follows: In order to obtain the maximum allowable net revenue from any system of public utility rates, the lowest rate or schedule of rates should not be less than the reasonable differential cost of producing the supply furnished thereunder; and all rates or schedules of rates higher than the lowest should be within the marginal demand price of each class of customers and preferably should make some contribution toward overhead costs. But we have not resolved the question of how much of the burden of overhead costs should be apportioned to each customer classification. This is governed by what the older economists used to call the *value of the service basis*. Value of the service is for the largest part a historical category, subject to modifications with the changing economic scene. The process is an experimental one in which the initiative should rest with the management who are in closest touch with their own market. It is a matter of informed judgment resting upon observation of the way in which the market behaves.

Diagrammatic Presentation of the Theory
of Monopoly Price

The considerations outlined above may be shown by means of diagrams. We will first take the case of a public utility which charges uniform prices. In Chart XVII the line *DD'* indicates a condition of fairly elastic demand. While the demand price decreases with increased supply, the price does not break or decline abruptly, as it would were the demand very inelastic. The

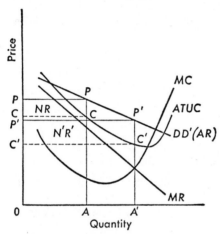

line *ATUC* indicates that as the supply increases, the cost per unit of supply decreases. If the quantity *OA* is put on the market, the cost per unit becomes *AC*. The total cost of production therefore is equal to *ACCO*. That amount of supply can be sold at the price *AP*, making the gross revenues *APPO*. The net revenue therefore is *CPPC*, or the quadrilateral *NR*. If we suppose that the quantity producd is *OA'*, the cost per unit falls to *A'C'* and the total cost becomes *A'C'C'O*. This quantity can be sold at the price of *A'P'*,

Chart XVII   Uniform Monopoly Price.

making the gross revenues *A'P'P'O*. The net revenue then becomes equal to *C'P'P'C'*, or the quadrilateral *N'R'*. The area of *N'R'* is greater than the area of *NR*. Under these conditions—that is, of elastic demand requiring some reduction in price as more supply is sold but resulting also in more than proportionate reduction in the cost per unit—the net revenue can be increased by producing a larger quantity.

Presumably the monopoly will seek to maximize this net revenue, and this would be accomplished at an output *OA'* and a price *A'P'*. For any scale of output less than *OA'*, say, *OA*, the net addition to revenue (marginal revenue *MR*) for an additional unit of sales exceeds the net addition to cost (marginal cost *MC*). Expansion of sales under these favorable circumstances is clearly desirable. However, if output is increased to an amount greater than *OA'*, net additions to cost (*MC*) would exceed net additions to revenue (*MR*), and net revenues would decline. This, for the monopolist, would clearly be undesirable. The optimum scale of operations for the concern would therefore be where marginal cost equals marginal revenue, at an output OA'. This diagram illustrates the situation where (1) the total cost includes a full normal return, and (2) where cost is represented as an average cost per unit for the full quantity actually disposed of, and (3) where a single uniform price is charged.

Now let us take the case of a public utility which discriminates in the prices to its customers. In Chart XVIII it is assumed, first, that the quantity OX can be sold to a group of customers whose demand price for this quantity is at least equal to XP, or a demand price of 10. If all the costs of produc- ing that much supply were included in the price, it would have to be XC; that is, the supply price would be 12. The quadrilateral NL represents the net loss occasioned by the sale of that much of the supply. But the utility is operating a plant with a capacity greater than OX. We shall assume that it increases its output to the quantity of OX'. The quantity lying between X and X' cannot be sold at the price XP but must be sold to

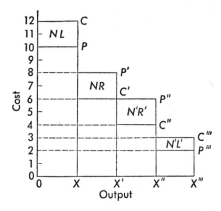

Chart XVIII   Discriminatory Monopoly Price.

customers whose demand price as a group does not exceed XP', or a de- mand price of 8. By increasing the quantity of supply, the *additional cost* of putting out XX' units of supply is at a cost of $X'C'$ per unit; that is, the sup- ply price of the increased quantity is 6 per unit. The quadrilateral NR repre- sents the net return realized upon the sale of the increased supply. Provided the quantity OX can still be disposed of at a price of 10, the price $X'P'$, or 8, is fixed in order to secure this additional business. It yields a net profit which offsets the net loss occasioned by the sale of the first quantity of supply. We shall next assume that the capacity of the plant is such that supply can be increased to the total output OX''. The cost of the increased supply $X'X''$ is $X''C''$ per unit, or 4. This increment of supply, we shall assume, cannot be sold at the price of $X'P'$ but can be sold at the price $X''P''$, or equal to 6. The quadrilateral $N'R'$ represents the net return realized from the sale of the last increment of business, provided the preceding increments of supply can con- tinue to be sold at the old prices. The net return $N'R'$ is not required to offset any accumulated net loss upon preceding increments of supply. It therefore becomes a true monopoly profit, made possible by discriminating among customers by the device of exacting a class price and by securing the increased output at lower unit costs in accordance with the behavior of overhead costs in relation to increased supply. The result of these transactions is tabulated below.

Transaction	Quantity	Supply Price	Sold at Demand Price	Profit or Loss per Unit
I	OX	12	10	Loss of 2
II	XX'	6	8	Profit of 2
III	X'X''	4	6	Profit of 2

It may now be assumed that the capacity of the plant has not yet been reached. Additional unutilized capacity is still available. But the additional output will have to be sold at a further reduction in price. The cost per unit of the last increment of supply $X'X'''$ is equal, we shall say, to $X''C'''$, or to 3. In order to sell this increment, however, the monopolist finds that he must fix a price equal to $X''P'''$, or a price of 2. The demand price of customers who could take the last increment of supply is less than its separate unit cost of production. If the sale is made, the monopolist realizes a net loss equal to the quadrilateral $N'L'$. The fourth transaction would therefore not only give him no net return for his trouble of manufacturing but would go also in part to reduce the monopoly profit realized from his third transaction. $N'L'$ would in part offset $N'R'$. As a true monopolist seeking to obtain a maximum net return, the utility would refuse to extend its output to X''' and would content itself with the output X''.

The Self-destructive Nature of Competition

In ordinary business undertakings like farming and merchandising, the force of fair competition serves to protect customers against unreasonable prices and inferior goods or services. Producers are, therefore, left to themselves with only that minimum of governmental interference which is imposed when public health, safety, or morals come to be adversely affected. Experience has proved, however, that competition functions abnormally in the public utility field. It has been demonstrated that under modern conditions such competition is slow to arise, that it is limited in its operation, and that it tends to destroy itself.

The comparative reluctance of competition to assert itself is due to the fact that large sums of capital are required and that the complexity of operations makes great demands upon managerial skill. Added to this is the consideration that specialization of capital has made competition hazardous because of the capital losses which inevitably accompany business failure.

Moreover, before enterprises may be pronounced successful, a long time is required in building up a market sufficient to absorb the product. This is especially true if the enterprise must compete with one already operating.

In the transportation industry, carriers compete for traffic moving between large centers, but they do so usually by operating over separate routes, thus tapping new traffic territory. While this is an aid toward a successful financial outcome for each of them, the local traffic along these routes is placed entirely at the mercy of the carrier. In fact this characteristic appears in all industries (like gas, water, electric, and telephone utilities) which require that customers, in order to be served, must be directly connected with the plant. The very evident costliness and inconvenience to customers of disconnection from one plant and of reconnection with another, together with the heavy cost to producers and the confusion in public thoroughfares arising from parallel facilities, tends to prevent that complete paralleling of facilities which would make competition more pervasive.

The self-destructive nature of competition rests upon the fact (already referred to) that, given a certain plant facility, the expenditures for operation are to a varying degree constant, regardless of increases in the rate of output. Thus, when there is unused capacity, producers in their desire to secure full utilization of the plant will try to secure an increased volume of business. The incremental cost attributable to increased traffic is relatively small, which sets up an irresistible inducement to get additional traffic. Competition for this traffic will be at rates which aim to cover the marginal cost and as much more as competition will permit. This opens the door to discriminations and to rate wars in which rates go below even the level of actual out-of-pocket costs.

Another fact that makes competition difficult is that costs are not accurately ascertainable for separate units of traffic. Even that portion of operating expenses which varies with output is segregable only with difficulty. Thus, the determination of the proper basis of charge has often become a matter of the "interaction of intelligent guesswork and external pressure." Out of this struggle for traffic have come either receiverships or an inevitable trend toward cooperation, culminating in consolidations or formal and informal understandings as to the prices to be maintained.

We may look at the situation from another point of view. Where two competing producers are operating in the same market, it is usually the case that their combined capacity is in excess of actual or potential requirements. As a result, neither producer is able to supply his share of the total requirements under conditions where the cost per unit is as low as it can be made. The supply of product is wasteful of producing capacity. One producer may be fully capable of supplying the total requirements. Under competition, both producers are trying to charge prices equal to their separate costs. If they are successful, by agreement among themselves, or by means of discriminatingly high prices upon the output not subject to competition, as is now the case in the transportation industry, consumers in the aggregate are paying more than the necessary cost of production.

The difficulties arising out of competitive production and out of the consequent discrimination in price adjustments have led to the adoption, as far as possible, of a policy of complete integration of supply in a given market. Thus the principle of monopoly was introduced. The reasoned conclusion, that the cost of production would be less under monopoly if there were no waste of surplus-producing capacity, has had much to do historically with the adoption of the new policy. Was this change, although dictated by economic considerations, also in the public interest? There can be no doubt upon that score at the present time, provided the monopoly is regulated. The only questions remaining relate to the scope, character, and intensity of regulation, and to the question whether public ownership and operation ought to be substituted for a policy of regulated private monopoly.

While most discussions of monopoly approach the problem from the point of view of the monopolistic control over price, it is important to note that monopoly is also a way of organizing production, which has its own peculiar advantages. This is our chief interest in it from the point of view of public utility economics. It is, of course, important to understand the theory of monopoly price so that we may know why a monopolist is in a position to increase his gains over and above what would come to him if he were required to sell in competition with other equally efficient producers. This provides the economic reason why his power must be limited by regulation. But it is equally important to understand the advantages of monopolistic organization of an industry which operates as a public utility and is thus limited by law in its power over prices. In the latter case, monopoly operates as a *beneficent* principle of organization which makes possible the conservation of productive capacity, the limitation of profit, and the systematizing of rates.

The Bearing of Regulation upon the Theory of Monopoly Price

What, it may now be asked, is the effect of governmental regulation upon the price policies of a public utility which operates as a monopoly?

In the first place regulation can prevent a public utility from charging all that the traffic will bear. Regulatory policy does permit the utility to classify its customers, thereby recognizing monopolistic class prices, but it does not permit experimentation with quantity supplied and with the rates in order to determine the point of maximum return from the point of view of the producer alone. Since public policy seeks to ensure the utility a total reasonable earning power, sufficient to compensate all the factors of production and no more, the adoption of a differential price policy under regulation is dictated by considerations other than those which arise out of the desire to secure the maximum net revenue. This should make clear that if regulation imposed a uniform price policy upon public utilities, it would not be aiding consumers as a whole. For, in classifying customers and in fixing class rates, regulation is seeking to extend supply to all customers who can pay rates at least equal to the separate cost of producing the increased supply and who in addition can make some contribution toward the necessary return. This appears clearly in Chart XVIII, where it was assumed that the unit cost of production was sufficient to cover all reasonable operating expenses, including a reasonable return upon the investment in the fixed plant.

It is, therefore, incumbent upon regulation so to fix prices, or permit the monopolist so to fix them in the first instance, as will enable the plant to attract sufficient custom to realize the maximum economy in production. If it is cheaper or more convenient for customers to supply themselves, their demand prices will reflect these considerations. Such customers should not be served. If customers are willing and able to use cheaper substitutes, whether they be substitutes produced by another monopolistic public utility or substitutes produced by competitive producers, their demand prices will likewise reflect these considerations. The public utility must be permitted to compete for this class of custom, but not at the expense of placing an additional burden upon its other consumers. Therefore the sale must not be at prices below the separate costs of producing these additional quantities of output. To produce at less than the separate costs not only throws the burden upon other consumers but also demoralizes the market for the substitutes.

In the case of customers able to supply themselves, the adoption of a price policy calculated to secure their demand, but which results in a net loss to the public utility, will not only make matters worse for other consumers but will put those who have hitherto supplied themselves in a position of dependence upon a business which cannot, in the long run, maintain its economic capacity to render this service continuously.

Returning once more to Chart XVIII, after the utility has extended its output to the quantity OX'', it will be satisfied, barring other considerations, to let matters rest, for that is the point of maximum net returns. But, by hypothesis, the area of $N'R'$ represents gross income in excess of necessary supply price of the quantity OX''. It therefore becomes the duty of the regulating authority to reduce the earning power to the point of reasonableness, economically defined. Obviously, rates may be reduced until the excess net return represented by $N'R'$ disappears. This can be done in three ways:

1. By reducing prices for all units of output comprising the quantity OX''. This should be done pro rata because under the theory of overhead cost all units of output are equally efficient in bringing about the degree of utilization which results in the cost level of $X''C''$ for the final increment.

2. By requiring the monopolist to extend his supply in the direction of X''' until full utilization is reached, even though the added supply must be sold to customers whose marginal demand price is less than the supply price of the added increment.

3. By combining the first method with the second method so that the benefit of a lowered price will be extended to existing customers and service extended to new customers with a lower demand price.

Improvements in the quality of service without change in price is another means of carrying off excess revenues. It is important to note that the *option* of pursuing any one or a combination of these methods is in the hands of regulating authorities and not in the hands of the public utility. Under any well-conceived plan of regulation the *obligation* to do something to carry off accrued monopoly profits falls upon regulating authorities. It is conceivable, also, that the surplus net revenues may be divided between the patrons and the monopolist by using some of it as a management bonus. The chief consideration is that *public purpose* and not private commercial purpose shall control the disposal of the excess. In this way, monopoly is limited by regulation. Instead of being an instrument of extortion, as is popularly assumed, monopoly becomes a beneficent method of organizing industry and of eliminating the risks and wastefulness of competitive production.

25. COST ANALYSIS
IN ITS RELATION
TO SELLING POLICIES

The first step in the practical determination of rates consists of an analysis of the cost of production. Having determined what the probable future and total cost of the service should be (including in such cost the proper allowances for ordinary operating expenses, taxes, and depreciation, and a reasonable return on the invested capital used and useful in rendering service), it is necessary to relate this estimate of total costs to an estimate of the units of service which may be said to occasion these costs. What we are after is to get some idea of costs per unit of service. We shall use the electric power industry for purposes of illustration.

We have seen in Chapter 10 that the most fundamental physical ratio for measuring economy in the use of plant capacity is the load factor. This relates the average rate of use to the maximum rate of use. The closer the average rate of use of plant capacity during the hours of the day is to the maximum hourly use (the peak) for that day, the nearer will the ratio approach 100 per cent load factor for that day. Were it ever achieved, it would constitute the "perfect day" as far as economy in the use of the plant is concerned, assuming that the reserve capacity above the peak is no more than necessary to assure continuity of service. It is turning out the maximum number of units of service (kilowatt-hours) of which the plant is capable. When total costs are related to total units of service, the cost per unit of service will be at a minimum. When sales are so manipulated as to achieve this ideal relationship in the use of plant, the going plant and the going business are perfectly adjusted to each other, and we have an ideal going concern. To be sure, selling policies—that is to say, the rates and conditions of service—are based upon the cost of production, yet upon the effectiveness with which rates marshall the users into a cooperating group in the use of plant will depend the level of average unit costs achieved. The dynamic factor, therefore, is the way in which individual rates generate customer response; that is to say, how they adjust to the value of the service to the

419

user. This is the function of differential rate-making, which in turn is determinative of the level of unit costs achieved.

Classifications of Revenues and Costs

Classifications of costs and revenues are provided by the uniform systems of accounts prescribed by state and federal regulatory commissions. These cost classifications usually follow the functional lines on which the business is organized. They are useful for general accounting and financial accounting purposes, but provide an inadequate basis for cost analysis incident to the rate-making process. They must be reanalyzed into the cost categories deemed necessary for rate-making and cost-finding purposes. Accounting classifications are, however, useful in ascertaining the reasonableness of the total cost of service and hence of the general level of rates.

In making such calculations of the total reasonable cost of service, commissions are faced with the difficulty that, though it may be possible to determine whether earnings have been adequate to cover necessary outlays for some past year or other test period, it becomes a troublesome matter to predict what the earnings and expenses will actually be for some future period. They may over- or underestimate these costs. This is a risk inherent in all rate-making by commissions. Unless provision is made for a revenue-stabilizing and equalizing device, such as the "barometer funds" or "stabilizing reserves" of service-at-cost contracts, the articulation of earnings and costs will always be by approximation only.

Earnings under a prescribed schedule of rates depend upon the volume of sales and the distribution of this volume among the various customer rate classes. Volume of sales depends first of all upon general business conditions. It grows during periods of prosperity and declines again during periods of depression. Besides the business cycle, other influences affecting volume are fortuitous circumstances like epidemics, public calamities like strikes, floods, and—most important of all—wars. The influenza epidemic in 1918, for instance, decreased the patronage, and hence the earnings, of electric railways throughout the country, due to the reduction in social intercourse. The effect of wars in stimulating some kinds of traffic in certain locations and in depressing others is sufficiently familiar not to require detailing here. These influences may have only a local effect, but they are nevertheless important in their effect on the volume of sales of some single concern.

Technically, the most direct influence upon consumer buying inheres in the rates which stimulate the demand of different classes of users. However, when important adjustments are made in particular rates, sales under old rates are no certain index of what may be expected under the new rates. Apart from general customer reaction to rate changes, it becomes a matter of carefully weighing the chances that customers may serve themselves, use substitutes, or modify their consumption in accordance with their ability to pay.

Under some circumstances, earnings alone need not be depended upon to meet all costs of operation. Public policy may provide that deficiencies in earnings be made good out of public funds. Subsidies augment the earnings of the post office, shipping companies, air-line carriers, and some publicly owned water and sewage utilities. This was also true of the railways during the period of federal lease and operation in World War I. Price fixing will then combine the principles of *private finance,* which distribute charges in proportion to user cost, with the principles of *public finance,* which allocate costs to public agencies in accordance with criteria of special or general benefit.

Cost Analysis and Particular Rates

In fixing particular rates we pass from a consideration of cost of service in terms of the total amount necessary to cost of service in terms of customers' responsibility for such outlays. Cost analysis from this point of view concerns itself with the extent to which each class of customers and each individual of a given class should share in bearing the burden of cost. It proceeds upon the hypothesis that each consumer should contribute toward total earnings *at least* in the amount that costs are definitely traceable to him. For this purpose, a statistical analysis of cost, as distinct from an accounting analysis, is employed. We shall again draw our illustrations from the electric industry.

Capacity (demand), output, and customer costs. We begin with two categories employed in the preceding chapter, namely, fixed and variable costs. These costs are now reanalysed into (1) capacity, (2) output, and (3) customer costs. They supply the principal criteria for cost differentiation.

The maximum daily system demand for electricity in kilowatts for the year (usually coming in December) determines the size of the installation, making some allowance for the necessary reserve capacity. By isolating the investment in power plants, substations, transmission and distribution system, the fixed expenses (return, taxes, depreciation, maintenance, etc.) can be computed. These represent demand or capacity costs. Demand (also called *readiness to serve*) costs are not of equal importance for all utilities. Utilities may be divided into two classes, furnishing service either with or without storage. When water is stored in a reservoir or gas in a holder, it is not necessary that these utilities have a producing capacity at least equal to the maximum demand. Peak demands can be supplied in part from storage, and the necessary supply can be produced at a relatively uniform rate of output. During periods of minimum demands, the plant may be shut down and the stored supply again drawn upon. It should be noted, however, that storage represents additional investment made necessary by irregularities in the daily demand. It is thus a demand or readiness-to-serve cost. The need of securing full utilization still remains, but the need is less accentuated. The fact that storage is possible has some influence upon the form of the rate for these utilities, as we shall see.

Electric railway and bus utilities, with their morning and evening rush hours, and electric and telephone utilities are the best illustrations of enterprises whose capacity costs depend upon the unavailability of peak storage. Telegraph utilities have characteristics which place them intermediate between these types. They need not give instantaneous service but may spread the peak demand over some longer interval of time as long as service is rendered without undue delay. Railroads in times of emergencies may declare embargoes upon particular types of freight movements, thus affording them some relief from the trials and costs of abnormal peak demands.

Some share of the expenditures for fuel, water, oil, and operating labor consumed in the steam plant of an electric utility is sometimes apportioned to the demand costs on the theory that maintaining banked boilers is a cost attributable to getting ready for the maximum demand.

It should be noted that most of these fixed expenditures vary with the growth in the maximum demand. They are, however, "sunk costs" because they do not decline with a drop in the total maximum demand.

Output costs are exclusively variable costs. They consist of the fuel, oil, and operating labor attributable to the generation of the kilowatt-hours of output, less any allowance apportionable to the demand costs, as indicated above. Sometimes they are also called *energy* costs. After segregation, output or energy costs are designed to record the ebb and flow of expenditures as generation decreases and increases. They are as nearly traceable to the use of electricity by individual customers and classification of customers as the minutiae of recording them will permit.

Customer costs consist of expenditures in reading and maintaining meters, billing, collecting, and keeping customers' accounts. To these should be added fixed expenses in connection with a utility's property on customers' premises. These properties usually include all the distribution system, beginning with the transformer that serves the customer, through to the customer's meter. They are reserved for his use alone. Beginning with the transformer, all other property is somehow used jointly with other customers and must be apportioned.

At this point it is convenient to call attention to the fact that some customers (notably industrial customers) use so much energy and make so large a demand upon the generating and transmission facilities of the utility that they are given special treatment. This special treatment will be arranged for in separate contracts which will include the rates and any special costs arising from the peculiar conditions under which service is supplied them. They are not customer costs in the above statistical sense, but they are costs segregated to individual customers for cost-finding and rate-making purposes. Properties so reserved may include transmission lines, transformer stations, and distribution lines, along with complex arrangements for metering, billing, and serving on the customers' premises.

For some rate-fixing purposes, especially when confronted with competitive situations, utilities employ a distinct category of costs not ordinarily used in their normal cost-finding procedures. This is the category of *incremental costs*, analogous to the marginal cost concept discussed in the previous chapter. However, the incremental-cost concept is used in a more practical way. We shall return to the use of the incremental-cost basis of allocation later, but we shall introduce it here in order to distinguish it from the demand, output, and customer-cost classifications.

Demand, output, and customer costs are the principal kinds of cost differentiation employed in setting up the basic rate structure and in testing its adequacy from time to time. In relating these costs to the form of the rates, it is assumed that each customer should pay a fixed amount ascertained as a customer cost by dividing the total annual customer costs by the average annual number of customers. He should pay a variable amount as an output cost, depending upon the units of output which he consumes; and finally, he should pay a variable amount as a demand cost, depending upon the units of demand which his installation exerts upon the central source of supply.

Certain general and administrative costs remain unallocated, including also a return on the amount of working capital required. Some of these expenses may be assigned to the demand and the customer category, or they may all be treated as undistributed or overhead costs and allocated to the capacity, energy, and customer-cost groupings as a "burden" in proportion to the previously assigned totals. Because many of the facilities used for street lighting are segregable and the characteristics of rendering street lighting service are, on the whole, quite uniform, the variable and fixed expenses pertaining thereto may also be directly allocated to this branch of the business.

The procedures in cost allocation and unit-cost determination are highly technical, and no useful purpose would be served in detailing them or even illustrating them here. A general discussion of the applicable principles must suffice for present purposes. It is also obvious that the results of such analyses will vary with the character of the business, the efficiency of operations, and the nature of conditions confronting each operating organization. The final results of such analyses of costs will therefore be indicated only by certain figures designed to give purely arbitrary values for monthly billing purposes, to wit:

Average capacity costs, $3.00 per kilowatt of demand per month
Average customer costs, 1.00 per customer per month
Average energy costs,   0.008 per kilowatt-hour

Differential costs of railway traffic. A cursory reference to the differential costs of railroad service and their relation to rate structure must suffice. Railroads have, in the course of time, developed numerous and highly complex service classifications, and rates are differentiated in accordance with them. Railroad traffic is first divided into freight and passenger train traffic, and separate costs for each branch of service should be determined. This allocation is made even more difficult than in the case of other utilities because of the dominance of joint costs and overhead costs. Since joint costs cannot be traced to specific joint products and overhead costs are untraceable to specific units of service, they are, so far as cost analysis is concerned, lumped together in making cost apportionments. For certain purposes it is also important to divide total costs into variable and fixed costs so that the "out of pocket" level of cost and the contribution which each service classification should make toward meeting the fixed expenses may be determined. For purposes of general orientation, the cost of conducting passenger train traffic may be further subdivided into mail, baggage, express, and passenger services. Freight train service may be similarly differentiated into costs allocated to terminal operations and the movement of trains, into the costs attributable to carload and less-than-carload operations, and other similar characteristics of service. Special cost studies may be made for dining car and Pullman services, for switching, refrigeration, and trucking services. In general, differential costs, along with value of service considerations, afford an economically sound basis for reasonable discrimination in the adjustment of transportation rates.

Some limitations of cost differentiation. The analysis of cost for rate-making is subject to some special limitations. While it may be practical to examine into costs with great minuteness for certain managerial purposes, especially those having to do with the efficiency of operations, the degree of refinement in cost analysis for rate-making purposes should not exceed that which can be made practically effective in rate differentiation. All variables of cost could not possibly be incorporated in rate schedules of general application without unduly complicating their administration and without giving rise to criticisms from customers who are unable to understand the reasons for the differentiation. Experience, for instance, has shown that standard electric rate schedules which go beyond a recognition of two elements, one depending upon demand or readiness to serve, another depending upon the actual consumption of energy, are too complex for practical purposes. With the progressive reduction in the cost of electric supply, it is no longer so necessary as it once was to measure all the characteristics under which the different customers take service. Rates should require a minimum of measuring, and changes in rates should not be too frequent. In measuring demand costs, for example, it might be desirable to distinguish three classes of customers: (1) those whose maximum demand normally comes at the time of the system peak, (2) those who take service entirely off the peak, and (3) those whose maximum demand may come at any time. Usually, however, "on-peak" customers are not specifically recognized in the construction of rate schedules, utilities preferring instead to practice promotional rate-making by inducing such customers to extend their use of service into "off-peak" periods.

Classification of Customers

It is now the universal practice to group the customers of public utilities into certain basic classifications which reflect the uses to which the service is put. By means of these classifications the rate analyst tries to take account of the fact that the value of the service to customers differs. Each customer classification is next provided with a schedule of rates which further takes account of the varying quantity of service purchased by the individual customer. If all customers were treated alike and were sold service under the same schedule of rates, this seeming equality of treatment would nevertheless be discriminatory because there is no greater inequality than the equal treatment of unequals. In any event, because the purchase is voluntary, the amount of service thus taken would be restricted and would not bring about full development of the business. Costs would have to be higher for all concerned. The criteria which must be considered are alternative costs of the same or substitute service, the elasticity of the demand for service, variations in customers' load factors and diversity factors, and perchance, the location and density of customers.

Basic classifications. The first customer classification is usually designated as residential or domestic service. Here customers are numerous, taking service in small quantities with high diversity factors and low load factors; there are few customers per mile of line in rural service, and hence they show with low density relatively high distribution investment and customer costs. A second conventional classification is of small commercial and industrial customers. These exhibit lower diversity factor but higher load factor characteristics, greater density, are much less numerous, and unlike residential customers use the service in the further production of goods and services. A third classification consists of the least numerous but large industrial and commercial customers with low diversity but high load factors. Characteristically, they consume service in large quantities. Finally, special classes of consumers should be distinguished, with peculiar service characteristics requiring separate and individual contracts. Street-lighting customers, large customers like electrometallurgical and electro-chemical companies taking service in wholesale quantities, and other utilities with whom contracts are negotiated for the interchange of electric service will illustrate these special classifications.

Rate Systems

The development of rate systems reflects the progress which has been made in the analysis of the conditions of demand and supply that lie back of the actual sale of public utility services. Again, only the more important aspects of this development will be touched upon in these pages.

Flat rates. The oldest form of rate was the so-called flat rate. According to this, each customer paid a fixed sum for some convenient period—the month, the quarter, or the year. It was extensively used by water utilities and in the infancy of the electric and gas utilities when they conducted a lighting business almost exclusively and when there was a rough equality

of use as between individual customers. Meters were either not available or
were costly and inefficient. Billing and collecting was a simple operation. As
customers' uses and variations therein increased, the growing inequality
of flat rates was recognized. Nevertheless, some forms of the flat rate have
maintained themselves in the water supply and urban transportation business, and, notably, in the telephone industry. The monthly charge of $4.50
per residence telephone is a survival of the flat-rate system of charging for
service.

Some differentiation was recognized in even the earlier flat rates when
these were made to vary with the size of the premises. The size and character of the premises seemed to give some indication of the probable demand for and consumption of service. In this form these flat prices were
usually termed *rentals*.

Fixture rates.   Differentiation really began when these flat rentals were
changed into fixture rates. They were called *fixture rates* because the price
became a specified sum per fixture, a different sum being charged for each
type (say, candlepower of lamps, diameter in inches of service pipe).
Water utilities best illustrate this practice during that rather long period
when the quantity of water consumed was less generally metered than it
now is. It sometimes took the form of a fixed sum paid semiannually for each
tap, with some differentiation whether the tap was in the kitchen, the bath-
room, or outside for hose connection. The amount paid under fixture rates
was thus roughly proportional to the amount of service which it was estimated could be furnished by means of the fixtures.

With these early rough approximations of quantifying output, it was
presumably considered that overhead costs, not varying with output, were
best apportioned equally or proportionately to an estimated quantity.

Early rate differentiation was thus founded upon inchoate cost differentiation based only on estimated variation in quantity. Flat rates and fixture
rates were uneconomical and conducive to waste because they failed to take
accurate account of the true variation of consumption among customers.
Excessive consumption was not penalized by a higher charge upon the customer causing the waste. They also failed to distinguish between the short-
and long-hour user. Even after meters became available, the change to a
new system could not be accomplished at one stroke because of the expense
of installing meters and because the influence of custom in fixing prices was
very strong. This was particularly true of water utilities where the sale of
water in large quantities on a flat-rate basis was condemned as unbusiness-
like, but the flat-rate sale of water for domestic use was continued for the

reason that requiring small householders to install meters might work a hardship upon them.[1]

Meter rates. With the introduction of cheap water, gas, and electric meters, various forms of meter rates were developed. First came the *uniform* or *straight-line meter rate.* The customer paid the same fixed rate per unit of quantity (per thousand gallons of water, per thousand cubic feet of gas, per kilowatt-hour of electricity) regardless of differences in their respective demands (rate of use) and the total quantity consumed. Hence it was called a *straight-line rate.* Large or small consumers, short- or long-hour users, heavy or light users, all paid the same rate per unit.

These rates had at least two defects. Early cost analyses by commissions and utilities showed that this rate form was ill-adapted and inequitable for those utilities where capacity and customer costs were important. It treated all costs as if they varied only with output. No rate could long serve an industry that failed to take account of cost variations so significant. The second defect was that uniform rates failed to develop the business to a maximum. Only consumers who put the service to its highest uses could be induced to buy. Lower valued uses or those capable of being met by cheaper substitutes remained unserved.

Step meter rates. Realization of these defects led to the adoption of a variant known as the *step meter rate.* Step rates provide a scale of charges whereby a larger quantity of output can be purchased at a lower price per unit than can a smaller quantity. One form of the step rate utilizes a uniform meter rate but applies a step system of quantity discounts. The more common form is illustrated in the following scale:

Less than 50 kilowatt-hours per month, 8¢ per kilowatt-hour
From 50 to 150 kilowatt-hours per month, 6¢ per kilowatt-hour
Over 150 kilowatt-hours per month, 4¢ per kilowatt-hour

The foregoing scale remedies the second defect in that it furnishes a greater quantity of service at lower unit rates. Its outstanding defect, however, is that it results in regressive charges, since it is possible to reduce the total bill by increasing the quantity consumed. According to the scale, 40 kilowatt-hours would cost a consumer $3.20 per month. By running up, if not wasting, his consumption to 50 kilowatt-hours per month, the monthly bill could be reduced to $3.00. This objection of regressivity could have been overcome by providing that the charge would never be less for a larger quantity than

[1] *Cf. Leavenworth v. Leavenworth City and Ft. Leavenworth Water Co.* (P.U.R. 1915B), p. 611.

for a smaller quantity. A better alternative, however, was the adoption of another variant in the scale of charges.

Block meter rates. By adopting a scale of charges which requires each customer to pay the rates set forth for successive blocks of energy consumed, the regressive nature of step rates is eliminated, larger usage of energy is encouraged, and differentiation in rates in accord with a descending scale as to both cost of service and value of service is achieved. The following scale of *block meter rates* goes a long way toward eliminating the defects of uniform meter rates.

First 50 kilowatt-hours per month, 8¢ per kilowatt-hour
Next 100 kilowatt-hours per month, 6¢ per kilowatt-hour
All in excess of 150 kilowatt-hours per month, 4¢ per kilowatt-hour

The block type of rates commends itself for its simplicity, and its use is now almost universal for residence service. By combining with it a provision for the payment of a minimum bill of $1.00 per month to cover at least some of the customer costs, further recognition is given to the cost-of-service basis of rate-making. A "fixed charge" of 60 cents per month, in addition to the charges calculated in accordance with the above scale, is a device used by the Wisconsin and other commissions to reflect more adequately and definitely the category of customer costs.

Demand or readiness-to-serve rates. From the earliest days of the electric industry it had always been realized that in standing ready to serve customers, the maximum demand had some influence upon the cost of service and that this element should be recognized in rate-making. The determination of a single customer's peak demand, however, required the use of demand meters. This was too costly except for very large users or for many customers taken as a class. It would also have been useful to know the time of customers' peak demands, and particularly whether these peaks were coincident with the peak demand of the system, which was likely to last for a considerable period of time. This would require the use of recording demand meters.

The difficulties and expense of demand metering led to the adoption of substitute devices for the increasing numbers of residential users and the small commercial and industrial customers. For the former, a room count was introduced on the theory that a customer living in a larger house, but using the same quantity of energy as a customer living in a smaller house, should pay at a higher rate per unit because he is bound to exert the higher demand upon plant capacity. Other primitive devices for measuring the demand were the ascertainment of the area of the residence, or a load count in terms of a percentage of the active connected load of all utilization devices. The room type of demand rate may be illustrated by the following scale, which also uses the block type of energy rate:

> For the first 5 kilowatt-hours per room, 8¢ per kilowatt-hour
> For the next 10 kilowatt-hours per room, 6¢ per kilowatt-hour
> For all additional kilowatt-hours, 4¢ per kilowatt-hour

Thus an eight-room residence customer would be required to use 40 kilowatt-hours at 8 cents per unit as compared with 20 kilowatt-hours for a four-room customer before getting the benefit of the next lower rate in the schedule.

Wright demand rates. The above rate forms have now largely disappeared with the introduction of heavy-duty appliances into the home, such as electric stoves, refrigerators, and water heaters. Only the rate form using the measured or estimated demand in kilowatts has maintained itself in some smaller commercial and industrial installations, where it has become known as the *Wright demand rate,* after the engineer who first conceived it. In its more recent formulation it stresses the use of the highest rate for the first block of kilowatt-hours per kilowatt of demand. It thus emphasizes the customer's load factor. In its earlier form it was expressed as a certain number of hours use per month of the active connected load. But with the cheapening of demand-indicating meters, it usually reads as follows:

For the first 60 kilowatt-hours per kilowatt of demand per month, 6¢ per kilowatt-hour
Excess consumption per month, 3¢ per kilowatt-hour

Its primary weaknesses are that it is not sufficiently promotional and that it does not assure that the demand costs will be recouped.

Hopkinson rates. The above deficiencies do not inhere in the rate form named after Dr. John Hopkinson, a professor of engineering at Kings College, London, who wrote the first scientific treatise upon the subject of electric rates.[2] This rate consists of two parts. One part, the so-called demand charge, makes a specific charge for the fixed capacity costs, and the other part, the *energy* charge, takes into account the variable output costs. The following schedule illustrates this form:

___

[2] Pioneer papers upon this general subject have been reprinted in *Reprints of Selected Original Rate Papers,* Edison Illuminating Co., Detroit, 1915. Special attention is directed to a paper describing the Dougherty form of demand rate which recognizes besides capacity costs, energy and customer costs. It is a three part rate schedule and needlessly complex; hence it aroused customer opposition and is of only historical importance.

Demand Charge

First 50 kilowatts of demand, $2.00 per kilowatt per month
Next 150 kilowatts of demand, $1.50 per kilowatt per month
Over 200 kilowatts of demand, $1.00 per kilowatt per month

Energy Charge

First 3,000 kilowatt-hours per month, 1.5¢ per kilowatt-hour
Next 17,000 kilowatt-hours per month, 1.0¢ per kilowatt-hour
Over 20,000 kilowatt-hours per month, 0.8¢ per kilowatt-hour

It should be noted that both the demand and energy part of the schedule are blocked and that the rate for energy is lower than in the single part rate. The Hopkinson type of rate is best adapted to the larger commercial and industrial consumer, for whom it is economical to measure the demand by computing it from the rating of the connected equipment or by reading a recording demand meter. When using the latter, the billing demand is usually the highest or the average of the three highest demands registered for any 15-minute or 30-minute interval during any three-month or six-month period.

Some Special Observations

A full treatment of the techniques employed and the policies envisaged in the pricing of public utility services can be provided only in extended monographs. There is also much intuitive knowledge obtainable only from experience. We will, however, venture some orienting observations with respect to rate-making for particular utilities.

Gas and water rates. Not unlike the electric industry, gas and water supply industries are also subject to capacity, output (also called *commodity*), and customer-cost classifications; but the rate-maker does not have available so practical a method for ascertaining and classifying demands as in the case of electricity supply. Moreover, storage exerts a strong influence in making capacity costs of lesser importance. For this reason gas and water rates for general service usually take the form of block meter rates with promotional features.

Water service is usually subject to a minimum charge, graded according to the size of the meter. The use of water for fire protection calls for a special rate because the quantity of water used is minimal, while the adequacy of the protection afforded depends upon the pumping capacity available. Hence, rates for fire protection usually take the form of a fixed charge per hydrant per year.

In supplying gas to the large industrial users, blocked demand and output rates of the Hopkinson type have been introduced, with demand meters determining the maximum hourly use for the year. The recent widespread introduction of natural gas, particularly for space heating, has caused a shift from the measurement of gas supplied in cubic feet to the *therm* basis. A therm is a unit of heating value equivalent to 100,000 British thermal units (Btu). Manufactured gas was usually required to have an average heating value of 550 British thermal units; hence, 1,000 cubic feet (Mcf) would have the equivalent heating value of 5.5 therms. With natural gas having a heat content of more than twice that of artificial gas, natural gas rates measured in Mcf would deliver over twice the heating value of artificial gas in the same cubical content. However, rates for the delivery of natural gas at the end of interstate pipelines to local utilities, the so-called city gate rates, continue to be measured in Mcf, but its local distribution and sale, particularly as mixed artificial and natural gas, usually is stated in therms during the transition period.

Urban and suburban transit rates. The normal unit for measuring passenger service is the *passenger mile*. This unit is recognized in the fixing of the station-to-station rates in intercity service by railway and highway carriers. Generally speaking, long distance transport has been placed upon a mileage basis. Where competition obtains, the short-line distance rate of one of the competitors becomes the rate which the other carrier with a more circuitous haul must meet. The first departure from a mileage scale appears in the zone rates, where a haul entirely within one zone is charged a fixed amount. Passengers riding into or through a particular zone will pay a zone rate which has some relation to distance, but which does not discriminate between hauls shorter than the full distance. Mileage and zone rates disregard terminal costs, spreading them uniformly over distance components, since passengers require little in the way of special terminal facilities.

In the case of urban and suburban mass transportation, where the average haul is a relatively short distance and the density of traffic over the lines is great, costs have been spread over the *passenger* as the fundamental unit. As the lines lengthened beyond the central city area, modifications were introduced which recognized distance to some extent. Suburban lines of lower traffic density were treated in accordance with the zone principle in which an additional charge was made for transfer to another conveyance to complete a longer or differently circumstanced journey. This was the beginning of differentiation on the distance principle, carried to a much greater extent in the zone system obtaining in European cities. Custom, the ease of fare collection, and the speed of loading and unloading have thus far committed American practice to the uniform flat fare, limiting the zone system to cautious experiments in areas of low traffic density.

But there is an unquestioned cost component, depending upon the demand in the cost of conducting metropolitan mass transport, which arises from the extreme demands for service during the morning and evening rush. It is illustrated in the daily load curve of a transit company shown in Chart IX. The load factor and diversity factor problem thus obtrude themselves into the operation of this utility and have given rise to new types of rate differentiation. The higher cash fare in contrast with the lower token fare (available only in quantity) aims to differentiate between the occasional and regular rider. Were it possible to differentiate them, passengers riding during rush hours ought to pay more than those using the facilities during nonrush hours. Despite the higher cost of this service, it was and still is the practice to grant lower fares to rush-hour patrons because they are the *regular* patrons, while the *occasional* patron, though riding off the peak, is penalized with a higher cash fare.

With the appearance of competition in the shape of "jitney" and later of "bus" transportation, the electric railway, besides experimenting with the motor vehicle, began to experiment also with rates that had promotional features in them. Sweet are the uses of adversity, but in this case they came too late. Two significant departures should be recorded. The *weekly pass,* first tried in Racine, Wisconsin, in 1919, found a limited application to meet bus competition in the transition period before the entire industry was overwhelmed by the private motor car. Priced a little above the regular rates (twelve rides per week) the holder of the weekly pass was entitled to an unlimited number of rides. Although subject to some abuse, it represents a return to the principle of the flat rate and was, indeed, a very effective device to fight competitors who could not adopt the same plan. Besides creating good will and speeding up the traffic schedules, it was designed to improve the load factor because such additional riding as it induced had to come at a time when the carrier had unutilized capacity and would therefore mean little additional outlay.

A second departure was a variant of the pass system known as the *permit card.* It sold for a fixed sum per month and entitled the holder to ride at less than the regular rate, usually the customary nickel fare. It thus represented an application of readiness-to-serve costs combined with a low incremental cost. The low rate per ride was designed to stimulate the riding habit and to meet competition. The occasional or convenience rider was required to pay the higher cash or token fares. Under the conditions obtaining in the 1920's and 1930's, it did not gain wide customer acceptance.

The disappearance of the electric railway from the smaller cities, its conversion into the trolley-bus and motorbus in urban street transportation are facts of recent technical evolution. Despite continuous experiments with fare systems, the patronage of urban mass transport has declined. There was a brief revival during the war when gasoline and tire rationing temporarily drove the competing private motor car off the streets. But adversity has again set in, aggravated by the higher postwar costs and the growing preponderance of short-term variable operating costs as the conversion from car to bus spreads. Still the need for an organized system of mass transportation in all except the smaller cities continues to be felt.

The underlying maladjustment seems to be that the industry is passing into the twilight zone where it cannot by itself rely upon equating costs with revenues derived from the patrons alone. The convenience, speed, and adaptability of self-supply by way of the motor car is undermining the transit industry as a business. An offsetting factor is the growing traffic congestion and the problem of terminal parking, representing costs which have been shifted to the taxpayer. In response, parking meters and off-street parking facilities have appeared and have created what in some communities are called *parking utilities*. It has been suggested that urban transit utilities and parking utilities be operated jointly. The hidden truth seems to be that urban transport creates two values, movement values and site values. These must, in some way, be associated by a dual system of pricing: fares to reach the transport values, and of tax exemption, subsidies or special assessments to reach the socially created site values. In order to effect the combination, public ownership may prove to be the better alternative under some local situations.

Telephone rates. In dealing with telephone rates difficulties in the analysis of costs and in metering service have stood in the way of differential rate-making. Commissions have, however, always carefully distinguished intercity toll business from the local exchange business of telephone plants. Toll service was placed upon a combination of message-time and zone-distance basis for daytime calls, with lower rates for off-peak evening and Sunday service. Another form of discrimination, reflecting in part the differences in cost but in greater part what the traffic will bear considerations, is the distinction between the higher person-to-person toll rate and the lower station-to-station rate.

Exchange service has been developed on the theory that while the industry has some decreasing cost tendencies, the major trend has been one of increasing costs because as the size of the community increases, both the quality of the service and the cost per telephone increases. This feature is usually explained by pointing out that two subscribers require but one connection. However, if the number of telephones is doubled, communication between them will require six connections; six subscribers will require fifteen connections. Pursuing this principle further, we derive the general conclusion that as the size of the community increases, more expensive and complicated switchboards and trunk lines become necessary, thus increasing the cost per station. At the same time the potential value of the service to the subscriber is likewise increased because of the larger range of possible communications. Thus, historically, exchange rates were developed on a flat-rate basis with differentiation between higher priced single-party and lower priced multiparty service, especially for urban residential and rural service. However, in recognition of the necessity of telephone service to businessmen, they are charged correspondingly higher flat rates in recognition of their greater ability and willingness to pay because they use the telephone as income-producing property.

The invention of devices for recording the number and length of calls in ordinary exchange service has made possible the introduction of metered rates for exchange service. They are used primarily for business and residence service in our larger cities. They consist of a flat minimum charge per month, which includes a minimum number of allowed free calls, and an additional charge per call at a rate low enough to encourage increased use. This form of measured service rate must be carefully adjusted in order not to make customers "cost conscious." The underlying psychology of marketing telephone service is to build the telephone into a freely used tool for commercial and social communication.

A concluding observation. With the increasing spread in the area of operations including communities of all sizes and the rural territory between them, the factor of density and its effect in creating unit cost differentials has come to the fore. Should rate systems be applied uniformly in area-wide operations, neglecting cost differentials due to differing densities? As it is sometimes phrased succinctly: Should the center carry the fringe? With this question we have arrived at one of the frontiers of rate-making. We meet this problem in all utilities, but it appears in its most advanced form in the telephone and electric industries. The question of the optimum geographic unit in rate-making has been answered differently by commissions. In the telephone industry the Bell system argues for company-wide rate-making neglecting cost differentials and basing rates on value of service principles. Most state commissions have adopted the Bell system's argument that company-wide rate-making promotes the maximum development of the service by permitting the larger communities in effect to subsidize the smaller one. With unit rate-making by exchanges, the service in smaller communities will be underdeveloped if not abandoned. The Wisconsin and California Commissions, in following unit rate-making, contend that rates in smaller communities can be kept within the limits of customers' ability to pay by permitting a lower rate of return. The question has not been resolved. The maintenance of uneconomic rate differentials, such that high cost areas do no equate revenues and costs, may lead to the misallocation of resources by the utility, where greater reliance upon cost analysis and the introduction of metered rates may give to geographic areas the comparative advantages and disadvantages of their geographic environment.

Rate systems for the different types of common carriers, especially railways, are so complex that no useful purpose would be served to pursue further these procedures and policies of rate-making in this preliminary orientation. We will add only that in place of the regional freight classifications of the past, national uniformity has now been achieved, thereby reducing somewhat the bewildering complexity of railway rates. In the Select Bibliography we include some references in which this subject is given detailed treatment.

3. PLANNING
AND
COORDINATION

In the remaining chapters of this book we shall attempt a discussion of some of the special problems which have developed in the public utility sector of the economy. These problems arise out of what appears to be a trend toward a planned coordination of the utilities with each other and with economic activities, both public and private, in the economy as a whole.

We shall present these somewhat disjointedly, but they nevertheless will have a common focus. Beginning with a discussion of the movement for public and co-operative ownership, we shall next consider in a series of chapters the part which public utilities have played in the development of certain regional resources. These discussions are in the nature of case studies from which certain conclusions and interpretations may be derived which should be useful in developing the lights and shadows of the current public utility picture. We shall close with the problem of public utility taxation and subsidization, and then attempt to present by way of summary some concluding observations.

26. THE
DEVELOPMENT OF PUBLIC
AND COOPERATIVE
OWNERSHIP

Anyone approaching the public utility problem with an open mind must admit that there never has been a time when public utility industries were conceived to be reserved only for private ownership. Their pivotal importance in any economy has always raised the question whether the institution of public or private property is best suited to ensure a supply of these services. For reasons which are peculiar to the history of English-speaking countries, they are the classic home of private initiative and hence of private ownership of public utilities. But even in these countries public ownership has in recent years been ever more widely extended. We shall restrict ourselves to record the facts about this extension of public ownership in the United States. We shall also neglect the railway industry because federal ownership of railways has been restricted to Alaska and the Canal Zone.

The Government as Public Service Enterpriser

When we speak of public ownership in this connection it is important to observe the various forms which such public ownership may take. Any governmental unit—federal, state, municipal, town, county, village, district —may become an owning unit. When utilities were small local enterprises, public ownership was almost exclusively municipal or village ownership. But the expansion in the market for utility service has made it necessary to consider also that counties, specially created districts, states, and even the federal government may become owning units. In recent years states and the federal government have used the device of the public corporation for ownership and operation of public utilities. Although not, strictly speaking, a form of public ownership, we should mention the cooperative in this connection as an owning unit that has been developed as an alternative to the private corporation.

It is not necessary that public ownership should also mean public operation. It is conceivable that a governmental unit might content itself with obtaining the title to public utility properties and then leasing these properties to private agencies for private operation. Under these circumstances the lease will not only fix the rental payment which must be paid but it will also seek to fix other terms and conditions in accordance with which the properties are to be operated. This mode of procedure is, however, resorted to so infrequently that we may pass it by with a mere mention. Normally and dominantly, public ownership as a policy means both ownership and operation.

The historic battleground upon which the issue of public versus private ownership has been fought in this country has been in local politics. As a policy, public ownership is neither foredoomed to fail nor foreordained to succeed. Since the unfortunate experiences with state ownership and operation after the panic of 1837, there has been little evidence of a movement with the state as the owning unit. As a combined result, however, of the conservation movement and the growing interconnection of public utilities into regional systems, renewed proposals for large-scale public ownership have been made. The example of the Province of Ontario, Canada, in creating in 1906 the Hydro-Electric Power Commission to own and operate electric power systems, has proved contagious.

Some historical antecedents. The progenitors of our modern public utilities were built and managed by the state. In both ancient and medieval times they were treated as public functions. The issue of private ownership did not arise until democratic forms of government undertook to carry into practice those liberal economic ideas of the eighteenth century which sought to provide more room for individual initiative. The industrial revolution, beginning at about the same time, brought in its wake a great increase in the number and kind of public service enterprises. What was more natural, therefore, than that these new economic developments, involving as they did a lengthy period of technical experimentation and of ripening for economic use, should be left to private initiative? This was particularly true of English-speaking countries. On the continent of Europe, however, the monarchical tradition helped to preserve the accustomed scope of governmental initiative. For this reason and despite recent changes, England and the United States remained, until the outbreak of World War II, the classic examples of public utilities privately owned.

The idea that public functions may be left in private hands dates from the "farming out" system first applied to taxation by ancient Rome. As applied to modern public utilities, it began with the highways of England in 1663 when the counties of Cambridge, Hereford, and Huntington were permitted by act of Parliament to levy tolls for the maintenance of trunk roads. The turnpike trusts thus sanctioned by law developed into corporations which later extended their activity into the canal and railroad fields. On the Continent, on the other hand, except for a brief initial period, the construction of railroads was principally by the state. Accordingly, in the nineteenth century there began that discussion of the comparative merits of public and private ownership and operation of public utilities which has from time to time elevated this question to the rank of an issue in practical politics.

The history of public ownership in this country begins in the early part of the nineteenth century when systems of inland transportation were promoted as part of Henry Clay's American system of development. With tariffs to encourage manufacturing, it was believed that the growing nonagricultural part of the population would be available to consume the surplus products of the farm. This interdependence and balance between industry and agriculture would require better transportation systems of roads, canals, and later railroads to create greater national strength and unity. Since private capital was not yet sufficiently plentiful and the strict constructionists of the Constitution raised doubts regarding the propriety of Congressional appropriations for internal improvements within the boundaries of states, it devolved upon the states to organize and to finance them by means of public loans, especially from abroad. By 1837 in excess of $170 million of state indebtedness had been incurred by the states of the Atlantic seaboard, as well as the lake and interior states, to open their territories to rapid settlement. Since much of the money was spent on unremunerative undertakings, the burden of the deficits devolved upon the taxpayers. When some of the states, chiefly in the South, repudiated both principal and interest of their debts, the consequence was injury of American credit abroad and a reaction in public opinion against state ownership and management and even against participation by states in the financing of such enterprises.

Municipal Ownership

Enabling legislation. Municipalities, as well as other subordinate units of government, are creatures of the state and derive their powers from the state either by means of constitutional or statutory enactments. If a municipality desires to engage in a public utility enterprise, authority to do so is now commonly granted in express terms through city charters or general statutory or constitutional authority. In view of the diversity of the legal situation in the different states, it is necessary to consult the laws of each state to make sure whether specific authority has been conferred. The courts have been called upon to decide whether such authorizations are constitutional. It is now well established and confirmed by the Supreme Court of the United States that such authority may be expressly conferred. It should be noted, however, that in some jurisdictions this power is not implied from a general grant of power unless the language of a statute is sufficiently clear to permit making the implication. If a special procedure is laid down in the law, such procedure must be followed. It should also be noted that the authority must specify whether the initiation of public service may be by construction of a new plant or acquisition of existing plant.

The most important procedural step, usually, is the submission of the question to a vote at a referendum election where the consent of a majority or more of the qualified electors voting thereon is necessary. If, as is usual, the construction or acquisition of the plant is to be financed by the issuance of bonds by the municipality, the proposition of their issuance must likewise be submitted for approval by the voters. It is in these election campaigns that proponents and opponents alike vie with each other in presenting their respective sides of the issue by means of arguments that are sometimes the despair of intelligent citizenship.

Whether the proposal is for construction or acquisition of a plant depends upon the legal situation. If the community is as yet unserved, or if, as is more likely, the private utility serving the particular market does not have an exclusive franchise (at least as against the city), the city may undertake to construct a new plant. In the latter event this may mean a period of intense competition and of duplication of service which may well be disastrous to all concerned. If, on the other hand, the franchise is exclusive (i.e., the incumbent has a legal monopoly), a method of municipal purchase may be provided in the franchise itself or in a general statute. But what if no provision has been made for municipal purchase and the municipality in conferring the franchise has agreed not to compete? Any attempt to build a competing plant would be met by an injunction from the courts because such action would be a violation of constitutional safeguards against impairment of the obligation of a contract. Would the municipality then be helpless to effect a change to public ownership? It is for situations such as this that municipalities have been authorized to exercise the power of eminent domain. They need not await the expiration of the franchise in order to make this change in public policy, but may begin condemnation proceedings which require that the necessity of the taking and the amount of the "just compensation" be judicially determined, after an affirmative vote by the electorate in a referendum election.

A distinctive method of converting from private to public ownership grew out of the indeterminate permit. As we have seen, the limited terms of old franchises were changed by statute into indeterminate permits if a public utility voluntarily surrendered its *old* franchises. Other utilities were deemed to have surrendered their old franchises and accepted indeterminate permits by operation of law if they had not expressly elected to retain their old franchises before a certain definite date. Of course, all *new* franchises were issued as franchises of indeterminate duration. It is a distinctive feature of indeterminate permits that under them the municipality concerned could *at any time* hold a referendum election to decide whether the property of the local utility should be purchased. If the referendum favored purchase, the utility and the commission were notified that the municipality was authorized to take over operation. The purchase price could then be fixed by agreement, or the city was empowered to apply to the administrative commission for a determination of the "just compensation" to be paid by the city to the utility.

In some cases public ownership might come automatically through the expiration of a franchise which provided that the property revert to the city. The more common provision, however, was that the city might purchase the property at a price, the determination of which was fixed in the franchise itself. A frequently used method of computing the price was that of capitalizing the net income for the last year or years of private operation at a definitely fixed capitalization rate. In other franchises it was provided that the purchase price be determined by arbitration or court action. In still other cases as in Cleveland, Ohio, municipal ownership was the result of the annexation by the city of a suburb which already owned a public plant. Operations could then be extended to serve additional customers in the enlarged marketing area.

Obstacles to government ownership. However much the way may have been cleared of legal obstacles, the policy of municipal ownership met two important financial obstacles. The first of these arose out of severance damages. Private owners whose properties extended beyond one municipal area into other municipal areas could claim compensation for severance damages if a single municipality purchased only the property within its own municipal boundaries. The threat of substantial severance damages and the fact that if the purchase were consummated, a city would have on its hands a less efficient operating organization than that which had achieved the larger economic unity, proved to be serious stumbling blocks in the way of city ownership. In some cases this defect was remedied with enabling legislation providing for the purchase by cities of utility properties extending beyond their own limits. In other cases resort was had to the device of setting up a new public corporation with an enlarged administrative area whose sole purpose was the acquisition and operation of these larger entities. The metropolitan water districts and public utility power districts of some of our western states are cases in point.

The second obstacle was that municipalities were unable to finance the purchase of private utilities. In order to purchase these properties it was necessary that the entire amount of the "just compensation" be paid in cash, unless other arrangements could be made by voluntary agreement whereby outstanding bonds were assumed by the city or a plan of installment purchase was provided for. If the entire amount was payable in cash, municipalities would have to borrow the money by issuing general obligation bonds. But the power of cities to borrow upon their general credit (which is the taxing power) was limited by statutory or constitutional limitations, usually restricting the amount of the bonds to from 5 to 10 per cent of the assessed value of their taxable properties. Since expanding municipal expenditures for streets, schools, and sanitary purposes had brought many cities close to their limits of indebtedness, the remaining margins were often insufficient to consummate the purchase.

To remedy this situation several suggestions have been made and carried into effect. In Montana, where the normal bond limitation was 3 per cent, a popular vote may increase the limit to 10 per cent in the acquisition of water and sewer facilities. In Kentucky a higher limit has been fixed for the larger cities, those of the first and second class having a rate of 10 per cent while others have only 5 per cent. In other states higher limits are specifically provided for the acquisition of public utilities. In defense of these higher limits it is urged that the usual grounds for limitation upon municipal expenditures do not exist because utilities are revenue-producing enterprises and therefore self supporting.

Another type of remedial legislation is that of authorizing states and local units of government to issue revenue bonds where principal and interest is payable solely from the revenue proceeds of the utilities. Revenue bonds are also given a first lien upon the property of the utility. This is tantamount to a loan upon the credit of the utility alone, the city operating the property under its proprietary power. Investment bankers contend that although revenue bonds are not as saleable as general obligation bonds having the full faith and credit of the city behind them, they can, nevertheless, be advantageously disposed of because the bonds are exempt from federal and state income taxes. These bonds are also accompanied by covenants stipulating minimum requirements as to maintenance, depreciation, insurance, and requirements for rates. They have been used extensively by the City of Los Angeles in financing the expansion of its Department of Water and Power as a supplement to original financing by means of general obligation bonds. As one of the pioneers in the promotion of this type of financing, the Department has now been authorized by charter amendment to issue this type of bond without having each issue submitted to a vote of the electorate.

Progress of the Movement for Public Ownership

Statistics shown in Table XI afford some idea of the extent of the movement for municipal ownership at the present time. One cannot fail to be impressed by the number and variety of economic services which municipal government has undertaken to render. However, the public investment in strictly public service enterprises in comparison with private investment, while growing in absolute amounts, is by no means dominant. Only in the field of water supply and of irrigation utilities does government initiative and cooperative initiative appear to play a predominant role. It should be noted also that some facilities such as highways, canals, waterways, bridges, and sewers have not been managed as commercial enterprises, at least not for considerable periods of time. Other public enterprises like printing establishments, heating plants, and street-lighting plants have been operated as government facilities, accepting no private customers. Other forms like housing, state insurance, flour milling, and coal yards are not public utilities strictly so-called and compete in the same market with like enterprises that are privately owned. In fine, the United States is still the classic home of privately owned utilities.

Gas utilities.   Nevertheless, public ownership has some significant results to record. The outstanding example of municipal ownership of the artificial gas industry is that of Philadelphia, established in 1841 and operated until 1887, when the plant was leased to a private company. An early and apparently successful gas utility was established in Richmond, Virginia, in 1852. This plant has continued under public ownership and operation to the present time. Other important municipal gas utilities are located in Duluth, Minn., Holyoke, Mass., Omaha, Neb., Long Beach, Cal., and Colorado Springs, Col. Eighty-three public plants operate in cities of less than 50,000. All told, public ownership has not made much progress in gas supply, electricity taking its place, and is practically nonexistent in the natural gas branch of the industry.

Table XI   Municipal Ownership and Operation of Utilities, 1953 *
(in Cities over 5,000)

Type of Utility	No. Reporting Utility	Percentage of Total Cities Reporting
Auditorium	406	16.6
Bus or trolley-bus system	38	1.6
Electric generation and distribution	290	11.9
Electric distribution only	212	8.7
Gas manufacture and distribution	42	1.7
Gas distribution only	66	2.7
Incinerator	421	17.2
Port facilities	78	3.2
Street railway	9	0.4
Sewage-treatment plant	1,203	49.3
Slaughterhouse	26	1.1
Water supply and distribution	1,648	67.5
Water distribution only	151	6.2
Airport	510	20.9

* *The Municipal Yearbook, 1953,* p. 67, Chicago. 87 cities of less than 25,000 population not reporting; 300 cities, practically all of less than 50,000, report having no utilities publicly owned.

Telephone utilities.   Another industry with few examples of public ownership and operation is that of telecommunications. Although there are numerous small telephone systems, they are mostly privately or cooperatively owned and managed. Unlike Canada, where there are numerous municipal systems, the United States has only a few scattered systems, the largest and most successful being that of Brookings, South Dakota.

Urban transit.   The supply of mass transportation by street railways in our larger cities has fallen upon evil days with the widespread ownership of the automobile, the appearance of fleets of taxicabs, and the competition of the motorbus. There has been some growth of municipal ownership of bus and trolley-bus systems, with twenty-eight of them in the medium sized cities of the country which still need common carrier service of the mass transportation kind. In the larger cities, coordination of service by electric railway, gas busses, trolley busses, and elevated and subway lines is the order of the day. Beginning with the rise of prices during and after World War I, electric railways found themselves in financial difficulties, with bankruptcies and reorganizations leading to experiments with mixed systems of public and private ownership, service-at-cost plans, public trusteeship plans, and outright public ownership and operation. The electric railways of Seattle and of Detroit were completely municipalized in 1919 and 1923, respectively. After years of competition between a municipal and a private electric railway, San Francisco adopted full-fledged public ownership and operation. Of the nine municipal systems, all but two operate in cities over 100,000. New York and Chicago are other recent examples of public ownership. The Chicago Transit Authority of 1947, a unique self-regulating public corporation, serves as an especially interesting experiment to provide an integrated mass transportation service in a city which cannot get along without one.

Electric utilities. At the present time, of the cities in excess of 5,000 population, 502 cities own and operate electric utilities, with 212 operating only distribution systems. Only fifteen municipally owned plants are found in cities in excess of 100,000, and most of the municipal plants are located in the smaller communities. The first municipal plants were established early in the 1880's and were mostly for street-lighting purposes. By 1892 the number had increased to 235. From 1902 to 1922 the number increased from 851 to 2,581, the high-water mark of the number of instances. These plants were usually established because the smaller communities did not hold out much promise to private enterprise that the plants could be made to pay. With the construction of transmission lines and the interconnection of power sources, both steam and hydro, the extension of service to the smallest communities and to rural areas was made possible. This also had the effect that many municipally owned properties were sold to private companies or discontinued the production of electric energy in small central stations, buying instead in wholesale quantities from privately owned transmission lines.

The above development illustrates the principal advantage of private enterprise, which is not confined to a single local market, and the principal disadvantage of municipal enterprise, which is thus restricted. The Ontario hydroelectric system of Canada, owned by the province, has overcome this disadvantage by producing hydroelectric power at Niagara Falls and other large and small central stations and by transmitting this energy for resale to many large and small communities and rural districts that own and operate only the local distributing systems. This publicly owned enterprise aims to distribute this power at cost, and thus it became the prototype of similar enterprises in the United States, notably the Tennessee Valley Authority. It was therefore drawn into the controversy over the comparative merits of public and private ownership in the United States.

There are other outstanding examples of publicly owned and operated electric utilities, of which those serving Los Angeles, Seattle, Tacoma, Pasadena and Glendale are perhaps the most prominent. We shall appraise the significance of these municipal enterprises in connection with our discussion of the regional development of our natural resources. We propose in a series of chapters to trace the gradual evolution of the regional economies of the Pacific Southwest, the Pacific Northwest, and the states in the Tennessee Valley region in order to show the impact of the river-basin planning movement upon both public and private ownership of public utilities. Before turning to these latter-day policies, however, we must discuss some of the more important aspects of rural electrification and the spread of the cooperative as an alternative type of ownership which sponsored rural electrification.

The Electric Cooperative and Rural Electrification

In contrast with Germany, France, Switzerland, Holland, and the Scandinavian countries, rural electrification in this country was ignominiously retarded. In 1919 only 1.6 per cent of the nation's farms had central station service. By 1935, with more active promotion by private utilities, one out of every ten farmers enjoyed electricity, a considerable increase. Thanks to the "Giant Power Survey" promoted by Governor Gifford Pinchot of Pennsylvania in the early 1920's, the first detailed studies of rural electrification were made. But it was the "New Deal," under the political leadership of Senator George W. Norris of Nebraska and President Franklin D. Roosevelt in promoting the Tennessee Valley project, which made the rural electric cooperative the carrier of this new phase of the rural electrification idea. To be sure, privately owned electric utilities in California and in certain other favored sections of the country had already spread electricity into rural areas. In most sections, however, it was the policy of "skimming the cream" in favorable territory, together with high rates and costly line extensions (often $1,500 to $1,800 per mile) that had held down the development. Municipally owned utilities likewise followed restrictive procedures in making rural extensions. The depressed condition of agriculture, beginning in 1921 with its low and unstable farm income, high tenancy rates, and heavy farm indebtedness, also militated against the spread of the movement.

The Rural Electrification Administration (REA). The Rural Electrification Administration, created by Executive order in May, 1935, and made over into a statutory agency by the Rural Electrification Act of 1936, changed all that. The Act provides for an administrator appointed by the President with Senate approval for a term of ten years at an annual salary of $10,000. Morris L. Cooke was the first appointee. It was the administrator's duty to authorize and make loans for rural electrification. He also made studies, investigations, and reports concerning the condition and progress of the electrification of rural areas. He obtains funds from the Treasury at the request and approval of the Secretary of Agriculture and in such amounts as may be determined by Congress. Loans are made for the purpose of financing the construction and operation of generating plants, transmission lines, and distribution facilities. They carry an interest rate of 2 per cent and must be fully amortized in thirty-five years. Loans may also be made for wiring rural premises and for the purchase and installation of electrical and plumbing appliances. In 1950 a rural telephone program was added to REA's responsibilities by Congress.

Funds may be loaned to states, territories, municipalities, utility districts, and cooperatives. Privately owned utilities may also borrow from REA, but they have not done so in any appreciable amount; however, their own rural electrification activities were remarkably quickened. Funds were allocated according to a formula which allots 50 per cent to the states in proportion to the number of farms *not* receiving central station service. The other 50 per cent is allotted by the administrator in a manner to advance most effectively the purposes of the Act but with no state receiving more than 10 per cent of the second allotment.

Chart XIX gives a picture of the percentages of farms electrified as of June 30, 1952, and Chart XX of farms having telephones as of April 1, 1950. The first of these charts also shows how the degree of electrification serves as a guide in the allocation of funds to states. In 1949 loans to the amount of $1.9 billion had been processed to 1,044 borrowers, 955 of them cooperatives, at that time. Public Power Districts had received 43 loans, other public agencies 22 loans, and private electric utilities only 24 loans. About 87 per cent of the dollar amount of the loans had been used in the construction of distribution systems, 12 per cent for generation and transmission facilities and only 1 per cent for the financing of consumer installations. By 1952 electric loans approved numbered 1,082 and had increased to $2.6 billion, though the program was slowing down. On the other hand, telephone loans were increasing. They numbered 190 and allocated over $82 million for 66,000 miles of pole lines serving 251,050 subscribers. Small, independent commercial companies represented 110 of the borrowers; the remainder were cooperatives.

It should be noted that the only security for the loans from the government were the physical facilities and the revenues which these distribution

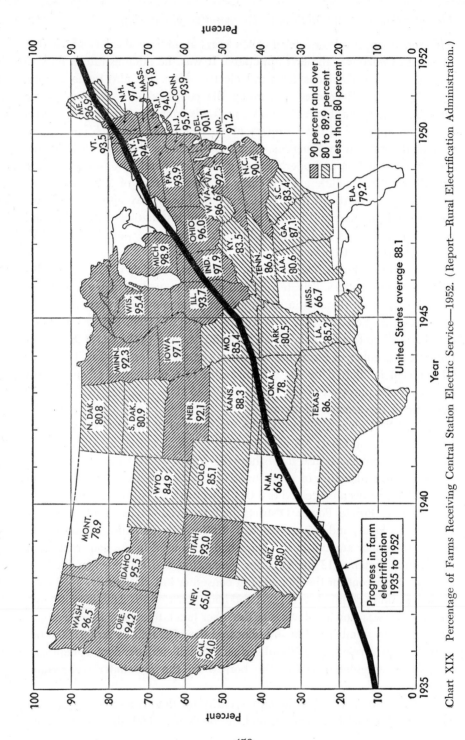

Chart XIX Percentage of Farms Receiving Central Station Electric Service—1952. (Report—Rural Electrification Administration.)

450

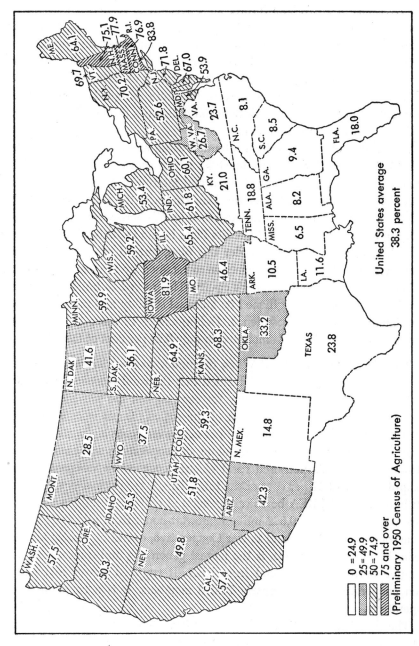

WASH. 57.5
ORE. 50.3
IDAHO 55.3
NEV. 49.8
CAL. 57.4
MONT. 28.5
WYO. 37.5
UTAH 51.8
ARIZ. 42.3
N. MEX. 14.8
N. DAK. 41.6
S. DAK. 56.1
NEB. 64.9
COLO. 59.3
KANS. 68.3
OKLA 33.2
TEXAS 23.8
MINN. 59.9
IOWA 81.9
MO. 46.4
ARK. 10.5
LA. 11.6
WIS. 59.2
ILL. 65.4
IND. 61.8
KY. 21.0
TENN. 18.8
MISS. 6.5
ALA. 8.2
GA. 9.4
FLA. 18.0
MICH. 53.4
OHIO 60.1
W. VA. 26.7
VA. 23.7
N.C. 8.1
S.C. 8.5
N.Y. 70.2
PA. 52.6
MD. 53.9
DEL. 67.0
VT. 75.1
N.H. 77.9
MASS. 76.9
R.I. 83.8
CONN. 71.8
ME. 64.1
69.7

United States average
38.3 percent

0 = 24.9
25 = 49.9
50 = 74.9
75 and over
(Preliminary 1950 Census of Agriculture)

Chart XX Percentage of Farms Having Telephones—1950. (Report—Rural Electrification Administration.

451

systems could produce—hence the importance of the Finance and Management Divisions of REA. The former kept account of loan transactions between borrowers and REA and between REA and the Treasury, while the latter gave advice and assistance in maintenance and operating procedures and in load building activities in particular. In many cases the directors and managers were without experience in operating electric utilities. Audits and inspections by these divisions were therefore designed not merely to verify records but also to forestall financial difficulties through improper expenditures and unwise commitments.

The degree of success which attended these efforts was borne out by the REA Administrator's Report for 1952 which showed that $361,898,705 had actually been paid on the principal and interest of all loans as against $314,422,633 actually due. Under the loan contracts the difference of $47,-912,558 constituted advance payments made by 674 borrowers on the principal of the loans under a Capital Credits Plan, begun in 1946 and supervised by the Management Division. Under this plan, instead of distributing patronage refunds, the excess payments were retained by the cooperative but credited to the individual member's equity. This served to build up the cooperative's net worth, strengthened its financial stability and paved the way for ultimate financial independence. Delinquencies of more than 30 days duration at the close of 1952 amounted to only 0.22 per cent of the total due.

The electric cooperative.   When the policy to electrify rural America was adopted in 1936, it was also decided that the rural electric cooperative should become the principal agency for carrying out the provisions of the law. At that time only 10.9 per cent of the nation's farms were electrified. In 1948, twelve years later, almost 80 per cent were receiving central station energy from some source, private, public, or cooperative; and among these distributors the REA-sponsored rural electric cooperative was preeminent by supplying about 57 per cent of the total. They were primarily purchasing distributors. In 1952 REA borrowers generated only 1,550 million kilowatt-hours while purchasing 9,622 million kilowatt-hours from other private or public sources. The Dairyland Power Cooperative, operating mostly in Wisconsin, Minnesota, and Iowa, is the largest generating and transmitting cooperative borrowing its capital from REA. It supplied power to twenty-seven cooperatives serving nearly 70,000 members. It is a cooperative of cooperatives.

The electric cooperative has become an important segment of the general cooperative movement in this country. It operates in accordance with the basic principles made famous by the Rochdale Pioneers of England. Briefly stated, these principles are: (1) Membership is open to all. (2) Control of the organization is democratic, that is to say, each member has only one vote. (3) It is based upon the principle of neutrality as far as political, religious, and racial considerations are concerned. (4) All trading is on a cash basis, cooperatives doing no credit business. (5) Only a limited interest is paid on the invested capital, the business not being conducted on the basis of a distribution of profits to members in proportion to their capital contribution. (6) Instead of the "profits" concept, cooperatives use the "savings" concept, the realized savings being returned to members in proportion to their patronage. (7) Cooperatives pursue an aggressive policy of education in the philosophy of cooperation.

Regulation.   Unlike privately owned utilities, the cooperative as a matter of state policy is not subject to regulation by state commissions. Only seven states (Kansas, Kentucky, Maryland, New Jersey, Virginia, West Virginia, Wyoming) regulate cooperatives as public utilities. The basic reason for this institutional difference is supposed to reside in the lack of conflict between the buyer and seller of public utility service in the case of the cooperative, which eliminates the necessity for state intervention. In other words, cooperatives are designed to practice self-regulation as far as their own sales policies or rates are concerned, although they may be subject to the jurisdiction of the commission as customers for the wholesale purchase of electric power from privately or publicly owned utilities. In Wisconsin, for instance, where municipally owned and privately owned utilities are alike subject to the jurisdiction of its state commission, contracts for power purchased from or sold to utilities come within the purview of commission regulation.

The Supreme Court of Utah, in holding that a cooperative was not a public utility and hence not subject to commission regulation, pointed out the difference between the two in *Garkane Power Co. v. Public Service Com.* [98 Utah 466, 470, *et seq.* (1940)] in rather definitive fashion:

The distinction between a public service corporation and a cooperative is a qualitative one. In a cooperative the principle of mutuality of ownership among all users is substituted for the conflicting interests that dominate the owner vender-nonowner vendee relationship. In a cooperative all sell to each. The owner is both seller and buyer . . .

In its argument the Commission contends that as a matter of policy it would be bad to allow cooperatives such as Garkane to escape the supervision and regulation on the theory largely, that they must be protected from themselves or the members be protected from mismanagement. On the contrary it appears that there is no need for regulation of true cooperatives. The theory of public utility regulation is based on a recognition that most public utilities are monopolistic, that their services are necessary or convenient to the residents of the area, and that because of the conflict of interest between the utility and its customers or consumers there are likely to arise situations where rates are so high as to deny service to many, or so low as to deny a fair return on its investment to the utility and its stockholders which in turn would tend to result in inadequate service. Therefore, regulation is desirable to harmonize and balance these interests. The services of Garkane may tend to be monopolistic in the area served because there is no other adequate utility to serve the residents there and its services will be convenient and useful if not vital to those residents, but the third element is totally lacking. There is no conflict of consumer and producer interests—they are one and the same. If rates are too high the surplus collected is returned to the consumers pro rata. If rates are too low the consumers must accept curtailed service or provide financial contribution to the Corporation. If service is not satisfactory the consumer-members have it in their power to elect other directors and demand certain changes. Resort to equity, as in the case of all mutuals, may be had if one group of members seeks to over-reach the others. The function of the Commission in approving rates, capital structure, etc., is unneeded by Garkane, its members, or the communities which it will serve . . .

We hold, therefore, that a non-profit electric cooperative which serves only its members, and is completely consumer-owned with each consumer limited to one membership, is not a public utility within the purview of our statute.

The principal remaining task is to coordinate the many units of public and cooperative enterprise with each other and with the private utility industry. This has already been done in various ways. The TVA has tied municipal ownership and cooperative ownership into an area-wide power system by being the sole supplier of electric power at wholesale under long-term contracts. Something like this has been happening in the Pacific Northwest where public and private utilities and cooperatives are purchasing power from the same source, the Bonneville Power Administration, under what amounts to a power-pooling plan.

27. LOS ANGELES
AND THE ECONOMICS
OF REGIONALISM

Los Angeles has the distinction of having developed the oldest and largest municipally owned public utility in the United States. Due to its location in a remote and arid region, the history of this city also provides an unusually clear illustration of the interdependence between natural resources and public utilities. Appropriation and utilization of soil and water, of minerals, forests, and marine resources would certainly have been slower and less intensive had not the utilities shown the way. Although the entire Pacific Southwest has attained a measure of fame as the Mecca of climate-conscious Americans (see Chart XXIV), it was the pressure of population upon resources that accelerated the development. Water for domestic, irrigation and industrial purposes is the *sine qua non* of economic life under desert conditions. To this has been added the demand for power which a mechanized and urbanized civilization makes. The region's economic watchwords have thus been "water and power" ever since it ceased being an appanage of Spanish culture in America. Appropriately, its municipally owned utility has come to be called the "Department of Water and Power."

With the integration of transport and the supply of gas and electric power inside and outside Los Angeles, the area was in a position to make rapid progress. There was, however, one cloud on an otherwise bright horizon. This was the uncertainty with respect to water supply for the area.

The use of local underground and surface waters for domestic, public, and irrigation purposes in supplying a rapidly increasing population was reaching the barrier which nature had interposed to expansion under semi-desert conditions. Many local water companies, the Los Angeles City Water Company among them, were beginning to show concern over the adequacy of future supply. It was under these conditions that the City of Los Angeles took over the private water company and proceeded with certain revolutionary plans of augmenting water and power supplies. Construction of the Los Angeles aqueduct between 1907 and 1913 and the arrival of this distant water supply inside the city on November 5, 1913, underwrote the expansion of the first four decades.

The immediate cause of this expansion appears to have been the continued exploitation of the oil and gas resources in the vicinity of the city, which gave rise to an oil refining industry that in turn inaugurated a southward trend in California manufacturing.

Industrialization which aimed at more than the supplying of local wants is definitely a development of the period beginning with World War I. Shipbuilding and the various phases of manufacturing, including aircraft construction, firmly established the goal of industrialization. An unwanted by-product was air pollution, which converted the beneficent and protective Los Angeles "fog" into the regional menace of "smog."

The industrial trend was a new factor in economic development. Extractive industry, resting more directly upon the exploitation of regional natural resources, continued its phenomenal progress. The salient facts are a matter of common knowledge. In livestock, dairy, and poultry production, in fruit, nut, truck, and field crops, there was continuous growth in the value of output, though there were significant shifts in their localization. In fine, the Los Angeles area during this period attained its status as a region of specialty crops.

Origin of the Department of Water and Power

The development of this municipal utility into one of the pillars of the economy of southern California can be quickly told. With the rapid population growth (see Table XII), beginning in the late 1890's, coupled with one

Table XII   Population of City and County of Los Angeles

Year	County	City	Per Cent City
1850	3,530	1,610	46
1860	11,333	4,385	39
1870	15,309	5,728	37
1880	33,881	11,183	33
1890	101,454	50,395	50
1900	170,289	102,479	60
1910	504,131	319,198	63
1920	936,455	576,673	62
1930	2,208,492	1,238,048	56
1940	2,785,643	1,504,277	54
1950	4,151,687	1,970,358	47

of those recurring periods of drought to which the region is subject, and with the inactivity of the private company in constructing new facilities, the conviction was borne in upon the citizens of Los Angeles that the private water supply system should be owned and operated by the city. A negotiated price of $2 million was fixed for the complete system of ditches, tunnels, reservoirs, distribution system, pumping plants, and infiltration galleries. Bonds to complete the purchase were voted in 1901 by a majority of five to one. On February 13, 1902, a municipal organization, known as the Board of Water Commissioners, was set up, and it proceeded to extend the system in all directions both by construction and by the purchase of other private systems that were having "water troubles."

Some early water utility problems. The most important of the city's acquisitions was William Mulholland, who had served the private company in the capacity of engineer and who was retained as superintendent together with the old personnel. The new management was conservative. Civil service principles were applied. The shortage of water led to the rapid introduction of meters and the substitution of meter rates for flat rates in order to check the reckless waste of water by many newcomers unfamiliar with conservation practices. Los Angeles was using more water per capita than any other city.

From the outset, due to the large city area of 43 square miles (now over 450) and the dispersion of settlement, there was a disproportion in the miles of main to population served. As the Board remarked:

The city early acquired the inconvenient habit of growing in spots, first in one locality and then another, jumping over broad intervals of space just as eligible for residence purposes between the two, in a manner most exasperating to those who had to follow up these capricious movements with the necessary public utilities.

The elevations to which water had to be pumped constituted (and still is) a distressing problem. The daily and seasonal peak demand required storage which was hard to find in the vicinity. The difficulties of financing expansion by means of general obligation bonds requiring a two-thirds vote forced a policy of financing through earnings, thus keeping rates high. But the principal difficulty was the threatened inadequacy of water supply.

Moisture falling as rain or snow upon the mountains to the north of the coastal plain on which the city lies is subject to rapid run-off, although it is also absorbed rapidly by the detritus of the valleys. These gravel beds afford convenient underground storage by retaining the water whence it may be recaptured through wells. Climatological records beginning in 1877 indicate that the water supply is markedly cyclical and seasonal. (See Charts XXI, XXII, XXIII, and XXIV.) The months from December to March normally yield two-thirds of the annual precipitation which must be stored in antici-

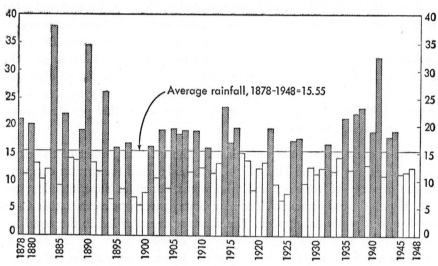

Chart XXI   Comparative Annual Rainfall—City of Los Angeles, 1878–1948.

pation of the heavy irrigation demands later. By 1904 pumping operations by the city and the irrigators in the surrounding territory had so lowered the plane of saturation (water table) that the continued growth and pros-

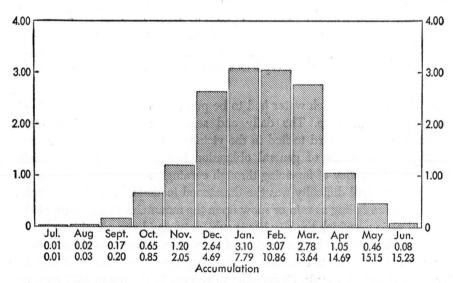

	Jul.	Aug	Sept.	Oct.	Nov.	Dec.	Jan.	Feb.	Mar.	Apr	May	Jun.
	0.01	0.02	0.17	0.65	1.20	2.64	3.10	3.07	2.78	1.05	0.46	0.08
	0.01	0.03	0.20	0.85	2.05	4.69	7.79	10.86	13.64	14.69	15.15	15.23

Accumulation

Chart XXII   Average Rainfall by Months—City of Los Angeles.

perity of the city was threatened. To divert water supplies from the tributary agricultural areas was robbing Peter to pay Paul. Hence the Board reported that the time had come when the flow of the Los Angeles River would have

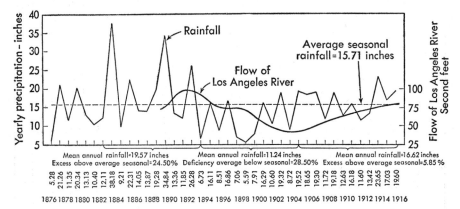

Chart XXIII   Relation between Rainfall and Flow of the Los Angeles River, 1876–1916.

to be supplemented, and it authorized an investigation of all available water resources by Superintendent Mulholland and J. B. Lippincott, a hydraulic engineer from the Reclamation Service. The report covered exhaustively the hydrography of Southern California and concluded that no adequate supplies were available south of the Tehachapi Mountains.

A solution of the problem was suggested in 1905 by Fred Eaton, former Mayor and city engineer. Having secured purchase options from ranchers in Owens Valley, 250 miles away, the plan was to bring this water to the

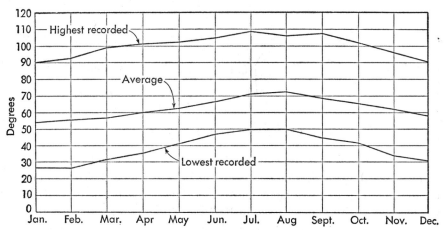

Chart XXIV   Maximum, Minimum, and Average Monthly Temperature. Los Angeles Weather Bureau.

city. It flowed down the eastern slope of the Sierra Nevada Mountains to the valley, where some of it was used for irrigation. The rest was drained off by the Owens River into Owens Lake, a dead sea of the Inyo Desert. (See Chart XXV.) After a detailed study of the proposal by Mulholland and

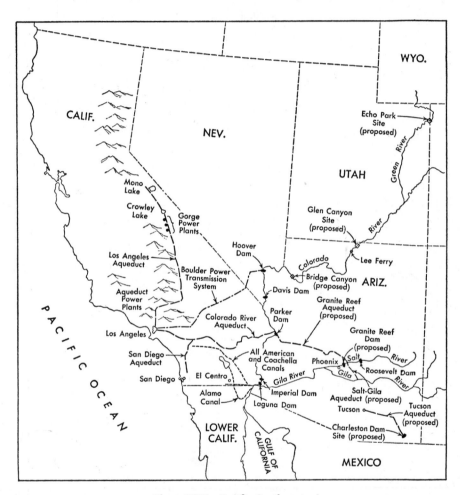

Chart XXV   Pacific Southwest.

others, who found that the construction of an aqueduct and reservoir system was feasible, an election was called in 1905 to vote $1,500,000 in bonds for the purchase of these lands and water rights. The bonds carried overwhelmingly, as did another issue in 1907 for $23 million for the actual construction of the aqueduct. A record-breaking undertaking for so small a city, the job was completed by the city's own construction organization headed by Mulholland at a cost within the original estimate. When the gates at the south portal of the terminal tunnel were opened and a flood of clear water plunged down the cascade into the San Fernando reservoir, Mulholland, in presenting the water to the people of Los Angeles on that memorable November 5, 1913, made what is probably the shortest dedicatory speech on record: "There it is. Take it."

Origin of the electric utility. Despite certain frustrating disagreements between Mulholland and Eaton, the latter wanting to exploit the power privileges for himself, the opportunity to develop hydroelectric energy along the line of the aqueduct was utilized by the city, thereby making this venture one of the first multiple-purpose projects on record. It is at this point that the power utility known as the Bureau of Power and Light had its inception and that the figure of E. F. Scattergood joins Henry Huntington and Mulholland as among the titans whose lengthened shadows are the series of great public and private works upon which rests the economy of southern California, if not of the entire Pacific Southwest.

The power opportunities are made possible by the differences in elevation between the source of the water in Owens Valley and the point of utilization in the Los Angeles area. Since these differences are greater than the necessary gradient for sustaining a gravity flow of water into the aqueduct, the gross head available at four points for power production was 1,960 feet. With a constant flow of water between 400 and 430 second-feet, these four aqueduct power plants, together with other additional power sites on tributary creeks and in the Owens River Gorge below Long Valley reservoir site, were estimated to be able to develop about 200,000 horsepower. Unfortunately, though a part of the original Scattergood plan, the Owens River Gorge plants were not built until 1951, owing to the aforementioned differences between Mulholland and Eaton. Only power from aqueduct plants of less than half this capacity and within 47 miles of the city became the first nucleus of public power transmitted to the city.

The Owens Valley tragedy. The somewhat devious procedures (often characteristic of public utility purchases of land and water rights) by means of which these water rights were acquired and consolidated for the city raised a storm of protest among the pioneer irrigators in Owens Valley who faced the prospect of having the valley dried up. A series of bombings of the Los Angeles aqueduct, which was carrying what the raiders regarded as *their* life-giving waters to the burgeoning metropolis on the other side of the mountains, gave tangible expression to these feelings of resentment and frustration. The city and the valley residents could have been spared this hu-

miliating experience if a more comprehensive plan of natural resource utilization had been inaugurated. Due to the exigencies of time and circumstances,
the Scattergood plan of developing water and power tributary to Long
Valley reservoir (now Lake Crowley) could not be brought to fruition. In
order to mollify some of the resentment in the valley, the City of Los Angeles
made extensive additional purchases of land and water rights and of commercial establishments in the urban communities. But absentee landlordism
was no substitute for some "grass roots" planning to meet the reasonable expectations of valley residents who wanted some irrigation water.

Period of conflict over power.   Meanwhile funds for the construction
of aqueduct power plants were authorized in 1910 in the amount of $3,500,-
000. However, the inadequacy of this original power-bond issue, the delay
through court proceedings in making even these funds available, the need
for charter amendments to reorganize the municipal agency, the authorization of additional power bonds in 1914 in the amount of $6,500,000, pro-
tracted negotiations with private utilities to purchase their distribution systems inside the city—all these being untoward incidents of a promotional
period—stalled the construction of power plants and of a transmission system and the inauguration of municipal distribution of electricity on a competitive basis until 1916. There was no material opposition to a publicly
owned water supply system, but the public development of a power supply
incidental to the aqueduct met determined opposition, chiefly from the private utilities then supplying the city. As the city's program developed into
one contemplating the retail sale of energy over a municipally owned distribution system, the opposition became more intense.

More growing pains.   The most immediate effect upon the city of the
new water supplies was a tremendous growth in area to over 450 square miles,
due to annexation of surrounding territory particularly in the San Fernando
Valley. These lands were being subdivided and required aqueduct water for
irrigation purposes. The subdivision of the original ranches into ever smaller
agricultural and residential units gave a renewed harvest to those real estate
operators fortunate enough to be within reach of the new supplies of water
and power. Such enrichment of the speculative and fortunate is an inevitable
by-product of private land ownership. Only public land ownership or "excess
condemnation" could prevent it. The systematic promotion of the city as a
residential, commercial, and industrial center, the discovery of important
oil and gas fields in 1921, the notoriety accompanying the development of
the motion picture industry, all ushered in an unprecedented period of growth
along many lines, especially after World War I. Once again the renewed

concentration of population raised fears as to the adequacy of the water resources. A series of dry years, of which 1924 (see Chart XXI) represents a particularly aggravated sample, brought on renewed agitation for an additional water supply from outside sources. In this new movement Los Angeles was joined by other communities in southern California where the water table had been falling and where the intrusion of ocean water was threatening. Under the leadership of Mulholland and Scattergood these efforts were directed this time toward bringing in the neglected water resources of the Colorado River, usually called "the last water hole" of the Pacific Southwest. With these developments the quest of Los Angeles for water, inevitably accompanied by the quest for power, passes on to a national stage where it has challenged the attention of the entire country.

Development of a Market Area

An amendment of the city charter in 1911 had created the Board of Public Service Commissioners and had given it full charge of the operation, maintenance, and extension of all works having to do with the production and distribution of water and power. Within the department were created the Bureau of Water Works and Supply, with Mulholland as chief engineer, and the Bureau of Power and Light, with Scattergood as chief electrical engineer. It was this simple organization built around two dominating personalities that made this municipal utility into a real going concern. With the aid of loyal and effective assistants, an organization was built up in which the "Power Bureau" more and more developed the earmarks of a fighting organization. While the "Water Bureau" easily achieved the position as sole distributor of water through a policy of purchase, the Power Bureau for years shared this market with the Los Angeles Gas and Electric Company and the Southern California Edison Company. After earlier efforts had been defeated, first to lease the aqueduct power sites for development to private companies, and later to induce the city to sell its power at wholesale to private franchise holders, Los Angeles undertook to build its own distribution system. On March 30, 1916, the first pole for the overhead distribution lines was set in the northeastern section of the city.

The competitive period. The Power Bureau began serving only a few thousand customers in territory competitive with the "Edison Company." By 1929 it had expanded the area of service to 220,710 customers. During this thirteen-year period, energy sold increased from about 15 million kilowatt-hours to 587 million kilowatt-hours. The Power Bureau's earlier operating history consisted of a seven-year period of competitive beginnings to 1923 and another period of stabilized competitive conditions during which the results of managerial and financial policies began to appear. By 1910, with the voting of the first power-bond issue, municipal policy had definitely settled down to developing its water and power resources under public ownership. It was officially declared and firmly embedded in the municipal charter by 1913. By amendment, the legal power to dispose of electric properties was withheld, as was the power to sell energy at wholesale, although surplus energy could be sold. Even the disposal of surplus was limited to municipalities and hedged about by means of revocable contracts. The power of sale to persons or corporations for redistribution was specifically denied.

In 1914 bonds to the amount of $6,500,000 were voted for the construction of power plants and a transmission system and for the construction or acquisition of a distributing system. As a preliminary, city officials, cooperating with civic organizations, undertook negotiations to acquire the lines of existing private electric utilities. Since the response to these overtures was deemed unsatisfactory, condemnation proceedings to acquire the property of the larger of these, the Southern California Edison Company, were determined upon. These proceedings [1] before the Railroad Commission of California were begun to determine a valuation of the Company's property within the City. To avoid the delay which would result from formal condemnation proceedings, especially since the completion of the first aqueduct power plant was within sight, the City proceeded with the construction of distribution lines paralleling those of the Edison Company in certain parts of the City. It is claimed that, upon being solicited, 80 per cent of the consumers along the City's lines signed up and were connected. It seems that this showing of determination on the City's part speeded up negotiations with the result that a purchase contract was finally obtained.

The purchase contract of 1917 gave the City the right and option to purchase the complete distribution system within the City consisting of lands, local distributing substations, low voltage distributing lines, poles, conduits, services, meters, and records. The option contract was necessary in order to give the City time to obtain authority to issue bonds. Essential to the purchase contract was an operating agreement, also negotiated between the parties at the same time and covering with its extensions the period of time between the taking of the option and the coming into possession of the property upon payment of the purchase price. The purchase agreement, as later modified, fixed a price of $11 million as of July 1, 1919, with allowance

---

[1] II California R.C. 83; *ibid.*, p. 588, Sept., 1916.

for extensions and betterments, less depreciation to the time of actual purchase.

The operating agreement also served as a legal device permitting the City to dispose of surplus power in excess of energy required by its own customers and thus obtain a revenue therefrom. During the term of the agreement the Company acted as the agent of the City in distributing such surplus to consumers served through the distributing system subject to purchase. The agreement further provided that the Company should have charge and control of the operation of such distributing system, collecting all bills and paying to the City the net proceeds after making certain deductions. These deductions covered (1) the actual costs of operation, maintenance, taxes and licenses; (2) the price of energy furnished consumers by the Company, representing demands not supplied through the City's surplus power; (3) a fixed monthly allowance of 8 per cent upon the option price for use of the Company's property; (4) a monthly allowance of 3.36 per cent for depreciation on the optioned property together with its extensions, such depreciation to be segregated in a special reserve and to follow the final ownership of the property. In addition, reciprocal standby or emergency services were provided for as between the Company and City plants. Under the agreement the City was, of course, empowered to complete the development of aqueduct power capabilities. The possibility of acquiring the steam generating plant and electric distributing system of the Los Angeles Gas and Electric Corporation was likewise contemplated and authorized.[2] A power purchase clause was designed to protect the Edison Company by supplying a market for its distant power plants not included under the option. The City agreed, on the other hand, not to construct electric distributing lines paralleling or duplicating the Edison system without its consent, except for street-lighting purposes.

[2] "The power purchase feature of the purchase agreement . . . provides that for a period of ten years, while the City may purchase and operate the existing steam plant of the Los Angeles Gas and Electric Corporation, it will otherwise confine its regular power generation to hydro-electric plants owned or controlled by it. That the Company will sell and deliver and the City will purchase from the Company, for a period of thirty years, all electric energy it may require for its own uses and for general distribution within the limits of the City in excess of the amount it may generate at such hydroelectric and steam plants, at rates to be fixed from time to time by the State Railroad Commission, and for supplying the City of Pasadena; that the Company shall have, for a period of fifteen years, the right and option to purchase upon written notice, any surplus electric energy the City may generate over and above such requirements and that the City may, with the approval of the majority vote of the people, terminate the whole agreement at the end of ten years from the date of purchase, or any time thereafter."

Eighteenth Annual Report, Board of Public Service Commissioners of the City of Los Angeles, p. 30, June 30, 1919.

Because of war conditions and delay occasioned by litigation instituted in behalf of hostile power interests, the bonds to consummate purchase could not be sold. Not until May 15, 1922, did the City finally come into possession of the property. While the $13,500,000 of power bonds had been voted in 1919, they were not actually sold and delivered until February, 1922. Thus, for more than four years, the Company operated the property subject to acquisition under the option contract.

Nevertheless, the favorable rates for service, and particularly power service put into effect in 1917, so aided the industrial growth of the City that all aqueduct power was easily absorbed, and the search was begun for additional power resources in the Sierra Nevadas and on the Colorado River. The principal reason assigned for this search for means of extending the municipal generating system was that the electric power generated by the municipal system was said to cost about .45 cents per kilowatt-hour, while that purchased from the Southern California Edison Company cost approximately 1.05 cents per kilowatt-hour. At the close of the fiscal year, June 30, 1922, 70 per cent of the power supplied to municipal consumers was generated at municipal plants, while the remaining 30 per cent had to be purchased.

The period of stabilized competition. It has always been a fixed point in the City's policy to achieve complete monopolization of the electric distributing facilities within the City. The Los Angeles Chamber of Commerce especially, among the civic organizations, sponsored this program in order to avoid the economic waste which would follow duplication of investment and operation. The city officials responsible for the management of the properties were likewise anxious to bring about city-wide monopoly in electric service because it was hoped that thereby the constant temptation for private power interests to interfere with the City's general development program would in large measure be abated. The failure of friendly negotiations during the early 1930's toward this end prompted the City to undertake the condemnation of the electric properties and business of the Los Angeles Gas and Electric Corporation. While earlier efforts at paralleling had abated, this form of competition, together with the haphazard and uncontrolled expansion in facilities by rival utilities into newly annexed territories had left the City with a hodgepodge of market areas. Hence the opinion was held by many that the full measure of benefit from public operation would not be achieved until monopolization of electric service within the City was complete.

Municipal management. On December 1, 1928, after more than fifty years of service with the water supply system, Mr. Mulholland resigned as general manager and chief engineer of the Water Bureau. He was succeeded by H. A. Van Norman who had been in the service of the Water Bureau since the days of aqueduct construction. For a short period, that is to say, for the fiscal year 1929, the bifurcated division of responsibility was eliminated, and Mr. Van Norman served as general manager of both utilities, with F. E. Weymouth serving as chief engineer of the Water Works and E. F. Scattergood as chief electrical engineer. However, the original organization and division of responsibility was again restored. This temporary reorganization was a reflection of a political upheaval in the Board which for a time was divided into a pro- and anti-Scattergood faction. On the whole the Board was remarkably free from outside political interference and from internal frictions. Much of the credit for this must be given to a number of outstanding members of the Board who were imbued with a high sense of public service and of local patriotism and who gave long years of service to the organization. Among this number, Dr. John R. Haynes, a migrant to Los Angeles of an earlier day, was outstanding. It was his political astuteness, social vision, and ability to conciliate and arbitrate that again and again kept the concern going. He also must be numbered among the titans.

The Board of five members, now known as the Department of Water and Power, is in effect both a regulating and managing agency, subject to the control of the municipal Council but protected by provisions of a Home Rule charter. The commissioners serve terms of five years, with staggered expiration dates. They are appointed or removed by the Mayor subject in both appointment and removal to approval by majority vote of the Council.

The general powers and duties of the Board are such as are usually exercised by the board of directors of a private corporation. They are empowered to hold, regulate, and control all property for the production and distribution of water and electric power. It is their duty to construct, operate, maintain, extend, manage, and control such utilities, and they are empowered to acquire and take property by purchase, lease, condemnation, or otherwise. Since publicly owned and operated public utilities in California were not subject to the jurisdiction of the California Railroad Commission, the Board also fixed the rates to be charged for water or electric energy, for use within or without the City, subject, however, to the approval of the Council by ordinance. A general rule for the guidance of the Board in fixing rates is provided, the material part of which reads as follows:

Such rates shall be so fixed at least every two years; provided that, except as hereinafter otherwise prescribed, such rates shall be of uniform operation, as near as may be, and shall be fair and reasonable, taking into consideration, among other things, the nature of the use, the quantity supplied and the value of the service; provided, further, that the rates inside the City may be less, but not greater, than the rates outside the City for the same or similar uses.

It is, therefore, important to note that the Board is, in effect, both a regulating and a managing agency subject to the superior control of the municipal Council as the legislative arm of a public corporation, the City of Los Angeles.

The Department as a Going Concern

With the acquisition of the electric distribution system of the Los Angeles Gas & Electric Company in 1936, the economic goal was achieved which enabled this municipal electric system to operate as a true public utility with monopoly in supply. This had long been the economic position of the municipal water system. The economic and financial facts of this long history since 1902 have been presented in an unbroken series of reports which present all the needed detail. Since 1916 these reports were significantly improved through the adoption of a "business type" audit by Price, Waterhouse and Company first for the Bureau of Power and Light under the leadership of Scattergood. These audits were later extended to the Bureau of Waterworks and Supply. Together with the adoption of the standardized classifications of accounts prescribed by commissions, the audited accounts tell a reliable story of the financial progress made by this going concern.

The end result of a financial history. In order to show what has been achieved, we present the balance sheets for fiscal 1952 (the fiftieth anniversary) in condensed form, together with appropriate comment. Table XIII and Table XIV show respectively the balance sheet for the water system and for the power system.

Comments on financial and accounting policies. It should be noted that the plant in service is carried at original cost and that accrued depreciation has been deducted from cost new, thus making the amount of book cost a net figure.

Funded debt still contains a relatively large amount of general obligation bonds, but the amount of revenue bonds outstanding is increasing while that of general obligation bonds is declining. First used by the power system, the revenue bond has also become a flexible means of financing the water utility. The department was a pioneer in the introduction and first use of the revenue bond, the principal advantage of which is that it can be issued without calling for a referendum election. Revenue bonds are obligations only of the department, payable out of the water revenue funds. They usually carry a call privilege and may thus be retired and new revenue bonds issued at lower interest rates. On the other hand, general obligation bonds cannot be called for redemption. Revenue bonds had recently been issued at a premium with an over-all effective interest rate of 2.75 per cent per annum.

Depreciation has been accrued in the case of the water system on a straight line basis, with minor exceptions, on all items of depreciable property, and the assignment of lives has been reviewed from time to time. Power system depreciation, on the other hand, has been computed, again with minor exceptions, on a 5 per cent sinking-fund basis, both the annuity and interest being credited to the reserve. In both cases the reserve is charged with the cost of retirements less salvage plus cost of removal.

The tax situation. No state or local taxes are paid on the operations of the Department inside the city, only as *local* taxes are assessed against property located outside the city. Nothing in the way of an equivalent to the federal corporate net income tax is assessed against the city. Each year, however, there is a transfer from net income of the water and power utility to the general and reserve funds of the city. This represents a payment in lieu of taxes. At one time considerable amounts in the way of free water and power service was being rendered to other city departments. These have now been eliminated. Payments in lieu of taxes appear to be a variable amount. In 1943, for instance, $440,900, or 3.2 per cent, of gross revenue was so transferred by the water system, while only three years later $1,860,000, or 11.3 per cent, was so transferred. Transfers from the power system for the same years were $2,060,000, or 5.5 per cent, and $2,400,000, or 5.6 per cent, respectively, a much more regular schedule of payments. This may be compared with total of all taxes of Southern California Edison Company which paid about $34 million in 1952, or more than 26 per cent of gross revenues, while the Los Angeles power system was paying only $2,674,000, or a little over 4 per cent.

The accumulation of an equity. A very important aspect of the public ownership movement is the gradual accrual of an equity by the owning entity. This is best illustrated by utilities having a long and financially successful history, like the Department of Water and Power which celebrated its Fiftieth Anniversary on February 6, 1952, although its tap root goes back to 1781, the founding of the City. From precarious beginnings this concern developed under municipal management into one of the most successful public enterprises. With the full faith and credit of the City behind it, general obligation bonds were issued for the original purchase price of $2 million in 1902 and from time to time for extensions and purchases of additional units

Table XIII   Balance Sheet, Department of Water and Power
Water System, June 30, 1952

Assets 1952

UTILITY PLANT, AT ORIGINAL COST:
Plant in service (excluding lands) $210,686,887
Less accumulated provisions for depreciation .... (65,820,801)

$144,866,086
Lands 36,767,573
Construction work in progress 2,122,471

$183,756,130

CONSTRUCTION FUNDS:
United States Treasury obligations and cash deposited with City
Treasurer .... $ 7,229,343
Less amount payable to revenue fund (see below) .... (647,494)

$ 6,581,849

LONG-TERM RECEIVABLE:
From Power System of the Department due in equal monthly installments to October, 1974, plus interest at 4½% .... $ 1,015,269

BOND REDEMPTION AND INTEREST FUNDS:
Deposits with City Treasurer for payment of—
Matured bonds and interest coupons .... $ 82,186
Bonds and interest coupons maturing subsequent to year end 357,765

$ 439,951

CURRENT AND WORKING ASSETS:
Deposits with City Treasurer .... $ 1,361,606
Amount receivable from construction funds (see above) 647,494
Cash on hand and revolving funds 157,810
Customers and miscellaneous accounts receivable, less allowance for
losses 2,053,999
Construction and operating materials and supplies, at approximate cost 4,660,957

$ 8,881,866

DEFERRED CHARGES:
Preliminary survey and investigation expenditures .... $ 459,096
Deferred stores, shop, and miscellaneous expenses 327,625
Unamortized bond issue expenses, less bond premiums received 44,399

$ 831,120

$201,506,185

of water and electric utility properties. With its credit established, the department was authorized to issue revenue bonds, thus freeing both the water and
electric system from dependence upon municipal credit.

The water and electric utility also had the benefit of financial contributions from the taxpayers in earlier years. Except in the case of the water
system, these have now been completely repaid, albeit without allowances

Table XIII   (*Continued*)

Liabilities 1952

FUNDED DEBT:
General obligation bonds .... $ 32,021,000
Revenue bonds 35,350,000

$ 67,371,000

> Note: Funded debt at June 30, 1952, included $2,879,000 regular ma-
> turities occurring in the succeeding fiscal year and $22,000 matured
> but not presented for payment.

ACCRUED INTEREST ON BONDS:
(Including at June 30, 1952, $60,186 matured coupons not presented
for payment) .... $ 597,251

OTHER CURRENT LIABILITIES:
Accounts payable, accrued expenses, payrolls, etc. .... $ 2,181,946
Customers' deposits 1,996,813

$ 4,178,759

INVESTMENT FROM PROCEEDS OF GENERAL TAXATION .... $ 10,068,501

CONTRIBUTIONS IN AID OF CONSTRUCTION .... $ 41,670,481

INCOME RETAINED FOR USE IN THE BUSINESS (EARNED SURPLUS) ...... $ 77,620,193

PURCHASE COMMITMENTS:
For construction and purchase contracts and materials, etc.:
At June 30, 1952 .... $7,696,000

$201,506,185

for interest. In 1952 only $10,068,501 remained as "investment from the pro-
ceeds of general taxation" in a balance sheet showing assets of $201,506,185
in the water utility.

Another item of importance is represented by contributions in aid of
construction, which were of special importance in the case of the water
utility. In 1952 they aggregated $41,670,481 for the water system but only
$3,077,778 for the power system.

Table XIV   Balance Sheet, Department of Water and Power
Power System, June 30, 1952

Assets 1952

UTILITY PLANT, AT ORIGINAL COST:

Plant in service (excluding lands) $350,280,227
Generating facilities in process of retirement 6,196,710
Less accumulated provisions for depreciation .... (88,110,508)

$268,366,429

Lands 20,010,677
Construction work in progress 21,462,556

$309,839,662

CONSTRUCTION FUNDS:

United States Treasury obligations and cash deposited with City
Treasurer .... $ 18,768,286
Less amount payable to revenue fund (see below) .... (2,603,636)

$ 16,164,650

BOND REDEMPTION AND INTEREST FUNDS:

Deposits with City Treasurer for payment of—
Matured bonds and interest coupons .... $ 64,571
Bonds and interest coupons maturing subsequent to year end 663,224
Principal and premium on bonds called for redemption in November
1952 (see contra) 5,793,750

$ 6,521,545

SPECIAL DEPOSITS:

For acquisition of land and rights of way, etc. .... $ 93,436

CURRENT AND WORKING ASSETS:

Deposits with City Treasurer (part invested in United States Treasury
obligations) .... $ 7,064,419
Amount receivable from construction funds (see above) 2,603,636
Cash on hand and revolving funds 234,796
Customers and miscellaneous accounts receivable, less allowance for
losses 4,736,634
Construction and operating materials and supplies, at approximate cost 11,052,796

$ 25,692,281

DEFERRED CHARGES:

Unamortized bond redemption and issue expenses—
Premiums paid on bonds refunded .... $ 3,899,170
Premium required on bonds called for redemption in November 1952 168,750
Bond issue expense, less premiums received 681,375

$4,749,295

Advance contributions to employees' retirement fund 1,502,746
Advance payment of generating charges for Hoover power plant 5,004,721
Preliminary survey and investigation expenditures 438,990
Deferred stores, shop, and miscellaneous expenses 1,163,819

$ 12,859,571

$371,171,145

Table XIV   (*Continued*)

Liabilities 1952

FUNDED DEBT:
General obligation bonds .... $ 14,343,000
Revenue bonds, excluding bonds called for redemption in November
1952 137,825,000
Long-term obligation to Water System of the Department 1,015,269

$153,183,269

Revenue bonds called for redemption in November 1952, including
$168,750 call premium (see bond redemption and interest funds—
contra) 5,793,750

$158,977,019

Note: Funded debt at June 30, 1952, included $5,402,000 regular ma-
turities occurring in the succeeding fiscal year and $2,000 matured
but not presented for payment.

ACCRUED INTEREST ON BONDS:
(Including at June 30, 1952, $62,571 matured coupons not presented
for payment) 797,917

OTHER CURRENT LIABILITIES:
Accounts payable, accrued expenses, payrolls, etc. (including at June
30, 1952, $775,860 payable from construction fund) 4,647,180

DEFERRED INCOME:
Received from cities of Burbank, Glendale, and Pasadena, for rentals
of transmission and other facilities, applicable to future periods 3,732,175

CONTRIBUTIONS IN AID OF CONSTRUCTION 3,077,778

INCOME RETAINED FOR USE IN THE BUSINESS (EARNED SURPLUS) 199,939,076

PURCHASE COMMITMENTS:
For construction contracts and materials, etc.
At June 30, 1952 .... $35,250,000

$371,171,145

Although both the water and power systems have charged rates sufficient to pay all the fixed and variable costs of operation, these rates, especially in the case of the power utility, were at times set with the view of financing extensions out of earnings. This has served to expand the equity of the City. At the end of fifty years of operation the income retained for use in the business was $77,620,193 for the water system and $199,939,076 for the power system. As a result of this management policy, the City now has an equity of $277,559,269 in utility properties, conservatively estimated to have cost $572,677,330.

The foregoing estimate of cost is conservative because the balance sheets reproduced in Tables XIII and XIV carry the utility plant in service at original cost, in accord with the requirements of the California Public Utility Commission. They are also conservative because the accumulated provision for depreciation on all properties except lands has been deducted from these original cost figures. The amounts of depreciation accumulated were $65,-820,801 for the water system and $88,110,508 for the power system, or $153,-931,309 for the department as a whole. These amounts have been collected from rate-payers because they represent an estimate of the amount of pecuniary capital which has been used up. Until needed for retirement purposes, this total, along with the aggregate earned surplus, is available for internal financing of extensions and improvements, and thereby reduces the outside indebtedness of the two utilities.

As already stated, the figures reproduced in the balance sheet can be relied upon as representing the facts because they have been audited for many years by independent auditors. Since the long-time controller of the department, Clyde Errett, has been responsible to the City Council, this arrangement has produced one of the finest and most reliable municipal utility accounting and record-keeping system in America.

A concluding observation.   This municipally owned utility is now run on a business basis with a minimum of political interference and with good civil service standards. Earlier accounting deficiencies due to the youth of the enterprise have been corrected. Except as it enjoys the tax advantage of freedom from federal and state taxation, which is inherent in the institutional setup of all public agencies, this utility can serve as a yardstick of comparison with respect to the cost of many of its operations. This capacity to be used for comparison purposes by regulating agencies is the most important contribution privately and publicly owned utilities can make toward each other's efficiency of operation under dominantly monopolistic conditions.

28. CALIFORNIA
AND THE COLORADO RIVER

Explorations

In 1856, one Thomas H. Blythe settled in the Palo Verde Valley, the first Californian to irrigate with Colorado River water. About twenty years later he made the first filing to use its waters on his Rancho. Meanwhile, Lt. Ives in 1857 had explored the lower Colorado, as far as the Black Canyon, for the War Department, pronouncing it "altogether valueless"; and Major J. W. Powell in 1869 explored the dangerous canyon section for the Geological Survey, the first white man to traverse the Grand Canyon. In 1860 Dr. O. M. Wozencraft, a dentist, and Ebenezer Hadley first proposed the irrigation of Imperial Valley's rich but desert lands, lying 250 feet below sea level, with water drawn from the elevated Colorado River. They contemplated using a canal route which followed the Alamo River through Mexico in order to avoid shifting sand dunes on the American side of the border. However, the project simmered for a long time, and construction was not started until the late 1890's by the California Development Company. By 1901 water from the Colorado was transforming a desert into a winter vegetable and fruit garden with a year-round growing season.

The primary need for flood control. Disaster struck the valley in November, 1905, when a flash flood coming from the Gila River, a lower tributary of the Colorado, swept through a break in the diversion dam and poured the full flow of the Colorado River into the valley for sixteen months. The flood inundated 30,000 acres of crop lands to form Salton Sea, destroying homes, highways, and railways. The breach was finally closed and the river once more coursed through its delta cone to the Gulf of Lower California, thanks to the heroic efforts of E. H. Harriman and his Southern Pacific Railway. But the flood menace remained because the silt-laden river when in flood was hard to confine within its levee-protected banks.

Other irrigation developments had also started on the Arizona side in Indian reservations and at Yuma, and at the confluence of the Gila and Colorado Rivers; most significant for the future was irrigation on the rich delta lands across the international boundary in Mexico. The attempt to fight a swollen river, depositing millions of tons of silt in its channel, with levees as the only defensive measure, was proving costly in the extreme. Yet again there were times when the river was dry, and the irrigated crops were withering for lack of moisture. It was a vicious cycle of flood and drought so characteristic of that section of the great American desert.

Enter the Reclamation Service.   At this point the Reclamation Service came forward with a proposal to control the river at its source. It had been studying and planning since 1902 an economically feasible approach to the central problem of the arid West, that of equating a deficient rainfall with a more than sufficient land supply. In 1914 Congress appropriated $50,000 for a study of the entire Colorado basin. Interrupted by war, these efforts finally bore fruit in 1918 when an agreement was executed between the United States and the Imperial Irrigation District for the construction of an entirely new All-American Irrigation Canal. This would avoid the sharing of a deficient water supply with Mexican irrigators as was true of the old Alamo Canal. In the same year, J. T. Whister, an engineer from the Bureau of Reclamation, recommended storage projects on the upper Colorado River of from 10 to 12 million acre-feet to regulate the stream flow. This proposal to build dams so far away, while of some help toward the control of floods, appeared inadequate, considering that the need was for flood control *and* irrigation in the lower reaches of the river. At this juncture a new series of reports by Director A. P. Davis of the Reclamation Bureau and by a Board of Engineers (among them J. L. Savage, the designer of Hoover Dam) showed that natural conditions favored a high dam at the lower end of the canyon section, where storage in excess of 30 million acre-feet was physically practicable and financially feasible. A dam in either Boulder or Black Canyon would master the river by creating a reservoir large enough to store two years' flow.

However persuasive may have been the urging of Congressman Phil Swing, representing the Imperial Irrigation District, that the federal government lend a hand in controlling the river, nothing happened until the demand of the Los Angeles basin for more water and power secured the passage of the Boulder Canyon Project Act which started that nation-wide movement in Congress for regional development of natural resources. The more important steps in this process should be noted.

By 1920 the population in the Los Angeles basin had grown well beyond a million. The area outside the city had been depending upon its bountiful supplies of underground water, but the rate of extraction became too great.

Where 2,500 artesian wells and thousands of pumped wells were flowing in 1900, by 1930 the water table was falling so rapidly that only 22 artesian wells remained. It was estimated at the time that these underground sources were being overdrawn at the rate of 600 acre-feet per day.

Enter the Metropolitan Water District. Yet the wealth built upon the foundations of these vanished flows could not be abandoned. Although the central city once again assumed the leadership, the threat of a water famine was so widespread that a new type of public corporation was needed to spark the movement. In 1927 the California legislature passed a Metropolitan Water District Act, the uniqueness of which was that it authorized an *association* of municipalities and other political entities whose areas *did not need to be contiguous.* Thirteen cities joined in 1928 to organize the Metropolitan Water District of Southern California by virtue of this enabling legislation.

The Act is entitled:

An act providing for the incorporation, government, and management of metropolitan water districts, authorizing such districts to incur bonded debt and to acquire, construct, operate and manage works and property, providing for the taxation of property therein and the performance of certain functions relating thereto by officers of counties, providing for the addition of area thereto and the exclusion of area therefrom and authorizing municipal corporations to aid and participate in the incorporation of such districts.

In effect, the Metropolitan Water District, abbreviated as MWD, is a government, set up to carry on a public utility function which is deemed to be governmental in character. For this purpose the district is given the power of eminent domain. It is authorized, subject to a 15 per cent limitation of the assessed value of taxable property, to borrow money and to issue bonds and other evidences of indebtedness. More important, it is authorized to *levy and collect taxes* for the purpose of carrying on operations and paying the obligations of the district. This power to tax is without limitation of rate or amount for the purpose of meeting both principal and interest requirements of bonded indebtedness and to pay obligations to the United States.

The district is empowered to acquire water and water rights within or without the state; to develop, store, and transport water, and to sell and deliver it at wholesale for municipal and domestic uses. Looking toward the Colorado River, the district is specifically authorized to contract with the United States or any board, department, or agency thereof.

The district is empowered to fix water rates which must be uniform for like classes of service and which in so far as practical will result in revenue sufficient to pay operating expenses, provide for repairs and maintenance, and meet interest and principal requirements on the bonded debt. To meet any deficiency in revenues, apart from the requirements of bonded indebtedness and obligations to the United States, the District also has the power to tax but is subject to a limit of 5 cents on each $100 of assessed valuation.

The Metropolitan Water District as a legal concern. The foregoing powers are vested in and exercised by a board of directors consisting of at least one representative from each municipality of those comprising the district. They are appointed by the chief executive officers of municipalities with the consent of the governing bodies. In 1928 the electorates of eleven municipalities (Beverly Hills, Burbank, Glendale, Los Angeles, Pasadena, San Marino, Santa Monica, Anaheim, Santa Ana, Colton, San Bernardino) voted to include their respective areas in the MWD. Other municipalities and water districts have since voted at an accelerating rate to join the MWD as the scarcity of water has borne in upon public consciousness. San Diego dropped its original plan of service via the All-American Canal and is now a part of the MWD as the San Diego County Water Authority. As of 1953 the estimated area comprised within the MWD is 1,751 square miles; its estimated population, 4,342,000; and its assessed valuation subject to taxation, over $6 billion. In this aggregate Los Angeles represents about one-half of the total in population and assessed valuation. Of 29 directors, Los Angeles is represented by 7 directors, but its voting power based upon the assessed value of property is limited to 260 votes in a total of 520 votes, although the assessed value of its taxable property is 52 per cent of the district total.

The constitutionality of the enabling Act was tested in *City of Pasadena v. Chamberlin* (204 Cal. 653) and upheld by the California Supreme Court. The Court held, in effect, that the supply of water from an outside source and its distribution in accordance with some common plan may, like the supply of sanitation, be a matter of broader scope than can be adequately handled by single municipal authorities. It "falls within the class of public purposes, such as irrigation and reclamation, for which the Legislature has the undoubted authority to provide governmental agencies or districts by general laws."

But the main objection to the Act was that the taxes authorized to be imposed were in the nature of assessments to be levied and collected upon the people of a municipality and upon their individual properties for benefits received. They were, however, to be imposed without an opportunity for property holders to be heard on the question of whether or not they wanted the burden imposed or whether they wanted their property to receive such benefits. The Act, therefore, was in violation of the due process clause of the state and federal constitution. In rejecting this contention the Court distinguished between taxes and special assessments. It could see no difference between taxes levied by municipalities for municipal water-supply purposes and taxes imposed by municipal water districts or public utility districts or metropolitan water districts. In the former

public taxation is imposed and collected upon the inhabitants of the municipalities *regardless of the benefits conferred upon particular property* [emphasis supplied] and by the same method by which taxes are generally levied and collected for the carrying on of the governmental functions of incorporated cities and towns.

In the case of the specially organized districts, "while these may not exercise all of the functions committed to municipal corporations, strictly so called, [they] *have come to be recognized as at least quasi governmental in character*" [emphasis supplied].

A final contention was that the board of directors provided for in the Act constituted a special commission and as such according to state law could not exercise the taxing power. This the Court disposed of by holding the board of directors to be governing officials in the same sense as the city council of a municipality and not a special commission. With the disposal of this litigation the legal path was cleared for the joint construction of a second great water carrier to the Los Angeles coastal area.

The Colorado River Aqueduct. Assuming the costs of the preliminary investigations which had been incurred by the Los Angeles Bureau of Waterworks and Supply, the MWD in 1930 began the planning and construction of an aqueduct along the route recommended by its chief engineer, F. E. Weymouth. Actual excavation started in January, 1933, and the first delivery of softened water was made to Pasadena in June, 1941. Beginning at a diversion point 155 miles below Hoover Dam, water released from Lake Mead storage is impounded in a reservoir of 717,000 acre-feet capacity created by Parker Dam. This raises the water level by 72 feet and regulates and clarifies the supply. It is pumped into an aqueduct system having 92.1 miles of tunnel, 28.7 miles of inverted siphons, 54.4 miles of covered conduit, and 62.8 miles of open, concrete lined canals. The flow terminates in Cajalco Reservoir (now Lake Mathews) of 225,000 acre-feet capacity, from which water is distributed to the gateway of local water systems after passing through a filtration and water-softening plant. Along the main aqueduct are five pumping plants, providing a pumping lift of 1,617 feet so distributed along the rising portion of the route as to secure the most economical fit between the aqueduct and the ground level. It is to these points that Hoover Dam electric power is transmitted.

Parker Dam was designed by and constructed under the direction of the Bureau of Reclamation with funds furnished by the MWD. This arrangement avoided the complications involved in the damming of an interstate stream, such as the opposition of Arizona which declared martial law to prevent construction by a California agency. The federal government retains title to the dam but operates it for the benefit of the MWD. Half the power privilege of a total capacity of 120,000 kilowatts and a limited right to regulate the top 10 feet of storage are reserved to the United States. The remaining 60,000 kilowatts belong to the District and are used in pumping. We must now turn to other developments on the Colorado River without which these water diversions to the coastal plain would have been impossible.

The Colorado River Compact

The rate of economic development in the states of the lower part of the basin, particularly in southern California and Arizona, had been outstripping that of the states in the upper part of the basin. It became apparent that the normal flow of the river might not be sufficient to meet both the accelerated appropriation in the lower basin and the future demands of the states that had been lagging behind. With the proposal to create such extensive water storage in the lower canyon section, it was feared that under the law of prior appropriation, lower basin priorities might thwart the water use plans of Colorado, Wyoming, and Utah. Since the law respecting the use of water from interstate streams was indefinite, it was felt that the jurisdiction of the federal government should be invoked to set up guaranties to protect these future interests in water. The Swing-Johnson Bill (Senator Hiram Johnson of California had undertaken to sponsor the plans of Los Angeles) authorizing the Boulder Canyon Project and the All-American Canal would have met the determined opposition of these upper basin interests unless these water uses were regulated and apportioned. Accordingly, Congress in 1921 authorized a compact between the states comprising the Colorado basin. A commission was at once set up under the chairmanship of Secretary of Commerce Herbert Hoover. Hearings were held and a Colorado River Compact was signed at Santa Fe on November 24, 1922. The allocation of water thus arrived at requires the states in the upper basin above Lee's Ferry (see Chart XXV), i.e., Wyoming, Colorado, New Mexico, and Utah, to guarantee the delivery during each 10-year period of not less than 75 million acre-feet to the lower basin. Thus, the lower basin states, i.e., Arizona, California, and Nevada, were apportioned an average annual amount of 7½ million acre-feet for beneficial consumptive use, to which was added an additional 1 million acre-feet of beneficial water use per year from sources below Lee's Ferry. With 7½ million acre-feet per year apportioned to the upper basin states, a *minimum* annual use of 16 million acre-feet has thus been definitely allocated.

The compact further provided that, if the United States should by some future treaty allocate water to Mexico, the Mexican portion should first be derived from any surplus available above the allocated 16 million acre-feet, and if this surplus be insufficient, then the deficiency was to be supplied equally by the two basins.

The Boulder Canyon Project Act

The way was now cleared for the actual construction of the necessary hydraulic works. However, Congress had always looked askance at the proposal because of the heavy costs involved. Accordingly, proponents suggested that the proceeds from the generation and sale of the large blocks of power that would become available would eventually return all the costs of the project to the federal government. In 1923, Los Angeles, through its Bureau of Waterworks and Supply, had begun investigations and surveys of the possible routes and designs of an aqueduct from the Colorado River. Eliminating the alternative of a gravity route, Mulholland came to the conclusion that the most practical diversion from the river was below Boulder Dam at an elevation which would require an aqueduct with five pumping lifts to bring the water to a terminal reservoir. (See Chart XXV.) It also appeared that the passage of the Swing-Johnson bill would be facilitated if the federal government could contract with financially competent agencies empowered to contract for these large quantities of water and power. This was the fundamental reason for setting up the Metropolitan Water District.

After a long, political battle Congress passed the Boulder Canyon Project Act which was approved by President Coolidge on December 21, 1928. It authorized the construction of Boulder (now Hoover) Dam and power plant and the All-American Canal at an expenditure limited to $165 million. The latter project was planned to supply an irrigable area of about 1 million acres in the Imperial and Coachella Valleys. This irrigation system was to be located entirely within the United States and was designed to save the costs and complications of maintaining the old delivery canals in Mexico.

The California Limitation Act. Before the Boulder Canyon Project Act could become fully effective, the signature of the basin states had to be secured. This proved to be difficult only in the cases of Arizona and California. Congress had approved the compact in the Act itself, but because it was feared that Arizona might not ratify, an alternative was provided for. Congress declared that the Act should not take effect unless ratified by at least six states, including California. Moreover, California was required irrevocably and unconditionally to agree with the United States for the benefit of the other states, including nonratifying Arizona, that its total annual consumptive use would not exceed 4,400,000 acre-feet out of the 7,500,000 acre-feet available to the lower basin, plus California's one-half share of the unapportioned surplus water. In 1929 California passed this so-called Limitation Act in direct response to this alternative, so that the Project Act could be declared fully effective by Presidential proclamation on June 25, 1929.

It is important to note the reasons assigned by Arizona for refusing to ratify the compact as stated by the chairman of its Colorado River Commission. In the first place, Arizona objected to the inclusion of the run-off of the Gila River under the compact, regarding that river as peculiarly its own. Second, Arizona objected because it contended that the prior appropriation doctrine remained in full force and effect as between California and Arizona. While the compact with its allocation of water supply had been substituted for this doctrine as between the two basins, thus ending the fear that California would appropriate great amounts of water through the All-American Canal or other aqueducts, yet this danger still confronted Arizona as far as the apportionment of supply among lower basin states was concerned.

Financing Colorado River development.   The financially conservative Coolidge administration had insisted that the Act provide that construction could not begin until the Secretary of the Interior had procured and executed water and power sale contracts which would assure repayment of the cost of the dam and power plant to the Treasury within fifty years and with interest at 4 per cent. Similar repayment provisions for a term of forty years, but without interest as provided in the Reclamation Act, were to be applied also to the All-American Canal. Pursuant thereto Secretary Wilbur entered into power contracts with public and private power users for the sale of hydraulic power at the dam site. The power contractors were to arrange for their own transmission lines to carry the energy to the market. The Secretary also contracted with them as agents to provide at their own expense for the installation, amortization, operations, and maintenance of the necessary electric power-producing machinery. It was planned that the

Reclamation Service operate only the dam to supply the energy of falling water, leaving its conversion to electric power to the contractors. The Southern California Edison Company acted for the private contractors and the Bureau of Power & Light of Los Angeles for the public contractors. This arrangement is in marked contrast with those adopted later in developing and selling the power of the Columbia and Tennessee Rivers.

These power contracts, particularly those with California interests, are proving to be the paying partners for this part of the undertaking. Permanent water contracts for the delivery of water from Hoover Dam storage for municipal water supply at 25 cents per acre-foot have also been negotiated, but these are contributing only a very minor part of the reimbursable costs. Water for irrigation purposes and that supplied in satisfaction of already perfected rights does not pay an additional water charge.

The annual water requirements for California irrigation interests aggregate 4,150,000 acre-feet and relate to the Palo Verde Irrigation District, the Yuma Project of California, the Imperial Irrigation District, and the Coachella Water District. To these should be added contract requirements of 1,100,000 acre-feet for the Metropolitan Water District and 112,000 acre-feet for the City of San Diego, or a grand total of 5,362,000 acre-feet. Another water contract with the state of Nevada calls for a maximum annual delivery of 300,000 acre-feet. In the end, after certain amendments had been enacted by Congress in 1940 favorable to Arizona, that state also ratified the Colorado River Compact in 1944. It immediately negotiated a water contract for an annual maximum delivery of 2,800,000 acre-feet plus one-half of any available surplus which the compact had left for apportionment between the two basins after October 1, 1963.

In order to assure repayment of All-American Canal costs, and hence the beginning of construction of this part of the project, a contract was negotiated between the Secretary and the Imperial Irrigation District in December, 1932. The federal government agreed to build both Imperial Dam and certain desilting works to divert water from the lower Colorado River and also the All-American Canal and to conduct this water by gravity into the Imperial and Coachella Valleys. (See Chart XXV.) The cost of these structures was not to exceed $38,500,000. The Imperial Irrigation District on its part agreed to repay its share of this investment in forty annual, interest-free installments and to operate and maintain the works, including some power-producing capabilities along the aqueduct. Similarly, the City of San Diego, the holder of 112,000 acre-feet of annual water rights, agreed to pay its share of this investment ($433,476) because at the time San Diego's plans called for the joint use of the All-American Canal and an extension westward to the city. Now San Diego receives its share of Colorado River water through an extension of the Metropolitan's aqueduct. (See Chart XXV.) Finally, another contract was entered into between the government and the Coachella Valley County Water District because the irrigators of this valley wanted to manage their own Coachella Canal system independently. For its share of the cost of joint user of the All-American installations, the district agreed to pay $13,128,078. All the water deliveries under the foregoing California contracts were subject to a scale of priorities, in which the agricultural areas of the Imperial Valley, of Palo Verde District, and other early appropriators held first priority. Under the terms of an agreement between California users the following is the arrangement of priorities:

1st priority	Imperial Valley, etc.	3,850,000	acre-feet
2nd "	Metropolitan Water District	550,000	acre-feet
3rd "	MWD and San Diego	662,000	acre-feet
4th "	Imperial Valley	300,000	acre-feet
	Total California water rights	5,362,000	acre-feet

The power contracts. When Secretary of the Interior Wilbur began negotiations for power contracts in September, 1929, applications were received for more than three times the energy actually believed to be available from Hoover Dam. It was necessary to apply the system of priorities which had been agreed upon in the compact. Accordingly, the Secretary allocated 36 per cent of the available firm energy to the Metropolitan Water District of Southern California to pump Colorado River water to the coastal area. There is thus being delivered to the wholesale customers of the district water costing 25 cents per acre-foot plus the guaranteed cost of Hoover Dam power allocated to and contracted for by the MWD. Because it was believed that neither Arizona nor Nevada would be able to absorb more of the available power, they were each allotted a minimum of 18 per cent of the firm energy on an "if and when needed" basis. The remaining firm energy was allotted 15 per cent to the City of Los Angeles, 4 per cent to Pasadena, Glendale, and Burbank (all owning municipal plants), and 9 per cent to the Southern California Edison Company, the Los Angeles Gas & Electric Company, and the Southern Sierras Power Company. First call on all secondary energy was given to the District with the Los Angeles Department of Water and Power and the private utilities entitled to one-half of any residue. It was also taken for granted that Arizona and Nevada would use very little of the allotted firm energy in the beginning. Hence, the Department of Water and Power and the private utilities made definite commitments each to pay for one-half the unused Nevada and Arizona energy.

The MWD was able to dispose of much of its unused firm energy, particularly after 1942 when the energy was absorbed by a huge metallurgical plant at Boulder City for the production of wartime magnesium. The California contracts of 1930 and 1931 thus made these Colorado River developments financially feasible.

Rate policy. In formulating the power contracts to assure liquidation of costs, it was necessary to determine the costs to be amortized, the quantity of energy to become available, and the value of that energy at the market. Only the southern California power market was capable of absorbing these large blocks of power.

Using the statutory amortization period of fifty years and deducting the statutory allocation of $25 million to flood control and deducting also the cost of power machinery, a conservative estimate of reimbursable costs was as follows:

Repayment Hoover Dam and Reservoir	$ 82,675,000
Interest at 4 per cent	108,107,007
Operation and maintenance	7,262,557
Depreciation	8,875,553
Total	$206,920,117

Firm energy annually available was estimatesd at 4,330,000,000 kilowatt-hours and secondary energy at 1,550,000,000 kilowatt-hours. Using the above costs plus estimated transmission costs to Los Angeles (to be borne by the contractors), the unit cost of Hoover Dam energy at central receiving substations was determined to be about 3.921 mills per kilowatt-hour. This compared with the cost of steam-generated energy at the market of 3.920 mills which was to be used as a yardstick for making periodic adjustments in the power contracts. Translating these costs back to the charge necessary to meet the cost of energy in falling water, the rate for firm energy was fixed at 1.63 mills per kilowatt-hour and for secondary energy at 0.5 mills per kilowatt-hour. According to the original Act the allocation for flood control was to be made reimbursable out of 62½ per cent of any surplus power revenues, the other 37½ per cent was to be paid to Nevada and Arizona in equal proportions in lieu of taxes. Remaining surplus revenues were to be paid into a Colorado River Dam Fund to be used in making investigations of additional projects and as Congress might direct.

Under a contract awarded by the Bureau of Reclamation on March 11, 1931 to the Six Companies, Inc., the construction of the world's highest dam (726.4 feet) was begun. Water storage in Lake Mead was started on February 1, 1935, which may be taken as the date when the rampaging river was placed under control. The reservoir has a capacity of 32,359,000 acre-feet, which was not achieved until June 1941. The structure was completed on March 1, 1936, and the installation of generators in the powerhouse had begun. It was designed for an ultimate generator installation of 1,332,300 kilowatts, 15 of them 82,500 kilowatts in size. It was contemplated that the upper 9½ million acre-feet of storage capacity would be kept available on April 1 of each year for flood control, unless there were additional upstream development.

It is appropriate at this point to recount the other works on the lower Colorado River and the utilization with which they are associated. Davis Dam, 67 miles below Hoover Dam, which is the keystone of the whole development, creates a reservoir capacity of 1,600,000 acre-feet and has an installed power capacity of 225,000 kilowatts. It reregulates the power producing discharges from Hoover Dam and is designed to meet the water requirements of the Mexican Water Treaty, to be discussed below. Parker Dam, 88 miles below, impounds Lake Havasu, the diversion reservoir for the MWD aqueduct. Headgate Rock Dam, 14 miles below Parker Dam, is a diversion dam for the Colorado River Indian Reservation in Arizona, the oldest appropriator on the lower river. A diversion structure, 43 miles below, is Palo Verde Weir, serving the Palo Verde Irrigation District of California. Imperial Dam, 90 miles below, is the diversion point for the All-American Canal in California and the Gila Canal in Arizona. Laguna Dam, 5 miles below and only 17 miles from the Mexican border, is the diversion structure for the Yuma Irrigation Project in Arizona. (See Chart XXV.)

In the interval between 1931 and June 1, 1937, the date of first delivery of power under the Boulder Canyon Project contracts, there had occurred significant reductions in fuel and construction costs. The price reductions combined with improvements in steam generation technology had lowered the competitive value of Hoover energy in Los Angeles. Moreover, in the TVA and Bonneville Power Administration legislation, the new rate policy was adopted of amortizing original costs instead of the maximum competitive return principle. In competing with the low industrial rates fixed by TVA and the Bonneville Power Administration to attract new chemical and metallurgical industries, the utilities in Los Angeles found themselves at a decided disadvantage. Pressure was therefore exerted upon Congress to extend the same treatment to the older federal project.

This was accomplished in the Boulder Canyon Project Adjustment Act of 1940. By stabilizing rates for the period of amortization, i.e., from 1937 to 1987, new reduced rates were put into effect of 1.163 mills for firm energy and 0.34 mill for secondary energy. The adjustment was accomplished by

(1) reducing the interest rate from 4 per cent to 3 per cent upon reimbursable advances; (2) deferring the amortization of the flood control component until 1987; (3) paying $300,000 annually to Arizona and Nevada in commutation of their somewhat uncertain rights to receive a share of the surplus revenues; (4) paying $500,000 annually into the Colorado River Development Fund in substitution of a "separate fund" provision of the earlier act. Under certain revised regulations the Los Angeles Department of Water & Power (the City) and the Southern California Edison Company (the Company) became the operating agents instead of lessees and accepted the responsibility of maintaining and operating the generating equipment—the City generating requirements for the public agencies and the Company for the private utilities. Meanwhile, the City had purchased the electric properties of the Los Angeles Gas & Electric Corporation and had thus acquired that company's share of the power allotments. Firm energy was redefined as 4,330 million kilowatt-hours for the first year, with an annual diminution of 8,760,000 kilowatt-hours to allow for silt accumulation and upstream projects. Secondary energy was defined as all energy in excess of firm energy.

The unique position of MWD among the allottees is that it was known that the District would not need the 36 per cent of the firm energy for which it was obligated. Arrangements were therefore made that the government sell as much of the District's unused energy as possible to other users. Since much of the firm energy was not resold, or was sold at less than firm power rates, the District experienced losses. During the first five years of operation, 2,295,274,051 kilowatt-hours of District energy was not resold, which involved a charge of $5,886,263. This was absorbed in MWD operating costs and had to be covered by supplementary tax levies.

The Mexican Water Treaty

We come now to the most controverted aspects of these lower Colorado River developments, the Mexican Water Treaty and the conflict between California and Arizona over water rights. Previous to the availability of Hoover storage, Mexican uses of Colorado River water, principally for irrigation of cotton-growing lands, had reached the limit of safe and profitable development. Together with American diversions, these uses consumed the entire flow during the dry season, and there were severe shortages during dry years. Mexican uses had averaged about 600,000 acre-feet. Moreover, they were dependent upon structures located in the United States and upon

canals and protective levees furnished by American capital. With no storage
sites available to Mexico in the flat delta area and with her agriculture men-
aced by devastating floods, the unregulated condition of the river gave no
promise of a permanent agriculture. As Senator Pittman said during the
debates in 1928 on the Boulder Project Act:

The natural flow of that river today will not irrigate any more than 240,000 acres
of land in Mexico. That is all it will irrigate . . . If this dam is never built, if
there is no water impounded on that river, Mexico a thousand years from now
will be where Mexico is today with regard to irrigation in Mexico.

After the construction of Hoover Dam this situation was changed radically. With the removal of the flood menace and with the regulated flow of
the river, Mexican landowners could benefit from the ample water supplies released for power production from Lake Mead storage. American
irrigation and domestic requirements, while growing, have not fully appropriated the contractual allotments nor will they do so for some time.
Even after full utilization has been obtained, Mexico will still be in a position
to make use of all the return water, excess flood flows, or seepage that
reaches the international boundary. Under these circumstances the beneficial use of water on Mexican lands had grown rapidly until it was estimated
to have reached 1,800,000 acre-feet. This was the reason for coming to some
final understanding with our southern neighbor.

The negotiators of the compact had foreseen this international com-
plication. After allocating water to the upper and lower basin, the compact
provides that:

If as a matter of international comity, the United States of America shall
hereafter recognize in the United States of Mexico any right to the use of any
waters of the Colorado River system, such waters shall be supplied first from the
waters which are surplus over and above the aggregate of the quantities specified
in paragraphs (a) and (b) [the 16 million acre-feet per annum definitely allocated]
and if such surplus shall prove insufficient for this purpose, then the burden of
such deficiency shall be equally borne by the upper basin and the lower basin.

To this availability clause of the compact all water delivery contracts
under the Project Act are made subject. It is therefore important to examine
the provisions of the treaty. Discussions with Mexico regarding a treaty
disposing of boundary waters began under a Congressional act of May 13,
1924, and was concerned only with the waters of the Rio Grande. The distribution of the water in this river between Mexico and the United States
is accomplished by dividing the river into two sections. The upper section
terminates at Fort Quitman, Texas, about 80 miles below El Paso. In accordance with a treaty ratified in 1906, the water in this section, derived ex-

clusively from American sources, is stored in Elephant Butte reservoir, 125 miles above the boundary line, and delivered to Mexico at El Paso for use by irrigators in the Juarez Valley who had beneficially applied this water for a long time. The amount so delivered is limited to 60,000 acre-feet and constitutes a recognition of perpetuity of use on Mexican lands in accordance with the doctrine of prior appropriation.

Because Mexico was unwilling to discuss the problem of the equitable use of the waters of the lower Rio Grande without considering also the same problem on the lower Colorado River, the scope of the investigation was expanded by a joint resolution approved March 3, 1927, to include also the Colorado and the Tijuana Rivers. The latter is a small boundary stream near San Diego, California. The treaty does little more with respect to the Tijuana than to reach an agreement that the two countries will at some future time allocate its available waters.

From El Paso to the Gulf of Mexico the Rio Grande constitutes the boundary, and it is this 1,200-mile long lower section with water contributions from tributaries in both countries that was the principal subject matter of the negotiations along with the lower Colorado. Mexican tributaries contribute 70 per cent of the supply while tributaries in the United States, notably the Pecos and Devils Rivers, furnish only 30 per cent. Apart from scattered minor irrigations at the northern end, the main development of this international river on the American side was in the citrus fruit and vegetable growing area at the lower end in Cameron, Hidalgo, and Willacy Counties. This development dates back to 1904, when the completion of the Missouri-Pacific Railway to Brownsville ushered in a period of rapid irrigation expansion in the lower valley, which had reached the approximate total of 400,000 acres by 1940.

Except for the recent construction of two large storage structures for irrigation and flood control, water use on the Mexican side was distinctly minor. On either side there were millions of acres capable of irrigation if some 4 million acre-feet of flood waters now wasting into the Gulf could be beneficially applied. Alternating periods of drought and flood made the unregulated supply deficient for even the then existing minor developments. Hence the negotiators of the treaty contemplated the joint construction of three storage reservoirs on the main stream to protect these improvements and to expand the irrigable area on both sides. On the Mexican side, development on the tributaries had expanded from about 100,000 acres at the beginning of the century to more than 500,000 acres. In the United States, except on the Pecos River where full development had already been obtained, the upper irrigated area lagged far behind that on the Mexican side.

Under the treaty as finally drafted, Texas retains the flow of its own major named tributaries, is allocated one-half of the water in the international boundary section of the river, and obtains one-third of the flow from six Mexican tributaries. The Mexican contribution was subject to an assured annual minimum of 350,000 acre-feet. With the coming of upstream development it was estimated that average stream flow into the reservoirs would aggregate 3,400,000 acre-feet, of which about 2 million acre-feet were allocated to the United States.

The reservoirs on the main stream would, of course, also afford benefits of flood and silt control and of electric power production. Besides affording dependable irrigation for some 500,000 additional acres in the lower reaches, there were benefits from hydroelectric power, the allocation of which followed procedures usually adopted for multiple-purpose structures. The energy and costs were divided equally between the two governments. Revenues from power sales were expected to be sufficient to cover operation and maintenance costs, to amortize the strictly power investment and to amortize also a portion of the costs of the storage dams. Only one of the reservoirs, Falcon Dam, has been completed and recently dedicated by President Eisenhower.

These benefits to Texas are offset by certain disadvantages to the states in the lower Colorado basin. The treaty, as finally drawn up by the two State Departments, conceded to Mexico a minimum quantity of 1,500,000 acre-feet per annum. The water was to be delivered in accordance with Mexican irrigation schedules and subject to an increase of 200,000 acre-feet if and when available as adjudged by the United States. In order to make possible these deliveries in accord with Mexican irrigation requirements, the United States agreed to build Davis Dam located between Boulder and Parker Dams, at its own expense. This dam was completed in 1949 at a cost of $104 million with an installed capacity of 225,000 kilowatts. Its reservoir of 1,600,000 acre-feet of active storage capacity serves the purpose of reregulating the outflow from Hoover Dam, the releases from which are dominated by electric power requirements. With the signing of the Mexican Water Treaty in 1945, the pressure to appropriate the remaining water supplies of the Colorado basin became more intense. It showed itself in a new phase of the controversy between California and Arizona over water rights.

The California-Arizona Controversy

The most recent aspects of the California-Arizona controversy involves the so-called Central Arizona Project (CAP). When Arizona after a delay of over twenty years finally ratified the Colorado River Compact, the Secretary of the Interior in 1944 entered into a contract with Arizona for the storage of 2,800,000 acre-feet of water from the main stream of the Colorado. At the same time, Arizona endorsed the Mexican Water Treaty, although her opposition to Mexican water claims had been as firm as that of California. She now proposed to divert 1,200,000 acre-feet to the Phoenix area in central Arizona.

The Central Arizona Project. The Bureau of Reclamation, using Colorado River development funds, began its study of the problem immediately after the war. In 1947 it issued its project planning report regarding the feasibility of the project in a revised form and found that the ratio of annual benefits to annual costs was 1.63 to 1. This proposal has been repeatedly submitted to Congress, where the bill has passed the Senate but has been held up in the House, owing to opposition from California.

The main elements of the project are a pumping plant at Parker Dam to lift the water from Lake Havasu, approximately 985 feet, into Granite Reef Aqueduct to be transported 241 miles to central Arizona. Power for pumping operations and for sale (principally in California) is to be obtained from a high dam and reservoir and power plant (750,000 kilowatts) at Bridge Canyon above Boulder. (See Chart XXV for this and other features.) The irrigation and water supply features are characterized as a "rescue" operation for central Arizona, where the rapidly increasing population is pressing upon the local water supplies of the Salt and Gila River basins. The main aqueduct and connecting canals are to supply water to replace the overdraft on the groundwater, to drain excess salts out of the area, thus maintaining a salt balance, and to furnish a supplemental supply to lands inadequately irrigated and to lands which have passed out of production. Municipal water supplies are also to be augmented for the City of Tucson. The cost of the entire project was estimated at $738,408,000, which includes several smaller dams, a power transmission system, and an irrigation distribution system.

After much maneuvering the parties to this controversy, including the Attorney General on behalf of the United States, have finally agreed to submit these issues to the United States Supreme Court. The suit of *Arizona v. California* was filed before that Court in January, 1953, and the question of the amount of Colorado River water available to Arizona and California may yet be judicially answered. California's objection to the Central Arizona Project on financial grounds will not be as easily disposed of. As compared with the self-liquidating arrangements in the Boulder Canyon Project Act and those relating to the Metropolitan Water District Aqueduct, the reimbursement plans for the Central Arizona Project are markedly defective. Only the sale of surplus power in the southern California market can bring about a substantial measure of cost repayment to the U.S. Treasury. Will that market absorb what promises to be high-cost hydroelectric power in view of the alternative cost of steam-generated electric energy from the mammoth plants now available in the Los Angeles market? Failing in their plans to make power the "paying partner" in this enterprise, its proponents have only two policies available to achieve their ends: One is a resort to the policy of subsidy by the federal government, and the other is to follow the example of the Metropolitan Water District of Southern California.

29. REGIONAL
DEVELOPMENT IN THE
COLUMBIA RIVER
BASIN

Another regional development centering in the planning for an entire river basin concerns the Columbia River and its tributaries. Since the days of the pioneers of the Oregon trail the treacherous waters of the lower Columbia had served as a natural waterway and gateway to an agricultural and lumbering empire unique in its productive potentialities. The Columbia drains an area of 259,000 square miles (39,000 are in Canada), equal to more than one-twelfth of the United States. It is a region of the heaviest but variable rainfall. The aggregate annual run-off is more than 180 million acre-feet, of which its principal tributary, the Snake, contributes about 37 million acre-feet, or about one-fifth. The major hydrologic divisions of the basin and their varying contributions to its run-off are shown in Chart XXVI, which also shows the political areas affected.

The Economy of the Region

The Cascade Mountain Range paralleling the Pacific Coast divides the area climatically. The valleys to the west have a mild and relatively humid climate, while the valleys and plains to the east have a colder, semi-desert climate. The rapid melting of the snow pack combined with warm rains creates severe flood conditions in May and June. In the drier and accessible sections of the basin, summertime irrigation is extensively practiced on about 3.7 million acres, 70 per cent of it in the Snake River Valley. Happily this coincides with a peak run-off of long duration. The steep gradient of the river, up to 2,700 feet on the main stem and up to 6,000 feet on the tributaries, provides the largest hydroelectric power potential in the United States. The humid mountains of the interior are forest-covered, and these

493

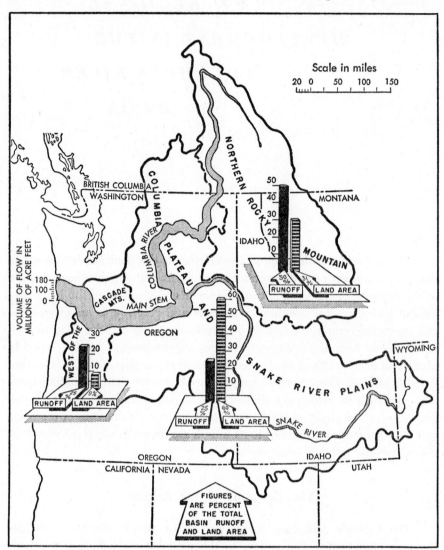

Chart XXVI   Major Hydrologic Regions—Columbia River Basin. (President's Water
Resources Policy Commission, Vol. II, 1950.)

together with the forests of the coastal area constitute our largest reserve of
standing timber.

The population of the Columbia Basin is about 3.3 millions, to which
should be added the more than a million people of the Puget Sound area,
which while not in the basin is really a part of the regional economy. Along
with California and the Pacific Southwest, the Pacific Northwest experienced

the greatest rate of population increase between 1940 and 1950. It was in excess of 40 per cent, as compared with a national average of less than 15 per cent.

This population is sustained primarily by extractive industry: agricul-ture, forestry, and fishing, and the processing industries based upon them. Of the 8 million acres of crops harvested, over half is devoted to the produc-tion of small grains by dry farming methods. Irrigation farming of the in-tensive type produces sugar beets, fruits, vegetables, and potatoes. Lum-bering, now rapidly converting to a sustained yield basis, produces 5.4 billion board-feet annually, or 15 per cent of the national lumber output. Livestock ranching on owned or leased grazing lands has been overex-panded and must be curtailed to regulate grazing, supplemented by irri-gated acreage to supply winter feeding. The Columbia River system, with its tremendous migratory runs of salmon to spawn in the cold, clear waters of the tributaries, is the basis of important fishing, both commercial and recreational. Mineral industries supply a long list of minerals of commercial importance. Their major concentrations center in Butte, Montana, for copper and in northern Idaho for silver, lead, and zinc. The greatest potentiality for the future resides in the world's largest phosphate reserves of some 5 billion tons in the southeastern corner of the basin.

Manufacturing plants processing these raw materials are widely scat-tered. Of most importance are the saw mills, paper and pulp mills, and the newly established electrochemical and electrometallurgical plants. The last named are located near water transport and where low-cost hydroelectric power is available. A growing recreational industry based upon scenic and other attractions in national parks, national forests, and wilderness areas is widely dispersed throughout the basin.

Multiple-Purpose Planning

Like other river systems the Columbia is both a promise and a menace. The promise resides first of all in the tremendous power potentialities which, according to some estimates,[1] might aggregate 34 million kilowatts of in-stalled capacity, an average annual generation of 168 billion kilowatt-hours and a potential water storage capacity of 75 million acre-feet. A second benefit arises from the use of stored water for irrigating dry lands or as sup-plementary water for lands now irrigated. The largest of these proposals now under development is the so-called Big Bend project on the Columbia of

[1] "Ten Rivers in America's Future," Report of the President's Water Resources Policy Commission, 1950, p. 19.

the Bureau of Reclamation, which will eventually irrigate about a million acres. This is associated with the completed Grand Coulee Dam, the largest man-made structure in the world, capable of developing in its eighteen large generating units in two powerhouses 1,944,000 kilowatts of electric energy. Other projects completed, under construction, or planned might add several millions of acres to the irrigable area.

The Corps of Engineers stresses the importance of the expansion of the present sea-going navigation of the lower Columbia River up to Portland into slack-water navigation by means of barges up the Willamette River, up the Columbia River, and up the Snake River as far as Lewiston, Idaho.

The menaces associated with these on-and-off river economic developments consist primarily of the danger of flooding, of stream pollution, and interference with the migratory run of salmon entering from the Pacific to spawn in the cold waters of tributary streams.

The earlier developments, generally by private enterprise, were of the single-purpose variety and mostly for power or irrigation purposes. The gradual realization, however, that the federal government must take a hand in the more comprehensive development and protection of the natural resource base of our economy, changed the incidence of these policies and gave them a federal orientation.

Inception of the Columbia Basin projects.   The first comprehensive investigation of the basin's potentialities was undertaken by the Bureau of Reclamation in 1914. But it was under authority granted the Secretary of War in 1925 to "formulate general plans for navigation, flood control, irrigation and the economic development of water power" that the first comprehensive planning was done for the rivers of America, among them the Columbia River. In one of the famous "308 Reports" (named after House Document No. 308) published in 1932 during the Hoover administration, water and power development of the Pacific Northwest in terms of the Columbia River system was fully explored. This report remained the basic plan until 1948. It recommended the construction of ten dams, the first one to be the Bonneville Dam, situated 42 miles east of Portland. (See Chart XXVII.) Construction was begun in September of 1933 by the Corps of Engineers as a Public Works project. It was formally authorized by Congress in the Rivers and Harbors Act of 1935. Dedicated by President F. D. Roosevelt in 1937 to the dual purpose of navigation and power production, it is now a completed structure providing a navigable channel for ocean vessels to the Dalles, with an installed generating capacity of 518,400 kilowatts. Its most significant features are a single-lift navigation lock, the largest in the world, and

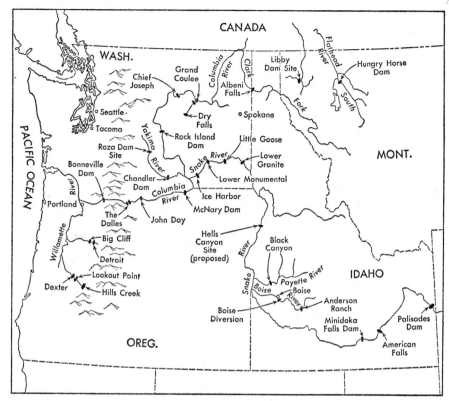

Chart XXVII   Pacific Northwest.

an installation of fish ladders and elevators to permit the migration of salmon.

Construction of a second unit under the plan, Grand Coulee Dam near Spokane, was also started in 1934 as a relief measure. It was authorized in 1935 and completed in 1941. This, as already mentioned, is also a multipurpose structure for irrigation and power, built and operated by the Bureau of Reclamation. Besides its unprecedentedly large power installation, this structure is notable because it represents the realization of a plan of Col. George Goethels, builder of the Panama Canal, who in 1921 supported the plan of early local promoters. By building a dam of inordinate height and size, the water is raised halfway up the canyon wall from where it can be pumped by using secondary or infirm power into a dry coulee or old river bed. Here the water is stored in a regulating reservoir to be used for irrigation purposes on fertile lands below in the Big Bend region, the return water again reaching the Columbia River.

The Bonneville Power Administration. With these initiating multi-purpose projects, the Columbia Basin development became a partnership between the Corps of Engineers and the Bureau of Reclamation when Congress in 1937 passed the Bonneville Project Act. This Act gave Secretary of the Interior Ickes the responsibility for marketing electric power generated at Bonneville Dam, supplemented by executive order in 1940 giving him the same responsibility for marketing surplus power at Grand Coulee. A new type of agency was created within the Department, known as the Bonneville Power Administration (BPA) headed by a single administrator. It was the administrator's function to build a network of transmission lines and connecting substations to collect the power from these and other sources of generation and to convey and sell power at wholesale to retail distributors of power.

Using the model or plan of administration already applied by the Tennessee Valley Authority, the BPA, with headquarters at Portland, developed marketing policies consistent with the mandate of Congress. The Administrator is required (1) "to encourage the widest possible use of all the electric energy that can be generated and marketed"; (2) to prevent its monopolization "by limited groups"; and (3) "to give preference and priority to public bodies and cooperatives."

Development of Utilization and Marketing Policies

The BPA's first effort was directed toward identifying its interests with the interests of the people of the region which it was ultimately meant to serve. Headed by J. D. Ross, the long-time superintendent of the Seattle municipal electric utility, the BPA endeavored to attract industry to the region which would be able to absorb the large blocks of power soon to become available. There were both friends and foes of the projects who were skeptical of the ability of the region to absorb these tremendous accessions to the regional power supply. Critics called them "white elephants" and "dams of doubt." As in the case of TVA, there were few municipally owned utilities to buy the power, and among these, few (Eugene, Oregon, Tacoma, and Seattle, Washington) had ample supplies of their own. An extraordinary series of exogenous events, however, in time dispelled these doubts.

The first and most important was the war emergency. The outbreak of war in Europe and our ultimate involvement in it created the underlying condition which in the end changed the power picture from one of a region of power surplus to one of power deficiency.

Another outside event of some importance was the drought condition of the middle 1930's, affecting particularly the high plains regions of the United States and giving rise to streams of refugees from the "dust bowl," who were migrating to the more humid and irrigable sections of the country.

Much credit for the final favorable results should be given BPA for its foresight in building transmission lines ahead of generator installations and in interconnecting its facilities with those of both private and public producers of power. The region was ready for an expanded network of hydropower supply because there were no supplies of oil or natural gas in the area. Moreover, its low-grade supplies of coal and of wood waste were utilized to only a limited extent. At first the actual building of the transmission system was slow in starting. Congress made no provision for that purpose in its initial appropriation for the agency. The first two generators at Bonneville Dam were completed a month before Congress provided funds for transmission. It was not until May, 1938, that the first appropriation provided for a 230-kilovolt transmission line between Bonneville Dam and Vancouver, Washington. With a grant of $10,950,000 from the Public Works Administration and a second Congressional appropriation in 1939, BPA was finally enabled to build 550 miles of line which expanded and completed a projected grid. Its main feature interconnected Bonneville and Grand Coulee Dams. By the end of fiscal 1945, the transmission system had grown to 2,720 circuit miles with adequate substation capacity. It operated 82 per cent of the region's high-voltage lines, tying together its own and other power sources, both public and private. As projected by Paul Raver, the new Administrator, it reached all major load centers in the Portland, Seattle, and Spokane areas.

With the war emergency, defense plants sprang up almost overnight and defense workers poured in by the thousands. To meet the increased demand for power the Northwest Power Pool was organized in 1942, with the view of conserving all the major power resources for an area extending from Puget Sound east to Fort Peck on the Missouri River and from the Canadian border to Salt Lake City.

Availability of an adequate and reliable supply of BPA power was an important factor in locating the extensive Hanford Engineering Works on its lines in Washington. This plant supplied important ingredients of the atomic bomb. In addition, power was supplied to several extensive aluminum plants, to seven Army camps and air bases, and to several naval establishments.

Following the mandate of Congress, BPA also gave special assistance to its preference customers. The laws of Oregon and Washington had authorized the organization of Public Utility Districts (PUD's) to go into the power business by purchasing or constructing distribution systems. With hydroelectric power available in wholesale quantities from BPA under the preference provision, these public agencies represented an outlet for power which would secure its wide utilization, stressing particularly residential and rural customers. A similar outlet under the same preference provisions developed from the rural electric cooperatives, which were being fostered by the Rural Electric Administration of the Department of Agriculture.

Although marketing policies contemplated sales to private utilities, such sales were not on a preference basis and were subject to cancellation on five years' notice if the power was required by preference customers. Contracts to the latter were for firm power and for twenty years but were subject to rate adjustments every five years. With much surplus power available, the preference provisions were not the subject of much criticism. At first sales to these outlets under preference provisions was slow indeed, but with the expansion of the transmission system this load increased, particularly after the war period. Table XV gives the number of public and cooperative distributors, the quantity of energy delivered to them, and their relative importance in the total of all deliveries for the fiscal year 1953.

Table XV   Power Sales to Public Agencies by BPA, Fiscal Year 1953

Class of Customer	Number	Kilowatt-hours Delivered, in Billions	Per Cent of Total Deliveries
Tacoma and Seattle	2	1.7	10.5
Other municipalities	15	0.3	1.8
Public utility districts	25	2.6	15.9
Cooperatives	35	0.5	2.8
Other	2	0.01	0.1
Total	79	5.1	31.1
Grand Total, all deliveries	. .	16.4	100.0

The major use of electric power generated by BPA, however, was by industries attracted to the Columbia basin by its low-cost energy base, that is to say, electrochemical and electrometallurgical industries. There were also industries contributing to the war effort, particularly aluminum manufacturing. On this account they gave some promise of permanence after war requirements had been met and would thus afford permanent employment and also broaden and stabilize the base of the economy. The main attractiveness of these industries (especially aluminum) to the BPA was that they were "high load factor" consumers of large blocks of power which could be served directly. The economic situation in the Columbia basin was similar in many respects to that of the Tennessee basin and the development and marketing program of TVA. The early aluminum industry, originating at Pittsburgh and locating at Niagara Falls and at Massena on the St. Lawrence River, had in 1910 come to Alcoa on the Little Tennessee River. During the defense and war periods of World War II, this industry expanded in the Tennessee Valley and moved into the Pacific Northwest. Besides the Aluminum Company of America, two new producers (Reynolds Metals Corporation and Olin Industries) entered the aluminum reduction business. After the war the Kaiser interests, the Anaconda Copper Mining Company, and the Harvey Machine Company also entered the field at various points in the Columbia basin. Firm power sales contracts to industry expanded from 65,000 kilowatts in 1940 to a peak of 740,625 kilowatts in 1944, dropped to a low of 280,275 kilowatts in 1946 after conversion, but rose again to 668,060 kilowatts in 1952. Almost all this power was used for aluminum manufacturing, as Chart XXVIII shows. This chart, showing monthly and yearly energy sales by type of customers, affords the best over-all view of the power marketing performance of BPA and should be consulted. It also shows the effect of the power curtailment as a result of the drought of 1952.

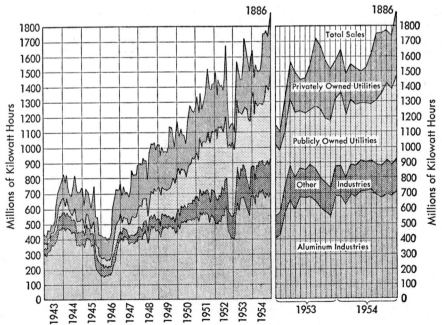

Chart XXVIII   Electric Energy Sales by Type of Customer. (Report—Bonneville Power Administration.)

Planning for the Ultimate Development of the Basin

In order to appreciate the general problem of planning for the ultimate development of the Columbia basin, it is necessary to have a comprehensive view of the electric power situation in the region as a whole. Here,
as elsewhere, power is the paying partner and therefore of primary importance in the coordination of the various public purposes involved in river
basin planning.

The Northwest Power Pool.   This is best shown in terms of the Northwest Power Pool to which the principal generating utilities, both public and

Table XVI   Power Produced by the Major Electric Generating
Systems of the Pacific Northwest

Name	Kilowatt-hours Produced, Billions	Per Cent of the Total	Kilowatt-hours Contributed to Pool, Billions	Kilowatt-hours Withdrawn from Pool, Billions
Portland General Electric Co.	0.7	2.3	. . .	1.9
Tacoma City Light *	0.8	2.6	. . .	0.7
Pacific Power & Light Co.	0.8	2.6	. . .	1.0
Washington Water Power Co.	1.4	4.6	. . .	0.7
Seattle City Light *	1.4	4.6	. . .	1.2
Puget Sound Power & Light Co.	1.5	5.0	. . .	0.1
Idaho Power Co.	2.1	6.9	0.4	. . .
Montana Power Co.	3.1	10.2	0.3	. . .
U.S. Columbia River Power System *	18.6	61.2	5.1	. . .
			5.8	5.6
Total publicly owned	20.8	68.4		
Total	30.4	100.0		

* Publicly owned power projects
Source: 1952 report of the Columbia River Power System, U.S. Department of the
Interior, pp. 28–29.

private, belong. Table XVI shows, for fiscal 1952, the amount of power contributed *to the pool* by its members and the amount supplied *by the pool*
to them. Utah Power and Light Company and British Columbia Electric
Company, though members of the pool, are not included because their importance is minor and their major service area lies outside the region.

The two multiple-purpose projects, Bonneville and Grand Coulee, producing 18.6 billion kilowatt-hours, dominate the situation. Together with

the municipally owned electric utilities of Tacoma and Seattle, themselves substantial producers, public agencies generate over 68 per cent of the total. In the fourteen years from 1939 to 1952, BPA generation grew from 35 million to 18,555 million kilowatt-hours, an unprecedented performance approached only by TVA.

A program of dam construction. With the coming of peace and the recession in power requirements, the unified development of the Columbia basin seemed to be halted; at least no new federal projects were begun until 1947. The development of a power shortage during the winter of 1948 to 1949, however, appeared to break the congressional log jam in appropriations. In quick succession the Corps of Engineers secured the funds to begin the construction of McNary Dam on the upper Columbia, designed for power, irrigation, and navigation. It adds 980,000 kilowatts to the installed capacity. A year later the Bureau of Reclamation started the construction of Hungry Horse Dam on the Flathead River in western Montana. This is a storage project to produce 285,000 kilowatts of power at the site, but intended mainly to "firm up" the power system downstream with its 2,980,000 acre-feet of usable storage. Although two different agencies were seeking appropriations from Congress, BPA as the potential marketing agency for the power was providing the needed coordination and integration. Flood control, river regulation, and recreational developments are also kept in mind, though there is no one agency for unified control. Yet one part of the public's desire for more electrical energy frequently clashes with another part of the public's serious objection to the inundation of land to provide storage sites. Such clashes occur whether prospective dams are to be constructed by the federal government, by local public agencies, or by pri-

Table XVII   Regional Power Projects—A 1953 Summary

| Stage | COLUMBIA BASIN PROJECTS | | | OUTSIDE BASIN PROJECTS WASH., OREG., IDAHO Private & Local Public, KW |
	Federal, KW	Private & Local Public, KW	Total, KW	
Completed	2,897,300	1,709,630	4,606,930	1,318,970
Under construction	3,438,600	116,000	3,554,600	62,000
Authorized for construction	3,779,000	. . . . . .	3,779,000	
Proposed for 1955	. . . .	902,500	902,500	
Proposed after 1955	. . . .	355,000	355,000	218,000
Planned but unauthorized	897,500	. . . . . .	897,500	
Total	11,012,400	3,083,130	14,095,530	1,598,970

vate utilities. Authorization of Glacier View Dam is opposed by the Park Bureau of the Department of the Interior because it would inundate a part of Glacier National Park. Fishery interests have been holding up two dams of the City of Tacoma totaling 460,000 kilowatts, and one dam of Portland General Electric designed for 120,000 kilowatts. Other objections relate to dam construction which would inundate zinc-lead mines. There are objections to relocation of major highways, to inundation of small communities and of Indian lands. Unified development must thread its way against such objections by compromise if necessary, by overriding or giving way to them. As of 1953, the present and prospective development for power purposes of the Columbia River basin by all agencies and all levels of government are summarized below with the details set forth in Tables XVII, XVIII, and XIX. We are also adding installed capacity data from outside the basin, especially from the heavily populated area of Washington west of the Cascades where major private and local public dams constitute an integral part

Table XVIII   Status of Power Development of Columbia River Basin, Federal Hydroelectric Projects, December 31, 1953

Dam	Stream	Usable Storage (Acre-Feet)	No. of Generators	Total Installed Capacity (Kilowatts)	Construction Agency *	Date in Service First Unit	Date in Service Last Unit
		COMPLETED					
1. Grand Coulee	Columbia	5,118,000	18	1,944,000	R		
2. Bonneville	Columbia	Pondage	10	518,400	E		
3. Hungry Horse	S.F. Flathead	2,980,000	4	285,000	R		
4. Detroit	No. Santiam †	340,000	2	100,000	E		
5. Anderson Ranch	S.F. Boise	464,200	2	27,000	R		
6. Minidaka	Snake	95,200	7	13,400	R		
7. Black Canyon	Payette	Pondage	2	8,000	R		
8. Boise Diversion	Boise	Pondage	3	1,500	R		
Total		8,997,400	48	2,897,300			
		UNDER CONSTRUCTION					
9. Chief Joseph	Columbia	Pondage	18	1,024,000	E	9–55	6–59
10. The Dalles	Columbia	Pondage	16	1,119,000	E	11–57	11–60
11. McNary	Columbia	Pondage	14	980,000	E	12–53	12–56
12. Palisades	Snake	1,200,000	4	114,000	R	12–56	9–57
13. Lookout Pt.	M.F. Willamette †	368,000	3	114,000	E	10–54	2–55
14. Albeni Falls	Pend Oreille	1,140,000	3	42,600	E	8–54	4–55
15. Big Cliff	No. Santiam	Pondage	1	18,000	E	4–54	
16. Dexter	M.F. Willamette	Pondage	1	15,000	E	4–55	
17. Chandler	Yakima	Pondage	2	12,000	R	9–55	
Total		2,708,000	62	3,438,600			

Table XVIII (*continued*)

Dam	Stream	Usable Storage (Acre-Feet)	No. of Generators	Total Installed Capacity (Kilowatts)	Construction Agency *	Date in Service First Unit	Last Unit
AUTHORIZED FOR CONSTRUCTION							
18. Priest Rapids	Columbia †	2,100,000	23	1,219,000	E	12–62	12–67
19. John Day	Columbia †	2,000,000	14	1,105,000	E	12–64	12–67
20. Libby	Kootenay	6,480,000	6	660,000	E	9–59	1–61
21. Little Goose	Snake	Pondage	4	195,000	E	12–61	8–62
22. Ice Harbor	Snake	Pondage	4	195,000	E	12–57	8–58
23. Lower Monumental	Snake	Pondage	4	180,000	E	12–60	8–61
	Snake	Pondage	4	165,000	E	12–62	8–63
24. Lower Granite	Snake	1,700,000	3	30,000	R	10–56	2–57
25. American Falls	M.F. Willamette †						
26. Hills Creek		221,000	1	20,000	E	12–59	
27. Roza	Yakima	Pondage	2	10,000	R	10–56	
Total		12,501,000	65	3,779,000			
PLANNED BUT UNAUTHORIZED							
28. Hells Canyon	Snake	3,880,000	8	800,000	R	9–58	6–60
29. Lower Scriver	Diversion from N.F. Payette	Pondage	2	60,000	R	9–57	11–57
30. Upper Scriver	Diversion from N.F. Payette	Pondage	3	37,500	R	9–57	1–58
Total		3,880,000	13	897,500			
Grand Total		28,086,400	188	11,012,400			

* Corps of Engineers signified by "E"; Bureau of Reclamation by "R."
† Includes flood-control storage.
Sources: Bonneville Power Administration, *Advance Program 1953*, Appendix, Tables 7 and 9.

of the regional power pool. The figures are kilowatts in Nameplate rating.

Thus the over-all situation is that federal hydroelectric power has obtained, and will in the future continue to have, a dominant position in the electric energy pattern for the region. After wartime expansion came postwar civilian demands and later Korean War requirements. Federal agencies in time also supplied an increasing share of the requirements of local private and public agencies. This is especially true of the Portland Electric Company, Pacific Power and Light Company, and Washington Water Power Company, with the Portland utility drawing over 70 per cent of its requirements from the pool.

Power planning for the future. It is paradoxical that the Pacific Northwest, with a plethora of power potentialities, should be a region of power shortage. The major reason is that the region was caught between the two contending forces in the controversy over public versus private generation of electric power. No doubt the uncertainties created by the conflict between PUD's and privately owned utilities to take over the latter's properties had something to do with the reluctance displayed by private utility systems to construct adequate generating capacity. The major reason, however, was that all the local utilities in the end preferred to depend on federal dams as a cheaper source of power than to build dams of their own. Coupled with this was the belief that the postwar years would be years of power surplus. Witnesses for the National Association of Electric Light Companies testified before the Senate appropriations committee in December, 1945, that by 1947 the country including the Pacific Northwest, would experience a power surplus.

Table XIX   Status of Power Development of Columbia River Basin, Private and Local Public Projects, December 31, 1953

Dam	Stream	Total Installed Capacity (kilowatts)	Agency	DATE IN SERVICE First Unit	Last Unit
COMPLETED					
Total of private and locally owned public utilities		1,709,630			
UNDER CONSTRUCTION					
Box Canyon	Pend Oreille	60,000	Pend Oreille PUD	7–54	10–54
Kerr, addition	Flathead	56,000	Montana Power Co.	10–54	
Total		116,000			
PROPOSED FOR COMPLETION BY 1955					
Mossyrock	Cowlitz	300,000	City of Tacoma	2–55	9–55
Round Butte	Deschutes	225,000	Portland Gen. Elec.	9–55	12–55
Mayfield	Cowlitz	160,000	City of Tacoma	12–54	6–55
Pelton	Deschutes	120,000	Portland Gen. Elec.	9–54	12–54
Dike	Snake	67,500	Idaho Power Co.	4–54	8–54
Guffey	Snake	30,000	Idaho Power Co.	10–53	12–53
Total		902,500			
PROPOSED FOR COMPLETION AFTER 1955					
Noxon Rapids	Clark	150,000	Washington Water Power Co.		
Trout Creek	Clark	120,000	Montana Power Co.		
Swift Creek	Swift Creek	50,000	Pacific Power and Light		
Muddy Fork	Muddy Fork	35,000	Pacific Power and Light		
Total		355,000			
Grand Total		3,083,130			

Source: Adapted from Bonneville Power Administration, *Advance Program 1953*, map on page 23 and Appendix, Table 10.

Local private utilities at first took the same position. The president of the Washington Water Power Company testified in 1946 before appropriations committees against a federal power expansion program. Representatives of this company and of Pacific Power & Light Company, in appearances before the Natural Resources Development Committee of the state of Washington early in 1946, predicted a power surplus by 1950 and opposed construction of Chief Joseph Dam, now under construction. BPA, on the other hand, urged construction of McNary and Chief Joseph on the Columbia and certain dams on the tributaries—Hungry Horse on the Flathead River and dams on the lower Snake River. When, as a result of increasing population and the migration of low-priced power using industry, power shortage came to the Pacific Northwest in 1947, the private utilities changed their position and joined with public power agencies in support of the federal expansion program in hydropower facilities. In fact, they joined with public agencies at a Northwest Utilities Conference at Tacoma on January 22, 1947, in adopting the basic principle of federal responsibility for providing regional power needs from multiple-purpose projects and interconnecting transmission lines.

This experience suggests that it is one of the special problems of this sector of the public utility economy to come to some basic understandings as to procedure and principle for working out coordination between public and private agencies in the public utility field. Integrating on a basin-wide scale all hydroelectric power facilities and providing adequate storage capacity for the proper management of stream flow in the interests of the primary objectives of power production, flood control, and navigation (in descending order of their economic importance) is the lesson of experience in the Pacific Northwest. Will the capitalist economy be able to rally sufficient collective wisdom to encompass these objectives?

Financial Aspects

When President Franklin D. Roosevelt dedicated Bonneville Dam in 1937, he gave expression to a rate policy which had already been adopted by TVA:

. . . in developing electricity from this Bonneville Dam, from Grand Coulee Dam and other dams to be built on the Columbia and its tributaries, the policy of the widest use ought to prevail. The transmission of electricity is making such scientific strides today that we can well visualize a date, not far distant, when every community in this great area will be wholly electrified.

Administrator J. D. Ross expressed himself similarly:

I like a rate as uniform as it can be. I do not know just how uniform you can make them, but over the whole district, the big towns and the little towns, or the big districts and the small districts, they have the same hours of use, have all of the current made in the same way, running out on the line in the same way, and if they are close together, there certainly is no differential between them possible.

Local interests, particularly those centering in Portland, speaking through the majority report of a "Bonneville Commission" set up by Oregon in 1933, took the position that the market area for Bonneville power would be restricted to an area within about 150 miles of the dam and that rate-making policy should reflect transmission distance. The minority, on the contrary, took the long-range view that Bonneville would not remain an isolated project and would have to be considered as a component of a regional power system. Others, like the Portland Chamber of Commerce, however, opposed the blanket rate or postage-stamp system of charging, contending that rates should reflect transmission distance and that federal policies should enable each separate project to afford each separate location its inherent economic advantages. The proposal was to develop new large industries at tidewater in order to have them absorb the major share of the power. One area should not be "discriminated against for the benefit of other areas." After public hearings had been held by Ross early in 1938 throughout Washington, Oregon, and Idaho, the weight of the testimony was overwhelmingly against the Portland proposal and in favor of uniform wholesale rates throughout the transmission area.

Wholesale and resale rates.   In conformity with this policy, BPA set a basic wholesale rate, available anywhere on the transmission system, of $17.50 per kilowatt-year. This rate was designed to increase the "load factor" and to keep power steadily in use throughout the day. It reduced to 4.0 mills per kilowatt-hour at 50 per cent load factor to 2.66 mills at 75 per cent load factor and to 2.0 mills at 100 per cent load factor. Such a rate is feasible, where, as in the case of Bonneville or other hydrosystems generally, most costs are capacity costs and output and customer costs unimportant. In accordance with the Bonneville Act, this rate as well as others fixed later were approved by the Federal Power Commission.

The administrator, in order to encourage the widest possible use of energy for domestic and rural uses, also fixed the resale rate at which purchasers were required to sell energy at retail. These schedules are shown in Table XX.

Table XX BPA Energy Sales, Revenues, Unit Revenues, 1953

Type of Rate Schedule	Energy Sales, Kilowatt-hours in thousands	Revenues	Mills per Kilowatt-hour
Kilowatt-year rate *	11,950,921	$24,974,606	2.09
Demand-output rate *	246,422	1,062,336	4.31
At-site power rate *	23,552	74,438	3.16
Resale power rate *	2,792,770	8,884,047	3.18
Developmental rate *	14,621	36,552	2.50
Emergency service	144,471	361,178	2.50
Exchange service	1,208,933	3,022,332	2.50
Total	16,381,960	$38,415,489	2.35

* Firm power including energy subject to interruption.

Energy deliveries for fiscal 1953 to BPA's various types of customers, together with revenue yields and the average rate per kilowatt-hour are summarized in Table XX.

Area distribution. Of equal importance with rate policy in marketing is the coverage of an area with transmission and distribution facilities. To prevent monopolization of power at the dam site or in the immediate vicinity, the statute developed the concept of "transmission distance." With the realization that power sources, both steam and hydro, can be organized territorially, the concept of "transmission distance" became that of a superpower system, and finally, as a result of war emergencies, that of a "power pool." Both private and public suppliers of power are subject to these technological imperatives. Beginning in 1940 with 142 miles of line there was continuous expansion of the transmission system to 5,707 miles of line with 145 substations by 1953. The main stem of this extensive power grid consisted of 3,060 miles of 230-kilovolt line and was interconnected throughout the Northwest with the transmission lines of privately and publicly owned utilities.

The new power policy, announced by the new federal administration in August of 1953, asserted that the federal government would continue construction and operation of transmission facilities where economically feasible and necessary for proper connection and operation of additional federally owned generating plants.

Conflict over preference provisions. Recently, the preference provisions in the Bonneville Act of 1937 have been under attack by the Washington State Industrial Development Committee as discriminatory against private companies who do not get the benefit of the long-term twenty-year contracts going to public and cooperative agencies. Preference clauses of some kind have been authorized since the Reclamation Act of 1906, and the same policy embodied successively in the Raker Act of 1913, the Federal Water Power Act of 1920, the Boulder Canyon Act of 1928, the TVA Act of 1933, the Rural Electrification Act of 1936, the Fort Peck Act of 1938, the Reclamation Project Act of 1939, and the Flood Control Act of 1944. The reason for the preference policy was to give the small and often struggling public agencies access to the economies of large scale and integrated public power systems.

Under the new dispensation, contracts with private companies may be for twenty years instead of only five years. It would make this power unavailable to preference customers, especially to the rural electric cooperatives. Appearing for their national association at a hearing early in 1954 before the House Committee on Interior and Insular Affairs on the need of Clarification of this policy, its executive manager summarizes their apprehensions:

. . . we feel it will result in smaller quantities of firm power being made available to the preference customer due to the announced limitations on type of projects on which construction will be undertaken and due to the fact that transmission facilities for the delivery of such power as is developed will be minimized. We also fear that any policy which allows commercial utility companies to develop the most profitable hydro-electric dam sites in accordance with their own wishes is bound to raise the average firm-power rate on such remaining less profitable projects, construction of which is undertaken by the Government. We also fear that the new policy portends additional increases in the cost of Federal power from the arbitrary assignment to commercial power production of bigger portions of project construction costs. And finally, we fear that power rates may be raised in accordance with the Assistant Secretary's speech of September 29, 1953, for the purpose of reducing "the spread in price between federally produced power and locally produced power" and to "materially reduce the *unfortunate* [emphasis supplied] pressure on local communities to establish local public power entities just to make Federal hydro-power available to themselves."

Later in the same statement the forebodings with respect to the new interpretation of the preference clause are stated as follows:

By contrast, the new criteria allows the Secretary of the Interior the discretion of contracting firm power to commercial utility companies on a 20-year nonwithdrawable basis. This discretion allows the Secretary to establish a quasi-preferential class of customers which we believe is outside of the law and outside of the intent of the Congress.

The foregoing statements thus reveal what are the contending elements in the application of the new power policies.

Cost Allocations and Reimbursement Policies

The most important focal center of conflict resides in allocations of the construction cost of multipurpose projects because these will govern reimbursement policies and will also be reflected in the rate schedules. Ordinarily, rate schedules should in the long run be based upon cost considerations taking into account the useful life of the projects.

Bonneville, Grand Coulee, and other cost allocations. It seems that in the Bonneville case, cost allocations followed no scientific procedures. The Act provides that the FPC prepare this allocation. After the basic rates had been approved a tentative cost allocation was made in 1938 and revised into a final allocation in 1945. The tentative allocation assigned 32.5 per cent of the joint or common costs to power production and the remainder to navigation. With the completion of generator installations and the river regulation afforded by Grand Coulee storage, the Commission made a final allocation in which it assigned 50 per cent to each function. Taking into account that power production was incidental to navigation and that experience with rate schedules already established was yielding a margin of revenues above directly assignable costs, the Commission, in the exercise of an administrative judgment, adopted the 50 per cent allocation. In other words, revenue margins were deemed adequate to amortize all the fixed power investment (direct costs and 50 per cent of joint costs) over a fifty-year reimbursement period.

In the case of Grand Coulee Dam a more definite procedure of cost allocation was adopted by the Secretary of the Interior. Using the "alternative justifiable expenditure basis" which was being used by TVA in its own allocations, a final allocation was made which assigned cost components to irrigation and power as major functions, and to river regulation, flood control, and navigation as minor functions. In thus assigning costs it was considered that power facilities used in pumping irrigation water should be assigned directly to the irrigation function. These allocations are shown in Table XXI as derived from the relevant schedules of the 1953 Report of the Bonneville Power Administration on the Columbia River Power System. Costs include interest during construction.

Hungry Horse Dam, now completed, had not been subjected to definitive allocation procedures by the Secretary of the Interior. Based upon a tentative allocation of estimated costs by the Bureau of Reclamation, the BPA, in the above report, has undertaken to allocate current construction costs for its own purposes. All the fixed investment of the Bonneville Power

Administration itself are exclusively power costs, since they consist of transmission lines, substations, and other facilities used in marketing power.
These allocations are likewise shown in Table XXI, which thus affords a
comprehensive, though incomplete, summary of the magnitude and functional apportionment of these expenditures.

Table XXI   Original Cost Allocations of Federal Investment in
Columbia Basin Projects as of June 30, 1953

Items	Total	Amounts Allocated To Nonpower	Power
Bonneville Dam			
Specific power facilities (power houses, generating equip.)	$38,620,787	$	$38,620,787
Specific navigation (ship lock)	6,343,034	6,343,034	
Joint facilities (dam, reservoir, fishways)	41,881,606	20,940,803	20,940,803
Subtotal	86,845,427	27,283,837	59,561,590
Grand Coulee Dam			
Specific power facilities			
Commercial power	110,722,374	....	110,722,374
Irrigation pumping	1,598,482	1,598,482	
Joint facilities			
Commercial power	54,697,782	....	54,697,782
Future downstream river reg'n.	41,474,142	....	41,474,142
Irrigation	70,918,216	70,918,216	
Flood control-navigation	1,000,000	1,000,000	
Specific Irrigation (reservoir, canals, pumping plant)	183,412,597	183,412,597	
Farmland for resale	4,327,145	4,327,145	
Subtotal	468,150,738	261,256,440	206,894,298
Hungry Horse Dam			
Specific power facilities	26,360,109	....	26,360,109
Joint facilities			
Commercial power	45,619,892	....	45,619,892
Future downstream river reg'n.	13,018,474	....	13,018,474
Flood Control	19,288,520	19,288,520	
Subtotal	104,286,995	19,288,520	84,998,475
Plant and Equipment BPA	299,094,735	....	299,094,735
Grand Total	958,377,897	307,828,797	650,549,098

Based upon the foregoing allocation, Table XXI shows that the original
construction cost of federal facilities in service as of June 30, 1953 aggregated $958,377,897, of which $650,549,098, or 68 per cent, was allocated to
wholesale production, transmission, and sale of power. Of the remainder of
$307,828,797 allocated to nonpower uses, $255,929,295, or 27 per cent of to-

tal cost, was allocated to the other major function of irrigation. To this should be added $4,327,145, representing the cost of farmlands held for resale. As the project now stands, only about $27,783,837 was allocated to navigation, or 3 per cent of the total, and only $19,788,520, or 2 per cent, to flood control.

Another interesting comparison, which emphasizes the multiple-purpose aspect of the projects, shows that of the grand total of over $958 million, $287,898,632, or 30 per cent, represent the cost of facilities used jointly. In allocating this joint cost, based upon the several theories employed, $175,-751,093, or 61 per cent, was charged to power; $70,918,216, or 25 per cent, to irrigation; $21,440,803, or 7 per cent, to navigation; and $19,788,520, or 7 per cent, to flood control. It may be anticipated that the proportions chargeable to navigation will be materially increased as dams on the lower river, whose major functions are navigation and power, are completed.

Earning capacity of the power system. Revenues are primarily from the sale of the power output, with only a minor share derivable from the irrigation facilities. Operation of the power system is the function of the BPA. According to its report for fiscal 1953 the current year's surplus from power operations and the cumulative total from the beginning of operations is shown in the following tabulation:

	Fiscal 1953	*Cumulative Total*
Operating revenues	$39,175,209	$304,429,094
Operating expense	10,856,179	82,619,508
Depreciation expense	9,410,048	54,135,668
Interest deduction	8,983,109	72,635,203
Misc. deductions	358,281	1,628,722
Total deductions	29,607,617	211,019,101
Net revenues from power	$ 9,567,592	$ 93,409,993

It would be confusing to insert at this point repayments made by BPA of reimbursable power costs because they are independent of actual power output from the different projects. Reimbursable power costs agreed upon by BPA and the Corps of Engineers for the Bonneville project are being paid into the U.S. Treasury according to a schedule designed to return plant costs allocated to power, including necessary replacements, over a fifty-year period beginning July 1, 1944. Payments also include annual interest at 2.5 per cent.

Surplus revenues are paid into either the United States Treasury or the Reclamation Fund. The allocation of costs to power operations is too complex for detailing here. The report for 1953 contains a calculation designed to show how much of the investment in power facilities has been repaid. (See Table XXII.)

Table XXII   Reimbursement of Federal Power Costs, Columbia River System

	Gross Power Investment	Less unexpended Appropriations	Net Power Capital	Repayments to June 30, 1953	Net Power Investment	Per Cent Repaid
BPA	$335,928,323	$50,737,393	$305,190,930	$ 81,964,087	$223,226,843	26.86
Bonneville	59,923,979	99,193	59,824,786	20,343,163	39,481,623	34.00
Columbia Basin	220,414,852	813,193	219,601,501	43,100,278	176,501,223	19.63
Hungry Horse Dam	87,328,204	2,448,781	84,879,423	449,556	84,429,867	0.53
Total	723,595,088	54,098,448	669,496,640	145,857,084	523,639,556	21.79

The future of the Bonneville Power Administration is beclouded with some uncertainties. One of these is the power shortage and another is the possibility that the very low wholesale rates may have to be increased. It is also of some concern that the aluminum industry is the largest consumer of power (see Chart XXVIII) and is not an intensive employer of labor. To this must be added the uncertainties created by the questions of policy now being debated as to the future of the "preference provisions" and as to the agitation over the question of public versus private production and distribution of electric power.

30. THE
ST. LAWRENCE SEAWAY
AND POWER PROJECT

The oldest utility project of regional importance in the western hemisphere concerns the waterway by which the Great Lakes drain into the sea. This greatest of all inland waterways extends from the Strait of Belle Isle into the heartland of the continent. It is of both regional and national significance. The fourteen-states tributary to this waterway comprises an area stretching west from Ohio to Montana and Wyoming, south as far as Missouri and Kansas, and north to the Canadian border. It is richly endowed with agricultural wealth, constituting the most productive food producing region of the world. In mineral wealth the area contains the largest coal and iron deposits and extensive potential energy resources in forests, gas, oil, oil shale, and hydraulic power. Combined with these natural resources are the human resources of an industrial and farm work force, trained, experienced, and skilled to the manifold tasks of industrial and agricultural production. Similar though less developed resources are tributary to this waterway from the Canadian side.

History of the Waterway

The initial improvement of this natural waterway first utilized by fur traders dates back to 1795 when, in order to get their cargoes of furs around the rapids without portaging, a fur trading company constructed wooden locks at Sault Ste. Marie. (See Chart XXIX.) Another barrier to commerce was overcome in 1829 when the first Welland Canal was built by private interests to by-pass Niagara Falls. It was equipped with forty wooden locks. Successive improvements by the Canadian Government of the canal in 1845 and 1887 provided a channel with 14-foot locks in order to handle a growing traffic which by 1914 had increased to 3,860,000 tons. At this time there was no ocean traffic. River channel dredging, the construction of more locks at the Sault, and harbor improvements made the Great Lakes–St. Lawrence sys-

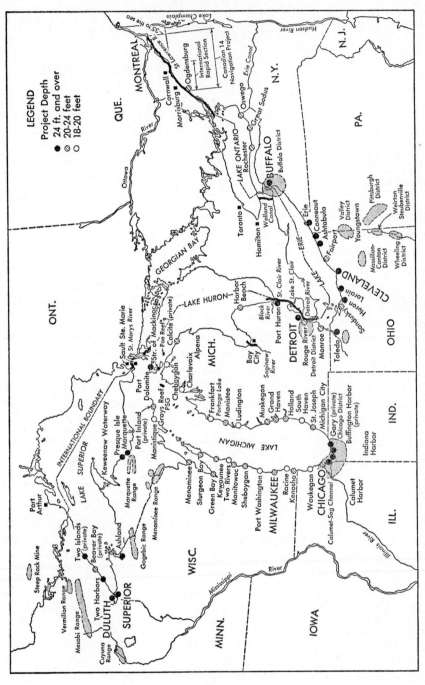

Chart XXIX St. Lawrence Basin. (Report—U.S. Army Engineers.)

tem into an interior waterway 2,300 miles in length. Early in the present century it boasted a minimum 14-foot navigation all the way from tidewater to Duluth.

In 1932 Canada completed a significant new improvement of the Welland Canal to 27 feet with locks to a depth of 30 feet over the sills. When in 1943 the United States finished the installation of the MacArthur locks at Sault Ste. Marie with a depth of 31 feet over the sills, the foundation had been laid which really started the agitation for a seaway for large ocean-going craft. The remaining obstacles in the upper waterway from Duluth to Lake Erie, it was felt, could be overcome by dredging to seaway specifications of 27 feet in the Detroit River, in Lake St. Clair, and in the St. Clair River. For the most part the Great Lakes provided a natural deep water channel, except where connecting channels in the Straits of Mackinac and the St. Marys River require deepening.

The most formidable obstacles are in the 160 miles between Lake Ontario and the deep-sea harbor of Montreal, now passable only to vessels through shallow 14-foot canals built by Canada around rapids. These obstacles are in the International Rapids section, where they are of joint concern to both the United States and Canada, and in the Lake St. Francis, Soulanges and Lachine sections which concern only Canada.

Political Background

The earliest planning and agitation for the present seaway and power project began in 1895 with an inquiry and first report upon the prospect of a "deep waterway." A basic step was taken when in 1909 the United States and Canada signed an International Boundary Treaty which created an International Joint Commission as administrative agent of the two governments. This body issued several reports on needed improvements, all favorable to the eventual consummation of a seaway plan. In 1923 the power phase became important when the American Superpower Corporation applied to the recently created Federal Power Commission for a license to develop some of the power in the international rapids section, but the application was turned down because the proposal was deemed to be in conflict with the seaway aspects. Henceforth the dual purposes of navigation and power appeared to be indissolubly joined. On the technical side, the Corps of Army Engineers became the United States agency which was usually called upon to supply engineering plans. By 1926 the Corps had settled down to recommend the single-stage development now being utilized.

Up to this time Canada showed much less interest in this dual-purpose project than was exhibited on the American side because the Province of Ontario was surfeited with hydroelectric power as a result of the operations of its Hydroelectric Power Commission. In the United States, interest in the project was running high, especially in New York where Governor Franklin Roosevelt in 1931 had set up a State Power Authority, first of its kind, to serve as the promotional and action agency. Meanwhile Canada had rebuilt the Welland Canal, opening it to traffic in 1932 with its 30-foot locks.

The treaty phase. In 1932 the Joint Board of Engineers issued the final report which became the basis for a proposed new treaty between the United States and Canada. It was signed in Washington on July 18, 1932. The following year the New York State Power Authority and the U.S. Army Engineers reached an accord on plans for power development, on the disposition of the United States share of power and on cost reimbursement. Hearings on the treaty were conducted by the Senate Committee on Foreign Relations, which voted fifteen to five to recommend approval of the treaty, including the accord on power. In addition to the usual opposition from the railroads, the Atlantic and Gulf ports, and the coal mining interests, there was also opposition in Congress to making the accord a part of the treaty. The House favored the proposition of turning power development over to the State of New York, while the Senate was opposed. To smooth the way for the treaty in the Senate, the ever-versatile Franklin Roosevelt created an Interdepartmental Board (consisting of representatives of the Departments of War and Commerce, the Federal Power Commission, and the New York Power Authority) to report on the treaty. In a special message submitting the favorable report, President Roosevelt urged Senate ratification. After prolonged debate the treaty was defeated by a roll-call vote of forty-six to forty-two, thus lacking the necessary two-thirds majority.

The executive agreement phase. Between 1934 and 1940 the legislative stalemate continued. Reports and surveys by various planning agencies continued to be made, all favoring the project except the Niagara Frontier Planning Board, which represented private power interests and which opposed construction. In 1936 discussion of a new treaty to include Niagara Falls redevelopment was started. At this time the national defense issue was injected by President Roosevelt in a speech at the dedication of the Thousand Island Bridge. Meanwhile, the need for power in both Canada and the United States developed in response to the renewed war emergency. President Roosevelt in a message urged construction at the International Rapids section because of its special value to national defense, allocating

$1 million of special defense funds for the purpose of preliminary engineering surveys and investigations by the Corps of Engineers and the Federal Power Commission. Canada made similar and corresponding preparations. These renewed mutual efforts finally bore fruit on March 19, 1941, when the United States and Canada signed an Executive Agreement at Ottawa, subject to approval by concurrent legislation. It provided for immediate construction in the International Rapids section and completion of navigation improvements elsewhere by 1948. The executive agreement was submitted to Congress for approval. It should be noted that the objective (international section improvement) had become a limited one, and the procedure had changed from treaty to legislation by both houses, thus requiring only a bare majority. The new plan also included the Federal–New York State accord providing for a joint cost allocation of $93,375,000 to be assumed by the New York Power Authority and to be reimbursed to the Treasury by the self-liquidating power project over a fifty-year period. The House was favorable but the Senate was opposed, and finally, late in 1944 defeated the proposal by a vote of fifty-six to twenty-five. In the meantime, July, 1942, MacArthur Lock of 31 feet over the sill had been completed as a fifth lock at Sault St. Marie. Hope of construction under the executive agreement had disappeared after Pearl Harbor in view of the shortage of steel and manpower, as President Roosevelt himself admitted.

The joint resolution phase. A third start to effectuate construction was begun in 1945 when Governor Dewey of New York and President Truman expressed themselves as favorable to the project. A new approach was finally initiated in 1947 when Senator Vandenberg introduced Joint Resolution III providing for *self-liquidation of navigation costs* by authorizing the *collection of tolls.* But the Senate remained obdurate by defeating the measure in 1948 with a vote of fifty-seven to thirty to recommit the measure to the Committee for further investigation.

The final formulation. Once more conferences were held to rejuvenate the project to the accompaniment of additional studies, surveys, and report. In July, 1948, separate applications were filed by the New York Power Authority and by the Hydroelectric Power Commission of Ontario for an order of approval from the old International Joint Commission under the Boundary Waters Treaty of 1909 of the joint project for *developing power.* Simultaneously, the New York Power Authority applied to the Federal Power Commission for a license to carry out the American portion. Later in the year a competing application for *private development* was made to the Federal Power Commission by the Public Power and Water Corporation of New Jersey.

While the applications were pending, Congress renewed consideration of the entire project. Canada was becoming increasingly restive under these delays. In repeated messages President Truman urged action, and in his budget message of 1950 recommended an appropriation for preliminary work because the Seaway was urgently needed for access to Labrador iron ores, so necessary for defense. A new note was supplied by the Canadian Minister of Transport when in a radio address he suggested that an *all-Canadian* route be considered should agreement not be reached with the United States. The project once more landed in the lap of Congress when early in 1951 the Federal Power Commission denied the application of both the private corporation and the New York State Power Authority, but *recommended* federal construction of the entire project. Like a cat with nine lives, the Seaway Project survived all these legislative vicissitudes, emerging finally as the Wiley Bill.

The Present Project

Certain preliminary but definitive steps should first be noted. On June 30, 1952, Canada and the United States submitted concurrent applications to the International Joint Commission for an order of approval of the power project. After hearings, the order was issued in October, 1952. Also concurrently, the Federal Power Commission was reconsidering the application of the New York Power Authority for a license to construct, in conjunction with the Ontario Hydroelectric Power Commission, the dams and necessary power works in the International Rapids section as approved by the International Joint Commission. The license was granted in July, 1953. Under the Wiley Bill the *navigation facilities* in the International Rapids section will be constructed in United States territory by the St. Lawrence Seaway Development Corporation. Corresponding facilities in the Canadian section will be completed by the St. Lawrence Seaway Authority of Canada, thus providing a seaway of 27-foot depth from Lake Erie to Montreal. From here, a minimum 35-foot channel is available to the open ocean. The work in the Thousand Islands section will consist of deepening and improving the channel to the specified depth at scattered locations. By withdrawing Senate amendments which called for the deepening of several channels above Lake Erie, as already explained, the legislative issue was restricted to United States participation in only one improvement but which was the major limiting factor, and to secure which, Canada was prepared to go it alone. Navigation improvements in the upper basin are to be incorporated in separate legislation to be dealt with in the future on their own merits. (See Chart XXX for a water level profile of the Great Lakes–St. Lawrence System.)

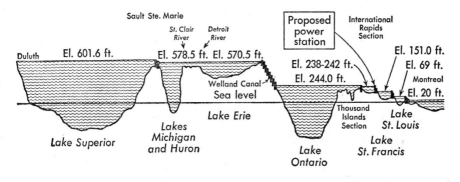

Chart XXX   Water Level Profile—Great Lakes—St. Lawrence System.

Provisions of the Seaway Act of 1954.   As finally passed on May 7 and signed by President Eisenhower on May 8, the Seaway Act adopts some of the principal provisions of the Tennessee Valley Project Act of 1933, although differing from it in certain essential respects, especially as these relate to power policies. Although an integral part of the underlying conception of multiple-purpose development, the Act in its terms separates the navigation function from the power production function, handing the latter over to the state of New York or some other licensee of the Federal Power Commission. The national security is an ambient purpose surrounding the entire enterprise, as is the economic development of the entire Great Lakes–St. Lawrence River basin.

The Act creates a public corporation, with the usual powers, to be known as the St. Lawrence Seaway Development Corporation, as an instrumentality of the United States, subject to the direction and supervision of the President or the head of such agency as he may designate. It is generally understood that the Corps of Engineers will be the construction agency and that the Secretary of the Army will supervise the corporation. Management, instead of being vested in a board of directors as the original bill provides, was placed in the hands of an administrator and a deputy administrator. An advisory board of five members is set up who are not to act in an administrative but in a consultative capacity. All are to be appointed by the President with Senate confirmation. Administrator and deputy are to be paid annual salaries of $17,500 and $16,000, respectively.

The corporation is authorized, in cooperation with the St. Lawrence Seaway Authority of Canada, to construct, operate, and maintain the single-stage navigation project in the International Rapids section and to do the necessary dredging in the Thousand Islands section. But it must first receive satisfactory assurance from Canada that the navigation works in the Canadian section of the river will be completed as authorized by Parliament in 1951. It is also required to coordinate its activities with the New York Power Authority, which was licensed by the Federal Power Commission to construct and operate the power works authorized by the International Joint Commission in 1952.

The corporation is directed to borrow $105 million through the sale of revenue bonds bearing interest at the current average rate of interest on current marketable bonds of the United States with comparable maturities. To make the project self-liquidating, the corporation is directed to negotiate an agreement with some agency designated by Canada governing the tolls to be levied on the Seaway and an equitable division of the revenues. If no agreement is reached, the corporation is directed to establish rates *unilaterally* after public hearings for the use of the United States-owned portion of the Seaway. Tolls or changes in tolls must be approved by the President and are subject to rehearing by the corporation upon complaint; the corporation's final orders are subject to review in the courts.

A yardstick for liquidation.   The yardstick for establishing tolls is laid down in five specific rules: (1) the rates shall be fair and reasonable, with consideration being given to the special character of cargoes such as bulk agricultural, mineral, and other raw materials; (2) rates shall vary according to the character of the cargo; (3) rates for vessel and ballast may be less than rates for passengers and cargo; (4) the rates shall be calculated so as to cover the costs of operating and maintaining the works of the Corporation, including depreciation, interest on obligations, and payments in lieu of taxes; and (5) rates shall be calculated with a view to providing sufficient revenue to amortize principal and debts and obligations of the Corporation over a period not to exceed fifty years. The spirit of the proponents of the Seaway is succinctly put in the words of Senator Wiley, Chairman of the Foreign Relations Committee: "At long last our efforts are crowned with victory." And the general conclusion was best expressed by the Senate Committee on Foreign Relations, in recommending "that the bill (S. 2150) do pass," which concluded as follows:

The committee is profoundly aware of the extensive studies, surveys, debates, and discussions which have attended the St. Lawrence project throughout the years, and of the many arguments advanced for and against the Seaway. After careful consideration of all the arguments, the committee is convinced that the United States' participation in the St. Lawrence Seaway project, Lake Erie to Montreal, is in the interest of the security of the United States, is economically desirable and sound, will pay for itself out of its earnings, and is a wise undertaking for the United States and Canada to build and operate jointly. Its true perspective is continental and its final results must inevitably be continental in their impact.

The power project. The power portion of the combined project may be summarized as follows: A fifty-year license to construct, operate, and maintain the power facilities on the American side of the International Rapids section was issued on July 15, 1953, to the New York Power Authority by the Federal Power Commission. It is required to cooperate with the Corps of Engineers in constructing and improving navigation facilities associated with the power project and to furnish power free of cost for the operation and maintenance of the navigation facilities. The use, storage, and discharge from storage of waters affected by the license are made subordinate to the reasonable rules and regulations as prescribed by the Secretary of the Army in the interest of navigation, or by the Commission for the protection of life, health and property, and for recreational purposes.

Under this license the Federal Power Commission will determine the "actual legitimate original cost" of the initial project, and any improvements thereof, upon which the Power Authority is entitled to earn 6 per cent per annum on the net investment after the first twenty years of operation. Earnings above this specified rate of return are regarded as surplus earnings, one-half of which may be used to make up any deficiency in the stipulated return in the past or to establish amortization reserves to retire the investment. In addition the licensee must pay fees based upon power output to reimburse the United States for the costs of administration. The license also requires the Power Authority to make a reasonable portion of the power capacity and of the power output available for use within the economic market area in neighboring states. The Federal Power Act also makes the projects recapturable by the United States upon termination of the license or transferable to a new licensee, in either case upon payment of the net investment.

Construction will be undertaken jointly with the Ontario Hydroelectric Power Commission and will be in accordance with the requirements of the Order of Approval of the International Joint Commission issued in October, 1952, which follow the plans outlined in the joint agreement of 1941 between this country and Canada. These include the power house and spillway dam at Barnhart Island, together with supporting structures for a reservoir providing some 80-odd feet of head. One-half of the available power, computed at 1,250,000 horsepower, is assigned under the license. Construction must begin within a year and be completed within seven years.

Estimated Cost of the Project

The Army engineers, thoroughly familiar with this project and increasingly conservative in their estimating, have placed the cost of the United

States portion of seaway construction at $88,074,000. Including the Canadian share of construction cost of $174,950,000, the total cost of the 27-foot channel from Lake Erie to Montreal is estimated to cost $263,024,000 at December, 1952, cost levels. The following tabulation breaks these costs down in accordance with the significant sections.

Section	Canada	United States	Total
Welland Canal	$ 2,000,000	. . . . .	$ 2,000,000
Thousand Island section	. . . . .	$ 1,766,000	1,766,000
International Rapids section	. . . . .	86,308,000	86,308,000
Canadian section	172,950,000	. . . . .	172,950,000
Total	$174,950,000	$88,074,000	$263,024,000

According to a "normal schedule" of construction, the time is estimated at six years, while an "accelerated schedule" would require five years. The amount appropriated for the project of $105 million will benefit a section of the country which has not been the recipient of federal aid to the same degree as have other sections. The Senate Committee compares it with the costs of the Suez Canal of $80 million, the Chicago drainage canal of $53 million, the Welland Ship Canal (already constructed by Canada) of $131 million, the Panama Canal of $375 million. Since the project is expected to be self-liquidating through shipping tolls, it will not be a burden upon the taxpayers and the Committee anticipates that substantial profits may continue to accrue to the federal treasury after the payoff period of fifty years or less.

Estimates of annual costs and revenues. The foregoing conclusion as to the financial capacity of the navigation project to reimburse the Treasury rests upon the following estimates:

Item	Canada	United States	Total
First cost of navigation work	$174,950,000	$88,074,000	$263,024,000
Add int. during construction 3%	15,746,000	7,927,000	23,673,000
Total navigation investment	190,696,000	96,001,000	286,697,000
Annual interest and amortization 3%	7,418,000	3,734,000	11,152,000
Annual maintenance and operation	2,000,000	1,460,000	3,460,000
Annual carrying charge	$ 9,418,000	$ 5,194,000	$ 14,612,000

To meet the annual carrying charge of $14,612,000, the Committee estimates that bulk traffic consisting of iron ore, grain, coal, and petroleum will be rapidly available, with substantial amounts of traffic in other commodities. As estimated by the Department of Commerce, a traffic ceiling of 50 million tons may be assumed as wholly reasonable, based upon the amount of traffic presently using the 14-foot channel. The required toll revenues to meet average annual carrying charges could be obtained from an average toll of 29 cents per ton if 50 million tons of cargo are available. With only 45 million tons available, average tolls would have to rise to 32½ cents per ton, and to 36½ cents per ton, with only 40 million tons available. With additional revenues forthcoming from the deadweight tonnage of ships returning empty, the Committee was convinced that the revenue potentials from the Lake Erie to Montreal section of the Seaway would make the project self-liquidating. Earlier revenue estimates by the Department of Commerce with tolls ranging from 25 cents to $1.25 per ton forecast annual revenues varying between $36 million and $49 million.

Some reservations. In presenting these estimates of seaway finances, attention should be directed to the fact that the burden of carrying the joint costs has all been allocated to the power phase of the joint project. Since the International Rapids power section affords the most economical power site in North America, these joint costs can be added to the power costs and still keep unit power costs well below the level of other power costs of the region. The failure to allocate some of these joint costs (hitherto assumed to be one-half) to the navigation phase was the reason assigned by Commissioner McWhorter of the Federal Power Commission for his dissent from the order of approval by the International Joint Commission. Chief of Engineers, Lt. General Pick, had estimated that facilities having joint value for navigation and power development would aggregate $212,807,000. This failure to allocate has served to reduce navigation costs and to ease their eventual liquidation.

The Committee deemed it inadvisable to suggest legislation which would provide for the deepening of the connecting channels of the Great Lakes because that portion of the Seaway project should be considered separately on its own merits. Since this phase of the Seaway project is already being considered by Congress, some estimates of the probable cost of these improvements should also be shown. (Authorizing legislation has now been passed.) Furthermore, we shall include the power phase in these estimates in order to give a complete picture of this dominantly dual-purpose project. Beginning with the project in its present state of improvement, the following calculations of cost are derived for the remaining work to be done to convert the 14-foot waterway into a 27-foot waterway with coincidental power production.

Item	Canada	United States	Total
		(*in thousands*)	
Total cost of remaining work	$457,369	$471,574	$928,943
Less allocation to power	223,076	223,076	446,152
Balance chargeable to navigation	234,293	248,498	482,791
Add interest during construction	21,086	20,871	41,957
Investment in navigation	255,379	269,369	524,748
Annual interest and amortization	9,934	10,093	20,027
Annual maintenance and operation	2,306	2,192	4,498
Annual carrying charge	12,240	12,285	24,525

By estimating benefits to a minimum traffic aggregate of 64 million tons in terms of savings in transportation charges, calculated as the differential between the cost of water transport without tolls and the cost of the cheapest alternative means of transport, the staff of the Deputy Chief of Engineers derived a figure of $60 million annually. This, in the opinion of General Robinson, establishes the economic feasibility of the over-all Seaway project because the ratio of benefit ($60 million) to cost ($24.5 million) is 2.45. Comparing an estimated potential toll revenue of $36.5 million with the same cost establishes a revenue-cost ratio of 1.49.

As to one's faith in these prognostications, we can do no better than once more to quote the Committee, whose makeup was essentially conservative:

The Great Lakes–St. Lawrence Seaway stands in a class by itself in that it can be made self-liquidating. No such potential traffic could be visualized for either the Panama Canal or the Suez Canal as is now anticipated for the St. Lawrence Seaway. While in the initial stages the project is to be financed with the assistance of the Federal Government, the seaway ultimately will be built and operated at no cost to the taxpayer. The tolls on the traffic using the navigation facilities will make the project self-liquidating. The related power phase will represent no cost to the Federal Government, since the State of New York has been granted a license to construct the power facilities jointly with the Hydroelectric Power Commission of Ontario and to share the costs previously classified as common to power and navigation.

The representative of the railroads opposing the project made much of these "omitted costs" and of the fact that the waterway will not be available for about five months of the year. There can be no doubt that these negative considerations are of some importance. The deepening of lake harbors is certainly an essential part of the ultimate unfolding of the project. What these costs will amount to and how they will be borne is problematical. Railroad interests reckon them as considerably in excess of $100 million. Until sufficient experience has been had with actual operations, making more facts available, resolving some doubts and perchance creating others, one must reserve judgment on long-range calculations such as these. Yet the action taken was undoubtedly wise because the present project has reduced these risks to a minimum. That has been its strength.

The Iron Ore Situation

In evaluating the economic feasibility of the present project and its future impact upon the region, the situation with respect to iron ore should be briefly reviewed. Much of this production is now concentrated in the Great Lakes region, making this the greatest industrial area in the world, since it produces over 35 per cent of the world's steel. (See Chart XXIX.) The Ruhr of Germany "is not even a close second." This concentration has been made possible by the fact that iron ore has been at one end of the Great Lakes water haul and coal at the other. Since 1910 over 80 per cent of the ore requirements has come from the Lake Superior regions, depleting these high-grade supplies at such a pace that the industry estimates—and these estimates are confirmed by the findings of the Paley Commission—that only thirteen years' supply of high-grade (50 per cent) ore are still available. Of estimated United States iron ore reserves of 79 billion long tons, 64 billion tons are in the Lake Superior district, but only 1.6 billion tons are first grade. Ores of 25 to 35 per cent content, called taconite, aggregate 60 billion tons, but this cannot be used economically without "beneficiation" (eliminating impurities) at the mines. This is now being done and the development of taconites will be expanded, although increasing reliance is being placed upon the development of high-grade foreign ores in Liberia, Venezuela, and Labrador.

Since most of the Labrador ore is owned by steel companies in the Great Lakes region, it is this ore which will provide tonnage for the haul from Seven Islands port through the improved St. Lawrence River channel, canal, and lock section. In the event of another war emergency, these shipments could be greatly increased. Even in peace time it is estimated that 80 per cent of the traffic would originate or terminate in the United States, making our participation in the construction and control of the project imperative.

The Seaway and Competition

It would seem that in the long run the fear that competing facilities will be irreparably injured will not be realized. The Seaway is expected to stimulate both the regional and national economy by unlocking natural resources, by reducing transportation costs for commodities that should move by water, and by providing a new and auxiliary transport route that should develop new channels of trade. While North Atlantic ports may initially suffer some loss from traffic diversion, as will their connecting carriers, this will be more than offset by the growth of new traffic.

Opposition to the Seaway is particularly virulent in the Atlantic and Gulf ports because it would decrease their traffic and cause a drop in employment. The Port of New York Authority estimates the drop in employment at 200,000 for the metropolitan area. It also points to the seasonal effect upon its business because the Seaway will be ice-bound for five months. Boston contends that it will lose 30 per cent of its port traffic, while New Orleans and Houston estimate even larger losses. Buffalo argues that its grain business will suffer, though it admits that there may be some compensating gains from increases in iron and steel production. The deepened channel may have the effect of revitalizing the shipbuilding industry in the Great Lakes area and elsewhere, though it is believed that the major competitive advantage will first accrue to the smaller foreign vessels because only a small percentage of American flag vessels will be able to use the Seaway. Canadian water transport will be greatly advanced because it will help unlock its undeveloped natural resources. Even Canadian railroads have favored the Seaway because of its effect in promoting general economic development in Canada. It is, of course, impossible to properly assess these contending claims based upon a static economy because both the American and Canadian economies are highly dynamic.

The railroad and coal interests have been the hard core of opposition to the Seaway and power projects. The railroads, in particular, voice their criticisms that it would be a useless addition to our transportation system, vulnerable to air attack and designed only to provide low-cost transportation of iron ore for steel companies. The Department of Defense does not agree with this argument, pointing out that the Seaway is almost submarine proof, that it will not require naval convoys as the all-ocean routes from Venezuela, Liberia, Brazil, Sweden, and others would and that it can be defended from air attack. Military experts regard reliance upon rails alone as inadequate to meet wartime needs. Moreover, these facilities have been decreasing since World War II, and without seaway transportation the price of iron ore would increase. Also, in the event of a hot war, water transport facilities, being more flexible, can be more rapidly expanded than rail facilities. If the Seaway is not constructed, the next twenty-five to fifty years will see the migration of the steel industry to the seaboard, where costs will be higher and where the relocation of steel will have a dislocating effect upon other industries.

The economic position of railroads with terminals on the Great Lakes is different from that of railroads in the rest of the country, although all made a common cause of opposing the project. It should be recalled in this connection that railroad executives of northwestern rail lines favored construction of the project in the 1920's. Not only did they point to the internal economy obtainable from the relief of traffic congestion in the East, but they also saw revenue improvement due to increased car efficiency from the quicker return of rolling stock from lake ports. But even more important was the effect they foresaw of lower cost deepwater transportation in extending the marketing radius of goods, thus developing railroad traffic to and from the ports.

31. THE

TENNESSEE VALLEY PROJECT—

A CASE STUDY

It is generally conceded that the most thorough-going example of the planned development of the natural and social resources of a region is afforded by the Tennessee Valley Authority. Its distinguishing characteristic is that it was the first federal agency to be given a comprehensive regional planning job by Congress, and that it has become the "ideal type" of a public corporation set up to develop and conserve the natural resources of a specific region. It has also done this job without sacrificing local interests to the centralizing trends and absentee controls that seem to be inherent in the electric power industry under holding company control. It has found the key to the solution of the problem of centralization versus decentralization of state and federal functions in a rational and step-by-step development of public policies, some of which were not taken without a sharp clash of pecuniary interests and personalities. It will be the primary purpose of this brief discussion to set forth the long-run objectives of this evolutionary trend.

Genesis of the TVA

The Tennessee River is formed by the junction of the Holston and French Broad Rivers four miles above Knoxville, Tennessee. It flows in a general southwesterly direction across the state of Tennessee and across northern Alabama. It then turns sharply to the north (deflected perhaps by uplift in its geologic past), recrosses western Tennessee and joins the Ohio River above Paducah. A map of the Tennessee Valley region and of the water control system is shown in Chart XXXI. The river watershed comprises an area of about 42,000 square miles with a population of about three million, the eastern half of which is largely mountainous. The median rainfall is about 51 inches, while rainfall in the 80's is recorded in the Great Smoky Mountains. The population is dominantly white and of Anglo-

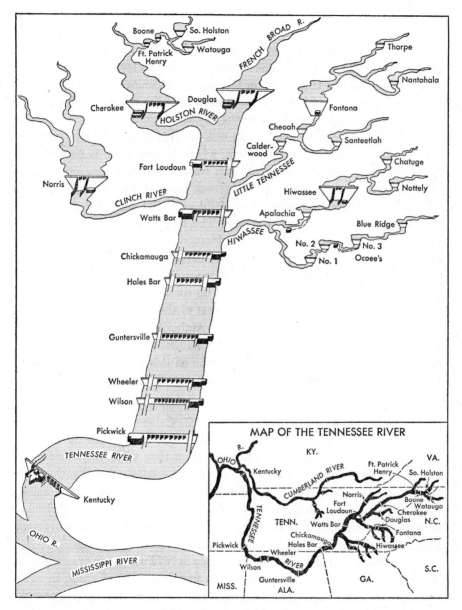

Chart XXXI Diagram of TVA Water Control System. (Annual Report—Tennessee Valley Authority.)

Saxon origin. Settlement of the Valley began during the last decades of the eighteenth century as the population followed the water courses.

As elsewhere, the heavily forested regions were cut over rapidly, and the economy developed primarily on an agricultural basis. Cotton was the major crop in the lower and level reaches of the Valley, with corn and tobacco in the bottom lands and on the sloping hillsides of the eastern part. Industrial development lagged behind the rest of the country; only the cities of Chattanooga and Knoxville showed any considerable concentration. The river, though capable of navigation, was divided into two major parts by the impassable Muscle Shoals section, where Wilson Dam is now located. The Civil War and Reconstruction Era further retarded development, the plantations giving way to a system of tenant farming. Though well endowed with certain mineral resources, especially coal and phosphates, economic exploitation of these resources lagged. The fertility-consuming methods of tillage of the cotton and tobacco kingdoms, combined with the soil erosion caused by rainfall and topography, ultimately produced agricultural distress, with depressed areas of subsistence farming unrelieved by significant urban industrial expansion. It could all be summed up in the statistic that the per capita income was only 42 per cent of the national average. In 1933 Congress created the Tennessee Valley Authority as a federal agency to bring such aid in the development of its natural resources as might prove economical. To understand the importance of this project, we must begin by tracing, in merest outline, its historical antecedents.

History of the project. The history of the Tennessee Valley project begins in 1824 with a suggestion by John C. Calhoun, President Monroe's Secretary of War, that a survey be made of Muscle Shoals with the new idea of improving the navigation of the river. At a time when the country was looking for easier means of access to the virgin territory then known as the "Southwest," this river with its tributaries commended itself as a natural waterway. After a preliminary survey made in 1827, Congress authorized an expenditure of about $700,000 to canalize Muscle Shoals, improvements which turned out to be largely evanescent.

The river attained renewed prominence in 1872 when surveys conducted by Army engineers recommended further improvements, affecting this time primarily the open channel of the stream but including the construction of a canal around Elk River Shoals, begun in 1875. Subsequently, there was much back-and-forth discussion with the result that these and other navigational improvements were not finally completed until 1900 at a cost of approximately $3 million.

Between 1905 and 1912, with renewed interest in our inland waterways and with the movement for conservation of natural resources then at its height, there were further reports touching not only needed navigation improvements but also reflecting new public interests in the development of water powers. In 1915, at a cost of $150,000, a new detailed survey of Muscle Shoals was made. This 37-mile long section continued to divide the stream into an upper and lower reach where navigation was relatively unimpeded. Muscle Shoals was the bottleneck above and below which there was considerable traffic in heavy and bulky commodities such as sand, gravel, and lumber. Very little traffic could pass Muscle Shoals because of poor water conditions.

World War I developments. With the European war in progress, the availability of Muscle Shoals as a site for the development of hydroelectric power was recognized. This could be turned to good account in the production of "fixed nitrogen" for explosives, for it was feared that the German submarine might at any time interfere with the supply of Chilean nitrates. Linked with this wartime demand was the increasingly urgent requirement that the loss of nitrogen in the soil, due to cropping and soil erosion or leaching, be restored, not only upon the once fertile lands in the Valley but countrywide as well.

In the National Defense Act of June 3, 1916, Congress appropriated $20 million for the production of nitrates. After some investigation, the process of the General Chemical Company was taken over. This company thought it had a modified form of the process developed by Professor Haber in Germany. Nitrate plant No. 1, including a direct-current steam plant, was constructed to test out this process on a commercial scale. It was a complete failure, worth only its salvage value.

In the meantime, nitrate plant No. 2, designed to use the well-known cyanamide process of nitrogen fixation, had been completed. This process consumed about four times the amount of electric energy as did the synthetic or Haber process. Lands for the construction of a dam (rechristened Wilson Dam) to flood out Muscle Shoals were acquired in 1917 from the Alabama Power Company (in effect a gift). Because the construction of Wilson Dam would require too much time, the Sheffield steam plant was completed to supply ad interim power. Nitrate plant No. 2 was ready to produce when the end of the war came. With additional wartime appropriations, dam construction was actually begun in 1918. By 1921, when the dam was about 35 per cent completed, the work was brought to a halt due to lack of funds, but with renewed appropriations in 1922, Wilson Dam and the appurtenant power plant were finally completed in 1925 after a total expenditure of $45 million. The two nitrate plants, the associated steam plants, the Waco limestone quarry, and the connecting railway had cost about $80 million.

Congressional struggles over Muscle Shoals. Beginning also in 1922 with successive appropriations, Congress authorized a complete survey by the Army engineers of the entire Tennessee River basin. At a cost of $1,090,-000, data and reports became available upon which general plans for the development of the river and its tributaries could be based. With these efforts to liquidate this wartime investment, the history of the project passes into that atmosphere of political conflict which enshrouded it until it emerged in terms of Senator Norris' bill.

In the congressional struggle over who should be the agent to operate these facilities, three interest groups are to be distinguished. The farming interest, mobilized through the American Farm Bureau Federation, advocated private operation under a fifty-year lease for the production of fertilizer. Bids by the American Cyanamide Company and by Henry Ford represented this point of view.

The public utility industry stood to a man for private operation. The proposal of a joint committee of Congress in 1926, embodying a fifty-year lease to thirteen allied electric power companies in the Valley area, had this solution in view.

Under the leadership of Senator Norris of Nebraska, the proponents of public ownership and operation of water power resources were as resolutely opposed, and his first bill to this effect was introduced in 1922. This group was twice successful in securing passage through Congress of bills designed to set up public ownership and operation by a public corporation. President Coolidge thwarted the first in 1928 with a pocket veto. The second attempt in 1931 was given an outright veto by President Hoover.

Effect of the national campaign of 1932. Increasingly, the transcendent issue was between public and private ownership and operation, other interests receding temporarily into the background. It was caught up in the national political campaign of 1932 in which the ineffectiveness of public utility regulation and ways of fighting the depression became major issues. With F. D. Roosevelt and Herbert Hoover the contending candidates, the Norris bill in its final formulation gave evidence of this revised orientation. Federal ownership and operation of Muscle Shoals was demanded so that there might be provided a "yardstick" to measure the economy of private operation of power utilities and the effectiveness of their regulation. After the election, President Roosevelt's approach, however, brought these various interests into a more comprehensive plan and gave them a greater co-ordination. Viewed in their historical perspective, the objectives of the project as finally formulated recapitulated the various public purposes which the past one hundred years had evolved. The plan began with putting into general use the great wartime electric generating station at Muscle Shoals; but it was intended in its ultimate unfolding to be a lesson in both the conservation of natural resources and the potentialities of national planning. As succinctly described by President Roosevelt in a now famous announcement from Warm Springs, Georgia in 1933:

It is clear that the Muscle Shoals development is but a small part of the potential public usefulness of the entire Tennessee River. Such use, if envisioned in its entirety, transcends mere power development; it enters the wide fields of flood control, soil erosion, afforestation, elimination from agricultural use of marginal lands, and distribution of and diversification of industry. In short, this power development of war days leads logically to national planning for a complete river watershed, involving many states and the future lives and welfare of millions. It touches and gives life to all forms of human concern.

Many hard lessons have taught us the human waste that results from lack of planning. Here and there a few wise cities and counties have looked ahead and planned. But our nation has "just grown." It is time to extend planning to a wider field, in this instance comprehending in one great project many states directly concerned with the basin of one of our greatest rivers.

This is in a true sense a return to the spirit and vision of the pioneer. If we are successful here we can march on, step by step, in a like development of other great natural territorial units within our borders.

The Program of Resource Development

A new type of federal agency. The public corporation (TVA) organized in June, 1933, was clothed with the required powers of government but was designed to have the flexibility and initiative of private corporations. It was to plan for the proper use, conservation, and development of the natural resources of the region and was allowed wide discretion as to how this was to be carried out.

The first board of directors, appointed by the President with the advice and consent of the Senate, consisted of three men carefully chosen for their special qualifications. Arthur E. Morgan, an engineer with experience in dam construction and river regulation, was named as chairman and given a full term of nine years. He was President of Antioch College and had shown a great deal of interest in the problems of planning for the development of our natural resources. A second member was Harcourt A. Morgan, an agriculturist who had spent a lifetime in the study of the problems of southern agriculture and who was President of the University of Tennessee. He was given a six-year term. The third member was David E. Lilienthal, an attorney with experience in public utility law, who had served as a member of the Public Service Commission of Wisconsin. His term was three years; thereafter all appointments were to be for nine years. The annual salary was fixed at $10,000.

Some significant departures from past practices.   It was a significant departure from past practices that the new corporation was freed from civil service laws of the United States in the appointment and promotion of all employees. In the development of its organization it was, however, charged with the duty of recognizing merit and efficiency and was specifically prohibited from applying any political test or qualification. Indicative of President Roosevelt's personal interest in this project was the power given to the President to remove any member who violated this general injunction of strict nonpartisanship. Otherwise, the directors could be removed from office only by concurrent resolution of the Senate and House. A directorship of TVA was, of course, to be a full-time job, and the incumbents could have no financial interest in any business likely to be adversely affected by the success of the project. The ultimate in conscientiousness was probably reached when Chairman Morgan turned over to the Secretary of State a list of all personal property owned by himself and members of his immediate family, with the promise to file a comparable statement upon leaving office.

The sponsors of the project realized that the corporation would very likely be operating in an atmosphere of open or covert antagonism. Hence they took the unusual precaution in the Act that the directors must profess a belief in its feasibility and wisdom. Moreover, the corporation was protected by stiff penalties against any false entries on its books, false reports, or statements made on its behalf, and most important of all, against conspiracies and collusive arrangements with intent to defraud it or defeat its purposes.

In general, the corporation was responsible to Congress, to which it looked for appropriations. Only for the future construction of facilities to be used in whole or in part for the generation or transmission of electric power was it empowered to issue and sell, with the approval of the Treasury, government bonds to the amount of $50 million.

In its accounting arrangements it was to conform as nearly as practical to accounting systems prescribed by the FPC. As a preliminary in accounting for fixed capital the board was to make a thorough investigation of the "present value" of Wilson Dam and of the steam plant appurtenant to the nitrate plants. This "present value" was then to be allocated to five principal functions, to wit: flood control, navigation, fertilizer, national defense, and power. In like manner the "cost" of all future construction was to be ascertained and so allocated. When approved by the President, these findings were to be the basis for keeping the "book values" of the properties. This provision raised an "allocation problem" of unusual novelty and great difficulty. TVA's transactions were also to be subjected to an annual audit by the Comptroller General, the costs of which were to be charged to the operating expenses of the corporation. This also created some difficulties later in working out the degree of autonomy to be vouchsafed this new type of public agency.

Publicity as to operations was provided for in an annual report to the President and Congress. One specific requirement should be mentioned because it was evidently prompted by the "yardstick" idea: The report was to include an itemized statement of the cost of power at each power station.

The board, through the President, was authorized to secure the services and assistance of other government departments. It has made liberal use of this power. In the first rush of applicant job seekers, it sidetracked much inconvenience and political annoyance by handing its ordinary personnel problems over to the United States Civil Service Commission. Recruitment was primarily from Valley residents. For supervisory personnel, as well as for consultants of varying experience and talents, it has gone far and wide. Other federal agencies and state governments have been called upon to loan the services of specialists. The Federal Reclamation Service, for instance, loaned the services of John L. Savage, the designer of Boulder and Maddon Dams, to prepare final surveys and plans for the Norris Dam.

In the earliest phases of its construction activities, TVA was of great service in helping to lift the depression, as were the CWA, PWA, and WPA. Yet it wisely resisted much local and congressional pressure to speed up construction activities unduly so that the new organization might have time to plan comprehensively with an eye to safety, reliability, and economy. During the infancy of these alphabetical agencies, a local wag, restive because employment was not picking up fast enough, said that evidently TVA stood for "tain't very active." Nevertheless, by salvaging construction equipment assembled at Muscle Shoals and putting it to productive use, the Authority was soon able to make rapid headway on its immediate and ultimate program.

Realizing the Planning and Action Program

In this brief interpretation of TVA's activities since 1933, we must, of course, be highly selective and restrict ourselves only to essential facts and to those events and decisions of policy which will best portray the essence of TVA as a regional project and will reveal something of the spirit that animated it. To gain perspective, we shall distinguish between its various programs; and between the time interval from 1933 to 1938, which may be designated the "fighting years," during which the basis for later activity was laid, and the period from 1938 to the present when the program is being rapidly realized.

The Fighting Years—1933 to 1938. The Tennessee Valley Project Act specified that the board at once make certain definite public improvements which constituted the immediate program. It also provided in more general language for certain long-range objectives representing the ultimate program. These envisaged the program of public planning, promotion, construction, marketing, and, at the same time, coordination with private enterprise that represented the new departure in public policy.

In the first place the board was empowered and directed to complete the installation of additional power units at Wilson Dam and in the steam plant at nitrate plant No. 2. Next, the statute authorized the construction of a dam in and across the Clinch River in eastern Tennessee, together with an appurtenant power plant and the necessary generating equipment. The dam was once locally known as Cove Creek Dam but has since been rechristened Norris Dam. It was to be connected with Wilson Dam by one or more transmission lines. In the third place, the board was authorized to sell all *surplus power* to public or private organizations; in order to effect such sale it was authorized to construct, purchase, or lease marketing transmission lines. Surplus power was defined as all power not needed in its own operations (construction and fertilizer) or required in the operation of navigation works. The Army had been selling electric energy at Wilson Dam to the only available purchaser, the Alabama Power Company, at very low rates as steam-replacement power. Finally, the board was directed to explore all the possibilities for the development of fertilizers.

General objective of the immediate program. Although the Authority did not regard itself primarily as a recovery-promoting agency, its early activities had much importance in this connection. Disclaiming that the dam was then required for power development, the board undertook the construction with PWA funds of General Joe Wheeler Dam at a point about 16 miles up the river from Muscle Shoals, where navigation locks were already under construction by Army engineers. The dam would impound water for a distance of 88 miles and submerge the last ledges of Muscle Shoals. The dam therefore had immediate importance for both navigation and flood control purposes and would eventually also serve for power production.

The general purpose of this immediate program was to further improve navigation on the river, especially by providing for the release of water from Norris Dam at times of low river flow. More importantly, it provided a very substantial element of flood control at Norris Dam and of power development at both Norris and Wilson Dams. In order to appreciate the situation, it is necessary to bear in mind the original variability of stream flow in the Tennessee River drainage basin. The average raianfall of 51 inches was so distributed that the high-water season came in the late winter and early spring. During the three fall months of the year, the stream flow was deficient. There was no natural or artificial water storage because the Wilson reservoir was sufficient only to meet daily fluctuations in the load. The periodicity in rainfall and run-off conditions was such that the maximum variations in daily flow in thousands of cubic feet per second (Mcfs) was of the order of 481 to 9 in an extreme year like 1898, or 215 to 8 for a more normal year like 1923.

Under these conditions the power capable of being developed at Wilson Dam was not all primary power; that is to say, power available 100 per cent of the time. Secondary power, available only part of the time, was distinctly less useful and valuable. In other words, Wilson was a "run-of-the-stream" power plant. In order to make secondary power more valuable, it would have to be supplemented by steam power or additional water storage. The installed hydroelectric horsepower at Muscle Shoals was 260,000, and steam-electric horsepower at Sheffield steam plant was 80,000. By the construction of Norris Dam and Reservoir on the tributary Clinch River, some 200 miles up the river system, the stream flow was equalized by impounding 3 million acre-feet of water in a reservoir 83½ square miles in extent. This provided for the release of water during low flow to help out navigation, for cutting down flood crests during winter and floods in spring, and for converting secondary power into additional primary power. In addition to 100,000 kilowatts of electric power capable of development at the Norris Dam site, the stored water would more than double the primary power at Wilson Dam. This was the *immediate* development program undertaken by TVA in 1933.

Before taking up the marketing and power policies of the TVA during the developmental years, we shall first take a look at the ultimate program of development, then only in the planning stage.

The Ultimate Development Program

At this point the immediate program of dam and reservoir construction was merged into the ultimate objective of complete regulation of the Tennessee River system, and this in turn was meshed with the board's program of fostering an orderly physical, economic, and social development of the area. The first comprehensive planning report dealing with the unified development of the Tennessee River system was issued in 1936 and has since been supplemented by more detailed studies. All the reports were to aid in planning for the proper use, conservation, and development of all the natural resources of the region. All the states, or subdivisions and agencies thereof, as well as cooperatives and private organizations affected by these activities, were to be drawn within the ambit of such planning. It was specifically laid down that these plans were to assist Congress and the several states, "in guiding and controlling the extent, sequence and nature of development that may be equitably and economically advanced through the expenditure of public funds or through the guidance or control of public authority."

Navigation, flood control, and power. The board was directed to construct such dams on the Tennessee River and its tributaries as might be required to provide a 9-foot channel from Knoxville to the mouth of the river, a distance of 650 miles. (See Chart XXXI.) Associated with navigation was the objective of flood control as a primary purpose. Owing to the annual and seasonal variation in stream flow, the Valley was subject to annual floods, some of which caused much damage. The severest floods on record occurred in 1867 and 1898, but the amount of damage is not known. A lesser flood in 1926 was estimated to have caused a property loss of $2,650,000, while the average annual loss was estimated at $1,780,000. These estimates did not include indirect losses from interrupted traffic and business, from unsanitary conditions and the spread of disease, and from the depreciation of lands as a result of the overflow.

The area around Chattanooga usually bore the brunt of these floods and had been pressing for flood control for some time. It was a fact, however, that any purely local improvement such as levee construction designed to give only flood protection would cost more in carrying and maintenance charges than the savings in property damage. Floods on the Mississippi and Ohio Rivers, where this type of protection was the only one feasible, were mainly though imperfectly controlled by levees to contain the river within its channel. On the Tennessee, however, the building of dams in the mountains offered the most effective approach to the local flood-control problem, and by controlling the flow of water from its very source, contribute also to flood protection in the highly developed main river valleys below. Additional flood protection could be provided also by constructing higher dams in the Tennessee River itself, thereby providing increased navigation benefits with fewer dams and locks and wider navigation channels. Finally, by utilizing a fall of nearly 3,000 feet from the mountains of western North Carolina to the junction of the Tennessee with the Ohio, through the merger of power production with this basin-wide system of navigation and flood-control works, the well-known principle of the economy of joint cost could be enlisted to make economically feasible expenditures which single-purpose structures could not sustain. This was the origin of the multiple-purpose type of development of an entire river system of which the TVA is the first and foremost example. It is of some though paradoxical significance that Arthur Morgan as the planner of this first multiple-purpose development should also have been the chief engineer of the Miami Conservancy District, boasting single-purpose flood-control dams with holes in them now protecting Dayton, Ohio.

From the point of view of navigation, the 650-mile long Tennessee is now a year-round water highway and an important component of a midcontinent network of waterways some 13,000 miles in extent. The Tennessee water storage system is also a component of a gigantic flood-control program for the Mississippi River system which embraces storage dams, levee systems, and other river-regulation works. The estimated 3 million kilowatts of continuous power which the Tennessee system of hydroelectric dams can generate represents a regional natural resource which can be combined in an integrated system of power supply with other power sources, both steam and hydro, for regional and interregional utilization.

Other developmental activities. There exists, however, an insidious danger to reservoir capacity in the excessive soil erosion with which Tennessee Valley lands are afflicted. It is known that the quantities of silt carried along by the stream and deposited in the reservoir and slack-water pools is considerable, though the actual rate of siltation is as yet not definitely known. It has, therefore, been deemed important to extend water control in the channel to water control on the land itself. Besides contributing to the protection of reservoir storage, such activities as reforestation and the improvement of agricultural techniques and soil conservation are avowed objectives of the TVA's program for social and economic development.

Why had certain lands become marginal lands from the point of view of their economic utilization? Originally, a large portion of the 42,000 square miles in the basin was forest-covered. But for upwards of a hundred years the Valley had been subject to uncontrolled and unplanned exploitation of its natural resources, more particularly its resources in soil and forests. As the protective forest cover was removed to make way for agricultural operations, the process of soil erosion began. Erosion is usually associated with gullying, but it is, in fact, a progressive process. It begins with sheet erosion, the washing away of the top soil so important to agricultural operations, and ends with gullying as its ultimate stage.

Portions of the basin were fast becoming the "bad lands" of the East. This was revealed in a survey of the lands of the Norris Dam watershed by the Federal Bureau of Chemistry and Soils. Of the 1,856,000 acres in this watershed, approximately 60 per cent was in forests. Of the remaining 742,-000 acres which had been cleared for cultivation, some 60 per cent had been "absolutely destroyed for farming." It was waste land with the soil washed away and was a serious menace to the reservoir below. The economic situation of such lands in the Valley was well described by a member of TVA's Department of Forestry and Soil Erosion in this jingle:

> Hordes of gullies now remind us
> We should build our lands to stay,
> And, departing, leave behind us
> Fields that have not washed away;
>
> When our sons assume the mortgage
> On the land that's had our toil
> They'll not have to ask the question
> Here's the farm, but where's the soil?

The Authority began its program of erosion control by locating the most critical soil-erosion areas in the Norris Dam watershed. Twenty-five Civilian Conservation Corps camps were brought into the area to check the process of erosion by building "check dams" in the gullies and by reforestation.

As a demonstration, lands were inventoried and the soils classified according to the uses for which they were best adapted. Hill farmers, who were working their submarginal farms against heavy economic odds, were induced to move to more cultivable soils, and their abandoned lands were consolidated into compact reforestation areas under public ownership. Other upland farmers were shown how sheet erosion could be minimized by terracing, by strip cropping, and by shifting from row crops to closer growing crops. Even wild lands, incapable of any sort of agriculture or even silviculture, were made over into recreational lands through a program of fish and game development.

The place of fertilizer development. It was well known in 1933 that the feed necessary to support a given livestock population in Tennessee could be more economically produced from sod-forming crops than cultivated crops. But the conversion of lands into permanent meadow and pasture lands would mean the liberal use of fertilizers, especially those containing phosphates and lime. It was also known that farmers had been forced to curtail their purchases of fertilizers since the depression of 1921 because prices of farm products had been falling faster than the prices of fertilizers. As a result, crops throughout the Valley were showing the effects of reduced supplies of essential plant foods.

The production of fixed nitrogen for fertilizer purposes had been, next to its manufacture for explosives, a principal reason for the development at Muscle Shoals. It was one of the early crucial policy decisions by the President that instead of leasing the fertilizer-producing facilities to some farm organization, as he was authorized to do, he chose the TVA. Accordingly, the board announced that it would use the facilities "to point the way toward a revival of fertilizer production and use on a basis commensurate with the farmer's ability to buy and the need of a readjusted system of agriculture." Instead of producing a nitrogenous fertilizer which could as well be supplied by nitrogen-fixing plants like clover and Lespedeza, the Authority built a new fertilizer plant as an addition to nitrate plant No. 2 to manufacture phosphates. Phosphate rock was available within a hundred miles of Muscle Shoals and surplus quantities of secondary as well as primary power were also available for operations.

Social and economic planning. While the hard core of TVA operations would continue to be the program of dam construction and power marketing, it was another important early policy decision that in promoting the economic and social well-being of the people living in this river basin, it was necessary to advance on a broad front. Only an integrated and balanced program of mobilizing the natural and human resources of the watershed and of the territory economically connected therewith could bring the desired result. This was the outstanding contribution of Harcourt A. Morgan. And it was as an outgrowth of this developmental approach that the scope of operations had to be primarily regional and the methods cooperative in character. There were times when a departure from these procedures seemed imminent, but the right switch was always thrown. When the choice came of using either national or local agencies in carrying out the program, it was state, county, and municipal organizations (private, public, and cooperative in character) that were usually selected. Mr. Lilienthal once called it "grass roots" administration. It was slower, to be sure, and fraught with set-backs, but it was essentially democratic in nature. Director Harry A. Curtis, another of the early architects of the TVA program, especially in its chemical engineering aspects, underscored the correct relationship between national and local functioning in one happy simile. In a recent article [1] he writes:

A federal agency may help and encourage and accelerate the pace of local organizations but no such agency can effectively replace or assume the role of local organizations. Federal aid is like a blood transfusion; it may, for the time being, save a patient's life, but the continued survival of the individual still resides in the ability of his bone marrow to produce normal blood.

In working out this experiment in planned and controlled development of a limited area, a program of agricultural and industrial research and development had to be undertaken. The program included: (1) a study of Tennessee Valley resources with a view to their use in industry and agriculture; (2) experiments and demonstrations in agriculture aimed toward putting farming on a more stable basis; (3) creation of limited areas demonstrating the possibilities in the use of TVA power; (4) cooperation with financial interests in the promotion of small industries in some places and large ones in others to demonstrate the interrelations between industry and agriculture.

The guiding principle in the plan was to foster the decentralization of industry and to balance agriculture with industry. As Chairman Morgan said: "Mass production will have a place in the design, but it should be servant and not master."

[1] "The TVA and the Tennessee Valley—What of the Future?" H. A. Curtis, *Land Economics*, Vol. 28, Nov., 1952, p. 334.

32. *POWER*
POLICIES OF TVA

With respect to its power policies the TVA has both proprietary functions and governmental functions. Proprietary functions are incidental to the primary governmental functions of providing flood control and navigation by building dams.

A New Approach to an Old Problem

It has been the historic policy of the federal government to provide navigation and flood-control benefits without requiring beneficiaries to pay for them. Private enterprise could not be expected to supply these benefits under such conditions. Under a unified plan of river resource development it was inevitable that these nonvendible governmental functions would be continued along with power production that had always been considered a vendible commodity. A new approach combining governmental function with proprietary ones in one agency was likewise inevitable. Here was the incidence of the most fundamental element in the power policy adopted by Congress, which was that the sale of power should help liquidate the cost of the projects in the best interests of the taxpayers of the United States. If navigation benefits, in some future reversal of our historic policy, should be made a vendible commodity through the imposition of tolls, then navigation would also become a proprietary function. If flood-control benefits, instead of being considered a charge against all taxpayers, were made a charge only against immediate beneficiaries, this charge would be a compulsory special assessment, but the function would still remain governmental in character. With power policies, therefore, we enter the domain of price economics.

The Sale of Surplus Power

TVA power policies begin with the provision in Section 10 of the Act that the board be empowered to sell surplus power and that in doing so it give preference to certain agencies. Preference agencies were defined as states, counties, municipalities, and cooperative organizations of citizens or farmers, not organized or doing business for profit but primarily for the purpose of supplying electricity to themselves. To assure that preference customers would get these benefits at the lowest possible costs, the board was authorized to include in the contract of sale such terms and conditions, including resale rate schedules, as were necessary to realize the purposes of the Act. Section 11 set up the further requirement that in distributing and selling surplus power to preference users the Authority do so equitably to all within economical transmission distance. This enlarged the area to be influenced by the preference provision. In further elaboration of the policy this section provided that the surplus power "be considered primarily as for the benefit of the people of the section as a whole and particularly the domestic and rural consumers to whom the power could economically be made available." In other words, the chain of preference was to be so extended as to promote as far as possible widespread use in the home and on the farm.

Sale of power to industry, especially large-scale industry, was to be regarded as a secondary purpose to be helpful principally in securing a sufficiently high-load factor and revenue returns which would permit domestic and rural use at the lowest possible rates and in such manner as to encourage increased domestic and rural use of electricity. Similarly, sale of surplus power to privately owned public utilities was authorized even though such power was "to be resold for a profit." However, such contracts were required to contain a provision authorizing the board to cancel the contract upon five years' written notice if the power were needed by preference customers. On the other hand, interconnection contracts with other power systems were authorized without limitation for the mutual exchange of unused excess power, for the conservation of stored water, and for emergency or breakdown relief.

The term of the contracts with distributors was not to exceed twenty years except when preference customers, singly or in concert, built and maintained their own transmission lines to the power source, in which case contracts might be for thirty years. In reselling to ultimate consumers, the distributing utility must do so without discrimination as between consumers in the same class. In case a distributor violated these terms and conditions, the contract would be voidable at the election of the board. The framers of the Act had particularly in mind the promotion of rural electrification. To this end the board was empowered in its discretion to construct transmission lines so that service might be extended to farms and small villages not then supplied at reasonable rates. From the beginning, the Authority emphasized these promotional activities, because the board was specifically

. . . authorized and directed to make studies, experiments, and determinations to promote the wider and better use of electric power for agricultural and domestic use or for small or local industries, and it may cooperate with state governments, or their subdivisions or agencies, with educational or research institutions, and with cooperatives or other organizations, in the application of electric power to the fuller and better balanced development of the resources of the region.

This, quite correctly, was interpreted by Director Lilienthal as "taking from the backs of men and women in the valley some of their ancient and arduous burdens."

The TVA Power Policy in Action

From the foregoing it is evident that the TVA power program was to be in the main involved in producing and transmitting electricity, selling it at wholesale and by means of long-term contracts. The distribution and sale at retail was to be, so far as possible, in the hands of local governments and cooperatives, or alternatively, private utilities. In many respects the Hydroelectric Power Commission of Ontario, Canada, was its prototype.

To put the Authority in a position to contract for the sale of power, it was expressly authorized to use appropriations from Congress, its own earnings or funds secured from the sale of bonds to *purchase, lease,* or *construct* transmission lines and to operate them. And in order to give effect to the priority arrangements it would be necessary to make possible the acquisition by preference customers of distribution facilities. To this end the board was authorized to advise and cooperate with them and assist them by extending credit. Since the retail market was largely occupied by the subsidiaries of holding companies either of the Commonwealth and Southern Corporation or of the Electric Bond and Share system, these marketing policies at once raised the question of what should be the relation between TVA operations and the utilities now serving this territory. A few small municipally owned and operated utilities were scattered here and there. At least in part, the answer was provided in section 12a where a policy of acquisition was suggested which would "at the same time preserve existing distribution facilities as going concerns and avoid duplication of such facilities."

The policy of sale to preference customers was further implemented by an early announcement by TVA of certain fundamental principles in accordance with which it proposed to carry out the power policy of the statute. First of all it recognized the public utility nature of these relation-ships. If private interests in maintaining existing relationships conflicted with the public interests in carrying out the Congressional policies (such as securing the widest possible use of electric power), the latter would have to prevail. In the second place, where such a conflict of interests could be recon-ciled without injury to public interests, the Authority would stand ready to make such reconciliation. Potential and actual injury to private interests, while deserving of serious consideration, would not, however, deter the board from executing its power program. Such injury was not a decisively prohibit-ing factor. The public interest in making power available at the lowest rate consistent with sound financing would have to come first. In the third place, the Authority recognized the right of a community to own and operate its own electric plant as a protection against unreasonable rates. This might take the form either of acquiring the existing facilities or of setting up a competing plant.

The board also indicated its intention of confining its marketing opera-tions, at least initially, to certain definite areas in order to get a compact, workable, and economic basis for its operations. This area was described as the region in the vicinity of Wilson Dam and Norris Dam and the region immediately proximate to the route of a connecting transmission line then under construction.

At a later stage it contemplated serving, roughly, the entire drainage area of the Tennessee River and all eastern Tennessee. This area, said the board, should include several cities of substantial size like Chattanooga and Knoxville and ultimately, "at least one city of more than a quarter million, within transmission distance, such as Birmingham, Memphis, Atlanta or Louisville."

In working out this unified area the board indicated that it would "avoid the construction of duplicate physical facilities, or wasteful competitive practices." If the lines of privately owned utilities were needed, a genuine effort would be made "to purchase such facilities from the private utilities on an equitable basis." The board warned, however, that this was not "to be construed in any sense [as] a commitment against extending the Author-ity's power operations outside the area selected," if public interests required. As justifying it in receiving applications to go outside, the board specified "unreasonably high rates and a failure or absence of public regulation to protect the public interest." Another reason which might force the Author-ity to go outside would be, "if the privately owned utilities in the area do not cooperate in the working out of the program."

An attempt at cooperation. It seemed at first that cooperation would be quickly forthcoming. On January 4, 1934, a contract was entered into between the Authority and the Commonwealth and Southern and its subsidiaries for the interchange of electric power and for the sale of certain power facilities consisting of lands, transmission lines and substations, distribution lines, etc., within definite areas. With the physical properties went franchises, contracts and the going business. The purchase price to be paid to the several companies was as follows:

Mississippi Power Company	$ 850,000
Alabama Power Company	1,150,000
Tennessee Electric Power Company	900,000
Total	$2,900,000

Only the contract with the Mississippi Power Company covering the properties in the northeastern part of the state was duly executed. The Alabama contract conveying transmission lines in seven counties of northern Alabama and serving about 10,000 customers became the subject of a suit by certain preferred stockholders in the Federal District Court to enjoin the performance of the contract between TVA and the Alabama Power Company and to restrain the other activities of the Authority as unconstitutional. This is the famous Ashwander case in which TVA won a final victory in 1936, as we shall see. The lower court, however, enjoined the transfer of the properties and also enjoined the municipalities concerned from contracting to purchase surplus power from TVA. Until this injunction (as well as others) was lifted and the question of the constitutionality of all of TVA's activities definitely settled, marketing activities were severely restricted.

Meanwhile, negotiations were also begun for the purchase of the distribution system in Knoxville, Tennessee, owned by the National Power and Light Company, another holding company. But the actual purchase of this as well as other properties was delayed by legal and negotiational skirmishing. It was a period of political propaganda, with battles at the polls, before commissions and legislatures, and in the courts. The hard core of opposition came from the utilities, the coal interests, and ice dealers. At the end of its first year of operation over 98 per cent of the output of Wilson Dam was still being sold to the Alabama Power Company at low rates as "steam replacement" energy. TVA distributors sold to only 6,500 customers.

Development of a market for TVA power. Service to distributors of TVA power was initiated on February 7, 1934, with the sale of wholesale power to Tupelo, Mississippi, a municipally owned utility in the northern part of the state. Energy from Wilson Dam was delivered over the facilities of the Mississippi Power Company. In the course of time, similar sales were made to other municipally owned or cooperatively owned utilities in the vicinity. With the passage of state enabling legislation, new cooperatives were set up in predominantly rural areas, and a program of rural electrification was begun. The first of these was the Alcorn County Electric Power Association of Mississippi. No comprehensive program of valley-wide distribution of power was possible, however, until the legal hurdles set up by private power interests in the shape of constitutional litigation had been overcome. But the ultimate favorable result of a low rate policy accompanied by aggressive merchandising methods was foreshadowed in the scattered instances of local distribution where TVA was able to gain a foothold. The growth in revenues and kilowatt-hour sales for the first twenty-year period is shown in Charts XXXII and XXXIII.

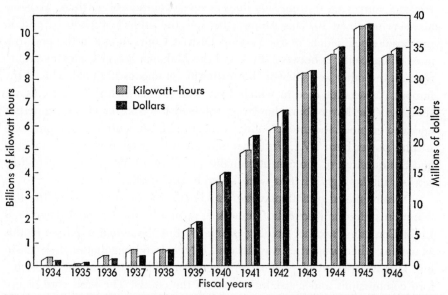

Chart XXXII   TVA Power Sales and Revenues—1934–1946. (Annual Report—TVA.)

The constitutional issue.   The constitutional issue was at least partially allayed by the United States Supreme Court in 1936 in *Ashwander v. TVA* (297 U.S. 288). The Court narrowed the decision down to the sale of Wilson Dam power. Since the construction and operation of Wilson Dam and power plant was a legitimate exercise of the federal war and interstate commerce powers, the electric energy derived from falling water was property which the government could sell; the acquisition of transmission lines and sub-stations to dispose of this power was also constitutional. This decision fore-shadowed but did not bring complete victory.

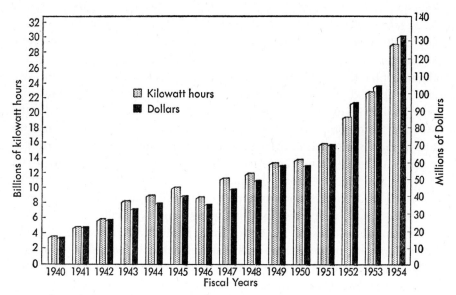

Chart XXXIII   TVA Power Sales and Revenues—1940–1954. (Annual Report—TVA.)

The constitutional issue from the point of view of constituting a barrier to TVA marketing policies was finally laid to rest in the "Eighteen Power Companies" case of 1939. In this case [*Tenn. Elec. Pr. Co. et al. v. TVA* (306 U.S. 118)], these southern utilities brought suit to restrain the Authority (1) from generating, transmitting, and selling electric power in competition with them, (2) from financing potential distributors, and (3) from regulating retail rates by means of these wholesale purchase contracts. Although the companies sought to challenge the entire TVA program of disposing of surplus power, the lower court once more narrowed the decision to the question of the legal power of the TVA and potential distributors to sell and buy surplus electric energy. It decided the question by announcing what has been called "the brutal doctrine of Chattanooga." Since the companies did not enjoy exclusive franchises, the cities, by invading this market, inflicted damages without committing a legal wrong. (*Damnum absque injuriae.*) The Supreme Court, in affirming the lower court, stated the case somewhat more gently by holding that the utilities had no legal standing to bring the suit because they had not been given a monopoly in their franchises.

The Achievement of Control of the Market

The decisions briefly referred to above, together with the decision of the Supreme Court establishing the validity of PWA loans [*Alabama Power Co. v. Ickes* (302 U.S. 464; 1938)] put the cities in a legal position where they could effectively compete with private utilities in their service areas. To forestall destructive competition, the private companies one after the other accepted the proffered opportunity to negotiate with TVA and its associated cities and cooperatives for the sale of their properties as going concerns. In a series of transactions beginning in 1936 and ending in 1945, the following major properties were acquired at prices generally reputed to have been fair prices: from Alabama Power Company, certain properties in northern Alabama; from Tennessee Public Service Company, properties in Knoxville and vicinity; from Memphis Power and Light Company, all its properties in Memphis and western Tennessee; from Tennessee Electric Power Company, properties in Chattanooga and Nashville and generally in the central sections of the state; from Kentucky-Tennessee Light and Power Company, properties in southwestern Kentucky; from East Tennessee Light and Power Company, properties in the northeastern section of the Tennessee valley. These physical properties were then divided, the TVA acquiring generation facilities, both steam and hydro, together with transmission and substation facilities, while cities and cooperatives absorbed the distribution systems. Where the purchase was jointly made, this step involved the redivision of the local distribution systems among municipalities and cooperatives, giving each an adequate service area. The negotiated prices aggregated about $125 million, the local agencies paying for their share in revenue bonds or REA loans. The importance of these purchases in expanding the marketing of TVA power may be gauged from the fact that 345,000 ultimate consumers were added to those who already purchased through retail distributors. In 1946 they amounted to about one-half the consumers taking TVA service.

Beginning in 1936, TVA also contracted to supply surplus power to large electrochemical and metallurgical companies who were expanding in the valley region, attracted by the large blocks of low-cost power which were becoming available through the continuous expansion of the dam construction program. The Aluminum Company of America, already located at Alcoa, Tennessee, and drawing power from its own plants on the Little Tennessee River, contracted for a generous supply of firm and interruptible power. The Monsanto Chemical Company, the Victor Chemical Company, the Electro

Metallurgical Company, and the Reynolds Metals Company were other large industries that built new plants in the Valley and absorbed large blocks of power under twenty-year contracts.

From hydraulic to steam power. With the beginning of the war, the Defense Department loads at Oak Ridge and elsewhere were added, further accelerating the construction of dams and steam plants. The growing scarcity of power in wartime, aggravated by occasional droughts, made necessary full utilization of the steam plants which had been acquired from the private utilities (four in number) and the steam plant at Sheffield, Alabama, which 'had been transferred to TVA from the War Department in 1933 but had been idle since World War I. To the war emergency, therefore, both hot and cold, can be traced the construction of many of the units in TVA's new steam plants, beginning with a steam plant at Watts Bar in 1941.

When the Atomic Energy Commission (AEC) announced that it was doubling its power-eating atomic capacity at Oak Ridge, Tennessee, TVA was called upon to supply the additional power requirements. With the expansion of additional atomic capacity at Paducah, Kentucky, both TVA and a private utility were called upon to share equally in supplying these new power requirements. By this time it was not possible that these tremendous accessions to power requirements might be supplied by further expansion in the hydroelectric capacity of the TVA power system. Only resort to the building of additional steam-electric capacity could assuage these new demands. Electric Energy, Inc., a private corporation formed by a consortium of five private utilities to supply its share of the new AEC loads, was also using the same alternative. And so it has come to pass that the natural scarcity of hydraulic power has made necessary the evolution of TVA from a dominantly hydroelectric utility to a dominantly steam-electric utility if it is to continue to supply the energy requirements of its service area on a basis of economy and efficiency. In 1946 only 2.5 per cent of the TVA system of power production was steam generated. In fiscal 1954 the percentage coming from steam was 51. (See Chart XXXIV.) In fiscal 1955, upon the completion of new steam units, steam-electric power was 62 per cent of the total.

TVA as a public utility. Early in its development of marketing policies, the directors of TVA decided that, except for limited and transient occasions, it would not and should not engage in the retail distribution of power. By enacting special legislation authorizing cities to establish municipal systems and to enter into power-purchase contracts with TVA, the states in the Valley area gave effect to this policy. It meant the holding of referenda and long, wearisome negotiations with private utilities looking toward the purchase of their properties at fair prices. Similarly, legal arrangements by way of enabling-legislation were developed in Mississippi and Alabama for the rural distribution of TVA electricity through consumer cooperatives. They became the prototypes of similar arrangements elsewhere.

In 1955 there were 97 municipal power systems and 51 rural electric cooperatives operating in a compact territory in the seven Valley states in

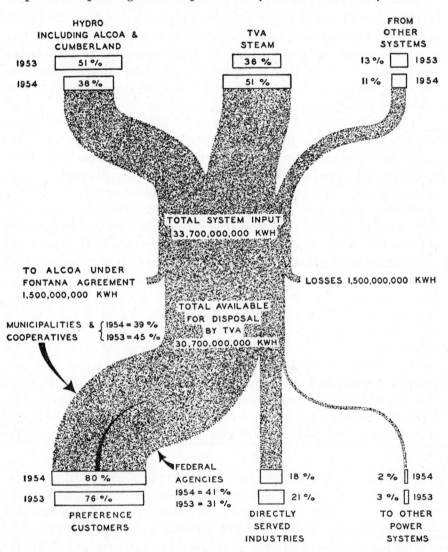

Chart XXXIV   Sources and Distribution of Electric Energy—TVA System
1953 and 1954.

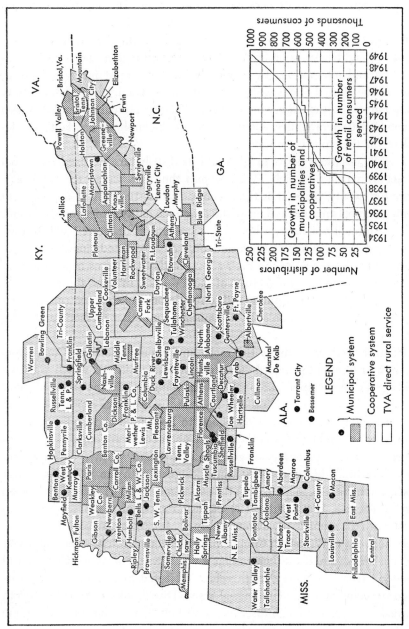

Chart XXXV   Municipal and Cooperative Distributors. (Annual Report—TVA 1949.)

distributing TVA power. (See Chart XXXV.) Two small privately owned electric systems are doing likewise. The economics of the arrangement is that distribution is a local function and can be efficiently performed by smaller units. Distribution may be decentralized. On the other hand, the production and transmission of power is a regional matter and requires centralization and integration. TVA has become the largest integrated power system in the United States which is rooted in local soil. It is a public utility with monopoly status upon which over 1,400,000 retail customers in an area of some 80,000 square miles, about the size of England and Scotland, are dependent for their power supply.

Legally, relations between TVA and its distributors are fixed by formal contract by virtue of which TVA becomes the *exclusive* source of electric energy for twenty years. It is these contracts that tie TVA as a producing organization to its market and make the economic entity into a going concern. There is mutuality of interest but also some conflict of interest which must be resolved through negotiations and mutual accommodations. But these contracts are also regulatory in their effects in that the terms of the contract seek to achieve the broad objectives of the TVA act. In brief, these contracts are also the repositories of public utility regulatory policies, controlling service, resale rates, financial policies, accounting, and other methods and practices.

Control of resale rates is the most fundamental element. Contractors are required to adopt standard schedules of resale rates of which we have already given an example. These rates at the time of their first announcement had almost revolutionary effects and became the center of a prolonged and vehement agitation. They were designed to be simple and understandable in construction, promotional in their effect upon consumption, and as low as the prospects of liquidating all costs would permit when these costs are based upon full utilization. They were designed with the following object lessons, among others, in mind: (1) the experiences of the municipally owned utility at Tacoma, Washington; (2) the experiences of the Wisconsin Commission with the municipally owned utility at Manitowoc, Wisconsin; (3) the experiences of the Wisconsin Commission with the privately owned utility at Madison, Wisconsin. It was known that it would take time to realize their full economic effects; the rates were therefore subjected to a developmental surcharge on commercial and industrial rates. Distributors were subjected to the usual requirement of no discrimination between customers of the same class. Rebates and special concessions were prohibited.

Distributors are required to keep their books according to a uniform system of accounts prescribed by TVA which follows the national models.

They furnish accounting statements and give TVA access to their books of account. The distributing utility, if a municipality, must keep its operations, funds, and accounts apart from the city's other affairs.

In delineating service areas an attempt is made to include some leaner territory, so that the centers of higher density will carry some fringe territories. The ruling purpose is to assist in the economic development of the region.

The policies guiding this joint attempt at economic partnership and utility control appear best from a perusal of the way in which distributors are required to apply their revenues: (1) to meet all operating expenses; (2) to meet interest requirements on all public utility indebtedness; (3) to meet all requirements for amortization of indebtedness; (4) to build up reasonable reserves for new construction and contingencies; (5) to make payments in lieu of taxes at equivalent rates; (6) to yield an annual return not in excess of 6 per cent upon any investment of a municipality's general funds.

Relations with private utilities. Having stabilized its economic relations within the territory naturally tributary to its developing power system, relations with the surrounding private utilities could also be stabilized and become less competitive. The Act permits the sale of surplus energy to private utilities but only for a secondary purpose; the purchase contracts may run for only five years. Such a contract was entered into rather early with the Arkansas Power & Light Company because delivery could be conveniently combined with the construction of a transmission line to reach Memphis, which was negotiating for the purchase of its private utility. In a different category still are sales of "dump" or "at will" power which can be used only by customers like utilities who have complementary steam or hydro sources of their own. Another type of sale is on an interchange agreement, which may be beneficial to both parties because they can thus exchange surplus power, paying only for their respective deficiencies of interchange. These arrangements are economical because of seasonal variation in stream flow or variations in the load and in load growth.

By establishing strong transmission interconnections with neighboring power producers, the systems can be operated to maximum levels of efficiency and power supply. The more rationally and comprehensively organized of such interchanges are known as "Power Pools." TVA soon established such interconnections, which have been expanded until the TVA power system is part of a transmission network which extends from the Great Lakes to the Gulf of Mexico and from west of the Mississippi River to the Carolina coast.

Internal uses.   Mention should also be made of the direct but minor sale of electric energy to ultimate customers on TVA construction projects or on a temporary basis. In addition there is power supplied the War Department in operating the navigation system. The use of energy by TVA directly in construction operations is charged at regular rates and enters the cost of fixed property by way of property accounts. This was an important outlet in the early years of TVA operations. Finally, we must mention the sale of power in operating the chemical plant, particularly the use of electric energy in fertilizer operations which was charged out at regular rates. We are now ready to examine the development of the TVA power system as a going plant.

Power System of TVA

In 1933 the power system of the TVA was comprised of Wilson Dam hydroplant, with an installation of 184,000 kilowatts, and the potentially useful but unused Sheffield steam plant of 60,000 kilowatts. The construction schedule of the Authority, as authorized and appropriated for by Congress, called for the gradual installation of additional dams in the main stem of the Tennessee River and of water storage dams in the tributaries, all in accordance with a plan for unified development of the river system as reported by TVA in 1936. Subject to later emendations and accelerations in the construction schedule, the principal objective was the completion of a navigable channel from Knoxville to Paducah as prescribed by Congress, the development of a comprehensive system of reservoirs for water storage for flood control and for the maximum production of hydroelectric power consistent with priority for the other objectives. Beginning with Norris and Wheeler dams (see Chart XXXI), placed in operation in the summer of 1936, the navigation channel was expanded and improved until completed in 1945. Concurrently, an increasing measure of real flood control was being achieved. In accord with these fundamental requirements, hydroelectric power was made available as required by growth in the load by installing units of generating capacity. During the earlier course of these construction operations, power supply was continuously in excess of the demand, until the marketing operations, as explained above, had developed a load sufficient to absorb the surplus. Meanwhile, the construction program was carried out steadily even in the face of constitutional questions regarding the legality of the Act.

At the present time these constitutional questions have been resolved, the market of the TVA service area is being developed, and the national defense requirements have forced the further expansion of steam generation in order to meet these requirements with a minimum margin of reserve capacity. The demands of federal agencies now served by TVA have grown from 400,000 kilowatts in 1951 to nearly 3,800,000 kilowatts in 1955. The 1955 power requirements of the federal agencies amounted to 45 per cent of the total system demand and more than one-half of the total energy sales.

In view of these defense considerations and potentialities of growth, it is important to have a picture of the present power system and of the contemplated enlargements now under construction. The following tabulations give these facts in summary form.

Power Sources	Installed Capacity, Kilowatts, End of Fiscal 1955	Net Generation, Kilowatt-hours, Fiscal 1955
Total TVA hydro plants	2,668,000	10,963,496,599
ALCOA hydro plants	375,735	1,478,119,800
Cumberland Basin hydro plants	459,000	1,277,546,000
Total hydro plants	3,502,735	13,719,162,399
TVA fuel plants	4,307,250	28,783,932,340
Total all plants	7,809,985	42,503,094,739
Purchased power		1,085,741,300
Interchange received		2,539,586,376
Total system input		46,128,422,415
Disposition of power		
Delivered under Fontana Agreement		1,481,941,100
Interchange delivered		683,217,984
Net energy supply		43,963,263,331
Shops and internal uses		2,916,400
Transmission and transformation losses		1,915,392,876
Total sales of electric energy		42,044,954,055

The foregoing tabulation shows the net generation available to the power system from its various sources and how it has been disposed of for the fiscal year 1955. Since this was a year of subnormal stream flows, generation from hydro plants was lower, and generation from fuel plants was higher than it would otherwise have been. Principally because of the need of AEC for power before generating facilities could be installed for that purpose, TVA also had to expand its purchases at higher cost and draw power extensively from its interconnections. This aspect of the year's operation is also reflected by the average load factor, which was only 45.93 per cent for the hydro system but 98.58 per cent for the fuel-burning system. Neglecting the small plants, the TVA hydro system now comprises 27 plants, with 5 more plants of the Aluminum Company of America generating for the system and 3 more plants of the Cumberland River operated by the Army Engineers but with their output marketed by TVA. The largest hydro plant in the system is still Wilson Dam, with 436,000-kilowatts capacity. A transmission system of 10,500 miles, with voltages ranging from 44 to 154 kilovolts interconnects these power sources and delivers the supply to TVA customers. Strategically located on the transmission network are seven large steam plants; the largest is Kingston steam plant with nameplate capacity of 1,440,000 kilowatts. Kingston also is the largest known steam plant in the world. In 1955 it operated at about 98 per cent capacity factor.

According to plans, the prospective growth in the load through the winter of 1958 to 1959 will be supplied by the following scheduled additions of generating capacity:

	Kilowatts
TVA hydro plants	74,500
Cumberland River plants	136,000
Alcoa hydro plants	50,000
Total hydro plants	260,500
TVA fuel plants	2,705,000
Total additions	2,965,500

All TVA hydro capacity and 1,395,000 kilowatts of the TVA fuel-plant capacity shown in the foregoing table is already in operation.

Financial Results of Operation

No over-all picture of the financial results of operation is available for both TVA and its distributors. They must, therefore, be shown separately. We shall show first the operating results for TVA for fiscal years 1954 and 1955. This will be followed by a summary of financial results for all municipal and cooperative distributors of TVA power as a group. This summary covers a wide range in financial returns between the best and the poorest of the individual distributors.

Financial returns for TVA's power program. Total revenues from power were $188 million in 1955, an increase of $54 million over fiscal 1954. Operating expenses increased by $35 million, leaving net operating revenues of $48 million, an increase of $19 million over 1954. The rate of return on the average depreciated investment in power for 1955 was 4¼ per cent, as compared with 3¼ per cent for 1954, a year of severe drought. The average return for the full twenty-two years of operation was 4 per cent. Reference to Chart XXXII will show that from 1934 to 1938 inclusive, the scale of operations was clearly abnormal. This five-year period represented the "fighting years" when TVA was beset by injunctions, with operations largely in the construction stage, and with its marketing and organizational programs undeveloped. (See Table XXIII.)

Table XXIII   TVA Operations as a Power Utility

	1955	1954	22 Years 1933–1955
Revenue			
Municipalities and cooperatives	$ 58,204,000	$ 52,733,000	$ 427,241,000
Federal agencies	102,963,000	54,369,000	266,003,000
Industrial	23,555,000	23,669,000	234,887,000
Interdivisional	2,494,000	2,422,000	29,673,000
Retail sales	. . . .	. . . .	2,606,000
Electric utilities	145,000	127,000	50,122,000
Other revenue	802,000	628,000	6,265,000
Total Electric Revenue	$ 188,163,000	$133,948,000	$1,016,797,000
Operating Expenses			
Production	$ 91,131,000	$ 65,313,000	$ 361,187,000
Transmission	7,837,000	7,050,000	63,103,000
Payments in lieu of taxes	3,878,000	3,579,000	37,208,000
Other operating expenses	7,323,000	6,226,000	55,059,000
Depreciation and amortization	30,093,000	22,960,000	189,353,000
Total Operating Expenses	$ 140,262,000	$105,128,000	$ 705,910,000
Net Income before Interest			
Earned by federal government on investment in power program	$ 47,901,000	$ 28,820,000	$ 310,887,000
Average depreciated investment assignable to power	1,130,000,000	890,000,000	353,000,000
Annual Return on Investment *	4¼%	3¼%	4%

* Net operating revenue and interest income divided by the average investment that produced the income.

Financial returns to distributors.   Municipal and cooperative distributors of TVA power also established some new records. For the first time sales by these distributors averaged more than a billion kilowatt-hours a month. The total sales of nearly 12.5 billion kilowatt-hours was an increase of 13 per cent over 1954. The over-all rate of return for distributors as a group was about 7.5 per cent. Residential sales averaged 5,206 kilowatt-hours per customer in 1955, a far cry from the 600-kilowatt-hours average annual use of 1933. It was approximately twice the national average. At the end of fiscal year 1955, residential customers numbered 1,214,000; commercial and industrial, 161,000; and street lighting, 1,200. The region continued to be a heavy purchaser of electric appliances. Electrical house heating and air conditioning showed marked increases. More than 145,000 homes in the service area were electrically heated. These electrical development activities are a joint contribution of TVA—the wholesaler—and of the distributors. (See Table XXIV.)

Table XXIV   Income Statements of TVA Municipal and Cooperative
Distributors Year Ended June 30, 1955

	Combined	Four Largest Municipalities *	Other Municipalities	Cooperatives
Kilowatt-hours sold, in thousands	12,482,894	5,880,579	4,185,971	2,416,344
Operating Revenue	$138,816,335	$58,278,793	$46,541,642	$33,995,900
Operating expense				
Purchased power	$ 58,204,118	$25,105,425	$19,777,782	$13,320,911
Distribution	15,715,145	7,318,896	4,162,536	4,233,713
Consumers' accounting and collecting	5,641,082	1,822,253	1,760,004	2,058,825
Sales promotion	1,563,021	756,824	324,221	481,976
Administrative and general	6,744,103	2,865,275	1,915,102	1,963,726
Total	$ 87,867,469	$37,868,673	$27,939,645	$22,059,151
Taxes and tax equivalents	6,391,206	2,817,541	2,921,585	652,080
Depreciation	15,723,828	4,988,839	4,368,827	6,366,162
Total	$109,982,503	$45,675,053	$35,230,057	$29,077,393
Net Revenue from Operations	$ 28,833,832	$12,603,740	$11,311,585	$ 4,918,507
Interest Earned and Other Income, net	381,856	85,102	54,319	242,435
Gross Income	$ 29,215,688	$12,688,842	$11,365,904	$ 5,160,942
Other Deductions				
Interest and debt expense	$ 4,070,870	$ 939,842	$ 776,920	$ 2,354,108
Amortization of acquisition adjustments	580,330	. . . .	527,555	52,775
Extraordinary items	22,765	117,000	32,751	126,986 †
Total	$ 4,673,965	$ 1,056,842	$ 1,337,226	$ 2,279,897
Net Income for the year	$ 24,541,723	$11,632,000	$10,028,678	$ 2,881,045

* Chattanooga, Knoxville, Memphis, Nashville.
† Credit.

A 1955 Reappraisal

As a result of TVA power policies the retail distribution of TVA power has expanded from two distributors in 1933 to 151 in 1955, including 97 municipalities, 51 rural electric cooperatives, two small private systems, and the town of Oak Ridge, Tennessee. The number of retail customers served by TVA distributors increased from 12,000 in 1934 to 1,388,000 in 1955. The 1955 figure exceeds by more than a million the number of customers for the same area twenty-two years ago. Since the Congressional emphasis was upon the expansion of electric use in the home and on the farm, it should be noted that in the TVA area in 1933 about 225,000 homes used some 130 million kilowatt-hours. In 1955 an average of 1,210,000 residential consumers used 6,340 million kilowatt-hours. This means that the average use was less than 600 kilowatt-hours per consumer in 1933 but grew to over 5,240 kilowatt-hours in 1955.

Where the original applications were restricted to a sparing use for lighting, with some incidental use for electric irons and radios, now these original uses have become incidental, and the major use is for electric refrigerators and electric ranges and house heating. Over 140,000 homes in the area are now electrically heated, and most new ones are now so equipped. In 1933 the average domestic use was about the same as for the nation as a whole. In 1955 the average use had increased almost nine times, while that of the nation, though expanding rapidly, increased only by less than four and a half times.

The differential is distinctly favorable to the Valley users. For some favorable cases these averages conceal the spectacular increases that have taken place. Rural electrification increased from about 15,000 farms in 1933 to over 400,000 in 1955; this was an increase from 3 per cent of total farms electrified to 93 per cent. It is estimated by TVA that *total* consumption, including industrial use but excluding use of large federal defense agencies, jumped from 1½ billion kilowatt-hours to 20 billion kilowatt-hours. This rate of growth was at least double that of the rest of the country. We have already discussed the economic principles underlying the phenomena so effectively illustrated by this response to TVA rates and policies. But what about the contagion of example or the "birchrod in the cupboard" idea? Despite some earlier extravagant claims for what might be called the "naïve yardstick idea" inherent in the "birchrod" concept of TVA rates, the effectiveness of the example set by TVA to other utilities, both private and public, cannot be gainsaid. Even though many utilities are not as favorably situated and could not be expected to achieve the same degree of saturation, TVA promotional methods have also achieved results elsewhere. This influence by example, rather than the "birchrod" concept of regulation, continues to be one of the public purposes inhering in TVA.

It is significant to note David Lilienthal's comments regarding what was frankly an experiment in determining the elasticity of demand at the outset. In his recent interpretation of "TVA—Democracy on the March," the former chairman of TVA and AEC writes:

What had proved to be a good business principle for Henry Ford in the pricing of his first automobiles, what was good business in the mass production field generally, would be good business in electricity supply. It would, moreover, add to the strength and the richness of living of the people of the valley. The particular rates the locally owned distributors of TVA power were to charge their customers, as embodied in those early TVA schedules, were not designed, nor were they advanced, as an absolute standard of precisely what should be charged for electricity anywhere and everywhere in the country, with the implication that any company charging more than the TVA rate was therefore proved an extortionist. The country is far too diverse, conditions are far too varied, for any such oversimplification of the idea of a "yardstick." The example this valley has supplied is a yardstick in a much more important sense. It has been demonstrated here, to the hilt, to the benefit both of consumers and utilities, that drastic reductions in electric rates result in hitherto undreamed of demands for more and more electricity in homes and on farms. That the yardstick, in this vital sense, has established its value and validity is no longer even challenged.

The demonstration did not stop with the adoption by TVA distributors of low resale rates. By the fortunate concurrence of many circumstances, fifty-one distributors have since been able under their contracts to reduce rates still further, in some cases as much as one-fourth. Although, as David Lilienthal suggests, the "sharp controversy" can now be given over to historians, it should not be dismissed with the cavalier notion that it was "only an incidental part of the TVA story." The low-rate policy so favorable to consumers was the vital and dynamic spark which furthered the other economic developments in the Valley area, centering in the natural resources of this river and its watershed. The contractual relations which tie 150 distributors and at least fifteen large-scale users of TVA power to their integrated power source, constitute the economic backbone of this enterprise as its financial statements abundantly attest. The depreciated cost of plant plus materials and supplies and working capital averaged about $385 million for the municipal and cooperative distributors during fiscal 1955. If this figure is related to the gross income of $29,215,688 shown in Table XXV, it will be seen that the return on the capital employed during 1955 was about 7½ per cent.

One of the real accomplishments of TVA which has received widespread recognition is the development of a system of accounts which records the monetary values of its transactions. After a somewhat inauspicious start, when its published statements were held up to public ridicule, but when TVA was actually laying the factual basis for its financial statements, the financial affairs of this public corporation have been brought to book completely and accurately. It is testified to by T. Coleman Andrews, Director of the Corporation Audits Division of the General Accounting Office, that since 1938 TVA "probably has the finest accounting system in the entire government." And then he adds, "There is no private enterprise in this country that has any better."

Is the taxpayer getting his money's worth? As far as investment in power facilities is concerned, TVA and its distributors have adopted the accounting system prescribed by the Federal Power Commission. These are the only expenditures made in behalf of a product designed to be sold on a self-liquidating basis. Its other expenditures are in behalf of benefits which are not returned to the taxpayers in dollars but in indirect benefits to a region or the nation as a whole. It is in recording these nonreimbursable expenditures that TVA has blazed a new accounting trail. It is now possible to say how much the annual benefits of the navigable channel and of flood control are costing the taxpayers. Similarly, expenditures for fertilizer and munitions development, for agricultural, forest, mineral, and other resources are shown, together with necessary overhead costs, so that Congress may judge whether the public is getting its money's worth.

The results of these operations are shown for a recent year (1955) in Table XXV, which summarizes the cumulative result of these activities in a condensed balance sheet. We shall attempt to explain only the more important items, giving further details.

Table XXV   Tennessee Valley Authority Condensed Balance Sheet, June 30, 1955

Assets		
Cash		$ 159,716,263
Current receivables		34,363,847
Inventories		29,168,097
Fixed assets	$2,034,418,811	
Less reserves for depreciation	222,271,657	1,812,147,154
Total Assets		$2,035,395,361
Liabilities		
Current liabilities		$ 55,379,719
Deferred credits		720,715
Funded debt		14,000,000
Contributions in aid of construction		303,417
Appropriations	$1,905,214,581	
Property transfers	45,203,448	
	$1,950,418,029	
Less net expense	159,290,652	
Less payments to Treasury	127,563,390	
	$ 286,854,042	1,663,563,987
Cumulative Net Income, Power Operations		301,427,523
Total Liabilities		$2,035,395,361

The item of *Cash* looms large among the assets because practically all is held in the U.S. Treasury in checking accounts, having been appropriated to TVA for extensive construction purposes. Only a continuing fund of $1 million is kept available for emergency purposes.

Current receivables are all accounts receivable, the bulk of it for power sold to federal agencies and other customers. *Inventories* represent mostly coal and oil for power production and other materials and supplies for power and chemical operations. The dominating element, *Fixed assets,* is represented by the cost of fixed plant. Since this reflects the comparative importance of the various statutory purposes in the history of TVA, we give the details of this item.

Multiple-use dams	$ 736,318,877
Single-use dams	60,544,644
Steam production plants	568,419,302
Other electric plant	355,685,847
Chemical plant	35,246,434
General plant	18,356,877
Construction in progress	258,531,063
Investigations for future projects	1,315,767
	$2,034,418,811

Much of TVA property is not depreciable, being represented by land and land rights and expenditures in connection with reservoir sites such as railroad and highway relocations. The balance is subjected to a depreciation charge based upon life expectancy. The accumulated depreciation of $222,271,657 thus accrued has been deducted in Table XXV, leaving a net plant investment of $1,812,147,154. Certain properties, not constructed by TVA but acquired from a predecessor or other public agencies, have been appraised. Thus, the net value assigned to Wilson Dam was $31,300,000.

Attention should be directed to the item for multiple-use dams. While the investments made in single-purpose facilities have all been assigned to the particular purpose, multiple-use dams were required by section 14 of the TVA Act to be allocated by the board of directors, subject to Presidential approval, to navigation, flood control, and power. This was done on a system-wide basis as dams were completed. Thus, ten allocations have been made, the last one coming in fiscal 1953 when Boone Dam was added to the system. Such joint- or multiple-purpose costs and the expenses for maintenance and depreciation relating to them, have been distributed, with the result that 42 per cent of the capital cost is now allocated to power, 27 per cent to navigation, and 31 per cent to flood control.

Little need be said regarding the *Liabilities* except to explain the financial relations between TVA and the Treasury. The item of *Funded debt* is represented by serial bonds issued under section 15c of the TVA Act, sold to and held by the U.S. Treasury, requiring interest payments at rates specified each year by the Treasury. According to the provisions of the Government Corporations Appropriation Act of 1948, TVA is required to pay from its net power proceeds not less than $2,500,000 per year of its outstanding bonds. In addition it is required to make stated repayments to the Treasury of its power investment from appropriations. With respect to new Congressional appropriations for power, the Act requires that these be repaid over a period not to exceed forty years after these facilities go into operation.

With the foregoing in mind, the equity of the United States in TVA as it appears in the foregoing balance sheet may be explained. Congressional appropriations from the beginning of operations on June 16, 1933, to June 30, 1955, plus the net appraised value of property transfers have amounted to $1,950,418,029. From this must be deducted expenditures, including depreciation made for nonincome-producing programs (navigation, flood control, resource development, etc.) aggregating $159,290,652. Repayments made to the Treasury, aggregating $127,563,390, leave a net investment from appropriations of $1,663,563,987. To this should be added net income from power operations for the period of $301,427,523, making an equity of $1,964,-991,510. Since TVA is authorized to utilize the proceeds derived from power sales and other sources in the conduct of its power business, in the operation of dams and reservoirs, and in the production and disposal of fertilizer, the net income from power operations is regarded as a reinvestment.

The answer to the question of whether the taxpayer has derived his money's worth depends upon the answer to several other distinct but related questions. The first of these is whether the navigation, flood control, and resource development programs from 1933 to 1955 have been worth what they cost. To answer this question we must first split up these costs into their respective categories. For purposes of simplification we shall restrict ourselves to navigation and flood-control operations as separate ventures, lumping the others under the heading of *"Other Programs."* Navigation operations from 1933 to 1955 cost $37,136,610; flood-control operations cost $29,541,790; and other programs (fertilizer and munitions development, resource development, etc.) cost $92,612,252.

The second question is whether there has been an adequate separation of the cost of performing the power function from the other programs. This question may likewise be split up into several subordinate questions: Has the allocation of cost between power and the other functions been made upon a reasonable basis? Has power been charged with its fair share of taxes and the costs of capital?

It is obvious that these questions cannot be answered within the limits of this brief discussion. It is, however, possible to mention some criteria for judging the reasonableness of the policy decisions which have been made. We shall not restrict ourselves to the problem as presented by TVA but shall take account of the problem as it comes to us from other federal projects and from the private branch of the utility industry. Before we do so, however, we must first take account of the principles and methods in accordance with which public utilities and other economic enterprises share in the overhead cost of government.

Benefits of flood control.   To explain TVA methods of achieving flood control, it is necessary to recall that the period of heaviest run-off in the Tennessee River watershed comes between late December and early April. The present system of dams on the main river and on tributaries provides 11,802,900 acre-feet of storage space available for flood control on January 1. The amount held available for flood storage declines to 10,399,700 acre-feet by March 15 and to 2,473,900 acre-feet for the summer. The difference between these minima represents storage capacity which can with safety be used for power development. To maintain these minima during 1952, for example, nearly 1 million acre-feet of water were spilled, about two-thirds of it in December. Were the system operated for power production alone, the equivalent of about 560 million kilowatt-hours of electric energy might have been produced by discharging this quantity of water through the generators. By retaining the required quantity of water in flood storage, especially in Kentucky Dam flood storage, the discharge into the Ohio River can be reduced during flood season, thereby reducing the river stage at Cairo, Illinois, and at points below on the Mississippi River as far south as the mouth of the Arkansas River. During 1952 it was estimated that the storage in Kentucky Dam averted a flood damage estimated at $400,000. The cumulative total of such estimated damages averted from the beginning of TVA flood-control operations aggregated $53,316,000. In contrast, the cumulated net expense of flood-control operations amounted to only $29,541,790. Hence benefits have exceeded costs by nearly $24 million. It is by means of such calculations that the social value of flood control must be gauged.

Navigation benefits.   Development of the water and other resources of the Valley by means of an integrated program had its principal and historic focus in the improvement of one artery of low-cost water transport as part of our historic system of inland waterways. The first fact to note is that navigation benefits supplied by TVA represent only a small part of the total benefits to be derived from our national water highways. They are therefore dependent upon the development of a national policy with respect to water transport. Like TVA's flood-control operations, navigation of the Tennessee has both regional and national importance. When the Kentucky Dam was dedicated by President Truman in 1945, a 630-mile long canalized stream was added to an improved inland waterway system, variously estimated as 7,000 to 10,000 miles in extent. As Chart XXXVI shows, this superior transportation artery, available the year round, penetrates deep into the heart of the south-eastern region of the United States and connects it with such industrial centers as Pittsburgh on the Ohio, Chicago on the Great Lakes, St. Louis and the Twin Cities on the upper Mississippi; with the grain fields of the lower Missouri; and with port cities like New Orleans on the lower Mississippi and like Houston along the Gulf intracoastal waterway.

With the completion of a small amount of clean-up dredging by November, 1952, the channel of the Tennessee attained its full project size: a minimum depth of 11 feet for barges of 9-foot draft, and a minimum width of 300 feet. The modernized barge lines now using this navigation channel carried 9½ million tons and 1½ billion ton-miles of traffic in 1955, about a 45-fold increase over the 33 million ton-miles of traffic (mostly short-haul sand and gravel) carried in 1933. Shipments of coal and coke accounted for more than half of the year's tonnage. Other major freight components were 1,871,-000 tons of sand and gravel, 850,000 tons of petroleum products, 615,000 tons of cereal grains, 107,000 tons of steel products, 116,000 tons of pulpwood and other forest products, and miscellaneous cargoes of motor vehicles, salt, sulphur, and fertilizer. Estimated savings to shippers in freight charges were claimed to be about $15 million. Since all costs to the federal government (i.e., TVA operating costs, including depreciation plus expenditures by U.S. Coast Guard and U.S. Army Engineers) aggregated only about $4 million, the difference of $11 million between estimated savings and costs incurred represents a return of over 8 per cent on the depreciated investment in the navigation facility. It should be noted that the return must cover the imputed cost of interest on funds borrowed by the federal government.

Measuring collective as opposed to private benefits. Calculations such as the above for each year since the beginning of navigation improvements by TVA in 1939, as shown in Chart XXXVII, seem to indicate a growing favorable relationship between pecuniary costs and pecuniary benefits. Similar computations of the cumulative annual expense of TVA flood-control operations and cumulative flood damages "prevented" are likewise shown in Chart XXXVIII. Viewed from the standpoint of liquidation, a sense of un-

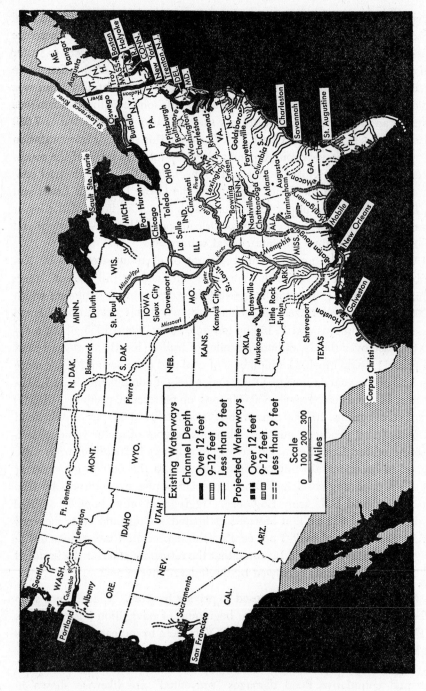

Chart XXXVI Inland Waterways System. (President's Water Resources Policy Commission, Vol. 1.)

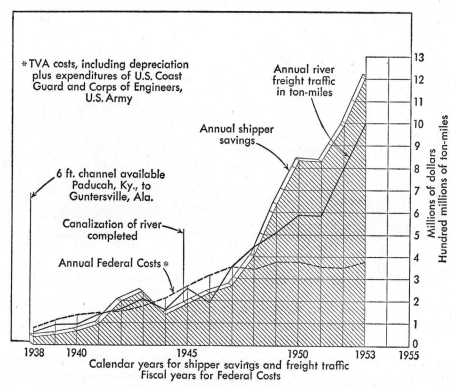

* TVA costs, including depreciation plus expenditures of U.S. Coast Guard and Corps of Engineers, U.S. Army

Annual river freight traffic in ton-miles

Annual shipper savings

6 ft. channel available Paducah, Ky., to Guntersville, Ala.

Canalization of river completed

Annual Federal Costs *

Millions of dollars
Hundred millions of ton-miles

Calendar years for shipper savings and freight traffic
Fiscal years for Federal Costs

Chart XXXVII   Tennessee River Navigation. (Annual Report—TVA 1954.)

reality seems to pervade these calculations. Measuring of benefits in pecuniary terms is entirely putative because no revenues are actually collected either as tolls for transport services or as special assessments for flood-control benefits. Of the two, navigation benefits come closer to being allocable to individual beneficiaries because these can be estimated as a private saving in expense. By using toll-free government plant (the navigable channel) instead of an alternative but competitive railway plant, the difference between normal railway freight charges in mills per ton-mile and the cost of water transport can be called a saving in the cost of transportation to the shipper. To be sure, the cost is borne by the general taxpayer. If, as will be done in the case of the St. Lawrence ship channel, Congress should require liquidation of waterway costs in whole or in part by imposing tolls, the comparatively higher cost of railway transport seems still to provide some margin of advantage to a waterway shipper, if the tolls remain within this margin.

Another defect in this measuring technique is that if the water-borne

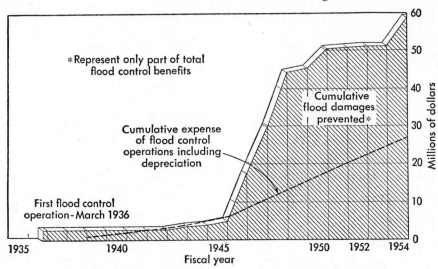

Chart XXXVIII   Flood Control Operations. (Annual Report—TVA 1954.)

traffic is diverted from the rails, such traffic losses may injure the internal economy of the rail lines and require them to raise rates on noncompetitive traffic. Only the coordination of water transport with the other forms of transport, especially railway transport, may affect a reconciliation of these conflicting public interests. Coordination in this connection must mean either charging carriers by water the full cost of water transport as tolls or permitting land transport agencies to take advantage of the subsidized facilities.

Transactions arising out of flood-control operations are of an entirely different order. There is no competitor offering to furnish flood protection. The federal government is rationing flood protection and imposing the pecuniary burden of these benefits upon the collectivity. Such expenditures are not unlike an insurance premium. In some years there may be no floods of consequence because of scant rainfall. Hence the total cumulative flood damage will remain at what it had been the year before, namely, $51,266,000, although the cumulative *cost* of flood-control operations to 1953 increased to $24,500,000.

However, according to TVA estimates, a serious flood menace still obtains at Chattanooga. Were a flood of the highest recorded dimensions (1867) or higher to strike the city, the damage to low-lying urban areas, despite existing reservoir protection, could still be about $12 million or more. While reservoir storage would reduce the potential damage from $100 million to $12 million, it would, to secure complete protection, be economical, according to TVA and Army engineers, to build local protective levees. Though

Congress has appropriated $500,000 to start construction, the City has failed to provide the necessary rights of way and otherwise to do its share under federal legislation. It chooses to run the risk of a damaging flood.

Another circumstance should be noted. It is pointed out by TVA that the downward swing in the rainfall cycle in recent years has reemphasized the value of reservoir storage in regulating *low* stream flow. Storage releases provide incidental benefits when made in the interests of sanitation, local water supplies, and the supply of hydro power.

Another phase of the juxtaposition of public and private interests with respect to navigation arises from the need for public-use terminals and public shipping facilities to meet the requirements of small shippers of bulk or package freight. TVA provided four such terminals at Decatur, Guntersville, Chattanooga, and Knoxville, and a public-use coal terminal at Harriman, Tennessee. All of these except the Harriman terminal have been leased to private operators. Private carriers or contract carriers for large private shippers (such as the coal, oil, grain, and steel companies employ) use private terminals. But these also involve waterfront planning by TVA. Similarly, TVA facilities (boat docks) were required for recreational boating, now grown to large proportions in connection with the recreational use of the reservoirs. All these facilities were provided and operated by TVA only on an interim basis.

The most basic barrier to securing optimum use of inland waterways, however, arises from the competitive element in our transportation policies. As presently established by Congress and administered by the Interstate Commerce Commission, rates for waterways, railways, and highways are not related to each other according to the relative cost of rendering service. The granting of "fourth section relief" to railroads from the long- and short-haul principle in order to meet water competition appears to be the factor which prevents a test to be made of the claim that water transportation has certain inherent advantages of low cost for bulk traffic when that traffic pays full user charges. It is by this maneuver that shippers are able to play waterways and railways against each other. Our 1940 declaration of national transportation policy by Congress sets up the target of "developing, coordinating and preserving a national transportation system by water, highway and rail, as well as other means, adequate to meet the needs of the commerce of the United States, of the Postal Service, and of the national defense." To this end Congress has decreed that regulation of all modes of transportation should be "so administered as to recognize and preserve the inherent advantages of each." This makes the establishment of reasonable rates "without unfair or destructive competitive practices" a national rather than a regional problem.

Among the more complex and difficult subjects with which a general outline of public utility economics must deal, not the least complex and difficult is that of taxation. The problem almost defies condensation within a single chapter because the historical development of tax policy has produced both great diversity of tax legislation by different governments and varying methods and effectiveness in their administration. To these considerations should be added another which must be remembered in reading this chapter. The taxation of public utilities proceeds under the taxing power. It is, therefore, subject to the constitutional limitations imposed by the rule of equality. Taxation of the various tax subjects, public utilities included, should be equal. This means that the central problem is one of determining what methods will produce equality of tax burden for all tax subjects. Definite conclusions as to public utility taxes can, therefore, flow only from a study of a particular tax system and the comparative burdens which these taxes impose upon public utilities as compared with the taxes upon other industries.

A beginning should nevertheless be made in our consideration of this problem because taxes have become an increasingly important cost component in the total "cost of service" which regulatory authorities take into account in fixing rates. We must also acquire some familiarity with the more or less distinct methods of public utility taxation which have been and are still being used as a result of this separate classification.

Methods of Utility Taxation

Past experiences with public utility taxation had convinced legislators that utilities as a class could only be made to pay their fair share of the overhead costs of government by subjecting them to special kinds of taxes, adapted to the nature of their property and operations. New methods of utility taxation were introduced. The more common types of special taxation were (1) a modification of the general property tax as applied to corporate property using centralized *ad valorem* assessment, (2) gross earnings taxation, (3) net income taxation, and (4) franchise taxation. We must consider briefly each of these types before turning our attention to more current problems.

The ad valorem system. In taxation the term *ad valorem* is used to designate a method of property taxation by which assessment takes place under the "unit rule" and by means of centralized assessment machinery. The aim of the new system was to include, in addition to the assessment of physical property, intangible elements of value arising from the treatment of the enterprise as a going concern. The "unit rule" has already been explained in Chapter 17. Centralized assessment was put into the hands of administrative commissions. These had a more permanent tenure and were protected from political influences, and their assessments were presumptively nonpartisan and scientific in character. As compared with local assessors, a state board would adopt uniform methods and be removed from local influences and prejudices. The immediate result was that assessments were substantially increased. In Indiana, for instance, the assessment of one railroad was increased from $8,538,053 in 1890 to $22,666,470 in 1891, although the assessment of other property in the same districts was increased only 43 per cent.

The use of "physical valuation" in connection with *ad valorem* taxation was begun by Michigan. A constitutional amendment in 1900 provided that "the legislature may provide for the assessment of property of corporations at its true value by a State Board of Assessors . . . The rate of taxation of such property shall be the rate which the State Board of Assessors shall ascertain and determine is the average rate levied upon other property." Legislation in 1901 provided for a physical valuation of all the railroads of the state, using as a base the cost of reproduction new less depreciation. The appraisal was made by Professor M. E. Cooley of the Engineering Department of the University of Michigan, while the intangible property was separately appraised by Professor H. C. Adams (later statistician for the ICC) of its Economics Department. The average state rate was applied to the combined assessment of tangible and intangible values and greatly increased the tax burden of railways in the state.

Wisconsin began to displace its gross earnings taxes by the *ad valorem* method in 1899, when express, sleeping car, freight line, and equipment companies were assessed by the State Board of Assessors under the new plan. The average rate applied was a consolidation of state and local rates and the resulting taxes were in lieu of all other taxes. In 1903 *ad valorem* taxation was applied to railways, and the methods of assessing them by the new state tax commission was modeled closely upon the Michigan plan. In 1905, telegraph companies, street railway companies, and electric light and power companies operated in connection with electric railways were brought within the scope of the system. Now light, heat, and power utilities through consolidations and the development of transmission lines have assumed statewide proportions and are likewise subject to *ad valorem* taxation.

At the present time "physical value" as evidence of market value has given ground to the market value of outstanding securities, as evidenced by security sales, and to a computed value based upon the capitalization of current and past net income at rates based upon the cost of attracting capital. In arriving at a single-value assessment, the tax commission uses these evidences of market value together with other statistical information deemed relevant (previous assessments, gross revenues, ratio of taxes to gross dividend record, etc.) in making a preliminary assessment. Taking into consideration arguments by taxpayers at hearings over preliminary assessments, the commission's deliberations produce a final assessment, the outcome of what has been called the "huddle system." A tax base is thus an administrative device for giving reasonable weight to relevant facts in a continuing process of equalizing the tax burden between utilities and other tax subjects. These methods of successive approximations have been characterized by Professor H. M. Groves as arriving at a figure "within the range of valuation within which reasonable men may differ but in which nothing is gained by the substitution of one competent opinion for another."

Allocation of assessment. Having ascertained the assessed value of a utility under the "unit rule," the next step is to allocate such value to the state or local taxing district. These allocations make use of rules of apportionment based upon certain criteria of property location or business done. Expressed as ratios, the Wisconsin rule in the case of railways uses (1) traffic-units/ton-miles and passenger miles, (2) total track mileage, (3) locomotive miles and car miles, (4) amount of physical property, (5) gross income, (6) net income. A simple average of these ratios determines the amount of tax base allocable to the state or subordinate taxing district.

With the extension of *ad valorem* taxation to other types of utilities, similar criteria of allocation to taxing districts were employed. Usually these were based upon the situs or locations of physical property modified by some index of business actually transacted, such as sales of product or service. Location of property gives expression to the benefit theory of taxation, while gross revenues take some account of ability to pay. In working out the allocation problem, utilities are in a neutral position as far as the apportionment of their total assessed taxes to expenditure units (state and local) are concerned. This aspect of the problem is more appropriately one of public finance and need not concern us here. On the other hand, the assessment of taxes by sovereign states upon corporations doing an interstate business is of much concern to the individual utility because it may result in double taxation. This arises out of diversity in methods of assessment adopted by contiguous states. Since each state determines for itself the details of its tax system, it is not an infrequent occurrence that the same property and earnings will be given a situs for purposes of taxation in more than one state. That is to say, the aggregate assessment of the separate states of the same utility will often materially exceed the sum which would be obtained if a single assessment were made because each state will adopt the rule of apportionment most favorable to itself. Only cooperation of states with substantial uniformity of method or federal assessment for state purposes can overcome this defect in tax administration.

The gross earnings tax. In certain states the difficulties in applying property taxation to railroads and other utilities led them to experiment with a tax based on gross earnings or gross receipts. It was first levied as a supplement to the property tax in order to derive more revenues from public utility sources. Utilities doing an interstate business contested this tax on the constitutional ground that it was an interference with interstate commerce. It was, however, upheld by the courts as not burdening interstate commerce (1) if levied in lieu of all other taxes or in lieu merely of taxes on intangible personal property, or (2) if levied only on gross earnings from *intrastate* commerce.

Applied tentatively to railways as early as the 1860's by a few states, its scope was so widened in the course of time as to constitute a substantial element in the tax system of thirty-two states and the sole basis for taxing public utility industries in the states of Maine, Minnesota, Connecticut, and California. In the latter state it was inaugurated in 1911 after an elaborate investigation by Professor Carl C. Plehn, of the University of California, of the relative burden of taxation on various classes of property.

What commended gross earnings taxation was the ease with which this tax can be administered. Gross revenues are more readily ascertained from the accounts than are the net revenues or the value of the property. It was argued that if the rates are properly adjusted, taxes on gross earnings can be made to cover both tangible and intangible property. Receipts from non-operating property are easily deducted and set aside for local assessment under the general property tax. Furthermore, the yield from gross earnings taxation is more regular from year to year because this base fluctuates less than does one based on net earnings. It was also deemed to have merit because it reached utilities that had little physical property but high earning power, such as express companies. Moreover, what appealed to legislatures was the ease with which revenue yields could be increased and diminished by varying the *rates* of taxation.

The greatest objection to the gross earnings method is that it does not measure the real ability of a tax subject to pay. This is reflected much more accurately in net earnings or in the commercial value of a business as ascertained under *ad valorem* assessment. Gross earnings give no indication of the margin of net income which may be available to pay taxes due to characteristic variations between utilities in "operating ratios" or in the amount of investment required per dollar of gross revenues.

The net income tax. In order to meet objections to gross earnings taxation, a tax on net income has been proposed as more nearly measuring ability to bear. But the fatal defect of the net income tax is that the receipts will fluctuate widely from year to year and vary markedly between different utilities. States have therefore used net income taxes only as supplementary or have followed the Wisconsin example of exempting public service corporations from its general income tax of 1911 but subjecting them to the *ad valorem* tax. Extensive utility properties enjoying the protection and services of state and local governments should participate in sharing these social overhead costs.

Federal income and excess profits taxes. The federal government, on the contrary, has been more inclined to use the net income as a measure of ability to pay. Beginning in 1909 with a federal corporate excise tax on net earnings in excess of $5,000 (taxed at a rate of 1 per cent), it has continued to use various forms of net income taxation because the broader base of federal taxation makes the distortion of revenue yield from changing net income less onerous. Since 1913, when the above corporate excise tax was repealed, public service corporations have been subjected to net income taxation at varying rates which now constitutes by far the largest single tax paid by public utilities. It should be noted that interest payments are deducted in ascertaining taxable net income, which therefore constitutes a modifying factor in the taxes paid by utility corporations with heavy margins of indebtedness.

During World Wars I and II, the federal government also levied excess-profits taxes as emergency revenue measures. The first of these was a graduated tax upon net income in excess of a return of 8 per cent upon the invested capital. This tax was soon repealed after the war. The excess-profits tax of World War II was designed to tax away 95 per cent of what were regarded as war profits. After an exemption of $10,000, excess profits were defined as net income in excess of the average for the period 1936 to 1939, or alternatively, as net income in excess of 8 per cent on invested capital (defined as capital stock plus surplus plus 50 per cent of borrowed capital). This tax was so difficult to administer and was so discriminatory in its operations that it, too, was repealed in 1946. The federal income tax, however, with its normal tax rates and its surtax rates, has remained as the most important single element in the burden of public utility taxation.

Miscellaneous Forms of Public Utility Taxation

Franchise taxes. The method of franchise taxation remains to this day as an important component in utility taxation. It first developed as supplementary to general property taxes when these were locally assessed, while the former was assessed by some state agency. Massachusetts, a pioneer in franchise taxation, levied such a tax upon *all* corporations in 1864 in the form of a tax upon what was called the "corporate excess." In an effort to reach intangible values then escaping under the general property tax, the franchise was selected as peculiarly "available" because a tax upon the value of the franchise was regarded with favor by the courts as taxation of a "special privilege." New York was another early state to adopt franchise taxation, though restricting it to public service corporations holding *special* franchises. As Governor Theodore Roosevelt said in a special message in 1899: "A corporation which derives its powers from the state should pay to the state a just percentage of its earnings as a return for the privilege it enjoys." In New York, franchise value was also defined as "corporate excess" but was handed over to local taxation by defining the franchise as real estate. Its assessment was to be equalized with the assessment of other property. California, before adopting gross earnings taxation in the constitutional amendment of 1910, had likewise used franchise taxation in reaching the corporate excess. Many other states adopted some form of franchise taxation, usually as supplementary to other taxes. Its popular appeal was that it seemed to be aimed at monopolistic profits which were then escaping control under the police power.

Diverse bases were adopted for measuring the value of the franchise. In its Massachusetts form of the corporate excess, it was measured by means of the capital stock of the corporations. The state tax commission determined the assessed value of the capital stock by taking into account its aggregate market value and the capitalized value of the company's profits. From this total corporate assessment was deducted the value of tax-exempt securities held, the value of tangible property located outside of the state, and the value of "real estate and machinery" locally assessed for taxes. The remainder was the "corporate excess" and considered to be the value of the franchise. It was taxed since 1865 at the average rate of taxation of other property throughout the state. The law was upheld as an excise tax on the corporate franchise [*Western Union Telegraph Co. v. Mass.* (125 U.S. 530; 1888)] and hence not subject to the constitutional requirement of uniformity applicable to property taxation.

Excise taxes. During the depression when the revenues of the federal government were declining, public utilities, on account of the steadiness of their income as compared with other businesses, recommended themselves to Congress as tax collectors and as additional sources of funds. Hard-pressed legislators in 1932 began the levy of excise taxes by imposing a 3 per cent tax on sales of electric energy for domestic and commercial purposes. At first intended to be paid by consumers, it was later (1933) imposed upon the utilities, although most state commissions have usually included these taxes among operating expenses in fixing rates. The telephone industry was also subjected to a federal levy of 15 per cent on local exchange revenues and 25 per cent on toll revenues. Similarly, a 25 per cent tax was collected on domestic telegraph, cable, and radio messages, one of 15 per cent on passenger fares above a 35-cent minimum, and one of 4½ per cent on the revenues of oil pipelines. Municipalities in New York and Washington have joined the procession by imposing sales taxes on the revenues of utilities operating within their borders.

Perhaps the oldest form of excise taxation was begun by Pennsylvania in 1831 by imposing taxes on the capital stock of all corporations. Many other states, as well as the federal government in 1916, followed this example by imposing varying rates of taxation on the nominal or market value of outstanding capital stock.

These so-called nuisance taxes, while not an important component of governmental revenue systems, manage to maintain themselves as incidental sources of much-needed government income. Only the excise tax on electric energy has been repealed. They have all been criticized as discriminatory because they impose higher burdens upon certain classes of customers while exempting others. In particular is this criticism directed against the almost universal practice of exempting publicly owned and cooperatively owned utilities from the burden of such sales taxes.

License taxes and quasi-tax burdens. We must not leave this subject without mentioning, however briefly, certain license taxes which are usually, though not exclusively, levied as a local tax and most frequently associated with franchise grants. Local transportation companies, especially the vanishing electric railway, have been subjected to car, pole, wire, and track licenses. The development of commission regulation has somehow rendered such taxes an anachronism because their original purpose was to force utility companies to divide monopoly profits with the community and to exact some recompense for the use of streets.

Other odds and ends of indirect imposts and quasi-taxes still survive in some of our cities. Chief among these are free services such as water, electricity, and gas supplied for municipal purposes, free transportation of public employees. They represent public burdens imposed on public utilities as if they were taxes since they operate to relieve other taxpayers of equivalent payments.

Taxes as Operating Expenses

Until 1922, the question of allowing income taxes as a deduction before determining the amount available as a return upon the rate base had not been definitely decided. All other taxes, except those capitalized as a part of the plant accounts, had been regularly deducted from operating revenues by commissions in setting up their rate-of-return calculations. With respect to income taxes, however, the practice varied. In the case of *Galveston Electric Co. vs. Galveston* (258 U.S. 388,399) the question was answered in the affirmative. Justice Brandeis held definitely:

In calculating . . . a proper return it is necessary to deduct from gross revenue the expenses and charges; and all taxes which would be payable if a fair return were earned are appropriate deductions. There is no difference in this respect between state and federal taxes, or between income taxes and others.

Some Current Policies of Tax Exemption and Subsidy

If there is one consensus as to tax policies among tax authorities today it is that the rate of public utility taxation, meaning thereby the burden upon their net income, should be no higher than the tax rates on other industries. This conclusion is derived from the realization that utility taxes are for the most part shifted to consumers who should bear no more than their fair share of the cost of government in the prices they pay for utility services. This also means that the same authorities do not favor the policy of tax exemption or tax limitation. To these authorities the "taxless town" or the untaxed utility is an anomaly. Ratepayers and taxpayers are not identical groups, so that excessive rates will not redound to their advantage as taxpayers. There is no necessary correspondence between property ownership (the benefit basis of taxation) and the earning of net income (the ability to pay basis of taxation) and the quantity of water, gas, telephone, electric, and transportation service consumed. The criteria of tax assessment or exemption should rest upon their own special facts. If there is need for financial support from government to establish utilities or keep their services running, this should be done openly and avowedly through a policy of outright subsidy. In such an arrangement, tax exemption functions as a form of subsidy.

The taxation of municipally owned utilities. A majority of the states exempt all forms of public property from taxation. Unless there is specific legislation to the contrary, this would apply to municipally owned utilities, and their services could therefore reach the consumer tax-free. In like manner municipally owned utilities are also exempt from the payment of the federal corporation net income tax.

This generalization, however, needs to be modified because municipally owned utilities may be authorized to pay tax equivalents into the public treasury, or they may make cash contributions for the support of the municipal government. To these payments should be added the cost of free or underpriced services rendered to various municipal departments. Municipal electric plants often make no charge for the lighting of streets, public parks, and public buildings. Similarly, municipal water systems furnish water service free or at reduced rates to public parks and public buildings and for street cleaning and fire protection.

Another type of contribution made by a municipally owned utility arises when they pay liberally for the use of public buildings and when their funds are earmarked for a specific public improvement such as a swimming pool or city park.

These haphazard relationships are in part a result of inadequate governmental accounting. Without separate accounting systems for their utility operations, revenues and expenses and cash funds become merged with the city's governmental operations so that their earnings lose their identity.

In a study of the "Comparative Rates of Public and Privately Owned Utilities" made by the Federal Power Commission (Rate Series No. 5, 1936, p. 31 *et seq.*), it investigated the amount of taxes, cash contributions, and free services supplied to the cities by 1,618 municipally owned utilities. For 1933 the Commission found that taxes were 0.9 per cent, cash contributions and free services were 14.2 per cent or a total of 15.1 per cent of annual operating revenues. These figures compared favorably with total taxes paid by reporting private utilities of 12.5 per cent of revenues for 1933. However, this favorable comparison came at a time before federal income taxes had become a dominating element in the tax bill of private utilities.

In 1936, according to the same study, 537 municipal electric systems contributed 17.3 per cent of operating revenues in taxes and contributions and 8.5 per cent in the value of free services. Taxes and cash contributions varied widely, running about 12 per cent of gross revenues in the northern states and up to about 30 per cent in the southern states. In the South, municipal electric plants were then run on a policy of high rates with maximum contribution to city finances. These were reduced by TVA in its service area to a tax-equivalent basis as part of a policy favoring low rates to consumers.

It should be noted that states, counties, and the federal government do not share in these cash contributions and tax equivalents. The customers of such municipally owned plants do not pay their fare share of state, county, and federal taxes. These deficiencies will have to be made up by other taxpayers.

In recent years there has been legislation in some states requiring municipally owned utilities to pay state and local taxes equivalent to those paid by privately owned utilities. This corresponds to the practices introduced by TVA in negotiating its wholesale power contracts with distributors. But these arrangements do not in all respects meet the valid objections of the critics of public ownership. They point to the discriminatory effect upon their operations of the exemption from federal taxation of all public agencies set up by the state governments. This tax advantage relates to the avoidance of the federal income tax upon the net income of the publicly owned utilities as well as to the cost advantage arising from the tax exemption of the income from securities issued by public agencies to finance themselves. The lower interest rates on these public issues, made possible by the value of the tax exemption feature to the recipients of large incomes, provides a further cost advantage to their public competitors.

The drive for public ownership uses as one of its chief arguments against private ownership the lower service rates made possible by the foregoing cost advantages. These rate comparisons, so say these critics, are made invalid by the bounty of such discriminatory federal taxation. Moreover, heavier tax burdens should not be placed upon all other tax subjects so that the ratepayers of Omaha, Tacoma, Los Angeles, and Knoxville can be supplied with utility service at lower prices. It must be admitted that this institutional disparity is inherent in our federal system, which only a constitutional amendment or a decision of the state courts can remedy.

The taxation of federal power projects. Greater progress has been made in eliminating disparities in taxation in connection with federal power projects. This can be exemplified best by means of the Boulder Dam tax payments and the arrangements for tax payments by TVA.

In accordance with the Boulder Canyon Project Adjustment Act of 1940, each of the lower basin states of Nevada and Arizona will receive an annual payment in lieu of taxes until 1987 of $300,000. These payments will be made out of revenues derived from the sale of surplus power. A statutory allocation of $25 million for flood control is to be amortized from the sale of electricity, but the amortization has been deferred until 1987. Another public cost to be met from the sale of power is that of planning and investigating future river improvements in the upper basin states of Colorado, Wyoming, New Mexico, and Utah. To this end an annual transfer of $500,000 is to be made until 1987 from the Colorado River Dam Fund into the Colorado River Development Fund to be used in formulating a comprehensive plan for further irrigation, electric power, and water control improvements in the basin. These allowances from federal revenues in lieu of taxes, while not in all respects the full equivalent of a local tax assessment, move in that direction.

In planning the construction of multiple-purpose projects for an entire watershed, as in the case of TVA, the problem of tax payments by the federal government acquires a new significance. It is obvious that the state, county, and local governments in the region will lose the tax revenues when large water reservoirs cover taxable land. The problem is less important in the case of other dams like Boulder, Grand Coulee, and Fort Peck, located in less populous areas, where less valuable land is displaced. Again, if the federal government and its distributors acquire the properties of privately owned electric utilities, state and local governments would lose the tax revenues hitherto paid by these companies.

To meet this problem, TVA at first made certain voluntary payments in lieu of taxes to state and local governments. After the purchase of the private utilities in the Valley region had been consummated, and after the dam construction program was fully under way, a definite policy had to be adopted in order to make the transition to complete public ownership. Beginning with payments of 10 per cent of gross revenues in 1940, these payments in lieu of taxes to state and local governments were gradually reduced until in 1949 and thereafter they again aggregated only 5 per cent. One-half of the total payment is distributed among the several states in proportion to TVA revenues received in these states during the preceding years. The other half is distributed in proportion to the electric utility property located in them.

The total is subject to an annual minimum apportionment to each state in proportion to the average two-year property taxes paid by the private utilities before TVA acquired their properties. Counties receive minimum payments out of the state minimum apportionment on the same average basis as did the states. In the case of counties where reservoirs are located, the "in lieu" payments are equal to 40 per cent of the average annual taxes paid during the two years before TVA acquired the reservoir lands. The 40 per cent restriction is explained by the fact that this percentage represents the allocation to power of the reservoir investment.

Taxes paid by distributors. The retail distributors of TVA electricity likewise pay taxes at rates agreed upon in their wholesale power contracts. Electric cooperatives are subject to property taxation in the TVA area except in the state of Mississippi, where the law grants practically complete tax exemption. Municipalities operating electric distribution systems are uniformly tax-exempt; hence arrangements were made in the contracts with TVA for "in lieu" payments. By applying the current state and county property tax rates to the book value of the property and the current municipal tax rate to that portion of the property located within the city, tax payments are equalized but also restricted. No longer can taxpayers benefit from excessive tax contributions from ratepayers. It is, however, the usual thing that the entire tax payments find their way into the general funds of the cities.

It would require a special study to determine whether these tax payments are the full equivalent of what they would be if the distribution systems were privately owned. The case of Memphis may be indicative. In 1947, Memphis, Tennessee, collected tax payments from its municipally owned electric distribution system of $341,774, which compares with $210,390 paid by the former private utility in 1939.

It should be noted that the tax burden borne by electricity users in the TVA service area consists of two items. In fiscal 1943, for instance, taxes paid by TVA amounted to $1,960,472, to which must be added payments made by municipalities and cooperatives of $1,957,614, making a total tax bill of $3,918,086. According to the annual report of TVA these payments exceeded taxes paid formerly by 48 per cent. One item is, however, not included. Neither TVA nor its distributors pay anything as federal taxes on their electric power operations. A federal tax component is not provided for in the basic rate structure.

One category of general benefits is supplied by TVA to residents in the area affected without requiring any contribution whatsoever. These are the benefits of flood control and river navigation, the costs of which have been segregated from power operations through an allocation process. Hence they are borne by the federal government.

34. A SOCIAL BALANCE SHEET OF PUBLIC UTILITY ECONOMICS

We have arrived at the close of our survey of public utility economics. It has been for the most part directed toward obtaining an understanding of its present-day problems. Necessarily, this has involved both a historical and institutional approach to the subject matter because one cannot achieve a meaningful appraisal of our present policies without an appreciation of the past conditions whence these problems are derived. But we have not neglected those aspects of the subject matter, especially those derived from our changing technology, which are also capable of analytical treatment.

Institutional Foundations

In drawing up this social balance sheet, which we are about to summarize, and which indicates where we stand in handling the problems of public utility economics, we have made use of the methodology perfected by one of the pioneers in the development of institutional economics, John R. Commons of Wisconsin. To be sure, we have not obtruded the method, but the time has come to recognize it formally. In his summarizing work, *Economics of Collective Action* (see Bibliography), he presents five simplified assumptions, analogous to elementary principles, which may be used as mental tools of investigation. They are custom, sovereignty, scarcity, efficiency, and futurity.

Custom for our purposes is that phase of collective action represented by the compulsory rules which have become embodied in the common law. Customs change only slowly because they are the rules of action to which mankind in the mass has become habituated. They are the most abiding rules with respect to which it has been said that the rule-makers are undiscoverable. *Sovereignty* is that phase of collective action whereby "the state" issues the compulsory rules of action, usually embodied in constitutions, statutes, decrees of courts, and administrative orders. Sovereignty, as distinct from custom, represents the active, conscious power of regulation which makes the working rules to which individual activity must conform.

Scarcity as a concept manifests itself in the legal control of natural resources deemed to be necessary in the process of supplying our economic wants. In terms of jurisprudence, scarcity is property, public or private. *Efficiency* means capacity to produce the goods and services required. Efficiency is thus the means employed for overcoming scarcity. For our purpose it may be taken to mean the technological means of production.

Futurity implies the time concept in its future aspects. Our economic activities of production and consumption take place in time. Past activities in production are for the enjoyment of consumption in both the present and future. But the motivation is derived from expectations of enjoyment in the *future*. The rationale of our economic activities thus resides in developing a process of continuous production which will give us security of expectation in the enjoyment of goods and services in the future. Working rules are a means to this end.

We may now summarize the institutional arrangements which have been set up as working rules for collective action. They have come down from the past and operate in the present, but they are designed to give us security of expectations for the future. They are subject to modification, of course, as we adjust ourselves to the changing facts in our environment, but we do not change them radically.

The most fundamental of these principles is the public utility status originating in the customs of the common law but elaborated and adapted by the processes of sovereignty. Whenever the technical conditions of the production of common necessities like telephonic communication require monopolistic organization, the opposition of interests between producers and consumers requires that their business relations be regulated as a public utility. Even when furnished by public agencies, as telephone service is in Great Britain, prices are fixed by independent public authority. When electric power was furnished by TVA through multiple-purpose projects in conjunction with navigation and flood control, an allocation of costs, both joint and direct, was made so that the power enterprise might be made self-liquidating as a public utility. Although the appearance of these federal projects was interpreted by some to mean that the public utility concept was passing, the policy of the Congress belied this assertion. Congress continued to require the reimbursement of power costs to the government by the users. Again, when power production was combined with the supply of irrigation water and of flood control, as in the Boulder Canyon Project, power was treated as a public utility and irrigation moved into the twilight zone requiring reimbursement of fixed irrigation costs, though without the payment of interest by the land users of the Imperial Valley Irrigation District. Reimbursement of flood-control expenditures was deferred and may ultimately be borne by all the taxpayers.

The public utility status is thus predicated upon the weaknesses of competition as a regulative force. Where regulated monopoly cannot be substituted, the ameliorative processes of the Sherman Anti-trust Act of 1890, the Clayton Act of 1914, and the Federal Trade Commission Act of 1914 have been invoked to make competition workable.

Another fundamental institution adopted was the device of the Public Service Corporation (with its companion piece, the administrative commission) as the incumbent of public utility franchises of perpetual, limited term, or indeterminate duration. In the course of time, franchise-fixed rates gave way to more flexible rates fixed by independent and mandatory state and federal commissions because the marketing area of utility companies had been enlarged in order to achieve economies and efficiencies, and these new economic areas transcended the older political areas of social control. The jurisdiction of state and federal commissions was accordingly enlarged, or new commissions (like the Atomic Energy Commission) were created to regulate new industries which a rapidly changing technology introduced. When the holding company was invented as a device for eliminating competition or expanding the territorial scope of utility operations, the Securities and Exchange Commission was created and given jurisdiction over holding companies to restore the effectiveness of regulation. In parallel with the private corporation, public agencies like states, counties, the federal government, municipal corporations, and public corporations like TVA were utilized to carry on the work of furnishing these utility services.

Somewhat later a new agency appeared, the cooperative, to render public utility services to its membership. The cooperative has taken root principally in the irrigation, telephone, and electric power fields, and almost exclusively in rural service where the low density of traffic made investment by risk-bearing private corporations especially hazardous. Since 1900 the federal government has become active in these areas to promote agricultural production and to ameliorate the conditions of rural living. In 1902 the Reclamation Service was set up as a promotional agency in the irrigation and electric power field in the arid West, and this has given a great impetus to the cooperative movement. Another federal agency to stimulate the cooperative movement was the TVA, which used the cooperative vehicle beginning in 1933 as a device to organize the rural distribution of electric power. This was followed by the REA in 1936, which used the cooperative in bringing electric and telephone service to those rural markets as yet untouched by the private corporation. The latest development is the power cooperative, of which the Dairyland Power Cooperative of Wisconsin is the most outstanding example. This is a cooperative of twenty-seven distribution cooperatives and other patrons who use this agency to generate electric power and transmit it to themselves in wholesale quantities.

From an institutional point of view we thus have these agencies of collective action: (1) the quasi-private corporation operating as a public utility and regulated for the most part by administrative commissions; (2) public agencies operating as arms of government but also as public utilities, with commission regulation the exception rather than the rule; (3) cooperatives operating not as public utilities but as agencies of self-help, with federal assistance in financing.

Between these three kinds of agencies with their institutional differences, there is competition for markets and a general rivalry in promoting social objectives. Comparisons of their activities are being made constantly as they strive for the approval of public opinion. This collective competition is the essence of liberty in a democratic state, and all are agencies of modern capitalism. They constitute social yardsticks for the measurement of relative performance. There is no one social yardstick which, like the physical yardstick, can be deposited in the Bureau of Standards at Washington and used as a standard of comparison. Econometrics provides no yardsticks of such absolute validity.

Atomic Energy

The working rules of society are being continually disarranged and made unworkable by changes in basic natural science. The social scientist must "pick up" behind the natural scientist to see if he can keep his concatenation of the social world intact. It is a much more difficult task.

From this point of view the development of the internal combustion engine, for example, has revolutionized the transportation industry, with the results which we have already noted. A new disturbing element is the arrival of atomic energy.

When the world's nuclear physicists in the 1920's and 1930's began to mobilize their growing knowledge of the structure and behavior of the atom and in the 1940's developed the chain reaction, their immediate purpose and the end product of their activities was the atomic bomb. But it was also their purpose to so direct and control the process of nuclear fission as to release more energy than was consumed, and to use these energy releases gradually as heat to generate steam and drive a turbine. This was accomplished when the Atomic Energy Commission reported that a reactor-powered generator at the Argonne National Laboratory had turned out 5,000 kilowatts of electricity. AEC now predicts that by 1957, with the cooperation of Westinghouse Electric and Manufacturing Company in building an electric generating plant, the first large-scale (60,000 kilowatts) commercial atomic power plant will go into service at Shippingport, Pennsylvania.

The Commission reports an estimated expenditure of $141 million for reactor development in fiscal 1955. Domestic uranium mining, now risen to new heights, will produce the necessary supply of uranium ores. But the cost of atomic power will be too high to be competitive with power from plants using coal, oil, or natural gas. Recent estimates contrast construction costs for atomic power plants of $300 or more per kilowatt of installed capacity with $150 or less for the conventional power plants.

In Chapter 10 we referred to the potential use of atomic energy along with the actual use of fossil fuels (coal, oil, and gas) and of hydraulic energy in the production of electricity. In addition to the use of some forms of atomic power for medical and other nonweapons purposes, its economical use in the widespread generation of electricity has moved measurably nearer within recent years. It has passed the pilot-plant stage, and experimental plants are being constructed (as we have seen) under the supervision of the Atomic Energy Commission with the cooperation of other public and private interests. While private contractors had already been used in the development of the weapons program, this program was being carried out under a strict security system. A significant change affecting the use of fissionable materials by public utilities was made by Congress in a 1954 amendment of the Atomic Energy Act of 1946.

When the AEC was first set up in 1946 the aim was to make the utilization of fissionable materials, technical knowledge in relation thereto, and the relevant plant facilities the sole property and monopoly of the government. With the utilization of atomic power no longer a "well-kept" secret, when the hope of securing adequate international control under the Baruch plan faded the question was raised whether maximum progress in securing technological improvements for *civilian* needs could be best attained under the government monopoly system.

The 1954 amendment is based upon the belief that greater progress can be made by relaxing the strict controls of federal monopoly and ownership in order to secure wider participation in the development of nuclear energy for peaceful purposes. Utilities, both publicly and privately owned, may apply to the AEC for permission to construct, operate, and own a nuclear power plant and to secure the use as licensees of what the act calls "special nuclear materials," meaning in this case nuclear fuel. Scientific information and economic data remain restricted except that the new regulations provide for the flow of information to licensees, consistent with national security. Nineteen applications have been received by the Commission for the use of nuclear materials. The law provides that the "special nuclear materials" may be distributed free to those engaged in research and development but will ultimately be distributed at a price to commercial users. Important applications accepted have been from the Yankee Atomic Electric Power Company of New England and from groups headed by Consolidated Edison Company of New York, by Commonwealth Edison Company of Chicago, and by Detroit Edison Company. It is contemplated that the "nuclear reactors" of the plants will be of different types in order to determine relative costs of production of electricity, the yardstick principle.

It is a significant fact that the fuel cost of a nuclear steam plant will be much less than the fuel cost of an ordinary steam plant using coal, oil, or gas, but the operation of such a plant will also be less flexible. Costs have been variously estimated, but the cardinal point is that a pound of uranium fuel contains as much energy as 1,500 tons of coal, thereby saving in transportation costs. Nuclear fuel costing $20 may be the equivalent of coal costing $10,000. However, the fixed investment costs will be correspondingly high. As a task force of the Hoover Commission on Organization of the Executive Branch of the Government, reporting on *Water Resources and Power* (see Bibliography), remarks (Volume II, p. 589):

This high investment cost is necessary because of the special problems encountered in the construction of the atomic plants, which must be built to stand high temperatures, to absorb the proper proportion of neutrons given off, to stand exposure to intense radiation and stand up against corrosion. These problems will call for the use of highly expensive metals and minerals, many of which will be used for the first time in connection with power generation. The control of the potential energy and the handling and disposal of fuel elements and waste are matters of utmost importance in determining the total investment cost of the plants. The operating of the plants by remote devices, under water or behind shields, and the disposal of waste in ways which will eliminate chances of contamination in the vicinity of the plants will require, at least during the early stages, the expenditure of large sums of money much beyond the financial requirements of the present-day steam plants. As in many new developments, the rate of obsolescence will be high.

Not unlike other investigators, the task force concluded that, despite the accelerated rate of progress, it will require from five to fifteen years to achieve economic nuclear power which can compete cost-wise with the conventional steam plant. A significant barrier to private investment in atomic power plants stems from the nonavailability of insurance coverage. When economic nuclear power is finally achieved, it is forecast that the present investment in the boiler plant and generating station will not be superseded. Neither will the investment in transmission and distribution plant to reach the market be imperiled. Construction plans now going forward suggest that in order to be economical, atomic power plants will be units of large capacity and carry the base load. They will very probably be introduced gradually into power systems as energy requirements expand first in areas of high-cost power. They will thus not constitute a risk threatening the integrity of existing investments in the electric industry, nor affect its public utility status.

Regulation

The processes of public regulation as a substitute for competition have encountered difficulties peculiarly their own. Assuming that a given utility has been assigned a service area in which it enjoys a monopoly by virtue of its franchise, how can service be made adequate and continuous and the price reasonable? This is the supreme function of the commissions. The process of administrative regulation combines the negative aspect of restraining the inherent powers of monopoly over service and price in private property, while at the same time providing the positive aspects of the requisites for economy and efficiency in production. Scarce natural resources and labor must be joined in an efficient working mechanism which will keep all the needed elements in a state of cooperation for the future. This is the purpose of the going-concern theory of regulation.

Basic in this theory is the much abused rate-making rule of *Smyth v. Ames,* which merely expresses the economic truism that for a business concern to retain its financial health it must be able in the long run to balance cost with income [$R = E + (V - D) r$]. To be sure, the rule had to be refined; some dross eliminated and new elements added. Even in its original unrefined form, the rule, properly interpreted, combined cost of service with value of service because the capacity of a utility to extract revenues from its market to meet total cost of the service is limited by "what the services are reasonably worth." The consumer is still sovereign.

The main elements of dross which had to be eliminated were in the fair-value formula, if it were to function effectively as a rate-making rule for the future. Replacement cost predicated upon either the identical plant or a sub-

stitute plant was the will-of-the-wisp which led protagonists of both producers and consumers astray. On a declining price level, reproduction cost
was favored by consumers because it validated a lower rate base, while on a
rising price level, replacement cost was favored by producers. In the meantime the development of monopoly and the absence of direct competition in
the service area of most utilities made replacement cost by means of a substitute plant or an identical plant irrelevant. The decision of the federal Supreme Court in the Hope case of 1944 ended the forty-six year sovereign
sway of the theory.

In certain state jurisdiction, however, the reproduction-cost standard
of rate-base determinations still has legal standing, although the amount of
weight to be accorded it remains uncertain. Ohio comes closest to giving it
primacy. Other states like Pennsylvania and Illinois, known as fair-value
states, have again given it some emphasis as a corrective factor against price
inflation. In this form, reproduction cost merely means a repricing of the
items of property in a property record—perchance by the use of index numbers; hence it has been given a new name, "current cost." Whether current-
cost computations would also be used to give due weight to deflationary
price movements, its protagonists do not say. Their rule of action seems to
be: "Sufficient unto the day is the evil thereof." This was the question raised
by the chairman of the Interstate Commerce Commission, B. H. Meyer, in
the O'Fallon case of 1927, when he indicated his fears that it would amount
to a rule of "heads I win, tails you lose."

From the point of view of strict theory, in markets where the rule of free
competition obtains, the competitive norm is set by the most efficient producer; that is to say, by the cost standards of a substitute plant, to which
other competitors must conform. Competitive standards of this type, based
upon reproduction of the service, may be reintroduced piecemeal by a regulating commission, in so far as deemed applicable under monopolistic conditions. They impinge upon the regulatory process as an efficiency factor—
which brings us to the general subject of depreciation as a component of the
rule of rate-making.

This new element, which was added in the fair-value formula, was first
recognized as a subtraction of the accrued depreciation from the gross cost to
yield the net value for rate-making purposes. By virtue of the Knoxville case
of 1909 and later cases the fair value thus became the "fair present value."
Another adjustment, following the Lindheimer case, was the elimination of
"observed depreciation" and the substitution of "age life" as a method of
accumulating depreciation accruals. This tied the method of estimating accrued depreciation to a detailed record of actual experience in plant retire-

ments. Another innovation making headway among some commissions was introduced by the California Commission. It attempts to achieve a higher degree of probability in estimating total service life by a periodic reappraisal of future life expectancy by means of the "remainder life" method.

The main achievement, however, has been that the allowance of depreciation as an operating expense and the amount to be deducted from the rate base as accrued depreciation are basically the same quantities. If, therefore, depreciation is to be estimated on the basis of replacement cost (in order to reflect the so-called real values), then this is also the amount to be deducted from the rate base as accrued depreciation.

The Limits of Regulatory Jurisdiction

A question which from time to time obtrudes itself into the workings of regulation has to do with how far regulatory jurisdiction should be extended. The general rule is that price-fixing should be extended only as far as may be necessary to provide a basis for price-fixing in the factor costs of the open market. This issue has come to the fore in connection with certain suggested amendments of the federal Natural Gas Act of 1938. In the first case decided by the Federal Power Commission under the 1938 legislation, the Columbian Fuel Corporation case of June 29, 1940 (2 FPC 200), the Commission held that it had been the intent of Congress to restrict the jurisdiction of the Commission to the transmission of gas at wholesale in interstate commerce and to prohibit the exercise of jurisdiction over the production and gathering of natural gas as well as the sale of such gas as incident thereto. At the other end of the pipeline it was the intent of Congress to preserve the regulatory jurisdiction of the state commissions over the retail distribution and sale of such gas in intrastate commerce.

In 1951 this jurisdictional question was presented once more in the Phillips Petroleum Company case (10 FPC 246), involving an independent producer and gatherer of oil and gas in Oklahoma and Texas. Phillips was not the owner of a pipeline transmitting gas over long distances in interstate commerce. It did sell its gas to pipelines (among others to the Michigan-Wisconsin Pipe Line) which served retailing utilities in these states and drew its supplies exclusively from the reserves available to the Phillips Petroleum Company. The Commission again decided that the Phillips Company was an independent producer of natural gas, that the sales involved were sales in interstate commerce for resale for ultimate public consumption, but that such sales, though made after the completion of production and gathering, were incidental to production and gathering. They were therefore excluded from FPC jurisdiction under the Natural Gas Act. The states of Michigan and Wisconsin, where the retailing utilities were located, challenged this interpretation in the courts in an attempt to force the FPC to take jurisdiction. Upon final review of the Commission's interpretation by the United States Supreme Court in *Phillips Petroleum Co. v. State of Wisconsin et al* (347 U.S. 672; 1954) the Court held that the Federal Power Commission must exercise jurisdiction over independent natural gas producers and gatherers like the Phillips Company.

Following the Court's mandate, the Commission issued orders prescribing new regulations requiring producers and gatherers who sell gas in interstate commerce to file rate schedules and to make applications for certificates of convenience and necessity. This order has affected thousands of independent suppliers not hitherto deemed to be subject to the Act and has given additional momentum to the drive for a Congressional amendment to exempt them.

In the past, when these producing and gathering facilities were owned by the pipeline companies themselves or by affiliates, the FPC had included these facilities and operations along with the investment in interstate pipelines as property used and useful in utility operations. According to the Hope case, these properties entered the rate base at their actual legitimate cost as a part of the net investment upon which a reasonable return was allowed. On the other hand, natural gas acquired for pipeline transportation from non-affiliated independents had been included in an estimate of the cost of service at higher contractual costs considered as "fair field prices" and presumably fixed at competitive levels. On April 15, 1954, the Federal Power Commission departed from this policy in an opinion titled, "In the Matter of Panhandle Eastern Pipe Line Company (3 P.U.R. 3d 396). It pointed out that not applying the "fair field price" standard to the Company's own production of natural gas, but only to gas purchased from independent producers, resulted in "indefensible discriminations" between pipelines as producers and independent producers. In the case of Panhandle this discrimination had resulted, so the Commission argued, in a decline in its own production from 52.4 per cent of sales in 1942 to only 22.6 per cent in 1952. The Commission contended that it was in the public interest that pipelines retain a substantial production of their own. This decision has now been appealed to the U.S. Circuit Court of Appeals for the District of Columbia. However, Senator Paul Douglas of Illinois has introduced a bill which would also require the use of the original cost basis of rate-making for the producing and gathering facilities owned by the pipelines.

These two decisions (the Phillips decision of the Supreme Court requiring the Federal Power Commission to regulate the price of natural gas moving in interstate commerce as far back as the well-head, and the Commission's own decision in the Panhandle Eastern case to use the "fair field price" as determined by competitive forces in fixing the price of the commodity) raise the question as to what the proper conservational policy should be for the country to follow. The Harris bill passed by the House in the 1955 Session has come before the Senate in the 1956 Session, as did the bill of like tenor by Senator Fulbright. As finally passed, the bill was vetoed by the President on account of improper use of campaign contributions to secure its passage. These bills, if enacted into law, would amend the Natural Gas Act and make certain that the production and gathering of natural gas would not be subject to federal regulation as a public utility and that the Commission may use the fair field price as influenced by conditions obtaining in terminal fuel markets.

Opposition to the bills comes from the consuming states who contend that the FPC must protect the consumers against the exaction of monopoly charges because there is no "vigorous competition" in the natural gas market.

The conditions of supply make for a natural monopoly from the well-head of the producer to the burner tip of the consumer. A natural gas consumer with his specialized appliances cannot shop around for his supply. He is dependent upon a single distributor who has been granted a monopoly subject to local or state regulation. He is legally free to use other fuels, but his freedom of choice is restricted by the loss of investment involved.

The distributor's freedom of choice is restricted by the fact that he can buy from only one or two pipelines whose supplies are complementary rather than competitive. In most cases the supply comes from one pipeline serving under long-term contracts. The distributor's only alternative is to fall back upon his former manufactured supply if it is still available. With the passage of time this has become an inaccessible opportunity. He is therefore dependent upon the reasonable gateway prices fixed by the federal commission.

The pipeline transporting the natural gas in wholesale quantities is dependent upon its own source of supply and upon the long-term supply contracts with producers in the natural gas fields. At the consuming end, the transporter is dependent upon a limited number of retail distributors whose fixed or growing requirements he has undertaken to meet under long-term contracts. The prices in these contracts are fixed by the FPC on a cost-of-service basis, including the cost of the gas and the cost of transportation. The cost of the gas is fixed by means of long-term contracts with a limited number of producers in a limited area of supply. Pipelines costing $100 million or more cannot be moved about at will "like a garden hose." The question of policy which must be resolved by the Congress is whether the lack of competition is such as to require regulation to take its place.

Opponents of the proposed legislation attribute the lack of competition to the operation of state conservation measures, like the fixing of minimum well-head prices and the protecting of correlative rights by requiring ratable takings. Though there may be thousands of producers, they do not offer effective competition because a limited number (six) of oil companies control over one-half the natural gas reserves, since most natural gas is found in the search for oil. Those favoring the regulation of the production of natural gas as a utility also contend that the high risk attending the exploration for gas has been exaggerated. While it may be true that wildcatters will drill only one producing well for every nine holes drilled, the scientific methods employed by the highly skilled explorations departments of major oil companies have success ratios of 27.6 per cent. After initial discovery has been made, the success ratios of producers in development wells climbed to 90.4 per cent, according to data obtained from annual reports with respect to exploratory and development wells. This is taken to mean that these methods can also be employed in developing the gas reserves of the future under regulation. Only an actual experiment with federal regulation of natural gas production can tell whether the gloomy forebodings of the producers are justified.

The Crisis in Transport Policies

In Chapter 9 we sketched the development of regulatory policies as related to the various segments of the transport industry. The attrition of traffic tributary to common carriers by intercity railroads was there briefly noted. The most serious aspect of this competition between the various modes of transport in its effect upon their earning capacity appears best from certain statistics of freight traffic, concerning which there is no dispute. In 1940, when Congress last legislated transport policy comprehensively, railroads were carrying 378 billion ton-miles of freight out of a total transport performance of 536 billion ton-miles, or 62 per cent. This total excluded coastwise and intercoastal traffic and highway traffic by motor trucks on purely local hauls. It did include all freight movements by electric railways, by motor trucks, shipping on the Great Lakes and on inland rivers and canals, by oil pipelines, and by air carriers. For 1954, in a total volume of 1,085 billion freight ton-miles, the railroads' share was estimated at 556 billion ton-miles, or 51.2 per cent. This shrinking of the relative share of transport performance by the railroads is markedly a postwar phenomenon, and the doubling of traffic by motor trucks and river and canal carriers is likewise. Even the traffic of oil pipelines as specialized carriers expanded from 9.7 to 15.7 per cent of the total. Spokesmen for the railroad industry place the blame for the decline in their industry upon the existence of subsidized competition (the user charge problem) and upon the ineffectiveness of regulation in curbing the excesses of competition.

One further characteristic which has been pointed to by railway spokesmen as explaining the ineffectiveness of transport regulation has to do with the existence of much unregulated transportation by highway and inland waterways. Of 206 billion freight ton-miles by highway carriers in 1953, only 73 billion ton-miles, or 35.3 per cent, were subject to regulation by the Interstate Commerce Commission. Only 31.5 per cent was fully regulated by the ICC as common carrier traffic, 3.8 per cent was subject to the attenuated regulation of contract carriers, while the balance of 64.7 per cent was either completely unregulated because they were private carriers or statutory exempt carriers for hire or because they were wholly intrastate. As to domestic waterway traffic, it was estimated that owing to the preponderance of private carriers and the liberal exemptions of "for hire" carriers, only 5.5 per cent was subject to economic regulation. The over-all result of the development of federal policies of regulating the transport industry has been to threaten its public utility status.

Obsolescent Regulation?

In the light of these developments which have long been recognized by students of transportation (as early even as the middle 1920's by Professor W. Z. Ripley), President Eisenhower on July 12, 1954, appointed a Presidential Advisory Committee on Transport Policy and Organization. It consisted of five cabinet officers,[1] the Director of the Office of Defense Mobilization, and the Director of the Bureau of the Budget, with Secretary of Commerce Weeks as Chairman. In its report of April, 1955, the Committee recommended the adoption of a revised transportation policy which would "permit greater reliance on competitive forces in transportation pricing" and would "assure the maintenance of a modernized and financially strong system of common carrier transportation adequate for the needs of an expanding and dynamic economy and the national security."

The sticking point in the critique which the Committee exercises with

[1] Cabinet officers were from the Department of Defense, Post Office, Agriculture, Treasury, and Commerce.

respect to the policy now embodied in the Act and its administration by the ICC is that the present policy authorizes "the substitution of the judgment of the regulatory body for that of management, especially in the adjustment of competitive rates between highway, rail and water carriers." The report emphasizes the fact that the federal government has played a decisive role in bringing about a revolution in transportation by providing improved highways, improved inland waterways, and a network of airways and airports, but that the regulation of transportation has failed to keep pace with these new developments.

With respect to railroad and motor carriers, for instance, the report points out that "their economic characteristics are virtually opposite, the one characterized by heavy investment and large elements of indirect and fixed costs while the other requires little investment and encounters a high proportion of direct and variable costs." It is obvious, the Committee finds, that "they are fitted for different roles in the development of the most effective and coordinated transportation system," railroads for heavy, long-haul, mass transportation at low rates and trucks for superior service in small units for shorter distances. In regulating competition between these agencies the ICC has permitted the railroads to meet the rates of truckers, but it has not permitted the railroads to fight it out by undercutting them. By removing these restraints, the Committee believes that the resulting "dynamic competition" will enable each kind of transport "to reflect its abilities in the market by aggressive experimentation in rates and service in order to demonstrate to the full its possibilities for service to the shipping and travelling public."

To carry this policy into effect, the Commission recommended the following changes in the statutory provisions:

1. As to maximum-minimum rate control, the recommendation is to limit the regulatory authority of the ICC to a determination of reasonable minimum or maximum rates with no change in existing provisions making undue discriminations and preferences unlawful.

2. As to suspension powers, the recommendation is to continue on a more restricted basis the Commission's authority to suspend proposed changes in rates, but to shorten the suspension from seven to three months and to continue the provision that places the burden of proof upon the carrier proposing a changed rate unless the protestant is also a carrier.

3. As to the long- and short-haul clause, the recommendation is to *remove* the requirement that common carriers by rail or water obtain *prior approval* for charging more than the aggregate of intermediate rates, and for charging less for longer than for shorter distances over the same line or route in the same direction, the shorter being included within the longer, if neces-

sary to meet actual competition and the charge is not less than a minimum reasonable rate.

4. As to volume freight rates, the recommendation is to make lawful such volume rates (including train-load rates) as are based on cost differences when such rates are established to meet competition. This would enable rail carriers to compete for the water-borne bulk traffic of private carriers.

The foregoing recommendations have been embodied in proposed legislation introduced in Congress during 1955 upon which preliminary hearings have been held, but no legislation has actually been enacted.

The Struggle for Survival

Against this program, highway and water carriers in particular are putting up determined opposition. Hardly had the report been released when the American Trucking Association commenced the raising of a "survival fund" to defeat the proposed legislation. The railroads contend that the new "regulatory philosophy" embodied in this program of "dynamic competition," which the Advisory Committee recommends, would allow traffic to move by the most economical and efficient mode of transport to the greater benefit of shippers and the consuming public. The American Trucking Association in an "Analysis" of the Weeks' Report, however, argues that "only the railroad systems would benefit from the new philosophy and (that) competing modes of surface transportation would be speedily driven to the wall and the railroad monopoly restored." They call the Report an "economic booby-trap for small business," and they contend that it "offers a hunting license and ammunition to the railroads to destroy competitors and disrupt marketing practices in agriculture and industry upon which our prosperity is based."

Spokesmen for the truckers also point out that if the financial picture is dark for the railroads, it is due to the annual passenger train deficit of over $500 million which freight traffic has had to absorb. They further contend that the adoption of a policy of dynamic competition would mean the emasculation of the present powers of the ICC, particularly the power to fix minimum rates in order to control competition, which was conferred in 1920. With respect to this they quote from Commissioner Aitchison's 1952 speech in Washington before transportation officials of eleven European nations:

This (conferring the power to fix minimum rates) was a distinct break away from the policy of freedom of competition, based on a realization that cutthroat competition in rates in the long run is a disservice to the public, and that to this public interest any private and selfish individual temporary gains must give way. Never-theless, the minimum rate making power has been exercised but sparingly, and with much circumspection.

The motive ascribed by the Trucking Association to the Advisory Com-mittee was to enable the railroads to practice "selective rate-cutting" as they had done previous to 1920, when coastal and intercoastal water carriers be-came a victim of the practice. By virtue of these amendments they would again be able to sharply reduce rates on selective competitive traffic "for the purpose of driving out of business a competitor" whose existence depends on the movement of the selected traffic. In other words, the railroads would be enabled to revert to the practices of the period previous to 1920 when they could once more exert the force of "cutthroat competition."

In certain other respects the recommendations of the Weeks' Commit-tee seem to receive the approval of the motor carrier industry and the small shipper. As the Committee indicated in its report:

A primary problem in transportation at present concerns the infringement of private carriers upon the field of common carriage and the need for remedial action in the form of more effective regulation of private carriers or enactment of legisla-tion to delineate more adequately the proper place and status of such carriers.

To this end the Committee proposes a redefinition of private carriage which would limit it to bona fide owners of the property transported, as distin-guished from those who, as a subterfuge, purchase the property for trans-portation purposes only, in order to escape regulation and the 3 per cent excise tax on freight charges levied against the for-hire carriers. Among other recommendations, one would repeal the exemption from regulation of water carriers handling only commodities in bulk; another would sharpen the defi-nition of contract carriage and require contract carriers to publish their actual rates rather than only minimum rates. It is clear that the aim is to protect the common carrier status and to assist those common carriers who are being left with the residual and often less lucrative traffic in protecting themselves against the raiding of private or contract carriers.

One problem which the advisory committee fails even to mention, although it is at the base of all policy determinations with respect to trans-port planning and coordination, is that of allocating fairly the cost of pro-viding and maintaining highways and waterways between private, contract, and common carriers. Spokesmen for the railways, on the other hand, never fail to dwell upon the hidden subsidy this affords their competitors. With respect to selected inland waterways, the Association of Southeastern Rail-roads has computed the annual cost of federal aid to navigation. These

annual costs include both capital and maintenance costs and are reduced to
federal aid per traffic unit. According to this calculation for the year 1954,
the federal aid was greatest on the Missouri River, being $0.27 per ton-mile
on the stretch between Kansas City and Sioux City and $0.057 per ton-mile
between Kansas City and the mouth of the river. On the Tennessee River
the federal aid drops to $0.0068 per ton-mile, while on the upper Mississippi
River from the Twin Cities to the mouth of the Missouri River, it drops to
$0.0036 per ton-mile. The lowest costs are, of course, achieved on the water-
ways of greatest traffic density, falling to $0.0016 per ton-mile on the Missis-
sippi from the mouth of the Missouri to the mouth of the Ohio, to $0.0013
on the Illinois River, to $0.0010 on the Ohio River, and to $0.0007 on the
Mississippi from the mouth of the Ohio to New Orleans.

Since most of the traffic on our inland waterways is now the bulk traffic
of private or contract carriers or of large pleasure craft, the Hoover Commission on Organization of the Executive Branch of the Government in its
Report to Congress of June, 1955, recommends that Congress follow the
example of toll charges for the Panama Canal and the St. Lawrence Seaway
and authorize a user charge sufficient to cover only maintenance and operation on our inland waterways. The charge is to be fixed by the Interstate
Commerce Commission, and small pleasure craft are to be exempted.

This has evoked violent opposition from all shippers now using our
inland waterways as contrary to our historic policy of toll-free navigation
and as breaking faith with those who have located investments on this
premise.

Taken in conjunction with conditions in our local transit industries, the
foregoing recital of the chaos in our national transport systems suggests
that our policies, regulatory and promotional, have failed to achieve that
degree of stabilization which the other branches of the public utility industries have attained. Here are the facts as ascertained by the Cabinet Committee:

The rates of return earned by Class I Railways in the United States show an increasingly gloomy picture as compared with other utility industries. For the postwar period from 1946–1954 the ratio of net railway operating income to the net
investment has averaged only 3.68 per cent. Railway credit is near the vanishing
point.

The Advisory Committee, in its report to the President, sums up its
estimate of the situation by saying: "The net result is a competitive system
of transportation that for all practical purposes has eliminated the monopoly
element which characterized this segment of our economy some thirty years
ago." From this writer's point of view it would have been truer to historical

fact to say that the monopoly element was never achieved in this segment of our economy because our transportation policy was dominated by a schizophrenic tendency which tried to operate on both a monopoly principle and the contradictory principle of competition at the same time. The inevitable result has been the present chaos in transportation. A much more comprehensive and thorough *investigation* and *study* of our transportation problem than we have *yet* had is indicated as a basis for ameliorative legislation.

Regional Planning

In the gradual evolution of regional planning we have also arrived at a point where the efficacy of various procedures in coordinating our collective activities must be appraised. It would be best for all concerned if such an appraisal could be conducted entirely apart from all partisan political considerations, at least as a first approximation. In the end, of course, conservation policies, regulatory policies, and planning policies must become a part of the warp and woof of politics and of economic statesmanship.

Let us review briefly where we stand as far as the essentials are concerned. In the Pacific Southwest we have used the compact approach to the problem of planning and coordinating the development of our natural resources. State and local governments in association with quasi-public agencies are cooperating with the federal government and its agencies in developing interstate compacts and legislative authorizations to do the job of planning and coordinating. As we have seen, this procedure has been accompanied by much litigation, and the promise of more, although it has contributed much in actual physical achievements.

In the Southeast we have the example of the TVA, which represents the federal corporation approach to the problem of planning and coordination. After considerable initial litigation with private interests, the initiative in planning and coordination has been in the hands of the federal government but with a definite sphere of action reserved to state and local governments and their agencies. In the actual achievement of physical development, this region is the most advanced, and the TVA has arrived at the point where it lays claim to federal public utility status. Here, the federal government is definitely in the power business.

The partnership policy. Federal policies associated with the conservation and reclamation of our water and power resources have recently undergone a reappraisal associated with the change in our national administration from Truman to Eisenhower. This has mostly affected multiple-purpose

projects in the northwestern part of the United States. Four principal mani-
festations of changes in policy have come as a consequence of the reappraisal.

　1.　There has come a decided slowing down in federal expenditures
for new starts in the construction of multiple-purpose projects.

　2.　Agreeable with this, there has come a revival of applications by private utilities and local public agencies to the Federal Power Commission for
licenses to develop reservoir sites. This is best illustrated by the application
of the Idaho Power Company to develop three single-purpose hydroelectric
power dams on the Snake River, in substitution for a multipurpose high dam,
Hells Canyon, which was a part of the comprehensive planned development
of the Columbia River basin.

　3.　A new policy has been adopted eliminating control over resale rates
from the contracts disposing of surplus power from multipurpose dams in
the Missouri basin.

　4.　A policy of containment is implied in the episode of the Dixon-Yates
contract with the Atomic Energy Commission for construction by private
utilities of a steam-electric plant near Memphis, Tennessee, in place of a
similar plant to be constructed by TVA with federal funds.

　The name finally given to the policy from which these acts stemmed was
the "partnership policy," since the federal government was to take care of
the dominant federal interest in flood control, navigation, irrigation, fishing,
wildlife, and recreation, while state and local agencies, private or public,
were to have the major responsibility for developing its power resources.
Only when local agencies were unable or unwilling to develop these power
resources should the federal government undertake to develop them for the
benefit of the people of the region.

　A further example of the partnership policy in action was the congressional authorization for the development of Priest Rapids Dam, another unit
in the comprehensive plan for the Columbia Basin by a public agency
(Public Utility District Number 2 of Grant County, Washington).

　Previous to the inauguration of the partnership policy, the Bonneville
Power Administration (BPA) assumed the leadership in planning a comprehensive power system, just as TVA had done in working out a unified plan
for the Tennessee watershed. Illustrative of the changed procedures which
may flow from the adoption of the partnership policy, we may take the
organization of the Puget Sound Utilities Council. Organized in 1954, the
Council is an association of Seattle City Light, Tacoma City Light, Puget
Sound Power & Light Company, Snohomish County Public Utility District
No. 1, and Chelan County Public Utility District No. 1. The council pro-

poses to plan for the integrated development of new power resources to supply the needs of their contiguous service areas, which comprise 60 per cent of the population of the state of Washington. The members of the Council already represent a producing capacity of 1,600,000 kilowatts in twenty-three hydro and steam plants. They hold long-term contracts for the purchase of power from the Bonneville Power Administration, and as members of the Northwest Power Pool, they have interchanged energy among themselves and with other members of the Pool.

As an organization, the Council is held together by means of inter-utility power contracts which guarantee a power market for the new facilities to be constructed. All decisions must be unanimous, with the chairmanship of the Council rotating annually. The only permanent employee is an executive secretary. The scheme is hailed as a new departure in the application of the public-private and federal-local partnership idea in the development of regional resources.

It is calculated that the Puget Sound–Cascade area will require 1,700,000 kilowatts of additional power within the next ten years. It is proposed to supply at least a portion of these requirements jointly by means of hydraulic power, fuel power, or nuclear power, depending upon which source is the cheapest at the moment. The new power installations will be financed by private means with federal assistance limited to nonpower installations such as fish ladders and navigation or flood-control facilities.

As an example of new projects to be undertaken jointly, the Council has under investigation what it calls "the most outstanding single project now known in North America." It is the Mica Creek storage-dam site on the Columbia River in eastern British Columbia, where the general course of the river is again southward. This $250-million upstream dam development would create a storage capacity of nearly double that of Grand Coulee Dam and would make possible a large increase in low-cost energy at dams in the United States, some of which would be available for distribution to members of the Council.

Concluding observation.   No one can say what the future trend in the development of policies will be. Only this can be said with some measure of assurance: The regional demand for the development of our natural resources will continue unabated as the far-flung plans of the Puget Sound Utilities Council and the plans for the further development of the Colorado River Basin sufficiently attest. Even staid New England, as a consequence of the St. Lawrence Seaway, is experiencing an "instinct within it that reaches and towers."

We have taken the reader to the boundaries of the public utility problem. We have been able to speak with professional profundity as to its present and past aspects because we have had known facts and experience to guide us. The future is a terra incognita with little in the way of guide-lines except as we hold fast to the institutional developments of the past. As Professor Commons said: "There are no statistics of the future."

Appendix A

Select Bibliography

The following brief bibliography of books, periodicals, and public documents has been selected as a ready reference of the more important sources from which the writer has drawn and which are available for additional reading in the area of public utility economics. Every student of the subject is indebted to Professor E. W. Clemens for the exhaustive bibliography in his notable treatise, *Economics and Public Utilities,* which should also be consulted.

General Treatises

Berle, A. A., and Means, G. C., *The Modern Corporation and Private Property* (Commerce Clearing House, 1932).

Berle, A. A., *The Twentieth Century Capitalist Revolution* (Appleton-Century-Crofts, 1954).

Ciriacy-Wantrup, S. V., *Resource Conservation, Economics and Policies* (University of California Press, 1952).

Clark, J. M., *The Economics of Overhead Cost* (University of Chicago Press, 1923).

Clark, J. M., *Social Control of Business* (McGraw-Hill, 1939).

Committee on Public Debt Policy, *Our National Debt* (Harcourt Brace, 1949).

Commons, J. R., *The Economics of Collective Action* (Macmillan, 1950).

Commons, J. R., *Institutional Economics* (Macmillan, 1934).

Commons, J. R., *Legal Foundations of Capitalism* (Macmillan, 1924).

Commons, J. R., *Industrial Goodwill* (McGraw-Hill, 1919).

Dewing, A. S., *Financial Policy of Corporations* (Ronald Press, 1953).

Ely, R. T., *Property and Contract,* 2 vol. (Macmillan, 1914).

Freund, Ernest, *The Police Power* (Callaghan & Co., 1904).

Grant, E. L., and Norton, P. T., *Depreciation* (Ronald Press, 1949).

Gruchy, A. G., *Modern Economic Thought* (Prentice-Hall, 1947).

Hall, J. P., *Cases on Constitutional Law* (West Publishing Co., 1913).

Holmes, O. W., *The Common Law* (Little, Brown, 1938).

Jensen, M. (ed.), *Regionalism in America* (Univ. of Wis. Press, 1951).

Pound, R., *The Spirit of the Common Law* (Marshall Jones, 1921).

Ripley, W. Z., *Main Street and Wall Street* (Little, Brown, 1927).

Wyman, B., *Control of the Market* (Moffat, Yard, 1911).

Wyman, B., *Public Service Corporations,* 2 vol. (Baker, Voorhis, 1911).

Special Treatises

Ayres, E., *Major Sources of Energy*, American Petroleum Institute.

Barnes, I. R., *Cases on Public Utility Regulation* (Appleton-Century-Crofts, 1938).

Bauer, J., *Transforming Public Utility Regulation* (Harper & Brothers, 1950).

Bauer, J., and Costello, P., *Transit Modernization and Street Traffic Control* (Public Adm. Service, 1950).

Baum, R. D., *The Federal Power Commission and State Utility Regulation* (American Council on Public Affairs, 1942).

Beckwith, B. P., *Marginal-Cost Price-Output Control* (Columbia University Press, 1955).

Biggar, E. B., *Hydro-Electric Development in Ontario* (Ryerson Press, 1920).

Bigham, T. C., and Roberts, M. J., *Transportation Principles and Problems* (McGraw-Hill, 1952).

Bonbright, J. C., *The Valuation of Property*, 2 vol. (McGraw-Hill, 1937).

Bonbright, J. C., and Means, G. C., *The Holding Company* (McGraw-Hill, 1932).

Buck, S. J., *The Granger Movement* (Harvard University Press, 1913).

Bussing, I., *Public Utility Regulation and the So-Called Sliding Scale* (Columbia University Press, 1936).

Clemens, E. W., *Economics and Public Utilities* (Appleton-Century-Crofts, 1950).

Cunningham, W. J., *American Railroads: Government Control and Reconstruction Policies* [McGraw-Hill (A. W. Shaw, 1922)].

Daggett, S., *Principles of Inland Transportation* (Harper & Brothers, 1955).

Dearing, C. L., and Owen, Wilfred, *National Transportation Policy* (Brookings Institution, 1949).

Doolittle, F. W., *Studies in the Cost of Urban Transportation Service* (American Electric Railway Association, 1916).

Dow, A., *Some Public Service Papers* (Privately printed, 1927).

(The) *Development of Scientific Rates for Electricity Supply, Being Reprints of Selected Original Rate Papers* (Edison Illuminating Company of Detroit, 1915).

Fair, M. L., and Williams, E. W., *Economics of Transportation* (Harper, 1950).

Foster, J. R., and Rodey, B. S., *Public Utility Accounting* (Prentice-Hall, 1951).

Frederick, J. H., *Commercial Air Transportation* (Irwin, 1951).

Gill, F. W., and Bates, G. L., *Airline Competition* (Harvard University, 1949).

Glaeser, M. G., *Outlines of Public Utility Economics* (Macmillan, 1927).

Golze, A. R., *Reclamation in the United States* (McGraw-Hill, 1952).

Greenwood, E., *Amber to Amperes* (Harper & Brothers, 1931).

Hoover, E. M., *The Location of Economic Activity* (McGraw-Hill, 1948).

Labatut, J., and Lane, W. J., *Highways in our National Life* (Princeton University Press, 1950).

Leopold, L. B., and Maddock, T., *The Flood Control Controversy* (Ronald Press, 1954).

Lilienthal, D. E., *TVA—Democracy on the March* (Harper and Brothers, 1953).

Locklin, P. D., *Economics of Transportation* (Irwin, 1954).

Mead, E., *Irrigation Institutions* (Macmillan, 1903).

Mortenson, W. P., *Milk Distribution as a Public Utility* (University of Chicago Press, 1940).

Nadeau, R. A., *The Water Seekers* (Doubleday, 1950).

Nash, L. R., *Public Utility Rate Structures* (McGraw-Hill, 1933).

Nash, L. R., *Anatomy of Depreciation* (Public Utilities Reports, 1947).

Putnam, P. C., *Energy in the Future* (Van Nostrand, 1953).

Ransmeier, J. S., *The Tennessee Valley Authority* (Vanderbilt University Press, 1942).

Robinson, W. W., *Ranchos Become Cities* (San Pasqual Press, 1939).

Ruggles, C. O., *Problems in Public Utility Economics and Management* (McGraw-Hill, 1933).

Ruggles, C. O., *Aspects of the Organization, Functions, and Financing of State Public Utility Commissions* (Harvard Univ. Press, 1937).

Schurr, S. H., and Marschak, J., *Economic Aspects of Atomic Energy* (Princeton University Press, 1950).

Sharfman, I. L., *The Interstate Commerce Commission* (Commonwealth Fund, 1931, 1935, 1936, 1937).

Smith, N. L., *Fair Rate of Return in Public Utility Regulation* (Houghton Mifflin, 1932).

Steinmetz, C. P., *America and the New Epoch* (Harper & Brothers, 1916).

Taff, C. A., *Commercial Motor Transportation* (Irwin, 1955).

Thompson, C. W., and Smith, W. R., *Public Utility Economics* (McGraw-Hill, 1941).

Trachsel, H. H., *Public Utility Regulation* (Irwin, 1947).

Troxel, C. E., *Economics of Public Utilities* (Rinehart, 1947).

Troxel, C. E., *Economics of Transport* (Rinehart, 1955).

Van Hise, C. R., *The Conservation of Natural Resources in the United States* (Macmillan, 1910).

Welch, F. X., *Cases on Public Utility Regulation* (Public Utility Reports, Inc., 1946).

Westmeyer, R. E., *Economics of Transportation* (Prentice-Hall, 1952).

Whitten, R. H., and Wilcox, D. F., *Valuation of Public Service Corporations*, 2 vols. (Banks Law Publishing Co., 1928).

Wilson, G. L., *Transportation and Communication* (Appleton-Century-Crofts, 1954).

Periodicals

Adler, E. A., "Business Jurisprudence," 28 *Harvard Law Review* 135, Dec. 1914.

Bonbright, James C., "Public Utility Rate Control in a Period of Price Inflation," *Land Economics*, Vol. 27, p. 16, Feb. 1951.

Clemens, E. W., "Some Aspects of the Rate-of-Return Problem," *Land Economics*, Vol. 30, p. 32, Feb. 1954.

Curtis, H. A., "The TVA and the Tennessee Valley—What of the Future?" *Land Economics*, Vol. 28, p. 334, Nov. 1952.

Glaeser, M. G., "Those Joint TVA Costs," *Pub. Util. Fortnightly*, Vol. 24, p. 259, Aug. 1939.

Gray, H. M., "The Passing of the Public Utility Concept," *J. Land and Pub. Util. Econ.,* Vol. 18, p. 8, May 1940.

Hale, R. L., "Conflicting Judicial Criteria of Utility Cases," *Columbia Law Review,* Vol. 3, p. 959.

Morehouse, E. W., and Baumeister, I., "How Will Atomic Power Affect the Electric Power Industry," *Land Economics,* Vol. 31, p. 93, May 1955.

Morton, Walter A., "Rate of Return and the Value of Money in Public Utilities," *Land Economics,* Vol. 28, p. 91, May 1952.

Thatcher, Lionel W., "Cost of Capital Techniques Employed in Determining the Rate of Return for Public Utilities, *Land Economics,* Vol. 30, p. 85, May 1954.

Government Documents

1. U.S. Reports of Federal Coordinator of Transportation: *Regulation of Transportation Agencies.* 73d Cong., 2nd Sess., Sen. Doc. 152, 1934. *Regulation of Railroads,* 73d Cong., 2nd Sess., Sen. Doc. 119, 1934. *Report of Federal Coordinator of Transportation.* 74th Cong., 1st Sess., H. Doc. 89, 1935. *Fourth Report of the Federal Coordinator of Transportation,* 74th Cong., 2nd Sess., H. Doc. 394, 1936.

2. National Resources Committee, *Energy Resources and National Policy* (Washington, 1939).

3. U.S. Senate, Report of the Joint Committee on the Investigation of the Tennessee Valley Authority (76th Cong., 1st Sess., Sen. Doc. 56, 1939).

4. U.S. Board of Investigation and Research, *Report on Practices and Procedures of Government Control of Transportation* (78th Cong., 2nd Sess., H. Doc. 678, 1944).

5. U.S. Board of Investigation and Research, *Public Aids to Domestic Transportation* (79th Cong., 1st Sess., H. Doc. 159, 1944).

6. U.S. Board of Investigation and Research, *The National Traffic Pattern* (79th Cong., 1st Sess., Sen. Doc. 83, 1944).

7. U.S. Board of Investigation and Research, *Comparison of Rail, Motor, and Water Carrier Costs* (79th Cong., 1st Sess., Sen. Doc. 84, 1945).

8. U.S. Board of Investigation and Research, *Report on Technological Trends in Transportation* (79th Cong., 1st Sess., Sen. Doc. 76, 1945).

9. U.S. Bureau of Reclamation, *Central Valley Project Studies* (Washington, 1947).

10. Report of the President's Water Resources Policy Commission. *Vol. I—General Report; Vol. II—Ten Rivers in America's Future; Vol. III—Water-Resources Law.* (Washington, 1950.)

11. Report of the 'President's' Materials Policy Commission. *Vol. I—Foundations for Growth and Security; Vol. II—The Outlook for Key Commodities; Vol. III—The Outlook for Energy Sources; Vol. IV—The Promise of Technology; Vol. V—Selected Reports to the Commission* (Washington, 1952).

12. Missouri Basin Survey Commission, *Missouri: Land and Water* (Washington, 1953).

13. Commission on Organization of the Executive Branch of the Government. *Vol. I—Water Resources and Power. A Report to the Congress; Vol. II— Separate Statements of the Commissioners* (Washington, 1955).

14. Commission on Organization of the Executive Branch of the Government. *Task Force Report on Water Resources and Power,* 3 vol. (Washington, 1955).

15. Hearings, Sub-committee, Interstate and Foreign Commerce, on *Transport Policy and Organization.* 84th Cong., House of Rep., Sept. 1955.

Appendix B

Chronology of Important Dates

I. The Promotional Epoch

1762   First pumping plant at Bethlehem, Pa.
1780's   Beginning of Canal Era
1794   Philadelphia and Lancaster Turnpike
1796   First "Aqueduct Corporation" in Boston
1807   Robert Fulton introduces steamboat on Hudson River
1816   First American gas utility chartered in Baltimore
1819   The Dartmouth College case
1824   *Gibbons v. Odgen*
1825   Completion of Erie Canal
1830   First railway operation by Baltimore and Ohio
1831   First street railway operation in New York City
1834   First railway mail contract
1836   Rhode Island sets up first fact finding commission
1837   Financial panic associated with internal improvements
1837   Charles River Bridge Company case
1844   First commercial telegraph service between Washington and Baltimore
1847   Mormons begin cooperative irrigation developments in Great Salt Lake Valley
1856   Organization of Western Union Telegraph Company
1858   Experimental operation of first trans-Atlantic cable

II. The Competitive Epoch

1850   First land grant to Illinois Central Ry.
1853   First use of underground railway in London
1861   First transcontinental telegraph line
1865   Atlantic cable begins continuous operation
1865   First natural gas utility at Fredonia, N.Y.
1865   Renewal of mail shipping subsidies
1869   First cable railway begins operation in New York City
1869   First transcontinental Pacific railway completed
1869   Beginning of trunk line competition as New York Central and Pennsylvania enter Chicago
1869   Organization of Mass. Railroad Commission
1871   Organization of Illinois Railroad and Warehouse Commission
1872   *Olcott v. Supervisors*
1873   Introduction of Lowe process of manufacture of carburetted water gas
1874   Report of Windom Committee to Congress
1875   Pioneer water filtration plant—Poughkeepsie, N.Y.
1877   *Munn vs. Illinois*

1877   *Peik vs. C. & N.W. Ry.*
1878   First Bell Telephone exchange at New Haven, Conn.
1878   First elevated railway (steam) at New York
1878   First introduction of electric arc street lighting system
1882   First steam electric central station (Pearl St.) at New York
1882   First hydro-electric central station at Appleton, Wisconsin
1883   First electric railway at Saratoga Springs, N.Y.
1886   First alternating current central station at Greensburg, Pa.
1886   Report of Cullom Committee to Congress
1886   Decision in the "Wabash" case reversing the "Peik" case
1887   Interstate Commerce Act
1888   First long distance electric transmission system at Portland, Oregon
1891   New Jersey enacts first state aid highway law
1891   Long distance transmission of natural gas—Indiana to Chicago
1893   First introduction of practical motor cars
1896–1898   Series of U.S. Supreme Court decisions weakening Interstate Commerce Act
1897   Post office inaugurates Rural Free Delivery Service
1900   A.T. & T. Co. organized as holding company

III. *Monopolistic Epoch with Planning and Coordination*

1898–1903   Era of railroad consolidations
1900   Organization of National Reclamation Association
1901   Convening of first National Rivers and Harbors Congress
1902   Reclamation Act setting up Reclamation Service
1903   New York converted Erie canal into modern barge canal
1903   Wright brothers flight at Kitty Hawk, N.C.
1904   Completion of first subway in New York City
1905–1913   New era of state commissions
1906   Sliding scale system introduced for Boston Consolidated Gas Company
1906   Hepburn Act
1907   First subway begins operation in New York
1909   Completion of Roosevelt Dam, Phoenix, Arizona
1910   Mann-Elkins Act
1910   Inauguration of Service-at-cost plan in Cleveland, Ohio
1912   Panama Canal Act
1913   LaFollette Valuation Act
1914   Clayton Act
1916   United States Shipping Board
1916   First Federal appropriation for air mail service
1916   First Federal highway aid law
1918   Federal Control Act for lease and operation of railways and telephone utilities during war
1920   Transportation Act
1920   Federal Water Power Act

1923   *Wolff Packing Co. v. Court of Industrial Relations*
1924   Organization of Inland Waterways Corporation
1925   Washington, D.C., sliding scale system of commission regulation
1928   Metropolitan Water District Act of California
1928   Passage of Boulder Canyon Project Act
1933   Emergency Transportation Act
1933   Tennessee Valley Authority Project Act
1934   Federal Communications Act
1934   *Nebbia v. New York*
1935   Rural Electrification Administration
1935   Federal Motor Carrier Act
1935   Federal Power Act
1935   Securities & Exchange Comm. gets jurisdiction over holding companies
1938   Civil Aeronautics Act
1938   Federal Natural Gas Act
1940   Transportation Act
1941   Organization of Office of Defense Transportation
1943   Acquisition of Postal Telegraph by Western Union
1945   First use of energy of atomic fission
1946   Federal Airport Act
1946   Atomic Energy Act
1954   Amendment to Atomic Energy Act authorizing civilian utilizations

Appendix C

Glossary of Technical Terms

1. *Acre-foot*—The volume of water required to cover one acre to a depth of one foot. One acre-foot equals 325,851 gallons.
2. *Connected load* on any system, or part of a system, is the combined rating of all the receiving apparatus on consumers' premises, which is connected to the system.
3. *Cubic feet per second* (cfs)—Streamflows and discharges of water through turbines and sluiceways or over spillways are measured in cubic feet per second. One cfs is the unit of flow equivalent to one cubic foot of water passing a point in a second. A cubic foot of water contains about 7½ gallons. Thus a discharge of 5,000 cfs equals 37,400 gallons per second and 1 cfs equals 1.98 acre-feet per day.
4. *Design flood*—The flood against which a given area is to be protected.
5. *Diversity factor* is the ratio of the sum of the maximum power demands of the subdivisions of any system or part of a system, to the maximum demand of the whole system or of the part of the system under consideration, measured at the point of supply.
6. *Dump power*—This is power in excess of all other classes of hydroelectric power, usually available for short periods of time and only during exceptionally favorable runoff conditions.
7. *Flood plain*—A smooth or relatively flat area bordering a stream and built up of sediments carried by the stream.
8. *Head*—Head is a term denoting the difference in height of water behind a dam and that in the stream below. The higher the head, the more power can be produced by running a given amount of water through the turbines; thus 5,000 cfs at a dam with a 100-foot head will produce twice as much power as at a dam with a 50-foot head.
9. *Horsepower and Kilowatt*—Horsepower and kilowatt are units measuring rates of doing work, the former usually applied to mechanical machines such as engines and turbines and the latter to electrical machinery such as generators. One horsepower is the power required to raise 550 pounds one foot in one second. A watt, which is equal to $\frac{1}{746}$ horsepower, is the unit of electrical power, but the term usually used is kilowatt, which means simply 1,000 watts. A kilowatt is about one and one-third (1.341) horsepower.
10. *Kilowatt-hours*—Electrical energy is measured in kilowatt-hours (kwh). One kilowatt (1,000 watts) of capacity in operation for one hour produces one kilowatt-hour, or an amount of energy sufficient to keep a 100-watt electric light bulb burning for 10 hours.
11. *Load or demand curves* are plotted between time and demand, the demand being averaged over any suitable interval of time. From these curves it is possible to determine the size of plant, the kind of plant, and the size and number of units required.
12. *Maximum demand or peak load* of an installation or system is the greatest

of all the demands which have occurred during a given period. It is determined by measurement over a prescribed time period.

13. *Multiple-purpose reservoir*—A reservoir designed to provide storage of water for more than one use; for example, storage provided for regulation of flow for navigation, irrigation, floods, and recreation.

14. *Primary power*—The power which is available to the consumer at all times except for very temporary interruptions due to mechanical failures.

15. *Runoff*—The discharge of water through surface streams. This term has a double use, being applied also to the quantity of water that runs off. Thus the runoff of a drainage basin is the water that is discharged from the basin as surface water.

16. *Secondary power*—The power which may be interrupted at the discretion of the producer within certain limits, which are ordinarily provided in a contract with the purchaser.

17. *Therm*—A new unit measuring the heat content of natural gas. A therm equals 100,000 B.t.u's (B.t.u equals heat required to raise 1 lb. of water 1 degree fahr.).

18. *Watershed*—The area contained within a drainage divide above a specified point on a stream, often called a drainage area, drainage basin, or catchment area in river-control engineering.

19. *Capacity factor*, sometimes also called plant factor, is the ratio of the average load to the total installed capacity of the equipment required to supply the load.

20. *Utilization factor* is the ratio of the peak load of the plant or power system to the installed capacity of the plant or system.

Index

Date Due